Mammals

OF THE SOUTHWESTERN
UNITED STATES

Mammals

OF THE SOUTHWESTERN
UNITED STATES

(WITH SPECIAL REFERENCE TO NEW MEXICO)

by

VERNON BAILEY

SENIOR BIOLOGIST,
DIVISION OF BIOLOGICAL INVESTIGATIONS
BUREAU OF BIOLOGICAL SURVEY

DOVER PUBLICATIONS, INC.

NEW YORK

This Dover edition, first published in 1971, is an
unabridged republication of the work originally
published by the United States Department of
Agriculture Bureau of Biological Survey as *Mammals of New Mexico*, No. 53 in the series *North
American Fauna*, in 1931.

International Standard Book Number: 0-486-22739-1
Library of Congress Catalog Card Number: 70-156908

Manufactured in the United States of America
Dover Publications, Inc.
180 Varick Street
New York, N. Y. 10014

CONTENTS

LIST OF PLATES

The plates appear together in a section following page 400

NORTH AMERICAN FAUNA - - No. 53

issued  by the

UNITED STATES DEPARTMENT OF AGRICULTURE
BUREAU OF BIOLOGICAL SURVEY

MAMMALS OF NEW MEXICO

By VERNON BAILEY, *Senior Biologist, Division of Biological Investigations*

INTRODUCTION

The results of the field work carried on at various times in New Mexico by the Bureau of Biological Survey have been published in part as North American Fauna No. 35, Life Zones and Crop Zones of New Mexico (Bailey, V., 1913).[1] This includes a map of the life zones of the State, descriptions of the physiographic features, and lists of characteristic zone-marking plants, birds, and mammals. These bird and mammal lists were not intended to include all the species, and they give no notes beyond a statement of their proper places in the life zones and distributional areas. The complete report on the birds of the State has been published (Bailey, F. M., 1928), and that on the mammals, which has been delayed for several years beyond the completion of field work, is here presented. Many supplemental notes have been added in both to bring them up to date.

---

[1] Citations in parentheses refer to Literature Cited, p. 395.

MAMMAL COLLECTORS AND COLLECTIONS

Since the expedition of Francisco Vasquez de Coronado to New Mexico in the years 1540 to 1542, trappers, explorers, surveyors, and naturalists have covered every nook and corner of the State and have gathered rich stores of specimens of the animal life for museum and private collections. This has been done without exhausting the resources in new, strange, and fascinating species. In 1820 Stephen Harriman Long, of the Army Engineer Corps, accompanied by Titian Ramsey Peale, Thomas Say, and William James, conducted an expedition from Pittsburgh to the Rocky Mountains, returning through northern New Mexico. The first account of some of the animal life of the region, including the first name for the Rocky Mountain form of the mule deer, *Odocoileus hemionus macrotis* Say, appeared in their report. In 1825 and 1826, James Ohio Pattie, of Kentucky, crossed New Mexico diagonally from northeast to southwest with his small party of free trappers, and in his journal narrative gives many graphic notes on the undisturbed animal life of that time.

In 1841 William Gambel visited New Mexico, mainly for the study of birds, but has left his name attached to mammals and plants also. In 1845 James William Abert explored northeastern New Mexico, and the following year with William Hemsley Emory traveled more extensively through the State, returning to Colorado on January 15, 1847. He did considerable collecting on this trip, and his name is commemorated by the beautiful tassel-eared Abert squirrel (*Sciurus aberti aberti* Woodhouse). In 1846 Emory accompanied Brig. Gen. Stephen Watts Kearny on a military expedition through New Mexico to California, entering the State over Raton Pass, and journeying via Las Vegas and Santa Fe, down the Rio Grande Valley, over the Mimbres Mountains, and down the Gila River into Arizona.

In 1851 Samuel Washington Woodhouse accompanied the expedition of Lorenzo Sitgreaves, of the United States Army, as physician and naturalist. From San Antonio he went to El Paso, Tex., then followed up the river valley to the Puerco, up it to Laguna, thence to Zuni and down the Zuni River into Arizona, collecting specimens and he later gave scientific names to some of the mammals encountered along the way. In 1853 Caleb Burwell Rowan Kennerly was attached as physician and naturalist to Lieut. Amiel Weeks Whipple's expedition to explore the route for a Pacific railroad near the thirty-fifth parallel. With Lieut. Joseph C. Ives he followed up the Rio Grande Valley from El Paso to Albuquerque, thence west to Laguna, Inscription Rock, and Zuni, and on into Arizona and later along the Mexican boundary. His mammal collections came to the United States National Museum and were described by Baird and others. *Ursus kennerlyi* Merriam was named from the skull of a grizzly bear that he collected just below the southwestern corner of New Mexico in Sonora. In 1854 John Pope crossed the Staked Plains of Texas, the Pecos River Valley, and around the southern Guadalupe Mountains of New Mexico back into Texas, collecting the type of the Mexican badger (*Taxidea taxus berlandieri* Baird) near the New Mexico line.

In 1864 Elliott Coues made a trip through New Mexico, stopping at Santa Fe, Albuquerque, and Fort Wingate, and while he devoted much of his attention to birds he gathered many specimens and much information on mammals.

In 1873 and 1874 Henry Wetherbee Henshaw, as ornithologist of the Wheeler survey, covered many localities in New Mexico, making extensive collections of birds and obtaining also specimens and notes on mammals. Again, in the summer of 1883, with Edward William Nelson, he made considerable collections of birds and a few of mammals on the upper Pecos, about 45 miles east of Santa Fe. Both Henshaw and Nelson later headed the Bureau of Biological Survey and both contributed important notes and information for the present report on the mammals of New Mexico.

From 1884 to 1888 Robert Wilson Shufeldt, of the Medical Department of the United States Army, was stationed at Fort Wingate, where he collected many specimens of mammals and discovered and named the large-eared deer mouse (*Peromyscus truei* Shufeldt). In 1886 and again in 1889 Alfred Webster Anthony collected birds and mammals in the Apache Hills a few miles south of Hachita and also covered much of the surrounding plains and both the Big and Little Hatchet Mountains. Most of his mammals went into the Merriam collection, now in the National Museum, and several species have been named from them.

In 1889 under the direction of C. Hart Merriam, the writer first entered New Mexico to collect and study mammals and birds for the Bureau of Biological Survey, then the Division of Economic Ornithology and Mammalogy, of the Department of Agriculture. A full account of ensuing field work at intervals over a period of 35 years, from 1889 to 1924, covering every part of the State, is given in the Birds of New Mexico, by Florence Merriam Bailey (1928, pp. 23–27).

Other members of the Biological Survey who have assisted in the New Mexico field work on mammals are Basil Hicks Dutcher, 1892; Albert Kenrick Fisher, 1892 and 1894; John Alden Loring, 1892, 1893, and 1894; James Hamilton Gaut, 1892 and 1893; Ned Hollister, 1902 and 1905; Arthur Holmes Howell, 1903; McClure Surber, 1903 and 1904; James Stokley Ligon, 1905, and later on predatory-animal control work; Clarence Birdseye, 1908; Edward Alfonso Goldman, 1908 and 1909; Ned Dearborn, 1910 and 1911; Ralph Todd Kellogg, 1912; Edwin Richard Kalmbach, 1913; and Alexander Wetmore, 1918.

Field naturalists not officially connected with the Biological Survey who have contributed materially in specimens and information on the mammals of New Mexico since the inception of the Biological Survey's explorations began, include many widely known for their activity in other fields of endeavor. Edgar Alexander Mearns, physician and naturalist of the Mexican Boundary Survey, made extensive collections of mammals along the southern border of New Mexico in 1892 and 1893. Ernest Thompson Seton did some collecting and gathered much information in 1893 and 1894, which has been placed on record in his various publications (1909–1925 and others). Charles M. Barber made collections in the vicinity of Halls Peak, at Mesilla Park, and in the Sacramento Mountains from 1895 to 1900.

Louis Agassiz Fuertes, artist and naturalist, joined the Baileys in camp at Carlsbad and in the Guadalupe Mountains in the summer of 1901, collecting mainly birds and making field sketches and studies of both birds and mammals. Theodore Dan Alison Cockerell, while at the Agricultural College at Mesilla Park, N. Mex., published extensively on the natural history of the State and collected some mammals, including a new subspecies of weasel, which he and C. M. Barber named in 1898 *Mustela frenatus neomexicanus*. James A. G. Rehn and Henry L. Viereck in 1902 spent about 11 weeks in the Sacramento Mountain region of New Mexico, and lists of the collections of mammals, birds, and reptiles they then made were published by Witmer Stone and James A. G. Rehn (1903, pp. 16–34).

The specimens and records of the predatory-animal and rodent-control field men of the Biological Survey have furnished a wealth of material for preparing this report on New Mexico mammals. The records of the Forest Service also, which have been placed at the disposal of the Biological Survey, have furnished an important record of the status of game and predatory animals on the forest areas of the State from year to year. Valuable information on mammals also was contributed by Aldo Leopold while inspector of game conditions on the national forests and later as secretary of the New Mexico Game Protective Association. Annual reports of the State game and fish commission, contributions from hunters, ranchmen, and residents over the State, as well as published records have provided much additional general and specific information that has been of service in the preparation of this report.

GEOGRAPHIC VARIATION

New Mexico is as rich in forms of mammal life as it is varied in types of environmental conditions. Hudsonian and Canadian Zone species extend down from the north through its mountain forest areas; Transition Zone species occupy its open yellow-pine forests; Upper Sonoran species of the semiarid Plains range over the eastern part of the State, and others from the Great Basin are found in the more arid sagebrush plains of the upper Rio Grande Valley and westward; while typical Lower Sonoran desert species occupy the Pecos, Rio Grande, and Gila River Valleys of the southern part of the State. Some typical Mexican species come into the desert ranges of the southwestern corner of the State and a few extend across into the Mogollon Mountain region. The mammals are mainly of the Rocky Mountain, Great Plains, Great Basin, and Desert types.

USEFUL AND INJURIOUS SPECIES

The native mammals of a State are one of its valuable assets; they figure largely in aiding pioneer settlement and development and, if wisely used and guarded, form a no less valuable source of revenue and recreation for the most highly developed sections of the country. On the other hand, predatory and crop-destroying species have caused a constant struggle on the part of residents from the time of the early settlers up to the present for the protection of their flocks, herds, and crops. Only recently, with the knowledge gained by years of study of the relationships of the species of mammals, of their characteristics, distribution, and habits, and of the methods of effectively protecting them or of controlling their abundance, has it been possible to solve many of the problems that will mean the greatest good to the greatest number of people in the State. Even with the necessary knowledge at hand nothing can be effectively done toward the protection, utilization, or control of the wild life without a full understanding of the facts and the full cooperation of those most vitally concerned—the resident population.

The many species and subspecies of mammals recognized in New Mexico may be grouped under useful species, such as game animals, fur-bearing animals, and destroyers of insects and rodents; or under harmful species, such as predatory animals and rodent pests.

The principal native game mammals are elk, mule deer, white-tailed deer, little Sonoran white-tailed deer, antelope, mountain sheep, peccaries, bears (black and grizzly), jack rabbits, varying hares, cottontails, and tree squirrels.

The principal fur-bearing mammals are the otter, mink, marten, striped skunk, spotted skunk, white-backed skunk, badger, ringtail, raccoon, opossum, coyote, wolf, gray fox, red fox, kit fox, desert fox, bobcat, beaver, and muskrat.

The mammals especially useful in preying upon rodent pests are the badger, skunks, the black-footed ferret, and weasels.

Those especially useful in destroying insect pests are the bats of all the 9 genera and 17 species; the shrews of the genera Sorex, Notiosorex, and Blarina; and the armadillo, all skunks, and the several varieties of grasshopper mice.

The harmful predatory species are wolves, coyotes, mountain lions, an occasional jaguar, bobcats, occasional cattle-killing grizzly and black bears, and some of the game and poultry destroying foxes.

The rodent pests include those conspicuously destructive to crops, forage, or forests, such as the four species and subspecies of the prairie dog; the numerous species of ground squirrels of the genus Citellus; and pocket gophers of the genera Geomys, Cratogeomys, and Thomomys, some of which are found in every part of the State.

There are also many rodents that may be slightly injurious and if overabundant would be destructive to crops, forage, or timber. These are porcupines (Erethizon), chipmunks (Eutamias), the numerous species of wood rats (Neotoma), cotton rats (Sigmodon), kangaroo rats (Dipodomys and Perodipus), meadow mice (Microtus), red-backed mice (Clethrionomys), white-footed mice (Peromyscus), harvest mice (Reithrodontomys), jumping mice (Zapus), and pocket mice (Perognathus).

GAME PROTECTION

Two of the largest, most abundant, and most valuable of the game mammals of the State, the buffalo and Merriam's elk, have been exterminated or pushed far beyond the borders. The Rocky Mountain bighorn and the northern elk have been almost if not entirely destroyed in the State, but if properly protected they have a chance of returning through the mountains from Colorado. The antelope are rapidly shrinking in numbers and can not last long unless given better protection than they have ever received. The Mexican mountain sheep have been almost or quite destroyed along the border of the southwestern corner of the State, but the Texas species seems to be holding its own in the southeastern part. The deer are holding their own better than any other large game, but both their range and abundance are being reduced. The peccary, or Mexican musk hog, has only a slight foothold in the southwest corner of the State, and while not an important game animal it should be guarded as an interesting type of the region.

Grizzly bears were once so numerous as to be a serious menace to human life and domestic stock, but now they are so scarce and so extremely shy that they may well be counted as game animals, unless, as occasionally happens, one gets back to the old habit of killing cattle. The black bear is still common in many of the mountain ranges, where it is usually harmless and is one of the most attractive forms of game and in addition yields a valuable coat of fur.

The small game mammals need only such protection as will render them of the greatest use and prevent either their overabundance or a too great a reduction in their numbers.

Fur-bearing species should be carefully guarded so that the greatest harvest of pelts may be gathered each season without curtailing the next year's crop. Skins taken when not at their best mean a partial or complete waste of time, labor, and material. A new industry of fur farming is slowly developing over the country and promises to add an important source of revenue for those who prove most skillful in some of its difficult details.

The matter of protecting and encouraging useful species other than those valuable for game or fur is of more importance than is generally supposed. Those valuable destroyers of insects, the bats, if provided with suitable roosting and drinking places, could doubtless be encouraged to remain where most needed. Such useful species as the badger and the armadillo, instead of being wantonly destroyed at sight by the unthinking and uninformed, should also be protected and encouraged in the good work they are doing. The cone-gathering pine squirrel is now becoming a valued assistant in reforestation by storing the seeds that are needed for extending the forests, and local sentiment is beginning to protect the bright little forester, formerly a target for wanton destruction.

CONTROL OF NOXIOUS SPECIES

In the past vast sums of money have been wasted in a fruitless warfare on predatory animals and rodent pests because the methods followed were ineffective or sporadic. At present, with carefully studied methods, efficient organization, and hearty cooperation of all concerned, rapid progress is being made in gaining control of the predatory species and putting into the hands of individual ranchmen and settlers the information necessary for economical control of such rodent pests as are occupants of their lands.

PROBLEMS IN MAMMALIAN STUDY

There are many problems presented for study in the mammal life of a State like New Mexico, but before any of the species can be handled intelligently as much as possible of the habits and life history of each must be known. The present report aims to give in condensed form such information as is available, and to arouse a local interest and a closer study of the habits and distribution of animal life and a more hearty cooperation in the protection of game and other useful species as well as in the better control of those that have proved locally injurious.[2] (See also Taylor, 1930.)

ANNOTATED LIST OF SPECIES

Under each species the distribution, habits, and economic status are treated as fully as the present state of knowledge will warrant. In many cases, however, the available information is meager, and comparatively little can be given.

Order MARSUPIALIA: Marsupials

Family DIDELPHIIDAE: Opossums

DIDELPHIS MARSUPIALIS TEXENSIS ALLEN

TEXAS OPOSSUM

Didelphis marsupialis texensis Allen, Amer. Mus. Nat. Hist. Bul. 14: 172, 1901.

Type.—Collected at Brownsville, Tex., April 13, 1892, by F. B. Armstrong.

General characters.—The Texas opossum is a true marsupial, about the size of a house cat, with soft gray or black fur, a pointed nose, naked black ears, and a long, naked, prehensile tail. The female has an abdominal pouch in which the young are nursed after birth until they are large enough to climb about and take care of themselves.

Measurements.—Type specimen (adult male): Total length, 820; tail, 410; hind foot, 70 millimeters.[3]

Distribution and habitat.—Opossums can be admitted to the New Mexico list only as rare stragglers along the eastern border, which lies just beyond their regular range. Hugh Campbell, of Monahans, Tex., wrote under date of April 14, 1909, that a few opossums had been taken there and that he knew of one instance of their occurring on the New Mexico side of the line. It seems most probable that this would be the southern long-tailed, black-eared form, *texensis*, extending up the Pecos Valley, rather than the eastern *virginianus*, which would not be likely to wander across the dry southern arm of the Staked Plains. It is not improbable, however, that *virginianus* may follow up the Canadian River Valley into New Mexico, as it has been reported from Tascosa, a short distance east of the line, and from Baca County, Colo., near the northeastern corner of New Mexico.

Slow and almost defenseless animals like opossums, which are usually fat and edible, are not well adapted to open desert country, as they depend mainly on cover for protection and for advantage in hunting their food. Opossums extend into the Great Plains region mainly along timbered or brushy stream valleys and are usually found within easy reach of water.

---

[2] Throughout the text acknowledgements of notes and records are given as they occur, but many duplicate notes have been made by different collectors and field naturalists, so that full credit is not always accorded in this way.

[3] The three regular measurements given are: Total length, from tip of nose to tip of tail in a straight line; length of tail, from the base, held at right angles to back, to tip of skin (not hairs); hind foot, from tip of heel to tip of longest claw. Unless otherwise noted, all measurements are in millimeters.

Order EDENTATA: Toothless or Peg-toothed Mammals

Family DASYPODIDAE: Armadillos

DASYPUS NOVEMCINCTUM TEXANUM BAILEY

TEXAS ARMADILLO

Dasypus novemcinctum texanum Bailey, North Amer. Fauna No. 25, p. 52, 1905.

Type.—Collected at Brownsville, Tex., June 10, 1892, by F. B. Armstrong.

General characters.—This armadillo, the only representative of the great order of Edentates occurring in the United States, is characterized by simple peglike teeth and a shell-like skin with nine transversely joined bands over the back.

Measurements.—Type specimen (an adult male) : Total length, 800 ; tail, 370 ; hind foot, 100 millimeters. An adult male topotype weighed 13 pounds.

Distribution and habitat.—This armadillo enters the southeastern corner of New Mexico as a rare animal on the extreme border of its range. In a letter of March 14, 1909, J. R. Holman, of Monahans, Tex., wrote:

Occasionally an armadillo is seen or captured in this region and for a distance of 70 miles or more north of this place. Their favorite haunts are the sand hills east of the Pecos Valley, but they are also occasionally found in the valley.

Hugh Campbell, of Monahans, Tex., also refers to the armadillo in a letter of April 14, 1909, as follows:

Antelope and javelines range both sides of the New Mexico line, and there are a few armadillos, but they are very scarce.

As Monahans is just below the corner of New Mexico, both of these records from well-known ranchmen furnish ample evidence on which to admit the species to the New Mexico list. As there are numerous records from the Texas side of the line, it is probable that armadillos will be found extending for some distance into Eddy County, N. Mex. Recent records show that their range has extended eastward and northward in Texas, but as yet they have not been found beyond the limits of the Lower Sonoran Zone.

General habits.—The question is constantly being raised whether to class armadillos as harmful or beneficial in their habits, and so many unsubstantiated charges of mischief are laid to them that it seems advisable to give some of the recent evidence in regard to their food habits that was not included in the report on Texas mammals. (Bailey, V., 1905, p. 51–56.)

Food habits.—In March, 1906, G. A. Schattenberg, a nurseryman of Bourne, Tex., sent to the Bureau of Biological Survey the stomachs of four armadillos from that place with the request that the contents be identified. He says of this animal:

I have found armadillos to be one of our most useful mammals in the way of destroying insects. They are slaughtered here by thousands for their shells by professional hunters. My aim is to create a sentiment among the rural population enabling me to submit a petition to our legislature asking for a law for their protection.

In a letter of April 24, 1909, Howard Lacey, of Kerrville, Tex., in sending to the Biological Survey the stomachs of three armadillos for examination, wrote:

Every housewife in the neighborhood declares that they break up hens' nests and most people consider them responsible for the scarcity of wild turkeys and quails for the last two years. In searching for grubs in the garden they dig up some plants, but this seems to be entirely unintentional mischief. Their usual method of hunting consists in nosing and rooting about under fallen leaves and vegetation or in rich mellow loam where insects abound. I have found places in rich moist soil where they kept the surface of the ground well stirred in repeated searching for food.

On examination of the stomachs sent in from Bourne one was found empty, but the other three taken January 13 were all well filled, and although it was the time of year when insect life is least in evidence, the determinations of the late F. E. L. Beal showed that the diet was mainly insects, worms, millipeds, and spiders. No. 1 contained identifiable remains of a large number of angleworms and ants, a few carabid and scarabaeid beetles and their larvae, and the larvae of tenebroid and lampyrid beetles and of cockroaches, several brown crickets, and a few spiders and millipeds. No. 2 contained about 80 per cent angleworms, several myriapods, a few carabid and scarabaeid beetles and larvae, young cockroaches, and a grasshopper. No. 3 contained about 70 per cent of angleworms, many myriapods, a few scarabaeid beetles and their larvae, and unidentified larvae of other beetles, young cockroaches, a spider, and a trace of a crawfish.

All three stomachs taken at Kerrville in May, 1907, were well filled. Their examination by W. L. McAtee showed the following contents: No. 1 contained 43 caterpillars, mostly cutworms, 36 beetles of 11 species, 11 grasshoppers of 5 species, a large number of ants, a few fly larvae, spiders, and myriapods. No. 2 contained a large number of fly larvae, caterpillars, beetles, and ants; a few grasshoppers and bugs; and a cicada, 7 spiders, 30 centipedes, and several myriapods. No. 3 was more than half filled with 120 caterpillars, mostly cutworms, a large number of beetles and their larvae, a lot of small ants, a grasshopper, a bug, a few crickets, fly larvae, earthworms, centipedes, myriapods, and spiders.

The wide range of insect food of armadillos seems to include most species with which they come in contact and to consist in greatest bulk of those most numerous and easily obtained. There is no evidence to substantiate the accusations that armadillos destroy garden vegetables or eat the eggs of poultry or game birds; moreover, the small and toothless opening of their mouths would render it difficult, if not impossible, for them to break or eat any but very small eggs or in any way to injure birds or young poultry. Although their food habits require further study, it now seems safe to conclude that armadillos are harmless and in a high degree beneficial mammals, and their extension of range should be welcomed rather than discouraged. The sale of their shells for baskets and curios should be severely condemned, as it threatens the extermination of these extremely interesting and useful little animals.

Breeding habits.—Some interesting notes on the breeding habits of the armadillo have been contributed. Howard Lacey writing from Kerrville, Tex., says:

I have twice found four young, and have heard of litters of four and two lots of six. Young ones are active from birth and have their eyes open.

In another letter he says:

A female killed last spring had four embryos neatly packed up in a single large round sack, which they filled to its utmost capacity. They would have been born in another day or so, and would, I think, have been able to run about as soon as they were born.

In a letter of April 4, 1911, the late J. D. Mitchell, of Victoria, Tex., wrote:

On March 28 a Mexican boy brought me a couple of young female armadillos dug from their den the day before. The eyes were still closed and the navel cords still attached, indicating recent birth. I am sending you one of these, thinking it may be of interest.

The young armadillo weighed, when received at the Biological Survey, 4¾ ounces, and measured 250 millimeters in total length. Although recently born it was very large for the size of the parent and well developed, with a tough, leathery shell.

In a letter of February 6, 1912, Mr. Mitchell wrote:

A dead female armadillo was brought to me by J. M. Fleming. There were four young in the uterus, all males, and gestation was apparently complete. This is the third litter that I have examined in the last two years in which all the young of the litter were of the same sex.

Two of these fetuses were sent to the Biological Survey and are preserved as specimens. Plate 1 shows one of them natural size. Again on March 20, 1918, Mr. Mitchell took an old female armadillo from a den and found as usual four nearly grown embryos in her single-cell uterus. All these were males and were preserved and sent to the Biological Survey just as they were in the sack. Apparently four is the regular number of young, always of one sex and developed in a single vesicle of the uterus.

Order ARTIODACTYLA: Hoofed Mammals

Family TAYASSUIDAE: Peccaries

PECARI ANGULATUS ANGULATUS (COPE)

TEXAS PECCARY; HAVALIN; MUSK HOG

Dicotyles angulatus Cope, Amer. Nat. 23: 134, 1889.

Type locality.—Guadalupe River, Tex.
General characters.—A small, wild pig with straight, sharp canines, a short tail, a large musk gland on the rump, coarse bristles of a dark gray color, and a light stripe or collar encircling shoulders.
Measurements.—Seton (1925–1928, v. 3) gives the total length as 34 to 40 inches; tail, half an inch; foot, 8½ inches. Ligon (1927, p. 97) gives the weight as 60 to 75 pounds.

Distribution and habitat.—The Texas peccary comes into extreme southeastern New Mexico in the sand dunes along the eastern edge of the Pecos Valley, where it was reported as abundant in 1892 by B. H. Dutcher; as common in 1901 by Royal H. Wright, of Carlsbad; and as common in 1902 by Merritt Cary, on the authority of reliable ranchmen and hunters.

In a letter of April 14, 1909, J. R. Holman, writing from Monahans, Tex., just south of the southeastern corner of New Mexico, says:

The peccary, or javeline, is still found in considerable numbers for a distance of 70 miles or more north of this place, but they seem to be disappearing as the country becomes more thickly settled by ranchmen. A goodly number of peccary hides are brought in by ranchmen from the surrounding country from time to time. The favorite haunt of these animals is the belt of sand-hill country east of the Pecos River, rather than the valley of the river not far away; still they may be encountered occasionally in the valley.

It is possible that a few remain at the present time, but this seems doubtful.

PECARI ANGULATUS SONORIENSIS (MEARNS)

YAQUI PECCARY ; HAVALIN ; MUSK HOG

Dicotyles angulatus sonoriensis Mearns, U. S. Natl. Mus. Proc. 20:469, 1897. (Advance sheets issued February 11, 1897.)

Type.—Collected at San Bernardino River, Sonora (near international boundary), September 8, 1892, by E. A. Mearns and F. X. Holzner.

General characters.—Similar to the Texas peccary, but paler gray in color. Weight of adult male and female from type locality, 46 and 44 pounds, respectively. (Mearns, 1907, p. 167.)

Distribution and habitat.—The pale peccaries of Sonora come into the southwestern corner of New Mexico, and in the summer of 1908 were said to be still common in places in the Peloncilla Mountains and Cloverdale Hills. In 1893 Mearns found them in the Apache, San Luis, and Guadalupe Mountains along the Mexican boundary line and in brushy places on the plains around the base and up to the summit of the San Luis Mountains (5,000 to 7,000 feet). (Mearns, 1907.) In 1912 J. E. Sheridan, of Silver City, reported to Aldo Leopold, of the Forest Service, that probably 25 were still ranging in the country southwest of Big Hatchet Peak. In New Mexico they range mainly on the Upper Sonoran Mountain slopes, where dense chaparral and numerous caves in the canyon walls furnish excellent cover and safe retreats and where the food supply is unusually abundant. Here oaks of at least seven species drop their acorns at different times of year, while pine nuts, juniper and manzanita berries, and cactus fruits abound, and wild potatoes grow in the gulches. In the neighboring valleys mesquite and acacia beans grow in abundance, and many of the thorny thickets are so dense as to furnish good cover. The peccary seems to be equally at home in the Upper and Lower Sonoran Zones if food and cover are satisfactory.

Economic status.—Although not important game animals, peccaries make fairly good food, and the skins and heads of old males are interesting trophies. Far more important, however, is the value of interesting native animals, unique in structure and habits, with a precarious foothold in one little corner of our great country, that will soon disappear forever if not given careful protection. A tract of otherwise worthless desert mountain range set aside for their maintenance would insure their perpetuation and eventually become famous as the only place in the country where a rare animal could be found on its native soil.

Family BOVIDAE: Bison and Mountain Sheep

BISON BISON BISON (LINNAEUS)

AMERICAN BUFFALO ; AMERICAN BISON ; KAH-NOO-NAH of the Taos Indians

[*Bos*] *bison* LINNAEUS, Syst. Nat. Ed. 10, v. 1, p. 72, 1758.

Type locality.—Mexico. Based on a captive buffalo in Montezuma's menagerie in his capital, now the City of Mexico, several hundred miles south of the range of the species. Seen and described by Cortez in 1521.

General characters.—The bison differs conspicuously from domestic cattle in the high hump over the shoulders, the woolly fur, and small tail.

Distribution and habitat.—In 1540 Coronado reached the city of Cibola [4] [Zuni] where he found " ox hides " and said of the Zuni Indians:

They travel eight days' journey into certain plains lying toward the North Sea. In this country are certain skins well dried, and they dress them and paint them where they kill their oxen, for so they say themselves.

Prior to this the Zuni Indians (according to Niça, 1539) traded buffalo hides to the Indians in the Gila Valley. From Zuni Coronado traveled northeastward across the Rio Grande Valley and first met with the buffalo 4 leagues beyond Cicuye (the pueblo of Pecos), probably close to where the little town of Ribera now stands, at the crossing of the Santa Fe Railroad over the Pecos River. Here, he says, "they met with a new kind of oxen, wild and fierce, whereof the first day they killed fourscore, which sufficed the army with flesh." From this point eastward through Texas to " Quivira " (village of the Wichitas in Kansas) through " mighty plains," he says, "All that way, the plains are as full of crooked-back oxen as the Mountain Serene in Spain is of sheep." (Whipple et al., 1856, p. 111.)

In 1582 another Spanish explorer, Antonio de Espejo, followed up the Rio Grande Valley to the Province of Tiguas (Puaray—near the present town of Bernalillo (Hodge, 1910, p. 748), and in two days' journey beyond came to another Province (probably near Santo Domingo), where he says " The country was fertile, and bordered on Cibola, where was abundance of kine." (Whipple et al., 1855, p. 114.) This probably also refers to the buffalo country east of the pueblo of Pecos, from which he was then only a few days' journey. In 1584 Espejo journeyed down the Pecos River Valley, a distance of 120 leagues, "all the way passing through great herds of buffaloes." (Davis, 1869, p. 260.)

For the following 200 years the Rio Grande Valley was traversed back and forth by Spanish and American explorers and expeditions without any mention of buffalo in the valley, but there were many references to the Rio de las Vacas (the Pecos River), named for its abundance of buffalo.

The Navajos and many of the Pueblo Indians of the Rio Grande Valley were great buffalo hunters, but so far back as the writer has been able to trace their records they journeyed east of the mountains to find their game or trade their wares for skins and meat. It is not improbable that for many centuries back the hunting population of the Rio Grande Valley helped to determine the western limit of range of the bison, but the more potent barrier of arid valleys seems to have marked the border line.

No good evidence is found that buffalo ever inhabited the Rio Grande Valley in New Mexico or the country west of it.[5] (Fig. 1.)

----

[4] " Cibolas " was a name applied by the early Mexican and Spanish explorers apparently to buffalo or to any buffalo-hunting Indians (Hodge, 1907, p. 299) and was probably applied to Zuni by Colorado as the first buffalo-hunting tribe or village that he encountered.

[5] In their Ethnozoology of the Tewa Indians, Henderson and Harrington (1914, p. 14) quote a note from J. A. Allen under date of Feb. 27, 1911, in which he says that Edward Palmer, the well-known natural-history collector, had written him in 1870 of finding " bison bones, some of them in a good state of preservation, about 20 miles west of Fort Wingate, N. Mex." This was on the route traveled by Whipple, Woodhouse, and Mollhausen 16 years before, and by many other naturalists since, and in a well-populated Indian country where the Indians seem to have no traditions of buffalo. On a military freight road between Fort Wingate and Fort Defiance it would not be strange to find bones of oxen, and it is not always easy in passing to say positively whether a few scattered bones are of cattle or bison. This record seems insufficient for extending the bison range to western New Mexico.

A Tewa Indian picked up by Whipple in 1853 along the Canadian River reported that many years ago his father had killed two buffalo at Santo Domingo, and a Mexican who accompanied this party of Indians said that in 1835 he had seen buffalo on the Rio del Norte. There is no clew to the Mexican's locality except that he came from the pueblo of San Juan (San Juan de Caballaros), 25 miles northwest of Santa Fe. It seems improbable that buffalo at this late date should occur in the midst of the most populous part of the Rio Grande Valley, unless as migrants or individuals lost or driven from the herds farther east.

A few buffalo bones, a horn, and a small piece of skin, found by Walter Hough in a cave near Tularosa River in the Mogollon Mountains of extreme western New Mexico, have been supposed to indicate the former occurrence of buffalo in this region (Lyon, 1907). The cave was connected with ruined walls and the bones from deep in the débris show traces of fire, so that human agency is evident in their location. From whence they were brought can be only conjecture. The distance to the known buffalo range east of the Rio Grande is about the same from this cave as from Zuni, and parts of the animals could have been brought back from the hunt. It is possible that small bands of buffalo may have strayed this far from their usual range, but if they were ever of common occurrence in this region it must have been at

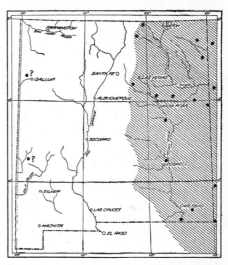

FIGURE 1.—Original distribution of Buffalo in New Mexico. The spots in the shaded area show actual records of former occurrence

very remote times, as there seem to be no other traces or records. In 1540 Coronado passed near this locality, which was about four days' journey south of Zuni, and first reported buffalo eight days' journey northward [northeast] from Zuni.

J. H. Byrne, en route east from El Paso, states that he found for the first time bois de vache at camp No. 10, February 26, 1854. (Pope, 1855, p. 55.) This was 1½ miles east of the "Salt Lakes" near the present Texas-New Mexico line at the west base of the Guadalupe Mountains, at a spring called Ojo del Cuerbo [Crow Spring]. It was a regular camping place on the wagon road around the southern point of the Guadalupe Mountains from the Pecos Valley to El Paso, and also a place from which, up to recent times, salt was hauled to supply the Rio Grande and Pecos Valley settlements. The oxen of freight teams camped in this barren desert valley were undoubtedly accountable for the bois de vache. It is still abundant there, and the writer used it as fuel as late as 1902.

Lieut. J. G. Parke (1855, p. 13) on his route from the Gila River eastward to the Rio Grande, speaks of using bois de vache at his camp of March 10, 1854. The camp was at a spring at the base of Cooks Peak, " Picacho de los Mimbres," about 18 miles north of Deming and 19 miles east of the Rio Mimbres, on the old military and emigrant road to Fort Webster, Ariz., and to California. He says the road is " equal to a turnpike " (p. 13) and "the only route traveled by the emigration to southern California " (p. 12). Tne next camp west of the Mimbres was at Ojo de Vache (Cattle Spring, now Cow Spring). As emigrant travel was then largely by oxen, the bois de vache at regular camp places is easily understood as no indication of buffalo. In 1823 Major Long's party found buffalo in northeastern New Mexico on the head of Cimarron Creek and near the eastern line of New Mexico on the Canadian River, where they recorded herds of bison, antelope, and wild horses. (James, 1823, v. 2, p. 77.) In 1824 Pattie mentions killing buffalo on Cimarron Creek in northeastern New Mexico, but records no more on the journey over the Taos Mountains nor along the Rio Grande Valley or westward. (Pattie, 1905, p. 73.)

In 1853 Lieutenant Whipple (1856, p. 34, 35) mentions buffalo signs and parties of Indian buffalo hunters near the Canadian River just east of the New Mexico line, but no more traces of the animal west of there. At this time, however, the Pecos Valley had also become well settled, and the village of Anton Chico was estimated to contain 500 inhabitants, while La Cuesta and other towns along the Pecos had long been established. The western border of the buffalo range was evidently shrinking even then.

In 1840 Allen (1876, p. 140) says they no longer ranged west of the Pecos River in either Texas or New Mexico, and in 1859 he was informed that there were no buffalo in New Mexico, and again in 1876 that none had been found for a long time in any part of New Mexico, although he gives the range of the southern herd as then occupying northwestern Texas and Oklahoma from the one hundredth meridian to the eastern line of New Mexico (p. 153), and maps them as overlapping the eastern border of the State. Here, close to the northeastern corner of New Mexico, Hornaday (1889, p. 525) estimates their number at 25, and Seton (1909, p. 296) records the killing of four that year about 25 miles east of the line.

Four buffalo were killed in 1884 near the southeastern corner of New Mexico, and one was killed in 1885 near the New Mexico line in the western part of Gaines County, Tex. (Bailey, 1905, p. 69.)

In 1899 at Portales, N. Mex., and in 1902 on the plains east of Carlsbad the writer found the old buffalo trails still conspicuous and deep on the well-grassed slopes leading to watering places.

In 1903 the writer talked with many of the Taos Indians, including their historian and the old men who in their younger days, up to about 1883, had hunted buffalo on the plains east of the mountains. These Indians at once grasped the importance of accuracy in giving information, and every record was thoroughly considered and given in the most careful detail. They said that the buffalo never ranged in their valley but were common on the plains along the east slope of the mountains and often ranged high up into the mountain valleys. The writer's guide and camp man, Sun Elk, who was then 36 years old, said that he was not old enough to go with parties for buffalo, but that his father, who was a great buffalo hunter, killed his first buffalo in Ponil Park (northeast of Elizabethtown), and killed others in the upper valleys of the Vermejo, and that the animals were occasionally killed in Moreno Valley, where he had himself seen their bones and horns. These valleys are high up on the east slope of the Sangre de Cristo Mountains and probably marked the extreme western limit of the buffalo in its original as well as its comparatively recent range. There seems to be no record of occurrence on the Rio Grande slope of these mountains for the hundreds of years that these Indians have lived here and handed down from generation to generation their history and traditions.

The Indians told the writer many stories of their hunting trips after buffalo on the plains to the east—trips that extended as far as extreme northeastern New Mexico, onto the Panhandle of Texas, and south to the Pecos Valley, where bands of hunters from hostile tribes were often met and many battles were fought. There are still strips of buffalo skin among the Taos Indians, used mainly for decorations and ornament and highly prized, and there is said to be one fine robe among them that an old Indian is keeping to be buried in. There is a buffalo clan in this as in many of the pueblo tribes. The buffalo dance is one of the principal dances of the tribe, and it is set to stirring music of drum and voice to represent now the low hum of the grazing herd and then the heavy thundering of the thousand-hoofed stampede.

The Indians recognized two species of buffalo—a larger northern and a small southern form. The southern form, from Texas and the Pecos Valley, called Zu-ke-ta kah-noo-nah, is said to have been small and slender, with thin hair, and rarely fat. They could run so fast that only a very good horse could catch one. The northern form called Zu-ta kah-noo-nah, ranging in the Arkansas River country and northward, is said to have been much larger, heavier, slower, longer-haired, and fatter. A cow of this form, it was claimed, was as heavy as a bull of the southern form. Since taking down this note direct from the Indians, the writer has been much interested in coming across a similar note published by Allen (1874, p. 55) in which he says:

One of my informants assured me that the mountain bison occurs in New Mexico, and that the Mexicans and Indians recognize it as different from the buffalo of the plains, with which they are also familiar, and that they call it by a different name.

On account of conflicting reports as to the characters of this mountain buffalo, Doctor Allen refused to recognize it as a valid form, but notes that the skulls that he found at 11,000 feet in the mountains of Colorado were larger, wider, and had longer horns than those from the plains country.

To-day a few tame buffalo and catalo (hybrids with domestic cattle) represent the species in the State. On June 21, 1918, J. S. Ligon reported a herd of 45 buffalo on the ranch of E. W. and R. E. McKenzie, 15 miles south of Fort Sumner in the Pecos Valley. These

are known as the "Buffalo Jones" animals and were bought by the
McKenzie brothers from the Jones estate at Portales, N. Mex. The
cows and young animals range by themselves, while five of the old
bulls are generally seen together. They are gentle and docile but
alert to all that goes on about them. They usually feed on the
higher ground. They are quick to discover the approach of a rider
and, though clumsy in appearance, are quick in action and run with
ease. In moving they go in a bee line in a rather compact herd.
When the writer saw the herd, at the end of one of the most severe
droughts the country had ever experienced, the buffalo were in good
condition, though the cattle were very poor and losses among them
had been heavy. It was said that buffalo remain fat under conditions
that would mean starvation to cattle.

In 1923 the tame buffalo on the McKenzie ranch near Fort Sumner
were reported to number 54 animals, and 33 were reported in 1925
on the Bell ranch, while several other private herds were kept in
western Texas. In the spring of 1924 a stray bull that had been
wandering up and down the Pecos Valley was driven into a corral
near Carlsbad, teased to a fighting fury to amuse the crowd of
spectators, photographed, and then turned out to roam again over
the valley to which the buffalo had given their name nearly four
centuries ago.

OVIS CANADENSIS CANADENSIS Shaw

ROCKY MOUNTAIN BIGHORN; MOUNTAIN SHEEP; PEAN QUA NA of the Taos
Indians

Ovis canadensis Shaw, Naturalists Miscel. 15: 610, 1804.

Type locality.—Mountains near Bow River, near Exshaw, Alberta.

General characters.—Size large, hair coarse with fine wool near the skin;
horns massive, and coiled in old males, slender and slightly curved in females.
Color in fresh fall and winter pelage very dark drab gray, fading in spring
to brownish gray.

Measurements.—Adult male from type region: Total length, 1,540; tail, 140;
foot, 460 millimeters.

Distribution and habitat.—The bighorn of the high mountains
of Colorado at one time ranged commonly down along the crest
of the Sangre de Cristo Mountains as far south as the Truchas Peaks,
Pecos Baldy, and Santa Fe Baldy on the east of the Rio Grande
Valley, and probably through the San Juan Mountains to the Jemez
on the west of the valley. There are few, if any, left in these regions
at the present time, but with adequate protection in New Mexico
the natural overflow from Colorado, where the sheep have been
well protected, should eventually restock these mountains.

In 1902, Dall DeWeese, of Canon City, Colo., prepared for the
Bureau of Biological Survey a map of the range of the Colorado
mountain sheep at that time, showing that they extended to the
New Mexico line in the Sangre de Cristo and San Juan Mountains.

In 1873, sheep were reported (Coues and Yarrow, 1875, pp. 68–69)
common in the mountains near Sante Fe and a skull was collected for
the United States National Museum.

In 1903, while camping on the head of the Pecos, the writer was
told that there were a few sheep farther north in the mountains but

that there were none in the Pecos region. He found tracks and signs, however, at 12,600 feet on the Truchas Peaks, which, while not fresh, were unmistakably those of mountain sheep. The Alpine Zone of these mountains affords the most ideal combination of cliffs and crags that can be imagined for these northern sheep. The only great disadvantage is their accessibility to hunters, for horses may be ridden over the open slopes far above timber line, and the usually difficult climb before reaching sheep country is eliminated as a factor in natural protection. In the Taos Mountains farther north the same conditions prevail with series of rugged peaks rising far above timber line, usually steep and rocky on one slope but all too accessible on the other. In 1904 the writer was told that mountain sheep had been abundant in these mountains up to 25 or 30 years before. He found old sheep horns near Blue Lake at the head of Pueblo Creek, but at that time the animals were practically exterminated; both ranchmen and Indians told him that none had been seen for several years. On the Culebra Peaks, still farther north in this range, he learned of one mountain sheep that had been killed in 1902, but this was the last that had been seen there. As these peaks are just south of the Colorado line, they would form the first steps in a natural restocking of the mountains of New Mexico from the Colorado herds; while from thence southward to the Pecos Mountains there is no pass lower than 9,000 feet, and the timberline crests of the range are but slightly interrupted.

In the San Juan Mountains, a lower and more accessible range west of the Rio Grande, mountain sheep probably disappeared at still earlier dates. In 1904 no recent record could be obtained from the ranchmen in the valley or the miners along the range south of the Colorado line. It is known, however, that in early days sheep extended as far south as the Jemez Mountains, where Bandelier reported them in 1880, where old horns were collected by Doctor Edwards in 1873, and where recently an almost complete skeleton of a fine large ram has been taken from an old Indian game pit in Frijoles Canyon. The skull of this specimen is now in the United States National Museum.

General habits.—These northern sheep are generally found above timber line on the high ranges and often in summer among the snow banks, or, farther north, among the glaciers, where they climb into the most inaccessible nooks and corners of the rocky peaks and cliffs. Their sure-footedness and skill in climbing are their great protection from natural enemies such as coyotes, wolves, and even cats, whose soft feet will not stand the rough stony slopes. Even hunters generally hesitate to encounter the necessary difficulty and danger of following them to the limit of their lofty ranges with but a slender chance of success. The sheep have thus persisted longest on the roughest peaks. Unfortunately, however, the deep snows of winter often force them down into lower country where food is obtainable and where numerous enemies surround them and sometimes in soft snow destroy whole herds of the defenseless animals. Only under conditions of rigid protective laws and a sympathetic public sentiment can they be expected to thrive on their most favorable grounds in our well-settled regions of to-day.

OVIS CANADENSIS TEXIANA Bailey

Texas Bighorn; Mountain Sheep

Ovis canadensis texianus Bailey, Biol. Soc. Wash. Proc. 25: 109, 1912.

Type.—Collected in Guadalupe Mountains, Tex., near New Mexico line, September 2, 1902, by Vernon Bailey.

General characters.—Similar to *canadensis*, but paler in colors with heavier dentition. Distinguished from *mexicanus* by narrower face, nasals, and palate.

Measurements.—From dry skin, adult male, total length, 1,490; tail, 70; hind foot, 370 millimeters.

Distribution and habitat.—The Texas bighorn comes just over the line into New Mexico on the west slope of the Guadalupe Mountains, where in 1901 the writer found their trails and tracks common over the steep slope east of Dog Canyon. There were also traces of them on the more barren desert ranges west of Dog Canyon, but at that time he could not learn of their occurrence farther north. In 1909 the Forest Service reported them extending 24 miles north of the Texas line. In the report of the State game and fish warden of New Mexico for 1912–1914 (de Baca, 1914, p. 112), the number of sheep in the Guadalupe Mountains was estimated at 200, but a careful examination of the range by J. S. Ligon in January, 1916, gave an estimate of probably not over 100 in this region. All the reports from the Sacramento, Capitan, and Jicarilla Mountains assert that no sheep have been known in these ranges in modern times.

In the San Andres Mountains in 1902 Gaut saw the skull of an old ram, killed about six years before at Grapevine Spring by a miner, who also reported two sheep seen on Sheep Mountain only a year before. Gaut made a special trip to this mountain, but failed to find any signs of sheep there at that time. In 1903 he reported a small bunch living in the mountains between Bear Canyon and San Augustine Peak. He followed their trail for several days, but finally had to give up the chase, as they kept along narrow ledges near the summit of the ridges, where they could see for a long distance. On the same trip he was informed that sheep formerly were found along the crest of the Organ Mountains, but that none had been seen there in recent years. The Huecho, Diablo, and Cornudas Ranges form closely connecting links of good sheep country between the Organ and Guadalupe Ranges. The steep southwestern slope of the Sacramento Mountains is also ideal sheep country, and it is highly probable that in the early days this desert-loving sheep practically surrounded the Tularosa Valley and in Texas extended almost continuously to the Chisos Mountains.

Late in December, 1914, Ligon made an unsuccessful trip in the San Andres Mountains for sheep, visiting localities where he had known of their recent occurrence, but finding no traces of them. Later he learned from an old trapper where 30 or more were located in another part of the range (letter of January 3, 1915). Apparently they were holding their own.

As most of the specimens of this species were taken in the Guadalupe Mountains just south of the New Mexico line, a full account of their habits and habitat was given in the report on the mammals of Texas. (Bailey, 1905, pp. 70–75.)

So far as known, the species inhabits mainly the Upper Sonoran Zone of the most arid desert ranges. In these low open mountains the sheep are so accessible to the neighboring settlements and so easily hunted that their range has been greatly reduced. It is doubtful if at the present time any sheep occur within the limits of New Mexico except in the Guadalupe and San Andres Mountains.

Food habits.—The food of these mountain sheep consists of leaves, twigs, buds, flowers, and seeds of a great variety of shrubs and native plants that are not eaten by domestic stock. In the examination of a number of stomachs no trace of grass was found, and it is doubtful if sheep are in the habit of eating grass to any extent. It is evident therefore that any number occupying these desert ranges would in no way conflict with the few cattle ranging over the same ground, for in most cases sheep range on slopes too steep and rough for cattle and horses.

The fact that the flesh of mountain sheep is the most delicious of wild game should furnish a strong argument for their protection, as it has been the most potent factor in their destruction in the past. In localities accessible to long-established settlements they have almost invariably disappeared.

Protection.—With adequate protection for a term of years, the mountain sheep could doubtless be brought back to its original range and abundance. The difficulty of enforcing game laws, however, in these uninhabited mountains is almost insurmountable, and wholly so without the full cooperation of the resident population. The fact that these sheep occupy land that will always remain practically worthless for stock raising or other agricultural purposes makes it doubly important that their numbers should be increased.

In the spring of 1924, while helping to explore the Carlsbad Cavern and neighboring caves of southeastern New Mexico, the writer covered some of the eastern slope of the Guadalupe Mountains near the line between New Mexico and Texas. Here the scattered herds of Texas bighorns that have so long struggled for existence were barely holding their own against predatory animals and man. The most optimistic estimates of their present numbers do not exceed a hundred individuals, although there is ample room and ideal range for several thousand in the Guadalupe Range. At present they are scattered along the heads of Slaughter, Big, Franks, Gunsight, McKitterick, and Guadalupe Canyons, mainly on the eastern slope of the range. Formerly they came down on the east slope to Rattlesnake Canyon and probably to Walnut and Dark Canyons, even below the level of the Carlsbad Cave.

On April 29 and 30, 1924, their fresh tracks and signs were found well up in Slaughter Canyon, with well-used trails leading into one of the large caves. For ages this cave has been used by the bighorns as a refuge from storms, and the spring, or drip pool, at the far end of the cave seems to be visited at all seasons. Fresh sheep tracks and beds showed in the deep layer of sheep manure on the floor of the cave and a few old skulls of sheep were picked up near the doorway. The great cave room, 100 to 200 feet wide, 75 feet high, and extending back some 400 feet into total darkness, was dimly lighted near the entrance by a great arched doorway on the west side and a small opening on the east, and afforded an ideal shelter for comfort and protection. No signs of human habitation were found in this cave, but it may well have been used as a game trap by the human occupants of neighboring caves as well as by predatory animals. Bear tracks are sometimes found in the cave, but the mountain sheep would have a fair chance to escape from bears or mountain lions, as the cave is wide and clear, and most of the sheep beds were on a great heap of flat rocks fallen from the roof between the two doorways. The old bleached skulls near the big doorway were undoubtedly the work of human hunters who had taken unfair advantage of them in their comfortable home.

Another large cave in the head of Franks Canyon is said also to be much frequented by the bighorns, and there are hundreds of smaller caves with wide open fronts along these high canyon walls, affording protection from storms and making this an especially favorable range for sheep. The mountain slopes are densely covered with chaparral, mountain plants, and grasses. The sheep are especially fond of the browse of mountain-mahogany (Cercocarpus),[6] syringa, ceanothus, and other common shrubs, and feed to a great extent on the tips and leaves and seeds of other smaller plants, and probably to some extent on grasses and roots. They have no competitors on the range except mule deer, as domestic horses, cattle, sheep, and goats do not penetrate to these steep, rough, upper slopes, and the forage is untouched except by game animals that at present make little impression upon it.

The whole summit and eastern slope of the Guadalupe Mountains from Guadalupe Peak in Texas north to Dog Canyon in New Mexico is now a permanent game refuge. It could easily support 1,000 bighorns and 5,000 mule deer, as the deer range lower and more widely than the mountain sheep. If the game were protected and its natural enemies destroyed, this range would soon be fully stocked. Under wise control and a definite plan for use of the surplus game, either for hunting or stocking other ranges, such an area could be made not only self-supporting but a valuable piece of property. (See recommendations by Ligon, 1927, p. 92.)

OVIS CANADENSIS MEXICANA MERRIAM

MEXICAN BIGHORN; MOUNTAIN SHEEP

Ovis mexicanus Merriam, Biol. Soc. Wash. Proc. 14: 30, 1901.

Type.—Collected at Lake Santa Maria, Chihuahua, Mexico, September 16, 1899, by E. W. Nelson and E. A. Goldman.

General characters.—Horns more slender and spreading, colors paler than in *canadensis* or *texianus*, face, nasals, and palate broader; hoofs and ears very large.

Measurements.—Type (adult male): Total length, 1,530; tail, 130; foot, 425 millimeters.

Distribution and habitat.—The only specimens of the Mexican bighorn from southern New Mexico in the United States National Museum are some old horns picked up by Mearns and Holzner in 1892 in the Dog Mountains, close to the Mexican line. Though these do not show good characters of the species, the locality is so close to the type locality of *mexicanus* (Lake Santa Maria, Chihuahua) that there can be little question about referring them to that species.

---

[6] The names of plants in this publication are for the most part those used by Wooton and Standley in their Flora of New Mexico (1915).

In 1892 Mearns found mountain sheep inhabiting the Dog, Big Hatchet, and San Luis Mountains in extreme southwestern New Mexico. He says:

It was found by our surveying party as far east as Monument No. 15, near which, on the northern border of the State of Chihuahua, two were seen by Señor Luis R. Servin * * * in June, 1892. * * * Edward Rector and Jack Doyle had killed many bighorns on the Hachita Granda Mountain in Grant County, N. Mex., where I saw six in 1892 in the canyon at the east base. Numerous horns were seen in the neighboring Dog Mountains of New Mexico, and a large ram was killed within 500 yards of Dog Spring, Grant County, N. Mex., September 11, 1893. * * * On another occasion Mr. Van Ormen saw four sheep, and at another time eight, always in rugged canyons of the Dog Mountains. In the San Luis Mountains, where horns were found on the east slope in 1893 and signs of sheep were plentiful at the summit, its range extended from 1,700 to 2,498 meters [5,500–8,100 feet]. (Mearns, 1907, p. 239.)

W. T. Hornaday (1901, p. 121) recorded sheep brought into Deming in 1900 from the mountains near the international boundary, 40 miles southeast of that town, and sold in a meat market.

In 1906 H. H. Hotchkiss told the writer that there were still some sheep in the Cloverdale range in the extreme southwestern corner of New Mexico. In 1908 E. A. Goldman found fresh tracks on the Big Hatchet Mountains between 6,500 and 7,500 feet altitude and was told by the ranchmen living in the valleys that there were at that time only a few sheep remaining in these mountains and probably none in the other ranges of southwestern New Mexico. In the country north of Deming there seem to be no recent records.

In 1907 Mrs. E. L. Fuller, of Lordsburg, reported that some years before her son had killed a mountain sheep at White Rock on the Gila and that there were then a few in the Burro and Carlisle Mountains, but in 1908 Goldman and the writer could get no recent records in that region.

From the Mogollon Mountain region there are no recent records of sheep, but in January, 1825, Pattie, with his party of beaver trappers, passed through the canyon of the San Francisco River and wrote in his journal that on the walls of these high and rugged mountains were "multitudes of mountain sheep. One of them that we killed had the largest horns that I ever saw on any animal." (Pattie, 1905, p. 91.)

In 1905 Hollister reported old horns of mountain sheep found in various parts of the little ranges of mountains from the Magdalenas to the Zunis during the previous 25 years. All were very old, and no one appeared to know when living sheep were found in the region. In the Zuni Mountains Hollister was told that very old horns and parts of skulls had been found at times, often when wells were being dug or in mine work, but no one living in that region could remember when there were sheep on the range.

In the great lava field south of the Zuni Mountains, some sheep heads with well-preserved horns have recently been found in the caves and among the Malpais, and two of these obtained by J. S. Ligon and sent to the Biological Survey resemble the type series of *Ovis mexicanus* more nearly than any other of the surrounding forms, and are referred to that species.

Family ANTILOCAPRIDAE: Pronghorned Antelope

ANTILOCAPRA AMERICANA AMERICANA (ORD)

AMERICAN ANTELOPE; PRONGHORN; TAH AH-NAH of the Taos Indians

Antilope americanus Ord, Guthrie's Geography, Amer. ed. 2, v. 2, p. 292, 1815.

Type locality.—Plains and highlands of the Missouri River.

General characters.—Size of a small deer, horns of male erect, with recurved tip and flat prong in front; deciduous annually. General color, buff with white rump and lower parts, and black markings on neck and face.

Measurements.—Adult male from North Dakota: Total length, 1,320; tail, 110; foot, 400 millimeters.

Distribution and habitat.—Up to about 1889, when Biological Survey work began in New Mexico, antelope ranged over most of its open plains and valley country, and in favorable places they were still found in large numbers.

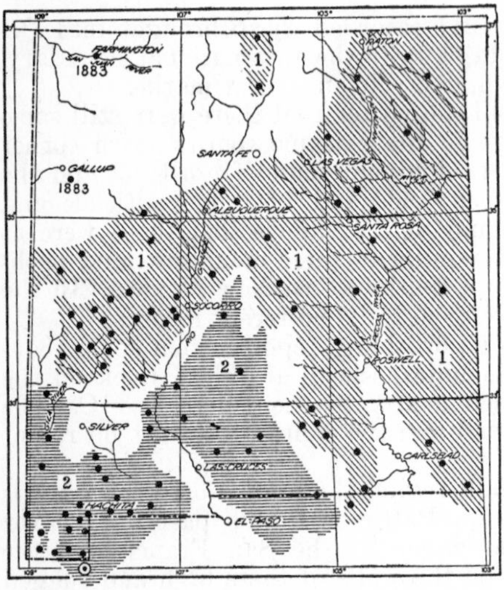

On the early expeditions they were encountered in great abundance over most of the plains country of New Mexico. In 1820 Major Long's party found them common within reach of watering places in the northeastern part, and in 1853 Whipple, on the survey of the thirty-sixth parallel, recorded them as unusually numerous in the Canadian River Valley in the region of Tucumcari and Cuervo, and also along the Gallinas River. Near Zuni, in 1853, Kennerly reported them as much hunted, scarce, and wild, but abundant a little farther west.

FIGURE 2.—Distribution of antelope up to recent times in New Mexico; the spots show actual records of occurrence: 1, *Antilocapra americana americana;* 2, *A. americana mexicana.* Type locality circled

The largest area from which they have entirely disappeared lies in the northwestern corner of the State, within the range of the Navajo Indians. In the early days of bows and arrows antelope were abundant over these great arid plains, and as late as 1883 they were still found in the San Juan Valley. (Fig. 2.) But L. C. Burnam, who has lived at Fruitland since 1881, told Clarence Birdseye that he had known of no antelope in that valley since 1883. In 1908 no recent record of antelope could be obtained in the Navajo region. The Navajo Indians are excellent hunters, and with their abundance of good horses and rifles have extirpated the antelope from their country. In 1904 a few were seen on the plains east of Tres Piedras and a few reported in the southern part of San Luis Valley close to the New Mexico line, but the Taos Indians could not remember when any had been seen on their side of the Rio

MAMMALS OF NEW MEXICO

Grande. One of these Indians told the writer that in 1886, while the snow was a foot deep on the plains, a band of 200 antelope gathered on the open mesa west of the Rio Grande opposite the mouth of Rio Hondo. About 30 Indians went after this herd, armed mainly with bows and arrows, but a few with primitive firearms. From this herd they killed 96 antelope, and the Indians with the bows and arrows got a fair share of the meat, for an arrow lodged in the animal held it for the owner of the arrow against any number of bullet holes. The Indians told of a later herd noted on this plain, apparently early in the nineties, when 40 were killed. The method of hunting antelope on horseback with bows and arrows dated far back with these Indians, before the time of firearms, as it did with the Navajos, but apparently had produced little effect on the abundance of the game, as all kinds seemed to be plentiful until rifles came into common use. The usual method of hunting with bows and arrows was to drive the antelope back and forth until they were exhausted or forced into narrow places where they could be shot at close quarters.

During the years from 1899 to 1918, when field work was being carried on in New Mexico by the Bureau of Biological Survey, the observed numbers of antelope underwent a marked decrease. In 1899 the writer found them still common over a great part of the Pecos Valley and Staked Plains country of eastern New Mexico, and from the towns of Portales, Roswell, and Eddy (now Carlsbad) he could ride out and see small bunches at any time.

In 1901 antelope were still found in small numbers in the Pecos Valley, 30 miles east of Carlsbad, and tracks were seen along the eastern base of the Guadalupe Mountains west of the Pecos, where the animals were said to be fairly common. In 1902 a few were seen at the southern end of this range and on the west slope on the edge of the great Salinas Valley. Farther north Hollister reported them as still common in the Pecos Valley, especially west of the river from Roswell to Santa Rosa. The same year Gaut was told that there were large numbers of antelope about 40 miles southwest of Santa Rosa, and he also reported them as common in the southeastern part of Galleo Canyon, 40 miles northwest of Corona.

As a result of Gaut's work in 1903 he reported a small number on the plains just north of the Jicarilla Mountains, and many east and north of the Mesa Jumanes. Farther south he found them in the Alamagordo Valley about Jarilla in small numbers and a few about Parker Lake, where on June 28 he saw a bunch of five. He also was told that 10 years earlier antelope could be seen at any time of year in great numbers about Parker Lake. In 1903, farther north, A. H. Howell saw two near Clayton, and a bunch of five on the mesa at the foot of Sierra Grande, and the writer was told that there were still a few in the country along the northern edge of the Staked Plains from Santa Rosa to Montoya. In 1904 a few were reported along the northern line of New Mexico west of the Rio Grande.

In 1905 Hollister reported that the antelope had long since disappeared from the Wingate and the Laguna regions in western New Mexico, but stated that they were still plentiful farther south. He found a few scattered over the plains north of the Gallina and Bear

Spring Mountains, and reported them as common on the plains of San Augustine west of Magdalena, where he saw several small bunches on a trip to the Datil Mountains.

Later, in 1906, in western New Mexico, the writer found small bunches of antelope on the plains south of Acoma. A band of five or six was seen along the road just south of Punta Malpais, tracks were seen near Lathrop Spring north of Quemado, and they were reported as common on the plains of San Augustine.

In 1908 antelope tracks were seen near camp at Beaver Lake on the Datil National Forest and at several places on the mesa south of the Elk Mountains. A bunch of 18 was seen at a salt trough near the head of Beaver Dam Creek at the east base of the Mogollon Mountains. There were said to be a few on the mesas at the head of Indian Creek south of the Corduroy Canyon and on the mesas north of Gila Hot Springs. They were most abundant, however, on the high plains .country north and east of Beaver Lake and along the south side of the Elk Mountains—areas that open out on the north to the plains of San Augustine. Hank Hotchkiss, who was with the writer at the time and had camped during the previous winter near Beaver Lake while trapping for wolves, reported the antelope as abundant in that section. He saw them every day and counted as many as 80 in a band, and estimated that 600 or 700 were in that vicinity. He said the Navajo Indians were hunting there at the time, and he saw one of them trying to stalk a bunch of antelope by holding before him a canvas stretched on a hoop and painted like an antelope. In this particular case the cowboys scared the antelope by firing at them, but as they went off over the hill the Indian started after and followed them until they were out of sight. Hotchkiss said that antelope hair was a foot deep on the ground where these Indians, one of the regular Navajo hunting parties of about 25, including women, had camped. The settlers in the region complained that these hunting parties were largely responsible for the rapid decrease of game.

In 1909 E. A. Goldman reported antelope as common over the eastern part of the San Augustine Plains, where he saw small bunches of from five to nine almost every day. From the antelope he saw and the information he could gather from the ranchmen he estimated that the animals numbered at that time several hundred, but all agreed that they were decreasing year by year.

In September, 1915, J. S. Ligon, in crossing the Continental Divide northwest of Chloride, reported 20 antelope near Eastwater, 7 on the Cooney Prairie, and a bunch of does and 4 bucks on the mesa east of the Elk Mountains, in addition to a few scattered individuals along the way. In October he made another trip over this route and reported 40 antelope on the ridge north of Corduroy Canyon, about 30 on the divide 23 miles northwest of Chloride, 29 about 30 miles northwest of Chloride, and 31 two miles farther to the northeast at Northwater. These were all very tame, and as the season for hunting deer and turkeys was then open, and there was no deputy game warden in that region, the antelope were being killed by hunters without restriction. More than 100 antelope were reported in a single drove in this region the previous winter, and as these are a part of the San Augustine Plains herd it was encouraging to find them still in such goodly numbers. On December 31 Ligon says:

My estimate is that there are 1,200 head of antelope in New Mexico at the present time. The greatest numbers are in the V+T Range, on the head of the Gila River, Datil National Forest. No doubt there are 300 head in this region, and in the pastures of the Victoria Land and Cattle Company (Geo. Warren, Manager, Engle, N. Mex.) between Engle and San Antonio, N. Mex. And right here I desire to state that this company, and Mr. Warren especially, deserve credit in giving these noble creatures such good protection. The general opinion is that in the pastures of this company (which are Spanish grants) there are between 250 and 300 antelope which for the present at least are safe.

On November 6, 1916, Ligon again visited this region in quest of wolves and ran into a bunch of five Navajo Indians with four pack horses loaded down with meat and hides of deer and antelope. Most of the meat was jerked and sacked, but two fresh antelope hides were seen among the deer hides tied to the packs, and, from the shooting heard in the open country where the antelope had been ranging and the fact that no more antelope were seen in that region for the two weeks of his stay, Ligon was led to believe that the antelope had been mostly killed or driven out.

In June, 1918, he wrote to the Biological Survey:

Such reports as I have received indicate that there are no antelope in the Pecos Valley proper, but there are some south and southwest of Dunlap, 25 or 30 miles west of the river.

The San Augustine Plains are the center of abundance of the antelope west of the Rio Grande and will probably be the scene of their last stand in the State. The location is ideal for an antelope preserve, which would be the only possible means of preventing the extermination of the species.

In the report of the State game warden for 1912–1914 (de Baca, 1914, p. 23), a small bunch of antelope was said to be well protected on the Urica ranch, owned by George H. Webster.

In a letter of March 14, 1917, O'Donel, manager of the Bell ranch, in San Miguel County, estimated the number of antelope protected in the pastures of this ranch at from 200 to 300. He stated:

I regret to say that they are not increasing, notwithstanding effective protection. The number that have been poached within the last 10 or 15 years is negligible, yet there are fewer antelope here than when I first knew the ranch 19 years ago. I am convinced that the antelope's natural enemies are sufficient to keep down the increase, and chief among these are the eagles and coyotes.

In 1916 Aldo Leopold, then in charge of New Mexico game and fish investigations of the Forest Service, gathered data on the number of antelope in New Mexico, using figures and estimates of forest rangers, game wardens, predatory-animal trappers, and ranch owners. He reported to the Forest Service a total of 1,740 antelope in the State, of which 250 were given as on national forests, 765 in fenced pastures, and 725 on open range.

Ligon (1927, p. 87) gave the number of antelope in New Mexico in 1926 as approximately 2,950 animals, and showed a carefully prepared map of the areas occupied and the number of animals in each of the 39 bands known to be in the State. Since the elimination of wolves and a great reduction of numbers of coyotes and bobcats in the State and the awakening of public sentiment to the importance of protecting and increasing the game animals, there seems reason to hope for the gradual increase and final restoration of these beautiful animals to certain parts of their old range in numbers to insure the perpetuation of the species. (See also Nelson, 1925.)

General habits.—Antelope are in every way a product of the open country, depending for protection on alertness, speed, numbers, and a clear field for escape. With a fair start no native animal can catch them on their own beat. Good race horses will overtake them on smooth ground, but as soon as they strike a stony surface the horses are left far behind. The great herds have always been on the wide plains and in the open valleys, where a few on guard could give fair warning, their white signal flashes showing far and their sharp snorting whistles still further warning the herds of approaching danger.

In part of their range the antelope migrated regularly from the high, cool, wind-swept plains where they spent the summer to lower, warmer, more sheltered valleys where they spent the winter, but the migrations were local and irregular. In the lower, warmer part of their range they were mainly resident, and many of the dwindling herds remained on the same valley slopes for generations, circling and soon returning when driven off by hunters, dogs, or predatory animals.

Food habits.—Antelope are generally considered grazing animals, mainly because they live out on open grassy plains or valleys and to some extent they are. Early in spring the writer has found the stomachs of those killed by coyotes filled with a combination of new green grass and the old dry grass of the previous year. In winter they will eat grass hay and alfalfa hay, but they seem to prefer the latter. They eat a great variety of plants, are fond of alfalfa, and are often seen picking the tips, buds, and leaves off the small bushes and low plants. At times they eat enough sagebrush leaves to flavor the meat, but apparently only when better food is scarce. Their delicate lips are well adapted to picking the seed-laden heads and capsules of grasses and other plants, and when food is abundant they are generally fat or in good condition. Even above the surface of the snow they find ample food if the range has not been overgrazed by sheep and other stock. They are fond of salt and often visit "salt licks" or come for a share of the salt placed on the range for stock. They usually visit watering places daily where these are conveniently located, but with the help of their succulent food often go for several days without water if they must go far to reach it.

Breeding habits.—Antelope are highly polygamous, and early in autumn the bucks, now with horns well hardened, begin to show signs of excitement. Fierce fights take place, and the victors exclude the vanquished from the herds of does, which are guarded and kept together until the rutting season is over. This generally lasts into or through the month of October. After the rut the horns of the males are shed, to be slowly renewed before the next breeding season. The young, usually two in number, are generally born in May, are without spots or other strong markings, and are largely dependent for safety on their excellent concealing coloration.

Economic status.—Aside from the unusual beauty and grace of the pronghorned antelope and their interest as the single representative of a unique family peculiar to North America, they have been of great practical value as one of our most abundant large game animals, which for generations have provided an important food supply to explorers, travelers, settlers, and hunters generally.

Their principal enemy has been man; but now with reduced numbers their old-time enemies—the coyotes, wolves, bobcats, and eagles—unless correspondingly reduced in numbers, will be able to get most of the young, while coyotes and wolves get some of the adults when deep snow or some unusual conditions give them the advantage. Sheep scab has also taken some antelope and possibly played an important part in their destruction but is now well under control.

With present knowledge and experience in game and wild-life control, there should be no difficulty in maintaining as many antelope as desired in any suitable areas where summer and winter food is available for them.

ANTILOCAPRA AMERICANA MEXICANA Merriam

Mexican Antelope; Mexican Pronghorn

Antilocapra americana mexicana Merriam, Biol. Soc. Wash. Proc. 14: 31, 1901.

Type.—Collected in Sierra en Media, Chihuahua, Mexico (about 10 miles south of the New Mexico border), October 4, 1899, by E. W. Nelson and E. A. Goldman.

General characters.—Colors paler than in *americana;* showing slight cranial differences.

Measurements.—Type (young adult male): Total length, 1,420; tail, 145; hind foot, 410 millimeters.

Distribution and habitat.—Upper and Lower Sonoran valleys and plains of southwestern New Mexico. Formerly abundant in the most arid parts of the State, but now becoming greatly restricted in numbers. (Fig. 2.)

Mearns (1907, pp. 226, 230) in his report on the Mexican boundary survey, said of this form:

The pronghorn antelope is already a rare animal in the region of the Southwest, where it ranged in thousands twenty-five years ago. * * * The antelope was not uncommon from the Rio Grande to the Animas Valley during the operations of the International Boundary Commission, and antelope and deer were largely depended upon for a supply of fresh meat. A trooper of the Second Cavalry, named Swartz, who was an excellent hunter, turned in more than 80 antelopes to the general mess from May to July, 1892. * * * Along the Boundary Line it was seen at every camp between the Rio Grande and the Animas Valley west of the San Luis Mountains (Monuments Nos. 1 to 68). In the vicinity of Dog Spring (Monument No. 55), New Mexico, 30 were shot for food between May 21 and June 13, 1892. * * * On our return to this region in 1893, antelope were abundant on the West Playas; some were seen on East Playas; and at Dog Spring, September 15 to 23 one herd of 30 and several small "bunches" of them were noted. About 20 were seen on the trip from Lang's Ranch to Cajon Bonito, September 8, 1893. * * * On the San Luis Mountains they were found up to 1,650 meters (5,412 feet).

In 1906 E. L. Munson, of Fort Bayard, in a letter to the Biological Survey, reported antelope as common along both sides of the Southern Pacific Railroad from the Rio Grande to the Arizona line, and several good-sized bunches between Fort Bayard and Deming. In the same year, J. W. Stafford, the writer's camp man, reported a few antelope between Palomas and Monticello and west of Engel in the Rio Grande Valley, and also two bunches that had been seen about 6 miles east of Carthage. In 1907 nine were reported along the road between Redrock and Lordsburg.

In 1908, with the assistance of Goldman and Birdseye, the writer covered a large part of the desert country south and west of Deming and obtained many notes on the range and abundance of antelope. On the train between El Paso and Deming he saw 4 near the station of Lanark, and at Deming the driver reported a bunch of 3 seen about 7 miles west of town, and said there were a good many on the plains south of Deming. In the Animas Valley Goldman and Birdseye saw 3 on the plain about 15 miles north of the Adobe ranch, and a few days later (August 6) the writer saw 3 in the same locality; on August 9, 3 were seen near the Gray ranch in the southern part of the valley, and the following day 4 single antelope were observed between the Gray and Lang ranches. On August 11 the writer saw 1 on the summit of San Luis Pass and another on the Cienega ranch in Playas Valley, and a few days before a cowboy reported a bunch of 13 near High Lonesome in the southern end of this valley. In the southern part of the Animas Valley at this time the ranchmen reported antelope seen in small bunches almost every day, and bunches of 16, 27, and 35 seen during the preceding winter. They estimated 200 or 300 animals in Animas Valley, and from reports the writer estimated 100 in Playas Valley and 50 in Hachita Valley and south of Deming at that time. Later in the season Goldman reported them as occurring in small numbers in the vicinity of Tres Hermanos, a group of desert mountains southwest of the Florida Mountains, and on the White Water Plain about 30 miles northwest of Deming.

In 1909 Goldman reported antelope as rather common on the plain 10 or 12 miles to the south of Lake Valley and thence southward; a few at the base of the Salada Hills about 15 miles west of Las Palomas; and also a few in the valley east of Socorro. The writer has not been able to examine any specimens from the Great Desert valleys, Jornada and Tularosa, east of the Rio Grande, but from the nature of the country he assumes that these also may be the Mexican form. Gaut reported a few small bunches in the southern part of the Tularosa Valley in 1903, and they were reported from the middle and northern parts of the Jornado Valley in 1906 and 1909 and from west of the Organ Mountains in 1908.

In this desert region in times past the antelope were hunted at all seasons, and were forced to rely mainly upon their speed and alertness for protection. In Ligon's report (1927) about 366 antelope are shown on his map within the range of this southern form. With an awakened sentiment for their protection, it would now seem probable that they may be able to hold their own or possibly increase in numbers over these great desert valleys, where they add so much to the interest and value of the region.

Family CERVIDAE: Deer and Elk

ODOCOILEUS HEMIONUS MACROTIS (Say)

ROCKY MOUNTAIN MULE DEER; PAHNA of the Taos Indians

Cariacus macrotis Say, Long's Expedition to Rocky Mountains 2: 88, 1825.

Type locality.—Mora River, near the present town of Mora, N. Mex.[7]

General characters.—Size large; antlers forked (pl. 2, A and B), deciduous; ears very large; glandular area on upper part of metatarsus about 4 or 5 inches long; colors dark gray in winter, dark reddish brown in summer; tail short and white with black tip, large white rump patches at sides of tail.

Measurements.—Adult male from Manzano Mountains: Total length, 1,690; tail, 221; hind foot, 490; ear, from crown (dry), 225 millimeters.

Distribution and habitat.—The large dark-colored mule deer of the mountains of all except the southern part of New Mexico (fig. 3), is represented in the National Museum collection by specimens from the Taos Mountains, the headwaters of the Pecos River, and from the Manzano, Sacramento, San Juan, Gallinas, and Mogollon Mountains. The deer are still found in considerable numbers throughout these ranges and over most of the rough and unsettled part of the State. In the valleys, especially in the more settled part, they have become very scarce or have entirely disappeared through persistent hunting. In northwestern New Mexico, in the Navajo country, they are conspicuously absent, as are antelope and other game not protected by the religious beliefs of these hunting Indians.

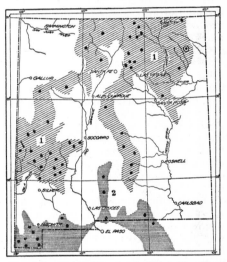

FIGURE 3.—Distribution of mule deer in New Mexico, the shaded areas showing approximate distribution, the spots showing actual records: 1, *Odocoileus hemionus macrotis*; 2, *O. hemionus canus.* Type locality circled

In the type region of northeastern New Mexico A. H. Howell found mule deer still present in small numbers in the canyons of the Raton Range in 1903, and in the same year the writer found them common a little farther south along the rough northern escarpment of the Staked Plains. At that time all the deer in that region were said to be mule deer, but in 1820 the hunter for Major

---

[7] The exact characters of *hemionus* and the consequent relation to *macrotis* will probably never be known, as there is little chance of ever securing a specimen of *hemionus* from near its type locality, the mouth of the Big Sioux River, southeastern South Dakota, but sufficient evidence is found to warrant recognizing the Rocky Mountain form as subspecifically different from the Plains form. Before the names of the mule deer can be satisfactorily settled, it is important that specimens be secured from near the type localities of the species that have been described, and any fragments of an old skull containing teeth may prove of great assistance in determining characters. Horns are of little value for comparison, and the skulls of does are more important than those of the bucks. Skins not too faded to show color are important for comparison, and even skins without legs, collected by hunters near the type localities, may be of great assistance.

Long's party reported two white-tailed deer in the bunch of five from which he obtained the type of *macrotis*. L. L. Dyche wrote that they were common in the mountains about the headwaters of the Pecos and Mora Rivers when he was there in 1881, and in these same mountains the writer found them still common in 1903, from 7,000 up to 12,000 feet. From the middle of July to the middle of August only does and fawns were found at the lower altitudes, while a dozen bucks were seen in different places between 11,000 and 12,000 feet, around Pecos Baldy and the Truchas Peaks. At that time the deer were all in the dark red coats and the bucks with well-grown velvety horns were generally alone, and keeping very quiet on the open slopes, where they were free from insect pests and, overlooking the country below them, they were comparatively safe from enemies. One old buck, a couple of thousand feet below, which the writer picked out with a field glass from the top of Truchas Peak, was so large that it had the appearance of an elk, and so a second trip was made around the peak for closer inspection. It proved, however, to be one of the giants of its species, with magnificent, nearly full-grown horns.

During the fall of 1903 and the summer of 1904 mule deer were found common on both slopes of the Taos Mountains and in the Culebra and Cabresto Ranges farther north. They were then most common in the dense windfalls and old burns high up on the slopes of the ranges, where they were protected from men and domestic stock. Late in the fall they were said to come down into the foothills and also the canyons, where a few years before they had been slaughtered in great numbers. McClure Surber, while in the mountains about Twining from October 7 to December 27, found no signs of deer high up in the mountains, but was told that during the winter of 1885, 263 mule deer had been killed in Hondo Canyon and almost as many during the fall and winter of 1886. During July and August of 1904 they were common about Wheeler Peak above 11,000 feet. A doe with fawns was seen above 10,000 feet but her presence was probably accounted for by the pressure of an overstocked range and thickly settled valleys below. The deer were conspicuously scarce in the parts of the range devoted mainly to sheep grazing, but they seemed to be on good terms with cattle and horses where the range was not badly overstocked.

In the San Juan Mountains west of the Rio Grande there were said to be a few mule deer, but in a week's work over the top of this range in 1904 the writer did not find a track or even an old horn. The range is so open and accessible that sheep and hunters have apparently excluded the deer. Still farther west in the Gallinas Range, or Mesa Prieta, they were fairly common that year, as they were also the following year in the Jemez Mountains. A fine buck killed on the Mesa Prieta on October 10 was estimated to weigh 300 pounds and was in the full bloom of its early winter gray coat with black breast and coal-black face band and a strong buffy suffusion of the lighter parts characteristic of this mountain deer. The great extent of steep, rocky slopes and the dense scrub oak of these ranges have furnished natural protection and the favorite food of the mule deer long after they were driven from the more accessible areas. The same favorable conditions prevail over much of the Jemez Mountains farther south, where late in August and early in September of 1906 the deer were common throughout the roughest and most densely forested parts. Here, as elsewhere, the does and fawns were on the lower slopes and the bucks mainly around the higher peaks. On Santa Clara Peak two does were seen down near the edge of the nut pines at 7,000 feet, while an old doe kept her fawn hidden in a spruce gulch near camp farther up the creek at 8,000 feet. The slender tracks of the does were common throughout the yellow-pine belt, while the heavy tracks of old bucks were frequently seen on Santa Clara and Pelado Peaks to the very summits. On Pelado Peak between 10,000 and 11,000 feet on September 6, four magnificent old bucks were seen together feeding in a little park. They were still in the rich red coat with full-grown velvet-covered horns, and though not more than 100 yards away they looked almost as large as elk. The next morning not far from camp in Valle San Antonio at 8,500 feet, another bunch of four large deer in the red coat came down to the creek to drink an hour before sunrise. All those seen up to September 10 were still in the red coat.

In the San Mateo or Mount Taylor group just north of Laguna a few old deer horns were seen in 1906, but no deer or tracks, and they were evidently scarce in this range as well as in the Zuni Mountains. In the Manzano Mountains in 1903, Gaut found mule deer common along the higher slopes and obtained several specimens in the dark-gray early winter coat. Usually in pleasant weather the deer were found on the open brushy slopes of scrub oak and mountain mahogany, and in snowy weather in the dense forests of spruce and aspen. During severe storms even in this narrow desert range the deer were said to come down low in the foothills. Gaut also found a few deer in the Mesa Jumanes and in the Jicarilla, Gallinas, and Capitan Mountains and the rough country surrounding them in Lincoln County. The same year (1902) the writer found mule deer fairly common throughout the Sacramento Mountains and on Sierra Blanca, where tracks were seen up to 12,000 feet. Over most of the Mescalero Indian Reservation the deer were scarce, as Indians are expert hunters and buckskin formed a part of their clothing and also a foundation for bead work; but in the remote corners of the reservation and over other parts of the range, especially along the heavily timbered summit, the deer seemed to be fairly common.

All the deer the writer has seen from high up in the Sacramento Mountains seem to be the dark northern form, but it is very probable that those keeping to the low desert spurs of the Guadalupe Range farther south are the gray mule deer. In 1900, M. H. Webb, of El Paso, Tex., told E. W. Nelson that the mule deer, then common in the Sacramento Mountains, often attained very large size, one which he had killed the previous fall weighing 375 pounds and another killed in the foothills the same season weighing 425 pounds after being disemboweled.

During the open season of 1914 reports from the Forest Service showed that on the Alamo National Forest 86 deer were killed; on the Lincoln, 34; on the Manzano, 11; on the Jemez, 16; on the Pecos, 3; on the Carson, 25; on the Datil, 243; and on the Gila, 600. No distinction was made as to species, but probably half of those killed on the Datil and Gila Forests were the little whitetail, while the others were mainly, if not all, mule deer. By this count a total of 1,018 deer were killed and accounted for on the national forests of New Mexico in one year.

In the 1915 open season the Forest Service reported on the Alamo National Forest 57 deer killed; on the Lincoln, 28; on the Manzano, 20; on the Carson, 8; on the Santa Fe, 40; on the Gila, 203; and on the Datil, 300, a total of 656 deer killed on national forests. Probably at least half of those killed on the Gila and Datil Forests were the little whitetail, the others mainly mule deer.

The Forest Service reports for 1916 show that on the Alamo-Lincoln National Forest 127 deer were killed; on the Manzano, 32; on the Santa Fe, 50; on the Carson, 34; on the Gila, 125; and on the Datil, 250.

The mule deer of the Mogollon Mountains is referred to the Rocky Mountain form, although in cranial characters a tendency is shown toward the lighter skull and dentition of the southern gray mule deer. It is a mountain-forest species with the gray heavily clouded with black, and the white markings suffused with buff as in those of the northern mountains. In 1906 this species was numerous in the mountains about the head of the Rio Mimbres and about the main Mogollon peaks in the Tularosa, western Datils, Elk, and San Francisco Ranges. In 1908 E. A. Goldman reported them from the western base of the mountains along the Gila and San Francisco Rivers, and in 1909 as occurring west of Chloride and Kingston on the east slope of the Mimbres, and in the San Mateo, Magdalena, Calluro, and Zuni Mountains. In 1905 Hollister reported them as then rare in the Zuni Mountains [8] and the low ranges between there and the Magdalenas, except in the eastern range of the Datils, where he found them fairly common.

On the head of the Mimbres River during the latter part of May, 1906, the mule deer were common about the writer's camp, singly or in small bunches of three or four. They were then without horns and were all in the dark-red summer coat. In August of 1908 they were still common through this region and to the north, about Beaver Lake and the Elk Mountains. The velvet-covered horns were then (August 28) practically full grown. During the latter half of October, 1906, while camped at 8,000 feet near the highest peaks of the Mogollons, the writer had a good chance to observe the range of these deer, which were then common up to the highest peaks, or at least to 10,500 feet, when the first snows began to fall. All the tracks seen at these high altitudes were large and evidently made by the bucks. A number of does and fawns were seen lower down between 8,000 and 9,000 feet. All were then in the fresh dark winter coat with a maximum of black on the breast and face. Even when seen in the woods at reasonably close range, the very dark colors were strikingly conspicuous.

In 1908 the mule deer, which were once common in the Burro Mountains, had entirely disappeared from that range, mainly through market hunting, and it is now impossible to say whether they were this northern species or the gray mule deer. Possibly the

[8] In 1856 C. B. R. Kennerly (1856, pp. 5–6) reported numerous herds of these deer both east and west of Zuni, where they are now very scarce or all gone.

southern form originally inhabited the foothill country around the southern border of the Mogollon Mountains, but, if so, it has been entirely killed or driven out from the valleys and low, easily accessible foothills. As the country becomes more densely settled, the deer will be exterminated from other mountains and rough country unless great care is taken to furnish them adequate protection.

In 1915 Ligon reported a few bunches of mule deer seen on a trip through the Mogollon Mountain country. He was told that they were not half so plentiful as they had been the previous year on account of the great number slaughtered in the region both in and out of season without regard to age or sex. During the open season hunters were so numerous that it was dangerous to be in the woods. In January of the next year he reported the species fairly common in the Guadalupe Mountains south of Queen, where he saw one doe and many tracks of others.

In the absence of State or Federal game refuges in New Mexico some of the large ranches have done their best to preserve a remnant of the native game. On the ranch of the Adams-Bartlett Cattle Co., in Colfax County, between 3,000 and 4,000 deer were estimated in 1914 (De Baca, 1914, p. 23) on more than 400,000 acres of well-fenced and guarded land. In 1918 William H. Bartlett reported several thousand deer on the ranch.

On another large ranch, that of the Bell Cattle Co. in eastern San Miguel County, C. M. O'Donel, general manager of the company, in a letter of March 14, 1917, reports 2,000 to 3,000 mule deer, but says that—

even so it does not appear that there are as many as there should be, considering that practically none have been killed for 18 or 19 years inside our fences, though they sometimes go outside and are slaughtered by hunters.

With the reduction in numbers of predatory animals, better enforcement of game laws, and the provision of suitable refuges and winter range these finest deer of the State should be maintained over the rough, mountainous areas in any abundance desired.

ODOCOILEUS HEMIONUS CANUS Merriam

Gray Mule Deer

Odocoileus hemionus canus Merriam, Wash. Acad. Sci. Proc. 3: 560, 1901.

Type.—Collected at Sierra en Media, Chihuahua, Mexico, October 7, 1900, by E. W. Nelson and E. A. Goldman.

General characters.—In color much paler gray in winter and more yellowish red in summer than *macrotis;* horns generally lower, wider, and slenderer.

Measurements.—Type (male adult) : Total length, 1,830 ; tail, 230 ; foot, 500 ; ear, from crown (dry), 215 millimeters.

Distribution and habitat.—The pale gray mule deer are still common in the desert ranges of southwestern New Mexico. (Fig. 3.) In 1908 Goldman and Birdseye found them in the Animas, San Luis, Peloncilla, Hatchet, and Hachita Mountains and in the surrounding foothills and adjoining gulches. Their range often extends down to the edge of mesquite and other Lower Sonoran vegetation, but is mainly Upper Sonoran. They were not found near the higher parts of these ranges where the little whitetail was most common. On the west slope of the Animas Mountains they were seen as low as 5,500 feet, and along the foothills of the Playas Valley they were reported, occasionally ranging out in the open valley. One was killed in the Hachita Mountains at one of the mining camps in July of that year, and a big buck was said to be frequently seen on Walnut Creek not far from High Lonesome at the southern end of the Playas Valley. They were reported in the foothills bordering Deer Creek near the Culberson ranch, and a fine head with antlers was picked up near the Lang ranch in the southern part of Animas Valley. In the San Luis Mountains Goldman reported them as occurring sparingly in the foothills from about 5,300 to 6,500 feet. In the Hatchet Mountains he found a few tracks at about 6,000 feet. He also reported them as occurring sparingly in the Florida Mountains, where they had formerly been more abundant and had ranged out for some distance on the plains.

All the specimens collected or examined from these mountains near the southern border of the State are typical *canus*, as would naturally be expected from the character of the country that they inhabit and from their proximity to the type locality of this desert species. Their northern limit, however, is not easily established, as the deer have disappeared from the low and open country north of Deming. In the Burro Mountains Goldman reported the mule deer as practically exterminated, except for a few still said to occur along the lower western slope. These and others of which he saw the tracks along the Gila Canyon near Redrock and those reported near the town of Gila ought to be of this species, but no specimens were obtained. Mule deer have been reported from the Franklin, Organ, and San Andres Mountains east of the Rio Grande, but no specimens have been taken. It is highly probable that these deer, as well as those occupying the desert spurs along the western base of the Guadalupe Mountains, can also be referred to *canus*, as the character of the country is identical with that in which the species is known. Its range seems to be mainly restricted to the extreme desert type of the Upper Sonoran mountains and foothills. In many places where the deer are most abundant there is no known open water for long distances, and it seems probable that they are able to exist on the moisture derived from fleshy and moisture-storing desert plants, such as agave, yucca, and sotol (Dasylirion). Their ability to live at long distances from water has been their greatest protection, both from hunters and from the crowding of the range by domesticated stock.

ODOCOILEUS VIRGINIANUS MACROURUS [9] (RAFINESQUE)

PLAINS WHITE-TAILED DEER; PAH-HU-MA'NA (STREAM DEER) of the Taos Indians

Corvus [sic] *macrourus* Rafinesque, Amer. Mo. Mag. 1 : 436, 1817.

Type locality.—Plains of Kansas River.
General characters.—Size large for a whitetail; horns with upright prongs from a single beam (pl. 2, D) ; leg glands small and low down on metatarsus;

---

[9] Until the deer of North America are more thoroughly studied, it seems best to use provisionally the name *macrourus* for the pale white-tailed deer of the mountains and plains of New Mexico east of the Rio Grande. The only specimens from the State available for study are a few skulls from the east slope of the Sacramento Mountains, but there are two good specimens from close to the southeastern corner in the sand-hill region north of Monahans, Tex. This name is also used for the Colorado whitetail.

tail long and bushy; ears small; color pale gray in winter, yellowish red in summer; lower parts and lower surface of tail white.

Measurements.—Female adult: Total length, 1,850; tail, 245; hind foot 425; ear from crown (dry), 145 millimeters.

Distribution and habitat.—White-tailed deer still occupy the eastern slopes of the Sacramento and Sangre de Cristo Mountains and the stream valleys and gulches, reaching out on the plains farther east. (Fig. 4.) In 1901 they were still common in the sand-dune country 30 to 40 miles east of Carlsbad, and there were a few on the west side of the Pecos Valley. In 1902 they were common along the east slope of the Sacramento Mountains, especially in the willow-bordered stream valleys. In the northeastern corner of the Mescalero Apache Indian Reservation they were especially abundant, and this section was known as the " whitetail " country. At Ruidoso,

near this corner, the writer examined 30 sets of deer horns brought in by the Indians from the vicinity, about half of which were whitetails. The same year Gaut reported white-tailed deer as common in Gallo Canyon north of the Jicarilla Mountains. He also reported them in the vicinity of Corona. In 1903 they were still common along the east slopes of the Pecos River and Taos Mountains, inhabiting the willow stream bottoms and aspen slopes of the range and being especially common along Coyote Creek north of Mora. In 1904 the Taos Indians told the writer that white-tailed deer were then very rare on the

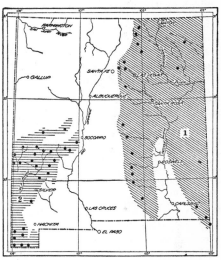

FIGURE 4.—Distribution of white-tailed deer in New Mexico: 1, *Odocoileus virginianus macrourus;* 2, *O. couesi*

west slope of their mountains but still fairly common along the east slope of the range.

On the Bell ranch, in San Miguel County, the manager, C. M. O'Donel, in a letter of March 14, 1917, wrote:

We used to have a bunch of 15 or 20 whitetail running in the river bottoms at the lower end of the ranch, but when the railroad was built through that part of the grant in 1902 they were all either shot or run out. I heard of one last year, but he has not been seen again.

Generally this species is found in the willow thickets of Upper Sonoran and Transition Zones, but it sometimes penetrates to the high mountain slopes where conditions are favorable for food and protection. On July 23, 1903, on the east side of Pecos Baldy, the writer saw a small whitetail buck in the red summer coat with half-grown velvet horns, at 11,400 feet, just below timber line. This habit of seeking the highest elevation during the time when their horns are soft and tender is common with the bucks of most species of deer in mountainous regions and has little bearing on the general distribution of the species. It is considered an effort to avoid the annoyance of flies and other insects lower down. While the does and fawns usually remain at lower altitudes during the summer, they also work gradually upward toward fall and descend with the first heavy snows. It is therefore difficult to assign zonal positions to most species of deer in mountainous countries, and the difficulty increases as the animals become more scarce and are more disturbed by hunting.

This white-tailed deer will soon become exterminated from the open country in New Mexico, and the only possible hope of keeping it from entirely disappearing from the State will be to give it a permanently protected breeding ground where conditions are suitable for food and shelter. Within its present range these conditions could be obtained in great perfection on the eastern slope of the Sacramento Mountains and along the southern and eastern slopes of the Sangre de Cristo Range.

ODOCOILEUS COUESI (COUES AND YARROW)

SONORA DEER; FANTAIL

Cariacus virginianus var. *couesi* Coues and Yarrow, Wheeler Survey 5: 72, 1875.

Type locality.—Camp Crittenden, Pima County, Ariz.

General characters.—The Sonora, or fantail, deer are about half the size or weight of the Virginia whitetail, which they resemble, in antlers (pl. 2, C) and general characters. The old bucks reach a maximum of about 100 pounds in weight and the does probably 75 pounds. They are graceful little deer with large ears and long bushy tails that spread when erect in great white fans, blending with the white of the inner surface of the hams and the belly until, as the deer go bounding away through the brush, the gray body is often lost to view in a series of white flashes that seem larger than the whole deer. From the stubby-tailed mule deer of the same region they are easily distinguished, even at long range, by their small size, long white tails and the gray summer coats of adults.

Measurements.—Large buck: Total length, 1,530; tail 270; hind foot 402; ear from crown, 203 millimeters.

Distribution and habitat.—In New Mexico the Sonora deer occupy the mountain ranges west of the Rio Grande as far north as the Datils and possibly to the Zuni Mountains. (Fig. 4.) There are specimens in the Biological Survey collection from the Animas, Mimbres, Mogollon, San Mateo, and San Francisco Mountains. In 1908 Goldman reported them as formerly abundant in the Burro Mountains, but at that time apparently all gone. In 1909 he was told by residents that there were a very few of them in the Zuni Mountains, but in previous years neither Hollister nor the writer had been able to get a trace of them in this range. Goldman also reported them as not uncommon in the San Mateo Mountains, where he saw their fresh tracks and picked up one of their characteristic little antlers at 9,000 feet altitude. In the Mimbres Range west of Chloride and Kingston he reported them as occurring in limited numbers. The same year officers of the Forest Service reported them in the Datil, Gallinas, Magdalena, and San Mateo Mountains.

In May, 1906, while camping on the head of the Mimbres River the writer found them common over the live-oak and pinyon slopes of the mountains, as well as up in the yellow-pine forest. They came into the little pasture around camp every night and were frequently seen over the slopes. H. H. Hotchkiss reported that he used to hunt them for the market at Silver City and had hauled in many wagon-

loads of their carcasses. He said that none of them weighed over
70 pounds dressed, and that the several heads of bucks picked up
around the camp for specimens were as large as any he had ever seen
in that part of the country.

During October, 1906, these little deer were common in the
Tularosa Mountains and at that season most abundant along the
crests of the high ridges from 8,000 to 9,000 feet altitude, in the
Transition and Canadian Zones. Their tracks were numerous, and
a number of deer were seen and a few old horns picked up. They
were also reported as common in the San Francisco Range west
of the town of Frisco, where in 1908 the writer found them still
common and picked up shed horns. Around the borders of Luna
Valley and over the slopes of the Escudilla Mountains on the
border between New Mexico and Arizona, they were also common.
During the latter half of October, 1906, while camping on Willow
Creek, which is the extreme head of the middle fork of the Gila,
the writer found them quite numerous over the wooded slopes of the
mountains from 8,500 feet up to 10,000 feet. The first snows were
then falling and he followed the deer tracks over the mountain
ridges to the crests of all but the few highest peaks where they
undoubtedly occasionally climb. At that season their principal
range seemed to be in the Transition Zone, but they would often
wander during the night through the Canadian Zone, and some were
started from their beds at altitudes of 9,000 and 9,500 feet, well
toward the upper part of this zone.

An adult doe shot October 20, for a specimen, weighed before
being dressed 61 pounds, and only 50 pounds after being eviscerated
for carrying to camp. She made a light back pack for the 2 miles
to camp a thousand feet below. Although she had raised a fawn
during the summer, she was in good condition, and her blue coat was
dense and glossy.

In crossing the Gila National Forest during the latter half of
August, 1908, the writer found these little deer common in the Mimbres or Black Mountains, at Beaver Lake in the Elk Mountains, and
in the Mogollon and San Francisco Mountains. Their tracks were
abundant throughout the region from the blue-oak and nut-pine
gulches up through timbered slopes of the mountains to the highest
point reached—the top of Elk Mountain at 10,200 feet. The deer
were frequently seen, and all the adults were then in the gray coat
in striking contrast to the mule deer that were then all in the red
summer coat. This substantiates the writer's previous conclusion in
regard to Texas specimens of the species that the adults are permanently gray at all seasons. (Bailey, 1905, p. 64.) The horns of
the bucks were practically full grown but still in the velvet with
soft tips. A 2½-year-old buck, taken August 30, showed well-developed 2-point horns and a trace of the red coat, which it was then
losing and which after that age would never return. The 3-year-old
buck collected in the Animas Mountains August 7, 1908, was in the
perfect gray coat of the adults, with velvet horns not fully developed. Its weight was estimated at 80 pounds, and though not fat it
was in good condition.

These Sonora deer were then numerous in the Animas Mountains,
mainly in Transition Zone above 7,000 feet, where the steep, rough,
and densely brushy slopes form an apparently safe retreat for them.

No stock and few hunters ever reach these difficult upper slopes, where the only trails are those made by deer and bears. The ridge tops of these mountains are parklike, with groves of pine and Douglas spruce on one side and orchards of oak, juniper, and nut pine on the other, while the lower slopes are densely covered with chaparral of scrub oak, manzanita, and mountain mahogany. Creeks and springs of pure cold water are found in the gulches and rarely extend down into the chaparral. Although the natural features of these mountains have protected the deer to a great extent, a few persistent hunters could easily exterminate them.

Food habits.—The stomach of the doe collected in the Mongollon Mountains October 20 was full of green leaves but without a trace of grass or acorns. Among the unchewed leaves in the paunch were recognized those of vetch, thermopsis, strawberry, geranium, aspen, two species of Senecio, and some lichens. The lower, or true, stomach was filled with finely masticated vegetable pulp in which nothing could be identified.

In the paunch of another young buck collected in the Mogollon Mountains in August only leaves and seed pods of hosackia were identified. The bulk of the contents was made up of various herbaceous plants that could not be recognized, but there was evidently no trace of grass in it.

The paunch of a 3-year-old buck collected in the Animas Mountains in August was filled mainly with twigs, leaves, and seeds of the abundant mountain mahogany (*Cercocarpus ledifolius*) so slightly masticated that stems, fruit, and uncut leaves were easily identified. There were also a few stems and leaves of geranium and other plants that could not be recognized but no trace of grass.

Better protection needed.—In September, 1915, J. S. Ligon reported Sonora deer still common in parts of the Mogollon Mountains, but much less so than formerly, owing to unrestricted hunting in season and out. On December 31, he wrote: "The number of deer killed in New Mexico during the season just closed far outnumbers the increase for the year, I am quite sure." These mountains now form the principal range of this species in New Mexico, but as the country fills up with settlers the deer will entirely disappear unless given better protection than they have received in the past. The sentiment among the ranchmen of the region is generally in favor of game protection, but in these remote sections it is difficult to enforce the laws. The many game refuges in these mountains will now doubtless insure the perpetuity of this interesting little deer, as well as the mule deer, Merriam's turkey, and Mearns's quail.

ODOCOILEUS CROOKI (Mearns)

Crook's Black-tailed Deer

Dorcelaphus crooki Mearns, U. S. Natl. Mus. Proc. 20: 468, 1897 (p. 2 of advance sheet, 1897).

Type.—Collected at summit of Dog Mountains, Grant County, N. Mex., June 9, 1892, by E. A. Mearns and F. X. Holzner.

General characters.—Mearns described this remarkable deer from a specimen that he collected on Dog Mountains near the international boundary line June 9, 1892. His type in the National Museum consists of a perfect skull of an adult doe, accompanied by the skin of its head and neck and a section of the back, the complete tail, and both hind legs up to the heel. Besides the type of this species, Mearns refers to a specimen from Bill Williams Mountain, Ariz., which he considers the same.

In his original description and the very full account of the species in his Mammals of the Mexican Boundary (1907), Mearns considered Crook's black-tailed deer a relative of the Columbia blacktail, which it strongly resembles. It occurs, however, in a region a thousand miles from the known range of the Columbia blacktail. Since Mearns's description was published the Biological Survey has carried on field work for several seasons in the country around the type locality, and frequent inquiry as to the occurrence of such a deer has failed to elicit any information in regard to it. The two well-known species of deer—the gray mule deer and the little Sonora whitetail—are common in these adjoining mountains. Every hunter and ranchman knows them well, and would be quick to recognize a form so strikingly different as Crook's blacktail. The only conclusion to be drawn is that this deer is either an extremely rare species or that the type is a hybrid between the gray mule deer and the little whitetail, and the characters fully justify the latter conclusion. The tail, which is the most striking external characteristic, is fully black above and white below, and is better haired and more bushy than in the mule deer and less so than in the little whitetail; it is also naked on the underside near the base for a greater distance than in the whitetail, but much less than in the mule deer. The metatarsal glands on the hind legs are also in size and position a fair average between the little low-down gland on the whitetail and the large high-up gland of the mule deer. They are about 2 inches in length, situated halfway from the dewclaw to the point of the heel. The full summer pelage of the type taken June 9 is somewhat unique, being a brownish gray, which is perhaps a good compromise between the bright tawny summer coat of the mule deer and the permanently gray coat of the adult little whitetail.

In skull and dental characters the compromise is equally perfect. This is seen most strongly in the long and somewhat narrow nasal bones, the medium depth of the lachrymal pit, the medium long and narrow symphysis of the lower mandibles, and the light and narrow molariform teeth. While most of these characters are shared to some extent with the Columbia blacktail, there are ample differences on which to separate it from that species. The lachrymal pit in *Columbianus* is almost as deep as in the mule deer and the nasals as short or shorter and equally wide and flat. The body color differs considerably also, and if *crooki* belonged to that group it should be considered a well-marked form. The fact that mule deer and white-tailed deer hybridize when without mates of their own species has been fully proved. A mounted specimen of spotted fawn in the United States National Museum collection was raised in the National Zoological Park from a mule deer and a Virginia whitetail. When only a few months old it showed the perfect compromise in relative size and position of metatarsal glands and had the medium long tail with wholly dark upper surface.

Measurements.—Type of *crooki* (adult female) : Total length, 1,440; tail, 195; foot, 400; ear from crown, 220 millimeters.

J. W. Griggs, of Goodell, Iowa, has successfully crossed these deer for many years and found the offspring hardy and fertile (Griggs, 1909). While hybrids are rare among unrestrained wild animals, it is not improbable that a pair of these two species of deer may have been stranded on some isolated peak or range during the rutting season and that a hybrid resulted. This seems the most probable explanation of a very puzzling specimen.

CERVUS CANADENSIS Erxleben

American Elk ; [10] Wapiti ; Tu una of the Taos Indians

[*Cervus elaphus*] *canadensis* Erxleben, Syst. Regni Anim. 1 : 305, 1777.

Type locality.—Eastern Canada.

General characters.—Next to the moose the largest of North American deer, with heavy and annually deciduous antlers, tail a mere rudiment, colors dark brown and buff with a buffy or whitish rump patch.

---

[10] To avoid confusion it seems necessary continually to reiterate that the American elk, or wapiti (Cervus), corresponds to the Old World stag, or red deer, while the American moose (Alces) corresponds to the Old World elk.

Distribution and habitat.—There is probably no museum specimen of the elk from northern New Mexico, but from its continuous range with the Colorado elk it may be safely considered the same form as that extending down through the Rocky Mountains from Montana and formerly reaching its southern limit in the Sangre de Cristo and Jemez Mountains approximately on a parallel with Las Vegas and Santa Fe. (Fig. 5.) There is slight probability that wild individuals of the native elk are still to be found in the mountains of New Mexico, but if they are it is probably in the San Juan and Sangre de Cristo Mountains just below the Colorado line. If not, the natural restocking of these wild and rugged mountains is entirely possible through adequate protection of the animals on both sides of the line and the natural increase and overflow of the present Colorado herds.

In 1902 Dall De Weese, of Canon City, Colo., in mapping the range of elk in Colorado, indicated their presence down to the New

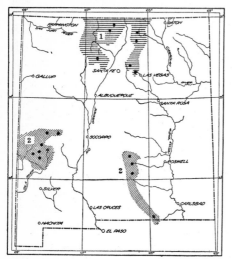

Mexico line in the San Juan Mountains, but in 1906 in crossing this range a little farther south the writer could find no signs of elk, although much of the country is ideal for them and they were reported by Pike as abundant in 1807 (Coues, 1895, p. 597) and by Cope as not uncommon here in 1874 (Cope, 1875).

In 1892 C. H. Fitch, of the United States Geological Survey, reported elk in the "Tierra Amarilla Mountains" (the San Juan), east of Tierra Amarilla.

In September, 1909, Harry C. Hall, acting supervisor of the Carson

FIGURE 5.—Original distribution of elk in New Mexico: 1, *Cervus canadensis;* 2, *C. merriami*

National Forest, reported two bull elk seen by forest rangers in the San Juan Mountains southeast of Tierra Amarilla.[11]

In 1906, the writer saw a fair-sized elk horn in a good state of preservation on the fence at a Mexican ranch near Jemez Hot Springs, and was told that it was picked up on Cebolla Creek in the central part of the Jemez Mountains. He could get no records of elk in the Jemez Mountains in recent years, but has no doubt that they once covered these mountains, which are in close connection with the San Juan Range.

In 1880 L. L. Dyche jumped a fine old bull elk in the mountains west of Las Vegas, near the head of Gallinas Creek, but on his hunt-

---

[11] Report transmitted by the Forest Service to the Biological Survey, accompanied by map showing locality.

ing trips in these mountains in the three subsequent years he found no trace of elk except occasionally old bleached horns. (Edwords, 1893, and letter from Professor Dyche of Feb. 10, 1911.)

E. W. Nelson, who in 1883 was staying near the head of the Pecos River, says that a few elk were reported in the mountains about there at that time.

While in these mountains in 1903, the writer could get only indefinite rumors that elk once were there, as apparently none had been heard of for many years. Farther north in the mountains northeast of Taos he was told by several reliable persons of an elk killed by a hunter in 1902. Still farther north in this range in 1904 he saw a fine large elk horn hanging on the Anchor mine just south of Comanche Creek. It was well bleached and probably 6 or 8 years old, but he was told that elk had been killed in these mountains only two or three years before.

On June 24, 1911, Thomas P. Gable, then Territorial game and fish warden of New Mexico, wrote to the Biological Survey that he had recently purchased from J. B. Dawson, of Routt County, Colo., 12 elk, including 9 cows and 3 bulls 3 to 4 years old. Four of these were placed in Potato Canyon, 15 miles northwest of Raton, another small herd in Cimarron Canyon, and another in Gallinas Canyon, 12 miles above Las Vegas Hot Springs. At the date of his letter four calves had been born and all were doing well. A year later (June 24, 1912) the succeeding game warden, Trinidad C. de Baca, wrote that he was arranging to place these elk on the Pecos National Forest, but apparently they did not all reach there, as in his 1912–1914 report (de Baca, 1914, p. 23) he mentions the elk planted in May, 1911, on the Uracca ranch having increased to 14, and those planted at the same time on the property controlled by William H. Smith, near Brilliant, having increased to 15. These were all under fence on excellent range and in good condition.

He further says: [12]

In Colfax County the Adams-Bartlett Cattle Co. purchased a few years ago a small band of elk, and in 1914 this had increased to a herd of about 50, which ranged at will in the great fenced pastures of this company.

In the same letter he reported 50 elk shipped from the Yellowstone Park at Gardiner, Mont. Three of these died en route, 6 were placed on the property of Apalonio A. Sena at Park Springs, San Miguel County, and the rest were kept in an inclosure on the Valley ranch at the southern border of the Pecos National Forest until such time as the roads should open so that they could be liberated farther up the valley.

Strong pleas for game refuges, especially for the protection of elk in the Pecos Mountains and other parts of the State, have been repeatedly made, and now there are many big-game refuges in the State of New Mexico. Public-spirited ranchmen are using their private holdings as real and effective game refuges, but there is little encouragement in introducing game to areas where, when it has become abundant and unsuspicious, it may be wiped out of existence.

---

[12] Letter from Trinidad C. de Baca, Mar. 25, 1915.

42

NORTH AMERICAN FAUNA

CERVUS MERRIAMI Nelson

MERRIAM'S ELK; CHYZE'-ZE-SCHA of the Hopi Indians (Mearns)[13]

Cervus merriami Nelson, Bul. Amer. Mus. Nat. Hist. 16: 7, 1902.

Type.—Collected at head of Black River, White Mountains, Ariz., in August, 1886, by E. W. Nelson.

General characters.—Size fully equal to *Cervus canadensis* of the Rocky Mountain region, with skull and horns more massive and horns more erect. Color paler and more reddish.

Distribution and habitat.—Merriam's elk is now probably extinct; certainly it no longer occurs in New Mexico. Forty years ago it was common in the Sacramento, White, and Guadalupe Mountains east of the Rio Grande, in the Mogollon group of mountains west of the Rio Grande, and in the White Mountains of Arizona. (Fig. 5.) There are old records for the Datil and Gallina Mountains of Socorro County and a doubtful record for the Manzano Mountains. To the north there are no more elk records until the Jemez and Pecos River Mountains are reached, where the Colorado elk comes down from the north.

In 1811 Humboldt wrote:

The enormous stag horns which Montesuma showed as curiosities to the companions of Cortez might have come from the deer [elk] of New California. I have seen two found in the monument of Xochicalco which have been preserved in the palace of the viceroy. (Translation.)[14]

Humboldt surmises that these horns may have come from the elk found near Monterey, Calif., of which he speaks, evidently being unaware that a much larger elk was common in the mountains of southern New Mexico whence Montezuma's specimens more probably were obtained.

In 1874 J. A. Allen in publishing some notes on mammals obtained from E. D. Mecham, of Ogden, Utah, who had spent 20 years as a trapper and guide in the Rocky Mountain region, quoted an interesting statement in regard to this elk. (Allen, 1874, p. 65) : " Mr. Mecham has seen them as far south as the Mexican boundary and speaks of having met with droves of 2,000 individuals in southern New Mexico."

In a letter from Blue, Ariz., dated May 26, 1906, D. B. Rudd, assistant forest ranger, wrote to the Forest Service:

In the year 1876 when my father moved to this part of the country the elk were very plentiful and could be found in large bands in the White Mountains and in the Blue Range, more particularly on the head of Black River. As late as 1890 elk could be found but not so plentifully. Since the year 1895 I can not find that any have been seen. Whether they were killed or whether the coming of cattle and sheep into their range caused them to leave might be a question.[15]

In a letter from Nutriosa, Ariz., dated May 25, 1906, G. B. Chapin, deputy forest ranger, wrote to the Forest Service:

While patrolling on a mesa between Black River and the higher plateau of of the Blue Range about two years ago I discovered bedding signs, then probably one year old, of a small band of elk. I also found a pair of antlers which I placed in a tree for protection from damage by fire or otherwise. The exact

[13] Mearns, 1907, p. 219.
[14] Cortez captured the city of Mexico in 1521 ; Humboldt lived there in 1803-4.
[15] From copy of letter transmitted to the Biological Survey by the Forest Service.

place as near as I can remember is on a little mesa facing a canyon known locally as Conklins Draw, between Fish Creek and Bear Wallow, about a mile east of Black River. I was told by James Warren, now deceased, of a band of elk ranging high up in the White Mountains on the southern slope of Baldy about four years ago. It would be possible for a remnant of elk to still be there.

In 1873 H. W. Henshaw, on a hurried trip into the Mogollon Mountains on the headwaters of the Gila, found tracks of elk but failed to find the animals.

In 1882 E. W. Nelson heard of elk from some prospectors at Chloride, N. Mex., who told him that they inhabited the Mogollon Mountains near the extreme headwaters of the Gila River. In 1884 he saw a doe and two young buck elk hanging at a hunter's camp in the mountains 10 miles east of Frisco, and was told that a good-sized band was then ranging on the head of Negrito Creek. Two years later he collected specimens in the White Mountains of Arizona, from which he eventually described the species.

In a letter transmitted by the Forest Service, June 12, 1906, Forest Ranger John Mundy, who has long been familiar with the Mogollon Mountains, said:

> To the best of my knowledge the elk is now extinct in the Mogollon Mountains, as I do not know of any being seen since the year 1888. Up to that time the elk were plentiful. In the winter of 1885 I was given a piece of bull elk killed by Phil Long, of Negrito. During that year there were three of these animals killed near Elk Mountains. At that time elk horns were scattered all over the country. Two elk were killed in the Elk Mountains in 1888 by some cowboys, and this is the last account I have of them.

A Mr. Delgar, living at Joseph, in 1906 told the writer that tracks of three elk were followed from the Tularosa Mountains to the Elk Mountains in 1883, but he had not known of a live elk in the country since. Their horns were common in the Tularosa Mountains in those days. In 1890 Spence Hill, who then owned the Gila Hot Springs, killed a cow elk and a bull elk in the Mogollons. The mounted head of the bull, which was said to be unusually large and perfect, was kept for several years in Silver City and then sent to Mr. Hill's father at Coffeyville, Kans., but the writer has not been able to locate it.

H. H. Hotchkiss, who came to the Mogollons in 1892 and has hunted and prospected there ever since, saw a fine bull elk on Lily Mountain, north of the main peaks of the Mogollons, in 1894, and says that later in the same year ranchmen reported tracks of three elk in the mountains. This seems to be the last trace of a live elk in the Mogollon Mountains, but old horns and bones were found in 1906 on the head of the Gila.

In the Mimbres Range it has not been possible to get a trace of even old elk horns from residents who have ridden the range there since 1886. In the Datil Mountains in 1905 Hollister was told by several ranchmen of old elk horns found there, but none of the oldest inhabitants remembered when elk were there. In the Bear Spring and Indian Spring Mountain country he was also told by ranchmen who had lived there more than 20 years that they had never known any elk there, but that in the early days horns in a state of good preservation were found. These mountains probably formed the northern border of the range of the species, as careful inquiry among the residents of the Zuni and Mount Taylor Ranges produces no record of even an old antler.

In 1903 Gaut heard from a ranchman living high up in the northern part of the Manzano Mountains that a fine old bull elk had been seen near his house in the fall of about 1901, but as this is the only record obtained from these mountains it was probably a very large mule deer, as Gaut suggested. Still it is possible that a stray elk from the White or Sacramento Mountains may have wandered up there after the last recorded appearance in those ranges.

In 1900 M. H. Webb, of El Paso, Tex., told Doctor Nelson that elk were formerly very numerous in the Sacramento Mountains, but had been practically exterminated. Two were killed in the fall of 1898, and in the fall of 1899 the track of a solitary individual was seen.

In 1902 while in these mountains the writer could get no records of elk killed or even seen later than 1893. Old elk horns (pl. 3, A) and parts of skulls were seen at a number of ranches throughout the mountains, and several fragments saved indicate that this was also Merriam's elk. So far as known, no complete specimen, nor even a mounted head of this elk is in existence from any point in New Mexico, although there are a few old horns and part of a skull from near Ruidoso, and horns have been seen at ranches east of Cloudcroft and in the Mogollon Mountains.

A set of the characteristic heavy horns of this elk for many years adorned the walls of the Cosmos Club in Washington, D. C., but the skin of the head on which they were mounted was from a Wyoming elk. The history of this head, which has since been placed in the National Museum collection, was furnished by C. H. Fitch, of the Reclamation Service, in 1911. The elk was killed in the Sacramento Mountains, N. Mex., and the horns, in the spring of 1881, were given to J. W. Sansem, who then had a store at Seven Rivers. Sansem gave them to Fitch on condition that they should be brought to Washington, which they were, by salt wagon to Roswell, burro pack to Santa Fe, and express to Washington. Mr. Fitch first saw them in May, 1881, and was told that the elk had been killed a short time before. He said that they were joined together by the top of the skull and weighed 46 pounds. Further detail concerning the horns was received from Sansem, who wrote on April 30, 1911, that when he first went to New Mexico in 1880 the settlers told him that there had been hundreds of elk in the Sacramento Mountains, but that not more than 20 were left. The horns in question, he stated, were given him by a stage driver, Billy Wilson, and came from a large bull killed between the Hondo and Sacramento Rivers, near the White Mountains, at about 7,000 feet altitude.

Examination of this specimen, now in the National Museum, shows that by the removal of the skin from the head and the basal portion of the skull three good measurements are afforded for comparison: Post-orbital breadth of skull, 171 millimeters; mastoid breadth, 176; diameter of brain case back of horns, 120. In the type skull of *Cervus merriami* these measurements are 160, 170, 115 millimeters, respectively. The horns measure, chord of curve from butt to tip: Right horn, 1,270 millimeters (50 inches); left, 1,170 millimeters (46 inches); over outer curve, right, 1,663 millimeters (65.5 inches); left, the same; inner brow tine from butt to tip, right, 407 millimeters (16 inches); left, 381 millimeters (15 inches); circumference of beam above brow prongs, right, 197 millimeters (7.75 inches); left, 193 millimeters (7.7 inches). Plate 3, B, shows how long and nearly upright these horns are.

Order LAGOMORPHA: Rabbits and Rabbitlike Animals

Family LEPORIDAE: Rabbits and Hares

LEPUS AMERICANUS BAIRDI HAYDEN

ROCKY MOUNTAIN SNOWSHOE RABBIT; Qua-ma-pe-wena of the Taos Indians

Lepus bairdii Hayden, Amer. Nat. 3: 115, 1869.

Type.—Collected in the Wind River Mountains, Wyo., June 2, 1860, by F. V. Hayden.

General characters.—A medium-sized mountain rabbit, larger than the cottontail and smaller than the jack rabbits, with medium-long ears and very large and hairy hind feet. Body brown in summer and feet and belly white; in winter pure white all over except the dark tips of ears.

Measurements (average).—Total length, 459; tail, 39; hind foot, 146 millimeters.

Distribution and habitat.—The Rocky Mountain snowshoe rabbits extend into northern New Mexico along the Sangre de Cristo Range on the high ridges along both sides of the Pecos River to about the latitude of Santa Fe and Las Vegas and down the San Juan and Jemez Ranges west of the Rio Grande. This is the extreme southern limit of range of a species that occupies an extensive area in the Rocky Mountain region and belongs to a still more widely distributed group of boreal rabbits. While mainly a Canadian Zone species, *bairdi* extends into the Hudsonian Zone nearly to timber line. In the Sacramento Mountains near Cloudcroft a rabbit was described that was said to turn white in winter, but in doing considerable work throughout this range the writer found no signs or other evidence of the presence of snowshoe rabbits and so considers the record as very doubtful. In the Pecos River Mountains their characteristic pellets and winter trails were found throughout the woods from the cold gulches at 8,000 feet along the upper Pecos up to the last timbered patches around the bases of the Pecos and Truchas Peaks.

One specimen in the brown coat was taken in July at a 11,000-foot camp on Jack Creek, and a few others were seen, but their habit of hiding in the thickets and dense coniferous forests, where their protectively colored brown summer coats render them inconspicuous, makes it difficult to collect specimens during the summer months. In the Taos Mountains they were common throughout the Canadian and into the Hudsonian Zone, but were rarely seen. In the Culebra Mountains a half-grown specimen was taken in August near the Anchor mine on Bitter Creek at about 10,000 feet altitude, and abundant evidence of their presence was seen throughout the range. Over the top of the San Juan Range between Hopewell and Tierra Amarilla, their unmistakable signs were seen in abundance throughout the spruce timber of the Canadian Zone. At Chama, J. A. Loring collected one on December 28, which was then pure white, although in October of the same year across the Colorado line near Silverton he had found them in the midst of the change from brown summer to the white winter coats. Over the top of the Gallinas Mountains in Rio Arriba County snowshoe-rabbit signs were abundant up to 10,000 feet, while a little farther south in the Jemez Mountains their characteristic pellets were found scattered through the deep forests of spruce and fir at 10,000 to 11,000 feet altitude where no other species of rabbit ever penetrates.

General habits.—These mountain-forest rabbits are largely nocturnal and when found during the daytime are generally startled from a form or resting place under some dense shrubbery or fallen timber. They can see perfectly well in the light, however, and are very shy and often difficult to approach after once being startled. Sometimes they are seen hopping along the edge of the timber early in the evening, but apparently their greatest activity is during the nighttime. After a light snow their tracks may be seen both in the timber and in brush patches, often indicating rapid flight and long leaps, and again marking a network of short hops among the bushes and small plants on which they are feeding.

Food habits.—The contents of their stomachs always show a finely masticated mass of vegetation. In the summer this is apt to be mainly soft green plants, but during winter and early in spring more woody fiber is included. The large flattened pellets nearly a half inch in diameter are found scattered along their runways and feeding grounds often in great abundance. These are compact and woody during winter, but in summer are often green, less definitely formed, and less compact, showing that the principal diet has been herbaceous vegetation. On their winter feeding grounds the cleanly cut twigs and stems of blueberry, rose, willow, and other bushes give some clue to the food selected. The bushes are usually cut at the surface of the snow; the height of the stumps indicates the depth of snow at the time. Those cut from the bare ground generally stand 4 or 5 inches high, but others cut from the surface of the snow often stand 2 or 3 feet from the ground. As the snow deepens or disappears the rabbits find a constantly changing level of twigs and an ever abundant food supply. Though never very fat, they are usually plump and often show two lines of white tallow along the back between the shoulder blades.

Breeding habits.—The normal number of mammae in adult females seems to be two pairs of abdominal and two of pectoral. The number of embryos in the few examined have been from 3 to 5, and there are records of 4 to 6 young, born in May and June. When first born they are well-furred, perfect little rabbits, with wide-open eyes, sharp incisor teeth and a soft woodsy color that would baffle the keen-eyed fox or lynx.

Economic status.—The fact that these rabbits nowhere live in agricultural regions has rendered them a measure of protection. In the coniferous forests their food consists entirely of deciduous shrubs or low vegetation, so that practically no harm can be attributed to them, either to forestry or to grazing. As a game animal they have considerable value, as they are among the best game and food rabbits of the country. To be successfully hunted they are often driven by dogs from one thicket or timber tract to another and shot as they cross the open spaces. They are extremely swift and afford good sport, and when properly cooked their meat is superior to that of most rabbits.

LEPUS TOWNSENDII CAMPANIUS Hollister

WHITE-TAILED JACK RABBIT, KA-PA-TUNA of the Taos Indians

Lepus campestris Bachman, Jour. Acad. Nat. Sci. Phila. (1) 7: 349, 1837.
Lepus townsendii campanius Hollister, Biol. Soc. Wash. Proc. 28: 70, March 12, 1915.

Type locality.—Plains of Saskatchewan, Canada.
General characters.—Readily distinguished from other hares by size of body and the large tail, which is pure white at all seasons; by the buffy gray upper parts in summer; and by the pure white coat in winter. The body is as heavy but the ears and legs are not so long as in the group of black-tailed jack rabbits.

Measurements.—Adults (approximately): Total length, 605; tail, 92; hind foot, 149; ear from notch, 95 millimeters.

Weight, 7 to 8 pounds.

Distribution and habitat.—A specimen of the white-tailed jack rabbit was collected on top of the San Juan Mountains west of Hopewell at about 10,000 feet altitude, and a few others were seen in that vicinity in the big, open parks over the top of the mountains. (Fig. 6.) Just north of Taos one was seen near camp at the edge of Hondo Valley, and the Indians said they were common in the valley near Taos. So far as known these are the only records

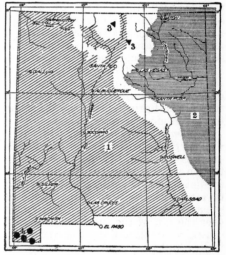

FIGURE 6.—Distribution of jack rabbits in New Mexico: 1, *Lepus californicus texianus;* 2, *L. californicus melanotis;* 3, *L. townsendii campanius;* 4, *L. gaillardi gaillardi*

for the State, but the rabbits are common in the San Luis Valley a little farther north and in Colorado east of the mountains, so that it is probable that they occur also in northeastern New Mexico.

General habits.—These large hares are preeminently prairie or plains animals, living always in the open, where their speed and keen sight and hearing protect them from most of their enemies. The greyhound will pull one down in a fair race and the golden eagle has them at a disadvantage, and sometimes forces them to take shelter in burrows. As one bounds out of the grass with striking white markings and long, high leaps its appearance is almost as spectacular as that of the antelope bounding over the prairie. Sometimes they will lie close until almost stepped upon, but generally they are very timid and wary. They are generally free from parasites or diseases and are considered good game and often sold in the markets.

In winter their fur becomes long and full and turns pure white, except the very tips of the ears, which are usually edged with black. The hairs on the feet become so long that they afford almost as good support on the deep snows as do the feet of snowshoe rabbits. On a firm snow or a slight crust they skim over the surface with great speed and evident enjoyment of their advantage over heavier enemies, while they gather their food from the tops of bushes and plants that stand above the surface.

Food habits.—During the summer the food of these jack rabbits consists of grass and a great variety of herbaceous plants and also such cultivated crops as they encounter. In winter it is largely buds, bark, and twigs of the prairie shrubs or any woody vegetation above the surface of the snow.

Breeding habits.—The white-tailed jack rabbits are less prolific than the jack rabbits of the low warm valleys, as they have a shorter season in which to reproduce their kind. The first litter of four or five young is generally born in May, and there may be later litters, as half-grown and small young are found up to the latter part of summer. The mammae are arranged in two pairs of abdominal and two pairs of pectoral, and a very copious supply of milk is supplied to the young. At first these are well secreted in some grass-covered form, slight depression, or shallow burrow, but before they are half grown they are out foraging for themselves and are able to outrun most of their enemies.

Economic status.—These rabbits are so well appreciated as a game animal that there are few complaints of any mischief or loss of crops from them. In most cases they need a certain degree of protection and encouragement to maintain themselves as a game and food animal. In rare cases, however, they become so abundant locally as to cause some loss to crops and even to winter haystacks. The greatest harm they do is to young orchards in winter when they skip over the top of the snow and nip off the twigs that rise above the crust. Under most circumstances their abundance is easily controlled and their depredations may be prevented by a little timely hunting.

LEPUS CALIFORNICUS TEXIANUS Waterhouse

Texas Jack Rabbit, Kah-tua-pua-na-ana of the Taos Indians

Lepus texianus Waterhouse, Nat. Hist. Mamm. 2: 136, 1848.

Type locality.—Unknown, but probably western Texas.

General characters.—This is the large, light gray jack rabbit with black upper surface of tail and black tips of ears. There is little difference in color between the summer and winter specimens, except that each coat fades to a lighter, clearer gray with age and the rabbit is palest just before renewing the fresh and somewhat darker summer and winter coats.

Measurements.—Adults average in total length, 606; tail, 85; hind foot, 133; ear from base of opening to tip in dried skins, 123 millimeters. The usual weight of adults when freshly killed is from 6 to 7 pounds.

Distribution and habitat.—The most abundant and widely distributed jack rabbit of New Mexico is *texianus*, occupying both the Lower and the Upper Sonoran Zones of practically the whole State west of and including a part of the Pecos Valley. (Fig. 6.) Along the Pecos Valley it grades into the darker, brownish gray *melanotis*, while in the southwestern part of New Mexico individuals show a slight gradation toward *eremicus* of the deserts of Arizona. While the range of the species is mainly Sonoran, individuals are occasionally found up in the open yellow-pine forests of the Transition Zone where they have strayed from their regular range. On the south slope of the Elk Mountains the writer shot a nursing female in the yellow pine woods at 8,700 feet altitude, but a run of 2 or 3 miles through open forest would have taken it down to its ordinary zone level.

These rabbits are common and at times numerous in the valleys and on the slopes and mesas below the 7,000-foot contour over more than the western half of New Mexico. Though often found among the scattered junipers and nut pines, they are generally more common in the open valleys among the various shrubs known as rabbit brush. Their distribution area remains the same, but their local abundance fluctuates from various causes. In time of drought they gather in sections where there is more moisture and a better supply of green vegetation, often becoming very numerous in certain valleys that have received enough rainfall to produce green vegetation while the surrounding country is parched and dry. Thus they are often abundant in one valley, scarce in another, and almost absent from a third. At times their numbers steadily increase until beyond the normal proportions, and again through the attack of some disease they are so thinned out that not a rabbit will be seen in an all-day's ride over the valleys. Normally, however, they are fairly abundant over the whole of their range.

General habits.—These rabbits perhaps supply the most conspicuous and characteristic animal life of the desert valleys. They are often most abundant where there is no possibility of getting water within a long distance and seem to be entirely independent of moisture, other than that obtained through their food plants. Though in part nocturnal, they also move about with perfect freedom in the daytime, and are specially active during the morning and evening hours. During the middle of the day they are usually seen only when started from their forms or concealed resting places in the grass or low vegetation. In hot weather they make their forms in the shade of bushes or cactus, or sit in the shade of some tree or fence post to avoid the heat and glare of the direct sunlight. If well concealed in their forms they will often lie until almost stepped on, and then bound away with long leaps and run with great speed. Often, however, they sit crouched in the half open, where they can not only be plainly seen but can see any approaching enemy and make good their escape. In riding through some of the valleys one can almost constantly see them, one after another springing up and bounding away from the sides of the road, sometimes a dozen running at a time.

In a 100-mile drive from Deming to Hachita and across into Animas Valley during August of 1908, the writer had an unusually good opportunity to observe the jack rabbits on some of their favorite grounds. In places they were numerous and again for a distance scarce. Their abundance depended largely on the distribution of the recent rains. They had left the dry and barren valleys and slopes that the rains had missed and gathered in great numbers in other sections that the heavy rains had visited. On some of the dry upper slopes across the range they were scarce and had evidently drifted into the areas of good feed. Along the east side of the Playas Valley, where a heavy rain had brought up an abundance of fresh grass and succulent vegetation, they were especially numerous, a dozen often being in sight at once along the road and many hopping into camp among the mesquites in the evening.

Food habits.—The food of these Texas jack rabbits includes a great variety of plants, but certain species are evident favorites. Alfalfa seems to attract them more than almost any other kind of food, while of the native plants they seem to prefer succulent young vegetation. Much grass is eaten, but as the grass becomes old and dry they seem to prefer many of the herbaceous plants, and in times of drought they feed largely upon cactus and the bark of mesquite and other desert shrubs. In winter their food consists largely of cactus, bark, and twigs. The pads of the large pricklypear (Opuntia) are first nibbled along the edges between the bunches of spines, but sometimes the whole pad is finally eaten, and often in times of scarcity the whole cactus plant is devoured, leaving only the bunches of thorns and the woody base. The bush cactuses (Cylindropuntia) are only attacked in times of great scarcity, but then are sometimes entirely peeled of their bark as high as the rabbits can reach, whole groves of them occasionally being killed in this manner. Many of the desert bushes, however, are so protected by thorns or other means that they are practically free from the attacks of rabbits. The leaves of some of the yuccas and agaves are occasionally found gnawed, but usually they are so well protected that the inner, fleshy parts can not be reached. For most domestic crops and fruit trees the jack rabbits show great fondness, and in farming areas they become a great pest unless kept well under control.

Breeding habits.—The Texas jack rabbits are very prolific and apparently raise several litters of young during the year. There seems to be a definite spring litter born in April or May. By the first of June many of the young are half grown, and later in the summer small young are often found or else the females are found to contain embryos or to be nursing young. As late as September 28 specimens of old females have been collected that were at the time nursing young, but the number of litters raised in a season is not definitely known and probably varies greatly with local conditions. The number of young in a litter varies from two to four, but in some cases it may be as high as six. The mammae are arranged in 3 pairs, 2 pairs of abdominal and 1 pair of pectoral, and the two long mammary glands are practically continuous along the sides of the belly.

Economic status.—In June, 1918, after two years of severe drought, J. S. Ligon found these rabbits unusually numerous in the Pecos Valley from Fort Sumner south for 160 miles into Texas. They apparently were more numerous there than in any other part of the Southwest and more numerous than he had ever known them there before. After careful observation he estimated an average of 400 to the square mile over several hundred square miles of the valley. After a light shower where green vegetation had started on low ground, great numbers could be seen feeding at any time during the day. They were of all ages, and one rabbit two-thirds grown ran across the road ahead of the automobile and disappeared in a large burrow in a prairie-dog town. Ligon was told that during the previous winter many had been killed and shipped to market from this valley at a good profit. In moderate numbers these jack rabbits are of some value as game animals, although not generally used as food among the ranch people. Many are infested with "warbles," or Cuterebra, the larvae of a fly, and also with tapeworm larvae, which appear under the skin in watery cysts. Neither of these parasites seriously affects the health of the rabbits unless unusually numerous, but they prejudice people against using the rabbits as food. To the Indians, as well as many other people in the State, the jack rabbits are a great source of food supply and in this way have a practical value. To anyone fond of shooting, when the rabbits are not too numerous, they offer excellent sport either with shotgun or rifle, and their flesh, if properly cooked, is fairly good. The half-grown young of the year are especially good and usually free from parasitic infestations.[16]

On the other hand, the damage that the rabbits do in an agricultural area is often so great as to render them one of the most serious of animal pests. On the stock range the grass and forage that they consume is often of serious consequence in limiting the number of domestic stock that can be maintained on the area. It has been estimated that 11 jack rabbits will eat as much green forage a day as one sheep, and allowing one rabbit to 2 acres, which is not an unusual local abundance, the rabbits on a 1,000-acre ranch would consume as much grass as about 50 sheep. To be sure, they do not live entirely upon grass, but a large part of their forage is such as would be eaten by sheep or cattle, and a large number of them on the stock ranch prove a serious drain upon its carrying power. In cultivated areas their depredations are often of a serious nature, especially where fields of alfalfa or grain are surrounded by extensive desert areas, as they gather from all sides for the green food. At Carlsbad, Dearborn found them doing considerable damage to melons and melon vines in August, 1910, and reported them also as destructive to young orchards in winter. At Garfield E. A. Goldman found them feeding in the alfalfa fields and found their stomachs full of the green alfalfa. At Mesilla Park in November, 1908, in company with Fabian Garcia, the writer examined a young orchard of apple and pear trees that had been set out on the experiment station grounds and found many of the trees peeled or cut off by the jack rabbits. A considerable number of trees had been injured, although the tracks did not indicate that there were many rabbits doing the mischief. Pieces of sweet apple with a little strychnine in each were placed on sharp sticks 4 inches above ground near some of the trees where the rabbits were working, and later Garcia wrote that he had picked up three dead rabbits in the orchard.

---

[16] At times of greatest abundance of wild rabbits a destructive disease called tularemia carries off great numbers of them. This is also dangerous and occasionally fatal to human beings when acquired through careless handling of infected rabbits. The disease may be conveyed by contact of the rabbit blood or body juices with the hands or skin, and also by the bites of ticks or flies that have been in contact with diseased rabbits. Experiments have shown that the germs of tularemia are not destroyed in lightly cooked or rare meat, but well-cooked rabbit meat may be safely eaten.

To make sure of protecting his trees, he had them wrapped with paper and they suffered no further injury during the winter.

In most cases where the rabbits are doing damage to crops they can be shot or their numbers otherwise controlled so as to prevent serious loss. Under ordinary circumstances their natural enemies—coyotes, foxes, eagles, owls, and hawks—keep them down to a reasonable abundance, but it so often becomes necessary for man to take a hand in their suppression that effective methods have been worked out for their control.

LEPUS CALIFORNICUS MELANOTIS Mearns

PLAINS JACK RABBIT

Lepus melanotis Mearns, Bul. Amer. Mus. Nat. Hist. 2:297, 1890.

Type.—Collected at Independence, Montgomery County, Kans., January 27, 1890, by E. A. Mearns.

General characters.—Distinguished from the clear gray *texianus* by its more brownish coloration. The upper parts are mainly of a light buffy-brown color; the black tail and tips of ears are conspicuous marks; and in size it is almost as large as *texianus*. The average length of adults is 582; tail, 80; hind foot, 131; and ear from basal notch in dried specimens, 104 millimeters.

Distribution and habitat.—The Plains jack rabbit is found in the Great Plains country, including the northeastern part of New Mexico east of the Rocky Mountains and Pecos River Valley. (Fig. 6.) Specimens from Clayton and Santa Rosa were referred by Nelson in his monograph of the rabbits (1909, p. 148), to this subspecies, while those from Roswell and Carlsbad were placed with the grayer *texianus*, but most of the specimens of the Pecos Valley are more or less intermediate between the two.

General habits.—In habits these Plains rabbits do not differ essentially from their near relative, *texianus*, except in adaptation to a different type of environment. Instead of living in the desert they occupy the grassy plains where for cover they have mainly grass, which gives a setting of more uniform green in summer and more of the yellow-brown tones in winter, in strong contrast to the light-gray tones of the desert. The darker colors of their environment are well paralleled by the darker tones of their own coloration. The Plains jack rabbits are generally less numerous than the desert jack rabbits, although at times they become very abundant and in places do considerable mischief. In this open country they are usually shyer than in the brushy regions. The speed with which one bounds from the grass and out of range makes quick work necessary for the collector with a shotgun, while with rifles they are excellent targets either for running or standing shots. In places where they are in the habit of following the same line of travel their runways are conspicuous through the grass and low vegetation, and in a good rabbit year these runways often show as well-defined crisscross lines over the prairie.

Food habits.—The food of the Plains jack rabbits consists not only of grass but any green vegetation of an edible nature that happens to come within their reach. They are also fond of most cultivated crops, including clover, alfalfa, grains, and vegetables, and will travel for a considerable distance to obtain a supply of these favorite foods.

Breeding habits.—Little is known of their breeding habits, but the young are out and often half grown early in May, and young of various sizes may be found throughout the summer and up to late autumn. Evidently several litters are raised during a season, but there are not sufficient data to show the average size of the litter. The mammae of adult females are arranged in two pairs of abdominal and one pair of pectoral. Three or four embryos have been noted in females, and it seems probable from the number of mammae that six is a possible maximum number of young.

Economic status.—In normal abundance these jack rabbits are a good game animal and are kept within harmless bounds by hunting and through check by natural enemies, but when they increase to unusual abundance they present a problem of some economic importance. In grainfields they do considerable damage, both in cutting down and eating the growing grain and in tangling the stems as they run through the fields, so that some of the grain is lost in reaping. In gardens and vegetable fields they attack almost all the crops, but are especially fond of cabbage, turnips, peas, and melons. They are also quick to find any young fruit trees that are planted, and when green food is scarce they are apt to cut or eat the bark from young trees. At times it has been necessary to organize rabbit drives or hunts to dispose of the surplus numbers.

LEPUS GAILLARDI GAILLARDI Mearns

GAILLARD'S JACK RABBIT

Lepus gaillardi Mearns, U. S. Natl. Mus. Proc. (1895) 18 : 560–562, June 24, 1896.

Type.—Collected at Mexican boundary line, near Monument 63, west arm of Playas Valley, southwestern New Mexico, June 17, 1892, by E. A. Mearns and F. X. Holzner.

General characters.—Distinguished from *texianus*, with which it is associated, by the strikingly white sides and flanks and by lack of black tips to the long ears. It is also more buffy or fawn colored over the back, while the light-gray rump patch blends into the white sides. The upper surface of the tail is black.

Measurements.—This rabbit is slightly smaller than *texianus*, average adults measuring in total length, 536; tail, 80; hind foot, 132; and ear from notch in dried skins, 109 millimeters.

Distribution and habitat.—Gaillard's jack rabbit is mainly a Mexican species extending into extreme southwestern New Mexico in the Playas and Animas Valleys, mainly in the Upper Sonoran Zone. (Fig. 6.) In the southern end of the Animas and Playas Valleys the ranchmen in 1908 reported white-sided jack rabbits, which they called antelope rabbits, and said they were frequently seen though not so commonly as the other species. The writer did not see any of them, although he was constantly watching for them, and several light-colored individuals of *texianus* were shot on suspicion that they might be *gaillardi*. There can be no doubt, however, of their occurrence and the correctness of the descriptions and reports of the local residents in that part of New Mexico. Mearns (1896, p. 560) records them as found on the east and west forks of the Playas Valley and on the east side of the San Luis Mountains, while, besides the type specimen that he collected, he secured a series of five from White Water just below the international boundary line.

General habits.—In habits there seems to be very little difference between Gaillard's and the common jack rabbit of the region.

Mearns records a female taken at the type locality June 16, 1892, containing three small fetuses and also mentions two half-grown young on the same date. Very little is known of this rare and interesting species, and any further notes on its distribution and habits would be of special interest.

SYLVILAGUS AUDUBONI NEOMEXICANUS Nelson

New Mexico Cottontail

Sylvilagus auduboni neomexicanus Nelson, Biol. Soc. Wash. Proc. 20: 83, 1907.

Type.—Collected at Fort Sumner, N. Mex., September 23, 1902, by James H. Gaut.

General characters.—This is one of the long-eared cottontails of the *auduboni* group, differing from the three other forms of the groups in the State in more brownish coloration of the upper parts.

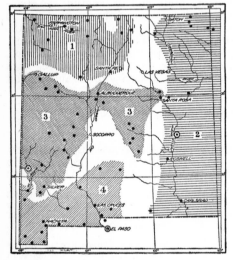

FIGURE 7.—Distribution of cottontail rabbits of the *auduboni* group in New Mexico: 1, *Sylvilagus auduboni warreni*; 2, *S. auduboni neomexicanus*; 3, *S. auduboni cedrophilus*; 4, *S. auduboni minor*. Type locality circled

Measurements.—Adults average for total length, 374; tail, 49; hind foot, 87; ear from notch at base to tip in dried skins, 55 millimeters.

Distribution and habitat.—The New Mexico cottontail occupies the plains country of eastern New Mexico, including most of the Pecos Valley. (Fig. 7.) Specimens from Clayton, Emory Peak, near Tucumcari, Roswell, Carlsbad, and the eastern slope of the Guadalupe Mountains are referred to this form, but do not necessarily mark the extreme western limit of its range. It inhabits the grassy plains country mainly below the border of junipers and nut pines and also the mesquite and creosote valley bottoms along the Pecos and Canadian Rivers. It is common in both the Upper and the Lower Sonoran Zones.

General habits.—Throughout most of their range these rabbits live in the open country, seeming to prefer places where they can see for a long distance, as they depend on flight for escape to some safe retreat. Their favorite haunts are the prairie-dog towns, which are thickly scattered over this plains region. Though they have long legs and make good speed for cottontails, they are no match for the coyotes and foxes and must depend on convenient cover for their protection. This is afforded by the burrows of prairie dogs, badgers, and even the large kangaroo rats, which inhabit their region. When startled the rabbits rush for the nearest cover, and if pressed for time dive into a burrow and disappear in a twinkling. If only moderately frightened they bound away with all speed, but before disappearing below usually sit up and look around to see if there is any real danger. So general is their habit of depending upon burrows for safety that they are commonly called, by the ranchmen, "prairie-dog rabbits," or merely "dog rabbits." Generally they are very wild and difficult to approach, but occasionally an individual will allow one to come close before running away. By whistling and talking softly to one, as it sat near the entrance of an old badger hole, the writer was able to approach and photograph it within 4 feet. Apparently they do not dig burrows for themselves, but are always able to find an abundant supply of unoccupied dens of other burrowing animals. Generally they are not very numerous, but in places over the open prairie where the short grass affords them little concealment they are frequently seen scampering from one burrow to another. Even at a distance when sitting up or running their long ears are conspicuous and readily distinguish them from the members of the *floridanus* group, which occurs farther east and in some of the mountain ranges in western New Mexico; but when they are on guard crouching upon the ground with ears laid low and colors blending into the surroundings, even in this short grassy country, they are inconspicuous and at times almost invisible.

In June, 1918, in the Pecos River Valley from Fort Sumner south, J. S. Ligon found these cottontails about as numerous as the jack rabbits and in greater numbers than he had ever seen them there before. This was after a 2-year severe drought during which the rabbits had apparently suffered no inconvenience or setback in breeding. He found young of all ages, some not yet out of the nest.

Food habits.—The food of the New Mexico cottontails consists of green grass and a great variety of herbaceous plants. They are fond of alfalfa, grain, and most garden vegetables. Occasionally when the snow is on the ground in winter they may be forced to browse upon twigs and bushes, but for most of the year they have ready access to the ground and can find enough green or cured vegetation to keep them well supplied.

Economic status.—In few places has this species been found so abundant as to be in danger of becoming a pest, but among the farms and orchards of the Pecos Valley, where it is comparatively common, there are some complaints of its injuring crops. At Carlsbad in August, 1910, Dearborn found the cottontails rather abundant and destructive to melon vines and young fruit trees, and the writer found them there in previous seasons fairly common in and about the alfalfa fields. They afford some good hunting, however, and in camp during the close season on other game they often provide the only fresh meat supply for long periods. Over most of their range their value as a game animal is probably sufficient to balance any injury they may do to crops, but in areas where they do serious harm they may easily be destroyed by hunting or by other methods of control. They have a host of natural enemies, including coyotes, foxes, badgers, hawks, owls, and eagles, and so long as these are numerous the rabbits have little chance of becoming pests.

SYLVILAGUS AUDUBONI MINOR (Mearns)

LITTLE COTTONTAIL

Lepus arizonae minor Mearns, U. S. Natl. Mus. Proc. (1895) 18: 557–558, 1896.

Type.—Collected at El Paso, Tex., April 28, 1892, by E. A. Mearns and F. X. Holzner.

    General characters.—A small, pale-gray rabbit with very long ears.

    Measurements.—Average adults: Total length, 351; tail, 52; hind foot, 80; ear from notch in dried skin, 59 millimeters.

    Distribution and habitat.—The little gray desert cottontails (pl. 4, A) are found mainly within the Lower Sonoran Zone of the Rio Grande and Tularosa Valleys and over the Deming Plain of south-western New Mexico and southward. (Fig. 7.) In many places they extend into the Upper Sonoran Zone around the edge of the mountains, but in their typical form do not range far beyond the Lower Sonoran. They are a valley species and prefer the open country where there is sufficient cover and protection.

    General habits.—Like all this group, the little cottontails are par-tial to burrows in the ground or to safe retreats among rocks or under ledges, where they can quickly escape from their enemies. Dense cover of weeds, brush, or cactus is accepted, but in most of the open desert country where they live the safest and most convenient retreats are apt to be badger holes or broken rocks at the base of some cliff. Prairie-dog burrows, when available, are often used by them, but over much of their range prairie dogs do not occur. The abun-dance of the species generally depends on the kind of cover that is available. In open situations where there are no badger holes or other burrows the rabbits are almost entirely absent, while in a section of valley infested with ground squirrels that have attracted badgers or in a half-abandoned prairie-dog town they may be swarming. At Deming, E. A. Goldman reported them as common on the surrounding plain, and often entering the small gardens and barnyards in the immediate vicinity of town, while on the east slope of the Big Hatchet Mountains he reported them as especially abundant on the stony lower slopes of the mountains up to 4,800 feet, beyond which they were less numerous, none being found much higher. At Redrock he reported them common in thickets and about fields along the river and in the brush along mesas bordering the valley. On a wagon trip from Deming to Hachita and through the Playas and Animas Valleys in August, 1908, the writer found them common over most of the valley country. Many were found in the open, where they ran to prairie-dog or badger holes, but others were seen in the brushy parts of the valleys, where they took refuge in the weed patches or among the bunches of mesquite and other low bushes. Goldman found them abundant in the Rio Grande Valley at Garfield and farther north along the river, while Gaut collected specimens and reported them as numerous on both sides of the great Tularosa Valley.

    Food habits.—These rabbits subsist upon green grass and a great variety of other vegetation, including in winter the bark and twigs of various shrubs and the juicy flesh of cactus, which they pick out from between the spines of the pricklypear and some other species. They are fond of most cultivated crops and sometimes injure young orchards by gnawing the bark from the trees or cutting off the twigs of newly planted grafts. At Mesilla Park in November, 1908, in one orchard containing 5 or 6 acres of choice young apple trees, they had injured nearly half and actually killed a few of the trees. The rabbits were rather numerous at the time and were doing some damage to vegetables and other crops. They were not being hunted to any extent, however, and little attention was paid to the damage they were doing.

SYLVILAGUS AUDUBONI CEDROPHILUS Nelson

CEDAR-BELT COTTONTAIL

Sylvilagus auduboni cedrophilus Nelson, Biol. Soc. Wash. Proc. 20: 83, 1907.

Type.—Collected at Cactus Flat, 20 miles north of Cliff, N. Mex., November 6, 1906, by Vernon Bailey.

General characters.—Slightly larger than *minor*, darker gray and more buffy or ochraceous over the upper parts.

Measurements.—Average of adults: Total length, 375; tail, 46; hind foot, 89; and ear from notch in dried skin, 60 millimeters.

Distribution and habitat.—The cedar-belt cottontails are characteristic of the cedar and pinyon foothills and elevated mesas in the Upper Sonoran Zone over central and west-central New Mexico. (Fig. 7.) Their range is not sharply defined, as on the east they grade into *neomexicanus*, on the south into the Lower Sonoran *minor*, and on the north into *warreni*, all of which are closely related subspecies, evidently the product of slightly different environments. With the present form the environment is somewhat peculiar in being usually an open orchardlike growth of low spreading junipers and nut pines interspersed with clumps and thickets of brush and bunches of cactus. Much of the country is rough, with sharp gulches, cut banks, and small, rocky canyons that afford considerable cover and protection and more shade than is found on the grassy plains or in the open Lower Sonoran valleys.

General habits.—The abundance of these rabbits depends much on the character of the country. In areas of rocky ledges, broken talus below cliffs, and especially lava fields, where they find safe shelter and protection from their enemies, they are usually numerous, while in more exposed localities they are generally scarce. A few may be found anywhere, however, among the junipers and nut pines in open parks, where the burrows of the prairie dog afford shelter and protection. In most localities there are some badger holes that the rabbits can use as safe retreats. Food is generally plentiful throughout their range, and the determining factor of their abundance is usually protection from the numerous enemies that they must avoid. Bobcats, coyotes, and gray foxes abound in this region, and together with the hawks by day and the owls by night they make life anxious for the rabbits. It is only by keeping close to their rocky or underground retreats that they are able to maintain an existence, and the speed with which they disappear attests constant practice. Locally they adapt themselves to various cover. On Cactus Flat, where the type was collected, they were common and took refuge under clusters of cane cactus and tall yuccas, while on the Rio Alamosa, E. A. Goldman found them rather common in thickets of Apache plume (*Fallugia parodoxa*) and of shadscale (*Atriplex canescens*). At Isleta Ned Hollister found them common

on weedy ground between the mesa and the river bottom, but whenever frightened they immediately ran for the rocks along the base
of the neighboring cliff. He found them in similar situations along
the Rio Puerco and other valleys; and he also collected specimens
in the Datil Mountains in the edge of yellow-pine timber, where,
with many other Upper Sonoran species, they extended up these
narrow, dry ranges beyond their usual zone. At Agua Fria Spring,
in the southern edge of the Zuni Mountains, Hollister reported them
as numerous along the borders of the lava fields and said that when
frightened they at once sought refuge in the many crevices and
holes of the lava beds. At San Rafael near the eastern base of the
Zuni Mountains the writer also found them numerous in the extremely rough and broken lava flow, for here the many caves and
cracks afforded absolute protection from any animals larger than
themselves. In a small valley in western Socorro County, J. S.
Ligon estimated their numbers at 1 to every 2 acres.

Food habits.—The food of the cedar belt cottontails consists of an
endless variety of green vegetation, most of which they are able to
find close to their safe retreats. In the little pockets and depressions
among the lava rocks, avoided by other grazing animals, the rabbits
hold almost complete possession. Some of these little patches are
grazed close by the rabbits and the scattered stems of plants from
which they have eaten the leaves are strewn over the ground among
their numerous characteristic pellets. Most of their excursions are
from the rocks or their dens in search of favorite food plants. Many
of the little shrubs and bushes where they have been browsing are
found with branches and stems cut off as smoothly as by a knife.
These cut bushes are especially noticeable where the rabbits have
spent the winter and depended on the shrubby growths while the
snow covered the lower vegetation. At Lake Valley, Goldman found
where they had stripped the bark from stems of bushes of Acacia
and Rhus, but this was probably done in winter or during a dry
season.

Breeding habits.—The mammae in this species are arranged in
three pairs of abdominal and one pair of pectoral, but the number of
embryos in two individuals were only two each. Both of these
records of two large embryos were at Albuquerque on July 23, 1889.
Another specimen taken at Santa Rosa on May 24 was nursing young,
but at the same place and time many half-grown young were seen.
At Wingate, Hollister reported in the latter half of June many tiny
young, as well as all sizes up to nearly full grown. As it is always
possible to find plenty of young of all sizes throughout the summer
and to at least the first of October, the rabbits must produce several
litters during a season, but there are too few data to show the actual
number of litters or even the average number of young in a litter.

Economic status.—To summer campers within the range of these
cottontails they are the most important game animals, as it is almost
always possible to obtain a supply of fresh meat by shooting the
young of the year along the roadsides. They are generally free
from diseases and are excellent eating. The young, properly fried
or broiled with a little bacon over the coals of a hot camp fire, afford
a meal that is usually welcome to hungry campers. The writer has
often decided that they are fully equal to quail or fried chicken,

but he may have been somewhat prejudiced in their favor at the time by a keen appetite. Even the old ones are good eating, especially if stewed with a little bacon or fat pork, but require more thorough cooking than do the young of the year.

Now that tularemia has become known as an occasional disease of rabbits to which human beings are also susceptible, care should be taken not to get the rabbit blood on one's hands and to cook the meat thoroughly.

Throughout most of their range there is little opportunity for injury to crops, as they occupy a region where agriculture is mainly confined to occasional garden patches. These can generally be protected by fencing or shooting. The natural enemies of the rabbits commonly hold them in sufficient check in open areas where crops can be grown. At Santa Rosa one half grown was found in the stomach of a large rattlesnake, and near Cuervo their bones were numerous under the nest of a pair of golden eagles on the cliff. At Conchas Creek the den of a coyote was discovered near camp by watching the old coyote carrying a cottontail to its young among the rocks. Pieces of cottontail skin were strewn over the ground around the mouth of this den, and evidently the family of coyotes was finding the rabbits an important food supply.

SYLVILAGUS AUDUBONI WARRENI Nelson

Colorado Cottontail; Gu of the Navajo Indians

Sylvilagus auduboni warreni Nelson, Biol. Soc. Wash. Proc. 20: 83, 1907.

Type.—Collected at Coventry, Colo., January 4, 1907, by C. H. Smith.

General characters.—A large, buffy-gray form of the *auduboni* group extending from Colorado into the northwestern corner of New Mexico.

Measurements.—Average adult specimens: Total length, 384; tail, 50; hind foot, 97; ear from notch in dried skin, 66 millimeters.

Distribution and habitat.—Specimens of the Colorado cottontail have been examined from several localities along the Rio Grande Valley north of Santa Fe, and westward over the San Juan Valley and south to near Juan Tafoya at the eastern base of Mount Taylor. (Fig. 7.) A large part of this area is open and very arid valley country, with scattered sagebrush and rabbit brush as the principal cover for such species. Their range is practically restricted to the Upper Sonoran Zone and a very distinct species, *S. nuttalli pinetus*, takes their place in the mountains of this region.

General habits.—These long-eared cottontails are common both in the open sagebrush- and rabbit-brush-covered valleys and on the nut-pine and juniper slopes around the base of the mountains. Along the densely brushed and timbered bottom lands of the San Juan River they are also common, but less conspicuous than out in the arid sagebrush valleys. At Fruitland they were abundant in the groves of cottonwood, buffaloberry, and bear brush in the weedy bottoms, where they made trails through the thickets and dodged so quickly out of sight that they were not easily collected. Out on the mesas they would run quickly to prairie-dog or badger holes or hide among the rocks along the low cliffs. They were most abundant, however, along the base of the cliffs in the great, dry washes that come down along the sides of the San Juan Valley.

In general habits they most nearly resemble their close relative and neighboring from *cedrophilus*, but are more commonly a valley species and more fully adapted to the open country at long distance from the scattered forests of juniper and nut pine. In actual habits there is apparently no difference except such as may be directly produced by the slight change of environment.

Economic status.—As food and game these rabbits are especially important to the Indians occupying their region, as well as to the white settlers and campers. Along the San Juan and Rio Grande Valleys they are common in a well-settled and productive agricultural region, and here, while of considerable value as game, they are often somewhat injurious in fields, gardens, and orchards. In most cases the farms are rather small, and under ordinary circumstances the rabbits can be kept in check by hunting or fencing, so that their depredations are of little consequence. As these methods are comparatively simple and inexpensive, no serious loss need be sustained.

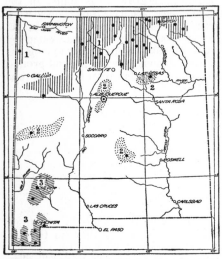

FIGURE 8.—Distribution of three cottontail rabbits in New Mexico: 1. *Sylvilagus nuttalli pinetis;* 2, *S. cognatus;* 3, *S. floridanus holzneri.* Type locality circled

SYLVILAGUS NUTTALLI PINETIS (ALLEN)

ROCKY MOUNTAIN COTTONTAIL; PE WE NA of the Taos Indians

Lepus sylvaticus pinetis Allen, Bul. Amer. Mus. Nat. Hist. 6: 348–349, 1894.

Type.—Collected in the White Mountains, Ariz., August 14, 1894, by B. C. Condit.

General characters.—These are rather large, heavy cottontails, with relatively short ears and with skull characters that separate them as a group from the forms of *auduboni*. The small audital bullae and slender rostrum of the skull are good cranial characters.

Measurements.—Adult specimens average in total length, 386; tail, 59; hind foot, 94; ear from notch in dried skin, 61 millimeters.

Distribution and habitat.—Common in the Transition Zone in mountains of Arizona, Colorado, and northern New Mexico, with an extreme vertical range from 7,500 to 10,000 feet, the Rocky Mountain cottontails are common also in the Transition Zone of the Zuni, Chuska, Jemez, San Juan, Sangre de Cristo, and Raton Ranges in New Mexico. (Fig. 8.) They occupy the yellow-pine belt, but stray into the edge of the junipers below and in places follow favorable slopes somewhat above the limits of the yellow pine. Like any species that completely fills a zone, they are occasionally found intruding into the borders of adjoining zones. They generally occupy the thickets and brush patches, log jams, and slab piles of the open timber, and often take refuge in hollow logs or under fallen trees and sometimes in old burrows and among broken rocks.

General habits.—The Rocky Mountain cottontails are usually not very abundant and in the thickets and brush specimens are not so easily obtained as are the more conspicuous species in the open country below. In the Jemez Mountains one half-grown individual was collected at 10,000 feet altitude in the lower edge of the Canadian Zone, and their trails and droppings were found scattered through much of the forest of the range. On top of the Chuska Mountain Plateau they were fairly common in the beautiful yellow-pine forest from 7,500 to 9,000 feet, where they lived mainly in the groves of aspens and Gambel's oak. In places they were found among the rocks, and two were shot on the face of a cliff where they were dodging back and forth from one crevice to another, but generally they hid in the brush and when followed ran from one thicket to another. In places where they are in the habit of running, they make fairly distinct trails, and their characteristic pellets are scattered in the thickets. In the Pecos River Mountains a few were seen from 8,000 to 10,000 feet, but they were not very common and the thick timber and brush hindered the obtaining of specimens. On the east slope of the Taos Mountains one was taken at 8,900 feet at the extreme upper edge of the Transition Zone in Moreno Valley and others lower down though still within the yellow-pine belt. On the west slope of these mountains specimens were taken at 7,700 feet and others seen as high as 10,000 feet, and on the west slope of the Culebras one was shot at 9,400 feet near the upper edge of its zone. In the San Juan Mountains they were common in the Transition Zone along both sides of the range, and specimens were taken on both slopes, while on the Gallinas Mountains of Rio Arriba County they were common throughout their zone in the abundant thickets of scrub oak and even up into the aspen thickets, where one was taken at 9,500 feet. In the region of Tres Piedras, both Loring and Gaut reported them numerous, the abundance of great bowlders and the oak thickets offering them unusual protection. In the Raton Range A. H. Howell found them rather scarce, but obtained a specimen in Oak Canyon and picked up an old skull in Bear Canyon. On the way from Catskill to Costillo Pass he collected five specimens in the timber along the mountain sides from 7,000 feet up to the summit of the pass at 10,500 feet, where one was trapped at the mouth of a burrow. At Catskill he found them living in and about the deserted cabins.

In the Mogollon Mountains a cottontail evidently of this group is common in the timber from 9,000 to 10,000 feet altitude, but neither Goldman nor the writer were able to obtain any specimens, as they kept out of sight in the extensive thickets. Even on a good tracking snow they would run ahead from one thicket to another, dodging and hiding so skillfully that no specimens were procured. It seems probable that the form inhabiting the mountains is typical *pinetis*, which is known to have the same range and habits in the White Mountains of Arizona, but until specimens are collected one can not be sure that they are not *cognatus* or *holzneri*, which are similar in habits.

Food habits.—The food of these cottontails evidently includes as great a variety of plants and green vegetation as that of any other species, but most of the plants are different from those on which the rabbits of the valley subsist, and there seems to be no record of the actual species eaten. Many of the shrubs and twigs of small bushes are cut along their trails and on their feeding grounds, indicating the nature of at least a part of their winter food, but even the species of shrubs have not been noted with sufficient care to indicate which kind the rabbits prefer.

Breeding habits.—Like others of the group, these rabbits have the mammae arranged in four pairs, three pairs of abdominal and one pair of pectoral, but there seems to be only one record of embryos examined to indicate the number of young to a litter. This record of three embryos noted by A. K. Fisher August 14, 1894, at Estes Park, Colo., is about all that is known definitely of the breeding habits of the species, and this probably is not the full normal number of young in a litter.

Economic status.—Throughout the range of these cottontails in New Mexico the writer has found them almost invariably healthy and in good condition for food. In the Chuska Mountain, in October, 1908, the rabbits were plump with little strips of fat conspicuous along the back and flanks, and furnished an important and greatly enjoyed addition to the camp fare. They seemed to be above the zone of the ordinary rabbit parasites and were as sound and healthy as the snowshoe rabbits and, except during the breeding season, were in excellent condition for food. In the forest area that they inhabit they rarely conflict with any agricultural interests, and though there are places where they might do slight damage to gardens and a few hardy fruit trees, these are so rare that the species should be considered as an important game asset and worthy of protection.

SYLVILAGUS COGNATUS Nelson

Manzano Mountain Cottontail

Sylvilagus cognatus Nelson, Biol. Soc. Wash. Proc. 20: 82, 1907.

Type.—Collected near summit of the Manzano Mountains, N. Mex., at 10,000 feet altitude, February, 1895, by A. Rea.

General characters.—A robust mountain form, probably of the *floridanus* group of eastern cottontails, distinguished by large size. Compared with the slender, long-eared valley species of the surrounding country it is large and heavily built. In color it is a light buffy gray, with a clear gray rump patch.

Measurements.—Adult specimens average in total length, 451; tail, 65; hind foot, 102; and ear from notch in dried skin, 67 millimeters.

Distribution and habitat.—The Manzano Mountain cottontail rabbits are known from four isolated mountain ranges in central New Mexico, where they occupy the full width of the Transition Zone from 7,300 feet altitude on the Mesa de la Yegua to 10,000 feet near the summit of the Manzano Mountains. (Fig. 8.) Specimens have also been referred to this species from the Capitan and Datil Mountains, but the limits of the range are not well known, and it probably occupies many of the scattered intervening mountain masses and covers much more of the country than is now indicated.

General habits.—The writer first encountered this species in June, 1903, on top of the Mesa de la Yegua, 40 miles southeast of Las Vegas, where one was taken and others seen in the scrub-oak thickets among the yellow pines at 7,300 feet altitude. Here at the lower edge of its range it seemed to be entirely confined to the Transition-zone summit of the plateau, and the difference between it and *neomexicanus*, which the writer had been collecting in the valley below, was so striking that he recognized it when the first one bounded away. The heavy body and short ears showed at once that he had encountered a very distinct species. In habits it was a brush rabbit, jumping out from one scrub-oak thicket and running to another with heavy, thumping gait. In 1903 Gaut reported cottontail rabbits in the Manzano Mountains ranging practically to the summit at 10,200 feet, but they were very scarce, and he was unable to obtain a specimen. In 1905 in these same mountains at 10,000 feet altitude, A. Rea collected a specimen that later became the type of the species. Apparently no report was made of them by Gaut in the Capitan Mountains, where he collected a specimen. In the Datil Mountains Hollister collected one and reported a few seen in the yellow-pine timber of both the Datil and the Gallinas Mountains.

SYLVILAGUS FLORIDANUS HOLZNERI (MEARNS)

HOLZNER'S COTTONTAIL

Lepus sylvaticus holzneri Mearns, U. S. Natl. Mus. Proc. (1895) 18: 554, 1896.
[*Lepus sylvaticus*] subspecies *rigidus* Mearns, U. S. Natl. Mus. Proc. (1895) 18: 555, 1896. Type from Carrizalillo Mountains, N. Mex.

Type.—Collected near summit of Huachuca Mountains, Ariz., August 29, 1893, by Frank X. Holzner.

General characters.—A light buffy gray rabbit of the *floridanus* group, with clear gray rump, conspicuously larger and more robust than the long-eared species of the valley and readily distinguished from it. From *cognatus* of the mountain ranges farther north it differs in slightly smaller size and relatively larger audital bullae, but resembles it in the gray rump patch and the long fur, especially noticeable on feet and tail.

Measurements.—Average of adult specimens: Total length, 425; tail, 71; hind foot, 98; and ear from notch in dried skin, 62 millimeters.

Distribution and habitat.—From its wider range in Mexico and southern Arizona Holzner's cottontail comes into New Mexico only in the mountains of the extreme southwest corner, where it has been taken in the Carrizalillo, Animas, San Luis, and Burro Mountains, and in the Pinos Altos Range back of Silver City (fig. 8). It belongs mainly to the Transition Zone with an extreme vertical range from 6,000 to 10,000 feet, a few scattering specimens occurring in the edges of both the Canadian and the Upper Sonoran Zones. Mearns also reported it from the Hatchet, Dog, Mule, and San Jose Mountains, near the Mexican boundary line, where he called it the wood rabbit to distinguish it from *minor* of the open valleys. He first met with it in the Carrizalillo Mountains in what he calls the red-juniper zone; and in the Animas Mountains E. A. Goldman and Clarence Birdseye reported it as ranging from 5,800 feet to the summit of Animas Peak in both the Upper Sonoran and the Transition Zones. They saw only two individuals but found plenty of signs of them under the dense chaparral among the oaks and pines. In the San Luis Mountains Goldman shot a nursing female on August 10, 1908, at 5,600 feet altitude among the Emory and Arizona oaks and saw signs of a few more to the top of the mountain. In September,

1911, B. V. Lilly, while hunting bears in the Animas Mountains, found where one of these rabbits lived on the extreme summit of the range and had a well-marked trail under some pines and bushes. He also saw them on the top of the San Luis Mountains south of the international boundary line. Of the actual habits of these rabbits very little is known, except that they live under the dense chaparral of the desert ranges in that region and often make well-defined trails through the thickets or from one patch of brush to another. It is an easy matter to find their trails and signs, but the rabbits are difficult to get sight of under their dense cover.

Family OCHOTONIDAE: Rock Conies

OCHOTONA SAXATILIS INCANA Howell

ROCK CONY; PIKA; LITTLE CHIEF HARE; TSA'-KA-NA of the Taos Indians

Ochotona saxatilis incana Howell, Biol. Soc. Wash. Proc. 32: 107, 1919.

Type.—Collected on Pecos Baldy, 12,000 feet, N. Mex., August 10, 1903, by Vernon Bailey.

General characters.—These little round-eared, tailless rodents are easily recognized by their guinea-pig-like form and squeaky voices. Their fluffy rabbitlike fur is of a brownish-gray color blending well with the rocks. Their legs are short, and the soles of the feet are covered with dense fur except on the naked toe pads.

Measurements.—Adult male: Total length from tip of nose to tip of where the tail should be, 180; hind foot, 30 millimeters.

Distribution and habitat.—Rock conies (pl. 4, B) are common on all the peaks of the Sangre de Cristo Range that reach to or above timber line. (Fig. 9.) They are found as low as 11,000 feet on some cold northeast slopes, but are more common from 12,000 feet to the summits of most of the peaks. In the Pecos River Mountains they were abundant in rock slides of the Hudsonian Zone over Pecos Baldy and the Truchas peaks from 11,000 feet to the very summits at 12,600 and 13,300 feet. In the Taos Mountains they were common from the camp at 11,400 feet to near the top of Wheeler Peak at 13,600 feet, and in the Culebra Mountains from timber line to the tops of the highest peaks. Their range is mainly in the Hudsonian Zone, but they also enter the Arctic Alpine and to some extent may be resident there. Where rock slides extend down the steep slopes of mountain sides well into the timber of the Canadian Zone the conies often follow down to the lower limits of slide rock, as do also many of the Hudsonian Zone plants among the cold shadows of the rocks. The cold air currents and icy streams under these open masses of broken rocks apparently carry the conditions of the higher zones below their usual limits.

General habits.—In habits the rock conies are timid, rabbitlike little creatures, but full of curiosity and with a confidence not difficult to win. They are quick and energetic workers and in the latter part of the short summer are so busy gathering their winter stores of food that they are much in evidence during the day and at times apparently work nights as well. In the Taos Mountains at camp near the head of Lake Fork at 11,400 feet they occupied the rock slide close around the tent, and finding that no attempts were made to injure them, they became comparatively tame. Up to August 8 they seemed not to take life very seriously, scampering over the rocks and picking out the various plants they liked best for food, but after a few freezing nights they began their haymaking and worked with frantic energy. Most of the day they were rushing back and forth gathering plants and storing them in sheltered nooks under the rocks, and even at night their little " yamp " note, like the bleating of a tiny lamb, was often heard not far from the tent. Whether they were actually at work at night is uncertain, but evidently they were awake and calling to one another.

In the Pecos River Mountains the writer had a good opportunity to study their habits at close quarters, as they lived in a rock slide at the east base of Pecos Baldy near his camp at 11,600 feet. A few adults and at least one family of nearly full-grown young occupied this rock slide and from August 7 to 17 were busily engaged in their haymaking. The old ones were full of energy, while the young occasionally helped with the work but spent most of their time ruuuing aimlessly over the rocks, playing and calling back and forth. They soon became accustomed to seeing the writer about and seemed to realize that he was not collecting specimens in that particular rock slide. During a pleasant Sunday morning he spent among them with a camera they became quite indifferent to his presence and gave him the opportunity desired for close study.

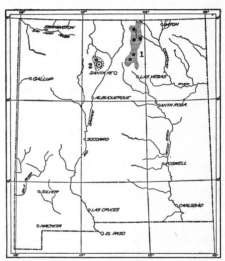

FIGURE 9.—Distribution of rock conies in New Mexico: 1, *Ochotona saxatilis;* 2, *O. nigrescens.* Type locality circled

A frosty night had stimulated them to activity, and one old fellow that had been watched for an hour was too busy to take notice. At 8 a. m. it was found hard at work gathering and stacking hay. It stopped for a few loud squeaks as it sat on the top of a gray-granite bowlder and then scampered over the rocks to the nearest weed patch. While it was busy gathering plants the writer crept closer to its rock pile, and as the cony came back with a big bunch of leaves of shrubby cinquefoil (*Potentilla fruticosa*) in its mouth and deposited them under a bowlder he located one of its haystacks, and while it went for another load he took his stand at a convenient distance for a photograph. In a minute the cony was back with a bunch of grass and a veratrum leaf in its mouth, making a bundle as big as its body and hiding it, but seeming not to interfere in the least with its rapid noiseless movements over the stones. It did not hesitate or stumble on its way to the cache, and after the green leaves were deposited under the rocks it bobbed up to the top of a rock, took a good look at the writer, settled itself comfortably for about five seconds, then jumped down and went bobbing over the rocks to another weed patch for more hay. This it kept up for an hour, bringing a load every one or two minutes, almost always of different material and depositing it now on one stack and now on another as happened to be nearest. Five of its haystacks were found in different parts of the rock slide. It came most frequently to the stack where the writer was situated and often ran past within 5 or 6 feet of him. Once it came within 2 feet and took a good look, but soon dodged back into the rocks. Occasionally it would squeak at the writer, but always seemed reassured when he talked softly to it. Below the surface the slide rock seemed to be open to it, and it would go down on one side and come up on the other, and the writer would hear little squeaks from the rocks directly under him, first on one side and then on the other. Apparently the cony ran as freely and rapidly through the caverns between the rocks as over the surface and just as noiselessly. From the furry soles of its feet there came no sound as it scampered over the rocks, and it never slipped or made a misstep even when it could not see over or around the bundle of green things in its mouth. Unlike the chipmunk, it did not use the front paws as hands, although once it was seen to put its forefeet on a Carex stem to hold it on the rock while it nibbled off the head. Usually its lips and teeth took the place of hands. Once the writer saw it reach out over the top of a stone, nip off a grass stem, and with its lips slowly draw stem and head into its mouth as it ate. At another time he watched it bite off the leaf of a Polygonum and chew rapidly at one end of it until the whole leaf had slowly disappeared into its mouth.

Its motions were so quick that the writer had much trouble in getting photographs, and he failed entirely in obtaining what he most wanted—a picture of the cony with a large bunch of plants in its mouth. It would run so fast and so irregularly over the rock that it could not be sighted in the finder. At last, by setting the camera in its runway and awaiting its return, the writer tried to get it as it came over a certain rock, but when it came to the rock it dodged down under it, and then before the writer could get the focus shortened, unable to see over its bouquet, it bumped into his foot. With a frightened squeak it dropped its load of cinquefoil and geranium leaves on his boot and dodged into the nearest crack in the rocks. For several minutes its excited complaints came up from deep down under the broken rocks, and when it did reappear it scolded from the top of a rock for some time before resuming its work. Evidently its success in running over the rocks without being able to see was due to its perfect familiarity with every stone and surface in the slide, and when it bumped into something it had never found there before it had cause for serious alarm.

After wasting many negatives, the writer turned his attention to the composition of the various haystacks, and, taking one of the best, opened it and examined it throughout. It was placed in the shelter of an overhanging point of rock and was composed of about a bushel of thoroughly dried, half-dried, and freshly cut plants, the last always on top. There were pieces of almost every plant growing around the edges of the rock slide or within easy reach. The stems and leaves were of the brightest gray green, like well-cured hay, and the stack was bright with flowers of purple Pentstemon, yellow Senecio and Potentilla, and blue Erigeron. There were several species of Carex and considerable grass, of which nine different species were distinguished, including timothy, redtop, awn grass, wild rye, and wild foxtail; and also thistles, asters, columbine, yarrow, Erigeron, Helenium, Pentstemon, Veratrum, Potentilla, Geranium, Polygonum, Heracleum, and Aralia. At another stack 400 feet higher up on the slope there were mainly wild clover, wild timothy, and other grass and sedges, with a few leaves of Caltha, Saxifraga, Geum, Silene, and a dwarf umbellifer.

Under most of these little haystacks were found the remains of stacks of previous years, woody stems not suitable for food that were left when the green foliage was eaten.

There is ample evidence that the conies do not hibernate, as they do not become very fat and are active until the deep snows bury their rock slides. In this particular slide at the steep east base of Pecos Baldy, the snow of the previous winter had not all disappeared by the middle of August, and the great drifts and avalanches must pile up to hundreds of feet in depth during the winter. Under this deep cover in the roomy chambers among the broken rocks the little animals are well protected from cold and enemies, and with abundance of winter food, which they have provided in safe and accessible places, the long cold winter has no terrors for them. The weasel or marten may occasionally get into their dens and cause terror and destruction, but the fact that the hay is usually all eaten when the snow disappears in spring or early summer would indicate a safe and prosperous winter.

Breeding habits.—Very little is known of the breeding habits of the rock conies except that by the 1st of August the young are commonly about half grown and that they have hardly reached maturity when the winter snows shut them in. There are probably three to six young to a litter, as the mammae of the breeding females are arranged in three pairs. In other species of the genus the writer has found three to five embryos, but when and where the young are born is as little known as the rest of the habits of these cave dwellers.

Economic status.—Too small for game and in a world too high for human industries, the conies are among the few animals of no economic importance. On the other hand, few of our wild animals have greater possibilities of delightful interest to those who care to penetrate to their mountain tops and study them at first hand. The opportunity for photographing them at work and play stands open to anyone with time and patience, while the chance of burrowing into their drifts and living with them long enough to learn something of their habits is one of the tempting phases of winter mountain work for those who are seeking new fields of interest and discovery.

OCHOTONA NIGRESCENS BAILEY

DUSKY ROCK CONY

Ochotona nigrescens Bailey, Biol. Soc. Wash. Proc. 26 : 133, 1913.

Type.—Collected in Jemez Mountains, N. Mex., at 10,000 feet altitude on Goat Peak at the head of Santa Clara Creek, August 28, 1906, by Vernon Bailey.

General characters.—About the size of *Ochotona saxatilis*, but much darker colored, with rich brown fur heavily tipped with black over head and back; throat and belly rich brown; outside of ears black; inside blackish toward tips.

Measurements.—Type: Total length, 200; hind foot, 30 millimeters.

Distribution and habitat.—The little dusky rock cony, or as often called rock rabbit, is common on the three main peaks of the Jemez Mountains—Santa Clara Peak on the north of Santa Clara Creek, Goat Peak on the south, and Pelado Peak still farther south. (Fig. 9.) Pelado Peak is about on a line with Pecos Baldy, the previously southernmost record of the genus in North America, but the Jemez Mountains are widely separated by the Rio Grande and Chama Valleys from any other mountain masses. The conies were found in rock slides of broken lava from 9,000 feet to the tops of the highest peaks mainly within the Canadian Zone. Their dark-gray color blends perfectly with the dark-gray lava slides in which they live, rendering them almost invisible to the naked eye as they sit on the rocks.

The writer succeeded in collecting only three specimens, but saw and heard many more. Those collected in the latter part of August were all adults, and no young of the year were found. Up to September 10 they had not begun to show much energy in making hay. There were abundant traces of the previous year's haystacks under sheltering rocks, but only in one place did the writer find a fresh heap of grass and red elder leaves. In voice and habits there seems to be no difference between this and the other various forms of the group, but long isolation in these high mountains under strikingly different environment has produced a well-marked local form, showing not only adaptation of color to environment but well-marked cranial characters by which it is easily distinguished from its nearest neighbor across the valley.

Order RODENTIA: Gnawing Animals

Family SCIURIDAE: Squirrels, Chipmunks, Prairie Dogs, and Woodchucks

SCIURUS ABERTI ABERTI Woodhouse

ABERT'S SQUIRREL; TASSEL-EARED SQUIRREL

Sciurus aberti Woodhouse, Acad. Nat. Sci. Phila. Proc. 6: 220, 1852.
Sciurus castanotus Baird, Acad. Nat. Sci. Phila. Proc. 7: 332, 1855. Type from Coppermines, N. Mex.

Type.—Collected on San Francisco Mountain, Ariz., October, 1851, by S. W. Woodhouse.

General characters.—A large squirrel with bushy tail and long ears that in winter bear tassels an inch or more in length. In color it is dark gray above and white below with a large brown patch on the back. In winter fur, with the bright brown back, long black ear tassels, gray sides, plumelike tail, and pure white lower parts inclosed by black side lines, it is certainly one of the handsomest of North American squirrels. Even in summer, with the brown back, long ears, and striking gray and white markings, these squirrels are wonderfully attractive animals. An interesting example of partial melanism is seen among them in the Mogollon Mountains, where the writer collected three specimens, and heard of others, with fully black lower parts, the tail and upper parts remaining normal in color. This produces an animal of striking appearance, even handsomer than the others, and very similar to the black-bellied Kaibab squirrel (*Sciurus kaibabensis*) from northwestern Arizona. In the Black

Range and San Mateo Mountains J. S. Ligon found a large percentage of these squirrels partly or entirely black, a case of dichromatism comparable to that of the gray and black squirrels of the Northeastern States.

Measurements.—Total length, 520; tail, 230; hind foot, 75 millimeters.

Distribution and habitat.—These handsome squirrels are usually abundant throughout the Transition, or yellow-pine, Zone of the Mogollon Mountain region (fig. 10) and westward over the plateau country of Arizona south of the Grand Canyon. Specimens examined from the mountains just north of Silver City, from both sides of the Black Range or Mimbres, the east base of the Mogollon Peaks, Frisco and Datil Ranges, and Magdalena Mountains are indistinguishable from typical *aberti* of the White and San Francisco Mountains of Arizona. Few animals are more narrowly restricted to a single zone than these squirrels, but the reason is obvious. Yellow pine furnishes their principal food. They are rarely found out of sight of these trees.

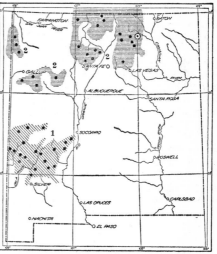

FIGURE 10.—Distribution of Abert's and tufted-eared squirrels in New Mexico: 1, *Sciurus. aberti aberti*; 2, *S. aberti minus*. Type locality circled

General habits.—Usually Abert's squirrels are very shy, but in some places, especially where abundant and undisturbed, they are often boldly conspicuous and even confiding. At the writer's camp in the yellow pines at the head of the Rio Mimbres in May, 1906, they were abundant and entirely undisturbed. In the early mornings as many as five were seen at a time running about on the ground in front of camp getting their breakfasts from buried treasures. They were so tame that one would often sit on a low branch within a few feet of the writer and gnaw the scales from a cone, picking out and eating the seeds, and one came down and drank at the brook close to where he was standing.

Their voice is not often heard, but is at once recognized as the husky barking of a big squirrel. Usually it is a soft chuff, chuff, repeated at intervals of a few seconds and only becoming animated when some enemy is sighted and other members of the family are to be warned. At times it may serve as a call note, but it seems to be mainly a warning cry. It is most commonly heard when the well-grown young are scattered and generally proceeds from the mother squirrel, but it is sometimes heard from isolated individuals and even from the young when not fully grown. The more conversational notes of these squirrels remain to be studied at close range.

Food habits.—In a good cone year the food of these squirrels seems to be almost entirely seeds of the yellow pine, at least during the fall and winter months, but in places some seeds of white pine and Douglas spruce are eaten. Even in May they may be found shelling off the scales of old cones and occasionally finding a good seed, but from this time on until the new cones begin to furnish seeds in August they depend on a varied diet. Many old acorns are dug up, while mushrooms, buds, and bark help out until the early acorns and then the pine seeds begin to ripen. But even in summer the yellow pine furnishes much of their food, mainly from the bark of its tender twigs and the male flowers, or staminate catkins. The half-grown young, when they first come out of the nest, feed largely upon these tender pollen-laden catkins, which are abundant during May. These are also eaten by the old squirrels, but not so extensively as is the bark from twigs. For a long time the writer was puzzled by the great number of tips of pine boughs scattered under the trees, in places carpeting the ground. Some of these bore young cones, some catkins, and some only the terminal tufts of leaves. As none of these were eaten or disturbed, he could not imagine why the squirrels were cutting them off until he discovered little sections of peeled branches scattered on the ground under the trees. The leafy tips of the sections were neatly clipped as with a knife. By watching the squirrels he soon discovered their method of operation. The leafy tip of the branch was nipped off and dropped, then a section just back of it convenient for handling was cut and carried to a comfortable perch, where the bark was removed and eaten and the naked wood thrown down. The thick white cambium of these branches is tender and sweet and has a pleasant taste. During the time of rapid growth it evidently contains much tree food, which also proves acceptable squirrel food, just as the cambium from the trunk of the yellow pine has been used for ages by many Indian tribes to carry them through times of scarcity.

The question has often been raised as to possible damage that this trimming may do the trees. In some cases, under a large tree, there are bushels of branch tips scattered over the ground, but this rarely causes a perceptible thinning of the branches overhead. It may be carried far enough seriously to injure an occasional tree, but the writer has never found any case where it had evidently done so. This food is largely depended upon from about the 1st of May until the 1st of August, but seems to be a last resort in case of scarcity of richer food. During the autumn months great quantities of acorns and pine cones are buried for future use, not in heaps as by many other squirrels, but scattered singly in shallow pits in the ground. The destruction of seeds is undoubtedly a detriment to the forest, but, on the other hand, this widespread annual planting of seeds must prove a great advantage. Each squirrel has its own set of trees and feeding and storing grounds, from which all others are excluded even to the extent of savage hostilities. Enemies are numerous, and it is doubtful if half the squirrels ever see a second summer. When one fails to use its buried stores they are left in the ground to grow. If it were not for the squirrels, the pine cones would lie on the ground or scatter their seeds to be eaten by mice and jays. Consequently, although many branches are trimmed and many seeds are eaten by these small tenants of the forest, it is still evident that they are great planters, and thus conservators, of the forest trees on which they depend for their living.

Breeding habits.—At the writer's camp on the Mimbres there were two nests of sticks and leaves in the yellow pines directly over his bed, one in the pine over the roof of the cabin near by, and other nests scattered through the woods. He climbed to one of them and found it composed of pine and cottonwood branches, gathered while green so the leaves were retained in a dense thatch that would shed any rain. It was placed in a fork of the branches up 30 or 40 feet from the ground and was nearly as large as a bushel basket. The branches were securely interlaced, making a firm structure, in the center of which was a nest cavity lined with soft bark and plant fiber and forming as comfortable a nest as any bird or squirrel could wish. Three doorways, just large enough to admit the squirrel and no larger animal, and through which a folded hand could slip in comfortably, opened from different sides of the nest cavity, so that from whatever side an enemy approached there was always an opposite door for exit. Other nests seen and examined were of the same general type; they were common wherever the squirrels were found. In a few cases, however, the squirrels took refuge in hollow cottonwoods and oak trees, which were scattered through the open forest, but a hollow pine is so rare that the leaf houses were depended on mainly for both summer and winter nests.

All the squirrels seen at this camp up to May 24 were adults, when the first half-grown young were seen out of the nests. After that the young were frequently seen. The stomach of one of these half-grown ones collected for a specimen was half full of curd, showing that it was still nursing, although also eating other food. This was in May, and farther north in the same mountains half-grown young were found common in October, and females have been found with milk in their nipples in August and September. It is therefore evident that two litters are sometimes raised, at least in a season of abundant food supply. The females have four pairs of mammae arranged in one pair of inguinal, two pairs of abdominal, and one pair of pectoral. The usual number of young is three or four, as in other species of squirrels with the same arrangement of mammae. Like other squirrels they are fully polygamous, and several males may be found pursuing a single female in the breeding season.

Economic status.—As game, if such beautiful animals should be considered game, there are no squirrels better worthy of the hunt, or better able to protect themselves from extinction. Their large size and good flavor render them always acceptable food, and the young of the year are particularly tender and delicious.

Mearns (1907, p. 252), camping with General Crook in the White Mountains of Arizona, said that this squirrel

furnished the hunters of our party with sport and agreeably supplemented our daily fare; indeed, under the régime of a clever camp cook it proved to be the favorite dish, although the menu included venison, bear meat, wild turkey, and pigeon, variously served.

When abundant and unhunted they are conspicuous and confiding, but on being hunted soon become the most wary and suspicious of squirrels. Once alarmed, they make off through the woods at a rapid rate, either on the ground or through the tree tops, to the tallest and thickest trees, where they show such skill and intelligence in hiding as to be almost perfectly protected from hunters. When located in the top of a tall tree they are usually able to protect themselves against a single hunter by keeping on the opposite side of the trunk or branch. It is noticeable that when they are scarce they are exceedingly shy, and only when abundant are they at all bold or conspicuous.

As an addition to city parks or private grounds where climate and conditions are suitable there is certainly no more attractive animal to be found, and the young could be easily taken from the nests and tamed for such purposes. In their native forests they are among the most attractive forms of animal life and worthy of careful protection.

SCIURUS ABERTI MIMUS Merriam

Tassel-Eared Squirrel; Tsla-qua'na of the Taos Indians

Sciurus aberti mimus Merriam, Biol. Soc. Wash. Proc. 17: 130, 1904.

Type.—Collected on Hall Peak, Mora County, N. Mex., January 16, 1895, by C. M. Barber.

General characters.—This form differs from *aberti* most noticeably in the restricted area of brown on its back; this is usually but a small spot or stripe, and in some cases it is almost or quite absent. The long black tassels of the ears are often mixed with brown but are just as striking, and in general appearance the squirrel is almost as beautiful as *aberti.* Specimens from the Mount Taylor, Zuni, and Chuska Ranges are somewhat intermediate, but can better be included with *mimus* than with *aberti.*

Measurements.—Type, adult female: Total length, 485; tail, 225; foot, 70 millimeters.

Distribution and habitat.—Tassel-eared squirrels inhabit the yellow-pine area of the Sangre de Cristo, San Juan, Jemez, Mount Taylor, Zuni, and Chuska Mountains of northern New Mexico. (Fig. 10.) Their range is not continuous in these mountains, and some slight variation in color is shown in different ranges, but not sufficient to warrant further subdivision. They extend into southwestern Colorado and northeastern Arizona. In all these areas the squirrels are at times abundant, again very scarce, apparently responding quickly to an abundant food supply and disappearing rapidly in seasons of cone and acorn failure. The writer has no evidence that they migrate, but their numbers correspond so regularly with abundance or scarcity of food that partial migration is strongly suggested. In September, 1903, they were common in Moreno Valley, where there was a good yield of yellow-pine cones, while at the same time in the Pecos Mountains both they and the pine cones were very scarce. In 1904 there was a failure of these cones in most of their range, and the squirrels were extremely scarce along the west side of the Taos Mountains, in the San Juan, Jicarilla, and Gallinas Ranges, although they were said to have been abundant the previous year, and the old cone cores showed that it had been a good year for squirrels.

General habits.—In habits as well as appearance these squirrels differ very little from *aberti.* They are rarely found outside the yellow-pine forest, and their big, rough nests of pine and other branches are generally placed in the forks of pine trees or occasionally in a Douglas spruce. These nests, well lined with soft grass, bark, and leaves, are comfortable summer and winter homes. The old squirrels rarely resort to them for protection, but usually select the top of some tall tree in which they can hide or dodge. When scarce they are very shy and difficult to find, and even where their cone scales are fresh and scattered over the ground it is often impossible to find the squirrels. Their work is easily distinguished from that of the red squirrel, as they cut off and carry a yellow-pine cone to a safe perch high in a tree and holding it between the hands neatly clip the scales and drop them to the ground, pick out a pine nut and, holding it between the thumbs, quickly shell and eat it, then clip another scale, and so on until the cone is finished and the naked core thrown down among the widely scattered scales.

The voice of these squirrels is rarely heard, but occasionally they utter a heavy soft bark not unlike that of the fox squirrel. This seems to be a warning cry, usually indicating danger of some kind, a passing hunter, coyote, cat, or hawk. The writer has heard one of the little animals become quite excited when a goshawk flew into a grove of yellow pines. The western red-tailed hawk is often found hunting through the pines where these squirrels live, and one that the writer shot had its crop well filled from a squirrel it had just eaten.

Food habits.—Under the feeding trees of these squirrels the ground is often strewn with scales and cores; while the little spruce squirrel, if feeding on yellow-pine seeds, must rest the cone on a log or branch and gnaw off the scales, which are left in a little heap. In times of need these big squirrels sometimes feed on the cones of the Douglas spruce, acorns, buds, catkins, and the bark of yellow-pine twigs. Even in case of a total failure of the cone crop a few of the squirrels survive on what they can pick up until another year. Usually some of the several species of oaks within their range bear acorns, and these seem to be the principal substitute for more desirable food. The contents of their stomachs generally show whether their food consists of pine nuts, acorns, or other materials.

Breeding habits.—The increase and decrease of the squirrels following upon the fluctuations of the food supply is no doubt due to the possibility of two full litters of young in a fruitful season or the restriction to one litter or none in a lean year.

Hibernation.—These squirrels do not hibernate, and their large tracks are conspicuous in the snow under the pines; the Indians hunt them most successfully on the first snows, when they can be located in their nests or trees.

In the Chuska Mountains early in October, 1908, the writer made the following notes:

These squirrels are common all through the yellow-pine forest of the Chuska Mountains. They are occasionally heard barking, but are more often seen running over the ground from tree to tree or heard scratching up the far side of a pine trunk. Often when on the ground, if pursued, one will run a long distance to get up some favorite tree and hide in its branches.

They are feeding now almost entirely on seeds of yellow pine, although the cone crop is poor and only an occasional tree has a good yield of cones. In places they get some cones of Douglas spruce, but the acorn crop seems to have been a failure. Under many of the pines are numerous freshly cut branch tips showing that the squirrels are still feeding in part on the bark of these twigs, which will probably help to carry them through the winter.

There are many half-grown young of the year and other full-grown young, evidently from first and second litters. Some of the old males are getting their winter pelage and long ear tufts, but the females are still ragged and worn, and neither they nor the young begin to show their ear tufts.

The series of specimens collected in these mountains furnished an important part of the camp food and next to the mallard ducks were the best game procured. It is a wonder that they are not exterminated by the Navajo Indians who inhabit these mountains in summer, unless, like the birds, the squirrels are considered sacred.

SCIURUS ARIZONENSIS ARIZONENSIS Coues

Arizona Gray Squirrel

Sciurus arizonensis Coues, Amer. Nat. 1 : 357, 1867.

Type.—Collected at Fort Whipple, Yavapai County, Ariz., December 20, 1865, by Elliott Coues.

General characters.—This is a large, plain gray squirrel about the size of *aberti* but with relatively longer tail and shorter, untufted ears; body dark gray above, white below, tail dark gray with silvery margins.

Measurements.—A large specimen measures in total length, 552; tail, 284; hind foot, 73 millimeters.

Distribution and habitat.—In 1885 Nelson collected these big Arizona gray squirrels on the headwaters of the San Francisco River in the western part of the Mogollon Mountains near Frisco (the present town of Reserve), and on Negrito Creek 10 miles east of Frisco he collected two or three more and reported half a dozen seen. Farther down the San Francisco Valley at Glenwood, near the mouth of Whitewater Creek, in November, 1906, the writer saw one on the ground under the walnut trees, but before he could get through a barbed-wire fence it had taken refuge in the tall sycamores and cottonwoods and was completely lost. On inquiry among the ranchers he learned that the gray squirrels were fairly common along the canyon of the San Francisco River, where black walnuts and acorns are abundant and groves of cottonwoods and sycamores afford cover and protection. Apparently they are squirrels of the river valleys of southern Arizona and southwestern New Mexico, mainly in the Upper Sonoran Zone, but also in river bottoms and canyons where the zones are more or less mixed. Their range corresponds in part with that of the Arizona black walnut (*Juglans major*), but stops short of the open valley country.

General habits.—Mearns, the only naturalist who has had much experience with these squirrels, records them in several places in Arizona as coming into the lower edge of the pines, but generally found in the canyons and stream valleys. He says their habits and actions closely resemble those of the eastern gray squirrel, and their food "comprises seeds of pine cones, acorns, walnuts, berries, and green vegetation." (Mearns, 1907, p. 277.)

SCIURUS FREMONTI FREMONTI Audubon and Bachman

Fremont's Pine Squirrel; Gray Chickaree

Sciurus fremonti Audubon and Bachman, Quadrupeds North America 3 : 237, 1854.

Type locality.—"Rocky Mountains"; probably Colorado.

General characters.—A small, short-eared squirrel of the chickaree group, with dark olive-gray back and light-gray belly in the winter but in summer more of a brownish gray above with a black line along each side, and with whitish lower parts.

Measurements.—A large individual measures in total length, 337; tail, 140; hind foot, 52 millimeters.

Distribution and habitat.—The pine squirrel of Colorado (pl. 5, A) is represented among the New Mexico specimens by a single individual from Chama. This was collected by Loring, December 22, 1893, in the San Juan Mountains close to the northern border of the State and is a young of the year in perfect winter pelage. (Fig. 11.) In every way it agrees fully with the small dark gray *fremonti*, but in winter pelage there is less difference between *fremonti* and *mogollonensis* than in summer. It is not improbable that summer specimens from the same locality will show intergradation with *mogollonensis*, so there is still some doubt as to whether typical *fremonti* occurs in New Mexico. The doubt is suggested by the fact that specimens in late summer pelage from farther south in the San Juan Mountains are referable to the larger and redder *mogollonensis*. Until a series of summer specimens is obtained from the mountains about Chama the question will not be fully settled. This is the pine squirrel of Colorado and parts of Wyoming and Utah, in much of its range closely associated with the lodgepole pine (*Pinus murrayana*), and hence commonly known as the pine squirrel. The little cones of this pine, often available, furnish its favorite food, but in their absence the cones of spruces and firs are largely depended upon. Its distribution and

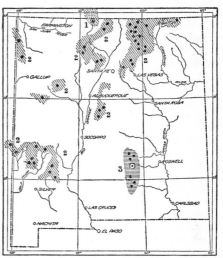

FIGURE 11.—Distribution of spruce squirrels in New Mexico: 1, *Sciurus fremonti fremonti;* 2, *S. fremonti mogollonensis;* 3, *S. fremonti lychnuchus.* Type locality circled

habits in Colorado have been so fully described by Warren (1910, p. 185) and Cary (1911, p. 69) that little can be added from its limited distribution in New Mexico.

SCIURUS FREMONTI MOGOLLONENSIS Mearns

SPRUCE SQUIRREL; ARIZONA CHICKAREE; TSU-WA-LA-AH-NA of the Taos Indians

Sciurus hudsonius mogollonensis Mearns, Auk 7: 49, 1890.
Sciurus fremonti neomexicanus Allen, Bul. Amer. Mus. Nat. Hist. 10: 291, 1898. Type from Rayado Canyon, Colfax County, N. Mex.

Type.—Collected at "Quaking asp settlement, summit of the Mogollon Mountains," [16] in central Arizona, May 25, 1887, by E. A. Mearns.

General characters.—Size slightly larger than *fremonti* with more fulvous in the gray of the upper parts and more black on the terminal portion of the tail.

---

[16] The Mogollon Mountains of Mearns are the western part of the White Mountains, in central Arizona, on recent maps called Mogollon Mesa.

Dark gray in winter, it is more of a reddish gray with black side stripes in summer.

Measurements.—An adult male measures in total length, 340; tail, 145; hind foot, 55 millimeters.

Distribution and habitat.—The name *mogollonensis* applies to most of the spruce squirrels of New Mexico as well as those of Arizona. Much to the surprise of the writer, the large series of specimens collected at different seasons in the mountains of northern New Mexico show no characters on which to separate *neomexicanus* from *mogollonensis*, although differing in well-marked subspecific characters from *fremonti*. Specimens in the Bureau of Biological Survey collection from the Sangre de Cristo, Raton, San Juan, Gallinas, Jemez, Manzano, Chuska, Mimbres, and Mogollon Mountains show no constant variation other than individual and seasonal. These squirrels are also common in the Mount Taylor, Elk, San Francisco, and Escadillo Mountains, but have not been found in the Datil Ranges. (Fig. 11.) In 1873 H. W. Henshaw collected one at El Moro (Zuni Mountains), but none have been taken there since. Their range is practically confined to the Canadian and the Hudsonian Zones and is more or less isolated in each of the mountains where they are found. The lack of greater geographic variation can only be accounted for by the great similarity of climatic and environmental conditions throughout the zones that they occupy.

The name pine squirrel, in common use for the dark gray chickaree farther north, is rarely applied to this species, which is commonly known throughout its range as the spruce squirrel. There is no common Canadian Zone pine in this region, and these squirrels are so closely associated with the several species of spruce and firs on which they depend for food that the name is peculiarly appropriate; moreover, in this region the big tufted-eared Abert's squirrel of the yellow pines is very commonly called the pine squirrel. These squirrels are associated mainly with the Douglas spruce, blue spruce, and Engelmann spruce, and also the two species of fir common to their zone and habitat. They rarely come down into the edge of the yellow-pine belt farther than the spruces extend on cold slopes.

General habits.—These bright, noisy little squirrels are generally abundant throughout their zone and if unmolested about camp soon become curious and finally fearless in their investigation of newcomers. Their energy and vivacity are boundless, but if alarmed they are as silent and wary as larger and more hunted game. Their stirring chr-r-r-r-r-r che-che-che-e-e-e-e begins with the sunrise, and the colder and frostier the morning the more energetically it rings from the tops of the tallest trees. Later in the day the squirrels are too busy to waste time with more than an occasional chr-r-r-r-r, unless some enemy appears in the distance. At any suspicious sound, a coughing bark with numerous variations begins and is kept up until the coast seems clear, but if the enemy approaches too near the bark ceases and is usually taken up by the next nearest neighbor and passed along until the intruder is heralded sometimes for miles through the woods, though not a squirrel is in sight. Occasionally you come upon one sitting on a branch only a few feet above your head gazing at you with wide-eyed surprise and curiosity. A few squeaks and whistles will usually coax it into frantic scolding and astonished antics. Often as you walk along under the trees a cone drops almost on your head, and making the bark rattle a squirrel climbs breathlessly up the tree to a safe height. Sometimes a low chr-r-r-r sounds like a chuckle, and you imagine that the rascal threw the cone at you purposely. Again, you surprise it on the ground among the logs and brush and give it a great fright, sending it flying with puffed tail over logs and from bush to bush until it reaches a safe tree, where it is soon out of reach and out of sight among the topmost branches, for it is an expert at hiding in the evergreen tree tops.

The nests of the spruce squirrels are numerous and conspicuous among the spruces, commonly placed on the branches several feet from the trunk and well fastened among the twigs and lateral branches. They are usually great balls a foot in diameter, made of twigs, grass, moss, and leaves. There is a hole at one side and a warm, soft, clean bed in the middle in a cavity just large enough for the squirrel to curl up comfortably. These nests apparently serve for both summer and winter homes, as hollow trees and logs are almost unknown among the spruces. In places the writer found three or four nests in a wide-spreading old Douglas spruce, but usually there are only one or two in a tree, and after the family of full-grown young breaks up the squirrels seem to be entirely solitary. This is no doubt a matter of necessity with them, as the life of each one depends upon his summer industry in storing food to last through the long cold winter. Social enough at a proper distance, they call, scold, chatter, and answer back and forth through the tree tops, but let one come on to the storing ground of another or into his tree or group of trees and there is war at once. The intruder seems always to know that he is in the wrong, and when discovered his only desire is to escape. Occasionally there is a fierce little contest—two squirrels mixed up in a furry ball—but usually it is only a race in which the stranger seems always to win; sometimes it is over the ground but often through the tree tops and to a good safe distance. The fights and chases are most vigorous during storing time in the fall months, but during the winter the storehouses are jealously guarded. During the spring and summer most of this vigilance is relaxed, as the males are then hunting much of their food at large, while the mother squirrels are caring for their young in the nests.

Food habits.—The food of the spruce squirrel varies with the time of year. When the young come out of the nests they begin to nibble and test every article that comes in their way, but finally settle down to a diet mainly of buds and leaves, which appear in their stomachs as a green mass mixed with the curd of their mother's milk. The writer has found this curd in their stomachs as late as August 17. At this midsummer time the store of last year's seeds is generally low, or entirely exhausted, so that the old squirrels are also depending upon buds, mushrooms, berries, and various seeds. Usually, however, some cone seeds are found throughout the summer and can be detected in the stomachs of the old squirrels by their oily consistency and strong characteristic odor. When the seeds of the spruce cones are nearly ripe the squirrels begin on them and it is rare to find anything else in their stomachs for the rest of the fall and winter.

If any preference is shown for the different spruces it may be for the Douglas, but the cones of Picea and Abies seem to be nearly as acceptable and always preferred to the large-coned pines. Occasionally the long heavy cones of the limber pine (*Pinus flexilis*) are found with the scales cut and the seeds eaten, and even the hard heavy cones of the yellow pine (*P. ponderosa*) are opened and the seeds eaten out or the cones buried for winter use. These large cones are not easily handled, however, and the spruce seems to be in every way more acceptable.

The cones are commonly eaten on one or two chosen branches in the squirrel's favorite tree. A cone is cut off or carried from the ground or from the winter cache to the branch where the squirrel sits, usually with its tail against the trunk of the tree, with the cone held stem upward in its hands. The basal scales are clipped off and dropped to the ground and each seed is eaten as it appears. When the cone is finished the core is thrown down, and in this way a little pile of scales and cores grows under the feeding branch until sometimes the season's accumulation is large enough to fill a bushel basket, and as time goes on year by year the pile of scales grows, until under some old spruces one may find 10 or 15 bushels. Sometimes these are from one species of cone, and again they may contain the scales and cores of Pseudotsuga, Picea, Abies, and Pinus. As these scale heaps accumulate year after year, the old scales at the bottom sink into the black mold of the woods' earth, or, spreading out and becoming scattered over a considerable area, form a favorite deposit for the winter supply of fresh cones. Holes are easily dug in these loose scales large enough to accommodate two or three to a dozen fresh cones, which are either lightly covered over or left in plain view.

During the cone season the regular early morning work of the squirrel is in the tree tops cutting off and dropping the cones to the ground, the tapping and thumping sounding almost continuously among the trees. After the sun is well up and the ground becomes warmer than the tree tops, the squirrels come down and work energetically in gathering and storing their crop. Every little hollow in the ground, or sheltered space under logs, or nooks and corners between the roots of trees is taken advantage of; also numerous holes are dug in the mellow earth to be packed full of cones for the winter's food. Bushels of cones are thus put away under and around a single tree, but rarely in large masses. Sometimes a quart or a peck may be found in a hollow that offered convenient protection, but usually they are stored in smaller cavities.

During winter a network of burrows is made under the deep, soft snow, and the cones are brought up as needed and eaten from a convenient perch on a branch. As the snow disappears in spring this network of runways over the surface of the ground is uncovered. Whether the squirrels complete their set of galleries to connect with all the chambers of the cache when the first soft snows fall, or whether they are able to extend them during winter before the snow hardens, has never been determined, but it seems more probable that most of the galleries are formed in the soft snow of early winter. The squirrels do not hibernate but may do some extra sleeping in the very cold weather. Their pantry is so protected and usually so close to the nest that there is little trouble in getting an abundance of food even during the storms. They do not become fat as do the animals that hibernate, but seem always to be plump and in good muscular condition.

During the busy season of cone harvest the faces and hands of the squirrels are generally smeared with pitch, which no amount of preening will take off until the fur loosens and comes out with it. This must be a great trial to such neat and orderly little animals, but it lasts only until the cold weather begins and the new winter coat replaces the old, worn, and soiled working suit. The pitch is then hard and brittle and that on the buried cones is covered over so the winter dress of silky fur is kept beautifully immaculate.

Breeding habits.—The breeding habits of the spruce squirrels are little known, as the young are born in spring or early summer, probably while the snow is still deep at the high levels in the mountains. By midsummer, or about the 1st of August, the half-grown young appear outside of the nests, and from that time until early in fall they keep together in families and are watched and warned of danger by the mother squirrel. The writer has never found more than four young in a family. Apparently the old squirrel takes no responsibility for feeding them after they are weaned, but the weaning does not take place until they are half grown and perfectly able to care for themselves. Before entirely weaned the half-grown young have been found with a mixture of curd, green food, and nuts in their stomachs. During October and November the half to two-thirds grown young are still in the fuzzy, immature pelage, but in November or December they get the full winter coat of the adults. They can be distinguished, however, during the first winter by their smaller size and by undeveloped cranial characters.

The father squirrel seems to have no place in the family group and has probably forgotten his family ties or has been banished as a superfluous member. Apparently there is only one litter in the year. In the many series of specimens collected the half-grown and immature individuals correspond closely in size and development when the dates at which they were taken are approximately the same.

Economic status.—The flesh of the spruce squirrel is of little value as food and commonly has a very perceptible flavor of turpentine; still, when camp is far away and there is no other food, it is very acceptable and even enjoyable if broiled over the coals, though without so much as salt to bring out the flavor. There have been many complaints of the destruction of tree seeds by these squirrels, and it is probable that they consume more than any other one animal of those seeds on which they are in the habit of feeding. On the other hand, they are the most diligent seed planters of these same trees. The cones are often stored in places well beyond the shade of the tree or carried a considerable distance from one part of the forest to another and usually buried to a favorable depth for germination, in case they are not dug up for food by the storer. Enemies, such as martens, minks, weasels, foxes, coyotes, cats, hawks, and owls, are numerous, and if half the squirrels survived the winters, their increase would be much greater than it usually is. Wherever a squirrel drops out during the winter his larder becomes in part a seed ground. It is impossible to say how much the forest owes to these planters, but it is certain that their planting has been going on for unknown ages.

Under the present forest management and the artificial methods of gathering and distributing tree seeds, the squirrels are important, if unwilling, assistants, for their stored cones are easily accessible and can be gathered rapidly in large quantities with the assurance that all those stored contain good seeds. As compensation for this robbery it is not only fair but wise conservation to protect the squirrels from all unnecessary destruction. But, aside from all utilitarian considerations, is it not well worth while to conserve one of the brightest, most cheerful, and interesting little animals of the forest for the enjoyment of those who can appreciate the wonderful out of doors?

SCIURUS FREMONTI LYCHNUCHUS Rehn

RUIDOSO CHICKAREE; RED SPRUCE SQUIRREL

Sciurus fremonti lychnuchus Rehn, Acad. Nat. Sci. Phila. Proc. 55: 18, May 7, 1903.

Type.—Collected in White Mountains, N. Mex., Forks of Ruidoso Creek, Lincoln County, August 18, 1898, by C. M. Barber.

General characters.—A well-marked subspecies of the size and general appearance of the Arizona chickaree but conspicuously redder in summer pelage—almost as red as the eastern red squirrel. The full winter pelage is not represented in any specimens examined.

Distribution and habitat.—Ruidoso chickarees are common throughout the Canadian Zone in the White, Capitan, and Sacramento Mountains, and possibly also in the Guadalupe Mountains south to the Texas line. (Fig. 11.) In going north through the Sacramento Mountains, Hollister and the writer first met with them 5 or 6 miles south of the little town of Weed, near the southern limit of spruces, and thence northward found them common throughout the spruce and firs for the whole length of the range and over the sides of the White Mountains (Sierra Blanca). Gaut collected them in the western part of the Capitan Mountains, and the writer found them in the eastern part. In the southern part of the Guadalupe Mountains in 1902 a small tree squirrel was reported as of very rare occurrence. but no trace of it could be found.

General habits.—In habits the Ruidoso chickaree differs very little from the spruce squirrel, to which it is more nearly related than to Fremont's pine squirrel. Possibly the more open forest in which they live has let more of the color of sunshine into their fur, or the mixture of red-leaved oaks (*Quercus novomexicana*) and yellow-barked pines in the lower edge of their range has afforded just the touch of protective coloration that has eliminated the darker individuals and preserved those of the brighter shades. On warm slopes the yellow pine straggles through most of their range, and its cones are often eaten, but generally the squirrels are found among the Douglas spruce or in the groves of blue spruce or firs, where their nests and heaps of cone scales show their real homes to be located.

Under some big Douglas spruces, just back of the delightful summer camp of Cloudcroft, in June, 1900, these squirrels were singing, scolding, and working every bright morning. The heaps of cone scales had accumulated all winter under the trees, until they were conical like wood-rat or muskrat houses, 2 or 3 feet high, and contained sometimes 5 or 6 bushels of scales. These were mainly of

Douglas spruce but contained also the scales of firs and a few white and yellow pine. Some were fresh and were being shelled daily on the heaps, showing that the last year's crop had tided over. The ground was filled with shallow holes where the cones had been taken out and hollow spaces under logs and stumps were empty. Later these would doubtless be filled again with the next crop of cones. Some mushrooms were also being eaten, and probably various seeds and berries would be drawn upon to tide over the next two months until the cone seeds would again be fit for food.

Up to June 1 the young squirrels were not yet out of the nests, or were not visible, but several nests were seen on the branches of the spruces. They were made of the usual twigs and leaves and the long green tree lichens, so common in the forest.

EUTAMIAS QUADRIVITTATUS QUADRIVITTATUS (SAY)

LARGER COLORADO CHIPMUNK; QUA-MHEÚ-NA of the Taos Indians

Sciurus quadrivittatus Say, in Long's Expedition to Rocky Mountains 2: note 27, 235, 1823.
Tamias quadrivittatus gracilis Allen, Bul. Amer. Mus. Nat. Hist. 3: 99, June, 1890. Type from San Pedro, N. Mex.

Type locality.—Arkansas River, 26 miles below Canon City, Colo.

General characters.—Of the two chipmunks found in the mountains of northern New Mexico, this is the larger species, with pure-white belly. From the smaller *operarius*, with which they are in many places associated, at the junction of the range, they are rarely distinguished except as specimens in the hand are compared; then the larger size, especially the larger feet and ears, more extensive and purer white of the lower parts, and darker under surface of the tail of *quadrivittatus* are very noticeable. Like so many species of western chipmunks, their backs are brightly marked with three lines of black, the central one extending usually to between the ears and bordered by two lines of light gray. Beyond the second lines of black are two conspicuous lines of pure white, and in summer pelage these are usually bordered by two short lines of dark brown or black. The winter pelage is much grayer throughout, but in summer with its golden brown sides and bright markings, this bush-tailed little half-squirrel is one of the brightest and prettiest, as well as commonest and most conspicuous, of the mountain animals.

Measurements.—Typical adults average in total length, 227; tail, 106; hind foot, 34 millimeters.

Distribution and habitat.—There are specimens of the larger Colorado chipmunk (pl. 5, B) in the Biological Survey collection from the Raton, Sierra Grande, Sangre de Cristo, San Juan, Jemez, Mount Taylor, Zuni, Sandia, and Manzano Mountains; also from the mesa north of Cabra Springs, the Canadian River near Liberty, and the northern rim of Llano Estacado near Cuervo. Its range is practically coincident with the Transition, or yellow pine, Zone of the mountains of northern New Mexico, generally from 7,500 to 8,500 feet altitude. (Fig. 12.) Occasionally one is found considerably above its zone on some warm slope where it has wandered during the summer months, and specimens of old and young were taken along the Canadian River near the lower edge of Upper Sonoran Zone where a few scrubby mesquite bushes could be seen on the opposite slope. They were living, however, in dense thickets on steep, cold slopes where conditions were undoubtedly similar to those 1,000 feet higher on warmer slopes. Generally they are found throughout the yellow-pine forest but are by no means restricted to forest cover.

Brushy and rocky slopes, scrub-oak gulches, old burns, berry patches, and thickets of second growth or any combination affording food and cover are accepted as a habitat.

General habits.—In habits the larger Colorado chipmunks are both tree squirrel and ground squirrel, as they climb readily and get a part of their food from the tree fruits and seeds, often taking refuge in tree tops to escape some of their enemies. Their real homes, however, are in the ground, among rocks or in hollow logs. At the approach of danger they usually seek protection in some of these strongholds, where they are comparatively safe. When seen by man they are generally running over the ground, along logs or fences, or sitting on stumps and rocks watching or feeding. Often they are seen in the tops of bushes or on branches of low trees gathering berries or seeds for food, and if suddenly surprised they are likely to disappear up the opposite side of the nearest tree.

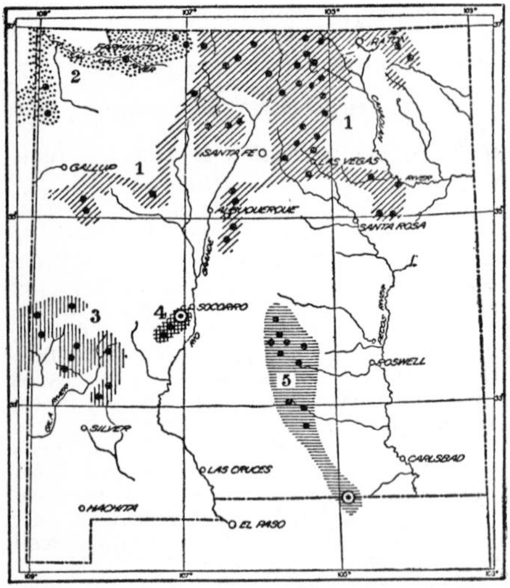

FIGURE 12.—Distribution of New Mexico chipmunks, in part: 1, *Eutamias quadrivittatus quadrivittatus*; 2, *E. quadrivittatus hopiensis*; 3, *E. cinereicollis cinereicollis*; 4, *E. cinereicollis canescens*; 5, *E. cinereicollis canipes.* Type localities circled

Voice.—In walking or riding through the woods, one frequently hears a shrill, rapid chipper as one of these little animals is suddenly startled and scurries for its burrow or the nearest tree. Apparently the warning is thus passed along to others of the family. Again, on a still day one often hears a l o w chuck - chuck - c h u c k repeated at intervals of about one second in a soft, faraway tone. By following the sound very quietly one generally locates the chipmunk sitting in a rounded ball on a stump or low branch of a tree, its tail waving gently as the soft barking note is made. This seems to be the regular call note, and it probably has many definite meanings in the chipmunk family circle. It often seems to imply peace and contentment rather than warning of danger. There are many minor notes and sounds that these chipmunks make, including a shriek of rage or fear when suddenly captured, but their language is little heard and less understood.

Food habits.—The food of these chipmunks comprises a great variety of seeds, grain, nuts, acorns, berries, tubers, and mushrooms, some green vegetation and occasionally insects. They are much more omnivorous than the tree squirrels, and for that reason are much more troublesome where there are fields of grain, gardens, or household supplies within their range; for the same reason they are more easily caught in traps, as they will accept a greater variety of baits. Like the ground squirrels, to which they are related, they apparently hibernate during the cold months, but they also lay up stores of food to be eaten in their burrows or dens when the weather is too cold or the snow too deep for obtaining a supply in the open. Much of the mischief that they occasionally do depends on this habit of storing food for winter, for each chipmunk established at the edge of a ripening grainfield works early and late from the time the grain begins to ripen until the last kernel is out of the field. The grain is cut down, shelled, tucked into the cheek pouches until they bulge out on both sides of the face, then carried on the scamper to the winter storehouse. This is kept up for a great part of each day, and the inroads on fields depend upon the number of chipmunks at work and the time elapsing from ripening to harvest. In many small fields of grain near the woods the ragged, half-eaten borders extend far into the grain before it is cut. Acorns and the seeds of other plants are also stored, but a grainfield always tempts the chipmunks from far and near. The food cache is often dug out by badgers, skunks, foxes, or other animals in search of a meal. An empty and torn up mass of soft grass fibers a foot or more below the surface of the ground and a scattered store of winter seeds are often found, showing where an unfortunate chipmunk served as a breakfast.

In spring, when the winter stores are exhausted and food is being sought far and wide, the chipmunks often find the hills of planted corn or gather the seeded grain from the fields; but the most serious mischief they do, or are likely to do, is to interfere with reforestation by digging up and eating the planted seeds of trees. So keen are their senses for the discovery of food that few seeds escape them, and it has been found necessary to destroy them over extensive planted areas to make the plantation successful.

Breeding habits.—The earliest breeding record reported was by McClure Surber from Rinconada in the Rio Grande Canyon, where, on May 11, he found a young chipmunk with the eyes not yet open. He succeeded in raising it as an interesting pet. This was at the extreme lower limit of range of the species where it has been reported active all winter and where it may breed earlier than it would at higher levels. By the middle of June, wherever the species occurs, many half-grown young are out, gathering their food, so the first of May may not be too early for the usual birth of the litters. The writer has never found small young in the autumn or late in summer, and specimens examined do not show any great variation in the development of the young at the same season. It therefore seems doubtful whether more than one litter is usually raised in a summer. The number of young as indicated by embryos varies from 4 to 6 but may be considerably more than this. The mammae of nursing females are generally eight, arranged in one pair of inguinal, two pairs of abdominal, and one pair of pectoral. The small or nearly half-grown young caught in traps or shot for specimens often show on stomach examination a mixture of curd from their mothers' milk with other food, such as green seeds, tender vegetation, or berries.

When the fall storing of seeds begins the families evidently break up and each stores its winter supply separately and close to its own warm nest chamber.

Hibernation.—Throughout most of their range these chipmunks hibernate or remain in their dens during the coldest weather. Unlike the true ground squirrels, they do not become excessively fat, and their period of hibernation is comparatively short and possibly incomplete. At Twining, in the Taos Mountains, at the extreme upper limit of their range Surber found them active until the first deep snows came about the 1st of December, after which no more were seen during the rest of the winter. At the extreme lower edge of their range in the Rio Grande Canyon at Cienequilla, however, he found them active during the whole winter. This would indicate that the hibernation is irregular and depends upon extreme cold; but it is possible that they do not hibernate at all, merely living on their ample stores of food in well-protected nests in the ground or among rocks. The fact of their failure to become very fat in fall would indicate imperfect hibernation, if any.

Economic status.—Though timid and quick to take alarm, these chipmunks are inquisitive and about camps often become tame enough to boldly enter food boxes and sacks. About regular camping places, if grain is scattered or other food is left where they can find it, they generally congregate in great numbers, and in such places newcomers with a fresh supply of food are forced to take means for its protection. If supplies are to be left in camps for any length of time they may be partially protected by storing them in tin-lined boxes or cupboards, or by suspending them from wires.

Seed planting.—In the economy of the forest the chipmunks have some value as seed planters, although differing from the squirrels in hoarding rather than scattering their winter stores. Their dens are more often in the open or in brush land well out from the shade of the forest. The seeds of bushes and small plants compose a large part of the stores, but tree seeds of oak, maple, juniper, and pine are also hoarded, and when the chipmunk is unearthed and eaten by some of its enemies the seeds are more or less scattered, planted, and left to grow. The forest has undoubtedly derived some benefit from the chipmunks in compensation for the great number of seeds that they annually consume; but of systematic reforestation they are probably the greatest enemies.

EUTAMIAS QUADRIVITTATUS HOPIENSIS Merriam

Hopi Chipmunk; Golden Chipmunk; Ko win'na of the Hopi Indians (Fisher)

Eutamias hopiensis Merriam, Biol. Soc. Wash. Proc. 18: 165, 1905.

Type.—Collected at Keam Canyon, Navajo County, Ariz., July 27, 1894, by A. K. Fisher.

General characters.—Differs from *quadrivittatus* mainly in the reduction of the dark stripes and the greater suffusion of golden colors; inhabits more arid, open, and scattered forests where, as usual, the lighter and brighter colors prevail.

Distribution and habitat.—In northwestern New Mexico the Hopi chipmunk occupies the scattered yellow-pine forests of the Chuska Mountains, the mesas and the canyon rims of the San Juan Valley, and the yellow pines of the western part of the Jicarilla Indian Reservation; but the greater part of its range extends over similar areas in southwestern Colorado, southern Utah, and northeastern Arizona. New Mexico specimens have been examined from the Chuska Mountains, Largo Canyon, Dulce, and La Jara. None of these are absolutely typical, but can much better be referred to *hopiensis* than *quadrivittatus*, toward which they are evidently grading.

General habits.—At the little town of Blanco on the San Juan River, Clarence Birdseye caught two specimens of the Hopi chipmunk in a trap set under a jointfir bush (Ephedra) at the base of a sandstone cliff in Canyon Largo, and was told that they were sometimes found in the open valley and even among the buildings of the settlement. In the Chuska Mountains they were common throughout the Transition Zone from 7,000 to 9,000 feet altitude, usually among the yellow pines and Gambel's oaks, and were often seen on rocks and cliffs. In these mountains their habits were very similar to those of *quadrivittatus*, except that they more readily took to the high trees and often escaped in the tops of the tallest pines. The writer found them active in 1908 up to the time of his leaving the mountains, October 12. There had been several slight snowfalls and the weather was very frosty, ice forming to considerable thickness almost every night at his camps near 9,000 feet elevation. At that time the chipmunks had not yet begun to show signs of hibernation and were busily storing food for the winter.

Specimens were taken in Largo Canyon November 19, 1908. In the yellow-pine forest of the Jicarilla Indian Reservation a few were found during September, 1904, and their soft, almost squirrel-like voices, so different from the shrill chipper of *quadrivittatus*, were noted. This was the first time the writer had encountered the species, and their habits as well as voices at once impressed him as quite different from those of *quadrivittatus* and *operarius*. After recognizing the difference in voice, it was some time before he could get sight of one of the Hopi chipmunks. They seemed to be fairly common but were so shy and so expert at climbing and hiding that only a few specimens were secured and most of these from the tops of tall trees. They were rapid and expert climbers and always succeeded in keeping on the far side of the trunk of a tree. Two that the writer surprised and cornered in the top of a nut pine finally escaped by keeping the tree between themselves and him until they got into the brush and reached tall timber.

Food habits.—In several places these chipmunks were found feeding on nuts of the pinyon pine, and several of those collected had acorns in their cheek pouches. They doubtless get some seeds from the yellow pine but the writer did not find any cones that were unquestionably opened by them. Berries and seeds of bushes and various plants form an important part of their food.

Breeding habits.—The breeding habits of this species are probably very similar to those of *quadrivittatus*, but there is little to judge from except the specimens. Almost full-grown young of the year are taken in July and August, and one small young just out was taken in the Chuska Mountains on October 3. This may indicate two broods a year occasionally in the mild climate where they are found.

EUTAMIAS CINEREICOLLIS CINEREICOLLIS (ALLEN)

GRAY-COLLARED CHIPMUNK; ARIZONA CHIPMUNK

Tamias cinereicollis Allen, Bul. Amer. Mus. Nat. Hist. 3: 94, 1890.

Type.—Collected in San Francisco Mountains, Ariz., August 2, 1889, by C. Hart Merriam and Vernon Bailey.

General characters.—The gray-collared chipmunk is about the size of, or a little larger than *quadrivittatus*, but is readily distinguished by its duller colors, more ashy neck and shoulders, and the broader black stripes of the back.

Measurements.—Adults from the type locality average in total length, 223; tail, 102; hind foot, 35 millimeters.

Distribution and habitat.—Though the greater part of the range of the gray-collared chipmunks lies through central Arizona, the animals are also the common chipmunk of the Mogollon, Datil, San Francisco, Tularosa, Elk, and Mimbres Mountains. They are found mainly within the spruce of the Canadian Zone but also in the yellow pine along the upper edge of the Transition. In the Mogollons the writer found them up to about 10,000 feet altitude, where they were just as common as at the lower edge of the zone. This seems also to agree with their range in the White Mountains and San Francisco Mountains of Arizona where they are mainly in the Canadian but also reach into the Transition Zone.

General habits.—The favorite haunts of the gray-collared chipmunks are log piles about old clearings, or the edges of burned forests, but they are also commonly found in the dense pine, spruce, or fir forests. They are good climbers, often taking to the trees for protection and escaping by hiding among the dense, evergreen foliage. When not alarmed they are often seen sitting on stumps or logs waving their bushy tails from side to side in slow serpentine motions as they utter a sharp chipper or low chuck-chuck-chuck. They are generally very shy and when alarmed will commonly disappear among the logs or trees, but one can usually secure specimens by waiting patiently until their curiosity brings them out to peer over the log or branch.

Food habits.—In the Mogollon and Mimbres Mountains, E. A. Goldman reported the chipmunks as apparently feeding on the cones of Douglas spruce, and he found one with a little mushroom in its cheek pouch. In the Datil Mountains the writer shot one with an acorn of Gambel's oak in its cheek and in the Mogollons found others busily gathering acorns and a variety of seeds for their winter stores. Currants, gooseberries, and shadblow berries are items in their bill of fare, and they dig many little holes in the ground, probably for tubers or starchy roots. The contents of their stomachs, most of which is unidentifiable, usually show a mixture of various finely masticated seeds, some green vegetation, and occasionally a trace of insects.

Breeding habits.—Little is known of the breeding habits of the gray-collared chipmunk except that by midsummer the young are half grown and in September and October almost full grown. Their uniformity in size would indicate but one litter a year.

Hibernation.—There is little evidence to show that these chipmunks hibernate, and it is certain that they do not become very fat in the fall and that they gather up stores of food for winter. They

have been found active in the Mogollon Mountains from 8,000 to
10,000 feet altitude, up to the end of October, with 2 inches of snow
on the ground and ice that would hold one up in crossing the streams.
Their tracks were abundant on the snow over the mountains, but it is
probable that during the real cold of winter they remain in their dens
under the deep snow, either sleeping or comfortably feeding on their
stores.

EUTAMIAS CINEREICOLLIS CANIPES Bailey

Gray-Footed Chipmunk

Eutamias cinereicollis canipes Bailey, Biol. Soc. Wash. Proc. 15: 117, 1902.

Type.—Collected in Guadalupe Mountains, close to the Texas–New Mexico line, August 24, 1901, by Vernon Bailey.

General characters.—This form of the *cinereicollis* and *bulleri* group from
the mountains east of the Rio Grande Valley, while widely separated geographically from *cinereicollis*, is so closely connected in general characters that
it is accorded only subspecific rank. The grayer feet and tail are the most
convenient characters by which to recognize it.

Distribution and habitat.—Specimens of the gray-footed chipmunk have been examined from the type locality in the southern part
of the Guadalupe Mountains; from McKitterick Canyon, Tex., and
Dog Canyon, N. Mex.; from Penasco Creek and Cloudcroft in the
Sacramento Mountains; Sierra Blanca; several localities in the
Capitan Mountains; and from the Jicarilla Mountains. They range
throughout the full width of the Transition and Canadian Zones, and
specimens have been taken from 7,500 feet on Penasco Creek to 11,880
feet at the summit of Sierra Blanca. In canyons and cold gulches
they often range as low as 7,000 feet. They are less common, however, in the lower, more open part of the Transition Zone and seem
to be more abundant throughout the spruce and fir forests of the
Canadian Zone.

General habits.—The gray-footed chipmunks are largely forest
animals and are usually found among the trees or in dense thickets,
but occasionally running along fences or over logs at the edge of
clearings and burns. They are fond of rocky slopes, where brush
and timber offer shade and cover and the cliffs afford runways,
convenient perches, and safe retreats. They are skillful at climbing
not only rocks and cliffs, but also trees and bushes. In search of
food they run through the tops of the scrub oak chaparral and the
various thickets in the gulches and climb such trees as afford pro-
vender for chipmunk pantries. Occasionally when alarmed they
take refuge in some convenient tree, but generally they rush for the
nearest burrow or crevice in the rocks, where they disappear and
keep quiet for a few minutes until the danger is supposed to have
passed. They soon reappear, however, and after carefully peering
about begin again to carry on their regular occupation of gathering
food. In the thick brush and in forests they are more often heard
than seen. Their note of alarm is a shrill, rapid chipper, like that
of *cinereicollis*, and not very unlike that of *quadrivittatus*. In case
of sudden alarm at close quarters it becomes so rapid as to blend
into a shrill squeak, but ordinarily it is a rapid trill, often repeated
several times in quick succession, or at short intervals. They also
have the low call note—a soft, slowly repeated chuck-chuck-chuck,

which is heard commonly from the top of a bowlder or a low branch of a tree.

Food habits.—Apparently these chipmunks feed to some extent on the seeds of the small cones of spruces and firs, but it is not always possible to be sure what is responsible for the scattered cone scales over the rocks and logs where they feed. Acorns of the various species of oaks seem to form their principal food supply during the late summer and autumn. These are gathered and stored from the time they begin to ripen until they are all gone or buried by the snow. Scattered acorn shells are the commonest mark of feeding grounds, and the cheek pouches of chipmunks collected often contain one large or several small acorns. Wild sunflower and many small seeds are gathered and eaten or stored. Gooseberries, currants, and other berries are eaten with evident relish, and fields of wheat, oats, and barley attract the chipmunks to their vicinity.

Along Penasco Creek, Hollister and the writer found them, in company with the smaller black-striped chipmunk (*E. minimus atristriatus*), busily carrying away grain from the margins of the fields. As little of their range, however, comes into cultivated country, their depredations of this nature are not likely to be serious. In areas where reforestation is necessary within their range, these chipmunks will probably have to be dealt with in advance to insure the safety of planted seeds. As the forest has been removed from much of their range, the question of reforestation is likely to be brought up in the near future.

Breeding habits.—At Cloudcroft, from May 28 to June 2, 1900, only the adults of these chipmunks were found, the young evidently being still in their dens. During August of the following year in the Guadalupe Mountains the young were nearly full grown and were busily gathering and storing food. In the Capitan Mountains the half-grown young were out and running about by the middle of June, and half-grown young were collected by Gaut during the early part of July and nearly full-grown young in August. There is evidently but one litter a year and none too much time for these to develop and lay up their winter stores before the cold weather begins.

Hibernation.—In the Gallinas Mountains near Corona, Gaut was told that the chipmunks were common during the summer, but when he was there late in October he reported that they had all hibernated. It is probable that they either hibernate or remain in their dens feeding on their winter stores during the cold weather of winter; but specimens collected late in fall show no indication of becoming extremely fat as do the animals that hibernate for long periods. The deep snow that lies every winter over their range would at least make it necessary for them to depend on their winter stores for food, and probably shut them securely into their underground dens.

EUTAMIAS CINEREICOLLIS CINEREUS Bailey

MAGDALENA CHIPMUNK

Eutamias cinereicollis cinereus Bailey, Biol. Soc. Wash. Proc. 26: 130, 1913.

Type.—Collected in Copper Canyon, Magdalena Mountains, N. Mex., September 1, 1909, by E. A. Goldman.

General characters.—This pale-gray form of *cinereicollis* is merely a color variety due to a restricted and arid habitat on the sparsely wooded ranges of the Magdalena and San Mateo Mountains. The series of specimens collected on these peaks by E. A. Goldman in September and October, 1909, are all in the bright post-breeding pelage, which is practically identical in the adults and young of the year. The duller gray winter coat had not begun to appear October 4, in the last specimen collected.

Measurements.—Type, adult male: Total length, 225; tail, 91; foot, 33 millimeters.

Distribution and habitat.—The specimens from the Magdalena Mountains were taken in Copper Canyon from 8,200 to 9,000 feet, in the San Mateo Mountains in Monica Canyon from 8,200 to 9,500, and on San Mateo Peak at the southern end of this range, at 9,500 feet. A specimen in the collection of the College of Agriculture and Mechanic Arts taken by O. B. Metcalf in the Organ Mountains, April 18, 1903, though much grayer and whiter than those of the type series, is apparently of this form in winter pelage.

General habits.—These chipmunks, E. A. Goldman says, were found along the bottom of Copper Canyon, where most of the vegetation belongs to the Canadian Zone. Here they were rather common and unsuspicious, and as he came along the trail on horseback one ran in and out among the rocks and finally sat in plain view watching him from a rock only 10 feet away. Another was sitting on a rock gnawing the cone of a Douglas spruce surrounded by fragments of numerous other cones. The number of cones of this tree freshly torn to fragments, apparently by these chipmunks, indicates that its seeds are a favorite food. In the San Mateo Mountains, Goldman says, the little animals were generally distributed from 8,200 feet upward, especially along rocky canyons. Here they were also found feeding on the seeds of the Douglas spruce, and in places cone fragments were found scattered among and over the tops of the rocks, which formed their favorite feeding perches. At the lower edge of their range they were also found feeding on the seeds of pinyon pine. Some of these cones had been brought from considerable distances to the rocks where the chipmunks were seen cutting them open and taking out the seeds. Judged from the number of cone fragments, these sweet little nuts are a favorite food.

This is the only form of the New Mexico chipmunks with which the writer has no personal acquaintance, but its habits are undoubtedly much the same as those of *cinereicollis* from which it is only narrowly isolated.

EUTAMIAS MINIMUS OPERARIUS MERRIAM

LESSER COLORADO CHIPMUNK; BUSY CHIPMUNK

Eutamias amoenus operarius Merriam, Biol. Soc. Wash. Proc. 18: 164, 1905.

Type.—Collected at Gold Hill, Boulder County, Colo., at 7,400 feet altitude, October 8, 1903, by Vernon Bailey.

General characters.—This is the little chipmunk of the mountains of Colorado and northern New Mexico. In color and markings it is very similar to the larger *quadrivittatus*, with which it is often found associated along the lower part of its range, but its smaller size and especially the smaller hind feet and ears distinguish it on comparing specimens. In summer pelage the belly of *operarius* is more buffy and the lower surface of the tail is lighter yellow than in *quadrivittatus*. Its small rounded skull is, however, the best distinguishing character.

Measurements.—Typical adults: Total length, 200; tail, 90; hind foot, 31 millimeters.

Distribution and habitat.—There are specimens of the lesser Colorado chipmunk in the Biological Survey collection from the Raton Mountains and numerous localities in the Culebra, Taos, and Pecos River ranges, from Halls Peak, the San Juan, Jemez, Gallinas, and Chuska Mountains. The altitudes at which these specimens were collected generally range from 8,000 to 13,000 feet throughout the Canadian and Hudsonian Zones. Specimens were collected on Truchas Peak at 13,300 feet; on the top of Pecos Baldy at 12,600 feet; in the Culebra Mountains at 13,200 feet; in the Taos Mountains at 12,500 feet, and chipmunks were seen up to 13,000 feet. The upper limit of their range reaches to the tops of the highest peaks, but at such heights they are so uncommon that they have probably strayed up from the timber line below. In a few places they range below the lower edge of the Canadian Zone, as at Tres Piedras, where specimens were collected in the yellow pines of the Transition Zone. Generally their range is above that of *quadrivittatus* but throughout the borders where the two species meet they are often found near together and in some cases slightly overlapping. *Operarius*, however, is a chipmunk of the spruces and firs, with which it is generally associated. (Fig. 13.)

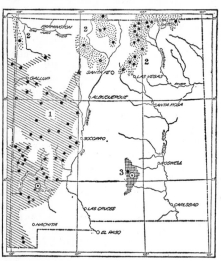

FIGURE 13.—Distribution of New Mexico chipmunks, in part: 1, *Eutamias dorsalis dorsalis;* 2. *E. minimus operarius;* 3, *E. minimus atristriatus.* Type localities circled

General habits. — These little mountain chipmunks, while common throughout timbered areas, are more partial to the edges of parks, burns, and windfalls, or to rock slides and brushy cliffs. They are generally seen running over logs, rocks, or the ground, and when alarmed they seem always to have burrows or safe retreats into which they can quickly disappear. They rarely take refuge in trees or climb about through the bushes in search of food, but are expert in running over the steep sides of rocks.

Voice.—Their little chippering voices are finer and sharper than those of the larger *quadrivittatus*, but otherwise are very similar. The writer has no record of their making any other sound and can not recall ever hearing them give the slow call note of the larger species.

Food habits.—In the Raton Mountains, A. H. Howell found the Colorado chipmunks feeding on wild cherries and the seeds of various weeds, including the ragweed (*Ambrosia trifida*), which were found in the pouches of several of the specimens collected. The writer has often watched them gathering the seeds of grass and small plants along the edges of the mountain parks and has seen them feeding on the berries of twistedstalk (*Streptopus amplexifolius*), and various species of gooseberries, currants, and blueberries. In the Gallinas Mountains they were feeding on acorns, but generally their range is above that of the oaks. At camp grounds they quickly gather to collect any scattered grain or kitchen refuse and unless discouraged soon become very tame.

Hibernation.—The writer has found them and has seen their tracks in the soft snow of October, but persons living in the mountains say there are no chipmunks about during the deep snow and cold weather of winter. They evidently spend a large part of the cold season in their burrows under the deep snow, but whether hibernating or merely enjoying the comforts of warm nests and plenty of food has never been determined. They do not become very fat in fall, and it is probable that their hibernation is not so complete as is that of the ground squirrels.

EUTAMIAS MINIMUS ATRISTRIATUS BAILEY

BLACK-STRIPED CHIPMUNK; PEÑASCO CHIPMUNK

Eutamias atristriatus Bailey, Biol. Soc. Wash. Proc. 26: 129, 1913.

Type.—Collected at Peñasco Creek, 12 miles east of Cloudcroft, N. Mex., at 7,400 feet altitude, September 6, 1902, by Vernon Bailey.

General characters.—The broad and strongly marked black stripes on the back of this chipmunk suggests the *bulleri* group, but its small size makes necessary a comparison with *operarius*, from which it differs in darker and duller coloration, more yellowish belly, and in its longer and narrower skull. Only specimens in post-breeding, or late summer, pelage, of September 6 and 7, have been examined.

Measurements.—Type: Total length, 220; tail, 114; hind foot, 32 milimeters.

Distribution and habitat.—In 1902 Hollister and the writer found these little yellow-bellied chipmunks throughout the Transition Zone along the east slope of the Sacramento Mountains, from 7,000 to 8,000 feet, ranging with *canipes* up to the edge of the spruce, and apparently a little below it to the junction of the yellow pines with the junipers. (Fig. 13.)

General habits.—Black-striped chipmunks were abundant in the open forest and especially along rail fences, but were rarely seen in dense woods. Dozens were seen on the roadside fences, often three or four at a time running ahead of our horses, and while many were shot for specimens, many more escaped into holes in the ground under logs, or among the weeds and brush. They were feeding on weed and sunflower seeds along the fences and on the wheat and oats at the edges of the fields. They were too busy to be noisy, but their chipper of alarm was constantly heard along the roadsides. At that season the young were about half grown and nearly uniform in size.

EUTAMIAS DORSALIS DORSALIS (BAIRD)

CLIFF CHIPMUNK; GILA CHIPMUNK; GRAY-BACKED CHIPMUNK

Tamias dorsalis Baird, Acad. Nat. Sci. Phila. Proc. 7: 332, 1855.

Type.—Collected at Fort Webster, now Santa Rita, Grant County, N. Mex., in 1851 by J. H. Clark.

General Characters.—This gray-backed chipmunk belongs to a group by itself, with one subspecies, *utahensis*, farther north. It is the largest of the New Mexico chipmunks and easily distinguished from all the rest by its light-gray back and sides, and obscure stripes. In winter pelage the dorsal stripes, except the central black one, are mostly concealed by the gray outer fur. In summer pelage the stripes are brighter though still obscure and the fulvous markings of other species are much reduced. The tail is long and full and richly colored below.

Measurements.—Typical adults: Total length, 234; tail, 106; hind foot, 35 millimeters.

Distribution and habitat.—The cliff chipmunk is common throughout most of the Upper Sonoran Zone of New Mexico west of the Rio Grande River and Jemez Mountains. There are specimens in the Biological Survey collection from the Animas, Burro, Tres Pinos, Mimbres, San Mateo, Magdalena, Bear Spring, and Datil Mountains, or from their lower slopes; also from Redrock, south fork of the Gila River, Upper Mimbres, Riley, El Moro, Fort Wingate, and Gallup, and from Fort Defiance, Ariz., close to the New Mexico line at the southern end of the Chuska Mountains. They are reported from the country around the base of Mount Taylor; and chipmunks that the writer saw on the walls of Chaco Canyon but failed to secure were undoubtedly of this species. They are common at Zuni and over the low country south of there to the Tularosa and Gila Rivers. Redrock is the only locality where they were actually taken in the Lower Sonoran Zone, and at this place the cold canyon slopes carry the Upper Sonoran species. In many of the arid mountain ranges they are found among the yellow pines where a Transition Zone slope faces, or is in close proximity to, a slope covered with the Upper Sonoran juniper and nut pines. In other words, the species fills the Upper Sonoran Zone to its limit, with the usual slight overlapping at the edges above and below, and is the only chipmunk common to that zone in New Mexico. It is closely associated with the nut pines and junipers, and its gray color goes well with its open, semiarid habitat. (Fig. 13.)

General habits.—The cliff chipmunks, more than any other species in New Mexico, are restricted to cliffs, canyon walls, and rocky slopes. They are perhaps the most expert rock climbers and will run over the perpendicular face of a smooth sandstone cliff with the ease and assurance of a lizard. Living as they do in an open and half-forested country, the numerous rock walls and ledges furnish safe retreats and give them cover close to an abundant food supply. The gulches and canyons are usually full of bushes, bearing seeds and berries within easy reach of the base of the rim rock, while the scrubby juniper and nut pine trees commonly grow in abundance along the upper edge of the rim. The chipmunks have long ago learned that their only safety lies in keeping within easy reach of their rocky strongholds and exercising the utmost vigilance in detecting enemies in time to escape. They are very shy and almost as difficult to hunt as mountain sheep, except that the collector can usually secure the specimen that has disappeared in the rocks by waiting from one to three minutes for it to reappear. They climb trees, especially the nut pines, junipers, and oaks, for food and occasionally, if no rocks are near, they take refuge in a tree; but usually at the approach of danger they rush to the nearest rocks or log pile. Along the edge of the timber they sometimes follow the logs and fallen trees or old fences and take refuge in holes in the ground underneath. They quickly gather at deserted cabins, which furnish all the requirements of safe retreat and many choice bits in the way of food. At such a cabin, on the head of the Mimbres, the writer collected a good series of specimens.

They are common over the great red-sandstone cliffs on which stands the Pueblo of Acoma, and around the base of the Enchanted Mesa, and are probably the chipmunks seen running over the walls of the Chaco Canyon. On the bare, black lava fields about San Rafael they completely eluded the writer by running faster than he could over the rough and broken surface of the malpais and either disappearing in the distance, or, if close pressed, taking refuge in one of the numerous crevices, to reappear, if at all, at some far distant point. In this open country, abounding in coyotes, foxes, cats, and other hungry carnivores, it is not difficult to understand where the chipmunks get their training in self protection. At Silver City, A. K. Fisher reported two seen in the vicinity of town and one secured; and at Pinos Altos, near there, the species was common but so shy that it was with difficulty that two specimens were secured. Hollister reported them in small numbers at Jara Peak near Riley and in the Bear Spring Mountains in the pinyon and juniper woods—usually about rocks, logs, brush, and fences— but they were very wild, and it was with difficulty that seven specimens were secured. In the high, barren cliffs bordering the mesa near the mouth of the Rio San Jose he also found them common, but so exceedingly shy that he was unable to trap or shoot a specimen.

Voice.—The usual chipper or alarm note of these chipmunks seems finer and shriller than that of the larger Colorado or gray-collared, and the slow call note is softer and more husky. Both of these notes are used in the manner of chipmunks in general, but during the intervals of the call note, the slow, serpentine waving of the beautiful bushy tail is more striking in this species than in any other New Mexico chipmunk. This motion and the voice and many of the habits strongly suggest the *merriami* group in southern California.

Food habits.—The nuts of the pinyon pine, acorns, and juniper berries are apparently the favorite and standard food of these chipmunks, but many seeds and berries are eaten, as well as the fruit of many species of cactus. The cones of pinyon pine are either cut off or picked up where they fall, then carried to the favorite feeding rock, where the seeds are taken out and eaten or stored for winter food; or else the fallen nuts are gathered up under the tree and tucked into the cheek pouches for food at a later time. The acorns of the Emory oak, blue oak, and many shrubby species, and the berries of several species of juniper trees, are gathered and the seeds cracked and eaten, or stored away for winter. In Arizona, Mearns says the chipmunks are very fond of the seeds of the hackberry tree. In the San Mateo Mountains E. A. Goldman found them feeding on the seeds of a dayflower (*Commelina dianthifolia*), and in the Magdalena Mountains near Kingston and at Redrock he found them feeding extensively on the fruit of various species of pricklypear. Their stomachs contained the pulp of these brightly colored fruits, and not only the mouths, but the stomachs and intestines were stained a deep purple from the juice. As he found only the pulp of the fruit in the stomachs, it is probable that the seeds were being stored for future use. On the south fork of the Gila River the writer found them eating the ripe, purple fruit of a large pricklypear (*Opuntia chlorotica*) which they had carried to the rocky points of the canyon. One chipmunk, shot while eating this fruit, had filled its cheek pouches with the seeds, but its stomach contained only the pulp of the ripe fruit. Its hands, nose, and mouth were stained a rich purple from the juice. They are very fond of the sweet yellow fruit of the wild currant, which grows in abundance along the canyons and gulches; and that a great variety of berries and seeds are acceptable food is indicated by the remains scattered on their feeding ground.

Breeding habits.—The cliff chipmunks breed considerably earlier than those of the higher zones. On the head of the Rio Mimbres half-grown young have been found running about by the middle of May, and by July or August they were almost full grown. Evidently two broods of young are raised in a season, as young have been collected on September 23, 26, 27, and November 27 just old enough to be out of the nests; while practically full-grown young of the year have been collected at much earlier dates. There seems to be no record of the number of young in a litter, but the females show the usual number of mammae—one pair of inguinal, two pairs of abdominal, and one pair of pectoral. As with other chipmunks the number of young is therefore probably from 4 to 6, with a possible maximum of 8.

Hibernation.—In the comparatively mild climate of the low zone in which these chipmunks live, there would seem little necessity for their hibernation. Near Silver City, D. D. Streeter collected them in 1892 up to November 27. It is doubtful whether they hibernate at all, or for more than the short period of a cold wave, and even then it is more probable that they remain in their dens to feed on their stores of seeds and nuts.

Economic status.—On account of the low altitude of their range, these chipmunks come more in contact with agriculture than any other species in New Mexico. In places along the Gila and San Francisco Rivers, they gather at the edges of the small fields in numbers sufficient to do some mischief to the grain, but the writer has never heard any complaints of serious depredations in this region, although the little gardens and grainfields of the Indians are easy objects for their attack. It is probable that the tree seeds that they plant and distribute and unintentionally leave to grow compensate for the great quantity of seeds they consume. If it ever becomes necessary to undertake artificial reforestation of these lower timber slopes, it will doubtless be necessary to destroy the chipmunks on such areas. This would not be a difficult task if undertaken in the right way, as they eagerly take any kind of grain that may be offered them as a bait.

AMMOSPERMOPHILUS LEUCURUS CINNAMOMEUS (Merriam)

Rusty Antelope Squirrel; White-Tailed Ground Squirrel; Hazecloy of the Navajo Indians (Birdseye); Iung-yai-ya of the Hopi Indians (Fisher)

Tamias leucurus cinnamomeus Merriam, North Amer. Fauna No. 3, p. 52, 1890.

Type.—Collected at Echo Cliffs, Painted Desert, Ariz., September 22, 1889, by C. Hart Merriam and Vernon Bailey.

General characters.—The short-eared, short-tailed, thickset little chipmunklike white-tailed ground squirrel differs from the true antelope squirrel, *Ammosper-*

mophilus leucurus, in having a brighter suffusion of cinnamon brown over the upper parts. It has the same white stripe along each side, and the short flattened bushy tail, usually carried curled up over the back, showing the white lower surface. In summer pelage the upperparts are grayish-fawn color; in winter, bright cinnamon, frosted with gray. The whole underparts are white, and in winter, silvery white.

Measurements.—An average adult male measures in total length, 230; tail, 70; hind foot, 42 millimeters.

Distribution and habitat.—This southeastern form of the antelope squirrel occupies the Upper Sonoran country of northwestern New Mexico, ranging throughout the San Juan and Chuska Valleys and across into the Puerco and San Jose Valleys west of the Rio Grande. (Fig. 14.) There are specimens from Fruitland, Rio Puerco, near the Pueblo of Jemez, and from 10 miles northwest of Socorro.

Hollister saw them near the junction of the Puerco and San Jose Rivers and near Laguna, and others are reported from near Cabezon, from Chaco and Blanco Canyons, Aztec, Shiprock, and the Chuska River. They come up the Zuni River to a little below the New Mexico line and probably to some extent above. They occupy the open desert country and delight in the sandiest, hottest, and driest areas.

General habits. — These little ground squirrels are typical of the desert, where they burrow into the mellow banks and mounds and scamper back and forth from bush to bush with their little white flags

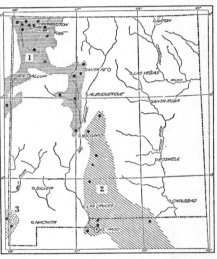

FIGURE 14.—Distribution of antelope squirrels in New Mexico: 1, *Ammospermophilus leucurus cinnamomeus;* 2, *A. interpres;* 3, *A. harrisi.* Type locality circled

always conspicuously shown when in retreat. There are no trees where they live, but they climb to the tops of greasebush and cactus, where they sit and watch for approaching enemies, or gather and eat their food. Often when alarmed they do not take to the nearest burrow but run for long distances dodging from bush to bush and hiding in the center of some thorny clump until hard pressed. If it is merely a collector on foot with a shotgun, they often escape by a long and speedy retreat until lost in the bushes. Like all ground squirrels they are strictly diurnal and retire at sundown to their burrows. These are usually shallow, and in the mellow soil do not afford safe protection from their worst enemies—badgers, coyotes, and foxes—unless protected by cactus, thorny bushes, or rocks. Broken rocks and the low, bare rims of desert gulches are always taken advantage of, if possible, as the burrows between and under them are far safer than those in the open. Usually the squirrels are silent, but occasionally one will utter a shrill, rapid chipper or trill somewhat like that of the 13-lined ground squirrel. Often when one of them is sitting on guard, the white tail is flicked in a way that quickly attracts attention, and it may be used as a signal or warning flashlight.

Food habits.—Their food consists of a great variety of seeds, fruits, green vegetation, and insects. The seeds and fruit of cactus are eagerly eaten wherever found, apparently that of all species with which the squirrels come in contact; even the fleshy parts of the cactus are sometimes eaten, as shown by the green, mucilaginous pulp in the stomachs of specimens examined; and it is probable that such moist food is what enables them to live in a country where long intervals elapse without rainfall and where no possible supply of water can be obtained. Cactus and yucca seeds are often found in their cheek pouches, but after having been eaten can rarely be identified in the stomach contents—a mass of clean, white dough. The rich, oily seeds of wild sunflowers and various related plants are eaten, and also the seeds of greasebush and a great variety of small desert plants. The squirrels eagerly take almost any kind of bait offered to tempt them into traps and are easily caught with rolled oats, whole oats, wheat, barley, or any kind of grain, prunes, or raisins. They are fond of fresh meat and often eat the mice and small animals left out in the traps during the day. The stomach contents commonly show traces of insects, but these have been so finely chewed that the species can not readily be identified.

Breeding habits.—The number of young produced at a litter is probably the same as with *leucurus*, six or eight, as shown by the number of embryos from that species. They are apparently born in the underground dens in May, as the small young are found running about in June and July. Evidently a second litter is sometimes raised, as half-grown young found in the latter part of August were probably born not earlier than the middle of July. In their warm valleys the summer is long and the winters mild.

Hibernation.—Apparently these ground squirrels do not hibernate for any great length of time, if at all. In the San Juan Valley, Birdseye reported them common and active up to November 20, 1908, and between Aztec and Laplatta, Loring saw them in December, 1893. During the winter of 1888–89 the writer found *leucurus* common in southern Utah during December and January, in places out on a foot of snow. They become moderately fat as the cold weather advances and probably hibernate to some extent during times of storm or unusual cold.

Economic status.—In the unoccupied desert country these little squirrels are harmless and attractive, but as irrigation reclaims the valleys they become one of the numerous pests to be controlled. They are at once attracted by grainfields and gardens and do considerable damage to both the planted and ripening grain. They are also fond of burrowing into banks, and the mellow earth of the lower side of an irrigation ditch is a tempting home site. If the burrow extends only half way through the bank, the seepage of water may do the rest and make a break of serious consequence. Fortunately, they are among the easiest of the rodents to trap, and with proper methods can be controlled at no great expense.

AMMOSPHERMOPHILUS INTERPRES (MERRIAM)

TEXAS ANTELOPE SQUIRREL

Tamias interpres Merriam, North Amer. Fauna No. 4, p. 21, 1905.

Type.—Collected at El Paso, Tex., December 10, 1889, by Vernon Bailey.

General characters.—The Texas antelope squirrel to some extent shows a compromise of the characters of *harrisi* and *cinnamomeus* but it is apparently distinct from both. Though it has almost the same dark-gray back and long tail as *harrisi*, the under surface of the tail is light gray or whitish—never dark gray as in *harrisi* and never pure white as in *cinnamomeus* and *leucurus*.

Measurements.—Adults from the type locality measure in total length, 225; tail, 79; hind foot, 38 millimeters.

Distribution and habitat.—There are specimens of the little Texas antelope squirrels from the southeastern foothills of the Manzano Mountains, from 10 miles northeast of Socorro, from several points along the foothills of the San Andres, Organ, and Franklin Mountains, and below the Texas line from the west base of the Guadalupe Mountains and from the Franklin Mountains near El Paso. They seem to be restricted to the canyons and rocky foothills of the desert mountains, not extending into the open valleys any great distance from rock. It is therefore difficult to say whether they belong to the Upper or Lower Sonoran Zone, as their range, so far as known, seems to follow the meeting line of the two. There may be here a compromise in distribution, as well as in characters, of the Upper Sonoran *cinnamomeus* and Lower Sonoran *harrisi*. The writer has seen no specimens from west of the Rio Grande, although Mearns records them from " Chihuahua near El Paso." There seems no logical reason why they should not inhabit the area from El Paso westward to Arizona, but very thorough collecting in this region has failed to discover any species of *Ammospermophilus*. To the northward near Socorro their range comes to within 20 miles of that of *cinnamomeus*, but specimens of *interpres* collected 10 miles northeast of Socorro are as distinct from those of *cinnamomeus* collected 10 miles northwest of Socorro as are those from the opposite extremes of their ranges. The Rio Grande Valley seems completely to separate the species at this point, as the Colorado River does the ranges of *harrisi* and *leucurus* farther west. It seems highly probable that at some past time of unusual abundance both *harrisi* and *cinnamomeus* extended their range to the desert valleys east of the Rio Grande River, and then as they receded to normal abundance the stranded individuals left behind intermingled the characters of the two distinct forms and perpetuated the blend in the present characters of *interpres*. In these characters the traces of *harrisi* seem to predominate. (Fig. 14.)

General habits.—More than any other species of the genus the Texas antelope squirrels seem to be restricted to rocky country, a fact that probably accounts for their absence from the Lower Sonoran valleys. While El Paso, Tex., is given as the type locality, no specimens were found in the river valley or nearer than the limestone ledges northeast of town. Throughout the Franklin and San Andres Mountains they seemed to be restricted to canyons and the lower rocky slopes, as they were also at the west base of the Guadalupe Mountains.   At a point 10 miles northeast of Socorro, E. A. Goldman collected one on the crest of a limestone ridge at about 5,000 feet elevation.   In the northern part of the San Andres Mountains, Gaut collected a series of specimens at the west base of Salinas Peak, others on the north and west slopes of Sheep Mountain, and a specimen near the west base of Capitol Peak, where, in December, 1902, he reported them numerous in the ledges and along rocky canyons.   He collected another, January 20, 1903, among the rocks in Bear Canyon of the same range.   In February he found them running about along the east base of the Franklin Mountains, where the temperature was close to the freezing point.   In a drizzling rain in December, 1889, the writer found them common in the Franklin Mountains; but they were then fat and lazy and kept in their burrows except during the warm part of the day.

Food habits.—The food of these antelope squirrels consists of a great variety of seeds, berries, and insects.   The seeds, fruit, and fleshy parts of many species of cactus are eaten.   The little hard beans of the mesquite and various other leguminous bushes are gathered for food, as well as the seeds of the creosote bush, sotol, and other seed-bearing plants.   In spring and early in summer considerable green vegetation is eaten.

Breeding habits.—Little is known of the breeding habits of these squirrels, except that near Boquillas, Tex., in May, the writer found the half-grown young out getting their own food, including various seeds and fruits.   This would indicate that they are early breeders, but there is no evidence of a second litter of young, notwithstanding the long season and mild climate of the country in which they live. The mammae of the females are arranged in five pairs, which indicates large families of five or more young.

Hibernation.—From the fact that they are found active at frequent intervals during the winter, it seems probable that these squirrels do not hibernate to any great extent.   But the quantity of fat they accumulate for winter would make it possible for them to sleep in their warm nests during a cold storm of considerable duration. Apparently every warm day brings them out for a fresh supply of food, which in desert regions seems always to abound.

Economic status.—The fact that this Texas species seems to avoid the mellow soil of the valleys practically releases it from the condemnation of the farmer.   It comes so little in touch with human interests and habitations as to be of slight economic importance.

AMMOSPERMOPHILUS HARRISI HARRISI (AUDUBON AND BACHMAN)

GRAY-TAILED ANTELOPE SQUIRREL

Spermophilus harrisii Audubon and Bachman, Quadrupeds of North America, 3: 267, 1854.

Type locality.—Unknown.   (See Merriam, 1889, p. 20.)

General characters.—This Arizona species of the antelope squirrel is readily distinguished by the slightly longer and wholly dark-gray tail and the dark gray upperparts; otherwise it is of the general size and appearance of the other members of the genus and has the single white line along each side.

Measurements.—An adult male from near Tucson, Ariz., measured in total length, 227; tail, 78; hind foot, 40; ear from notch to tip, 10 millimeters; and weighed 139 grams.

Distribution and habitat.—There is but one specimen of the gray-tailed antelope squirrel (pl. 6, A) from extreme southwestern New Mexico, taken by Ligon in May, 1920, 12 miles northwest of Animas, but the writer had a previous record from near the same locality in 1907 and 1908. At Pratt, a little station on the El Paso & Southwestern Railroad, located about 4 miles east of the Arizona line in the San Simon Valley, the gray-tailed squirrels were reported as common by H. H. Hotchkiss, who gave the writer a good description of them and told him that he had shot them there about his camp and that one was drowned in a tub of water in his blacksmith shop. So far as known, this is the easternmost limit of the range of *harrisi*, which is mainly a Lower Sonoran desert species.

General habits.—The habits of *harrisi* are similar to those of *cinnamomeus* and *interpres*, from both of which it seems to be separated geographically.

Its food is mainly the fruit and seeds of cactus, especially of the large bisnaga, but numerous other seeds and green plants are eaten. In Arizona, Mearns found it feeding on mesquite beans and seeds of yuccas. He noted that the mating season is from the middle of January to the middle of March. On March 20 he found a female containing six fetuses the size of small grapes, and by the middle of July found the young half grown.

CALLOSPERMOPHILUS LATERALIS LATERALIS (Say)

SAY'S GROUND SQUIRREL; NOO-YOO'-NA of the Taos Indians

S[ciurus] lateralis Say, Long's Expedition to Rocky Mountains 2: note 28, 235, 1823.

Type locality.—Arkansas River, a few miles below Canyon City, Colo.
General characters.—This forest ground squirrel resembles a large chipmunk but has a heavier body and shorter legs, tail, and ears. It is brownish gray with a buff and a black stripe along each side. The head, shoulders, and legs are suffused with bright chestnut in summer and brownish gray in winter. The under surface of the tail is clear yellow in both winter and summer pelage. In the young of the year there is often a trace of a second black stripe along each side.
Measurements.—Adults from Colorado measure, approximately, in total length, 290; tail, 100; hind foot, 44 millimeters.

Distribution and habitat.—Say's ground squirrels (pl. 6, B) are found throughout the mountains of northern New Mexico, mainly in the Canadian Zone and the upper edge of the Transition. (Fig. 15.) There are specimens from the Sangre de Cristo, San Juan, Jemez, and Chuska Mountains. They are often found among the yellow pines, more commonly toward the upper edge of the Transition Zone, but occasionally at its lower edge. Their greatest abundance seems to be throughout the Canadian Zone, but they often range up to extreme timber line. On Pecos Baldy they were found to the top at 12,600 feet, and in the Taos Mountains they were abundant about our 11,400-foot camp. While restricted to a timbered country, they avoid the deep forests and prefer open areas where rocks, old logs, and abundant vegetation afford cover and food.

General habits.—These are not typical ground squirrels but are nearer to that group than to the chipmunks. Though they rarely climb trees they always prefer some perch such as a log, stump, or rock. They lack the nervous energy and activity of the chipmunks and are even accused of being lazy, often sitting a long time motionless in the warm sunshine, especially in autumn when they are becoming heavy with fat. On a few occasions the writer has surprised them looking for food in trees or bushes, but on the instant they always rushed to the ground and away to the nearest burrow or rock pile. If possible, they dig their burrows or make their dens under or among rocks, but in the absence of such protection they burrow in the ground under some old log or stump, or even, occasionally, out in the open. The great rock slides or steep slopes of talus along the mountain cliffs, where deep under the broken mass of rock they find safe retreats and are well protected from numerous enemies, are their favorite strongholds. Generally they are silent and rather shy and suspicious, but occasionally one will give a clear, birdlike whistle, very shrill and piercing, entirely unlike the note of the chipmunks.

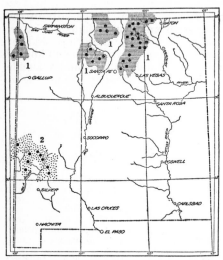

FIGURE 15.—Distribution of Say's ground squirrels in New Mexico: 1, *Callospermophilus lateralis lateralis*; 2, *C. lateralis arizonensis*

Food habits.—The food of these squirrels consists of a great variety of seeds, grains, nuts, and berries, some green vegetation, roots and bulbs, and occasionally insects or meat. One specimen collected in the Jemez Mountains in September had its cheek pouches full of the little bulbs of willow-weed (Epilobium), while its stomach was full of green vegetation and some brown substance, probably mushroom; another, shot in the Chuska Mountains, had its cheek pouches filled with seeds of the yellow pine; and still another, collected by A. H. Howell in Costilla Pass, had chokecherry pits, acorns, and small seeds in its pouches. In the Taos Mountains the writer found Say's squirrels with their pouches filled with unripe oats from the roadside. They have great appetites and seem, especially in autumn, to spend most of the day in eating, making their sides fairly stand out. They are fond of rolled oats or any kind of grain that may be used for trap bait and quickly gather at camping places to pick up what the horses have scattered, but they do not draw the line at scattered grain if they can find the sack, and nothing in the way of camp food seems to come amiss.

Breeding habits.—Apparently but one litter of young is raised in a season, and they are rarely seen out of the nest before the latter part of July or the first of August. They are then almost half grown and able to gather their own food. By September and October they are nearly full grown and are becoming fat for their winter hibernation, which takes place somewhat later than that of the adults. The number of young in a litter probably varies normally from 4 to 6, as with other species of the genus, but 4 to 7 have been recorded. The teats of the females are generally arranged in 4 or 5 pairs, the normal number probably being 5.

Hibernation.—Like most of the true ground squirrels and unlike the chipmunks, they become very fat in the fall and hibernate for a long period. The old males seem to acquire the proper quantity of oil inside of their skins earlier than the females that have raised young, while the young of the year are still later in laying up the necessary fat to carry them through the winter. Though the time of hibernation depends in part on the weather, it also depends largely upon the accumulation of sufficient fat. A few freezing nights in September send most of them to their winter beds, but the warm days sure to come later bring out those that are poorest to gather more of the rich harvest of seeds, with which they stuff their cheek pouches and large stomachs to their utmost capacity. In the Taos Mountains the writer found them out up to September 25; in the Costilla Mountains, A. H. Howell took them as late as September 27; and in the Gallinas and Chuska Mountains specimens were collected as late as October 5. These, however, were the last remnant, as the majority den up by the middle of September. The date of emerging from hibernation is not definitely known, as few naturalists or collectors are in the mountains at the time when they reappear. There are specimens in the Bureau of Biological Survey collection from Rayado Canyon collected April 1, and from Halls Peak collected April 24; but as another specimen from Martinez is labeled December 1 by the same collector (C. M. Barber), there seems some doubt as to whether these records were normal or whether these squirrels may not have been kept during the winter in captivity. No notes accompany the skins. It is probable, however, that the squirrels emerge from their winter quarters with the first bare ground of early spring. It is also probable that they come out of hibernation without much surplus fat, as late in spring and early in summer there is usually no trace of the thick layer of fat that lined their skins in the fall. The stores of food laid up in fall are probably in part used during the early spring and possibly help to tide over the breeding season.

Economic status.—Fortunately, these ground squirrels do not come much in contact with agriculture, but along the lower edge of their range there are some small farms or grainfields and garden patches. They are exceedingly fond of grain and sometimes collect in considerable numbers along the edges of fields, where they gather and carry away as much of the crop as the time between ripening and harvest will permit. Their cheek pouches are much larger than those of chipmunks and, when distended to the limit of their capacity, will hold several hundred kernels of wheat, barley, or oats. In a small field surrounded by woods they will sometimes take a considerable portion of the crop, but they are easily trapped or poisoned and need not be allowed to do serious damage. In the forest they gather up the seeds of various trees, especially of oaks, pines, and spruces, to be eaten on the spot or stored for future use.

Like the chipmunks, they store in underground chambers excavated mainly in the open or under logs, stumps, or rock piles. It is evident that many of these winter stores are never eaten and are often dug open, scattered, and buried in the earth by badgers, foxes, and bears, or other enemies in search of fat little squirrels for breakfast. This constant scattering and planting of tree seeds has undoubtedly been of sufficient benefit to the forest to compensate in part for the quantity of seeds eaten by the squirrels, but under modern methods of reforestation both squirrels and chipmunks will have to be destroyed over the areas to be planted. This will not be difficult to accomplish, as their numbers are easily controlled; but as extensive areas are likely to be involved, the most economical method of disposing of them should be employed.

CALLOSPERMOPHILUS LATERALIS ARIZONENSIS BAILEY

CHESTNUT-MANTLED GROUND SQUIRREL; YUNG-YI-UH of the Hopi Indians
(Mearns)

Callospermophilus lateralis arizonensis Bailey, Biol. Soc. Wash. Proc. 26: 130, 1913.

Type.—Collected in the San Francisco Moutains, Ariz., August 8, 1889, by C. Hart Merriam and Vernon Bailey.

General characters.—In general appearance this ground squirrel much resembles *lateralis*. Its principal points of difference are a slightly richer coloration in summer coat with invariable dark-gray under surface of tail in adults, in striking contrast to the clear-yellow under surface of the tail in *lateralis*. In the young of the year the tail is often pale chestnut along the central part of the lower surface. Although widely separated geographically from *lateralis*, this form shows such slight characters that it is accorded only subspecific rank.

Measurements.—Average measurements of seven adult male topotypes: Total length, 282; tail, 99; hind foot, 42 millimeters. Weight of type, 10 ounces.

Distribution and habitat.—The chestnut-mantled ground squirrel occupies the San Francisco and White Mountain region of Arizona and the Mogollon Mountain region of New Mexico, with a practically continuous range from the San Francisco Peaks to the Mimbres Mountains. It seems to be generally distributed throughout the Canadian and the Transition Zones, with its center of abundance in the Canadian. It is not so common in the lower part of the Transition Zone, but in places seems to come to its lower edge and to have a slightly lower range than has *lateralis*. This may well be due to the restricted area of the Canadian Zone in the region.

General habits.—In habits the chestnut-mantled are practically identical with Say's ground squirrels of the mountains farther north. In spring and summer they are active and busy, but in the warm days of early autumn these pot-bellied, lazy little philosophers of the woods spend much of their time sitting on stumps, stones, or logs in a brown study, as if thinking of the long comfortable sleep soon to begin. Early in September they are already very fat and their stomachs usually much distended with the rich meats of acorns and seeds of various trees and plants. They keep within easy reach of their large burrows, which are usually located under logs, stumps, and bowlders, and at the first alarm usually take refuge in them, often refusing to come out again for a long time, perhaps even until another warm day. Their slow, quiet manners are in striking contrast to those of the sprightly chipmunks, and while often seen they are rarely heard. Occasionally one utters a shrill, whistling call note either of alarm or warning, and when caught in traps they sometimes utter a sharp squeal.

Food habits.—In summer their food includes considerable green vegetation, berries, and half-ripe seeds of numerous plants, but in autumn it is for the most part restricted to nuts and seeds. Acorns and seeds of the yellow pine are favorite foods, but the seeds from cones of the Douglas spruce and probably other spruces are also eaten; and seed-filled capsules of Pentstemon, Gilia, and Frasera, together with the seeds of grasses and many other small plants are found in their cheek pouches or scattered over the feeding logs and rocks used by them. Like the chipmunks and many of the ground squirrels they will gather at camps for scattered grain and such scraps of food as can be found.

Breeding habits.—The young are evidently born late in spring, as they are not seen out of the burrows before early summer. By September they are well grown and while busily storing food are beginning to acquire their winter supply of fat. The writer has never found small young during the autumn, and it is probable that only one litter is raised during the summer. These have none too much time to develop and get ready for winter. The 8 to 10 teats of the females would indicate rather large families.

Hibernation.—Up to September 6 (1908) these ground squirrels were common and active in Luna Valley, and in the Tularosa Mountains at 9,000 feet altitude the writer saw one October 12 in the gray winter coat. At an 8,500-foot camp on Willow Creek in the Mogollon Mountains, one was seen by Mrs. Bailey on October 28, which was a warm day following two snows and many hard freezes. Its fatness and the gray color of its winter coat were noted as it ran to its burrow under a large log on the sunny slope. No others were seen at this camp, where they were evidently abundant earlier in the season, and this was an unusually late appearance as they commonly hibernate before the first of October.

CITELLUS VARIEGATUS GRAMMURUS (Say)

ROCK SQUIRREL; KO-AH-KE-NA of the Taos Indians; ZA-TET-ENA of the Navajo Indians

S[ciurus] grammurus Say, Long's Expedition to Rocky Mountains, 2: Note 37, 259, 1823.

Type locality.—Purgatory River, Las Animas County, Colo.

General characters.—The rock squirrel is about the size of an eastern gray squirrel, with equally long but less bushy tail, shorter ears, and coarser hairs. The general color is buffy gray with clear or silvery gray over the shoulders. The back is coarsely scalloped or mottled with crescent-shaped spots or wavy cross lines; the lower parts are soiled whitish, and the feet clear buffy.

Measurements.—An adult male from Trinidad, Colo., near the type locality, measures, total length, 493; tail, 217; hind foot, 58 millimeters. A female measures 480, 215, and 57 millimeters, respectively.

Distribution and habitat.—Rock squirrels are common and often abundant animals over most of New Mexico, where rocks, cliffs, and canyons furnish homes suitable to their needs. They are absent from the open plains and wide valleys and from the higher mountains.

Their range is mainly in the upper Sonoran Zone, but in places they enter the edge of the Transition Zone and to a slight extent the Lower Sonoran. (Fig. 16.) This, however, is no more than the usual overlapping of an abundant and wide-ranging species.

They shun both plains and forests but delight in the rim-rock border of an arid valley or the sunny ledges of a canyon wall. The great bowlders scattered along the bases of steep slopes furnish convenient watchtowers and cover for their burrows, and old buildings, bridges, and terraced roadways also supply their needs. Even old logs and stumps are sometimes accepted in place of rocks as cover and watchtowers, and "cut-banks," or steep earth walls, are often inhabited. Because of these squirrels' numerous enemies, their burrows are rarely found in the level open places where most ground squirrels would choose to live, and they are never found far from well-fortified cover.

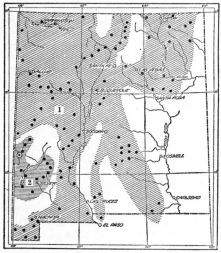

FIGURE 16.—Distribution of rock squirrels in New Mexico: 1, *Citellus variegatus grammurus;* 2. *C. variegatus juglans.* Type locality circled

General habits.—The habit of sitting for hours on top of rocks while basking in the sun and keeping watch for enemies has given these squirrels their common and appropriate name. They are neither tree squirrels nor ground squirrels, although t h e y climb readily into scrubby trees for nuts and often make their homes in burrows in the ground. Their favorite homes are clefts in rocks that will admit no larger animal, but when none of these are at hand and they are forced to dig back between or under rocks or bowlders, or under houses, logs, or stumps, they usually do so in such a way that the burrows can not be enlarged or dug out even by such enemies as the badger, wolf, or bear. The burrows are large, and judged by the bushel or more of earth often thrown out at a time must go deep into the ground. They are evidently used year after year and cleaned out or extended each season for breeding or hibernation.

Voice.—The call note of the rock squirrels is a loud, shrill whistle, sometimes prolonged with a slight quaver, but again so short and sharp as to resemble the call of a woodchuck or evening grosbeak. In the Apache Canyon near Clayton, A. H. Howell heard their loud whistling call a few times. In the Big Hatchet Mountains, E. A. Goldman recognized "their familiar whistle from the rocky slopes between 5,500 feet and the summit."

The call generally warns of approaching danger and is most commonly heard from the growing young. It is also used by the adults and in times of special danger becomes vigorous and excited, on rare occasions beginning high and running down the scale in quite a musical form. At times it is a low chuckle or chipper given as the squirrel vanishes into a stone pile or under a brush fence.

Food habits.—The unusually wide range of food accepted by these rock squirrels includes nuts, seeds, grain, berries, fruit, roots, green vegetation, insects, and fresh or old dried meat. The diet varies at different seasons according to the supply and demand. In spring and early in summer more green vegetation is eaten, later more fruit, and in autumn the richest seeds, grains, and nuts are sought. Often the stomachs of squirrels skinned for museum specimens show a large proportion of the food to be green foliage, which can not be more specifically determined. Finely chewed grain and seeds or acorns and nuts are the more usual contents, however. The pulp of cactus plants is sometimes recognized. Traces of insects are also sometimes detected and occasionally meat from the trap bait or from small rodents found in traps. At regular camp places they gather to collect scattered grain, and gardens and grainfields always attract them.

At Tularosa, Gaut reported the stomach of one taken November 6 (1902) full of ground-up seeds of saltbush (*Atriplex canescens*). At San Pedro, in July (1889), the writer found them feeding extensively on pinyon nuts, which were abundant and ripening. Climbing the trees, the squirrels brought down the cones to convenient rocks or logs, cut off the scales, extracted the nuts, and ate them.

At Riley, in September (1905), Hollister collected an old female whose cheek pouches were filled with fresh juniper berries.

At Tres Piedras, on August 1 (1904), Gaut shot one with its cheek pouches full of pine seeds.

In Hondo Canyon, on August 13 (1904), the writer found the emptied cones of nut pines scattered over the rocks where the squirrels lived, and one of the squirrels, which he shot near a field, had its pouches stuffed with the ripening wheat.

In Apache Canyon, near Clayton, in August (1903), A. H. Howell usually found their pouches filled with seeds, and one that he shot had been feeding chiefly on seeds of false gromwell (*Onosmodium molle*). Another that he killed in the Raton Range had its pouches stuffed with wild cherries and acorns, and still another was eating a large smooth caterpillar. At the ranches in Bear Canyon, August 23 to September 12, he found them quite troublesome to the crops.

On the lower slopes of Mount Taylor they were closely associated with the little blue oak and Gambel's oak, which on September 21 (1906) were loaded with ripe acorns. One was seen sunning itself on an oak limb 30 feet from the ground, and acorn shells were scattered at the feeding places.

In the foothills of the Jicarilla Mountains Gaut collected two with their cheek pouches distended with the berries of the cherrystone juniper (*Juniperus monosperma*). The squirrels also were very fond of the fresh meat and bread with which his traps were baited.

In the Capitan Mountains Gaut found one with seeds of the wild gourd in its cheek pouches, and one carrying four nuts of the Texas walnut (*Juglans rupestris*).

In Dark Canyon, west of Carlsbad, the writer shot one with 13 of these little walnuts in its pouches and a quantity of cactus fruit in its stomach. In a canyon of the Organ Mountains east of Mesilla Park he shot one in the act of filling its cheek pouches with the seeds of the big pricklypear (*Opuntia engelmanni*). Its stomach was full of the ripe pulp of the rich purple fruit, its hands and face were stained a bright purple, and even its flesh was strongly tinged with the purple dye. Skins of the cactus fruit were scattered over the rocks in great abundance near a heavily fruited cluster of cactus where the squirrel was in the habit of feeding. The seeds were evidently being stored for winter or spring food, as they had not been eaten. The squirrels have a habit of storing nuts, seeds, and grain whenever abundant and of using the stores when other food is scarce. Early in spring they seem to be always searching and digging for food, and any left-over stores are probably most acceptable then, especially during the early breeding season.

In the Animas Mountains the rock squirrels were feeding in part on the berries of checker-barked juniper, and Birdseye and Goldman were annoyed by their persistently getting into traps baited with meat for carnivores.

At Cuchillo, Las Palomas, Kingston, and Garfield, Goldman was told that they did considerable damage by carrying off peaches and other orchard fruits, climbing the trees and carrying the fruit to their burrows or feeding places. About some burrows near one peach orchard he found several quarts of peach pits, which not only substantiated the charge but showed that the fruits and not the seeds were sought.

At Garfield he shot one which was sunning itself 20 feet from the ground in a cottonwood tree and found its pouches full of muskmelon seeds from a garden near by.

In the foothills of the Capitan Mountains Gaut learned that the squirrels were doing serious damage to the little fields of corn and that many of the ranchers were compelled to poison the animals to prevent their destroying the entire crop.

Breeding habits.—Mearns, in his very full and interesting account (1907, p. 315) of the habits of this rock squirrel records two sets of five and seven fetuses found in breeding females collected for specimens. The mammae of the females are normally 10 in number, arranged in 3 pairs of abdominal and 2 pairs of pectoral, and it is probable that the number of young in a litter may run as high as 10.

The dates of the fetuses recorded by Mearns are June 14 and 23, but the squirrels often breed earlier. At Santa Rosa the writer saw young ones out of the nest on June 5, and on the northern point of the Staked Plains, between Cuervo and Montoya on June 17 he found the foot of a half-grown young in the stomach of a prairie falcon. Hollister collected half-grown young at Fort Wingate on June 29. The greater number, however, breed late unless there are two litters in a season. At Clayton, A. H. Howell collected half-grown young August 12, and in the Guadalupe Mountains the writer collected quarter-grown young August 9. Gaut collected quarter-grown and half-grown young in the Jicarilla Mountains on September 17 and 20, and Hollister took a half-grown young at Riley on September 24. They are prolific breeders and would increase at an alarming rate but for a host of enemies.

Hibernation.—In the northern and higher parts of their range these rock squirrels hibernate from early in October to the last of March, but in the lower southern part of the State they are more irregular, and some may not hibernate at all during mild winters. The date of hibernation depends on the weather and the quantity of fat stored up, and as the late young do not become fat until nearly full grown, they are often the latest to den up. Old females that have raised young are also late in acquiring a winter's store of fat and consequently in going into winter quarters, so a few late records may be taken when general hibernation has been going on for some time. In the Raton Range, A. H. Howell found these squirrels common and active up to September 12, and near Catskill up to October 1; and E. C. Thurber collected one at Chico, October 23. In Taos Creek the writer found them common to September 30 and on Chama River to October 15. In the Chuska Mountains a few were found from October 1 to 12, and along the San Juan River valley a few were seen October 15 to 20, but they had mostly disappeared. No more were seen by Birdseye, who remained in the valley to November 20. In Chaco Canyon none were seen October 23 and 24, but at San Rafael a few were found up to October 31.

In the West Datil Mountains the writer found them out to October 9, and in the East Datils Hollister reported them common to October 24. In the Manzano Mountains Gaut collected specimens October 10 and 27 and at Tularosa November 5 and 15, but failed to find any trace of them later during December and January in the San Andres and Organ Mountains. On November 9, in a warm canyon of the Organ Mountains, the writer collected one but saw no others.

E. A. Goldman found them common through October in the foothills west of the Rio Grande and a few still out at Kingston and Lake Valley up to November 7 to 14, and at Garfield, November 17 to 21. Two specimens caught in traps by McClure Surber January 12 and 28 under an old mill in Hondo Canyon are actual winter records, and it would not be surprising to find one or two out in the warm, sheltered canyons on mild days in winter.

There are few data to show when they emerge from hibernation, as collectors rarely reach the field until they are out and active. At Cienequilla, in the Rio Grande Valley above Sante Fe, in 1904, Surber reported them numerous but says, " I saw very few, however, until April 3, which was a beautiful day and brought them out in great numbers. I counted 23 during a short walk up the river." From that time on he reported them as common and the date of April 3 probably marked the general awakening from hibernation.

Economic status.—Although fairly good eating, these rock squirrels are rarely used as food or classed as game. The general feeling against animals that live in burrows in the ground seems to be responsible for this, as their habits are cleanly and their size is equal to that of the eastern gray squirrel. Their use as food should be encouraged, however, as this would aid in keeping down their numbers and protecting the crops. In a few cases they have been accused of burrowing into the banks of irrigation ditches and causing breaks, and the writer has seen many places in canyons and along hillsides where this might well happen.

Their large size, abundance, and wide distribution would make of them a very serious farm pest but for the fact that much of their range is unoccupied arid land. With increasing reclamation and agriculture their injury to crops and fruit will become greater and effective measures will be required to keep them under control. Shooting and trapping now usually suffice to keep their numbers down at the little canyon ranches, but as the country fills up and the hawks, owls, foxes, wild cats, and coyotes are thinned out or driven back the squirrels will increase. They thrive on civilization and appreciate its protection. They gather at ranches and about villages, and the writer has seen them sitting as at home on old house walls and chimney tops even where they had to go to the hills to get their food; for they have little fear of dogs or tame cats, but bobcats, gray foxes, coyotes, and hawks make life a burden to them.

CITELLUS VARIEGATUS JUGLANS Bailey

Walnut Rock Squirrel

Citellus variegatus juglans Bailey, Biol. Soc. Wash. Proc. 26: 131, 1913.

Type.—Collected at Glenwood, N. Mex., at 5,000 feet altitude on the Rio San Francisco at the southwest base of the Mogollon Mountains, November 2, 1906, by Vernon Bailey.

General characters.—This large, dark-colored form of the rock squirrel resembles typical *variegatus* from the valley of Mexico in external characters much more nearly than it does the light-gray *grammurus* from most of New Mexico. From *variegatus* it is distinguished mainly by cranial characters and especially by the lighter dentition.

Measurements.—The type, an adult male, measures in total length, 500; tail, 230; hind foot, 65 millimeters.

Distribution and habitat.—The walnut rock squirrels inhabit the valleys and canyons of the Gila and San Francisco Rivers and their numerous branches throughout the Mogollon Mountains, and extend over to the head of the Mimbres and into the Burro Mountains. In these warm canyons filled with luxuriant vegetation and abundance of nuts, fruits, and berries, they seem to have developed well-established characters, which distinguish them from the squirrels of the more open and arid country. They occupy both the Upper and Lower Sonoran Zones in the narrow valleys where these zones are more or less mixed or intermingled. The specimens that the writer refers to this form are from Glenwood, Gila, Redrock, Burro Mountains, head of the Rio Mimbres, and the east fork of the Gila River at the site of Old Fort Vincent. Their range is almost coincident with that of the Arizona black walnut (*Juglans major*), with which they are closely associated and the nuts of which furnish much of their food.

General habits.—In the narrow canyons that cut deeply into the Mogollon Mountains from the south and west, sheer rock walls and numerous caves and clefts furnish ideal homes and safe retreats for these squirrels. Here they can bask in the sun or dodge quickly into narrow crevices among the rocks, and find an abundance of food, furnished by the black walnuts, numerous oaks, nut pines, junipers, grapes, hackberries, cherries, and other fruit, and seed bearing plants. At the type locality the writer found them common and still active up to November 5 (1906). They were frequently seen and heard along the canyon sides, and their big burrows under rocks, logs, and banks showed signs of constant use. The type of this form, an old male caught at an opening under a bank of driftwood on the river flats, was very fat and in perfect, glossy winter coat, dark and heavily mottled. Its stomach was full of juniper berries—chewed-up seeds, skins, and all—which were easily recognized. It was in perfect condition for hibernating but evidently waiting for the cold weather, which had not yet begun in the low canyon. At Cliff, on the Gila, they were still active during the writer's stay from November 6 to 9, 1906, and in these low canyons it would not be surprising to find them out on any warm day during the winter. At a point 6 miles south of Chloride on December 16, 1915, J. S. Ligon reported three out sunning themselves. At Gila E. A. Goldman found them common among the rocks on the hillsides, under the drift logs in the bottom of the river valley, and under the cover of dense thickets; they were also living in holes in the ground along the steep banks of the arroyos. He found them common at Redrock and along the box canyon of the Gila just above.

Farther north along the Rio San Francisco they are abundant from Alma up through the canyon to Reserve and thence up the Tularosa Valley to Joseph; and up the Negrito Creek Canyon and in the numerous side canyons cutting back from the river. Up to October 14 they were abundant and active in the canyons between Frisco and Joseph, where they were seen feeding on the black walnuts, which in places carpeted the ground under the low-spreading trees. There was also an abundance of acorns, pine nuts, and juniper berries in these canyons, all of which probably supplied them with food. In the Burro Mountains E. A. Goldman found them common among the rocks from the foothills up to about 6,500 feet altitude. Along the east fork of the Gila and Diamond Creek Canyon they were abundant in the walnut groves at the base of cliffs and on the steep rocky slopes, and in places were occupying the old caves used long ago by cliff dwellers. In some of these caves were the remains of plastered walls and storage vaults where food supplies had evidently been securely inclosed to protect them from the ravages of the rodents.

In some of the canyons where there were gardens and small farms it seemed as if the depredations of these squirrels must be very serious. Up to the present time, however, so little agriculture has been attempted in this region that few complaints have been heard against animals smaller than wolves, mountain lions, and bears.

CITELLUS SPILOSOMA CANESCENS (Merriam)

Gray Spotted Ground Squirrel

Spermophilus canescens Merriam, North Amer. Fauna No. 4, p. 38, 1890.[17]
Spermophilus spilosoma macrospilotus Merriam, North Amer. Fauna No. 4, p. 38, 1890.

Type.—Collected at Wilcox, Ariz., November 16, 1889, by Vernon Bailey.
General characters.—About the size of the antelope squirrel or a large chipmunk, but instead of being striped is closely and irregularly dotted over the

---

[17] *Spermophilus canescens* Merriam was based on the gray phase of the spotted spermophile occurring at Wilcox, Ariz., before its dichromatism was discovered. In its red phase it is identical with *macrospilotus*, and as both species were described on the same page of North American Fauna No. 4 (Merriam, 1890b, p. 38) the name *canescens* is here adopted because of priority on the page.

back with white spots, which in unworn pelage usually show narrow posterior margins of black. The ears are very short; the tail is slender and slightly spreading. The ground color of the upperparts is bright ochraceous, light russet brown, or ashy gray; the underparts are white or soiled whitish. A few individuals are much more grayish.

Measurements.—An adult male from Oracle measures in total length 220; tail, 70; hind foot, 32 millimeters. Another male from near Tucson measured 208, 51, and 30 millimeters, respectively, and weighed 107 grams.

Distribution and habitat.—There are specimens of the gray spotted ground squirrel (pl. 7, A) in the Biological Survey collection from Deming, Faywood, Silver City, Mangas Valley, Hachita, and the southern end of Playas Valley. (Fig. 17.) Mearns collected them at Dog Spring in the Dog Mountains, at the Corner Monument No. 40 and Monument No. 15 west of El Paso on the Mexican boundary line.

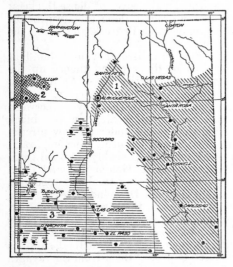

FIGURE 17.—Distribution of the spotted ground squirrels in New Mexico: 1, *Citellus spilosoma major;* 2, *C. spilosoma obsidianus;* 3, *C. spilosoma macrospilotus;* 4, *C. spilosoma marginatus;* 5, *C. spilosoma arens.* Type locality circled

Specimens from El Paso, Tex., Mesilla Park, and Alamogordo carry it over the Rio Grande Valley. There are also referred to this form a series of larger and grayer specimens collected by E. A. Goldman at Lake Valley, near Ojo Caliente, on the Alamosa River, at localities 10 and 15 miles southeast of Magdalena, and on the San Augustine Plains 12 miles north of Monica Spring, and by Hollister at the base of the Bear Spring Mountains. Over the Deming Plains these squirrels a r e restricted mainly to the upper division of the Lower Sonoran Zone, but in places they extend somewhat into the edge of the Upper Sonoran, and those of the San Augustine Plains are in straight Upper Sonoran Zone. They are desert-loving animals and most abundant in the barren arid valleys.

General habits.—In color and habits these little squirrels are perfectly adapted to desert conditions. With their spotted sand-colored backs, they are as inconspicuous as the lizards and horned toads, and are largely dependent on their coloration for protection. They run quickly over hot stretches of sand from bush to bush or burrow to burrow, and the instant they stop running are lost to sight. Their only sure protection from a host of enemies is found in numerous burrows entering the sandy banks of dry washes, the sides of sand dunes, or little sand blown mounds at the base of mesquite or creosote bushes or at the edge of cactus beds. They seem always close to some burrow and if pursued, in a twinkling disappear underground.

Generally, they are quiet and shy, endeavoring to keep out of sight, but occasionally one utters a long, quavering or bubbling whistle, so fine and piercing that it suggests a bird or insect. To human ears it gives no clue to direction, no hint of its author's location. It is evidently a warning note, but may also be used as a call note among the individuals of a family. Even when located, the little spotted squirrels are not easily kept track of, but when one has been seen disappearing down its burrow, after a few minutes of patient waiting the little black eye is almost sure to appear at the entrance, and a low squeak or fine whistle will make the head pop up like a jack-in-a-box. In desert valleys they may be located by their little spreading tracks around burrows. Besides the few burrows they dig for themselves, they use any opening that comes handy, from kangaroo-rat to prairie-dog and badger holes.

Food habits.—The food of the spotted ground squirrels consists largely of the seeds of the small desert plants among which they live and green vegetation and cactus. At Deming they were found feeding mainly on the seeds of wild sunflowers, which in December were abundant, but the stomach of one contained also considerable green mucilaginous pulp from a cactus plant. At Mesilla they were feeding on wild-gourd seeds. They will take any kind of grain used for trap bait and are especially fond of rolled oats. On the San Augustine Plains, Goldman found them feeding largely on the seeds of salt-bush (*Atriplex canescens*). They have been reported feeding extensively on mesquite beans, and it is probable that almost every bean bush of the desert contributes to their food supply, while the many species of cactus and other juicy plants furnish an ample supply of moisture in a region where water is rarely obtained. They also eat a good many insects and are fond of fresh meat.

Breeding habits.—The mammae of the females are usually arranged in 5 pairs—2 pairs of inguinal, 2 abdominal, and 1 pectoral. There is little evidence of the number of young in a litter, but it can be safely assumed to be five or more, as in other members of the group. A female collected by Mearns at Fort Hancock, Tex., June 15, contained 7, and another taken June 23, 6 small fetuses, and one on June 25 was giving milk. On June 26 at the same place Mearns also collected a half-grown young. The ages and the dates of taking of immature specimens in the Biological Survey collection indicate two litters in a year. Even in the upper part of their range on the San Augustine Plains, Hollister collected small and large young at the same date, September 17, which would indicate early and late litters; small young just out of the burrows were collected at Hachita by Goldman July 14, and others, of about the same size in Mangos Valley on October 4 of the same year, indicating at least two litters in that region. Mearns reports young seen out of their burrows as early as April 28.

Hibernation.—Before the cold weather begins the adults become very fat and disappear into their underground dens. The late young, which do not accumulate fat so early, are found out of the burrows on warm days until a much later time. At Deming several young of the year were collected on December 4 and 6, 1889. Most of those collected after the last of September are young, and it is probable that some of the adults enter hibernation early in September. In April they are usually out and active again, and Mearns collected them in March on the Mexican boundary line in southern New

Mexico and reported them out in February and March at El Paso in 1892. The mating season evidently begins as soon as they emerge from hibernation in March and April.

Economic status.—Over most of the valleys where these squirrels are common there is no agriculture, and their consumption of seeds and green vegetation is of no practical moment. At Mesilla Park, Fabian Garcia reports these little squirrels doing considerable mischief in the fields, especially in digging up the planted seeds. Their injury to growing crops and ripening grain will never be so serious as with larger species, but may in places cause considerable loss. As they occupy a valley region that is being brought under intensive cultivation by means of irrigation, their burrows are almost certain to cause considerable trouble in the ditch banks, and it will eventually be necessary to take measures to keep down their numbers.

CITELLUS SPILOSOMA MAJOR (MERRIAM)

LARGE SPOTTED GROUND SQUIRREL

Spermophilus spilosoma major Merriam, North Amer. Fauna No. 4, p. 39, 1890.

Type.—Collected at Albuquerque, N. Mex., June 22, 1889, by Vernon Bailey.
General characters.—Though this is one of the largest forms of the spotted spermophile in the United States, it is not a large animal and is only slightly larger than *canescens*. In the brightest summer pelage the upperparts are pale fulvous with large white dots scattered over the back; the underparts white. The early spring pelage is more grayish.
Measurements.—The type, an adult female, measured in total length, 234; tail, 80; hind foot, 30 millimeters.

Distribution and habitat.—Since first described by Merriam in 1890 from specimens collected at Albuquerque, the range of the large spotted ground squirrel has been found to extend north along the Rio Grande to Espanola, east to Santa Rosa, down the Canadian River Valley, and thence south down the Pecos River Valley to the Davis Mountains, Tex., where it seems to include the form described in 1902 as *marginatus*. Considerable variation is shown over this range, but the writer is referring to *major* specimens from Isleta, Espanola, Santa Rosa, Cabra Spring (about 30 miles north of Santa Rosa), from 8 miles north and 30 miles south of Fort Sumner, and 20 miles north of Roswell and near Carlsbad in the Pecos Valley and from Carrizozo and the north base of the Capitan Mountains farther west. Their range is mainly in the Upper Sonoran Zone of the Rio Grande, Pecos, and Canadian River Valleys, but seems not to extend far out onto the Upper Sonoran Plains.

General habits.—At Albuquerque, where this species was first taken in July, 1889, the squirrels were abundant over the dry mesa top and along the edge of the valley east of town, and some were seen even in the edge of town among the houses. Early in the mornings they could be heard calling over the mesa top and seen standing up like picket pins, watching the approach of the writer from as far as he could see them. During the hottest part of the day they were less in evidence and were evidently keeping cool in their burrows, which were small and inconspicuously dug out here and there, with the entrance often concealed by a bush or tuft of weeds. When alarmed the squirrels would quickly disappear into prairie-dog or badger burrows, or any opening offering a convenient retreat, and as usual in arid regions where burrows remain open for years after being abandoned, they abounded. The squirrels seemed to be uniformly distributed over the dry part of the valley but entirely absent from the irrigated land or the moist river valley where vegetation was abundant. In 1905 Hollister found them common near Isleta on the dry sandy hills near the river and up on the rocky slopes of the first mesa. They were very shy and not over four or five individuals were seen. These were generally seen during the cool morning or evening hours. In 1904 Gaut found them common over the dry part of the Rio Grande Valley about Espanola, where he collected a series of seven specimens. In 1903 a few were collected about Santa Rosa, but they were not very common here and were only occasionally seen or heard.

Food habits.—The large spotted ground squirrels feed on numerous seeds of the desert plants and even such weeds as the sandbur (*Cenchrus tribuloides*). They eat considerable green vegetation, and their stomachs are often found well filled with grasshoppers and beetles, but actual knowledge of their food habits is meager.

Breeding habits.—At Albuquerque half-grown young were found abundant in July. One old female taken July 16 contained 5 small embryos. The mammae of the females are arranged in 5 pairs and the number of young probably varies from 5 to 10 in a litter. Evidently two litters are raised in a season, as indicated by the July embryos and half-grown young.

Hibernation.—Most of the specimens collected have been taken during the summer months, but some are dated as late as September 27 and others as early as May 2. Though these dates suggest the time of entering and emerging from hibernation, it is more probable that the squirrels disappear late in October and reappear early in March.

At Corona, on October 10 (1902), Gaut was unable to find any of the squirrels, although they were said to be common earlier in the season. At Carrizozo, farther south, he collected one as late as October 29, but apparently most of them had hibernated. Near Roswell half-grown young of the year were collected as late as September 16, but the adults presumably were hibernating. These late young would indicate a second litter.

Economic status.—The range of this species lies almost entirely outside of the irrigated areas but comes within a dry-farming district. Locally the squirrels may do considerable mischief by taking the planted seeds from the ground before they come up, but the depredations in grainfields are not likely to be serious unless their numbers greatly increase.

CITELLUS SPILOSOMA PRATENSIS (Merriam)

Park Spotted Ground Squirrel

Spermophilus spilosoma pratensis Merriam, North Amer. Fauna No. 3, p. 55, 1890.

Type.—Collected in San Francisco Mountains (northeast base), Ariz., August 5, 1889, by C. Hart Merriam and Vernon Bailey.

General characters.—This small dark-colored ground squirrel is merely a dark-color phase of the *spilosoma* group, dull sepia brown, dotted over the back with small whitish spots.

Distribution and habitat.—The park spotted ground squirrels come into western New Mexico along the Puerco and Zuni River Valleys, as shown by specimens from Gallup and Thoreau and one from Ojo Caliente, near Zuni, which the writer examined in the field but could not save. Their range is probably much more general and extensive than is shown by these few records as the field work has not been very thorough over that part of the State.

They occupy the semiarid Upper Sonoran Zone among the scattered junipers and nut pines or the narrow open valleys between the areas of scrubby timber. Though usually not on actual malpais, as were those from the type locality, they are generally on dark soil, much of which is volcanic. Their dark color is here as protective as is the light sand color of squirrels of the sandy river valleys.

At Wingate, in June, 1905, Hollister found these squirrels exceedingly shy. Their burrows were usually on hill sides in small groups, and most of the squirrels disappeared in them as soon as seen and did not reappear. No specimens were taken at Wingate, but a week later three were trapped near Gallup, where they occurred in about the same numbers. At Thoreau, in June, 1909, Goldman took one specimen and reported the squirrels common on the plain near the station.

CITELLUS MEXICANUS PARVIDENS (MEARNS)

RIO GRANDE GROUND SQUIRREL

Spermophilus mexicanus parvidens Mearns, U. S. Natl. Mus. Proc. 18: 443, 1896 (advance sheets).

Type.—Collected at Fort Clark, Tex., March 21, 1893, by E. A. Mearns.

General characters.—Largest of the striped ground squirrels of Texas and New Mexico, although smaller than typical *mexicanus* from farther south. The whole back is striped with nine well-defined parallel rows of whitish spots over dull brown; the underparts are creamy or soiled whitish; the ears are very short; and the tail long and spreading.

Measurements.—Adult male from Roswell: Total length, 330; tail, 131; hind foot, 43 millimeters; adult female, 302, 118, and 39 millimeters, respectively.

Distribution and habitat.—The Rio Grande ground squirrel is a southern species coming into southeastern New Mexico along the Pecos Valley to Carlsbad and Roswell. (Fig. 18.) Its range seems to be restricted to Lower Sonoran Zone, mainly within the semiarid division. An alcoholic specimen recorded from Fort Bliss as collected by S. W. Crawford may have been incorrectly labeled, for, although a great deal of field work has been done in that locality, no other specimen has been secured, and the species apparently does not now inhabit the El Paso region of the Rio Grande Valley.

The first discovery of this species in New Mexico was by B. H. Dutcher, who collected specimens at Eddy (now Carlsbad) in 1892 and reported them common over the mesa in that part of the Pecos Valley. Later the writer found them common at both Carlsbad and Roswell. They seem to be invariably associated with the mesquite, which is abundant in the warmer parts of this valley, and it is not improbable that they follow the same plant formation somewhat farther north than Roswell.

General habits.—The burrows of these ground squirrels are generally situated at the base of mesquite bushes in the open valley, or sometimes in the shade of creosote or acacia or even at the edge of a cluster of cactus. They are strictly "ground" squirrels, climbing only into low bushes for seeds and fruit and depending entirely on their burrows for protection. They are shy and usually silent. In considerable experience with the species the writer has never heard one utter any sound or call note, but like all other species of the genus they undoubtedly have a note of warning.

Food habits.—The sweet pods of mesquite are found scattered around their burrows and evidently form one of their staple articles of food. They also feed on numerous seeds, grain, fruits, green foliage, lizards, and some insects. Their fondness for seeds gets them into bad repute with the farmer, as they often gather around gardens and grainfields, where they do considerable damage in spring by digging up corn, melons, beans, and various sprouting seeds, and in summer and fall by feeding on the ripening grain. Specimens examined at Roswell in June were feeding on about equal proportions of seeds and insects, so there is some compensation for the harm done.

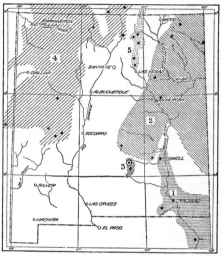

Hibernation.—Over most of their range the Rio Grande ground squirrels apparently do not hibernate but have the remarkable habit of closing their burrows and remaining inside during the coldest weather. Several times the writer has caught them in what he mistook for pocket-gopher burrows, but found that the single closed external mound marked the entrance of the ground squirrel's den.

FIGURE 18.—Distribution of the striped ground squirrels in New Mexico: 1, *Citellus mexicanus parvidens;* 2, *C. tridecemlineatus arenicola;* 3, *C. tridecemlineatus hollisteri;* 4, *C. tridecemlineatus parvus;* 5, *C. tridecemlineatus alleri.* Type locality circled

The habit, however, is not thoroughly understood, and little is known of the breeding habits or other phases of the life history of this species.

CITELLUS TRIDECEMLINEATUS ARENICOLA Howell

PALE GROUND SQUIRREL

Citellus tridecemlineatus arenicola Howell, Biol. Soc. Wash. Proc. 41:213, December 18, 1928.

Type.—Collected at Pendennis, Kans., April 22, 1897, by J. Alden Loring.

General characters.—This small pale form of the 13-lined ground squirrel is recognized by its alternating lines of spots and stripes over the light brown back. The six light stripes and five rows of dots are light-buff or cream color, in strong contrast to the intervening brown stripes. The underparts are white or soiled whitish.

Measurements.—Adult specimens from the type locality: Total length, 238; tail, 77; hind foot, 32 millimeters.

Distribution and habitat.—These little pale ground squirrels (pl. 7, B) of the semiarid great plains region come into New Mexico over the Llano Estacado and the plains to the north and west. There are specimens from Folsom, Chico, Clayton, and near Texline, from 6 miles north of Cabra Spring, from the highest northern point of the Staked Plains, the northwest base of the Capitan Mountains and near Roswell. They are practically restricted to the treeless Upper Sonoran plains. At Roswell they come into the edge of the Lower Sonoran Zone and those from the Canadian River Valley farther east are grading toward *texensis*.

General habits.—Over the open short-grass plains where these small squirrels abound there is little shelter or protection from enemies except what is derived from protective marking. As the squirrels stand up in the grass like sticks or picket pins, the fine lines of the back blend so perfectly with the grass blades that the animals are almost invisible. Indeed, they would rarely be noticed but for their sharp little trill, which is heard for a considerable distance over the prairie. Their small burrows enter the prairie sod at frequent intervals, and while scarcely visible to the observer are always conveniently located for the quick disappearance of their owners. The runways can often be traced through the grass from one burrow to another where the animals visit back and forth and explore for food. Sometimes the runways take the form of tunnels under the grass, but usually are mere trails worn by long use.

Food habits.—Like all ground squirrels they are fond of a great variety of seeds, including grains and many of those planted for farm crops. They also eat a great many insects, sometimes more than any other food. One specimen taken on the highest point of the Staked Plains June 17 had its stomach well filled with a variety of insects, largely larvae. Grasshoppers are often conspicuous in their stomach contents, and it is probable that the good they do in keeping down grass-feeding insects partly balances the harm they do in destroying vegetation and seeds, but when they enter the newly planted fields and dig up the seed of small grain, corn, or melons it becomes necessary to take control measures.

Breeding habits.—The pale ground squirrels are rather prolific breeders, as shown by the number of embryos in specimens examined, ranging from 6 to 10. Even a larger number may at times be produced as the mammae are normally arranged in six pairs, and there are records of as high as 14 embryos in the closely related *tridecemlineatus*. Apparently only one litter of young is raised in a season.

Hibernation.—These squirrels hibernate rather early and evidently for a long period during the cold season. A specimen collected at Folsom by A. H. Howell, on August 29, gives the latest date at which they are recorded in New Mexico, but it is probable that they do not all den up before some time in September. Their date of emerging from hibernation is not definitely known, but in this southern latitude it is probably early—presumably some time in March.

CITELLUS TRIDECEMLINEATUS PARVUS (ALLEN)

LITTLE STRIPED GROUND SQUIRREL

Spermophilus tridecemlineatus parvus Allen, Bul. Amer. Mus. Nat. Hist. 7: 337, 1895.

Type.—Collected at Uncompahgre Indian Reservation, northeastern Utah, November 2, 1895, by W. W. Granger.

General characters.—Smallest of all the striped ground squirrels; readily distinguished from *arenicola* by smaller size, almost pure-white stripes, and rows of spots, and white underparts. The stripes of the back are less continuous and often broken into a series of overlapping dots. The brown between the lines is also duller and has less of a chestnut tone.

Measurements.—An adult female from the type region in western Colorado measures in total length, 196; tail, 66; hind foot, 29 millimeters.

Distribution and habitat.—The little striped ground squirrel occupies the arid Upper Sonoran Plains of New Mexico west of the Rio Grande Valley and north of the Mogollon Mountains. Specimens have been examined from the San Augustine Plains and Datil Mountains; and others from Springerville, Ariz.; Antonito, Colo.; and localities farther west that carry its range over the northwestern part of New Mexico. A specimen in the National Museum collection taken by J. T. Rothrock at Tierra Amarilla, October 1, 1873, is the only actual specimen for northern New Mexico, but they are common just north of the line at Antonito, Colo., in the southern part of the San Luis Valley, and they were described by the Taos Indians, who said they were occasionally found near the pueblo. On the high plains about 15 miles southwest of Acoma the writer saw one but did not succeed in getting it. Some of the localities lie at the edge of Transition Zone, but the species apparently belongs to the Upper Sonoran, which it completely fills. It is apparently nowhere abundant or else is so inconspicuous that it is rarely taken or observed. Much of the collecting in northwestern New Mexico has also been done presumably after hibernation was complete, which in part accounts for the meager information concerning the species. Its habits are similar to those of *arenicola* farther east, except that in a more arid region it finds less vegetation for cover and is more exposed to light and enemies. Its burrows are so small and scattered that they are rarely seen, and most of the specimens secured have been taken in traps. They are often found on the same ground with the Arizona prairie dog (*Cynomys ludovicianus arizonensis*), but other than an accidental occurrence in the same kind of country there seems to be no association of the two species unless the vacant prairie-dog burrows form a convenient means of escape in time of danger. On the San Augustine Plains E. A. Goldman picked up one at a prairie-dog burrow where he had placed poisoned grain for the prairie dog. It was a half-grown young of the year and was lying at the entrance of the burrow with 11 kernels of poisoned wheat in its cheek pouches. He shot another as it was running along the roadside on the plains 15 miles southwest of Monica Spring. The voice of these squirrels is rarely heard, but it is a fine trill much like that of *arenicola.*

Little or nothing is known of the food or breeding habits of the little striped ground squirrel.

CITELLUS TRIDECEMLINEATUS HOLLISTERI Bailey

Mescalero Ground Squirrel

Citellus tridecemlineatus hollisteri Bailey, Biol. Soc. Wash. Proc. 26: 131, 1913.

Type.—Collected at Mescalero Indian Reservation, Sacramento Mountains, N. Mex. (8,000 feet), September 11, 1902, by Vernon Bailey.

General characters.—This little dark, brown-backed, striped ground squirrel of the Sacramento Mountains is about the size of *arenicola* but much darker colored. The brown of its back is as dark and rich as that of typical *tridecemlineatus* and much darker and richer than *alleni*.

Measurements.—The type, an adult female, measures: Total length, 232; tail, 70; hind foot, 32 millimeters.

Distribution and habitat.—In the fall of 1902, as Hollister and the writer were riding through the open yellow pine forest on Penasco Creek, about 12 miles east of Cloudcroft, they first heard the characteristic chr-r-r-r-r-r-r of *tridecemlineatus* along the roadside, and later, when crossing the grassy parks of Transition Zone on the Mescalero Indian Reservation, this was a common sound, but the animals were so shy they could not get sight of one. In the beautiful parklike valley known as Elk Park, in the southeastern part of the reservation near the Indian sawmill, they found the squirrels so common on the bright warm morning of September 11 that they were able to collect a series of seven specimens. Frosty nights had apparently driven the fat old males into hibernation, but a few females and many young were still out on warm days filling their stomachs with rich seeds and their skins with fat for the winter's supply of nourishment. Most of the specimens collected were immature and had accumulated but little fat. An adult female was obtained that had been nursing young and was late in getting in hibernating condition. Marsh hawks were common and scouring the parks evidently in search of ground squirrels for breakfast, and as they passed low over the earth a series of trills followed the course of each and indicated the location of the squirrels. Their striped backs rendered them so inconspicuous in the grassy and weedy parks that had it not been for their voices the collectors probably would have passed them by unnoticed. The warning of danger, which they were constantly passing along to one another, proved in this case their greatest danger. The species was at once recognized as different from any previously described, and the writer finds in his catalogue the note " sp. nov." entered at the time after the name.

This squirrel affords a most interesting example of the modifying influence of environment on a species. In more than 2,000 miles of open plains it shows no appreciable variation, but in the Sacramento Mountains in a 50-mile strip of half-forested country with changed climatic conditions it has acquired strongly marked characters. Its food, both plant and insect, in the mountains is almost totally different from that of the plains animals. Here the sweeping prairie winds are broken, snow lies deep and late in spring, the earth under which hibernation takes place is warmer in winter, the summer climate is cooler, and the air more moist at the surface of the ground. There is less light and more shadow, the breeding season is probably later and the growing period shorter. As a result of this changed environment there is the marked change in darker, richer coloration of the animals.

CITELLUS TRIDECEMLINEATUS ALLENI (Merriam)

Allen's Ground Squirrel

Spermophilus tridecemlineatus alleni Merriam, Biol. Soc. Wash. Proc. **12: 71,** 1898.

Type.—Collected in Bighorn Mountains, Wyo., September 18, 1893, by Vernon Bailey.

General characters.—Described by C. Hart Merriam from 8,000 feet altitude on the Bighorn Mountains of Wyoming; in size beween *arenicola* and *parvus* but darker colored than either, while the skull is slenderer and with smaller bullae than in *parvus*.

Measurements.—The type, an adult male, measures in total length, 211; tail, 74; hind foot, 32 millimeters.

Distribution and habitat.—The little dull-colored striped Allen's ground squirrel is especially common in Moreno Valley along the east side of the Taos Mountains, at Black Lake, and south along the yellow pine margin of the Pecos Mountains to near Las Vegas. In the Biological Survey collection there are four specimens from Moreno Valley, one from 10 miles south of Mora and one from 12 miles north of Las Vegas, all from the Transition Zone and from localities ranging from 7,100 to 8,700 feet altitude. The writer also saw them in the vicinity of Black Lake and presumes they have a much more extensive range in the mountain parks. In Moreno Valley they seem to be fairly common, and specimens were taken near Elizabethtown at the northern end and others near Taos Pass in the central part of this great open mountain valley. They were seen and shot along the roadsides as they ran to their little burrows under sagebrush and rabbit brush. The last specimens taken were shot on September 20, and after that none were seen, probably because they had hibernated. All those taken were very fat and evidently ready for winter quarters.

Only after critical comparison have these specimens been referred to *alleni*, as that species has never been recorded so far south by nearly the width of two States. The conditions, zone level, type of country, and general environment are very similar to those where the type of *alleni* was taken; and even if a continuous range can not be established there seems no escaping the identity of the specimens, especially those from Moreno Valley. A larger series of specimens at different seasons may show color differences, but none is shown in the present material.

CYNOMYS LUDOVICIANUS LUDOVICIANUS (Ord)

Black-Tailed Prairie Dog

Arctomys ludoviciana Ord, Guthrie's Geography, Amer. ed. 2, v. 2, p. 292, 302, 1815. (Reprint by S. N. Rhoads, 1894.)

Type locality.—" Missouri and throughout Louisiana." The Upper Missouri River.

General characters.—These prairie dogs are big fat buffy squirrel-like rodents with short ears, short legs, and short black-tipped tails.

Measurements.—Adults weigh 2 to 3 pounds and measure in total length about 388; tail, 86; and hind foot, 62 millimeters.

Distribution and habitat.—The Great Plains form of the prairie dog occupies the area east of the Pecos River Valley and the Sangre de Cristo Mountains, as shown on the accompanying map (fig. 19),

but the intergradation with *arizonensis* is very gradual, and specimens near the border line may be referred almost as well to one as to
the other.   Though irregularly distributed in colonies over this
Great Plains area, they may be said to occupy practically all of it,
although one colony may be miles from another.   Some of the
colonies are extensive, occupying many square miles, while others
are limited to a few acres or little groups of half a dozen or a
dozen animals.   The spots on the map indicate localities where
prairie dogs have been collected or reported, but the wide spaces
between are by no means devoid of them, and only indicate areas
from which no reports are available.   This species occupies mainly
the Upper Sonoran Zone, but crowds it to the limits or slightly
beyond, in places into the edges of both the Lower Sonoran and

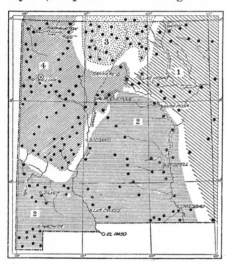

Transition Zones.   T h e
prairie dogs keep to the
open country, avoiding all
forested or brushy ground
and also the bottom lands
of rank vegetation growth.
Their habitat is mainly
short-grass open prairie
and mesa tops where their
favorite food is abundant
and where enemies a r e
seen at a distance.   Their
abundance has been greatly
reduced in certain localities
through many years of constant control efforts, but
while kept down in one locality they increase in
another.

General habits. — These
big, fat near relatives of
the ground squirrel are
among the most sociable
and friendly of the rodent
tribe and depend largely

FIGURE 19.—Distribution of the prairie dogs in
New Mexico: 1, *Cynomys ludovicianus ludovicianus;* 2, *C. ludovicianus arizonensis;* 3, *C.
gunnisoni gunnisoni;* 4, *C. gunnisoni zuniensis.*
Type locality circled

upon their social organization for their protection from enemies.
An old and successful prairie-dog town is usually located on
wide-open and mainly level ground where an unobstructed view is
to be had on all sides and no enemy can approach without being
discovered by some watchful sentinel.   The burrows are not far
apart and are always at hand for a quick retreat if danger appears.   They are home and fortress, and generally each well-com-
pleted burrow has an elevated rim around the entrance to prevent
the possible flooding of the underground nest chamber and living
quarters.   The prairie dogs are busy, industrious, and cheerful; out
with the first sunlight in the morning.   Hundreds of these plump,
sand-colored little animals scampering about digging up tender grass
roots, cutting and eating the short grass, or clearing away the larger
plants that obstruct the view, and even running and playing for
mere sport, produce an animated picture of wild life.   But let an

enemy appear and the picture quickly changes. The first prairie dog to make the discovery sets up a frantic barking or chattering, which at once arrests the attention of every one within hearing, and all are on guard against the danger. Some rush for the burrows, others straighten up on their haunches or hind feet at full length to discover and study the danger. The barking is taken up by others and continued as long as danger threatens, and when one animal becomes panic-stricken and takes to his burrow, others take up the alarm until the last prairie dog has been frightened below the surface. Then all remains quiet until the man or coyote or whatever the enemy may be has passed well beyond. Sometimes they will not reappear for an hour, but usually after half an hour of quiet they poke their noses cautiously above the surface and with great care inspect the surrounding country for any remaining traces of the enemy. A few reassuring barks here and there from the leaders and the prairie-dog town is again as populous and active as ever. They are strictly diurnal and generally most active during the morning and evening hours when the two prolonged meals of the day are being obtained, but in a well-regulated and populous dog town some are commonly seen moving about at all times of day. Even during the midday rest hours a few are likely to be busy with some needed repairs on their mounds, searching for dainty bits of food, or sitting or lying quietly on guard, so that in pleasant summer weather a totally deserted village is rarely seen.

The voice of these prairie dogs is somewhat between the shrill whistle of the marmot and the rapid trill of the prairie ground squirrels, being a continual nasal yap, yap, yap, repeated at one or two second intervals with greater or less energy as the occasion warrants, each syllable accompanied by a flip of the tail. Occasionally a prolonged chrrrr is heard, as one stretches to its full height and runs all of its notes into one long cry. Many little chirps and chuckles are occasionally heard at closer quarters, and a deep gurgle often comes up from below as the prairie dog retreats to the depths of his den.

Their little short legs prevent them from running very fast, but the long front claws make them sturdy diggers of deep and long burrows, though usually these have but one entrance. Old burrows that have been used for many generations can be distinguished by the greater accumulation of earth around the entrance and by the broader rim that slopes farther back than in the case of newer burrows.

Food habits.—Though highly specialized vegetarian rodents, the prairie dogs live so extensively upon the short rich grasses that they might almost be called grazing animals. Blades and stems and especially the basal portion of the low grass plants form most of their food, but many are dug up and devoured root and branch. In the more arid part of their range the ground thus cleared of its vegetation often remains bare, and in a dry season when plant growth has been greatly restricted by lack of moisture extensive areas are entirely denuded of every trace of vegetation so that the prairie dogs are forced to go to considerable distance from their burrows to procure a food supply. In normal times when plant growth is more rapid the new growth keeps them well supplied with fresh food close to their dens. They are hearty eaters, and their large stomachs are usually found distended to the limit of their capacity with finely masticated vegetation. The drain thus put upon the grazing capacity of land occupied by numerous prairie-dog towns has been variously estimated at 50 to 75 per cent of its value for stock. It is little wonder therefore that the stockmen consider prairie dogs one of their greatest enemies and use every possible means to destroy them.

Breeding habits.—Commonly in May four or five young are brought forth in the burrows, and early in June families of less than half-grown young begin to appear at the surface. For a long time the mother prairie dog is so solicitous for their safety that she is always watching for enemies. At her first word of warning the young rush for the burrow and either disappear without a moment's hesitation or pause and, standing erect in a little circle around the entrance, wait for the final word to dive to the soft nest below. The English equivalent of the final word that sends them head foremost below remains to be given, but it is always effective and until the young are well grown, parental authority is well obeyed. Families of small young are sometimes seen as late as the latter part of July, but that may not signify a second litter. More probably they are the first litter of last year's females, which in many species do not breed so early as the older individuals.

Hibernation.—In the northern part of the range of this species hibernation continues through all the long cold winter months, but in the southern part of its range, including eastern New Mexico, the dormant period is not so long or regular, but does include apparently three or four months of the coldest weather, while in the higher levels of its range the period may extend for considerably longer. Late in autumn the animals become excessively fat, so that hibernation is possible whenever a cold day comes.

Economic status.—The actual numbers of individuals on a given area can be counted or closely estimated in the smaller colonies, but the irregularity of distribution renders it impossible to give any adequate idea of the numbers over a wide area. Their numbers quickly run into the millions, however, and with the oft-repeated estimate of grass consumed by 32 prairie dogs equalling that required by one sheep and of 256 prairie dogs equaling that required by one cow, the loss sustained on the cattle and sheep ranges of New Mexico through devastation by prairie dogs is enormous. It has been estimated that this is spread over 6,000,000 acres of choice grazing land. But for natural enemies the increase of the prairie dog would be overwhelming. Badgers, coyotes, black-footed ferrets, eagles, and most of the larger hawks are preying upon them constantly throughout their active period, but the badger and the black-footed ferret are their chief enemies. The badger with its powerful claws quickly enlarges the burrows of the prairie dogs and feasts on the occupants, while the black-footed ferret runs in and out of their burrows at will and kills to its heart's content so long as a prairie dog can be found. The black-footed ferrets are rare, but the badgers are common wherever prairie dogs are found. These enemies, however, serve only to check the natural increase of the prairie dogs, and to reduce their numbers and free the range from their devastation artificial methods are necessary. Circulars and formulas giving directions for the best methods of destroying prairie dogs have been prepared by the Bureau of Biological Survey.

CYNOMYS LUDOVICIANUS ARIZONENSIS Mearns

Arizona Prairie Dog

Cynomys arizonensis Mearns, Bul. Amer. Mus. Nat. Hist. 2: 305, 1890.

Type.—Collected at Point of Mountain, near Willcox, Ariz., May 3, 1885, by E. A. Mearns.

General characters.—This subspecies is distinguished from *ludovicianus* by slightly longer tail and brighter coloration, in addition to obscure cranial characters.

Measurements.—Average of adult males: Total length, 388; tail, 89; hind foot, 62 millimeters. (Hollister, 1916, p. 20.) Weight, 2 pounds to 2 pounds and 8 ounces.

Distribution and habitat.—As indicated on the accompanying map (fig. 19), the Arizona prairie dog ranges over the southern part of New Mexico west of the Pecos Valley. Though some of the colonies are in the edge of the Lower Sonoran Zone and others in the edge of the Transition Zone, the range is mainly Upper Sonoran. On the mesa tops colonies are often found among the scattered juniper and nut pine growth, but the characteristic habitat and the short-grass slopes of the open valley sides are their favorite situations. Many of the colonies are in typical desert environment, which gives some peculiarities of habit not shared by the better-fed relatives of the grassy plains. In the Pecos Valley in 1899 prairie dogs were found abundant at frequent intervals from Portales to Roswell, down the valley to Carlsbad, and southward into Texas; also from Roswell west to the Capitan Mountains in numerous and extensive colonies. Two years later they were equally numerous in a line from Carlsbad west over the top of the Guadalupe Mountains and out for 35 miles east of Carlsbad to the edge of the Staked Plains. The following year they were found at frequent intervals over the plateau top and eastern slopes of the Guadalupe and the Sacramento and White Mountains, and Hollister reported them in abundance from Roswell all the way up the Pecos Valley to Santa Rosa. In May, 1903, the writer found them abundant in colonies all around Santa Rosa, a few in the edge of town, a large colony covering 200 or 300 acres near his camp at the wells east of town, and others a short distance to the north and west. Gaut reported them as in great numbers over the half-timbered mesa south of the Capitan Mountains, where they were doing considerable damage to the ranch crops. He also reported them along the eastern slopes of the Manzano Mountains and at localities on both slopes of the San Andres Mountains farther south. In 1892 Streator reported an extensive prairie-dog town about 3 miles south of Silver City, where in November and December the animals were apparently in a starving condition and feeding mainly on cactus. In August, 1908, on a trip from Deming to Hachita and through the Playas and Animas Valleys the writer found the prairie dogs numerous in many localities, especially along the elevated and more open margins of the valleys, but extensive colonies were also seen in the bottoms of these great desert valleys. Animas Valley was an almost continuous prairie-dog town for its whole length and breadth. In many places where rain had missed a part of the valley the prairie dogs had taken all the season's vegetation and had made barren deserts miles in extent.

Ten prairie dogs to an acre were estimated as a fair allowance for their numbers in the colonies, and apparently these colonies covered at least a third of Grant County, or approximately 1,000 square miles, which would give 6,400,000 prairie dogs to one county. This is but a rough estimate of their actual numbers, but may give some idea of the abundance of these animals in a region where the rainfall is very light and plant growth slow and uncertain. Extensive colonies were also found on the south, east, and west of Silver City and throughout the Gila Valley, at Cliff, along Duck Creek Valley and on Cactus Flat between the Gila and San Francisco Rivers, which marks the northern edge of their range in this section. In the vicinity of Lake Valley, E. A. Goldman found them in scattered colonies to the south and east and reaching in one place 8 miles north of the town. Most of this country is characterized by more or less desert vegetation, such as cactus, Spanish-bayonet, and mesquite, and in places an abundance of low grama and other grasses.

General habits.—In habits these prairie dogs do not differ from the typical species, except in degree of adaptation to their more arid environment. Their burrows are the same, with the same craterlike rims to prevent violent rains from running down and filling them up at every cloudburst.

In this arid region one is usually struck by the extreme bareness of the prairie-dog towns, for the vegetation has been killed out for a considerable distance from the burrows. In places the distance from the burrows to the grassland has become too great for safety to the animals, and the towns have been abandoned and new pastures sought by the colonies. It is often necessary in the arid regions for the prairie dogs to adapt themselves to unusual kinds of food, such as cactus, and the bark of mesquite and other available bushes growing within reach of their homes. Greater activity on the part of the animals is necessary in obtaining a food supply, and the colonies are often more open and scattered.

Breeding habits.—The small young begin to appear about the burrows in early June, and at Santa Rosa, in 1910, Lantz found the first family of young in May, but the first that the writer saw in 1903 in the same locality were two families of young on June 4. The mammae of the females are arranged in 4 pairs, usually given as 1 pair of inguinal, 1 abdominal, and 2 pectoral, but perhaps more properly classed as 2 pairs of abdominal and 2 of pectoral. The abdominal and pectoral mammary glands are separated and distinct on each side, making four large mammary glands each bearing two nipples. The usual number of young seems to be 4, but the number varies, and the 5 or 6 young often seen around the entrance of one burrow probably represent but a single family. There is no direct evidence to show whether more than one litter of young is raised in a season.

Hibernation.—There seem to be few data as to the hibernation of these southern prairie dogs. Streator collected specimens a little south of Silver City on December 1 and 4, 1892, and Gaut found them active along the east slope of the San Andres Mountains in January, 1903, but uninhabited prairie-dog towns, which he reported a little farther north in November and December, suggest that the animals may have been hibernating in those colonies. In other places where they range higher in the mountains and in localities where there is considerable snow they undoubtedly den up during part of the winter. Specimens collected in November, 1906, on Cactus Flat and along Duck Creek north of the Gila were very fat and in full long silky winter fur, but the weather was still mild and they were getting an abundance of green vegetation with which their stomachs were well filled. The writer estimated that each of these animals would yield a pint of oil, and they were certainly in good condition for a long period of hibernation.

Economic status.—In this arid section of the State, where vegetation is thinly scattered, a thousand prairie dogs require as much grass as in regions where it is more abundant. The colonies are generally in the best grazing localities, and in many places on the stock range the grass has been greatly thinned or entirely destroyed over miles of country. Where the prairie dogs are forced to move to new pastures the old prairie-dog towns grow up to worthless weeds or equally worthless foxtail grass, which furnishes forage for neither prairie dogs nor cattle. As prairie dogs of one species or another are abundant over most of the State, the total loss from their ravages on the stock range is enormous. Though their rapid increase is checked by natural enemies, chief of which are the badgers, coyotes, eagles, and large hawks, the reduction of their present numbers can only be accomplished through artificial means. Economical methods of control have been thoroughly worked out by the Biological Survey and demonstrated in many localities.

CYNOMYS GUNNISONI GUNNISONI (BAIRD)

GUNNISON'S PRAIRIE DOG; KE'OO UNA of the Taos Indians

Spermophilus gunnisoni Baird, Acad. Nat. Sci. Phila. Proc. 7: 334, 1855.

Type.—Collected at Cochetopa Pass, Colo., September, 1863, by F. Kreutzfeldt, under Captain J. W. Gunnison.
General characters.—In size Gunnison's is slightly smaller than the black-tailed prairie dog, its tail is relatively shorter without distinct black tip, and its coloration slightly paler buff.
Measurements.—Average of adult males: Total length, 340; tail, 53; hind foot, 56 millimeters. An adult male collected September 6 in the Jemez Mountains weighed 1½ pounds.

Distribution and habitat.—The typical form of Gunnison's prairie dog occupies the high plateau country of southern Colorado and northern New Mexico, including the Sangre de Cristo, San Juan, and Jemez Mountain Ranges. (Fig. 19.) Here they occupy the elevated open valleys mainly in the Transition Zone, but extending often into the Canadian Zone parks and in places down even to the Upper Sonoran valleys. In the Sangre de Cristo Mountains they were found abundant throughout the Moreno Valley, around Black Lake, and down the Guadalupita on Coyote Creek, and A. H. Howell found a large colony occupying the open parks at the summit of Costilla Pass at 10,000 feet. Along Comanche Creek and upper Costilla River valleys, the lower Costilla Valley, and out across the

Rio Grande Plain along the Colorado-New Mexico line, they were found in many localities and also in the Rio Grande Valley about Taos, Tres Piedras, and all along the east slope of the San Juan Range up to 9,700 feet; west of the San Juan Mountains they were again found in scattered colonies in the valley below Tierra Amarilla, at Chama and Navajo, and over the Jicarilla Indian Reservation. Farther south they were abundant throughout the Gallinas and Jemez Mountain region, occupying the open parks up to at least 9,500 feet and extending down into the valleys around the mountains down to Coyote at 7,000 feet and along the Chama River Valley even to near Espanola. They are generally scattered over the open country, but are often numerous in one park and scarce or wanting in another, their numbers, and distribution seeming to depend on the success and increase of each of the colonial units. At the lower western and southern edge of their range they grade imperceptibly into the slightly marked subspecies *zuniensis* of the western part of the State.

General habits.—These prairie dogs of the white-tailed group differ considerably from the black-tailed species, and are readily recognized as distinct in both form and habits. They are less closely colonial, and occasionally scattered individuals are found apparently living by themselves or starting new colonies, while the general prairie-dog towns are less compact and indicate less of the community spirit. The burrows are also noticeably different, the earth being thrown out commonly on one side and left there without an attempt to build up a waterproof rim around the entrance. It usually lies in a mound at the side of the burrow and serves the purpose of a signal tower, as in the other species. Living in a rougher, elevated, and sloping country these prairie dogs have evidently not felt the need of protection against the flooding of their burrows by heavy rains.

The voice and especially the barking note is slightly different from that of the black-tailed species, but not different enough for easy recognition. The lack of the conspicuous black tip of the tail as the animals sit barking by their burrows is noticeable at the distance at which they are generally seen, as are also the paler color and the more conspicuous black mark over the eye. To the experienced observer it is not difficult to distinguish the species in passing through a prairie-dog town, but to the uninitiated no difference would be noticed among any of the prairie dogs. The Gunnison form is less restricted to open country than is the black-tailed species, and often small colonies or individuals are scattered through the sagebrush and among the juniper trees where skulking animals might easily take them unawares. In this habit they are more individual, more like the closely related ground squirrels, and apparently less highly specialized for social protection.

Food habits.—The food of Gunnison's prairie dog consists mainly of grasses and other small plants that they cut or dig up around their burrows. They do a great deal of digging and apparently unearth some bulbs or the roots of plants that are favorite foods, but the bulk of their forage is the little short grama and other grasses, which constitute the choicest cattle range. These grasses are eaten top and bottom and often entirely destroyed over considerable areas within their reach.

Breeding habits.—In this group of prairie dogs the mammae are normally in five pairs, arranged in 1 pair of inguinal, 2 pairs of abdominal, and 2 pairs of pectoral. The young are usually five in number, but there are few records on which to base an average.

Hibernation.—In much of the high country where these prairie dogs live the winters are long and the snow deep, and they apparently hibernate for a great part of the winter. Specimens collected at 9,000 feet on October 9 were very fat and in good winter fur, but had been showing no signs of hibernating. In 1903, Surber reported the last seen in colonies near Taos about the first of December, but as the winter was unusually warm, this was considered a late date for them to disappear. He was told that generally in that region no prairie dogs were seen during the winter months, or after the first cold weather had set in. The time at which they emerge from hibernation is not known.

Economic status.—It is unfortunate that these good-natured, sociable, interesting little animals should conflict with man's interests, but so long as they insist on feeding upon the best range grasses the practical question is at once raised of the relative value of 32 prairie dogs to one sheep, or 256 prairie dogs to one cow. (Merriam, 1902, p. 258.) When the number of prairie dogs runs into the millions the reduction of carrying power of the range for domestic stock is a serious matter; so serious indeed that many thousands of dollars are expended yearly by the ranchmen in efforts to rid the range of this unprofitable grade of stock.

CYNOMYS GUNNISONI ZUNIENSIS Hollister

ZUNI PRAIRIE DOG; GLO-UN of the Navajo Indians; DIRK'QUAR of the Moki Indians (Fisher)

Cynomys gunnisoni zuniensis Hollister, North Amer. Fauna No. 40, p. 32, 1916.

Type.—Collected at Wingate, N. Mex., June 26, 1905, by N. Hollister.

General characters.—Similar to *gunnisoni* but slightly larger, brighter, and more cinnamon in color.

Measurements.—Adult male: Total length, 363; tail, 53; hind foot, 60 millimeters. Weight of adult male, 2 pounds.

Distribution and habitat.—Northwestern New Mexico, southwestern Colorado, and northern Arizona. In New Mexico the greater part of the range of this species lies in the Upper Sonoran Zone west of the Jemez and north of the Mogollon Mountains, but it also extends into the Rio Grande Valley at Albuquerque and south along the western side of the valley to Fairview. (Fig. 19.) Specimens have been taken in the Sandia Mountains near San Pedro and near Pecos on the upper Pecos River, actually on the same ground with the black-tailed prairie dogs, but throughout nearly the length of the State these two distinct species usually keep slightly apart.

General habits.—In habits the Zuni prairie dog does not differ from typical *gunnisoni*, except as the animals occupy more open and level country over the great arid plains of the western part of the State. In the more level country there is often an ill-defined rim encircling the burrow sufficient to keep out a moderate quantity of flood water, but in many cases the earth is all thrown out on one side without giving any real protection from floods. Over most of their range there is no permanent water within reach of the prairie-dog towns, and in dry periods they must be forced to go for months without a drink, but this does not seem to trouble them in the least, although after a shower they are often seen drinking at the little pools, and their tracks show on the muddy margins of any available water holes. The old theory that prairie dogs dig wells to a subterranean water supply has been proved to be without foundation. At Albuquerque, where they were numerous over the dry mesa, it would have been necessary for them to go 250 feet to water, and in many localities they would have to sink their wells much farther and through solid rock. The juice of their green food and occasionally of cactus and other plants enables them to keep up the necessary supply of moisture for their bodies.

Along the Rio Grande, where the country has been thickly settled for centuries, the prairie dogs are less numerous and live mainly in small and scattered colonies, but back over the wide stretches of unoccupied grazing lands to the west they are often numerous, living in extensive prairie dog towns or scattered groups. Near the Navajo Indian settlements they are generally scarce and very shy, owing apparently to the fact that they have long been counted an important source of food supply by these people. At Wingate, in 1905, Hollister found them the most abundant and conspicuous mammals of the whole region; the Puerco Valley was covered with their burrows, and they were plentiful in every mountain park, while over the Zuni Mountains they were scattered everywhere, chiefly in open parks and valleys in populous and noisy colonies. He also found them abundant from Laguna to Magdalena. In the big valley surrounding the Pueblo of Zuni in 1908 the writer found them scattered in more or less well-defined colonies where they were doing some mischief in the Indian fields and occasionally burrowing into the banks of the newly made irrigation ditches. Over the Quemado Valley still farther south they were equally abundant and in the same scattered formation of small groups or extensive colonies. Over the San Augustine Plain and through the Datil and the northern part of the Mogollon Mountains E. A. Goldman and Ned Hollister reported them as always present in varying numbers, and in many places extremely injurious to the stock range. At Fairview, in 1909, Goldman found them abundant and generally distributed throughout the valley and over the bordering hill slopes, although they were reported to have appeared there only five years prior to that time. The cattlemen estimated that over considerable areas they had eaten or destroyed at least half of the forage. Over the Chuska Mountains in the northwestern corner of the State the writer found them common locally over the whole range of the great mountain plateau, usually in grassy parks at altitudes ranging up to 9,000 feet. In some of these colonies, however, they were scarce and the ground showed evidence of their having been dug out by the Indians or drowned out of their burrows with streams of water turned into them from the neighboring creeks or springs. Numerous colonies were also found in crossing the arid plains of the San Juan Valley.

During October the prairie dogs were fat and sleepy and their long fur looked fuzzy and warm, as if they were ready for cold weather. Their burrows were constantly being dug out by badgers and in many places also by the Navajo Indians, and many little ditches were seen leading to their burrows, showing where the Navajos had forced them out with water. The Navajo Indians have always been great hunters, and now that larger game is scarce, they make excursions especially for prairie dogs. At Fruitland, Clarence Birdseye reported them coming in from the country on the north side of the valley loaded down with these fat little delicacies for the family fare. Some of the colonies had been almost exterminated in this way.

Food habits.—Grass seems to be the main source of food supply for this species as with other prairie dogs, but in autumn they seem especially partial to the grass heads, which contain an abundance of ripening seeds. Along the Alamosa River E. A. Goldman shot several whose pouches contained fragments of the heads of grama grass (*Bouteloua oligostachya*) and other grasses such as *Munroa squarrosa* and also a few seeds of the wild sunflowers (*Verbesina encelioides*). He reported also many plants and small shrubs cut down by the prairie dogs near their burrows, but probably to clear the view rather than serve as food. Two prairie dogs, which were shot for specimens in the Chuska Mountains in October, were very fat, and their stomachs were distended mainly with finely masticated grass, but contained also a large proportion of seeds of grass and other green plants. Another shot for a specimen on September 28 south of Acoma was moderately fat, and the stomach contents were largely seeds and heads of grama and other grasses and some other plants, parts of which also were carried in the cheek pouches. In most cases the prairie dogs find food abundant, but in dry seasons they are sometimes obliged to abandon a locality and move on to places where a fresh supply of grass can be obtained.

Breeding habits.—The arrangement and number of mammae in this species are the same as in typical *gunnisoni*, and the number of young is undoubtedly the same, varying from four to six. Near Reserve at 8,000 feet in western Socorro County J. S. Ligon reports the first prairie dog seen out of winter quarters on March 4, 1915; on March 12 many were seen and by the 20th apparently all were out. On March 30 they appeared to be in the midst of breeding activity, the males fighting and chasing one another in great excitement, and a female killed on May 4 contained four well-grown embryos. Groups of five and six small young are often seen running to a single burrow, where they disappear or sit up for a moment to watch an intruder. On the mesa near Albuquerque late in June, 1889, the writer found numerous families of young about the burrows, and at that time they were about half grown and were digging grass for themselves and, although they were still in family groups, were rapidly dispensing with parental care.

Hibernation.—In the San Juan Valley after the middle of October, 1908, the raw, windy days and cold nights with often half an inch of ice in the mornings kept the prairie dogs well out of sight until the wind went down and, for a short time, the sun shone warmly, when they would go out and dig for grass roots and fix up their burrows for winter; but they were fat and furry and worked in a slow, sleepy manner. They were evidently on the verge of hibernation and needed only a cold snap to send them to bed for the winter. In the mountain regions from 7,000 to 8,500 feet altitude J. S. Ligon reports that the prairie dogs go in about November 1 and do not come out again before about March 10, while at higher elevations they sometimes remain denned up under deep snow five or six months of the year. In the spring of 1915 he reported that they all came out about March 15, even though they had to scratch out through 6 or 8 inches of snow. At their appearance they were in most cases fairly fat. In November, 1914, Ligon dug into a number of prairie-dog burrows to learn more in regard to the hibernation of the animals, but unfortunately the burrows selected were not occupied at that time. He found the burrows with a number of branches below the surface of the ground and at the ends of some of these branches in excavated pockets he found grass nests. Some of the branch burrows extended only a short distance, while others made circles and came back to the main burrow, and they were arranged in a great variety of positions and angles from perpendicular to horizontal. Many of the side branches and even some of the nest holes were filled with loose earth, which in some cases seemed to be used as doors to close the burrow behind the occupant. Sometimes it was necessary for the prairie dog to dig through several feet of loose earth to reach a safe nest. One of the objects in digging into these burrows was to find if stores of food were laid up for winter use, but as none was discovered it was evident that they had either been used or had been deposited in other burrows. Unfortunately Ligon does not give the depth or length of any of these burrows, but in the Chuska Mountains, where the Indians had dug out the prairie dogs for food, the holes commonly extended 10 or 15 feet and in some cases 20 feet from the entrance, but usually they were so filled up with loose earth that it was difficult to say how deep they had gone. Apparently, however, in most cases they reach a depth of 6 to 8 feet.

Economic status.—Among the Navajo Indians the Zuni prairie dogs have considerable value as game and food. Their furry coats, if collected when prime, might be made into useful clothing, as the fur is soft, although not very dense, and the skins are strong and durable. The small size of the skins, however, seems to prohibit their use as fur in the present fur market.

When taken young and well tamed prairie dogs are said to make delightful pets for children, and this might give them a real value and fill a long-felt need. On the other hand, their great abundance and the extent of country over which they abound renders them one of the most injurious of rodent pests. (Taylor and Loftfield, 1924.) The cattlemen estimate that over considerable areas the prairie dogs eat or destroy at least half of the grass and on the public range, where it is no one's special business to kill them, they hold their own and continue almost to hold the range. As new farms are opened in valleys where they abound, the crops are often seriously damaged before they can be controlled. The following extract of a letter from John McDermott, of Laplata, San Juan County, in

August, 1888, gives a fair idea of what the pioneer has to contend with on prairie-dog range:

I wish to ask your advice as to the best way for stopping the ravages of prairie dogs. They have damaged my crops over $250 this season and in spite of all I could do to fight them. I have tried strychnine with wheat and corn, phosphorized wheat, and Paris green and bran. With strychnine I killed a few in late fall and early spring, but when there is anything green to be had they will not touch it. Drowning them by running water into their holes is the only successful method I have found, but it is both slow and costly, as their runways are often so long under ground as to take from one-half hour to an hour to fill a hole with water. Bisulphide of carbon is impracticable here from its cost. The dealers in our nearest town charge 75 cents per pound for it. Some of my neighbors have suffered even worse than I have, and the dogs seem to be increasing in spite of us.

In the course of time, however, it is always possible for the ranchman to clear his fields of prairie dogs, though often at considerable expense, but on the stock range they still flourish and will until concerted action wipes them out over extensive areas so that they will not quickly return.

MARMOTA FLAVIVENTRIS OBSCURA Howell

DUSKY MARMOT; WOODCHUCK; ROCKCHUCK; PEAN-CHE-HAH′N̄ of the
Taos Indians

Marmota flaviventer obscura Howell, Biol. Soc. Wash. Proc. 27:16, 1914.

Type.—Collected at west base of Wheeler Peak, 5 miles south of Twining, N. Mex., at 11,300 feet altitude, July 4, 1904, by Vernon Bailey.

General characters.—A large, dark, grizzled-brown woodchuck, with long, bushy, dark-brown or blackish tail.

Measurements.—Average total length, 655; tail, 204; hind foot, 91 millimeters.

Distribution and habitat.—Dusky marmots are common in the higher mountains of northern New Mexico and southern Colorado, mainly in the Hudsonian Zone. There are specimens from Pecos Baldy, Truchas Peak, Wheeler Peak, and Agua Fria Peak. In the Pecos River Mountains in August, 1903, they were common from a little below timber line at 11,400 feet to the highest peaks in that range or throughout the Hudsonian and even into Arctic-Alpine Zone. On the top of Truchas Peak at 13,300 feet one had dug a burrow under the triangulation monument, and whistled at observers from the rocks only a little below. In the Taos Mountains in August of the following year marmots were also abundant throughout the Hudsonian Zone from 11,000 feet up to extreme timber line, and a few old signs were seen on the very top of Wheeler Peak at 13,600 feet. Apparently no woodchucks are known in the low country of New Mexico.[18]

General habits.—In the Taos Mountains from a 11,400-foot camp at the west base of Wheeler Peak the loud characteristic whistle could be heard from the cliffs across the little lake, from the great

---

[18]A. H. Howell (1915, p. 55) in his monograph of the genus in North America, says: "Several lower jaws and fragments of crania, found in a cave on the Manzano Mountains by Archibald Rea, and broken pieces of a skull secured by Dr. Walter Hough from a cave near the Tularosa River near Old Fort Tularosa [in the Mogollon Mountains] indicate the former occurrence of this species in those ranges. The jaws from the Manzano Mountains agree essentially with recent material, but the fragment from the Tularosa River is not specifically identifiable."

A skin obtained at Santa Fe in 1874 by H. C. Yarrow and recorded in the Wheeler survey (Coues and Yarrow, 1875, p. 123), undoubtedly came from the Pecos Mountains.

terminal moraine back of camp, and more frequently from the long rock slides on the opposite slope high up on the side of the peak. Occasionally one would come down from the rocks and run along the edge of the lake, where afterwards fresh tracks on the muddy shore were seen. In the Pecos River Mountains at the 11,600-foot camp on the side of Pecos Baldy one lived in a little cave in the rocks close to camp and grew tame enough to let the writer pass within 25 or 30 feet in going to the creek for water. He was careful not to alarm the animal, as neighbors at that altitude were rare, and while specimens were needed, they could be found farther from camp. The furry neighbor, however, ignorant of the good intentions, after a few days moved over to the big rock slide across the small lake. In most places the marmots were as wild as deer and it was often difficult to get within rifle range of one. A warning chirp from the cliff above would set all within hearing to rushing over the rocks for their dens, and they moved surprisingly fast for such clumsy-looking animals. In one place a family of 6— 2 old ones and 4 half-grown young—after reaching their home in the rocks chirped for a long time. Often, however, they disappear almost as quickly as they discover you, and the cause is evident. Idle campers and would-be sportsmen try their rifles just for fun on every woodchuck they can get sight of, often leaving them crippled or dead where shot. It is little wonder that pursued by man and natural enemies, the woodchucks make their homes in the steep mountain slopes or hide in the safe retreat of seams and crevices of broken cliffs or the great slopes of talus, where they can be comparatively safe under the fathomless piles of broken rock. Sometimes they burrow under big bowlders out in the parks and meadows, where rich mountain vegetation affords an ample supply of choice food, and in some places they make fairly well-beaten trails from one bowlder den to another or across the meadow grass.

Food habits.—The food of the marmots consists entirely of green vegetation, and the stomachs of those collected for specimens were found distended with a great variety of plants so finely chewed that they could not be identified, although the color and texture of the different parts of the stomach contents indicated everything in sight, from bright-green grass to masses of yellow sedum, the heads of little pink clovers, and other colored flowers, together with the ripening seeds of many plants. Even by the middle of August the adults were beginning to lay on a store of fat for the long winter sleep, while the half-grown young were doing their best to grow up and get fat at the same time.

Breeding habits.—One old female that the writer collected near Truchas Peak on August 14 was with a family of half-grown young in the rock slide, but he could not be sure of the number of young. Apparently there were four or five in sight at a time. Her mammae, which had all been in use that season, were arranged in 5 pairs—1 pair of inguinal, 2 pairs of abdominal, and 2 pairs of pectoral. It is probable, therefore, that five young is about the minimum size of the litter.

Hibernation.—At Twining, in 1903, Surber reported marmots numerous in the vicinity and beginning their hibernation around the bases of the peaks about the 1st of October, but he said that they did not hibernate at the tops of the peaks for almost a month later. This probably means merely that the old ones, which became fat early, went into winter quarters as soon as they had accumulated their store of fat, while the younger animals, as is usual with this group and many of the ground squirrels, remain active as long as possible to accumulate enough fat to carry them through the winter, and do not enter their winter dens until actually forced to by the cold weather.

An interesting note on the hibernation of this species of woodchuck at Ophir, Colo., was made by S. E. Osborn. The animal was found in midwinter in the Silver Mountain Tunnel, where, Osborn says (1892), he—

had packed in grass for a nest, and taken up his winter quarters. He was rolled up like a ball, with his fore paws over his eyes; we pulled his paws away, and his eyes were closed; all efforts to awaken him were futile, he would yawn like a boy that had been disturbed when sleeping soundly, return his paws to his eyes, and curl himself up in his original position.

At the high altitudes where these animals live there are few observers at the time when they come out of hibernation in spring and no records to show just when they appear, but it is a long sleep between the 1st of October and the time when any bare ground can be found around these peaks.

Family MURIDAE: Old-World Rats and Mice

RATTUS NORVEGICUS (ERXLEBEN)

BROWN RAT; WHARF RAT

[*Mus*] *norvegicus* Erxleben, Syst. Regni Anim. 1: 381, 1777.

Type locality.—Norway.

General characters.—The nose of the brown rat is long and pointed, the ears are narrow, the tail long and tapering, half naked and scaly, the fur thin and coarse, and the color buffy brownish above, soiled whitish below.

Measurements.—A medium-sized adult male measures in total length, 455; tail, 210; hind foot, 44 millimeters, and weighs about a pound.

Distribution and habitat.—Introduced in the colonial days about 1775 from Europe, wharf rats have found their way over most of the settled parts of this country, except the arid desert regions. Woodhouse (1854, p. 48) reported them as found throughout all the white settlements of New Mexico in 1851. In 1889 the writer found them common at Albuquerque, in the Rio Grande Valley, and in 1902 Gaut reported them common at Santa Rosa, in the Pecos Valley. It is probable that they are found at most, if not all, of the railroad towns in the State, but fortunately in this arid region they do not spread far into the country, and many extensive areas seem to be entirely free from them. In an open country they are not able to protect themselves from numerous enemies and consequently are restricted in range to towns and dwellings where they can obtain cover and a supply of food and water.

General habits.—In habits the rats are generally filthy scavengers, keeping under floors and within the walls of buildings, where they are safe from enemies and can prey upon garbage and refuse as well as upon the stores of food and grain that are with difficulty protected from them. They burrow readily in the ground and often gain entrance to buildings by burrowing under walls and into cellars. They can also climb and will get over walls and wire fences that they can not get under or through. Their voices are often heard as they fight, squeal, and chatter in the walls or under floors, and in every way they deserve the disgust associated with the name of rat.

Food habits.—In food habits they are omnivorous, accepting anything in the way of grain, provisions, fruit, meat, vegetables, garbage, or any refuse of an edible nature. They drink a great deal and will not remain where water is not accessible.

Breeding habits.—Rats are prolific breeders, producing litters of from eight to more than a dozen young at frequent intervals throughout a large part of the year.

Economic status.—The continual destruction of grain, food, and various stores by rats produces an enormous annual loss throughout the country, besides that caused by fires, which they are instrumental in starting by gnawing the insulation from electric wires; but most serious are the diseases which they convey from place to place. Constant warfare on rats is necessary to keep their numbers within bounds, and a bulletin has been prepared by the Bureau of Biological Survey, giving the most effective and economical methods for their destruction (Silver, 1927).

RATTUS ALEXANDRINUS (Geoffroy)

Roof Rat

Mus alexandrinus Geoffroy, Description de l'Egypte, Mammiferes, p. 733, 1818.

Type locality.—Alexandria, Egypt.

General characters.—Smaller and slenderer than the wharf rat, with larger ears and longer, slenderer tail, which exceeds in length the head and body. Color, brownish gray above with usually a white belly.

Measurements.—An adult male measures in total length, 410; tail, 234; foot, 37 millimeters.

Distribution and habitat.—One specimen of the roof rat in the collection of the College of Agriculture and Mechanic Arts at Mesilla Park, taken at Las Cruces in October, 1914, by A. Archer, seems to furnish the only record for New Mexico. Mearns records the roof rat from El Paso, Tex., and points in southern Arizona, but usually this species is found near the coasts of the southern United States, where it has been introduced from ships and has spread but a short distance inland. It is less restricted to towns and buildings than the the wharf rat, and its possible occupation of the arid valleys of southern New Mexico and Arizona suggests a dangerous tendency in these areas of intensive agriculture.

MUS MUSCULUS MUSCULUS Linnaeus

House Mouse

[*Mus*] *musculus* Linnaeus, Syst. Nat., Ed. 10, v. 1, p. 62, 1758.

Type locality.—Sweden.

General characters.—This is a sleek little mouse with sharp nose, and long tapering tail, nearly naked and finely scaled; the color of the upperparts is buffy brown, the lower parts usually buffy gray.

Measurements.—An old male measures in total length, 165; tail, 98; hind foot, 19 millimeters.

Distribution and habitat.—The house mice were introduced from Europe with the early settlement of the country. Woodhouse (1854, p. 48) reported them as common about all the settlements in New

Mexico in 1851, and to-day there are probably few ranches or houses in the State where they are not found. In 1889 the writer found them common in the little mining camp of San Pedro in the Sandia Mountains east of Albuquerque at a time when that new camp was mainly a settlement of tents. They were also common at that time in and about Albuquerque, and in 1893 Loring found them in the meadows and along the irrigation ditches at Aztec in the extreme northwestern part of the State. They are not only abundant and troublesome in houses, storehouses, barns, and stables, but they have spread to the fields and meadows, where they are one of the most abundant and destructive of the small rodents in the farming districts of the State. At Redrock, E. A. Goldman reported one caught in a weedy field a quarter of a mile from the nearest house, and at Farmington and Fruitland Clarence Birdseye reported them abundant among the weeds and in the grain and alfalfa fields along the ditches, often in company with meadow mice, harvest mice, and white-footed mice. They readily adapt themselves to wild life, where vegetation or any old trash affords cover from their numerous enemies and where there is a supply of grain and seeds for food.

Food habits.—In choice of food they are as omnivorous as the rats, accepting anything in the way of grain, seeds, fruit, vegetables, meat, garbage, and any old refuse.

Breeding habits.—House mice are very prolific, producing large litters of young at frequent intervals and quickly increasing in numbers to the carrying capacity of any locality where they become established. It is only through a host of enemies that they are kept within bounds and from doing great injury.

Economic status.—These house mice, which are of no possible value, are among the most destructive of small rodent pests, and every effort is required to protect crops and foods from their ravages. So far as possible buildings should be made both rat and mouse proof, but it is not always possible to exclude these little intruders, as they are brought in under cover of boxes or crates, and they quickly establish themselves and multiply rapidly. The damage done by the mice is sometimes more than equaled, however, by that of domestic cats, which are usually kept to control their abundance and which in many cases feed to a far greater extent on the native song and insectivorous birds than upon the mice that run riot in fields and buildings.

Family CRICETIDAE: American Rats and Mice

ONYCHOMYS LEUCOGASTER MELANOPHRYS Merriam

GRASSHOPPER MOUSE; CALLING MOUSE; SCORPION MOUSE; HO-O-LA of the Moki Indians (Fisher)

Onychomys leucogaster melanophrys Merriam, North Amer. Fauna No. 2, p. 2, 1889.
Onychomys melanophrys pallescens Merriam, North Amer. Fauna No. 3, p. 61, 1890. Type from Moki Pueblo, Ariz.

Type.—Collected at Kanab, Utah, December 22, 1888, by Vernon Bailey.
General characters.—This grasshopper mouse is a bright-colored southern form of the northern grasshopper mouse *Onychomys leucogaster*. It is a plump little animal, with small ears and rather short, tapering tail. In fully adult pelage the upper parts are a bright cinnamon buff, with the upper middle portion of the ear blackish; the lower parts, feet, lower surface, and tip of

tail pure white. Immature specimens are pale slate gray above, becoming darker gray as they reach maturity and dark grayish buff during the first winter, often with considerable wash of blackish over the back. The skull, compared with that of *leucogaster*, is long and narrow, with relatively longer, slenderer rostrum.

Measurements.—The type, an adult male, measures in total length, 145; tail, 41; hind foot, 21 millimeters. Other specimens from various localities average 154, 44, 22 millimeters, respectively, and run as high as 163, 55, 23 millimeters.

Distribution and habitat.—The scorpion mice inhabit the whole Upper Sonoran Zone area of northwestern New Mexico, both on the open plains and valleys and in the scattered juniper and nut pine country. (Fig. 20.) They are animals of the open country, evidently preferring the more arid and barren areas, where they are in places abundant, although generally of scattered and infrequent occurrence.

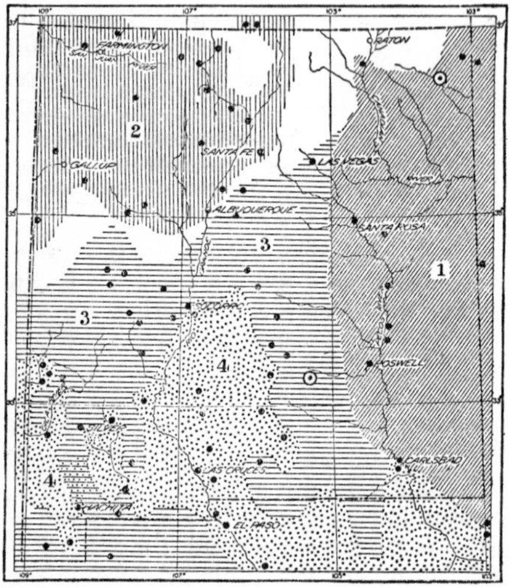

FIGURE 20.—Distribution of grasshopper mice in New Mexico: 1, *Onychomys leucogaster articeps*; 2, *O. leucogaster melanophrys*; 3, *O. leucogaster ruidosae*; 4, *O. torridus torridus*. Type localities circled.

General habits. — The names "grasshopper mouse" and "scorpion mouse" refer to the food of this little animal, while the name "calling mouse" refers to its very unusual voice. In camp on a still night one often hears a fine, shrill whistle or prolonged squeak, insectlike in attenuated quality but as smooth and prolonged as the hunting call of the timber wolf, and next morning often finds some of these little hunters in traps near by. In captivity the mice utter their calls from cage to cage, or if taken away from their companions, or if alone when the mating season arrives and warm nights stir their social instincts. Often from their cages in the evening the fine call note rings out, repeated at irregular intervals, and on a few fortunate occasions the writer has watched one throw up its head, and with open mouth and closed eyes send forth its call exactly as he has watched a lone wolf give its prolonged howl from the snow-covered crest of a far ridge. With the difference in size of the animals allowed for, the calls are not so different; it is merely that the voice of the calling mouse is so attenuated that only keen ears can detect it.

These little rodents are among the most interesting of their group, in that their highly carnivorous and insectivorous tastes have modified their rodent habits. Though they doubtless have definite homes, they are found so generally scattered over the country as to suggest the wandering traits of larger predacious mammals. They are caught in traps set almost anywhere over the open country, but the experienced collector rarely sets traps especially for them, as they leave· no trace or signs of habitation. In sandy spots their pudgy, round tracks may often be distinguished from the slenderer footprints of *Peromyscus* and *Perognathus*, but they seem never to lead to or from any definite place or abode. Where most abundant the mice are taken in traps set at the burrows of kangaroo rats, pocket mice, and ground squirrels, but perhaps most frequently in old deserted badger holes. They evidently occupy any burrow found deserted or from which they can evict the owner, although it is probable that they make burrows for themselves and for their nests and young. Old badger and prairie-dog burrows are probably fruitful fields of search for their insect prey.

Many are caught in traps set across little furrows made by dragging the heel through the sand, for they never cross such a mark without investigating it to its full length, and their omnivorous tastes and unsuspicious natures make them easy victims of any kind of small trap with almost any form of bait. If the trap already contains some other kind of mouse they at once fall to and feast upon its flesh, thus ruining many important specimens for the collector. Generally only a few scorpion mice are taken at one locality, not because they are rare but because there is no definite way of finding where they live. Occasionally, however, they are found in unusual abundance and fill the traps in advance of other species. At Wingate in June, 1905, Hollister found them extremely abundant in the valley of the Rio Puerco. They were caught at all places where traps were set in the open valley and evidently at their own burrows, which were usually under cover of low bushes in sandy soil. Several were caught in traps set for pocket gophers down to a depth of 20 inches below the ground. During his stay of 10 days at that locality he made up a fine series of 32 specimens, mainly adults, and threw away a large number of immature and imperfect individuals.

Along the Chama River, Gaut and the writer collected them at Stinking Spring Lake [Burford Lake], and others just above the Colorado line in the Rio Grande Valley near Antonito, Colo., which carries their range along both of these valleys in the Upper Sonoran Zone.

At Stinking Spring Lake one was heard almost every evening near camp. Its fine shrill whistle would sound repeatedly from the sagebrush just at dark in a prolonged note so thin and piercing that its vibrations must have been about the limit of rapidity to which human ears are attuned. This note was frequently heard at camps all over the plains country. It is heard mostly at night and frequently in the early evening, but occasionally at any time of night up to the dusk of early morning. It is doubtless a call note like the howl of the wolf, or possibly a warning or danger signal. The writer first became familiar with the note from a tame specimen of the northern grasshopper mouse kept in his room, and has never failed to recognize it since whenever heard. His reason for believing it a call note rather than a note of alarm is that the several individuals that he has kept alive showed no signs of fear or timidity. They were unafraid from the first, made no objections to being handled, and proved both gentle and interesting pets.

Food habits.—The stomachs of these scorpion mice are usually found to contain the remains of a great variety of insects, including grasshoppers, crickets, scorpions, mole crickets, beetles, caterpillars, cutworms, and insect eggs; also the flesh and hair of many small mammals that they kill or find in traps; occasional lizards, and numerous weed seeds. (Bailey and Sperry, 1929.) Near Acoma one ate a pocket mouse that the writer had trapped with great difficulty and needed for a specimen. Near Fruitland, Clarence Birdseye reported a kangaroo rat and another scorpion mouse eaten in his traps. Fresh meat seems to be a favorite food, but they will also take any kind of rolled oats or grain used for trap bait, and the stomach contents usually show more or less of the remains of seeds.

Breeding habits.—At Wingate, Hollister took two females on June 21, containing four and five embryos, respectively. The females have 3 pair of mammae, arranged in 2 pairs of inguinal and 1 pair of pectoral. Four and five seem to be the common number of fetuses in this group, but as these are usually arranged two on one side and three on the other, it is evident that six is the normal maximum to a litter. The breeding dates would indicate that more than one litter is produced in a season, and young of various ages from just large enough to be out to nearly full grown are often caught at the same place and time. Although rather prolific, the scorpion mice have enough enemies to keep down their abundance and their life in the open renders them especially exposed to nocturnal birds and beasts of prey.

Hibernation.—In winter the adults often become quite fat, and the tails swollen with a thick layer of fat under the skin, but in New Mexico they evidently do not hibernate, as they are caught at all times during the year. The actual type of *melanophrys* was caught at Kanab, Utah, December 22, 1888, while there was a little snow on the ground and the nights were freezing cold. They have not been found storing up food or carrying it in their cheek pouches, and there seems to be no evidence that they make any provision for the future. Even in midwinter they find some insects and mice with which to vary their diet, and in the deep burrows of larger animals where numerous insects gather to spend the winter they find abundance of choice food.

Economic status.—Usually these mice are not sufficiently abundant to be of any great economic importance, and if they were abundant their beneficial food habits would overbalance the slight mischief they might occasionally do. It is evident from the numerous cases in which the flesh and hair of other mice are found in their stomachs that they often capture and devour other species of mice as well as numerous insects.

For several years the writer kept and bred them at his home at Washington, where they proved useful as well as interesting. Two were given a nest box in the kitchen where they soon exterminated the cockroaches at night and so consistently slept through the day that they were unnoticed by the cook. They never climbed above the floor nor did any mischief, but legs and shells of cockroaches could be found all around the edges of the floor. They were then given the freedom of the basement with an open cage for a nest and well supplied with water and sunflower seeds. For more than a year they lived comfortably and so thoroughly exterminated all insect pests that no more cockroaches appeared again for a couple of years. The grasshopper mice made no trouble and were in no way objectionable in the basement. They seemed never to climb above the floor.

The experiment of using them to keep down insect pests in greenhouses and gardens is well worth trying and could easily be managed in any inclosure from which they could not escape. They are easily caught alive in small box traps, and in places where they are common tin cans sunk below the surface of the ground should catch them in considerable numbers. They seem to have no inclination to climb but in confinement would probably burrow into the earth or find any small openings through which to escape. If they could be made serviceable in dwellings and greenhouses as well as interesting and attractive pets for children, they would fill an important place in our domestic economy.

ONYCHOMYS LEUCOGASTER ARCTICEPS Rhoads

Southern Plains Grasshopper Mouse

Onychomys arcticeps Rhoads, Acad. Nat. Sci. Phila. Proc. 1898: 194, 1899.

Type.—Collected at Clapham, Union County, N. Mex., November 7, 1893, by Ernest Thompson Seton.

General characters.—Very similar to *melanophrys* but averaging slightly duller in coloration, more buffy and less cinnamon in adult pelage.

Measurements.—Average: Total length, 151; tail, 42; hind foot, 21 millimeters. Maximum measurements: 170, 53, and 23 millimeters, respectively.

Distribution and habitat.—The southern Plains grasshopper mouse is found on the Upper Sonoran plains of eastern New Mexico, including the Pecos Valley from Carlsbad to Santa Rosa, grading insensibly into *ruidosae* farther west. At Carlsbad and Roswell it enters the edge of Lower Sonoran Zone with a mixture of other Upper Sonoran species, but nowhere extends into pure Lower Sonoran. (Fig. 20.) It is a mouse of the grassy and weedy plains country.

General habits.—Like other species of the genus these pretty, soft-furred, clean little mice wander about like predatory animals rather than like ordinary rodents. They are caught in traps set for other animals in runways, burrows, open places, under the weeds and wolfberry bushes along the gulches, or out on the short grass plains where there is no cover. They seem as much at home as the badger, with only the good mellow earth to burrow in and plenty of game below the surface if not on top. They are nocturnal rovers, but are bright and lively in the daytime if captured and kept where they can be observed and handled, and, unlike most rodents, when captured they are unusually gentle and unafraid.

Like the scorpion mouse their shrill little voice is often heard at night, and in the morning round of the traps some choice catch may be found half eaten as evidence of their presence. They are easily caught if at all common, for they seem to have no fear of traps or man, and will blunder into any kind of trap that offers food or a mousy odor.

Breeding habits.—The mammae of the females are arranged in two pairs of inguinal and one pair of pectoral, and the number of young in a litter as indicated by the embryos is usually four, although five and six are sometimes found. As the females are found containing embryos in April, May, June, July, and August, evidently more than one litter is raised in a year.

ONYCHOMYS LEUCOGASTER RUIDOSAE Rehn

Ruidoso Grasshopper Mouse

Onychomys ruidosae Rehn, Acad. Nat. Sci. Phila. Proc. 55: 22, 1903.

Type.—Collected at Ruidoso (Hales ranch), N. Mex., September 19, 1898, by C. M. Barber.

General characters.—Similar to *melanophrys* and *arcticeps* but slightly darker in coloration; size about the same or slightly larger.

Measurements.—Average total length, 159; tail, 49; hind foot, 22.2 millimeters; maximum: 167, 55, and 24 millimeters, respectively.

Distribution and habitat.—The Ruidoso grasshopper mouse ranges over the Upper Sonoran mesas and foothills of central and southwestern New Mexico and west into Arizona and south into Mexico. (Fig. 20.) The animals are generally found among the desert shrubs collectively called sagebrush, greasebush, and rabbit brush, but also out on the sandy flats and even among the scattered nut pines and junipers . At Jarilla, Gaut caught one among the mesquite bushes, and at Lake Valley E. A. Goldman took one under a desert willow bush, but both were at the edge of the Lower Sonoran Zone. At Mesilla, Deming, and Hachita they were also at the extreme lower edge of their zone, but at such localities they were thrown with many species of plants that do not extend over much of their range, and were beginning to grade toward the paler *albescens* of Chihuahua. The mice were common in the foothill region of the White, Capitan, Jicarilla, Manzano, and Sandia Mountains, and west of the Rio Grande Hollister found them abundant near Burleigh, in the grassy parks of the Bear Spring Mountains up to nearly 8,000 feet, and also in the grassy parks and openings and sandy sections in the Gallina and Datil Ranges.

General habits.—Of the 24 specimens collected by Hollister some were trapped at the entrances of kangaroo-rat and ground-squirrel burrows and one deep down in a pocket-gopher burrow. On the San Augustine Plains E. A. Goldman found them common under the greasebush in the loose sandy soil of the open, and up into the edge of the pinyon belt. One was found in the stomach of the New Mexico desert fox, while some of those caught had been eaten by more fortunate companions. On Cactus Flat between the Gila and San Francisco Rivers, the writer caught three in one night near his camp in traps set at burrows of kangaroo rats. At Deming he found them abundant in December, 1889, and in August, 1908, Goldman found them still common near there and living in similar burrows in the sand dunes among the mesquite bushes.

Food habits.—At San Pedro in the Sandia Mountains the writer caught these mice in traps baited with cheese, bread, and rolled oats. In one trap he found the head and part of the skin of a harvest mouse (Reithrodontomys), and in another trap near by a grasshopper mouse whose stomach contained the missing parts of the victim. At Cactus Flat a grasshopper mouse ate about half of a five-toed kangaroo rat from one of the writer's traps before getting into another near by. Its stomach contained the freshly eaten flesh and hair of the rat, besides some insects and seeds. The stomachs of two others were full of about equal quantities of seeds and insects. At Deming the mice ate four or five kangaroo rats and three of their own kind from the traps, but the stomachs of most of those taken were full of sunflower and little wild-bean seeds with a mixture of indeterminable insect remains.

Breeding habits.—At Socorro E. A. Goldman caught a female on August 19, 1909, containing four embryos, and at San Pedro on July 10, 1889, the writer collected a female containing four well-grown embryos and at the same time caught several half-grown young. Apparently two or more litters are raised in a season under favorable circumstances, but the breeding season in this group seems to be very irregular.

ONYCHOMYS TORRIDUS TORRIDUS (Coues)

ARIZONA GRASSHOPPER MOUSE

Hesperomys (*Onychomys*) *torridus* Coues, Acad. Nat. Sci. Phila. Proc. 1874: 183, 1874.
Onychomys torridus arenicola Mearns, U. S. Natl. Mus. Proc. 19: 139, 1896. Type from Rio Grande, 6 miles above El Paso, Tex.

Type.—Collected at Camp Grant, Graham County, Ariz., June 10, 1867, by Edward Palmer.
General characters.—A small and relatively long-tailed grasshopper mouse, entirely distinct from members of the *leucogaster* group. The autumn and winter pelage of adults is a bright cinnamon buff over the upper parts, very similar in color to the corresponding pelage of *melanophrys*. The underparts, feet, tip, and lower side of tail are pure white. In spring and early summer the general color is slightly paler. The young and immature are bluish or dull gray. The skulls, compared with those of *melanophrys*, are small and slender and the interpterygoid space is evenly rounded against the posterior shelf of palate.
Measurements.—An adult female from near the type locality measures, total length, 151; tail, 54; hind foot, 21 millimeters. A male from near Tucson measures 148, 48, and 21 millimeters, respectively; ear from notch, 17 millimeters; and weighed 26.8 grams. The tail usually measures more than half the combined length of head and body, while in the *leucogaster* group it is commonly less than half.

Distribution and habitat.—The little Arizona grasshopper mouse (pl. 8, A) has a wide distribution in the Lower Sonoran valleys of southern New Mexico. (Fig. 20.) Specimens from Carlsbad, Tularosa, several localities in the Tularosa Valley, the base of the Organ, Franklin, and San Andres Mountains, Socorro, Hillsboro, near Hachita and Silver City, Redrock, Glenwood, and Pleasanton, N. Mex., and El Paso, Tex., carry its range practically over all the Lower Sonoran valleys of the State. At Silver City it comes into the edge of the Upper Sonoran. Its range meets that of the Upper Sonoran *ruidosae*, but the two do not overlap to any great extent, *torridus* occupying the most arid desert valleys of the mesquite and creosote-bush area.

General habits.—In habits the Arizona grasshopper mice do not differ greatly from their larger relatives. They seem to be generally distributed over the desert valleys, where they are caught at all sorts of burrows, some of which they evidently dig for homes, others being borrowed or appropriated. They seem to prefer sandy or mellow ground and are generally caught in traps set for other animals at the entrances of burrows or in little trenches made by scraping the foot through the sand.

At Glenwood the writer caught four or five specimens on the dry flats and mesquite-covered mesas, mainly in traps baited with rolled oats set for Perodipus and Perognathus. At Socorro E. A. Goldman caught several at burrows under creosote and mesquite bushes along the edge of the valley, and at Hillsboro he took one specimen at a small burrow under a bush of *Schmaltzia microphylla*. At Tularosa Gaut caught them both in the lower foothills and out on the flat valley south of town. He also caught them at various places along the lower slopes of the San Andres and Organ Mountains, and Hollister collected a specimen at the edge of the Lower Sonoran Zone in the Tularosa Valley south of the Sacramento Mountains. They are active at all times of the year, and specimens have been taken in the coldest winter weather.

Food habits.—The stomachs of those taken for specimens usually show a large proportion of insect remains, some seeds, and occasionally traces of the hair or flesh of other mice. The stomachs of five taken near Glenwood early in November contained about equal parts of seeds and insects, none of which could be identified. At Socorro, in August, the stomach of one that E. A. Goldman caught contained the remains of grasshoppers and a whitish pulp, which was apparently from some kind of seeds. Specimens caught in western Texas during the winter also showed a combination of insects and seeds in about equal quantities and several contained the remains of mice or kangaroo rats, which had been eaten from traps near the locality where they were caught. The legs of grasshoppers and parts of beetles, crickets, and scorpions are sometimes recognizable in the stomachs. In captivity the mice eagerly eat scorpions, grasshoppers, crickets, cockroaches, beetles, beetle larvae, flies, maggots, moths, wasps, spiders, and any fresh meat, refusing only hairy caterpillars, centipedes, and ants. They apparently do not carry or store up food for winter but always seem to be able to find abundance when and where it is needed.

Breeding habits.—A female that E. A. Goldman collected at Socorro on August 14 contained four fetuses, and this seems to be the usual number of young produced at a birth. The mammae are arranged in 3 pairs, 2 pairs of inguinal close together and 1 pair of pectoral. There are not sufficient data to show whether these mice breed more than once during a season, but apparently they are never abundant, and it is probable that they are not prolific breeders.

Economic status.—The Arizona grasshopper mice have no possibilities of injurious effect on agriculture, and their influence in holding in check the abundance of insects and other species of mice may be far more important than is generally supposed. A close study of their food and general habits shows them to be mainly if not entirely useful animals.

Genus PEROMYSCUS Gloger

The genus Peromyscus is represented in New Mexico by 10 recognized forms, including two subgenera, Haplomylomys Osgood and

Peromyscus Gloger. In the present treatment of the species and subspecies, Osgood's admirable revision of the genus is used. (Osgood, 1909.) A few additional records help to round out the ranges of some of the forms, as do also the collectors' field notes, while the maps are on a larger scale than hitherto published and permit a more detailed distribution. As a group these mice are undoubtedly the most abundant mammals of the region, both in species and individuals, and among the mammals small enough to be classed as mice they are in some ways of the greatest economic importance. Collectively they may be said to cover every part of the State and usually in great numbers. The habits of the different forms vary to such an extent that it is important to know which is responsible for any mischief in order that its depredations may be controlled in the most economical manner.

PEROMYSCUS MANICULATUS RUFINUS (MERRIAM)

TAWNY DEER MOUSE; KLA-TSE-HA'-NA of the Taos Indians; NA-ZON'-ZA of the Navajo Indians

Hesperomys leucopus rufinus Merriam, North Amer. Fauna No. 3, p. 65, 1890.

Type.—Collected at San Francisco Mountain, Ariz. (9,000 feet), August 22, 1889, by C. Hart Merriam and Vernon Bailey.

General characters.—This is a little short-eared deer mouse, with its tail decidedly shorter than its head and body. In adults the upper parts are rich ochraceous or rufescent, more or less mixed with dusky; the ears are covered with short, silky hairs and usually with a minute tuft of white hairs at the anterior base; the lower surface of the tail, feet, and lower parts are white, the tail sharply bicolor. Young and immature specimens are bluish or slaty gray.

Measurements.—Average of 15 typical adult specimens: Total length, 160; tail, 70; hind foot, 20; ear from notch, 15.5 millimeters.

Distribution and habitat.—The little bright-colored tawny deer mice inhabit the mountain country of northern and western New Mexico, reaching their southern limit in the Mogollon and Sacramento Mountains and their eastern in the Sierra Grande region. (Fig. 21.) In the typical form they are most abundant in the Transition and the Canadian Zones, but in places they extend slightly below the limit of the Transition Zone before blanching into the pale *blandus* of the lower country. To a slight extent they also reach into the Hudsonian Zone, and specimens have been taken on peaks in the Arctic-Alpine, but not in sufficient numbers to give them a permanent place in either of these higher zones. They seem to reach their greatest abundance in the open yellow-pine forests of the Transition Zone, but are also abundant throughout the open forests and parks of the Canadian. In the dense spruce and fir forests they are often taken, but seem to be less numerous than in the more open areas. More than any other species of Peromyscus in New Mexico, they are characteristically woods mice.

General habits.—Throughout the mountain forest region of New Mexico these are the most abundant mice, and often the collector is obliged to catch and throw away dozens of them before he is able to catch the more obscure and retiring species for which he is always searching. Traps set under logs and rocks, in banks, about old stumps, at hollows under the base of trees, or under brush heaps in mats of fallen grass and dense vegetation are usually filled up by these mice for two or three consecutive nights. From a good trap line of 75 or 100 traps extending over a couple of acres of rough ground, or for half a mile across a valley and up a steep slope the collector often takes two or three dozen of *Peromyscus* for several mornings. They then become so scarce along the trap line that more desirable species can be caught. By going to his traps morning and evening the collector will at first get several diurnal species of mice and shrews in the evening round, while these strictly nocturnal mice will be found only in the morning round. They seem to be in every nook and corner, and it is difficult to place a trap where they will not find it. They are excellent climbers, and traps set on logs or leaning tree trunks or on the large branches of low trees will catch more of them than of any other species.

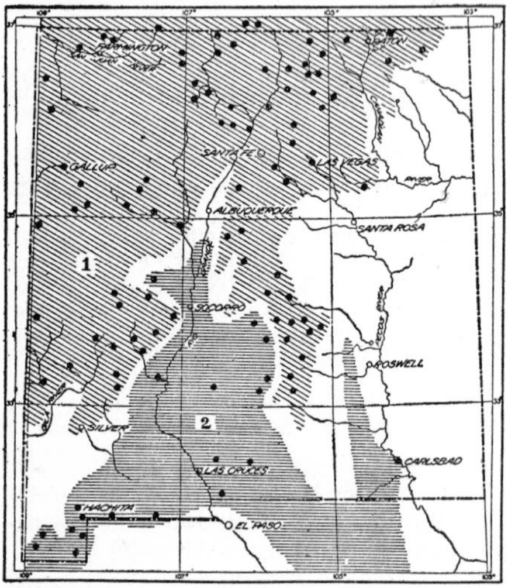

FIGURE 21.—Distribution of the small white-footed mice in New Mexico: 1, *Peromyscus maniculatus rufinus*; 2, *P. maniculatus blandus*

Where a tent is pitched in the woods they are sure to come in and will sometimes keep the campers awake by scampering over their canvas or trying to make nests in their hair at night. They are gentle little animals and never bite unless captured and held against their will, when they resist most vigorously and effectively. Their homes seem to be generally underground among the rocks, in hollow trees or logs, in camps, cabins or old buildings, or on the surface of the ground under dense cover. There is some doubt as to whether they dig burrows for themselves, but they certainly make numerous doorways into the abandoned underground tunnels of pocket gophers, which are commonly available. They also use the burrows of other small mammals in their locality. The conditions desired are cover, a dry place for the nest in summer, and a well-protected warm and dry home for winter.

Their nests are usually of the finest, softest, and driest grass stems and plant fibers and are often lined with wool, feathers, or the silky down of various plants. The nests in which the young are found are especially well made and carefully lined, often as neat and compact as the nests of many birds. One or two openings at the sides admit the owners to the central nest chamber, but unlike the nests of meadow mice, no runways or smoothly worn trails lead away from the doors. The nests, when occupied, are always fresh and clean, and apparently the summer and winter nests are quite distinct. Many of the summer nests are placed on the surface of the ground under some cover that will protect them from rain and dampness.

Any new cover is quickly taken possession of, and a camp wagon can not stand long where these mice are abundant without being occupied. At Stinking Spring Lake [Burford Lake] one made its nest under a harness, which was thrown on the ground by the side of the wagon and covered with canvas. For a nest it had taken a bunch of dry water plants that the writer had collected for specimens, and made a lining of duck feathers, which were abundant around the camp. The scattered grain and bits of food about camp apparently deceived them into thinking they had found a permanent food supply. At night their fine, squeaking voices were often heard. In southwestern Colorado, Cary heard their midnight squeaking in an abandoned cabin in which he was sleeping. He says: "A faint squeak in one end of the cabin elicited answers from other parts of the building, and the noise was kept up for some time." (Cary, 1911, p. 104.)

Food habits.—The food of these mice consists mainly of seeds, grain, acorns, berries, and occasionally insects and any fresh meat they can get hold of. The rich, oily seeds of many of the plants belonging to the Compositae seem to be a favorite food, but apparently almost every kind of seed that they can procure is eaten, as is shown by the chaff, scales, and shells often conspicuous on their feeding grounds. Though grass, seeds, and grains of many kinds are eagerly eaten, in striking contrast to the meadow mice, their stomach contents rarely show a trace of green vegetation. The seeds and pulp of bright-colored berries, such as raspberries, thimbleberries, strawberries, and blueberries, are often found in the stomach contents. Traces of the hard parts of insects are also sometimes found. Occasionally mice of their own and other species when caught in traps are found half eaten, indicating carnivorous and cannibalistic habits. They are readily caught in traps baited with bacon, salt pork, or any kind of fresh meat, and they will gnaw drying skins or bones whenever opportunity offers. Bread crust, cheese, cold meat, dried fruit, and miscellaneous refuse from the camp table are eaten or carried off and stored for future use. In a forest camp the grain sack is never safe and can rarely rest on the ground for a night without having little holes cut in the sides by the provident mice. They store in their dens or in conveniently accessible holes or pockets in the ground. Their mouths and cheeks are often found stuffed with seeds and grain, and while relatively less capacious than those of the ground squirrels, they serve to transport considerable quantities. Only the cleanest, soundest, and best of the grain and seeds are taken for storing, as is shown by the choice little deposits. These are not, strictly speaking, winter stores, as the mice are active at all times of the year and can usually find an abundance of food. In much of their range, however, the snow becomes deep in winter and the stores are probably drawn upon then more than at other seasons.

These deer mice do not hibernate, and late in the fall the writer has found their tracks in snow on the mountains at altitudes above 10,000 feet. During long winters of deep snows they live comfortably in chambers and runways under the surface of the ground and in cavities under logs and leaves above the surface. Here they are well protected from their enemies, but at night they often brave danger and come out to scamper over the white drifts, as is evidenced by delicate lines of miniature squirrel-like tracks in the snow in the mornings. Some of these tracks end with a blurred wing mark, for the small owls eagerly watch and wait to pounce upon them. Perhaps more than any other species of mice, they furnish the winter food of these owls.

Breeding habits.—The 6 mammae of the females are arranged, as usual, in 3 pairs—2 pairs of inguinal and 1 pair of pectoral. The usual numbers of embryos seem to be four to six, but there is one record of seven, which is probably an unusual number. There are no records to show how early the breeding season begins, but it certainly lasts until late in the autumn, as the writer collected one female on September 13 that contained five, and A. H. Howell collected one on September 27 containing six fetuses. As both of these were at localities high up in the mountains, they suggest that the breeding season may even continue through a part of the winter. In the Manzano Mountains Gaut caught half-grown and quarter-grown young in December. Young of various ages seem to be about through the spring, summer, and autumn months, but so little winter work has been done by collectors in the mountains that one of the most interesting chapters of animal habits remains to be studied and written.

Economic status.—Though a large part of the range of this species is above the agricultural zones, its lower part overlaps many fields of grain and other crops. Along the borders of fields of wheat, oats, and barley the mice in spring eat or carry away the planted seed and in fall feast upon the ripening grain until the last shock is hauled away and the last stack threshed or used up. Their actual destruction of grain, however, is usually not great and often remains unnoticed, but combined with other species they levy a small tax upon the farm returns. In new settlements within their range and in forest camps they quickly gather in and about buildings. The complaints of the forest ranger more often apply to these than to any other mice. In winter camps frequently left unoccupied the mice sometimes make use of the warm bedding for nest material. Provisions left in these camps have to be suspended from the ceiling by wires to protect them, and even then they are not always safe, for the mice are excellent climbers and fearless in making long leaps. As scarcely any kind of food is exempt from their attacks, the mischief a few can make in a camp is often of a serious nature.

But the remedy is simple: A few good mouse traps set in the corners of each camp to get the mice as fast as they come in. If the camp is to be abandoned for a considerable time, it will be well to leave a dozen or more traps set in different parts of the building to provide for the occasional newcomers. In a camp used at intervals they are more troublesome than in one long abandoned, as at each occupancy enough food is usually scattered to attract them anew. In such a camp in the Mogollon Mountains, where the writer spent a week, they were so numerous that although a considerable number were caught each night they were not all gone when he left. Here, besides helping themselves to his food, they found his string of the drying skulls of small mammals that he had collected and ate some

of them and carried off others. At one of his camps in the Jemez
Mountains they were so numerous about the grub box that the cook
set traps under the wagon and in one night caught 14.

As these deer mice are typical forest dwellers, their influence upon
the forest growth has been a matter of considerable study. Though
they can not compete with the squirrels and chipmunks in opening
and carrying away cones and tree seeds, there is little chance of any
fallen seeds remaining on the ground undiscovered. The seeds they
gather and store here and there in the ground may in some cases aid
in extending and reproducing the forest, but the mice are so numerous and so social in their habits that it is doubtful if the cache of
an individual that has been killed often escapes discovery by its
companions. It is even probable that they discover and confiscate
many of the more carefully secreted stores of squirrels and chipmunks, which would otherwise be left to grow. So far as the present
evidence would indicate, these mice are probably serious enemies
of the forest growth. In areas where reforestation is attempted by
means of seed planting they are unquestionably one of the greatest
enemies of the projects. Their abundance and keen sense of the location of edible seeds leaves little chance for a planted seed to escape discovery. Methods of protecting planted seeds from them
have not yet been perfected. Their greatest natural enemies are
owls, weasels, foxes, wild cats, badgers, skunks, and snakes, without
which the problem of their superabundance would be an extremely
difficult one.

PEROMYSCUS MANICULATUS BLANDUS Osgood

LITTLE PALE DEER MOUSE; FROSTED DEER MOUSE

Peromyscus sonoriensis blandus Osgood, Biol. Soc. Wash. Proc. 17 : 56, 1904.

Type.—Collected at Escalon, Chihuahua, Mexico, November 27, 1893, by E. A.
Goldman.

General characters.—Differs from *rufinus* mainly in paler coloration. In
adults the upper parts are buffy gray or dull ochraceous and in immature
individuals often very pale ashy gray.

Measurements.—Average of seven adults from the type locality: Total
length, 145; tail, 61; hind foot, 21; ear from notch, 14.9 millimeters.

Distribution and habitat.—Below the mountain forests in the arid
and unforested desert ranges and open valleys of southern New
Mexico, the little pale deer mice inhabit mainly the Upper Sonoran
Zone, and along its upper border grade into *rufinus*. In places they
also crowd down into the edge of the Lower Sonoran Zone, but
seem not to be generally distributed over it where the larger *tornillo*
holds the ground. They generally inhabit the open country rather
than the rocks and cliffs, which are fully occupied by larger species.
(Fig. 21.)

General habits.—Although inhabiting a rough country, these little
gray mice are generally found in the mellow spots of open valley
bottoms, sometimes under the protection of a moderate growth of
weeds and vegetation, but oftener in the open areas where vegetation is scarce and there seems little cover to protect them from
enemies. This exposed habitat may account for their being usually
less abundant than their better protected neighbors of the cliffs,

brushy bottoms and forest areas. A few specimens only are collected here and there. At Carlsbad, Dutcher collected one in the Pecos Valley and in the San Andres Mountains and the foothills surrounding Tularosa Valley Gaut collected a few; one was taken by C. M. Barber at Mesilla, and in the Animas Valley and the Hachita country they were collected by E. A. Goldman and Clarence Birdseye. Along the Mexican boundary line Mearns found the mouse on rocky hills and buttes as well as on the level plain, but says that " Grassy spots around springs are its favorite abodes, and in such places it is abundant." (Mearns, 1907, p. 390.)

Food habits.—In food habits these mice seem to be as omnivorous as their near relative *rufinus.* Seeds and grain of almost any kind seem to be eaten by them, and the writer has never yet found any trap bait that they would refuse. Mearns says they are " largely carnivorous, devouring insects or any animal food " and proving " an annoyance by eating small mammals caught in our traps."

Breeding habits.—In breeding habits this form probably does not differ materially from *rufinus,* but there are few data upon which to base conclusions. Mearns records two females taken May 13 and 14 each containing four large fetuses, and a half-grown young one taken May 15. In the collection are half-grown young collected in May, August, December, and January.

Economic status.—Over much of their range these mice do not come into contact with agricultural industries and are not of sufficient abundance to be of any appreciable economic importance. In habits they are as mischievous as any of the species, and may locally become troublesome about fields, gardens, grain stacks, barns, or houses. Their usual scarcity is probably due to the open country in which they live and the lack of protection from their numerous enemies. As they live mainly underground in the mellow soil of open valleys, they are an easy prey not only to owls and cats, which pounce upon them at night, but also to badgers, skunks, coyotes, and foxes, which dig out their nests by day. As with other species, it is only necessary to uncover and expose them to their enemies and they will quickly vanish.

PEROMYSCUS LEUCOPUS TORNILLO Mearns

Tornillo White-Footed Mouse [19]

Peromyscus tornillo Mearns, U. S. Natl. Mus. Proc. 18: 445, 1896 (p. 3 of advance sheet issued March 25, 1896).

Type.—Collected in Rio Grande Valley, 6 miles above El Paso, Tex., February 18, 1892, by E. A. Mearns and F. X. Holzner.

General characters.—A medium-sized Peromyscus with tail shorter than head and body, and ears smaller than in any of the long-tailed species. In adults the upperparts are dull grayish brown, the underparts and feet, pure white, and the tail indistinctly bicolor.

Measurements.—Average of 10 adults from near the type locality: Total length, 182; tail, 82.6; hind foot, 22.5; ear from notch, 14.5 millimeters.

Distribution and habitat.—The Tornillo white-footed mouse occupies the whole Lower Sonoran Zone of the Rio Grande, Pecos, and Canadian River Valleys in New Mexico, extending up the Rio Grande Valley as far as Santa Fe and up the Pecos Valley to Santa Rosa

---

[19] Tornillo is the Mexican name of the screw-bean mesquite, *Prosopis pubescens.*

and northeastward to Clapham and Clayton. It is a species of the open country and valleys, and not often associated with rocks and cliffs. (Fig. 22.)

General habits.—In the Rio Grande Valley above El Paso, Mearns (1907, p. 409) says, "The Tornillo mouse is very abundant under groves of the screw bean * * * ." At Las Cruces E. A. Goldman caught these mice among the grass and weeds along irrigation ditches near the river; at Garfield, in weedy patches and bushes along the edges of fields and on bottom lands; near Lake Valley in thick grass on moist land; and at Las Palomas, where they were common, among thickets of Baccharis, Pluchea, and weeds along the bottom lands near the river. At Hot Springs, 7 miles north of Las Palomas, he took them in the grass and weeds along the edge of the marsh at Socorro in thickets o f cottonwood, willow, Baccharis, a n d Pluchea on the river bottoms on both sides of the valley; at C u c h i l l o he found t h e m common in weedy fields in the bottom of the valley and also about rocks along the bluffs bordering the valley; and near the mouth of Water Canyon in the Magdalena Mountains he caught them under the cover of a dense growth of cactus. At the junction of the Puerco and San Jose Rivers, Hollister found them common in the tule marsh and the weedy thickets along the r i v e r bottoms; he also caught

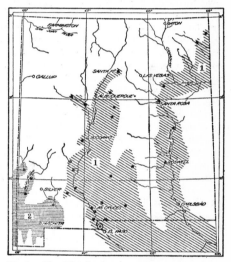

FIGURE 22.—Distribution of white-footed mice in New Mexico: 1, *Peromyscus leucopus tornillo;* 2, *P. leucopus arizonae.* Type locality circled

one in the Pecos Valley 8 miles north of Fort Sumner. Barber took one at Roswell, in the Pecos Valley; the writer caught them under mesquite bushes on the river flats a mile above Carlsbad, and also in the weedy bottoms near Santa Rosa, and in Conchos Creek Valley near Cabra Springs. A. H. Howell caught them in stony pastures and in an old cabin on the prairie near Clayton. Gaut took specimens in the ruins at the Gran Quivera and in many locations in canyon bottoms, in brushy and weedy places about the Organ, San Andres, and Manzano Mountains, and also in the Tularosa Valley.

From these detailed notes on habitat, it is evident that the species is mainly restricted to the brushy and weedy parts of the open valley country. Whether this is choice or necessity will perhaps never be known, but it suggests that the larger, more active species have taken possession of the favorite strongholds and that the humbler forms are forced to be content with the second choice of situations.

Food habits.—From the close association of these mice with the common mesquite, screw bean, and acacia bushes, it seems probable that they are attracted by the abundant crop of little beans yielded by these bushes, or possibly by the sweet, nutritious pods. Their range extends considerably beyond that of any of these bushes, however, and their food includes the seeds of other plants. Gaut reported them feeding in part on seeds of the creosote bush. They are eager for rolled oats or any kind of grain or seeds used for trap bait and are so easily caught as to become a nuisance to the collector who is in search of more desirable species. In the Carlsbad Cave they were feeding mainly on the large crickets found in all parts of the cavern but also eagerly devouring remains of lunches and the oatmeal used for trap-bait.

Breeding habits.—In this group the six mammae are arranged in two pairs of inguinal and one pair of pectoral. At Fort Hancock, Tex., Mearns recorded a female that on June 16 contained four fetuses. At Rio Puerco Hollister collected two females, September 5, 1905, one of which contained four large and the other nine small fetuses; and another specimen collected September 8 contained five large fetuses. The nine young are probably an abnormal number, as it exceeds by three the usual number of mammae. From four to six is probably the usual number of young. These few breeding records do not give any index to the length of the breeding season, but it is probable that several litters are produced in a year, or that the breeding season extends practically throughout the year. In the low hot country where these mice are generally found, there is usually an abundant food supply, and there is no reason why the breeding season should not be continuous.

Economic status.—These mice are generally found along the borders of fields, meadows, or standing or harvested grain, where they can do the greatest degree of mischief. They often gather in vacant houses or outbuildings and occasionally make their nests in occupied houses or in the camp wagon. As they are strictly nocturnal they are rarely seen. A host of night-prowling enemies prevents their living in open or exposed locations, and without the protecting cover of weeds, grass, or low vegetation they could not maintain their abundance. Where they become troublesome it is only necessary to remove their cover and expose them to their enemies.

PEROMYSCUS LEUCOPUS ARIZONAE (ALLEN)

ARIZONA WHITE-FOOTED MOUSE

Sitomys americanus arizonae Allen, Bul. Amer. Mus. Nat. Hist. 6: 321, 1894.

Type.—Collected at Fairbank, Ariz., March 13, 1894, by W. W. Price.
General characters.—Very similar to *tornillo* but seems to average slightly darker in color.
Measurements.—Average of five adult specimens from the type region: Total length, 186; tail, 82.6; hind foot, 22.6 millimeters.

Distribution and habitat.—The Arizona white-footed mice are abundant over the Deming Plains and in the Gila Valley of southwestern New Mexico, where they seem to be restricted to the Lower Sonoran desert. There are specimens from Deming, Redrock, Gila, and Glenwood. (Fig. 22.)

General habits.—In habits they seem to be identical with *tornillo*, occupying the weedy or brushy valley bottoms and corresponding in abundance to the cover that furnishes their protection. Their homes seem to be mainly under ground and generally in the burrows of other animals. The abandoned burrows of pocket gophers, kangaroo rats, and even badgers, are taken possession of, but it is not improbable that some of the nest burrows are dug in the mellow soil when abandoned burrows can not be found. At Deming they were not common on the open ground near the town where the writer trapped in December, 1889; but in 1908, at the sink of the Mimbres 8 miles farther east, E. A. Goldman found them numerous in the more weedy and grassy land.

Food habits.—The host of little seeds of desert plants that hang in the dry pods or scatter and lie for long periods perfectly preserved on or in the dry soil furnish an abundant food supply for these and many other mice. Rolled oats and all kinds of grain, seeds, and nuts used for trap bait are eagerly eaten by them, and they quickly fill the collector's traps.

Breeding habits.—Mearns records three females of this species, taken October 21 to 23, which contained 4, 5, and 7 fetuses.

Economic status.—As most of the range of these mice lies in unoccupied desert country, they are generally harmless, but along the few streams where irrigation is possible they are especially abundant at the edges of fields and in weedy places from which they can easily make inroads on the grain and garden crops or dig up the planted seeds. As they are active only at night they are rarely seen, and the mischief they do is not always recognized or attributed to its proper source. In clean fields with clean borders there is little danger from these or any other species of mice.

PEROMYSCUS TRUEI TRUEI (SHUFELDT)

LARGE-EARED DEER MOUSE; CLIFF MOUSE

Hesperomys truei Shufeldt, U. S. Natl. Mus. Proc. 8: 407, 1885.
Hesperomys megalotis Merriam, North Amer. Fauna No. 3, p. 63, 1890. Type from Painted Desert, Ariz.

Type.—Collected at Fort Wingate, N. Mex., March 14, 1865, by R. W. Shufeldt.

General characters.—One of the large, long-tailed deer mice or cliff mice of New Mexico. Its ears are relatively the largest of any of our native mice and are thin and nearly naked like those of some bats. The tip of the tail is unusually hairy for a Peromyscus; fur very long and soft; mustache long; eyes large and prominent. In adult specimens the sides are rich buff and the back slightly darker buffy brown. The feet and lower parts are pure white.

Measurements.—Average of 10 adult specimens: Total length, 186; tail, 92; hind foot, 23; ear from notch, 22.4 millimeters.

Distribution and habitat.—The large-eared deer, or cliff mice inhabit practically all of the Upper Sonoran Zone area of New Mexico where there are rocks, cliffs, or canyons to furnish suitable homes. (Fig. 23.) They are absent from the open plains country along the eastern edge of the State, and apparently reach their eastern limit of range in the little canyons along the northern rim of the Staked Plains and in the Sierra Grande region. They are not found in the Lower Sonoran valleys, where *eremicus* and *anthonyi* take their place in rocky situations. They are strictly limited to their zone both below and above. Of approximately 50 localities in the State from which there are specimens, none lies beyond the limits of the zone.

They are preeminently cliff dwellers and are rarely found far from rocks, cliffs, or walls.

General habits.—It is unfortunate that the name mouse should be attached to these beautiful, bright-eyed little cliff dwellers, for which the name squirrel would have been almost as appropriate. In appearance they are delightfully bright and attractive, although rarely seen in daylight except when captured for specimens. Along some of the canyon walls they are abundant and often fill the collector's line of traps before other rarer and more desirable specimens can be taken. Telltale trails of dainty footprints lead over the dusty shelves of caves and crevices in the rocks, for the rocks are their castles; but they forage along the bases of cliffs and back for a considerable distance among the nut pine and juniper trees, where they climb the trunks and lower branches to gather the seeds for food.

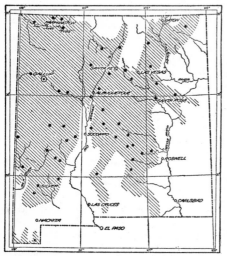

FIGURE 23.—Distribution of the large-eared deer mouse, *Peromyscus truei truei,* in New Mexico. Type locality circled

Near Santa Rosa, on the rim of a small side canyon of the Pecos River, they were common and associated with *rowleyi* and *nasutus,* both of which have somewhat similar habits. There is some question as to whether these three species live amicably together or whether they divide the ground among them so as to occupy different sections, but sometimes all three, as well as the little *rufinus,* were found in close proximity.

At the northern escarpment of the Staked Plains, *truei* was common in the rocks and cliffs from bottom to top and also among the junipers and nut pines wherever they grew, which was never far from the rocks. On Conchas Creek, a few miles north of Cabra Springs, they were also common among the cliffs and junipers, and in a hollow juniper tree near camp one had made a nest of bark and sheep's wool, which was thick, soft, and neat as that of a bird. Through a crack in the tree a little above the nest the writer could look in upon the black-eyed occupant, either curled up fast asleep or alertly watching his approach. When he rapped civilly on the trunk it would raise its head and look out at him inquiringly, but when he broke branches it would become alarmed and run up the hollow inside to a place of safety above the opening. It climbed the smooth inside of the trunk with perfect ease and great agility. It is probable that the species is much more arboreal than is supposed, its noctural habits having shielded it from observation. In 1892 A. K. Fisher found the mice so abundant at Fort Wingate that in a few nights' trapping he secured 32 specimens. His traps were set among the rocks and fallen trees in the pinyon and cedar growth, and a fine series of topotype specimens was secured of a species at that time little known. Since then their range has been very fully determined, as the species has been conspicuous and peculiarly interesting. In the San Juan Valley, Clarence Birdseye collected specimens in 1908 near Fruitland in the sandstone bluffs and ledges along the river and also secured three in and about an old log house in the brushy bottoms.

Food habits.—Like all members of the genus, these deer mice are typical seed eaters, although occasionally varying their diet with a little fruit or a few insects. Pine nuts and juniper seeds seem to be their favorite food, as indicated by the shells left in little heaps on their feeding grounds under rocks, in the cliffs, or in hollow trunks or branches. When these seeds are not available there are always others of numerous little plants that can be gathered before they have fallen, picked up from the surface of the ground, or dug from underneath even after they have begun to grow. The food supply, therefore, seems always to be abundant.

Seeds are rarely found in the cheek pouches, however, as the mice seem not to store any great quantity for future use, and the stomach contents are so finely ground as to give little clue to the kinds of seeds eaten. It is usually a mass of white dough from which every shell or hard part that might serve for identification has been carefully removed. The shells and remains of seeds scattered at their feeding places are the principal clue to their food habits, and as several species often occur together, this clue is not entirely reliable. The deer mice are fond of rolled oats, barley, or almost any grain used in baiting traps and often come into camp at night and cut holes in the sacks of barley used for horse feed. Occasionally they even invade the grub box in the wagon and sometimes find this such satisfactory quarters that they build a nest and temporarily abandon their cliff home for the camp wagon.

They never acquire much surplus fat and do not hibernate even in the coldest winter weather. Their tracks are as common on the snow in winter as in the dusty caves in summer, although it is difficult to understand how their delicate feet and half-naked soles can stand the cold.

Breeding habits.—The mammae of these mice are arranged in 3 pairs—2 pairs of inguinal, close together between the hind legs, and 1 pair of pectoral. The number of young in a litter is usually four to six. At Santa Rosa, Lantz took a female, May 15, that contained four embryos; at Fort Wingate, A. K. Fisher took two on July 3 containing four and five embryos, and others have been taken with six. The young are evidently produced and reared in the nests in safe retreats among the rocks, for they are rarely seen. Judging from the abundance of the mice and the fact that young in the blue coat and of various ages are caught in traps throughout the year, it seems probable that more than one litter is produced in a season.

Economic status.—Locally when very numerous these mice may do considerable mischief to crops planted near their cliffs or cause trouble by entering houses and barns situated near their homes. If the juniper and nut pine areas were to be reforested, they, with the

other species of their group, would render the planting of seeds a
hopeless task. Though they may do some good in distributing the
seeds of trees, it is doubtful if this counteracts to any great extent
the real harm they do in gathering and consuming a large part of
the tree seeds. Their enemies are legion, and include especially owls,
cats, foxes, skunks, weasels, coyotes, badgers, civet cats, and almost
every carnivorous night prowler of their region. Without the check
of these enemies their abundance would soon be of serious consequence, not only to native vegetation but to agricultural industries.

PEROMYSCUS BOYLEI ROWLEYI (Allen)

Rowley's Deer Mouse; Rowley's Cliff Mouse

Sitomys rowleyi Allen, Bul. Amer. Mus. Nat. Hist. 5: 76, April, 1893.
Sitomys rowleyi pinalis Miller, Bul. Amer. Mus. Nat. Hist. 5: 331, December,
1893. Type from Grant County, N. Mex.
Peromyscus boylii penicillatus Mearns, U. S. Natl. Mus. Proc. 19:139, 1896.
Type from Franklin Mountains, Tex.

Type.—Collected at Noland ranch, San Juan River, Utah, near the northwest
corner of New Mexico, April 20, 1892, by Charles P. Rowley.
General characters.—One of the largest and longest-tailed deer mice occurring
in New Mexico. Its body measurements are about the same as those of *truei*,
but it has a slightly longer tail and much smaller ears. The upper parts are
dull brownish gray; the lower parts and feet, white.
Measurements.—Average of 10 adults from the type locality: Total length,
191; tail, 99; hind foot, 21.6; ear from notch, 17.2 millimeters. Weight of
adult male 25.7 grams.

Distribution and habitat.—Rowley's deer mice have practically
the same range as *truei* and *nasutus* in New Mexico, covering all the
rough country in the Upper Sonoran Zone and all the zone except
the open plains along the eastern edge of the State. (Fig. 24.)
They do not occur in the purely Lower Sonoran valleys nor in the
mountains above the Upper Sonoran. Locally, their distribution
and abundance are modified by the character of the country, as they
are partial to trees, rocks, cliffs, canyons, and rough, hilly country.
They occupy practically all the juniper and nut pine country of
New Mexico and are closely associated with these trees, from which
they evidently derive much of their subsistence. The combination
of rocks and the low open forest of juniper, nut pines, and blue
oaks seems to afford a favorite habitat, as in such locations they are
generally abundant. Camps and deserted houses are accepted in
place of cliffs and even when not deserted are often invaded.
General habits.—The only noticeable difference between the habits
of Rowley's deer mice and the large-eared cliff mice is their adaptability to more varied conditions. The two are often caught at the
same place and in the same traps on succeeding nights, but this species
is also often taken in brushy and weedy ground where the others do
not occur.
In the Zuni Mountains Hollister found these mice abundant in the
lava beds about springs, creeks, old dwellings, and ranch buildings.
In the San Juan Valley Clarence Birdseye caught them on the brushy
river flats among the dense growth of cottonwoods and willows, and
also in the open at some distance from the cover of brush and timber.
He also identified this species in the stomach contents of a gray fox.

In the Animas Mountains they were common over the rocky and brushy slopes, where they were caught in traps baited with acorns and rolled oats. At Glenwood the writer found them common among the junipers and nut pines and also in the weedy bottoms along the river flats. In the Hondo Canyon Gaut caught one in an old deserted cabin and others in the clefts of lava rock forming the canyon walls. At the east base of the Capitan Mountains the writer found them abundant in the open forest of scrubby timber and caught them under logs and in the old brushy fence rows. In the Magdalena Mountains E. A. Goldman collected specimens from 6,500 feet to about 8,200 feet altitude. As the Upper Sonoran Zone in these arid ranges reaches to even a greater elevation on the hot slopes, it is probable that these mice were near the edge of their proper zone. Goldman also found them in abundance in the Mogollon, Burro, Florida, Big Hatchet, Animas, and San Luis Mountains, but no specimens were taken in the Lower Sonoran valleys between these ranges. Gaut took a large series of them in the Organ, San Andres, Capitan, Jicarilla, Manzano, and Sandia Mountains, and A. H. Howell collected them in the Sierra Grande and Raton Mountains.

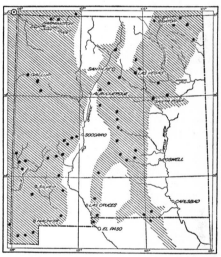

FIGURE 24.—Distribution of the Rowley cliff mouse, *Peromyscus boylei rowleyi*, in New Mexico

Like other members of the genus, these mice are strictly nocturnal in habits and are rarely observed in the daytime unless their nests are broken into among rocks, in hollow logs or trees, or when they occasionally come to live in the camp wagon. They do not usually burrow in the ground but appropriate any cavity that offers concealment and protection from their enemies, and long experience has taught them that rocky cliffs are the safest retreats. The fact that they feed extensively on seeds and nuts from trees and bushes and are so generally caught among the trees would indicate that they are partially arboreal in their habits, as are many of the members of the genus.

Food habits.—Apparently the favorite foods of these mice are hackberries, juniper berries, pine nuts, and acorns, as the remains of these are the most conspicuous in the localities they inhabit. It is evident, however, that a great variety of the smaller seeds that leave less conspicuous remains for identification are eaten. Their stomach contents usually show a mass of finely masticated white dough with rarely a trace of green vegetation, insects, or any material that can be identified. They are fond of rolled oats and almost any kind of grain or seed used as trap bait. At Kingston E. A. Goldman found one that had been feeding on the purple pulp of ripe cactus fruit until its hands were stained with the juice, and its intestines were bright purple. In the Burro Mountains, in September, he says they were feeding largely on acorns, as was shown by the quantity of freshly gnawed shells under rocks and logs near their holes.

Breeding habits.—The mammae of the females, as in other species of the genus, are in 3 pairs—2 pairs of inguinal and 1 pair of pectoral—and as with related species it is probable that the usual number of young to the litter is four to six. Mearns (1907, p. 419) records pregnant females taken on May 18, August 21, and October 26, containing two and three fetuses, and G. S. Miller, jr. (1893, p. 333) mentions a specimen taken in Arizona by W. E. D. Scott on December 4, which contained three two-thirds grown embryos. A female kept in captivity gave birth to four young on May 2, 1921, one of the litter weighing 2.2 grams. The nests and young of such rock-inhabiting species are rarely found, but nursing females are frequently captured at all times during the spring, summer, and autumn, and occasionally in winter, and it is probable that several litters of young are produced in a season. It is not unusual to find nursing females among those that have not acquired the adult pelage, but the age at which this change occurs is not positively known. They are certainly prolific breeders if one can judge by their abundance in localities where they are well protected from enemies.

Hibernation.—These mice do not usually acquire any surplus fat and are apparently equally active at all seasons. They may store up some food in the form of seeds and nuts for winter, but little is known of their storing habits. They seem to be able to obtain plenty of food, and the little pits over the surface of the ground where they have dug up seeds are in places numerous.

Economic status.—As these deer mice are usually abundant animals, able to adapt themselves to almost any environment where food and cover are available, they are likely to prove of considerable economic importance in agricultural districts within their range. They readily enter the borders of grainfields and feed both on the ripening grain and sprouting seeds. They may also live in grain shocks or stacks, or gather at granaries or bins that are not mouse proof, and in this manner cause some loss to the harvested crop. Only in cases of their unusual abundance would these depredations be of a serious nature, but with the destruction of their natural enemies such an abundance might be expected. They are preyed upon by nocturnal birds and mammals, from which their only protection is concealment. By removing all cover in the nature of weedy and brushy field borders, their enemies would be given a fair chance and their overabundance in most cases prevented.

Where they prove troublesome about camps and houses a few mousetraps kept set in unused corners will conveniently dispose of them and often prevent serious mischief.

PEROMYSCUS NASUTUS (ALLEN)

LONG-NOSED DEER MOUSE; COLORADO CLIFF MOUSE

Vesperimus nasutus Allen, Bul. Amer. Mus. Nat. Hist. 3: 299, 1891.

Type.—Collected at Estes Park, Colo., January 20, 1891, by W. G. Smith.

General characters.—One of the large long-tailed, long-eared species of Peromyscus, about the size and general appearance of *rowleyi*, with ears almost as large as those of *truei*. The general coloration is dull and dark buffy gray, as in *rowleyi*. The name "long-nosed" refers only to the skull and not to the external appearance of the animal.

Measurements.—Average of five typical adults: Total length, 195; tail, 99; hind foot, 23.2; and ear from notch, 19.7 millimeters.

Distribution and habitat.—The long-nosed deer mouse (pl. 8, B) has much the same range as *truei* and *rowleyi*, with both of which it is sometimes confused, but from which it seems to be entirely distinct. (Fig. 25.) It is rather a scarce species, although its range covers practically all the rough Upper Sonoran country of New Mexico except the extreme northwestern and southwestern parts. There seem to be no specimens from the San Juan Valley or the Mogollon Mountain regions, but the absence of specimens does not prove the absence of the species. Like *truei* and *rowleyi*, in its zone, it is a species of the rocks, cliffs, and canyons, not being found on the plains or in open valley areas.

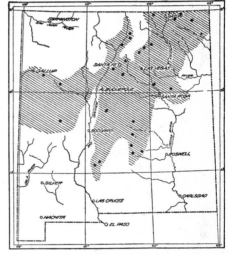

FIGURE 25.—Distribution of the long-nosed deer mouse, *Peromyscus nasutus*, in New Mexico

General habits.—Along the Pecos River these big-eared hairy-tailed mice range entirely through Upper Sonoran Zone from Santa Rosa to Ribera and Glorieta, and up the river 8 or 10 miles above Pecos to their upper limit, where Weller caught several at 7,400 feet altitude at the extreme upper edge of the Upper Sonoran Zone among the last junipers and nut pines. At these localities they were found living in cliffs or on rocky slopes or among the juniper trees not far from rocks. In the Raton Range A. H. Howell took specimens at Folsom, and others near the summit of Emory Peak and in Oak Canyon, in every case among rocks or in canyons. He also collected them on Sierra Grande and near Catskill in similar situations. In the Capitan Mountains Gaut collected specimens on the rocky slopes from the base up to 9,000 feet on southwest slopes and to about 8,000 feet on northwest slopes. None was found above these altitudes, although less trapping was done over the top of the range.

In this region he secured 20 specimens of *nasutus* among a much greater number of *rowleyi*. In the Jicarilla, Manzano, and San Andres Mountains he found them in about the same abundance and with similar range and habits. Surber took a few specimens in the Hondo and Rio Grande Canyons. Hollister collected them in the lava beds about Grant and also in the Datil Mountains.

In all these localities, so far as the records show, they seem to have been associated with rocks among the nut pines and junipers and to have the same general habits as the large-eared *truei*, which is generally found in the same cliffs.

Food habits.—In food habits *nasutus* is very similar to *truei* and apparently depends largely upon the seeds of juniper trees and nut pines. The stomach contents merely indicate that they are seed eaters like other species of the group.

Breeding habits.—At Grant, on July 29, Hollister collected an old female that contained four large fetuses and at Sierra Grande on August 20 A. H. Howell collected one containing six fetuses. As in other species of the group the mammae are arranged in three pairs.

Economic status.—Owing to the scarcity of individuals, this species is of less importance than *truei* or *rowleyi* of the same region, but for its numbers it is worthy of the same economic consideration.

PEROMYSCUS EREMICUS EREMICUS (BAIRD)

DESERT PEROMYSCUS

Hesperomys eremicus Baird, Mammals of North America, p. 479, 1859.
Peromyscus eremicus arenarius Mearns, U. S. Natl. Mus. Proc. 19: 138, 1896.
Type from near El Paso, Tex.

Type locality.—Old Fort Yuma, Calif. No type designated.
General characters.—A medium-sized Peromyscus with long and very slender tail, medium-sized and thinly haired ears, and wholly naked soles of the hind feet. The sides are bright buffy ochraceous and the back buffy gray. The tail is indistinctly bicolor, being a little lighter below than above.
Measurements.—Average of 10 adults from near the type locality: Total length, 183; tail, 101; hind foot, 20.5; ear from notch, 17.5 millimeters. Weights, 21 to 26.6 grams.

Distribution and habitat.—The desert Peromyscus inhabits the Pecos, Tularosa, and Rio Grande Valleys of southern New Mexico. (Fig. 26.) All the specimens examined are from localities in the extreme arid Lower Sonoran area. To a great extent they are also rock and cliff dwellers and are rarely found in the open valleys far from rocks or the protecting walls of canyons or cut banks.

General habits.—Along the foothills of the Franklin, Organ, and San Andres Mountains, Gaut found them abundant in canyons and in rocky places, but scarce at any distance from cover. At Carlsbad the writer caught them in the rocks along the river just above town and also in similar places near El Paso and in the canyons of the Franklin Mountains. In the Rio Grande Valley E. A. Goldman caught them on the stony mesa near Las Cruces, in the rocky foothills just north of Garfield, and one at the base of a ledge in Lake Valley. At Las Palomas he found them common about the clumps of cactus, mesquite bushes, and small-leaved sumac along the base of the rocky bluffs of the river; and at Cuchillo along the edge of the valley. They are most abundant where canyon walls furnish caves and shelves and numerous safe retreats in proximity to an abundant

growth of desert shrubs and cactus. Owing to its strictly nocturnal habits, the desert Peromyscus is rarely seen alive, but in its
region the collectors' traps set under rocks and along shelves and
in the small caves of cliffs usually yield more of this species of mouse
than of any other. In fact, the ground seems to be carefully divided
between it and the smaller species, which are almost invariably
caught under cover of vegetation and distant from the rocks where
eremicus never occurs. Active at all seasons of the year, in their
low hot valleys the desert mice seem to make no distinction between
summer and winter except in a fuller, more furry coat for the colder
season.

Food habits.—There is little to be said of the actual food of these
mice other than that it consists mainly of seeds. The hard shells
of hackberry nutlets are often found scattered over the rocks, but
most of their food consists
of small seeds and a few
insects, which leave little
clue to the species eaten.
They are readily caught
with rolled oats or any kind
of grain, nuts, or melon or
sunflower seeds, and
Mearns reports that they
are fond of salt pork. In
captivity they drink water
eagerly and often, but in
the wild state must procure
their moisture from succulent vegetation.

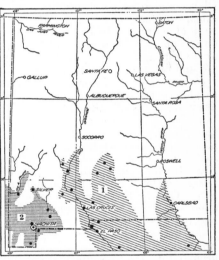

FIGURE 26.—Distribution of desert white-footed
mice in New Mexico: 1, *Peromyscus eremicus
eremicus*; 2, *P. eremicus anthonyi.* Type locality
circled

Breeding habits.—In this
group (subgenus Haplomy-
lomys) there are only four
mammae, arranged in two
pairs of inguinal at the
posterior part of the ab-
domen. Seven pregnant
females examined by
Mearns at dates ranging
from January 9 to April 15 contained, respectively, 4, 4, 3, 1, 4, 2,
and 3 fetuses, and it seems safe to assume that four young is the
normal maximum number in this group. Immature specimens of
various ages collected at all seasons would indicate a habit of perennial breeding that may make up for the small families and prevent
the possibility of race suicide. In the mild climate of their region
they are doubtless even more prolific than are the species of colder
zones having larger families.

Economic status.—As much of the country occupied by these mice
is uninhabited desert, their abundance is of little consequence.
Locally, however, where irrigated valleys are bounded by rocks and
cliffs, they may do some damage about buildings, in gardens, and
along the edges of fields. The clearing out of weedy and brushy
cover along the field borders so as to expose them to their natural

enemies, mainly the little owls, would in most cases prevent any further mischief.

PEROMYSCUS EREMICUS ANTHONYI (MERRIAM)

ANTHONY'S DESERT MOUSE

Hesperomys (*Vesperimus*) *anthonyi* Merriam, Biol. Soc. Wash. Proc. 4: 2, 1887.

Type.—Collected at "Camp Apache," near Hachita, Grand County, N. Mex., May 10, 1886, by A. W. Anthony.

General characters.—A slightly darker, richer-colored form of *eremicus*, with ears slightly smaller, and buffy pectoral spot usually present.

Measurements.—Average of 10 adults: Total length, 194; tail, 108; hind foot, 21.5 millimeters.

Distribution and habitat.—Anthony's desert mouse, a not very strongly marked form of the *eremicus* group, occupies the Deming Plains region of southwestern New Mexico, mainly in the Lower Sonoran Zone. (Fig. 26.) Most of the localities where specimens were taken are in foothills of the desert ranges or in rocky places on the plains. Its whole range seems to be close to the upper edge of the zone and in many localities it occupies ground where the Upper and Lower Sonoran Zones meet and to some extent mingle.

General habits.—In habits as in general characters these mice are so closely related to *eremicus* as to be almost indistinguishable. They are rock and cliff dwellers to a great extent, but at Deming a few specimens were caught in the mesquite-covered sand dunes along the waterless Rio Mimbres. E. A. Goldman found them common along the rocky base of the Little Florida Mountains 10 miles south of Deming and also near Redrock in the canyon of the Gila. Near Hachita he found them among the loose rocks and ledges along the slopes of the low mountains. One collected not far from Silver City by Streator is also referred to this form. Mearns took them at several localities along the Mexican boundary line where, he says (1907, p. 439), they were "restricted to bushy places and rocky buttes, none having been taken on the level sandy ground where most of our trapping was done." Beyond the nature of the ground that they occupy nothing has been recorded of the habits of these mice, but from their close relationship it is probable that their food and breeding habits do not differ at all from those of *eremicus*.

PEROMYSCUS CRINITUS AURIPECTUS (ALLEN)

BUFF-BREASTED CANYON MOUSE

Sitomys auripectus Allen, Bul. Amer. Mus. Nat. Hist. 5: 75, 1893.

Type.—Collected at Bluff City, Utah, May 14, 1892, by Charles P. Rowley.

General characters.—A slender, long-tailed, and moderately large-eared mouse with bright golden-buff upper parts and usually a buff patch on the white breast; tail very hairy and ears mainly naked.

Measurements.—Average of 10 adult topotypes: Total length, 178; tail, 93; hind foot, 20.8 millimeters.

Distribution and habitat.—The beautiful buff-breasted canyon mouse was described by Doctor Allen from Bluff City, Utah, not far from the northwestern extremity of New Mexico; and while there is but one actual record of occurrence in New Mexico, it undoubtedly inhabits the sandstone cliffs and canyons of the whole San Juan

River Valley. (Fig. 27.) There are four specimens from Chaco Canyon, N. Mex., and others from Noland ranch, Utah, only 2½ miles from the northwestern corner of New Mexico. They seem to be restricted to the Upper Sonoran Zone and apparently, more than any other species, are limited to cliffs and canyons.

General habits.—W. W. Granger, who collected them in Chaco Canyon, says they are—

relatively much less common than the other species of *Peromyscus* which were found associated with it, the ratio, as determined by trapping, being about 1 to 5. I have always found it confined to rocky places. In Chaco Cañon the pueblo ruins were its favorite abode. (Allen, 1896, p. 251.)

Though farther west these mice are extremely numerous along the walls of the Grand Canyon they seem to be scarce in the New Mexico part of their range. Judged from field notes by Granger, Loring, and Cary, however, their habits seem to be the same as those of *crinitus* living in the canyons farther west. Cary found them in the ruined cliff dwellings at Mesa Verde, and their whole range is closely associated with the region of abundant prehistoric cliff houses. In the Grand Canyon, Merriam discovered that they were excellent climbers and shot one by moonlight as it peered down at him from the branch of a tree. (Merriam 1890a, p. 62.)

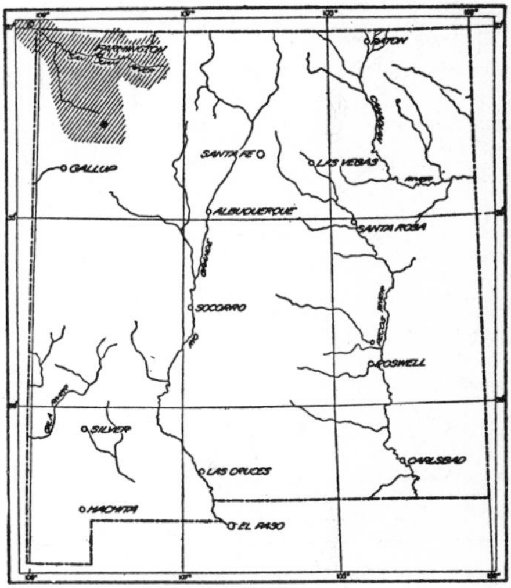

FIGURE 27.—Distribution of buff-breasted canyon mouse, *Peromyscus crinitus auripectus,* in New Mexico

Breeding habits.—Practically nothing is known of their actual food or breeding habits. The number of mammae is but four, and judged from other species in the group, the number of young may safely be assumed to be four or less in a litter.

Economic status.—In the days of the cliff dwellers these mice may have been of great economic importance, and have caused much loss to the hoarded stores of food, but at the present day most of their range is so inaccessible that they are mainly interesting because of their beauty and the bit of wild life they contribute to a region full of wonders.

REITHRODONTOMYS MEGALOTIS MEGALOTIS (BAIRD)

BIG-EARED HARVEST MOUSE

Reithrodon megalotis Baird, Mammals of North America, p. 451, 1859.

Type.—Collected between Janos, Chihuahua, and San Luis Spring, near border of Grant County, N. Mex., by C. B. R. Kennerly. Actual locality unknown but probably in Sonora. Specimen without date but entered in United States National Museum catalogue in 1855.

General characters.—In appearance very similar to a small house mouse, but distinguished superficially by the shorter and less tapering tail and more surely by the deeply grooved upper incisors. The upper parts are a rich brownish gray; the lower parts, feet, and lower half of tail, white.

Measurements.—Average of 6 adults from the type region: Total length, 140; tail, 71; hind foot, 17.6; ear from notch to tip, 12.5 millimeters.

Distribution and habitat.—The big-eared harvest mice occupy the Lower Sonoran valleys of all southern New Mexico, including the Pecos, Tularosa, Rio Grande, and Gila Valleys and extend over the Deming Plain. (Fig. 28.) Specimens from Roswell, from near the base of the Jicarilla Mountains, from the northern end of the San Andres Mountains, and from Silver City, Cliff, and the San

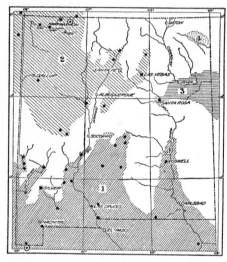

Francisco River Valley near Alma mark the northern limits of its range. Some of these localities, such as the Jicarilla Mountains, Mesa Jumanes, and Silver City, are above the limits of the Lower Sonoran Zone, but are in the area of intergradation with the more northern form, *aztecus*.

FIGURE 28.—Distribution of harvest mice in New Mexico: 1, *Reithrodontomys megalotis megalotis*; 2, *R. megalotis aztecus*; 3, *R. albescens griseus*; 4, *R. montanus.* Type localities circled

General habits.—Some of the harvest mice build nests in bushes, but *megalotis* and its subspecies seem to be entirely ground dwellers. They live under cover of grass, weeds, and such vegetation as will protect them from enemies above and at the same time furnish ample food for their needs. They are generally caught in dry meadows or grassy or weedy borders of fields and roadsides where their narrow trails may be found by carefully parting the grass and searching over the surface of the ground. They also may be caught by setting traps at random on little bare spots under the cover of grass and fallen vegetation where no trace of their runways are seen, in furrows along the edges of fields or the spaces between growing grain. Old haycocks, weed piles, or rubbish heaps often furnish cover for their nests and burrows and are favorite points from which to make their excursions for food. In suitable localities they become very numerous, but over much of the desert country they are so scarce and scattered that only an occasional specimen can be secured.

At Las Cruces E. A. Goldman caught them in grass and weeds along irrigation ditches in the valley, and at Las Palomas he took a few in patches of grass and weeds on damp ground near the river.

Near Fairview and Kingston he caught them among the weeds and grass in fields of the open valleys and in similar situations at the sink of the Mimbres, near Redrock, Gila, Pleasanton, Dry Creek, and on the Lang ranch in the southern part of the Animas Valley.

At Silver City the writer caught one in the weeds at the edge of an orchard just above town, and Streater caught a specimen by the side of a stone wall near there. At Glenwood the writer found them abundant in the dense weedy growth along the river bottom and had no trouble in catching them there and at Cliff on the Gila River.

In the Organ Mountains Gaut caught them in grassy gulches and under old rubbish around the ranches. At Tularosa he secured a series of specimens along the irrigation ditch at the edge of the valley, where they were taken in traps set in runways for cotton rats. At the northern end of the San Andres Mountains he took two specimens in a grassy bottom just west of the divide on the road to San Marcial, and at the southern end of the Mesa Jumanes he took two specimens in a patch of high grass. He also caught one in the Jicarilla Mountains near the rocks on one of the peaks, at about 8,000 feet, but was unable to catch any more in that locality. A few specimens that the writer caught in the southern end of the Guadalupe Mountains near the Texas-New Mexico line in Upper Sonoran Zone are also referred to this species.

Food habits.—Harvest mice are mainly seed eaters. Their stomach contents usually show only a white starchy mass of finely masticated dough from the various seeds eaten or occasionally a little green pulp of the foliage with which they have varied their diet. The cut stems of grasses and small plants along the runways and on their feeding grounds are the only clue to their preference in food. As some of the species are excellent climbers, it is not improbable that these also climb through the grass and weed tops for the seeds they prefer. They do not hibernate or become fat in autumn, but are active throughout the winter, when they probably get an abundance of ripe and fallen seeds from the surface of the ground.

Breeding habits.—Apparently these mice are prolific breeders, as young of various ages are caught throughout the summer. One old female taken by Gaut late in January, 1903, from among a pile of empty cans in the southern part of the Organ Mountains contained four fetuses. One collected at Silver City on May 10 and another taken at Fairview on October 13 also contained four fetuses each. The mammae of the females are in 3 pairs, 2 pairs of inguinal, and 1 pair of pectoral, and the normal number of young at a birth is probably 4 to 6.

Economic status.—These mice would seem too small to be of much economic importance, but where they become excessively numerous, as they do in some sections, their inroads on growing grass and grain crops cause considerable loss. But if their natural enemies, the hawks, owls, weasels, and skunks, are carefully protected, there is little danger of their becoming a pest, and in case of an abnormal outbreak it is only necessary to clear the weedy borders of fields and waste places and give their enemies a chance to reach them.

REITHRODONTOMYS MEGALOTIS AZTECUS Allen

Aztec Harvest Mouse

Reithrodontomys aztecus Allen, Bul. Amer. Mus. Nat. Hist. 5: 79, 1893.

Type.—Collected at Laplata, San Juan County, N. Mex., April 11, 1892, by C. P. Rowley.

General characters.—Similar to *megalotis* [20] but slightly larger, with larger ears, longer fur, and duller gray of upper parts.

Measurements.—Average of seven specimens from the type locality: Total length, 144; tail, 68; hind foot, 18; ear from notch, 13.8 millimeters.

Distribution and habitat.—The Aztec harvest mouse is an Upper Sonoran form of the *megalotis* group occupying the valley country of northwestern New Mexico and extending around the southern end of the Pecos Mountains and along their eastern base as far north as Guadalupita on Coyote Creek. (Fig. 28.) It extends up the Rio Grande Valley to Espanola but apparently does not reach northward into the San Luis Valley. It inhabits the open country, where there is sufficient low vegetation for food and cover, and so far as known is restricted to the Upper Sonoran Zone.

General habits.—The habits of this form do not differ noticeably from those of its near relative, *megalotis*, of the Lower Sonoran valleys except as modified by somewhat different environment. In December, 1893, Loring took 12 specimens in one night at Laplata, where he caught them among weeds and small willows in the center of a large field. At Aztec he found them common in a patch of high grass and cattails, which had evidently been marshy and wet during the spring, and caught them in traps set in Microtus runways. In 1908 Birdseye found them common at Farmington and Fruitland in the San Juan River Valley, where he also caught them in the runways of *Microtus aztecus* in grassy, swampy places, along ditch banks, and under the cover of tumble weeds, wild sunflowers, and scattered grain and alfalfa.

White-footed mice and house mice as well as Microtus were caught in the same traps and in the same situations with the harvest mice, as the abundant cover and food furnish the ideal conditions under which all these rodents thrive. Hollister caught them along the weedy bottoms of the Puerco River flats at Wingate, in a saltgrass and tule marsh about a spring at the mouth of the Rio San Jose, and in weed and grass patches along the creek at Datil. Along the Zuni River a few miles below the New Mexico line, the writer caught one in the greasebush along the dry wash, where there was no permanent water nor grass cover near, so it is evident that at times they wander away from safe cover. At Espanola Gaut found them common along the valley bottom, and in the Manzano Mountains he took one specimen at the edge of a little park high up on the east slope of the mountains where the growth of grass was dense over the surface of the ground.

The little runways of the Aztec mouse are easily distinguished from those of Microtus by being narrower and less worn, and by dis-

---

[20] The characters separating this form from *megalotis* are so slight that most authors have considered them indistinguishable, but Howell (1914), in a critical study of the group, has decided that they are sufficiently marked for the recognition of *aztecus* as a subspecies.

appearing in the more open growth. The nests are neatly formed balls of grass placed on the surface of the ground under cover of grass or weeds and entered by one or more tiny doorways at the sides near the ground. At Aztec Loring found these grass nests lined with soft down from cattails, but usually fine grass or plant fibers are used for lining the warm dry chamber within. These mice do not become fat or hibernate and seem to be equally active during the night and day both in summer and winter.

Food habits.—The harvest mice are easily caught in traps baited with rolled oats, rolled barley, wheat, or any grain, but their native food seems to be mainly seeds. Cut grass stems found along their runways or about the burrows would indicate that grass seeds are a favorite food. At times a little green vegetation is also eaten, as shown by the color of the stomach contents.

Breeding habits.—The Aztec harvest mice are prolific breeders apparently throughout the year. At Aztec on December 7 Loring caught a female containing one large fetus, and several of the others caught were apparently nursing young. At Fruitland Birdseye found a female October 31 containing seven large fetuses; at Espanola Gaut collected a female in June with four fetuses nearly ready for birth. Near Monica Spring on the San Augustine Plains E. A. Goldman took one September 18 that contained six fetuses. The 6 mammae of the females are arranged in 2 pairs of inguinal and 1 pair of pectoral and apparently the normal variation of young is from 4 to 6.

Economic status.—As this subspecies occupies one of the most extensive and important agricultural valleys in New Mexico, where it is particularly abundant, considerable economic importance may be ascribed to it. The dense vegetation along the irrigation ditches, field borders, and roadsides in the San Juan Valley furnish such perfect cover and protection that the mice multiply at a rate calculated to do considerable damage to the grain and hay crops. Their depredations, however, will rarely if ever be found sufficiently serious to warrant the use of poisons or artificial means of destruction. Ordinarily the mere cleaning up of waste places to expose them to their natural enemies will be found the most effective and economical means of controlling their abundance, with the added advantage of keeping down the weeds that are usually left to distribute seeds over the fields. Both mice and weeds can be kept under reasonable control by a little work in mowing or burning or by close grazing of the waste places.

REITHRODONTOMYS ALBESCENS GRISEUS BAILEY

GRAY HARVEST MOUSE

Reithrodontomys griseus Bailey, North Amer. Fauna No. 25, p. 106, 1905.

Type.—Collected at San Antonio, Tex., March 4, 1897, by H. P. Attwater.

General characters.—The smallest harvest mouse occurring in New Mexico, with relatively small hind feet, buffy-gray upper parts, and white lower parts.

Measurements.—Average of typical specimens: Total length, 142; tail, 60; hind foot, 15 millimeters.

Distribution and habitat.—A single specimen of the little gray harvest mouse taken at Santa Rosa marks the westernmost point

of range of a common Texas species. It undoubtedly extends up
the Canadian River Valley and across to Santa Rosa in the Pecos
Valley, or it may occupy the whole of the Pecos Valley up to this
point. (Fig. 28.) In Texas its range seems to be restricted to the
Lower Sonoran Zone, and at Santa Rosa it probably represents the
Lower Sonoran element, which is found there in dilute form.

General habits.—In October, 1902, Gaut collected a specimen of
this mouse among the mesquite bushes on the flats near Santa Rosa,
but in a large number of traps kept in the vicinity for some time
he secured no other specimens; nor were other collectors able to
secure any there the following year. It is evident that the species
was then not common in that locality, and that the record marks
an extreme limit of range. The species seems, however, to be rare
or not often taken in any part of its range and is represented in
collections by small series from widely scattered localities. It occupies the grassy prairies and field borders and seems to have much
the same habits as the other species of harvest mice.

REITHRODONTOMYS MONTANUS (BAIRD)

SAN LUIS VALLEY HARVEST MOUSE

Reithrodon montanus Baird, Acad. Nat. Sci. Phila. 7: 335, 1855.

Type.—Collected in San Luis Valley near San Luis Lakes, Colo., August 29
or 30, 1853 or 1854, by Mr. Kreutzfeldt under Capt. E. G. Beckwith.

General characters.—Size intermediate between that of *megalotis* and *griseus*,
colors paler than in *megalotis*, without dark dorsal stripe of *griseus*.

Measurements.—Average of adults: Total length, 126; tail, 58; hind foot,
17 millimeters.

Distribution and habitat.—A single specimen of the San Luis
Valley harvest mouse sent to the Biological Survey for identification
by D. E. Merrill from the State College of New Mexico at Mesilla
Park was collected by Fred I. Howarth on January 27, 1914, 3 miles
south of Raton. (Fig. 28.) It is a female and rather small, measuring in total length, 121; tail, 51; hind foot, 16 millimeters, but was
identified by A. H. Howell, who has monographed the genus (1914)
as *montanus*, which adds this species, previously known only from
the San Luis Valley in Colorado, to the State list of New Mexico.

SIGMODON HISPIDUS BERLANDIERI BAIRD

BERLANDIER'S COTTON RAT

Sigmodon berlandieri Baird, Acad. Nat. Sci. Phila. Proc. 7: 333, 1855.
Sigmodon hispidus pallidus Mearns, U. S. Natl. Mus. Proc. 20: 504, 1897 (advance sheets). Type from near El Paso, Tex.

Type.—Collected at Rio Nazas, Coahuila, Mexico, in 1853 by D. N. Couch.

General characters.—A full-grown cotton rat might easily be mistaken for a
half-grown brown rat, *Rattus norvegicus*, which it somewhat resembles in size,
color, and proportions, but with which it has no real relationship. The fur is
coarse but full and soft in winter and thin and hispid in summer. The upper
parts are buffy gray, the belly white, and feet light gray. The tail is thinly
haired, tapering, light gray below, and blackish above.

Measurements.—Average of five typical adults: Total length, 256; tail, 113;
hind foot, 32.5 millimeters.

Distribution and habitat.—The large gray Berlandier's cotton rat
extends into New Mexico from the south and east up the Pecos River

Valley to Carlsbad and Roswell, up the Tularosa Valley to Tularosa, and up the Rio Grande Valley from El Paso to Socorro and westward to near Deming. (Fig. 29.) It fills the Lower Sonoran valleys wherever there is sufficient grass or vegetation for food and cover but is absent from the more arid and barren areas. Its range is continuous along the river and stream valleys where bottom-land vegetation furnishes the conditions required by its mode of life; but some of the localities, such as the west slope of the Guadalupe Mountains, Tularosa, and Deming, probably represent more or less isolated colonies.

General habits.—Over a wide range corresponding closely to the cotton-growing area of the United States, these rats are so common in the fields that they have acquired the name of cotton rats. The name is less appropriate for the New Mexico form, *berlandieri*, although in both the Pecos and Rio Grande Valleys they occur close to the edges of fields of cotton. They are generally found in the grassy and weedy bottoms along the valleys, where they make numerous little roads or roadways under cover of grass or fallen vegetation. In fact their habits are very similar to those of the meadow mouse (Microtus) of the higher zones. They live in burrows underground or in nests of grass and soft fibers placed on the surface of the ground under cover of vegetation, and from these nests and burrows their little roadways extend in all directions, often into the edges of fields of grain and other crops. Their roadways frequently lead into marshes or on to damp ground, but always avoid the open where cover and food are not abundant.

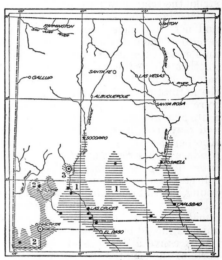

FIGURE 29.—Distribution of cotton rats in New Mexico: 1, *Sigmodon hispidus berlandieri;* 2, *S. minimus minimus;* 3, *S. minimus goldmani.* Type localities circled

Food habits.—Their food consists chiefly of green vegetation, leaves, stems, and seeds of various plants along their runways. The grass stems are cut off at the bottom and drawn down by cutting away the lower sections until the leaves, flowers, and seeds are within reach. The cut stems are left scattered along the way. Grain at any stage from the green blades to the ripening heads is a favorite food. Alfalfa, too, is a very acceptable article of diet, and wherever they can the rats extend their runways into fields of alfalfa to feed upon the tender leaves and stems.

Near Deming early in September, where E. A. Goldman found them common among the weeds and bushes around the sink of the

Mimbres, their well-marked runways extended from the burrows throughout the neighboring vegetation. The owner of an alfalfa field reported some damage from them especially when the alfalfa was large. On examining a recently mowed field Goldman found signs of their work in the alfalfa, numerous stems having been cut off and partly eaten. At Carlsbad in July the writer found them feeding mainly on grass and alfalfa, but a few grasshoppers were also found in their stomachs. At Tularosa, where Gaut collected a large series of them in November, he reported them as cannibalistic in their tastes, fully two-thirds of those taken in his traps being partly eaten by their comrades. They seem fond of rolled oats, or any kind of grain or seeds used for trap bait, and are easily caught either in baited traps or traps set across runways where they will strike the trigger in passing.

Breeding habits.—These cotton rats are extremely prolific breeders and not only have large litters of young but apparently produce several of them during a season. A female collected by E. A. Goldman near Deming, September 1, 1908, contained four fetuses, and another which the writer collected at Carlsbad, September 11, contained 11 nearly matured fetuses, which was probably more than the normal number for a litter, as she had but 10 mammae. These were arranged in 1 pair of inguinal, 2 pairs of abdominal, and 2 pairs of pectoral. The anterior pair were directly between the arms and may have been supernumerary although they were functional. Another female examined lacked this anterior pair. The young produced after September 9 would probably mean a second or third litter during a season. At Tularosa, on November 4 to 14, Gaut collected 4 adults, 4 full-grown young of the year, 4 half-grown young, 2 about one-third grown, and 2 about one-fourth grown, indicating very irregular breeding or two or three litters for each of the females during the breeding season. The breeding habits of these animals should be studied more closely, as they probably account for the excessive abundance of the species at certain times. In other parts of the country the cotton rats " have swarmed " in such numbers as to have gained the reputation of migrating in vast armies, but probably, through the lack of some normal check on their abundance, they have merely multiplied at a normal rate. In such cases they have done great damage to growing crops, resulting in heavy losses.

Hibernation.—So far as known cotton rats do not hibernate and over most of their range are active through winter and summer. They never accumulate any noticeable fat and apparently do not even lay up stores of food for winter. In the southern part of their range it is probable that they even continue to breed throughout the year.

Economic status.—The destruction of crops by cotton rats depends upon their abundance and their abundance depends largely upon the conditions affording cover and protection from their enemies. If wide borders of grass and weeds are left along the edges of fields and roadsides where they can safely multiply during a large part of the year, they will almost certainly enter the fields and do more or less damage as the crops develop. If the irrigation ditches are allowed to become a tangle of weeds and vines, they form favorite homes and breeding grounds for the cotton rats, which perforate their banks with great numbers of burrows and sooner or later cause leakage or breaks. By keeping the vegetation closely grazed or mowed in all waste places and exposing the burrows and runways to the keen scrutiny of hawks, owls, weasels, and skunks, the cotton rats will rarely do any serious damage. In cases of extreme abundance they can be partially controlled by artificial means, but the preventative means will be found much more economical and successful if taken in time.

SIGMODON MINIMUS MINIMUS Mearns

LEAST COTTON RAT

Sigmodon minima Mearns, U. S. Natl. Mus. Proc. 17: 130, 1894.

Type.—Collected at Upper Corner Monument of Mexican boundary line, Grant County, N. Mex., April 26, 1892, by E. A. Mearns and F. X. Holzner.

General characters.—This small, dark-gray cotton rat is readily distinguished from *berlandieri* by its coarser fur, more hairy and concolor tail, and buff-colored belly. Its relatively short wide skull places it with another group distinct from *hispidus*.

Measurements.—The type of *minimus* measures: Total length, 223; tail, 94; hind foot, 28 millimeters.

Distribution and habitat.—The least cotton rat has an irregular and probably broken distribution in the low mountains and valleys of southern New Mexico, Arizona, and northern Mexico. (Fig. 29.) The type and one other specimen taken at Monument No. 40, where the boundary line turns abruptly southward, a series of specimens collected at the Lang ranch at the southern end of the Animas Valley, and others collected at Silver City are at present all the records for New Mexico. These localities are all in the Upper Sonoran Zone, to which the species apparently is restricted.

General habits.—In Animas Valley E. A. Goldman collected three specimens August 10 and 14, 1908, at the Lang ranch. He found them living in thick grass on moist ground in the Cienega. They had conspicuous and well-worn runways leading from their burrows out over the surface of the ground. Sometimes their runways extended in opposite directions from a single hole and curved around crossing one another, or were connected by crosslines forming a network of trails apparently made by one animal, for when one was caught at a burrow no others were taken in that vicinity. Cut-grass stems were found scattered along these runways where the cotton rats had been feeding. At Silver City the writer found a colony living in a weedy field just north of town where the characteristic trails were found running under weeds and grass, and leading to numerous burrows in the ground under a big bunch of beargrass (*Nolina lindheimeri*). These runways were strewn with numerous stems of green plants, which had been cut for food. One of the females caught on May 10, 1906, contained three small embryos, and another four. Very little is known of the habits of this species, and as it lives in a region where agriculture is rarely attempted it is at present of little economic importance.

SIGMODON MINIMUS GOLDMANI Bailey

GOLDMAN'S COTTON RAT

Sigmodon minimus goldmani Bailey, Biol. Soc. Wash. Proc. 26: 132, 1913.

Type.—Collected 7 miles north of Palomas, N. Mex., October 28, 1909, by E. A. Goldman.

General characters.—Almost black over the upper parts, with black ears and tail and very dark feet; belly, rich fulvous.

Measurements.—The type measures: Total length, 256; tail, 107; hind foot, 31 millimeters.

Distribution and habitat.—The little hairy-tailed Goldman's cotton rat is probably local in distribution but with such marked characters that the specimens can not be referred to *minimus*. The type and two topotypes were collected by Goldman along the edges of the marsh at a hot spring 7 miles north of the town of Palomas. (Fig. 29.) They were taken from runways that extended from holes along the bank out into the marsh among the grass and sedges. Some of the runways led through shallow water to a nest of grass and plant stems out among the cattail flags. The nest, although not very old, was apparently unoccupied at the time he found it. The runway led from beneath up into an opening in the center about 4 inches in diameter, lined with small sections of salt grass (*Distichlis spicata*). Freshly cut stems of this grass were found in a few places along the runways and the stomachs of the specimens taken were filled with grain and white pulp in separate masses and varying proportions, showing that more than one kind of food was eaten.

Subfamily NEOTOMINAE Merriam

WOOD RATS, PACK RATS, TRADE RATS

General characters and habits of the subfamily.—This subfamily of native ratlike animals is represented in New Mexico by 10 species and subspecies, some of which occur in almost every part of the State. They belong to a purely American group of rodents, differing more widely from the introduced Old-World rats in structural characters and in habits than in general appearance. They are large-eared, bright-eyed, soft-furred little animals and of interesting habits, which have been the subject of numerous popular articles of somewhat sensational character. Two subgenera are represented in New Mexico, those with the short-haired, round tails of the subgenus Neotoma, and two species of the bushy-tailed subgenus Teonoma.

A passion for building houses is common to all the species and often induces them to carry away any article of convenient size for building material. This has given them their local names of "pack rat" and "trade rat" and has furnished the foundation for much romance regarding their habits of borrowing and returning property that does not rightfully belong to them.

Aside from their characteristic houses, which differ somewhat with the various species, their presence can almost always be determined by the elongated pelletlike excrement neatly placed in out-of-the-way corners under or near the houses or rock dens. This is so characteristic that it can rarely be mistaken for any other animal and so durable that it remains for years in dry situations, sometimes accumulating in caves or sheltered places under the rocks in masses of a bushel or more. Its appearance generally gives some clue as to its age and as to whether the rats are occupying the dens or not, and in this way it serves an important purpose to the experienced collector who places his traps where the freshest signs are found. Another peculiar and very characteristic indication of the presence of wood rats in rocky situations is seen in white streaking or capping of rocky points near their dens. This is a calcareous deposit from the urine of the wood rats, which, like that of many desert animals, is usually thick and milky with mineral salts. The sharp points and edges of rocks seem to be the favorite place of deposit of this liquid, which gradually builds up a whitish calcite layer over the rock surface that often extends down in long white streaks. A cross section of this deposit may be 2 or 3 millimeters in thickness, and it is as hard as the usual calcite formation around hot springs and of much the same general appearance. It remains for years, if not permanently, on the rocks, and a cliff or canyon wall well streaked or capped with white indicates an abundance of some species of wood rats. The habit seems common to all of the rock-dwelling species.

Wood rats are cleanly animals and if larger would be valuable as game, as their flesh is tender and of excellent flavor. With many tribes of Indians they are a popular game animal and by testing most of the species the writer has found them very good eating. An external musky odor does not penetrate beneath the skin.

In the present treatment of the species and subspecies of wood rats in New Mexico, Goldman's monograph (1910) of the group has been followed as to classification and nomenclature. The ranges have been worked out in somewhat greater detail and general habits of the species included.

NEOTOMA MICROPUS CANESCENS Allen

HOARY WOOD RAT

Neotoma micropus canescens Allen, Bul. Amer. Mus. Nat. Hist. 3 : 285, 1891.

Type.—Collected at North Beaver Creek, Beaver County, Okla., October, 1889, by Jenness Richardson and John Rowley, jr.

General characters.—One of the largest and palest of the New Mexico wood rats of the round-tailed group. The upper parts are pale, ashy gray; the lower parts and feet white, the white reaching to the skin on throat and breast; the tail, dark gray above and white below. From *albigula*, which overlaps the range of this species along its upper borders, it is easily distinguished by larger size, especially larger hind feet, thicker tail, and much grayer coloration.

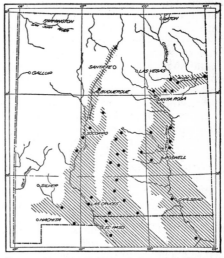

FIGURE 30.—Distribution of hoary wood rat, *Neotoma micropus canescens*, in New Mexico

Measurements.—Adults: Total length, 330; tail, 137; hind foot, 36 millimeters.

Distribution and habitat.—The hoary northern form of the wood rat of a wide-ranging Lower Sonoran species extends up the two great valleys of New Mexico, the Pecos, and the Rio Grande. (Fig. 30.) In the Pecos Valley it reaches to Santa Rosa and thence eastward down the Canadian Valley. Up the Rio Grande Valley it reaches commonly to Socorro and scatteringly to Rinconada, and extends westward at least as far as Deming. It occupies mainly open Lower Sonoran valleys, and unlike most of the species of wood rats, its home is rarely associated with rocks or cliffs.

General habits.—The hoary wood rats are abundant in the open arid valleys where cactus abounds and are usually found associated either with cactus or some of the thorny desert shrubs. Their favorite location for a house is in the midst of a bed of large prickly-

pears or thorny bushes, but they often build around the base of the
cane cactus (*Opuntia arborescens*), in a group of Spanish-bayonets,
or in an allthorn (*Koeberlinia spinosa*), where an abundance of
cactus can be found for building material. Sometimes their houses
stand in the open and, while protected only by their thorny walls, are
so well built that they become large and symmetrical and are rarely
broken into by enemies. A well-built house in the open is usually
conical in form, 3 or 4 feet high, and about as wide at the base,
but those built in or around cactus or in thorn bushes are less symmetrical and often lean against some natural support or are wide
and low to suit their surroundings.

At Carlsbad in 1892 Dutcher found a few of the houses and collected specimens of the wood rats. In 1901 the writer found them
abundant all over that part of the Pecos Valley living in stick,
thorn, and rubbish houses under mesquites, cactus, allthorn, blue-
thorn, and other thorny bushes, but they were not found reaching
into the foothills of the mountains where the white-throated wood
rat occupied the cliffs and rocky situations. A few hoary wood rats
were collected in the open valley near Roswell, and in 1902 Hollister
found them abundant along the Pecos Valley from Roswell to Fort
Sumner and Santa Rosa living in houses among the mesquite bushes,
and sometimes built over burrows of old kangaroo-rat dens.

At Santa Rosa they were fairly common, usually living in houses
built among the cactus and often close to cliffs occupied by *albigula*.
One small and very symmetrical house about 2½ feet high, built
among the low mesquite bushes, was composed largely of dry balls
of manure, a few sticks and bones, and a quantity of old shotgun
cartridges picked up at a duck blind near by. Near Cuervo, about
20 miles east of Santa Rosa, where low mesquite bushes and cactus
patches abound, these wood rats are as common as in the Lower
Pecos Valley. A dozen of their houses were within 30 rods of our
camp, while in the rocks just beyond, the white-throated was equally
common. Here their houses were usually placed under bunches of
cane cactus (*Opuntia arborescens*) and largely composed of its fallen segments, seed capsules, and tufts of dry thorns mixed with cow
chips, sticks, and bones. Some of these houses were entered by half
a dozen doorways, either at the sides or under the edges on the surface of the ground and leading to internal chambers both above and
below the surface of the ground.

Two of these houses were torn apart to make it possible to study
their internal structure. The occupants were driven out and photographed as they ran about half dazed in the glare of daylight. At
first they tried to run to other houses and when intercepted and
driven back ran about much bewildered, though they did not seem
greatly frightened. One climbed up a cactus bush, ran over the
branches, and jumped from branch to branch, paying no attention
to the thorns. When poked with a stick it ran about and then jumped
to the ground but quickly climbed back up the cactus over the mass
of thorns, its delicate pink feet apparently never getting scratched.
It was as bright and pretty as a squirrel or chipmunk and soon became
so tame that it would let the writer almost touch it. The chambers
in the house were perfectly dry, although there had been a hard rain
during the previous night. A badger had been digging close to one

of these houses but evidently had kept at a safe distance from the thorny structure, although it must have been sorely tempted by the knowledge of a savory meal within the walls.

In the Tularosa Valley the characteristic cactus houses of this species are common over practically all the open valley, but no wood rats have been collected except in its northern portion. Near Tularosa, Gaut found them common along the irrigation ditches and over the low foothills along the edge of the valley, and he found old houses near the salt marshes and lava beds in the middle part of the valley. Gaut also collected a few scattered specimens of this species in the edge of the Upper Sonoran Zone at the northwest base of the Capitan Mountains, at the western base of the Jicarilla Mountains, and at the east base of the Manzanos. Near the Jicarilla Mountains he caught two at a ranch house, where the ranchman informed him they had been living for some time. In the Rio Grande Valley houses built in the characteristic fashion of this species are common along the sides of the valley and out over the mesa east of Mesilla Park and northward along the valley. E. A. Goldman collected a specimen near the eastern base of the Magdalena Mountains at an altitude of 6,400 feet. It was shot while sitting at the entrance of its burrow under a large pricklypear, where it evidently had just begun a new house, a few pieces of cactus having been placed along the sides of its runaway a short distance from the burrow. Near Ojo de la Parida, 10 miles northeast of Socorro, he caught two of these wood rats at burrows in clumps of coarse grass in the sand dunes. Here little sand mounds were used as a foundation for the houses; one of these was entered by five or six openings, mainly near the base of the mound, while near the top were small accumulations of sticks and cow chips. In the rocks not far away lived the white-throated wood rats (*Neotoma albigula albigula*).

Over the mesa west of San Marcial the writer found the characteristic houses of the hoary wood rat under numerous bunches of pricklypear and about the base of banana yuccas (*Yucca baccata*) or Spanish-daggers (*Y. macrocarpa*). Near Deming, in 1908, E. A. Goldman collected one specimen of this species in a brush patch near the sink of the Rio Mimbres, but in the same general region he found the white-throated species much commoner. From Deming westward the white-throated rat seemed to adopt the habit of the hoary wood rat, living in houses built in the open valley. Many of these houses, however, were probably originally built by the hoary wood rats and later, when deserted, taken possession of by their white-throated neighbors. In 1908 both species were scarce over the Deming Plains, but the previous year when the writer passed through without stopping to collect, some species of wood rat was so unusually abundant that the houses were conspicuous on every side, and much of the vegetation had been gnawed and some of it killed by them. This was evidently one of the wood-rat waves of abundance, which occasionally sweep over the desert, soon followed by an unusual scarcity of the species. It is likely that the hoary wood rat reaches considerably farther west than Deming, although no specimens are available to prove it. Except as they adapt themselves to open country they do not differ greatly in habits from the white-throated, but the two species seem rarely, if ever, to occupy the same ground.

Food habits.—The food of these wood rats consists largely of the flesh and fruit of cactus, but includes also a great variety of green vegetation, fruit, and seeds. The sugary pods and little beanlike seeds of the mesquite bushes are always acceptable food where they can be found and are sometimes stored away in considerable quantities in the houses. Usually the wood rats live in wide stretches of arid valley, where no water can be had except at brief intervals following the occasional rains. At times many months must elapse when their only water is contained in their desert food plants. During the long dry seasons they seem to depend largely on the pulp of cactus plants for both food and moisture, but sometimes many of the bushes are stripped of their bark during the drought. Mearns says (1907, p. 472) that they are "usually found about streams and springs, often in the fringe of cottonwood and willow growth along rivers," but the writer's experience has been that they are also a wide-ranging open-valley species.

Breeding habits.—Mearns records a female, taken June 24 at Fort Hancock on the Rio Grande, that contained three large fetuses. As in the case of other species of wood rats the young probably vary from two to four in number. The mammae of the females are arranged in two pairs, close together between the hind legs.

In the Biological Survey collection there are specimens of nursing young taken at Rinconada, April 23; of about quarter-grown young taken at Cuervo, June 14; and at west base of Capitan Mountains, June 25; others a little larger at the same place, June 25 and 26; and others half and two-thirds grown, June 27 and 29 and July 2. At Carlsbad specimens of quarter and half grown young were taken, September 22 and 23; and at Fort Sumner a litter of three-quarter-grown young was taken, September 25. At Ancho a nursing young was taken, September 23, and a nearly full-grown young the next day. At Tularosa a half-grown young was taken, November 21. From these records it seems probable that two or more litters are produced in a season, or at least that the breeding season is continuous throughout more than half of the year.

Economic status.—As most of the country where these wood rats live is extremely arid and at present of little agricultural value, the animals are practically harmless and add an interesting feature to the deserts. Locally, however, they do considerable mischief along the edges of irrigated fields and about gardens, houses, and buildings. They have been accused of killing chickens, but this is far more likely to be the work of the common brown rat, which is a notorious chicken thief. The wood rats rarely remain about occupied buildings for any length of time, and they seem to be an easy prey to dogs and cats. Their houses are so conspicuous that they can be easily located and torn to pieces and the rats left defenseless against a host of eager enemies. If cactus ever becomes a farm product of the arid region, it will then be necessary to keep the number of wood rats reduced to a minimum, as they would certainly injure the cactus crop more than any other species of rodent.

Their principal enemies are wild cats, ringtails (Bassariscus), foxes, coyotes, hawks, and owls, and in the country where they abound their remains are more abundant under hawk and owl nests than are those of any other mammal.

NEOTOMA ALBIGULA ALBIGULA Hartley

White-Throated Wood Rat

Neotoma albigula Hartley, Calif. Acad. Sci. Proc. (2), 4: 157, May 9, 1894.
Neotoma intermedia angusticeps Merriam, Biol. Soc. Wash. Proc. 9: 127, 1894;
   type from Grant County, N. Mex.

Type.—Collected at Old Fort Lowell, Ariz., June 14, 1893, by W. W. Price and
R. L. Wilbur.

General characters.—Size medium for the group of round-tailed wood rats;
upper parts brownish or buffy gray; lower parts white or occasionally buffy;
throat and breast pure white to base of fur; tail bicolor.

Measurements.—Average total length, 328; tail, 152; hind foot, 33.5; ear from
notch, 30 millimeters; weight of adult female, 188 grams.

Distribution and habitat.—The white-throated wood rats (Pl. 9, A)
cover a large part of New Mexico, mainly in the Upper Sonoran Zone.
(Fig. 31.) In northwestern New Mexico they give place to *lepida*
and in northeastern to *warreni;* otherwise they occupy the whole Upper Sonoran area of the State, except the open part of the Staked Plains, where no species of wood rat occurs. In places their range extends into the edge of the Lower Sonoran Zone but not to any great extent, as that zone is mainly occupied by the slightly larger *canescens.* They show a strong preference for rough country and when possible choose rocks and cliffs for their homes. Where these are not available they often adapt themselves to such protective cover as is offered by logs, hollow trees, cactus patches, brush, and old buildings.

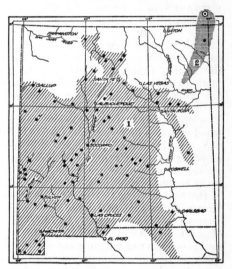

FIGURE 31.—Distribution of the white-throated and Warren's wood rats in New Mexico: 1, *Neotoma albigula albigula;* 2, *N. albigula warreni.* Type locality circled

General habits.—Like all wood rats these white-throated rats are
great builders, and whether the location selected is in the rocks or
in the cactus patches the building goes on industriously, but with
suitable adaptation to local conditions. Where rocks or cliffs are
to be found they are chosen, presumably for the protection they
afford. Clefts and shallow caves in the cliffs are favorite strongholds, and in some of these the rats have gone on building up their
piles of thorny rubbish until they have astonishing accumulations.
Caves containing 20 to 50 bushels of material that the rats have carried in bit by bit are not uncommon, and some are filled entirely with
thorny masses, barricades that prevent the larger animals from penetrating to the nest chambers back in the rocks. More commonly,
however, the dens chosen are cracks and narrow clefts, over the en-

trances to which their thorny building material is piled to block the way or conceal them from enemies. Some of their building seems useless and merely the result of an instinct to pile up whatever material can be found of a size convenient for handling. These useless beginnings are not carried very far, however, and the successful houses are occupied and added to by generation after generation of industrious tenants.

Houses in the open or away from rocks are usually begun about the base of a hollow tree, over an old log or stump, or in the center of a thorny bush or bunch of cactus. A house begun in a bush or cactus patch is more apt to grow into a symmetrical structure than one built in a more sheltered situation. It often rises in a peaked dome 4 or 5 feet high and as wide across at the base, with numerous doorways at the sides or underneath the edges. Such a house changes form in time, settling with wear if unused, or if occupied by a vigorous family rising with the accumulation of constantly added material into a higher and sharper peak.

The building material used by the rats is dependent on what is available in the vicinity and varies endlessly. Sticks, stones, bones, cow chips, horse manure, cactus stems, thorny branches, and shells of the various fruits and seeds are the commonest materials used. In many cases, however, stray articles found about camp sites or houses are taken—empty cartridges, forks, spoons, pieces of dishes, bits of cloth, rope, or any material that can be conveniently transported. The small traps of the collector are frequently gathered up by the wood rats and placed on the houses to help swell their height.

No two houses are alike, and some are so different as to be worthy of separate description. In the San Andres Mountains Gaut described one house as built mainly of dried horse manure, pieces of spiny cactus, and branches of ocotillo and allthorn, the spiniest bushes of the region. On Cactus Flat, between the Gila and San Francisco Rivers, these rats had large houses in almost every bunch of bush cactus (*Opuntia schottii*), and here they were made almost entirely of short spiny branches of the cactus and as many dried cow chips as could be gathered within a convenient radius. This grove of densely spiny cactus was a veritable paradise for wood rats, as it evidently furnished them unusual protection from enemies and the houses were large and well inhabited. During a night's camp on this flat the writer set five traps at the five houses and secured a good specimen in each trap.

Only a few miles distant from Cactus Flat, at Glenwood, on the San Francisco River, the wood rats living in the brushy banks of the gulches had habits so different that the writer could hardly believe they were the same species. The houses were placed in weedy or brushy places or under trees and were often 3 or 4 feet high, conical, and sharp-peaked, with several holes entering the sides and base. The building material consisted of cow chips, sticks, bones, stones, leaves, and such scattered rubbish as could be gathered together. Well-worn runways led off on various sides to the feeding grounds in neighboring brush and weed patches. One nest was found 20 feet from the ground among the grapevines on a willow tree, a location unusual with this species but common to some others.

On the plains about Deming rat houses attributed to this species, but from which no specimens were collected, were abundant in the cactus, mesquite, and allthorn bushes, and many were unusually large. Some were estimated to contain 6 to 10 bushels of material. They were made largely of sticks, stones, cow chips, bones, cactus thorn bushes, and the dagger-pointed leaves of the Spanish-bayonet (*Yucca radiosa*). The houses placed in cactus and allthorn bushes especially bristle with thorny points. One house observed by the roadside where the usual building material was scarce was composed largely of dry cakes of mud from the ruts of the road where wagons had passed after a rain.

At Gallup one of the houses photographed was built around the base of a hollow juniper tree, and was composed of 2 or 3 bushels of sticks, stones, bones, cactus, old rags, bits of rope, and other rubbish. Under the tree was a big nest of finely shredded juniper bark like a great ball of tow. There was an opening in the side and a warm soft nest in the center just big enough for the rat to curl up in. A good supply of food was cached in the cavity near the nest, and all preparations were made for a comfortable winter. It seemed too bad to catch this thrifty young bachelor, but it was needed for a specimen and also to decide which species was to be credited with this well-built house and nest.

At San Rafael the white-throated wood rats were abundant in the rough and broken lava beds, which furnish innumerable cracks and crevices for safe retreats. Here the houses of sticks and rubbish were merely filled into the cracks to block the opening against enemies larger than themselves. In the limestone cliffs near by their usual accumulations of building material were packed into the corners to suit each situation and serve as protection where it was needed. Other houses were found on the valley slope under the cane cactus (*Opuntia arborescens*). In the Burro Mountains E. A. Goldman found their nests among the foothills about the base of tree yuccas and one at the base of a hollow oak. In the Rio Grande Valley other houses were found placed in dense clusters of saltbush (Atriplex), small-leafed sumac (*Rhus microphylla*), and the three-lobed sumac (*Rhus trilobata*). In the Chama Valley near Abiquiu their houses were often placed about the base of juniper trees, and the burrows entered the ground underneath and between the roots of the trees from all sides. In the cavity under one of these trees the writer found a soft nest of juniper bark and rabbit fur from which the rat was driven out. Other houses were located in patches of cane cactus. These various examples show the wide range of adaptation to environment and the strong home-building instinct of these wood rats.

The internal structure of the house varies somewhat but usually consists of one or several rooms or nest cavities, sometimes all above ground and again part or all below the surface and well back along burrows, which reach under tree roots or under rocks. The nests are usually of finely shredded bark or other soft plant fibers and are often thick and warm and always soft and clean. Sometimes they are covered over but more often are open and cup-shaped like a robin's nest, just large enough for the rat to curl up in. Some of the house chambers are filled with food of various kinds brought in to be eaten at leisure or stored for future use. The rats dig extensive burrows, when necessary, but sometimes build their houses on old mounds of kangaroo rats and use the burrows thus provided for their underground nest and storage chambers.

The wood rats are expert climbers. Much of their food is gathered from bushes, trees, and vines, and occasionally they are found living in hollow trees at considerable heights from the ground. At Silver City A. K. Fisher saw one thrust its head out of a woodpecker's hole in a nut pine 10 or 12 feet from the ground, and the writer has shot them in oaks 20 feet from the ground where they were running about in the branches. They even climb the spiniest cactus trees and run over the thousands of needle-pointed spines without the slightest hesitation or inconvenience, notwithstanding the fact that the soles of their feet are as naked and delicate as the palm of one's hand. Though they are constantly running over a great variety of cactus plants, gathering and eating their fruit or gnawing the fleshy stems for food, the writer has never detected a scratch or thorn in the delicate feet and noses of the hundreds of specimens collected.

The wood rats are usually nocturnal but not entirely so, as they are often seen running about in full daylight, especially early in the evening. Apparently they are active throughout the night, however, and in a vacant house or camp where they have taken up quarters it is difficult to sleep on account of the noisy disturbance that they keep up, dragging and rattling their material over the floors. So far as the writer is aware they make no vocal sound except a sharp scream of rage or pain when caught in a trap or injured. A thumping or drumming sound seems to be used in signaling one another. This is often attributed to the striking of their tails upon the floor but is really made by striking with the soles of the hind feet.

Food habits.—The food of these wood rats as shown by the supplies stored, the remains of meals, and the contents of stomachs examined includes a great variety of plants and not only fruits and seeds but a large proportion of green vegetation. They are inquisitive and always ready to test any new substance that may prove edible, and camp or household supplies are likely to prove acceptable to their taste. The green pulp of cactus plants is one of their staple articles of diet, and in dry seasons when other moist vegetation is scarce and the wood rats are abundant the cactus plants often suffer and some are actually killed.

At Las Palomas, in the Rio Grande Valley in October, 1909, E. A. Goldman reported two species of pricklypear, *Opuntia macrocentra* and *O. cyclodes*, with many of the flattened joints cut off or eaten and the spiny rims or crescent-shaped fragments left piled on the houses for building material or accumulated about the entrances to the burrows. Many of the half-eaten joints of the cactus are left to heal over and keep on growing in their mutilated state. At Santa Rosa and many other localities the writer has found the cane cactus girdled and many of the plants killed by the wood rats, which had eaten the outer pulp from the woody stems. Near Socorro other species of cactus were found eaten by the wood rats, including the low fleshy Echinocereus, in which the stems were hollowed out from near the ground and the whole inside of the plant eaten. Cactus fruit of almost every kind and description is eagerly eaten and forms in places a large part of the food. The half pulpy fruit of the cane cactus is eaten, but the juicy fruit of many species of pricklypear seems to be preferred. In many cases wood rats have been found so permeated with the purple juice of these fruits that the intestines and even the muscular walls of the abdomen were stained a bright purple. The fleshy part of the cactus fruit seems to be preferred, but the seeds are probably also eaten or else stored for future use. The base of yucca and agave leaves are often cut out and eaten, and the tender tips of tall or arborescent yucca plants are occasionally reached by cutting a spiral stairway through the leaves. The leaves of beargrass (Nolina) and sotol are also cut off and the white starchy bases eaten, while the tough blades are used for building material. The bark of numerous shrubs and trees is often stripped off and eaten to such an extent as to kill the plants. Mesquite, acacias, allthorns, ocotillo, sumac, and other bushes are thus killed, especially during the dry seasons. At Cuchillo in October, 1909, E. A. Goldman reported a 5-year-old apple tree from the base of which the bark had been gnawed by the wood rats in a way to injure seriously the tree. A runway passed close by, and the wood rats had stopped to feed on the green bark. A trap set at the gnawed place proved the gnawer to be of this species. As no other trees in the orchard were found injured this could not be considered a regular habit of the wood rats.

Green leaves of various plants are extensively eaten, but usually the green mass in the stomach contents gives no clue to the species of plants. Berries, fruits, seeds, nuts, and acorns are also acceptable foods. Apparently every species of acorn coming within their range is taken whenever found and the empty shells left about the wood-rat houses. At Fairview, E. A. Goldman found a trail leading from one of the houses to the base of a walnut tree, where the ground was covered by a heavy crop of fallen nuts, which the wood rats were apparently gathering; and along the lower slopes of the San Mateo Mountains he was told that they gathered large quantities of pinyon nuts. A Mexican told him of gathering several bushels of these nuts by going from one house to another and robbing the storerooms in the interiors. He said that as much as 2 quarts were often found at one place. Juniper berries of various species are also a favorite food, and both the sweet outer pulp and the kernel of the hard-shelled seeds are eaten. The writer has found considerable quantities of these berries, sometimes still attached to the green twigs but generally separate as if gathered up from the ground, stored in cavities near nests or in the houses themselves. Great quantities of the old juniper-seed shells are often found under or near wood-rat houses, where they have been eaten during previous seasons. Mesquite beans in the sugary pods are often gathered for food and stored in considerable quantities in the houses. The seeds of the little wild gourd are eaten and the gourd shells used for building material, but it seems doubtful if the wood rats eat the intensely bitter flesh of the gourds. For trap bait they will take bread, biscuits, pancake, bacon, and almost any kind of meat, cooked or raw, prunes, raisins, rolled oats, barley, or any kind of grain or nuts. They can even be caught in traps without bait by setting the trap in their doorways or across their well-used runways. Mearns (1907, p. 477) accuses them of carrying off boxes of pills, bird skins, hen's eggs, candles, soap, and other household articles.

Breeding habits.—The mammae of the females are arranged in two pairs between the hind legs, so close together that the rats have been described by a ranchman as "having four teats just like a cow." The young are usually two to four in number. Mearns records 3 females taken March 31 and October 3 containing 1, 2, and 3 fetuses, and 4 others without date, 2 of which would have given birth to 2 young and 2 others to 3 each. E. A. Goldman took 1 in Mangus Valley, September 22, containing 2 fetuses, and 2 seems to be the commoner number of young to a litter. Small young are often taken so late in the autumn months as to indicate that more than one litter is usually raised in a season. There are specimens of very small, or about one-quarter grown, young, evidently not a month old, taken March 2, May 10, July 1, 6, and 23, and September 28; and of about half-grown young, taken March 10, May 6, June 25, 28, and 29, July 1, 6, 11, 13, and 29, August 10, September 3, 7, 9, and 10, October 5, and 14, and November 1.

Hibernation.—Apparently none of the species of wood rats hibernate, and unlike hibernating mammals they never accumulate any considerable fat under the skin.

Economic status.—During 1907 wood rats were excessively numerous over the Deming Plain and in parts of the Rio Grande Valley, N. Mex., but no field work was done there that season to prove whether the species was *albigula* or *canescens*. The habits would imply the latter, but the following year the commoner species there was *albigula*. Much of the desert vegetation had been killed during their abundance, but in the following year they had been reduced to normal numbers. It is probable that under favorable conditions these wood rats would breed more rapidly and increase to numbers of serious consequences. They rarely do much harm to grain or other crops, however, and can not be considered a serious pest except in very local and exceptional cases. On the experimental cactus farm at Mesilla Park they have been very troublesome, and E. O. Wooton reports that it has been difficult to protect the cactus plants from their ravages. A dense growth of cactus almost invariably harbors an abundance of them, and if cactus culture should become an industry, the wood rat would be the most serious animal enemy to contend with. They are easily trapped or poisoned, however, and it is only necessary to remove their protective cover to accomplish their complete destruction. As game animals they may some time have a real value as their flesh is as tender, sweet, and delicious as young rabbit or quail. Their food habits are exemplary and in every way they lead cleanly and wholesome lives, in striking contrast to the filthy habits of the house rat. Mearns says (1907, p. 479) that the Hopi Indians kill and eat them and pronounce their flesh a delicacy; and that Captain Martinez, of the Army Engineer Corps of Mexico, informed him that—

physicians of northern Mexico commonly order broth made from the wood rat for the Indians and peasants whom they are called upon to treat, just as our physicians prescribe chicken broth and beef tea.

NEOTOMA ALBIGULA WARRENI Merriam

Warren's Wood Rat

Neotoma albigula warreni Merriam, Biol. Soc. Wash. Proc. 21: 143, 1908.

Type.—Collected at the Gaume ranch, Baca County, Colo., November 28, 1907, by Merritt Cary.

General characters.—Similar to *albigula* but slightly larger and with the upperparts more gray and less buffy. To some extent it resembles the still lighter gray *canescens* of adjoining territory, but the skull shows that it does not belong in that group.

Measurements.—Average of six adult topotypes: Total length, 313; tail, 133; hind foot, 36 millimeters.

Distribution and habitat.—Warren's wood rats are known only from a limited area in the northeastern corner of New Mexico and southeastern corner of Colorado in the Upper Sonoran Zone. (Fig. 31.) The Gaume ranch, a little north of the New Mexico line in Baca County, Colo., and Clayton, N. Mex., are the only localities at which specimens have been collected. In Colorado Cary says they inhabit the rough juniper country, and at Clayton, A. H. Howell collected three specimens in a rocky pasture near town.

General habits.—Cary says (1911, p. 116):

At Gaume's ranch, in Shell Rock Canyon, I found these wood rats living among rocks along the canyon walls or in hollow junipers on the upper rims of canyons, and occasionally in large stick houses reared against the bases of junipers in the dense growth well back from the canyon rims. Whether among the rocks or in the junipers, the nests were fortified with a varied assortment of spines and thorns, the sharp spiny bundles of the tree cactus (*Opuntia arborescens*) always predominating. The stick houses averaged about 2 feet in height and often contained several bushels of dead juniper branches. Judging from the signs observed at the nest entrances, the rats were subsisting largely at this time of year (November) upon the berries of *Juniperus monosperma*.

At Clayton, A. H. Howell merely records the three specimens taken in a rocky pasture near town and supposed them to be the white-throated, from which their habits apparently do not differ noticeably. In fact, the specimens from Clayton are considered by E. A. Goldman as somewhat intermediate between *albigula* and *warreni.*

NEOTOMA MEXICANA MEXICANA Baird

Mexican Wood Rat

Neotoma mexicana Baird, Acad. Nat. Sci. Phila. Proc. 7: 333, 1855.

Type.—Collected in mountains near Chihuahua City, Mexico, by John Potts, without date, but entered in United States National Museum Catalogue July 6, 1854.

General characters.—A medium-sized round-tailed wood rat, about the size of the white-throated, but with more olive-gray upper parts and only the surface of the lower parts white, the base of the fur being plumbeous on throat and breast.

Measurements.—Adults: Total length, 327; tail, 149; hind foot, 34 millimeters.

Distribution and habitat.—The Mexican wood rat barely reaches northward into southern New Mexico on both sides of the Rio Grande Valley. (Fig. 32.) Specimens from the Guadalupe Mountains on the New Mexico–Texas line and others from the Animas Mountains in the southwestern corner of the State were taken among the yellow pines in the Transition Zone.

General habits.—In the Guadalupe Mountains these wood rats live among the rocks and cliffs from the lower edge of the yellow pines up to the highest peaks practically throughout the Transition Zone. They seem to be entirely rock-dwelling animals, as no independent houses were found, and their building was confined to filling the seams in the rocks with sticks and rubbish. Dense woods and chaparral furnish abundant cover close up to the rocks, so there is less necessity for building than with species occupying the lower, more open country. In these mountains their food seems to consist largely of the abundant acorns, and along the lower border of their range of the sweet berries of the alligator juniper (*Juniperus pachyphloea*).

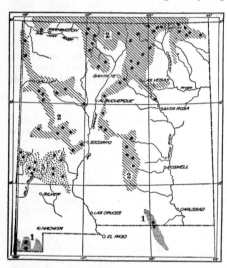

FIGURE 32.—Distribution of wood rats of the *mexicana* group in New Mexico: 1, *Neotoma mexicana mexicana;* 2, *N. mexicana fallax;* 3, *N. mexicana pinetorum.*

In the Animas Mountains E. A. Goldman and Birdseye caught them among the rocks from 6,800 feet to near the top of Animas Peak at about 8,000 feet. Most of the specimens were taken on the cold slope of the mountain throughout the Transition Zone; here also building operations were reduced to a minimum, usually being limited to a few sticks dropped among the cracks and clefts of the rocks. The dense chaparral of these mountains furnishes them a superficial cover, but evidently does not entirely protect them from enemies, as they were nowhere abundant.

NEOTOMA MEXICANA FALLAX Merriam

Colorado Wood Rat; Ka-it-za of the Navajo Indians

Neotoma fallax Merriam, Biol. Soc. Wash. Proc. 9: 123, 1894.

Type.—Collected at Gold Hill, Boulder County, Colo., November 1, 1889, by Denis Gale.

General characters.—Like *mexicana* but slightly larger; color clearer gray with less brownish. Readily distinguished from *albigula*, with which its range comes in contact, by the plumbeous base of the white hairs of throat and breast and by the darker gray of the upper parts.

Measurements.—Average of typical adults: Total length, 331; tail, 150; hind foot, 33 millimeters.

Distribution and habitat.—The Colorado wood rats are a mountain species, occupying the yellow-pine zone of all the mountains of northern New Mexico south to the Datil, San Mateo, and White Mountains; they fill the Transition Zone completely and where conditions are especially favorable occasionally penetrate into the lower edge of the Canadian Zone or down into the upper edge of the Upper

Sonoran. (Fig. 32.) They are generally confined to the rocks and cliffs but also build their houses over old logs or stumps or at the bases of hollow trees. Though mainly inhabiting the forest areas, they are not exclusively a forest animal except as brush and trees offer them protection. Great bare cliffs and long rock slides are their favorite haunts, and along some of the canyon walls they are particularly numerous.

General habits.—Like other species of the *mexicana* group they are not extensive builders but usually carry into their rocky dens a considerable mass of sticks, barks, stones, bones, leaves, and rubbish to close up openings and corners, thus rendering their retreats more secure. In brush heaps and around old logs they sometimes show great skill and industry in building houses. Over the yellow pine top of the Chuska Mountains they were common both in the cliffs and in the woods about old logs. In the cliffs they piled up sticks, stones, bark, cones, and rubbish at the entrance to their caves; and stuffed leaves and branches of green plants, evidently for food, into the corners about their nests. In the woods they built houses somewhat like those of the bushy-tailed wood rat, piling up heaps of rubbish under and around old logs. One house that the writer photographed was under a big yellow pine log lying 2 or 3 feet above the ground. The house consisted of about 10 bushels of sticks, pieces of bark, pine cones, and leaves. There were several doorways, and deep in the middle was a warm nest of bark fiber. Around the outside and in all the cavities of the house were stuffed well-cured green leaves of Gambel's oak, twigs and leaves and fruit of wild rose, Ceanothus, Frasera, and a quantity of dried toadstools. After examining the house the writer caught the wood rat to make sure of the species and found it to be an adult female. Traps were kept at the house for several nights but only the one was caught. This was late in October, and the little animal had evidently made good provision for a comfortable winter.

In the Manzano Mountains, Gaut reported these wood rats abundant throughout the Transition Zone, where houses were found about the roots of trees, hollow logs, and occasional brush piles. At Eastview sawmill dens were noticed about the logs and piles of lumber, and one of the employees of the mill brought in a fine specimen that he had killed under his cabin and claimed had been living there for several months and causing him considerable annoyance. All the deserted cabins visited in these mountains were occupied by one or more of these wood rats, as could be seen at a glance on entering them. Sticks, stones, bones, and leaves were found piled up in corners, under floors, and in boxes and old stoves, and wood-rat tracks were seen crossing and recrossing the dusty floors.

In the mountains along the headwaters of the Pecos River the wood rats were common throughout the Transition Zone, and specimens were taken from 7,400 to 8,500 feet altitude. At the fork of the Pecos and Mora Creeks they were common in the cliffs and in heaps of drift on the river banks, and in the narrow canyon they were frequently caught in traps set on old logs at the edge of the water. They make dens in the cliffs and among the rocks, usually marked by heaps of rubbish and the remains of food, while copious deposits of excrement cover some shelves or fill some niches in the rocks, and the edges of the rocks are whitened with the calcite deposit from their urine.

In the Raton Range, A. H. Howell found them in every cliff and ledge, extending even up to the summit of Emory Peak, and on Sierra Grande he says they range well up toward the summit, their signs being seen in the cliff at the upper edge of timber at 9,000 feet. He also found them common in the canyon near Clayton, where they had evidently followed down the canyon walls well into the Upper Sonoran Zone; in the sandstone cliffs at Catskill and Vermejo Park, and in Road Canyon, living under logs and old stumps as well as in the rocks. Hollister collected them in the Mount Taylor, Zuni, and Datil Ranges. In the San Juan Valley, Clarence Birdseye found them common along the river flats, living under logs, in deserted outbuildings, and about stables and stockyards. Near Fruitland he caught one in a meat-baited skunk trap set near a stable, and one in an old deserted henhouse surrounded by cottonwoods and brush. The one in the henhouse had built a large nest of bits of manure, straw, branches of wild rose, rabbit brush (Chrysothamnus), and other bushes between the roof and some old roosts. In the higher part of the Zuni Mountains Goldman found them common in rocky places from 8,200 feet, among yellow pines, up to the summit of the range. He caught one at a hole under a rock about which nearly a bushel of freshly cut leaves of Rocky Mountain maple (*Acer glabrum*) had been piled. In the Magdalena Mountains he took specimens from 6,700 to 9,200 feet and found their nests nearly to the top of the range. In the San Mateo Mountains he also took specimens from 7,800 to 9,000 feet and saw signs of their occurrence near the summits of the peaks.

Food habits.—The food of this species consists of a great variety of green plants, berries, fruits, seeds, nuts, acorns, mushrooms, and almost anything in the way of camp supplies of an edible nature. In the Pecos Mountains a great number of pine, spruce, and balsam cones were found in their houses, evidently carried in for the seeds they contained. Acorn shells are always abundant about their nests, if oak trees grow in the vicinity. Along the lower edge of their range pine nuts and juniper berries furnish food, and both the fruit and pulp of cactus plants are eaten when available. Much of their range, however, is above the limits of cactus, so that this does not form a great part of their general food. Their stomachs usually contain some green food, and the abundance of green leaves cut and carried into the houses indicate that these cured plants are an important winter food stored up in the form of hay. Oak, maple, poplar, rose, blueberry, and Holodiscus and Frasera leaves have been found in their houses.

In one large house a quantity of dried mushrooms was found, evidently gathered for the winter food supply. Around camps they will eat anything from rolled barley to a cake of soap, and for trap bait they eagerly accept grain, bread, nuts, and meat of any kind— fresh, cooked, or dried. They never become fat but always seem plump and well fed, probably owing to their wide range of food materials, some of which are available at all seasons.

Breeding habits.—The usual number of young in this species seems to be 2 or 3, with probably a maximum of 4 to correspond with the number of mammae. Cary records a female, collected May 1, near Loveland, Colo., that contained 3 small fetuses, while a female that he surprised in her nest among the rafters of a cabin near Boulder on July 23 glided silently from the nest with two young about quarter grown clinging to her teats. The breeding season seems to begin early in spring and to continue through the summer, as young about quarter and half grown and others almost full grown are taken during July, August, and September. It is probable that more than one litter is raised in a season, although part of the variation in age of young may be due to irregularity in the time of breeding.

Economic status.—The range of the Colorado wood rats is mainly in the mountains above the level of agriculture or permanent habitation, so that economically they are of little importance, although they often prove very annoying and cause some slight losses to campers and temporary residents in the mountain forests. A camp or cabin in the woods within their range rarely escapes their notice, and their building instincts are at once appealed to by the elaborate structure with great hollow spaces inside that need only to be filled up with sticks and stones to make ideal quarters. They proceed at once to put in such improvements as they think suitable and, aside from filling up bunks, cupboards, stoves, and pantries with rubbish, often partly destroy such clothing and furniture as may have been left in the buildings. Food is almost certain to be carried away unless suspended from the roof by wires. But a few traps or a little poisoned grain placed in a box in one corner, with a hole in the side and marked " poison " to prevent accident, would in most cases obviate the annoyance which they thus cause.

In the San Juan Valley, Clarence Birdseye was told that these wood rats were one of the favorite foods of the Navajo Indians. If some of the early explorers who starved to death in the country where they abound had known how easily they could have supplied themselves with an abundance of such delicate and delicious small game their journeys might have been rendered comparatively safe.

NEOTOMA MEXICANA PINETORUM Merriam

San Francisco Mountain Wood Rat

Neotoma pinetorum Merriam, Biol. Soc. Wash. Proc. 8: 111, 1893.

Type.—Collected at San Francisco Mountain, Ariz., August 16, 1889, by Vernon Bailey.

General characters.—The largest of the three forms of the *mexicanus* group occurring in New Mexico. In color it is darker and browner over the upper parts than either *mexicana* or *fallax.* The lower parts are pure white on the surface over the gray or plumbeous base of fur.

Measurements.—Average of 4. adults from the type locality: Total length, 357; tail, 164; hind foot, 36.5 millimeters.

Distribution and habitat.—The San Francisco Mountain wood rats inhabit the yellow-pine forests of the Mogollon and White Mountains, from the Mimbres and Black Range west to San Francisco Mountain, Ariz. (Fig. 32.) They even reach to some extent into the Canadian Zone, but seem not to come below the edge of the Transition.

General habits.—In the Mogollon Mountains they are common from about 7,000 feet to near the tops of the highest peaks. On Willow Creek, one of the headwaters of the Gila, the writer caught them at 8,500 feet among rocks and under old logs in the woods. There were also nests and signs of their presence in old cabins and often in heaps of drift along the creek. Some were caught in traps set on logs in the open woods where no rocks or wood-rat houses were to be seen, indicating that the animals wander a considerable distance from their dens. E. A. Goldman collected specimens near the top of the mountains and reported their houses of sticks and leaves under logs, among rocks, and around deserted buildings. One nest that he found under a log near a stream was more than 10 feet in length, built mainly of branches of willow, wild rose, hop vines, and fragments of various plants and leaves. In the Tularosa Mountains the writer found stick houses evidently of this species, built under the shelter of spruce and fir trees high up on the cold slope of the mountains but had no opportunity to collect specimens. One of these houses was unusually high and symmetrical and independent of any protection from logs and trees. It was composed mainly of sticks and leaves, and showed evidence of being freshly built and well occupied. In the Mimbres Mountains two of these wood rats were caught near the head of Powder Horn Canyon just below the lower edge of the Canadian Zone. Here they were living on a thickly timbered slope and in large houses of sticks and leaves built over big logs in the woods. Well-worn trails led from the houses down to the little stream near by, and the rats were caught in traps set along these trails. At camp on the head of the Rio Mimbres they were common among the rocks, under old logs and brush piles, in stick houses at the base of trees, or in clusters of cactus, and also in the several vacant cabins along the stream. In food and general habits *pinetorum* probably does not differ materially from the more widely ranging and better-known *fallax*.

NEOTOMA LEPIDA LEPIDA Thomas

Thomas's Wood Rat

Neotoma lepida Thomas, Ann. and Mag. Nat. Hist. (6) 12: 235, 1893.

Type locality.—Unknown.

General characters.—The smallest wood rat in New Mexico—a little soft, silky-haired, fuzzy-tailed species of the *desertorum* group. Though not approaching the condition in the bushy-tailed wood rats, the round tail is much more hairy than in the *mexicana* or *albigula* groups. In color the upper parts are bright buffy gray, the lower parts buff or whitish, often with a pure-white throat, or with a median white stripe on the throat; the feet are white; tail clear gray all around or sometimes slightly lighter below.

Measurements.—Total length, 286; tail, 136; hind foot, 29 millimeters.

Distribution and habitat.—Thomas's wood rat is mainly an Arizona species extending into the northwestern corner of New Mexico, where it apparently occupies the whole Great San Juan Valley south to the Zuni Mountains. It occupies the sandstone cliffs and canyon walls in the open valley country of the Upper Sonoran Zone. (Fig. 33.)

General habits.—Practically all of the specimens collected were taken in sandstone cliffs around the valley borders. At Gallup they were common, but so closely associated with the white-throated and Colorado wood rats that the habits and houses of the three could not be readily distinguished. Hollister collected specimens at both Wingate and Fort Wingate and here also found them associated with the white-throated. At another camp 35 miles north of Bluewater fresh wood-rat signs were noticed in the rocks close to where a camp-fire was built. After supper the writer placed a trap in the rocks and a little later hearing it snap took out one of the Thomas's wood rats and reset the trap. In the morning it contained a white-throated wood rat. This seems to indicate that the two species have similar habits and associate on friendly terms. At Blanco on the San Juan River Birdseye collected one specimen and reported that they were quite common in the sandstone cliffs around the village.

In passing over the San Juan Valley the writer saw many wood-rat h o u s e s about the base of juniper trees and in cactus patches in the open, but no specimens were collected. Over the wide valley south of Chaco Canyon their houses were common in the extensive beds of the fine-spined pricklypear. These were built entirely of cactus, several bushels of the spiny pads being heaped up in a place. One that the writer tried to dig out proved to have a hollow space and numerous holes under it, but he did not succeed in capturing any of its occupants. There was no water for a 2-day journey, and as it was necessary to make a dry camp that night, he could not remain longer to collect specimens, so the identity of the species is in doubt. These houses very likely belonged to *lepida*, however.

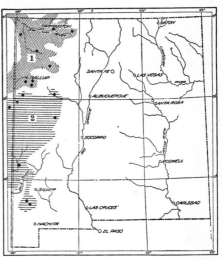

FIGURE 33.—Distribution of wood rats of the *lepida* group in New Mexico: 1, *Neotoma lepida lepida;* 2, *N. lepida stephensi*

The habits of *lepida* are, for the present, hopelessly confused with other species, and no generalization can be safely made in regard to them. Juniper berries seem to furnish a large part of the food of all the wood rats of this region and probably also of this species.

At Fort Wingate A. K. Fisher collected three half-grown young on July 5 and 6, 1892, so nearly of a size that they evidently were all of one litter. This is practically all the evidence available of the number of young and of the breeding habits, but on general principles they can be assumed to be similar to those of other closely related species.

NEOTOMA LEPIDA STEPHENSI Goldman

Stephens's Wood Rat

Neotoma stephensi Goldman, Biol. Soc. Wash. Proc. 18:32, 1905.

Type.—Collected in Hualpai Mountains, Ariz., July 1, 1902, by Frank Stephens.

General characters.—Size slightly larger and colors darker than *lepida;* fur soft and silky; tail round but well-haired and not distinctly bicolor. Upper parts dark buffy gray; feet and lower parts white; belly sometimes buffy but throat usually pure white. Tail dark gray above; slightly lighter gray below.

Measurements.—Adults: Total length, 305; tail, 135; hind foot, 31 millimeters.

Distribution and habitat.—Fuzzy-tailed Stephens's wood rat occupies the juniper and nut pine plateau region of middle-western New Mexico and westward through Arizona. (Fig. 33.) It is an Upper Sonoran species of a half-wooded canyon and lava-rock country. It shows as striking a color adaptation to its dark soil and rock environment as does the bright buffy *lepida* to its sandstone cliffs and valleys.

General habits.—This apparently is not an abundant species in New Mexico, where it occupies the same general region with the more abundant and larger *albigula*. In the Burro Mountains E. A. Goldman found Stephens's wood rat common, however, and collected specimens along the cliffs, about old logs and brush piles, from 6,400 feet to the summit of the mountains. Here they were living in stick nests placed about logs or brush, and in places their burrows entered the ground about the bases of rocks with many sticks piled about the entrances. In the cliffs the entrances to the burrows were often bare or marked by only a few sticks. Many well-worn trails extended from the houses and burrows over the surface of the ground or along the base of the rocks where they ran from one entrance to another.

At Glenwood on the San Francisco River they were evidently common along the canyon walls, but only one specimen was taken. On the Zuni River just below the Arizona line several were collected along the sides of a rocky ridge bordering the valley. Hollister collected specimens at Burley near the Datil Mountains and at Grant, but in both localities the species was so closely associated with the white-throated that the notes on habits are uncertain. In the Burro Mountains E. A. Goldman found freshly cut twigs of mountain-mahogany (Cercocarpus), Ceanothus, and oak in the rat houses, but whether these were building materials or the remains of food is uncertain. One of the specimens that he collected late in September contained two small fetuses.

NEOTOMA CINEREA OROLESTES Merriam

Colorado Bushy-tailed Wood Rat; Hena of the Taos Indians

Neotoma orolestes Merriam, Biol. Soc. Wash. Proc. 9: 128, 1894.

Type.—Collected in Saguache Valley, Colo., August 13, 1892, by J. Alden Loring.

General characters.—The largest wood rat in New Mexico, with very large ears, long mustaches, and wide, bushy, almost squirrellike tail. In adults the tail is usually an inch wide and the mustache about 4 inches long on each side of the nose. The upperparts are dark cinnamon gray, and the top of the tail dusky, or clear dark gray; the feet and underparts, including lower surface of tail, pure white. The young are slaty gray above with less bushy tail.

Measurements.—Average of adults: Total length, 394; tail, 169; hind foot, 40 millimeters.

Distribution and habitat.—The Colorado bushy-tailed wood rats (pl. 9, B) are mountain animals occupying the Transition and the Canadian Zones of the Sangre de Cristo, San Juan, and Jemez Mountains of north-central New Mexico and the mountains of Colorado and northward. (Fig. 34.) In the Pecos River Mountains specimens were taken from 8,000 feet at the junction of the Pecos and Mora Rivers up to 11,200 feet at the east base of Pecos Baldy and their signs were found up to 11,600 feet. Apparently they range throughout the width of the Transition and the Canadian Zones, but are either more common or more commonly taken in the Transition Zone. In the Taos Mountains they were taken up to 11,400 feet, and their nests and signs were seen under rocks up to timberline.

General habits. — These are rock and forest dwelling animals of the mountain slopes. The great stretches of slide rock that accumulate along the bases of cliffs on the mountain sides are almost invariably occupied by them, as are the cliffs and caves. Where no rocks are available they often build large houses of sticks and leaves over old logs or stumps or around the base of hollow trees and leave well-worn runways under brush and logs through the woods. They are often caught in traps

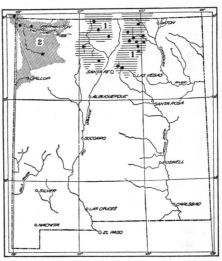

FIGURE 34.—Distribution of bushy-tailed wood rats in New Mexico: 1, *Neotoma cinerea orolestes;* 2, *N. cinerea arizonae*

set on logs, and the fact that they quickly find a cabin left vacant in the woods indicates that they are extensive travelers and not closely bound by home ties. Along the edges of Moreno Valley the writer found a number of their large houses in pine and spruce woods. One built over some hollow logs and another over a big bowlder, were 5 or 6 feet high and about as broad, with numerous holes and chambers in the sides and underneath the edges. They were composed of sticks, chips, cones, leaves, and much refuse from food material. At one of them a pair of adult wood rats were caught that were evidently occupying the house together. In an old cabin near camp on the east slope of the Taos Mountains one had made a very comfortable and convenient home by piling heaps of sticks and chips in three of the corners of the room and filling an old box with the green leaves and seed pods of various plants. In one corner on a beam close to the roof was a large soft nest made of wool, feathers, and a chewed-up gunny sack. It was as large as one's head, neatly built with a cup-shaped opening at the top, where the rat curled up to sleep.

Apparently every old cabin in the woods is occupied by one or more of these animals, as can at once be ascertained by the characteristic odor as well as by the piles of sticks and chips in corners, under floors, or in old bunks, and by the scattered pellets and the little pudgy round tracks in the dust or ashes on the floors.

Near Chama in the San Juan Mountains Loring found where one lived in an old slaughterhouse. There were two cup-shaped nests of soft dry grass on a board up near the rafters, and along this board, which was about 1 foot wide and 5 feet long, were distributed some 2 bushels of rubbish, sticks, cows' horns, and hoofs. He caught one of the wood rats in an abandoned camp and another in a marten trap, which he had set in the woods and baited with meat and crows' feathers.

High up in the Taos Mountains they were abundant everywhere among the big broken bowlders and the steep slide rock along the slopes, and in such locations they persisted in getting into traps set for martens and weasels. Usually in such rocky situations they do not build very extensive houses, but their presence can be quickly determined by piles of sticks filling the spaces between the rocks and by their characteristic black, cylindrical pellets and the white capping of the edges and points of sheltered rocks.

In the Jemez Mountains the writer found them from 8,000 feet in Santa Clara Canyon up to 11,000 feet on the highest peaks. Their nests were readily distinguished from those of the white-throated and the Colorado wood rats by their larger sticks and green branches. Frequently a bushel of well-cured green leaves and branches were found on a house or packed in among the rocks for winter food. These wood rats are excellent climbers and not only delight in running over the walls and rafters of cabins but also in climbing over rocks or up the trunks and branches of trees.

At one of the camps on the headwaters of the Costilla River, when the camp wagon had stood under some trees for a couple of nights, one of these rats took up its quarters in the wagon. On being disturbed it jumped out of the wagon, ran up the nearest tree and along the branches to another tree, and hid in a thick place high up in the small branches, climbing as nimbly and as rapidly as a squirrel or chipmunk.

In Colorado Cary reported that at one of his camps the wood rats continually climbed the tent walls and that in the mines the men told him that they often passed them on the ladders.

Very little is known of the winter habits of these animals except as they occasionally come into unoccupied hunters' or miners' camps. They do not become fat or hibernate for the cold weather, but much of the material stored is evidently intended for winter food, and in the well-sheltered caves and rock slides they doubtless have safe and comfortable winter quarters.

Food habits.—These bushy-tailed wood rats are as omnivorous as other members of the group, feeding on various green plants, seeds, nuts, berries, fruits, and any supplies which they can pick up around camps or cabins. Pine and spruce cones are often found in the houses, but whether these are gathered for food or merely for building material is uncertain. Acorn shells are often found scattered about, and mushrooms packed away in their houses may be stored for food. There are few things about camp that they will not eat or carry away if opportunity offers. All camp foods are welcome, while saddle strings and harness straps if left within reach are cut off and carried away for building material or as a possible food supply. Traps baited with rolled oats or any kind of grain, or with pieces of biscuit, dried fruit, and cooked or raw meat will catch them with as much certainty as if the traps had been baited with the nuts and seeds to which they are accustomed.

Breeding habits.—There is little known of the breeding habits of this species except that specimens of quarter and half grown young are collected through July and August and even into September. Young that are almost full grown are also collected through July and August, and most of the young in September and October are nearly full grown. It is doubtful whether more than one litter is raised in a season. The number in a litter is probably two to four, as is usual with other species of the genus with the same number and arrangement of mammae.

Economic status.—These animals are of practically no economic importance except as they cause occasional annoyance in camps or houses and destroy food and other supplies. Fortunately they are never numerous, and after one or two are caught in a locality others are not likely to appear for some time.

NEOTOMA CINEREA ARIZONAE Merriam

Arizona Bushy-tailed Wood Rat; Kar la of the Hopi Indians (Fisher)

Neotoma arizonae Merriam, Biol. Soc. Wash. Proc. 8: 110, 1893.

Type.—Collected in Keam Canyon, Ariz., May 21, 1888, by J. Sullivan.
General characters.—Slightly smaller than *orolestes* with less spreading bushy tail and lighter coloration. Upperparts clear rich buff; top of the tail ashy gray; feet and underparts pure white.
Measurements.—Adults: Total length, 347; tail, 146; hind foot, 36 millimeters.

Distribution and habitat.—The Arizona bushy-tailed wood rat comes into the northwestern corner of New Mexico in the San Juan Valley in the Upper Sonoran Zone. (Fig. 34.) Clarence Birdseye collected specimens at Farmington and Shiprock, and the writer took one at the Pueblo Bonito in Chaco Canyon. They live in an open desert-valley country, usually in sandstone cliffs and ledges.

General habits.—Birdseye described their nests among the rocks as composed of flat pieces of sandstone often 4 or 5 inches across, actually heavier than the wood rat, as well as of cattle and horse manure, bones of various animals, and the stems of plants, conspicuous among which being the spinescent branches of saltbush (*Atriplex confertifolia* and *A. canescens*), and some pieces of cactus. The nests were often built under fallen rocks at the base of cliffs or in crevices of the walls. At Shiprock he found a large house in the side of a dry wash and although there was abundant sign around the house he succeeded in catching only one specimen in several nights' trapping.

In the ruins of the prehistoric Pueblo Bonito in Chaco Canyon these wood rats were abundant. They were the only occupants of an old adobe house in which the writer camped one night late in

October to escape the cold wind that was blowing, and all night long they kept running over the floor and over his bed. Occasionally he would give the canvas a kick and send one flying, and then the animal would stay away for an hour or so but at each return it would wake him up by a great rattle and scratching. The house was built on one of the ruins of the old pueblo, and the wood rats came in at numerous holes under the floor. The white streaks on the old ruins and cliffs were geologic in suggestion and may have dated back to the days of an industrious Indian population of the canyon. As the range of these wood rats lies within the region of cliff dwellings in northwestern New Mexico, southeastern Utah, and northeastern Arizona, where they now inhabit both the cliffs and ruins, they were doubtless animals of decided economic importance in prehistoric times. They may have been important as food animals, but more probably were serious pests that the food-storing aborigines had to contend with in protecting their winter supplies.

CLETHRIONOMYS GAPPERI GALEI (Merriam)

Colorado Red-backed Mouse

Evotomys galei Merriam, North Amer. Fauna No. 4, p. 23, 1890.

Type.—Collected at Ward, Boulder County, Colo., July 14, 1889, by Denis Gale.

General characters.—The red-backed mice are small, compactly built, short-tailed, short-eared, and short-footed ground-dwelling rodents. The fur is long and soft, almost concealing the ears and general form. The whole back from the middle of the forehead to the tail is bright hazel or yellowish brown; the sides and face are gray, and the lower parts white.

Measurements.—An adult male from the type locality measures in total length, 146; tail, 40; hind foot, 18 millimeters.

Distribution and habitat.—The Colorado red-backed mice extend down through the mountains of northern New Mexico to the Pecos and Jemez Mountains, where the species reaches its southern limit. (Fig. 35.) One specimen was taken just south of Pecos Baldy at 11,000 feet in dense spruce woods. In the Taos Mountains others were collected from 10,700 feet to 11,500 feet, and in the Jemez Mountains a few were caught on the cold slope of Goat Peak at 8,600 feet. These are the only records for New Mexico, but they indicate a range throughout the Canadian Zone in the high mountains east and west of the Rio Grande Valley. They can hardly be said to be common in this area, however, as thorough trapping in many suitable locations failed to produce specimens.

General habits.—Although related to the meadow mice and having somewhat similar habits, these red-backed mice belong to the woods and not to the meadows. In the Pecos Mountains the one specimen secured after much trapping was taken under a log in dry spruce woods. In the Taos Mountains a few miles south of Twining they were caught in a similar location under logs and rocks in a dense grove of Engelmann spruce and corkbark fir at 10,700 feet altitude; and again, in similar situations a few miles farther south near the little lake at the head of Lake Fork at 11,500 feet. In the Jemez Mountains one adult and two young were caught under logs in the dry spruce and fir forest at 8,600 feet on the north slope of one of the main peaks.

In places their little runways may be traced along the surface of the ground under logs or from one log to another and occasionally out in the grass and weed patches where they feed. Generally, however, the ground is so open that they do not make runways or leave any visible trace of their presence, unless it be the half-eaten stems of grass and weeds near or under the logs or rocks where they live, or at the entrance of their little burrows, which enter the mellow woods earth.

Their nests are rarely found on the surface of the ground, and it is probable that the underground winter nests are used during the short cool summer at these high altitudes.

They do not become fat or hibernate and apparently do not lay up stores of food for winter. Their stomachs usually contain the remains of finely masti-cated vegetation, part of which is green. Often a large part is white, indi-cating that it is selected from the blanched tender base of grasses and plants at the surface of the ground. Such food is just as accessible under the snows of winter as in sum-mer, and with the advan-tage of perfect protection from enemies above. It is not improbable that even the roots of plants are eaten in winter either from the burrows or from close to the surface of the ground. The mice are fond of rolled oats or any kind of grain used for trap bait and also feed on seeds of various plants when they are to be

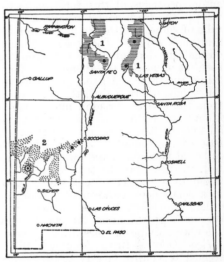

FIGURE 35.—Distribution of the red-backed mice in New Mexico: 1, *Clethrionomys gapperi galei;* 2, *C. limitis.* Type locality circled

had. The stomach contents, however, indicate that the bulk of the food is composed of growing vegetation.

Breeding habits.—The mammae of the females are arranged in 4 pairs—2 inguinal and 2 pectoral. The usual number of young seems to be four to six, but the writer has only the one record of four from New Mexico, that of a female caught in the Jemez Mountains September 2 contained four half-grown fetuses. At the same time two half-grown young were caught.

CLETHRIONOMYS LIMITIS (BAILEY)

SOUTHERN RED-BACKED MOUSE

Evotomys limitis Bailey, Biol. Soc. Wash. Proc. 26: 133, 1913.

Type.—Collected in Mogollon Mountains on Willow Creek at 8,500 feet alti-tude, October 27, 1906, by Vernon Bailey.

General characters.—This southern form of the red-backed mouse is distin-guished from *galei* by larger size and duller and darker coloration. The difference is conspicuous in the skulls, which are much larger, with relatively more elongated braincase.

Measurements.—The type, an adult male, measures in total length, 162; tail, 42, hind foot, 20 millimeters.

Distribution and habitat.—Specimens of the southern red-backed mouse taken in the Mogollon, San Mateo, and Magdalena Mountains of New Mexico and the White Mountains of Arizona indicate a range filling the Canadian Zone of this southern mountain region. (Fig. 35.) The range is probably somewhat interrupted by lower country lying between some of these mountains, but the characters of the species seem to be fairly uniform. It is widely separated by low country from *galei* and all the Rocky Mountain forms and marks the most southern distribution of the genus in America.

General habits.—At the type locality the writer collected seven adult specimens of this form on October 26 and 27, 1906. These were in the fresh winter pelage, as at that time there had been two falls of snow, and the ice had frozen over the creek thick enough to bear one's weight. They seemed to be abundant in the spruce woods on the cold slope of the deep canyon, and more would probably have been taken but for the abundance of other mice that were constantly filling the traps. All the specimens were secured under old logs in the woods, where their little runways could usually be distinguished from those of the meadow mice along the border. In the Mogollon Mountains E. A. Goldman caught one in Copper Canyon at an altitude of 9,000 feet, where the vegetation was mainly character-istic of the Canadian Zone; and in the San Mateo Mountains he collected two adults and two half-grown young October 5 at 10,000 feet altitude near the top of San Mateo Peak. One of these was taken in a thicket of currant, meadowrue, holodiscus, and grass in a small nook between rock slides on the southwest slope. The others were taken in aspen thickets on the summit of the peak where the undergrowth was largely honeysuckle (*Lonicera albiflora*). They were living in holes in the ground among the rocks and leaves.

Food habits.—In the Mogollon Mountains the food of these mice seemed to consist largely of the seeds of small plants that were being cut down along their runways. Their stomach contents showed little green vegetation. They were eager for the rolled oats used for trap bait, as was proved by the stomach contents of those caught.

MICROTUS MORDAX MORDAX (Merriam)

Rocky Mountain Meadow Mouse; Pah-klu'-lena-na of the Taos Indians

Arvicola (*Mynomes*) *mordax* Merriam, North Amer. Fauna No. 5, p. 61, 1891.

Type.—Collected at Sawtooth (or Alturas) Lake, Idaho, September 29, 1890, by C. Hart Merriam and Vernon Bailey.

General characters.—Ears mainly concealed in the fur; tail long, about one-third of total length; fur coarse; color of upper parts light brownish gray; sides clear gray; lower parts silvery gray.

Measurements.—Average of adult males: Total length, 186; tail, 64; hind foot, 21 millimeters; adult female: 182; 60; 20 millimeters, respectively.

Distribution and habitat.—The Rocky Mountain meadow mice are common in most of the high mountains of New Mexico, as well as throughout the Rocky Mountain region. (Fig. 36.) They range through the Canadian Zone and extend into the Hudsonian to some extent. In many places they follow down along the banks of cold mountain streams well into and even through the Transition Zone, but in such cases are almost invariably associated with an abundance of the Canadian Zone plants, which also follow down the cold stream borders. In the Taos Mountains specimens were taken from 8,200 to 12,500 feet and in the Pecos Mountains from 8,000 to 11,600 feet.

General habits.—Within their range they are generally the most abundant meadow mice of the mountain areas. The cold creek banks and frosty mountain meadows are their favorite haunts. The borders of ice-cold springs and meadows where spring-made brooks trickle through or larger streams go roaring over bowlder beds are almost certain to be marked with their burrows and runways. The borders of temporary streams coming from melting snow banks are often occupied by them, and when the streams become dry they dis-perse through the green vegetation and are often found at considerable distances from any water, even living under old logs and brush heaps in the edge of the forest, where they depend upon green vegetation for moisture until the early snows bury them for the winter. Where water is abundant they are semiaquatic in habits, and their runways often lead into the edge of the spring or creek, coming out again on the opposite bank. They swim and dive with perfect freedom and make their trails through marshy ground half in the water and half out. Numerous burrows, many of which are old and others freshly

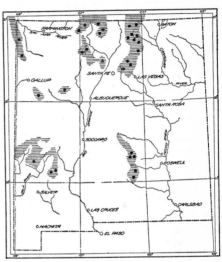

FIGURE 36.—Distribution of Rocky Mountain meadow mouse, *Microtus mordax mordax*, in New Mexico

excavated, penetrate the banks and lead to underground nests and chambers or into the hollows in the banks, from which they branch out in all directions to different feeding grounds, with numerous roads and short cuts to their burrows. The little roads leading over the surface of the ground from one burrow to another or off through the green grass are usually well worn and if much used are smooth and well kept. They are not merely paths worn by the repeated passing of feet, but deliberately made roads from which growing vegetation is cut and the old fallen mat of vege-tation lifted high enough to make tunnels between it and the smooth surface of the ground. Where there is an abundance of both fresh and dry vegetation their runways are well concealed, but in many places they are conspicuous from above as one looks closely down into the short grass and over the mountain plants. Their appearance generally shows whether they are fresh and well used, but better evidence is to be had in the abundance of cut plants scattered along the borders on the feeding grounds and the little dark-green pellets of excrement at the sides of the runways.

In the Pecos Mountains during July and August of 1903 they were found rather scarce through the Canadian Zone, but the surface of the ground over the mountain slopes was often marked with a network of their runways and perforated by numerous burrows. Evidently they had been much more numerous during the previous season and through the winter, but for some reason their numbers had been reduced below the normal. Such fluctuations in the abundance of these mice are very common and probably due to various causes. In winter they apparently spread out over more of the open ground under the protecting cover of snow, and with the disappearance of snow again gather into areas of better cover and where the spring vegetation furnishes the favorite foods. With the dry seasons they also gather more especially along the watercourses or into the marshes. In mountains with dry open slopes, such as the Capitans and Sacramentos, they seem to get through the dry season without any water other than the dew, occasional rains, and the moisture they get from the abundant succulent plants. In such locations they gather into the moist hollows or under logs in the cool, damp woods. In the Capitan Mountains Gaut collected a few specimens in high weeds and grass about a temporary rainwater pond near the summit of the range. Others were collected at cold springs on the different slopes of the mountains, and at such places they were found about old logs not far from the edge of water holes. In the White Mountains they were common along the streams of the lower slope, and abundant signs, probably of this species, were found to the summit of Sierra Blanca. In the Taos Mountains they were found on both slopes along all of the streams, and in Moreno Valley were especially numerous in a little springy meadow at the foot of the mountain slope.

A. H. Howell took specimens at 9,000 feet on Costilla Pass, and the writer found them abundant along streams in the Culebra Mountains. In the San Juan Mountains none were found in the parklike openings over the top of the range, but unmistakable traces were seen in the marshes on the west slope. Loring took one near Chama by a little stream in the meadow, and Gaut collected one on the headwaters of the Chama River and another near an aspen grove at Horse Lake, on the Jicarilla Indian Reservation. Other specimens were collected along the streams in the Jemez Mountains. In the Canadian Zone areas of Mount Taylor and the Zuni Mountains the writer found evident traces of this species, although none was collected. On the Chuska Mountains they were abundant on cold slopes and about springs along the top of the range. Here they were living on dry slopes as well as in wet places, and their runways and cuttings were abundant among the logs and under the dense grass and weedy vegetation of the upper gulches. In the Mogollon and Mimbres Mountains they were also abuundant in the Canadian Zone and were often found in woods and on waterless slopes, as well as along the margins of streams.

Food habits.—The food of these little animals consists almost entirely of green vegetation, largely grass. Their stomach contents usually show a green mass of finely ground food, and even their excrement is dark green. The stomach contents usually can not be identified, and the only clue to the species of plants eaten is found in the remains of those partly eaten on the feeding grounds. These include a great variety of species, in fact almost every meadow plant is cut down and sampled or partly eaten, and in the woods the species chosen seem to be those most convenient. Different kinds of grass are cut along the runways and when young and tender the green stems and leaves are partly eaten. Later in the season as the grass fills with seeds the stems are cut off at the base and drawn down by repeated cutting into sections until the seed-laden tops are reached. The heads are then eaten, seeds and all, and the little sections of the stems 1 or 2 inches long are left piled up as refuse. In this way a great deal of grass is cut in a night by a single meadow mouse, and where they are abundant in a meadow the total destruction of grass is considerable. Early in spring the tender shoots of grass are eaten as they come up, and in winter under the snow their favorite food seems to be the blanched inner folds of grass stems close to the ground. Under the snow their tunnels carried over the surface of the ground reach abundant vegetation. Green bark is also acceptable food and branches of trees cut in the fall are often found stripped of their bark when the snow disappears in spring. Even the trunks of small trees lying under the snow are often stripped of bark and the bases of many bushes and small trees are sometimes girdled so as to injure or kill them. The mice are fond of any kind of grain used for trap bait and also of fresh meat, salt pork, or bacon. In a trap line, where they are abundant and many specimens are caught in a small area, some of the mice in the traps are usually found half eaten by others that have come along and found them dead.

Breeding habits.—The 4 pairs of mammae of this species are arranged in 2 pairs of pectoral and 2 pairs of inguinal with a wide abdominal space between. The number of young in a litter as indicated by the embryos examined from various parts of the range of the species, varies usually from 4 to 6, and in one case reached 7. The breeding season extends over a considerable part of the year but its limits are not definitely known. In the Mimbres Mountains the writer collected an old female on May 24 that contained five small fetuses. It is probable that from two to several litters are raised in a season by the adult breeders and when conditions are favorable and food abundant reproduction probably goes on at a rapid rate. Females not fully grown during the same season in which they were born often contain fetuses but usually in small numbers. The power of very rapid reproduction probably accounts for the great abundance of these animals at times, as their host of enemies could easily account for their scarcity at other times in the same localities.

The young are brought forth and reared in well-made nests placed in chambers of the burrows or on the surface of the ground under cover of fallen vegetation. These nests are usually in the form of a somewhat flattened ball, composed of soft grass and plant fibers and often lined with bits of fur from the parents or other animals. They are well covered and are entered by one or two openings at the sides near the surface of the ground. A heavy rain seems never to wet the inner part of the nest unless the water rises from beneath to flood the chambers. The nests are very warm and when in use are always neat and clean.

Economic status.—Fortunately the Rocky Mountain meadow mice range almost entirely above the zones of agriculture, where little harm can be done to cultivated crops, meadows, or fruit trees, as otherwise they might be a very serious pest. At present their mischief consists mainly in slightly lessening the grass crop of the mountain meadows and parks and in destroying some small trees that otherwise might aid in the reforestation of the mountain slopes. They are so numerous and widely distributed that any form of artificial destruction or control of abundance would be very expensive. Their enemies, however, are legion, and quickly gather where the mice are most abundant. Hawks, owls, foxes, coyotes, wildcats, weasels, badgers, and skunks are constantly searching for them and pounce upon every one that shows himself above cover. The most effective means of controlling the abundance of such rodents is by giving protection to their enemies and so far as possible in removing the cover that affords them their only protection.

MICROTUS NANUS NANUS (Merriam)

Dwarf Meadow Mouse

Arvicola (Mynomes) nanus Merriam, North Amer. Fauna No. 5, p. 63, 1891.

Type.—Collected in Pahsimeroi Mountains, Idaho, September 16, 1890, by C. Hart Merriam and Vernon Bailey.

General characters.—Very similar in color and general appearance to *mordax* except for slightly smaller size and relatively much shorter tail. The tail is about one-quarter of the total length, or about twice the length of the hind foot. The color of the upper parts is light brownish gray; underparts, silvery gray.

Measurements.—Adult specimens from Colorado average in total length, 172; tail, 43; hind foot, 20 millimeters; females, 161; 44; 20 millimeters, respectively.

Distribution and habitat.—Specimens of the dwarf mountain species of meadow mouse (pl. 9, A) have been taken in New Mexico only on top of the San Juan Range from 8,700 to 9,900 feet altitude in pure Canadian Zone. (Fig. 37.) It is an abundant species in the mountains of Colorado and will undoubtedly be taken in the mountain parks along the Sangre de Cristo Range in New Mexico.

General habits.—In the San Juan Mountains specimens were taken in a springy marsh at the forks of Tusas Creek on the east slope of the mountains at 8,700 feet, and later in the springy marshes on the crest of the range west of Hopewell at 9,900 feet. In the open park on the crest of the range they were found living in weedy patches of ground around the springs or in the banks of little streams, as well as out on the drier parts of the park in the short grass well away from water. Along the edges of water pools in the half-dry creek bed the runways often ended at the water's edge and began again on the opposite side; while sections of cut grass lying in the water, runways in muddy places, and burrows in wet ground showed a fondness for the neighborhood of water. In several instances holes and runways were found where the ground was dry and dusty and only scattered tufts of short grass offered scanty food and cover. In dry places little roadways could be traced from burrow to burrow across dusty intervals, and the small round burrows entered the bare hard ground in perfectly open places. In some cases the mice had taken possession of old burrows of pocket gophers, making entrances of their own size all along the line of the underground galleries and using the pocket-gopher burrows for protected runways. They were also good burrowers themselves, and in many places dug their little round holes deep into the mellow banks, throwing out fresh earth in considerable quantities every night. Scattered remains of half-eaten grass stems along their runways show their food to consist mainly of grass, but rolled oats and whole oats used for trap bait were eagerly eaten. As many mice were caught during the daytime as at night and apparently at all times of day. More than half of those caught from September 7 to 14 were young of various sizes, some barely large enough to be out of the nest.

In food and breeding habits the dwarf meadow mouse apparently differs very little from the Rocky Mountain one, the only other species occupying the Canadian Zone of this region. The mammae in breeding females have the same arrangement in 4 pairs, and the number of young as indicated by the embryos varies from 4 to 6, although specimens have been recorded containing as many as 10. Owing to its limited and elevated

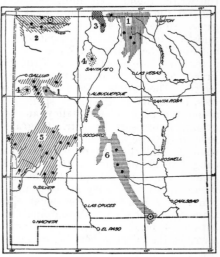

FIGURE 37.—Distribution of meadow mice in New Mexico: 1, *Microtus pennsylvanicus modestus*; 2, *M. azetecus*; 3, *M. nanus nanus*; 4, *M. montanus arizonensis*; 5, *M. mexicanus mogollonensis*. Type localities circled

range in New Mexico, it can be considered of little or no economic importance.

MICROTUS MONTANUS ARIZONENSIS BAILEY

ARIZONA MEADOW MOUSE

Microtus montanus arizonensis Bailey, Biol. Soc. Wash. Proc. 12: 88, 1898.

Type.—Collected at Springerville, Ariz., November 7, 1890, by E. W. Nelson.
General characters.—Resembles *nanus* but larger and darker colored with cranial characters that place it nearer to *montanus.* The tail is about one-quarter the total length and a little more than twice the length of hind foot. The color of the upper parts is darker gray and more brownish than in *nanus* or *mordax;* while the lower parts are washed with whitish or silvery gray.
Measurements.—The type measures in total length, 184; tail, 55; hind foot, 20 millimeters.

Distribution and habitat.—Up to the present time the Arizona meadow mouse is known only from three widely separated localities—Springerville, Ariz., and Nutria and the Jemez Mountains in New Mexico—mainly in the Transition Zone. (Fig. 37.)

At Nutria, N. Mex., near a large spring at the southern edge of the Zuni Mountains, Henshaw secured a specimen in 1874, which is still in the National Museum collection. No notes accompany it, but it was undoubtedly captured in the marshy ground near the spring, which from Henshaw's description seems admirably suited to the habits of the species.

Near Springerville, Ariz., E. W. Nelson collected a series of specimens in 1890 on wet ground bordering a small creek at the lower edge of the pine belt. In Valle San Antonio at 8,300 feet altitude, the writer found them numerous in the meadows along the creek, and on the slope of Pelado Peak one specimen was caught on a grassy slope near a spring at 11,000 feet. This was taken in the midst of the Canadian Zone, but seems to be the only specimen taken outside of the Transition Zone.

General habits.—Those in Valle San Antonio were in the rich grassy meadows near camp, and a considerable number were collected. Their runways and burrows could be seen all over the meadows, especially in the large springs, which come out of the banks along the edge of the valley and are full of grass because the ground is too soft for cattle to graze over them. The mice fairly reveled in these protected spots, and more got into the writer's traps than he had time to prepare as specimens. Most of them were caught in the daytime in traps baited with rolled oats, which they seemed eager to get. In habits they seem to be identical with *montanus* of the valley marshes and springs of Utah and Nevada, where they live under somewhat similar conditions. In fact, the skins from the Jemez Mountains are to some extent intermediate between typical *arizonensis* and *montanus*, but for the present it seems better to refer them to *arizonensis*.

MICROTUS PENNSYLVANICUS MODESTUS (Baird)

Saguache Meadow Mouse

Arvicola modesta Baird, Mammals of North America, p. 535, 1859.

Type.—Collected in Cochetopa Pass, Colo., by Mr. Kreutzfeldt and Lieut. E. G. Beckwith, undated but entered in Museum Catalogue in March, 1855.

General characters.—A large, dark-colored meadow mouse with very soft silky fur, and tail about twice the length of the hind foot and slightly more than a quarter of the total length. Color of the upperparts dusky brown; underparts, smoky gray in summer, less brownish above and more grayish below in winter.

Measurements.—Adult male: Total length, 178; tail, 46; hind foot, 23 millimeters; adult female, 179; 49; 22 millimeters, respectively.

Distribution and habitat.—The Saguache meadow mouse, a wide-ranging plains and Rocky Mountain species, comes into northern New Mexico along both sides of the Sangre de Cristo Mountains, and one colony has been discovered at San Rafael near the eastern point of the Zuni Mountains. (Fig. 37.) The species generally occupies both the Upper Sonoran and the Transition Zones, but the New Mexico localities except San Rafael lie mainly within the Transition. The few New Mexico localities represent a somewhat scattered and ragged southern edge of the distribution of the species. More detailed collecting along the upper Rio Grande and Pecos Valleys will doubtless round out the range and fill in some of the present gaps in our knowledge.

General habits.—This western form of the eastern meadow mouse more fully justifies the common name than does any other species in New Mexico. Its home is almost invariably in the meadows of low and middle altitudes where agriculture is important and settlements are abundant and where its habits are likely to be well known and feared. The mice are fond of wet ground, marshes, and stream banks, are good swimmers, and have no objection to running through water to and from their feeding grounds, but they thrive just as well in dry meadows, clover and alfalfa fields, or even in grainfields, where an abundance of growing crops furnishes cover and food. They are most conspicuous, however, in the high meadows, where they multiply rapidly until the hay harvest begins, when their cover is removed, and they are forced to find protection elsewhere and hide under haycocks or gather thickly into the grassy fence corners or uncut borders. In the hayfields as they run through the grass or stubble after being uncovered by rake or pitchfork they are conspicuously black and are evidently aware of their danger as they rush frantically to cover. If any small dogs are in sight the danger is very real, for the dogs often kill a large number during a day while following the hay wagons. There is just enough danger in the sport to keep up the dog's excitement, for the mice are pugnacious little fighters, and if one ever gets a dog by the nose or lip, a mingling of blood and howls is likely to follow.

Though specimens have been collected at only a few localities in northern New Mexico, these would indicate that the species undoubtedly has a much wider range and is much more common than at present known. In all the meadows examined in Moreno Valley the mice were abundant. They were also plentiful in the extensive meadows about Black Lake, along the Hondo River north of Taos, in the meadows just below the edge of the mountains, and at many localities in the San Luis Valley, Colo., above the New Mexico line. The southernmost locality at which they have been found is San Rafael, where there are extensive marshes fed by big springs. Here, although abundant and forming an extensive colony, they are probably somewhat isolated from the general range of the species. It is not improbable, however, that they will be found in many marshy localities along the Rio Grande Valley above Albuquerque. At San Rafael their habits were somewhat unusual, as it is one of the few known localities where they occupy alkaline meadows. They were abundant along the banks of irrigation ditches, along the little streams that drained the springs through the meadows, and through the dense patches of tules and saltgrass, as well as over the wet marshes and in dry areas of low dense saltgrass. Extensive areas of rank cat-tails and tules on soft ground where cattle could not graze furnished the safest cover from which they could not be driven by enemies, and in which they could take refuge after the hay was cut and the more extensive meadows left exposed for the winter.

Food habits.—Under normal conditions grass and various meadow plants form the principal food of these mice, but they are particularly fond of clover, alfalfa, and any kind of growing grains. In the meadows along the Rio Hondo early in August their runways extended into the wheat fields, and considerable ripening grain had been cut and eaten along the trails. In the marshes at San Rafael late in October the blanched bases of grasses and tules seemed to be their favorite food in the meadows where hay had been cut and no standing grass with seeds remained. Even the white base of the little hard spikes of saltgrass seemed to be relished. At that season, however, the grainfields had all been harvested and the alfalfa stubble grazed so closely that no cover and little food remained for the mice in the fields. The green bark of bushes and small trees is often eaten by these mice, especially in winter when other green food is scarce.

Breeding habits.—The mammae, as in other species of the group, are arranged in 4 pairs, and the number of young in a litter varies usually from 4 to 6, but occasionally reaches 7 and even 8 in number. Four females collected on the Rio Hondo in early August all contained fetuses of various sizes, the highest number being 7. In Colorado, Loring found litters of 6, 7, and 8 young in their nests.

Their summer nests are usually placed on the surface of the ground under cover of fallen vegetation or if in wet marshes on little elevated tussocks above the level of the water. Like those of most meadow mice they are hollow balls, often somewhat flattened by the rains, and usually composed of soft grass and plant fibers. One or two openings at the sides constitute the entrances to the nest chamber and connect with runways leading away to other nests, burrows, or feeding grounds. Tiny naked young are often found in these surface nests. Freshly made nests containing young are often found under haycocks that have been standing but a few days. Winter nests are placed in the burrows or under haystacks or any such cover that will afford warmth and protection during the cold season.

Hibernation.—Like other species of the genus they are active during the winter and enjoy their safest existence when buried under the deep snows.

Economic status.—Fortunately these mice cover but a small part of the State of New Mexico, but all their range lies in good farming country, and if irrigation extends their area will extend with it. The damage they can do to crops is in direct proportion to their abundance, and where conditions permit of rapid increase they are capable of practically destroying all the crops and fruit. They increase very rapidly, and without the check of their natural enemies their numbers would soon multiply to alarming proportions. At San Rafael hawk and owl pellets were found by the side of nearly every fence post in the meadows, composed almost entirely of the fur and bones of these mice. The droppings of coyotes and foxes along the trails were also filled with their fur and bones. Badger and skunk tracks were suggestively numerous in the cow paths over the pastures and meadows. The presence of the mice in a meadow can usually be predicted when marsh hawks are seen skimming low over the ground and pouncing at frequent intervals into the grass or mowed ground, for hawks quickly gather to feast on mice that are exposed by having their cover removed. Without the check of their natural enemies the mice would not only have a more extensive and continuous range but would be present in such numbers as to cause great losses to crops.

MICROTUS AZTECUS (Allen)

Aztec Meadow Mouse

Arvicola (Mynomes) aztecus Allen, Bul. Amer. Mus. Nat. Hist. 5 : 73, 1893.

Type.—Collected at Aztec, San Juan County, N. Mex., altitude 5,900 feet, April 23, 1892, by Charles P. Rowley.

General characters.—Slightly larger than *modestus* and more dusky or less brownish in color; the skull has the same tooth pattern, but a relatively longer, narrower brain case. Readily distinguished from *modestus* by skull characters but not always by external characters.

Measurements.—Adult male from Fruitland: Total length, 211; tail, 64; hind foot, 23 millimeters; adult female, 181; 51; 22.5 millimeters, respectively.

Distribution and habitat.—The Aztec meadow mouse, a well-marked form of the *pennsylvanicus* group, occupies the fertile areas of the San Juan River Valley in the northwestern part of New Mexico. (Fig. 37.) There are specimens from Aztec, Laplata, Fruitland, and Farmington, beyond which localities the range of the species is unknown. This is in the Upper Sonoran Valley, but many Transition Zone plants occupy the stream borders and bottom lands, and as these areas are occupied by the mice there is some question as to their actual zonal position.

General habits.—At Aztec, where Loring collected a large series of specimens in December, 1893, they were caught in runways along the banks of irrigation ditches and in a patch of high grass close to the river that evidently was flooded during high water. Loring says they were often caught in the daytime, and after setting a series of traps he would frequently return along the line and find several mice in them. At Laplata he also caught them in runways along the irrigation ditches. At Fruitland, in October, 1908, Clarence Birdseye found one of their runways in the mixed grass and alfalfa along a ditch and caught a pair of adult mice in it. At Farmington, in November, he found their runways numerous in a little swampy meadow back of town, where under a dense growth of saltgrass and tules he caught a few specimens. He was told by an old trapper living at Farmington that these mice were often caught in mink and muskrat traps set in swamps along the river.

Beyond these few brief notes practically nothing is known of the habits of this species. It is probable they are abundant in all the suitable meadows and swamps along the San Juan Valley and that they have a much wider range than is at present known.

Their habits seem to be very similar to those of *modestus*, their nearest relative. Of the 33 specimens collected at Aztec by Loring in December, six only were adults, the rest being half and two-thirds grown young of the year. The different sizes of young may represent successive litters and probably indicate that in this warm valley two or more litters of young are raised during the summer.

As more of the valley is brought under cultivation and valuable fruits are produced, there is danger that these mice will multiply and at times become very destructive. The alfalfa fields will furnish favorable food and protection for them, and under such conditions their abundance should be closely watched and if they become numerous at once reported to the Bureau of Biological Survey.

MICROTUS MEXICANUS MOGOLLONENSIS (MEARNS)

MOGOLLON MEADOW MOUSE

Arvicola mogollonensis Mearns, Bul. Amer. Mus. Nat. Hist. 2: 283, 1890.

Type.—Collected at Baker Butte, Mogollon Mesa, Ariz., July 26, 1887, by E. A. Mearns.

General characters.—The Mogollon meadow mice are small with short tail and feet, tail less than one-quarter of the total length and less than twice the length of hind foot. Color of upperparts dull rusty brown; lowerparts, cinnamon or buffy gray; feet and tail grayish brown.

Measurements.—Average of 10 adult specimens: Total length, 131; tail, 28.5; hind foot, 18 millimeters.

Distribution and habitat.—The little brown Mogollon mice are a northern form of the wide-ranging *mexicanus* group covering the plateau region of Mexico, western New Mexico, and central Arizona. (Fig. 37.) They occupy the parks and open places in the yellow-pine forest area of the Mogollon Mountain region, the Zuni Mountains, and Mount Taylor. Though abundant over this Transition Zone section they seem to be entirely absent from the surrounding low country to the south and from the Rio Grande Valley on the east. In other words, they seem to be entirely isolated by the lower zones.

General habits.—On the headwaters of the Rio Mimbres, where the writer camped under the big yellow pines, these small brown mice were gathered close to an old cabin, and their little runways were found in the weeds and grass leading out from among old logs and the branches of a fallen tree. Here several specimens were caught, always in the daytime, while at night the traps filled up with white-footed mice (Peromyscus). Near Elk Mountains, an isolated group in the northern part of the Mogollons, their runways were discovered in the open parks under the short rich grama grass, and a few specimens were taken. Others were taken in the west end of Luna Valley and others still farther north in the Datil Mountains, all in the yellow-pine country. In the Datil Mountains they were living in a small meadow surrounding a spring, as well as in the open grassy forest. There they were so numerous that the writer's traps quickly filled up with them and many more were taken than he had time to save for specimens.

In the East Datil Mountains, Hollister found a few of their runways near a small spring at 9,000 feet altitude, and later more of them in the dry grassy canyon at the same altitude. The runways were deeply worn and led to burrows either at the base of grass tufts or under dead logs or trees. In the Zuni Mountains he found a few of their runways and caught two of the animals in a damp grassy area at the head of Agua Fria Spring; and in the Mount Taylor Range in a similar situation at about 9,000 feet altitude he found them abundant and collected a series of 12 specimens. Here in a damp grassy spot near a small stream the ground was fairly covered with their runways leading back and forth between their small round burrows.

In the San Mateo Mountains near Monica Spring E. A. Goldman found them common on open grassy hillsides above 9,000 feet where well-worn runways led to and from the burrows. Sometimes the burrows were placed under the shelter of tufts of grass and in other places were fully exposed in the open. In the southern end of this range of mountains he also found them common at about 9,000 feet on dry slopes among the yellow pines. On the east slope of the Mimbres Mountains near Kingston he found them common from 6,200 to 9,500 feet with the characteristic Transition Zone vegetation. Here as usual their runways led from one burrow to another and the burrows were usually placed at the base of a tuft of grass, a bush, or a stone. A few were found among grass and weeds along a small irrigation ditch near the lower edge of the Transition Zone. He also found them in the Magdalena and Zuni Mountains, where their habits were much the same.

In most cases these mice seem to prefer the open semiarid parks or forests, where there is no permanent water and the only moisture is supplied by rain, dew, or green vegetation; otherwise their habits are similar to those of many other species of the genus, their little roads and burrows and characteristic excrement merely indicating the presence of some species of meadow mouse. Their homes are mainly underground in burrows and chambers that they excavate for themselves or else in the abandoned galleries of pocket gophers of which they often take possession.

Food habits.—The food of these meadow mice consists mainly of green vegetation, including a large proportion of grasses. The sections of plant stems left lying along the runways give a clue to the species selected for food, but many of those cut up and left have really been rejected, while others have been entirely eaten. The tender bases of certain grasses and the seed-laden tops of others seem to be the favorite foods.

Breeding habits.—The mammae in this as in other species of the *mexicanus* group are only 4 in number arranged in 1 pair of inguinal and 1 pair of pectoral. The young are usually 2, 3, or 4 in number, but 1 female caught near old Fort Tularosa on October 7 contained 5 large embryos, and another collected by E. A. Goldman October 6 on San Mateo Mountain contained 2 small embryos. Young of various sizes collected at different dates during the summer months would indicate that the species breeds several times during a season.

Economic status.—In most of the country occupied by these meadow mice there is practically no agriculture. Scattered stock ranches occasionally fall within their distribution area, but the mice are rarely sufficiently abundant to do serious injury. The open country in which they live gives a great advantage to the enemies that naturally prey upon them, especially to the hawks and owls, which pounce upon them from above. In the Datil Mountains the writer caught a badger near one of their colonies and found traces of their fur and bones in its stomach. Places where badgers and skunks have been digging out their burrows are frequently seen, and their fur and bones are often recognized in the droppings of coyotes and foxes.

MICROTUS MEXICANUS GUADALUPENSIS Bailey

Guadalupe Meadow Mouse

Microtus mexicanus guadalupensis Bailey, Biol. Soc. Wash. Proc. 15: 118, 1902.

Type.—Collected in Guadalupe Mountains, Tex., close to the New Mexico line at 7,800 feet altitude, August 21, 1901, by Vernon Bailey.

General characters.—In *guadalupensis* the size is slightly larger and the colors a little lighter than in *mexicanus* or *mogollonensis*. The upperparts are dull umber brown, the underparts buffy gray.

Measurements.—Type, adult male: Total length, 152; tail, 34; hind foot, 20 millimeters.

Distribution and habitat.—Specimens of the little short-tailed brown Guadalupe meadow mouse have been taken along the Guadalupe, Sacramento, White, and Manzano Mountains east of the Rio Grande Valley, mainly in the Transition Zone, to which the species evidently belongs. (Fig. 37.)

General habits.—In the Guadalupe Mountains, in the upper parts of Dog Canyon and McKittrick Canyon, these meadow mice were common over the open slopes of the mountain, in brushy or grassy places from 7,800 to 8,500 feet in the Transition Zone. In the head of McKittrick Canyon they lived in the grassy parks and open places in the woods, where their runways, burrows, and winter nests were abundant under tall grass and weeds. Higher up on the open ridges their runways were found winding about among stones, under the shinnery oak, and through low bushes on the driest slopes and even penetrating well into the edge of dry woods. The runways were very distinct and easily followed from one burrow to another or to the feeding grounds. During August the nests in use seemed to be entirely underground in the chambers of the burrows, but old nests of grass on the surface of the ground under cover of vegetation had evidently been used during the preceding winter, probably when the mountains were buried in snow.

In September, 1902, Hollister and the writer found these little mice common in various localities in the Sacramento and White Mountains, and specimens were collected in several localities ranging in altitude from 7,500 to 8,500 feet, mainly in open places in the yellow-pine forest. At the upper edge of their range specimens were collected in the same runways with *Microtus mordax*. Barber collected one at 10,000 feet in the White Mountains.

In the Capitan Mountains Gaut collected specimens on the summit of the main ridge near the west end of the range, where he reported them as found about decayed pine logs in timbered regions, always in dry situations. In the Manzano Mountains he also found them abundant at various altitudes from 8,100 to 10,200 feet, usually in dry woods, but in one case a colony was found in a marshy place at the edge of a small park. On one side of this little grassy meadow lay an old decayed log under which was their main runway, many side trails branching out in various directions through the short grass. He says:

My first discovery of this colony was in the afternoon of October 16, and at that time the little fellows were busily engaged in collecting food, and upon my approach scampered off through the grass in all directions. They did not appear to be very shy and one particularly bold individual sat up in a runway and watched me while I set a trap about 10 feet away on the same trail. A few minutes later the same individual was secured in a little out-of-sight mouse trap.

In other places he found their small trails or runways forming networks over the open slopes, and colonies were also found on rocky hillsides and under and about logs in the woods.

Food habits.—In food as well as other habits they seem not to differ from the closely related Mogollon meadow mice. Green vegetation seems to form their principal food, and the scattered stems of grass and various plants that they have cut along the runways furnished the only clue to their bill of fare. Rolled oats, grain, or meat are acceptable substitutes for their natural food and form very attractive trap bait. Occasionally one of the animals is found partly eaten in the trap, evidently having been discovered by others of its kind, but this does not necessarily mean that cannibalism is a natural habit.

Breeding habits.—In *guadalupensis* as in *mogollonensis* the mammae are arranged in two pairs, and the young probably range from two to four in a litter. In the Guadalupe Mountains old females were taken containing fetuses late in August. Young and immature specimens collected late in summer and in autumn would indicate that the breeding season is prolonged.

Economic status.—As most of the country where this species has been found is somewhat arid grazing or forest land where at present there is little or no agriculture, the mice may be considered of negative economic importance. If they should become excessively numerous at any time, their drain upon the grazing land might be somewhat serious, and in the future when some of this land will be of value for certain types of agriculture they may also do some damage, especially if the region proves to be valuable for tree fruits.

FIBER ZIBETHICUS OSOYOOSENSIS (LORD)

ROCKY MOUNTAIN MUSKRAT; PAH-HAH-NU-U'-NA of the Taos Indians

Fiber osoyoosensis Lord, Zool. Soc. London Proc. 1863: 97.

Type.—Collected at Osoyoos Lake, British Columbia, Canada, prior to 1863, by J. K. Lord.

General characters.—Size large; colors dark, in winter heavily overlaid with dark hairs on the back and with considerable dusky on belly. In summer, bright brown with little trace of black hairs; young, sooty brown.

Measurements.—Adult male from Farmington, N. Mex., measures in total length, 547; tail, 233; hind foot, 78 millimeters.

Distribution and habitat.—The Rocky Mountain muskrat, a large dark form, occupies the San Juan and Rio Grande Valleys of northern New Mexico. (Fig. 38.) There are specimens from Farmington, Costilla River, Rinconada, and Albuquerque, which agree perfectly with others from the mountain region of Colorado and northwestward to southern British Columbia.[21]

In marshy localities along the streams these muskrats are locally common, but not of very general distribution or great abundance in any part of New Mexico. At Farmington, Clarence Birdseye found them along the San Juan and Animas Rivers in several swampy marshes and in some of the main irrigation ditches. He says that owing to the nature of their habitat they seldom build houses, and,

---

[21] The specimen from Albuquerque, collected July 18, is in worn and faded summer pelage, with no trace of the black over-hairs and with but a thin layer of bright brown hairs above and below to obscure the pale under-fur. It is a little paler than an Aug. 23 specimen from Costilla River, but is not so pale as other summer specimens of *osoyoosensis* from localities farther north, which are considered typical of the species. The skull of this specimen has all the characters of *osoyoosensis* and shows no approach to either the little *pallidus* or equally small *ripensis*.

as might be expected they do considerable harm by burrowing through the banks of ditches and thus letting out the water. They are trapped to some extent for the fur market. Four specimens that Birdseye caught on November 20 are in fine dark, early-winter pelage. At Blanco farther up the San Juan River he reported a few along the river banks but did not secure specimens. At Taos, the writer saw a skin in one of the pueblo houses, and Sun Elk told him that there were muskrats in the meadows below the pueblo and also in the irrigation ditches. At Rinconada, on the Rio Grande River above Espanola, McClure Surber collected two specimens on April 17, which were somewhat faded but still in the dark winter pelage. One that the writer trapped in a beaver pond on the Costilla River on August 23 was in the clear brown summer coat, as was the one taken at Albuquerque in July.

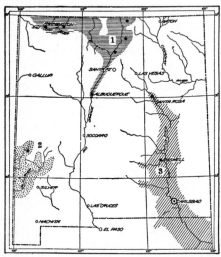

FIGURE 38.—Distribution of muskrats in New Mexico: 1, *Fiber zibethicus osoyoosensis;* 2, *F. zibethicus pallidus;* 3, *F. zibethicus ripensis.* Type locality circled

At Albuquerque they were common in irrigation ditches on the river flats, and tracks were also seen along the shores of the Rio Grande. At Socorro, E. A. Goldman was told that there were a few along the river valley, but he was unable to find any trace of them when there in 1909.

General habits.—In habits these muskrats do not differ from other races except as they adapt themselves to the character of the country. As they usually live along ditches, creeks, and river banks, they have no occasion to build houses as do those living in lakes, ponds, and larger marshes; but this is not a peculiarity of the species as in other parts of the country they build houses of considerable size. As far as possible they select grassy banks and deep, still water for their homes, burrowing into the banks from below the surface of the water and excavating commodious nest chambers above the water level. From these secure retreats they come out, usually in the evening, and forage after food of grass, tules, water plants, and various roots.

Food habits.—To a great extent their food consists of the tender bases or bulbs and roots of certain species of plants. The blades and stems of grass and tules left at their feeding places often accumulate in little mounds showing the nature of part of their food.

Economic status.—The fur of this large dark form commands a good price, and where the muskrats are abundant trapping is profitable. In many localities, however, the fur value does not equal the losses caused by the animals. In agricultural valleys dependent on irrigation, the muskrats should be destroyed, but in the higher parts of their range, especially in mountain valleys where there is little or no agriculture they are valuable fur-producing animals and should be protected, the open season for trapping being made to correspond with the time of the best fur. In many cases a large part of the fur of such animals is taken at a time when it is of little value, and it is only by proper restrictions that trappers are able to get the best returns for their time and labor.

FIBER ZIBETHICUS RIPENSIS BAILEY

PECOS MUSKRAT

Fiber zibethicus ripensis Bailey, Biol. Soc. Wash. Proc. 15: 119, 1902.

Type.—Collected along Pecos River at Carlsbad, New Mex., July 26, 1901, by Vernon Bailey.

General characters.—Size very small for a muskrat. Colors, pale dull brown in summer. Skull small and short with relatively large bullae.

Measurements.—Type, adult male: Total length, 470; tail, 202; hind foot, 67 millimeters.

Distribution and habitat.—So far as at present known the little Pecos muskrat is confined to the Pecos River and its tributaries. (Fig. 38.) Specimens have been taken at Fort Stockton, Tex., and Carlsbad, Roswell, and Santa Rosa, N. Mex. It probably also extends into the Rio Grande River along the Texas border, and may possibly reach into the southern New Mexico part of the Rio Grande Valley, but no specimens have yet been obtained in that region.

General habits.—Near Carlsbad the Pecos muskrats were common in 1902, and six specimens were collected along the banks of the river. They were caught on grassy shores along the still water, where they burrowed into the banks and found abundant food in the tules and grass at the margins of the stream. They were also living in the irrigation ditches and doubtless occupied some of the marshes fed by the ditches. At Santa Rosa, Gaut collected a series of seven specimens in October, 1902. These were just beginning to show the darker winter fur but had not completed their fall molt, and no specimens of the full winter pelage of the species are yet in the Biological Survey collection. Gaut's specimens were found in the marshes and small creeks leading out from the enormous springs near Santa Rosa and also along the neighboring river banks where still water and growing vegetation afforded favorable conditions. It is probable that the muskrats occupy many other situations along the valley of the Pecos River, but there are long sections of the river too irregular in flow and with barren banks that are unsuitable for them.

The animals are largely nocturnal in habits and are often found on their feeding grounds just before dark and again early in the morning. Occasionally they are seen swimming about in broad daylight, but at the first alarm they dive with a splash and generally keep out of sight for some time. They burrow into the banks of streams and ditches well below the surface of the water, and can pass from one burrow or bank nest to another without showing themselves. Their nest chambers in the banks are placed a little above the water level and usually have only the one entrance from below. Occasionally the nests are broken into from above, but in such cases the opening is quickly closed as a protection against enemies. Where the burrows are placed in the banks of irrigation ditches there is always danger of their penetrating to a lower level on the outside and causing breaks. A special effort is therefore necessary on the part of the farmers and those having the care of the ditches to destroy or keep the muskrats out of the main ditches. Various methods have been employed for fencing with wire mesh and various traps have been recommended for catching the muskrats as they enter the ditches.

Trapping with steel traps should always be done with heavily weighted traps near deep water to insure the prompt drowning of the muskrats and to prevent the cruel torture of their remaining alive with mangled feet or twisting off their feet and escaping.

Food habits.—The food of this as of other muskrats varies according to the locality in which they live. The roots and tender parts of sedges, grasses, and other plants growing in or near the water are selected, and numerous fragments left on the feeding shelves along the edges of the water show only a part of what has been eaten.

Economic status.—From its small size and the light color of its fur this muskrat is of less value than the larger, darker animals from the North. Its fur value probably does not compensate for the damage it does in this valley, which largely depends upon irrigation for agriculture. It is therefore generally considered as a pest rather than as a valuable game or fur animal.

FIBER ZIBETHICUS PALLIDUS Mearns

ARIZONA MUSKRAT; KHU-TO of the Hualpai Indians (Mearns); POM'-WE of the Hopi Indians (Mearns, 1907, p. 496)

Fiber zibethicus pallidus Mearns, Bul. Amer. Mus. Nat. Hist. 2 : 280, 1890.

Type.—Collected at Fort Verde, Yavapai County, Ariz., in 1885 or 1886 by E. A. Mearns.

General characters.—Size small; colors very pale in summer with no black hairs overlying the fur. Winter pelage apparently unknown, but summer fur the palest of any of the muskrats.

Measurements.—Average of nine topotypes measured by Doctor Mearns: Total length, 482; tail, 204; hind foot, 67 millimeters.

Distribution and habitat.—Hollister (1911, p. 28), in his Systematic Synopsis of the Muskrats, gives the range of the Arizona muskrat as extending into southwestern New Mexico along the branches of the Gila River, and also as occurring in the Rio Grande River at Albuquerque. (Fig. 38.) His conclusions are based on one specimen collected at Albuquerque in July, 1889, and on three broken skulls taken by Walter Hough from a prehistoric bone cave near the Tularosa River and not far from the present town of Reserve. Upon a careful reexamination of this material the writer finds it necessary to refer the Albuquerque specimen to *osoyoosensis.* The three skulls that Hough took from the ruins of cliff dwellings near the Tularosa River are not perfect enough to show unmistakable characters. They are rather large for the skulls of *pallidus,* and while not fossil, may not represent the species of muskrat at present found in the upper branches of the Gila. The admission of *pallidus* to the New Mexico list of mammals is therefore provisional, but muskrats undoubtedly occur in the Gila and San Francisco Rivers in the State, and if so, they should on geographic grounds belong to this little pale species, which occupies the Gila farther south in Arizona.

Family CASTORIDAE: Beavers

CASTOR CANADENSIS FRONDATOR Mearns

Broad-Tailed Beaver; Colorado River Beaver

Castor canadensis frondator Mearns, U. S. Natl. Mus. Proc. 20: 502–503, 1898. (Advance sheets published March 5, 1897.)

Type.—Collected at San Pedro River, Sonora, Mexico, near Arizona line, October 24, 1892, by E. A. Mearns and F. X. Holzner.

General characters.—Size about as in *canadensis;* colors lighter and brighter. Upper parts light chestnut; middle of belly reddish chestnut, brightest posteriorly and around base of tail; hind feet dark chestnut; colors slightly darker in winter; young very similar to adults.

Measurements.—Type, adult male: Total length, 1,070; tail, 360; hind foot, 185 millimeters. Weight of type, 62 pounds.

Distribution and habitat.— There seems to be no New Mexico specimens of beavers that can be referred to typical *frondator*, but the beavers occupying the branches of the Gila and San Juan Rivers undoubtedly belong to this form, as do all those examined from the drainage of the Colorado River system. (Fig. 39.) There are still a few beavers in the headwaters of the Gila where they were formerly exceedingly numerous. There are

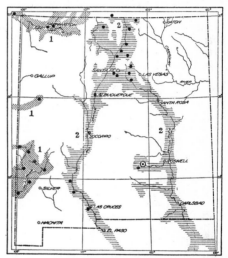

FIGURE 39.—Distribution of beavers in New Mexico: 1, *Castor canadensis frondator;* 2, *C. canadensis mexicanus.* Type locality circled

also some in the San Juan River and its tributaries. On the headwaters of the Zuni River they were so common in the early days as to give the name " Nutria " to one of the principal creeks on the south slope of the Zuni Mountains. It is to be hoped that specimens will be obtained from these localities to show whether *frondator* holds true to the sources of the streams, which it occupies lower down.

In 1825 Pattie and his party struck the Gila River near the Hot Springs in the Mogollon Mountains, and in his journal (December 15) Pattie says they caught 30 beavers the first night they were encamped on the river. Two weeks later they struck the San Francisco River and caught 37 beavers the first night. He further says that in one month's trapping along these rivers they secured 250 beaver skins. (Pattie, 1905.) During February, Pattie and his party continued down the Gila to the site of the present town of Redrock and westward into Arizona finding beavers all along the river, and at one place west of the New Mexico line they recorded taking 200 skins in one locality. Pattie also records great numbers of beavers taken on the trip farther down the Gila and in the Colorado River. In 1892, while at Silver City, Streater was told that beavers were still common about the headwaters of the Gila River. In 1906 the writer was told that some were still in the region, and he saw plenty of old dams and cuttings though no fresh signs on Willow Creek, one of the extreme head branches of the Gila. In 1908 on the headwaters of the San Francisco River the Luna Valley he saw fresh tracks and freshly cut branches of willow and cottonwood along the stream, but no other evidence of the presence of beavers in the various streams of the Mogollon Mountains. They have given their name, however, to one of the branches of the east fork of the Gila, Beaver Creek, and also to Beaver Dam Creek, a branch of the Negrito that flows into the San Francisco River from the east. Along Beaver Dam Creek many old dams and numerous old stumps of cottonwoods cut down years before were seen, but there were no fresh signs. One large narrow-leaved cottonwood had been cut half-way through at the base where it measured 26 inches in diameter.

The same year, 1908, E. A. Goldman reported a few beavers living along the Gila River near Redrock. Traces of their work were seen at various places along the river banks, and one nest cavity entered a low bank among the roots of a large tree. There was very little accumulated material at this place, but a small willow standing over the nest cavity had been cut until it fell, hanging with the trunk still attached to the stump. Two cottonwood trees about 18 inches in diameter standing on the bank near by had been partly cut through a short distance above the ground. The cutting on these trunks showed that the work had been carried on at intervals for some time. Another beaver nest was found in the bank of the Gila about 4 miles above Redrock. Here numerous cottonwood trees, willow bushes, and arrowwood stems had been cut and piled into holes along the steep bank. Some of the holes were below the water level and others 10 or 15 feet above the water in the face of the bank. Many of the cottonwood branches were completely stripped of bark and had apparently been cut on the opposite side of the river a hundred yards below, dragged 40 or 50 feet to the water and then towed upstream. Most of the branches were about half an inch in diameter and some were 3 or 4 inches through. Large cottonwood, willow, and sycamore trees near the nest showed old scars where they had been cut into at various times. A few slides were seen along the banks where the beavers were in the habit of coming from and returning to the water, and it was evident that a number were actively at work along this part of the river, although a party of trappers had systematically trapped them out only a few years before.

In 1915 J. S. Ligon was told by J. J. Pitts, who settled in Apache Canyon in western Socorro County in 1883, that there were then two large beaver dams across the canyon, a distance of about 200 yards, backing up the water in deep, smooth ponds surrounded by dense growths of willows. All the beavers along this stream as well as along the Frisco River were caught by an old trapper from Texas in

1884 and 1885, with the result that the canyon is now a barren, bowlder-strewn wash.

On April 21, 1916, Ligon reported a small colony of beavers on the East Gila River, west of the Black Range, and in the Middle Gila he found that there were a considerable number, one colony on the T. J. ranch being well protected.

In the San Juan River Valley in October, 1908, the writer found freshly cut willows stranded along the stream near Fruitland, and there were many old stumps left from earlier cuttings along the river flats. In this same valley Clarence Birdseye later found traces of them down the river at Liberty and near Farmington and Blanco; also along the Animas River and in some of the large irrigation ditches. They were reported as steadily increasing in numbers and he says:

> They had followed down the Farmington ditch from the Animas River to about a mile above town, where their work could be seen within 100 yards of the electric light plant. Their habit of entering the ditches has caused a strong feeling against the beavers, for they are continually either damming the ditches or letting the water out by burrowing through the banks. There is particular danger of this occurring in the main ditch because it runs for a considerable distance along a side hill and any break in the lower bank quickly enlarges and floods the country below.

At Blanco Birdseye found cottonwoods and willows cut along both banks of the river and numerous slides where the beavers came out on the banks. Here also he reported the beavers as following the ditches for a considerable distance from the river and sometimes cutting and damming the banks. In one place he saw several wagon-loads of cottonwood branches, willows, tumbleweeds, cat-tails and other material that had been removed from the ditch where the beaver had built their dam.

A very full and interesting account of the habits of this species of beaver is given by Mearns in his report on the Mammals of the Mexican Boundary Survey. (1907, p. 350–362.)

CASTOR CANADENSIS MEXICANUS Bailey

Rio Grande Beaver; Pah-ya'-nah of the Taos Indians

Castor canadensis mexicanus Bailey, Biol. Soc. Wash. Proc. 26: 191, 1913.

Type.—Collected at Ruidoso Creek, 6 miles below Ruidoso, N. Mex., September 29, 1899, by C. M. Barber.

General characters.—Size of *frondator*; colors duller and paler; upperparts dull rusty brown; belly clear drab or pale buffy gray, slightly darker in winter, paler in summer; young very similar to adults.

For some years it has been customary to refer the beavers of the Rio Grande drainage to *frondator*, but sufficient material has now come into the collections to show that they are markedly different from those of the Colorado drainage. The characters seem to be very constant throughout the Rio Grande and Pecos drainage in both New Mexico and Texas, although in the higher mountains of northern New Mexico they show a tendency to darker coloration, and probably a gradation toward *frondator* or *canadensis*.

Measurements.—Type, adult female: Total length, 1,070; tail, 400; hind foot, 174 millimeters. Weight, 47 pounds.

Distribution and habitat.—A few beavers (pl. 11, A) are still to be found at intervals along the Pecos and Rio Grande Rivers and on some of the tributary streams. (Fig. 39.)

In 1826, the younger Pattie, with his party of free trappers, trapped for beavers all along the Pecos River from 20 miles above its mouth up to the first Spanish settlement (probably Anton Chico), which was then a town of 500 inhabitants. (Pattie, 1905, p. 16.)

In 1898, C. M. Barber collected specimens of beavers on the Ruidoso Creek, a branch of the Rio Hondo, on the east slope of the Sacramento Mountains, and published the following note (Barber, 1902, p. 192):

In September of 1898, I located a large colony of beavers about six miles below Ruidoso Post Office, on the Ruidoso Creek, Lincoln County, New Mexico. After a period of probation spent in learning their habits and how to trap them, I succeeded in securing a series of eleven specimens, representing all ages. This species lives here in the creek bank, and little attempt was made to deepen the stream by damming it. I found old cuttings up the stream to an altitude of about 8,000 feet. At the time I visited the colony they were living among the Mexican ranches at about 6,000 feet elevation. At that season (September to November) they were feeding on corn alone, although a few scarred willows were to be seen along the bank. The Mexicans had planted their corn right down to the water's edge to utilize all the available ground in the narrow valley. The beavers were cutting and dragging the corn to the stream, then floating it to their dens. In places there was a wagon load of stalks in the water. Near the dens they had cleaned the ground for a hundred feet on either side and made great trails in dragging stalks to the stream. The Mexicans could not trap them, and as they never appeared in the day time and seldom in the twilight, very few were killed.

Five of Barber's specimens were obtained by the Biological Survey and one has served for the type of the species.

From 1881 to 1884, L. L. Dyche made several hunting and collecting trips to the headwaters of the Pecos River, and in a letter dated February 10, 1911, he writes that there were then a considerable number of beavers about 15 miles from the head of the Pecos River. He says:

From Beatty's cabin for a number of miles down the river beaver dams were quite common, and in the pools which were caused by these dams I found the best trout fishing of any locality I have ever visited in the Rocky Mountains.

In 1902 the writer followed down Ruidoso Creek and found that there were still a few beavers along this stream, which, with its sections of deep water and steep banks, is peculiarly adapted to the habits of beavers. In 1903 he also visited the headwaters of the Pecos River and found that they were still occupying some of the streams in that region. A family lived in the bank of the Pecos near Ribera, and a dam was reported near Willis where the animals were then at work. There were old cuttings along many of the other streams, but in most cases the beavers had been entirely trapped out. Near the headwaters of the Media River, northwest of Pecos Baldy at about 10,000 feet, a beautiful little beaver meadow was found where a large dam thrown across the creek had raised the depth of the water to 5 or 6 feet. In the pond which had been formed above this dam several large stick and mud houses had been built, and probably 100 poplar trees ranging from 4 to 8 inches in diameter besides a great amount of willow brush had been cut for building material along the margins of the meadow. The dam had been broken several years before, leaving the houses dry, and these had been broken into and the beavers were all gone. This little meadow, with its border of aspens and willows surrounded by the spruces of the mountain slope, must have been an attractive spot when occupied by the beavers. Without the beavers it was merely a dried-up marsh, overgrown with a tangle of willows, which had crowded out even the aspens from the 2 or 3 acres of creek bottom that had been occupied by the beaver colony.

Many similar places along the high mountain streams were found where beavers had formerly been common but had been trapped out, because in such localities the dams are easily broken and the beavers can be caught or killed without much trouble or even the skill necessary for ordinary trapping. In the deep water of the larger valley streams they are not so easily caught, and fortunately enough have escaped in spite of persistent trapping to prevent the complete extermination of the species.

In many places along the canyons of the Rio Grande above Santa Fe there were still some of the animals in 1903–4, and trappers were then catching them in considerable numbers. In 1889 the writer was told that there were a few in the Rio Grande River near Albuquerque, and in 1909, E. A. Goldman saw some old beaver cuttings near Socorro and was told that there were still a few along the river. He also saw signs of them at Garfield and found them common in the Rio Grande near Las Palomas, and they were reported near Las Cruces. At Las Palomas he found where nearly all the willows had been cut over an area of about an acre, and many cottonwood trees had also been cut, while along the river banks were numerous fresh tracks and places where the beavers had worn the banks in going in and out of the water. The trunks of the cottonwoods lay where they had fallen but were stripped of a large part of the bark, while the smaller branches had been cut and carried away. At another place, about 5 miles below Las Palomas, he reported 15 or 20 acres of willow and cottonwood bottoms that had been practically cleared by beavers. In 1915, J. S. Ligon reported them as becoming abundant in places along the Rio Grande above and below San Marcial, where there were some complaints of their felling trees across the fences.

In such localities beavers live entirely in the banks of the rivers and select the deepest water for their operations. They are not easily trapped and usually remain the longest where they do real damage, while in the higher mountains where they can do no damage they are easily caught and quickly destroyed. In the San Juan Mountains in 1904 the writer found a beaver house and dam that were not very old on the west slope leading down into the Brazos Canyon, but he found no fresh beaver work in these mountains at that time. In the Taos Mountains in the same year no fresh beaver signs were found, although beavers were said to have occupied Pueblo Creek, Hondo River, and the Red River only a few years before. Some old stumps and cuttings were seen along these streams but no fresh work, although beavers were then fairly common along the Rio Grande into which these streams flowed. Farther north in the Culebra Mountains an active colony was found in the upper part of the Costilla River at an altitude of 9,400 feet.

General habits.—The Costilla at this point was a narrow creek across which beavers had thrown several dams and along which they had built a number of houses, which had probably been used for generations. The locality was peculiarly favorable to their needs, comprising a narrow willow bottom stretching along the creek for a quarter of a mile and covering probably 6 or 8 acres of ground. On one side the mountain rose in steep wooded slopes covered with spruce and aspens, while on the other the open hillsides were dotted with yellow pines and Douglas spruce. At the time of the writer's visit, October 23, although the stream was low, averaging about 2 feet deep, with a width of only 20 feet, it had a strong current. The beavers had recently thrown a new dam across it from one edge of the valley to the other, a distance of about 15 rods, forming a pond of some 2 or 3 acres, which reached back to the edge of the old dam. The old dam had been cut with axes to let out the water, some of the beavers had been killed, and the carcass of an old male lay rotting in the pond. The old main house had been cut into and the beavers had partially abandoned the pond and built a new dam and a new house below, but they had also repaired the break in the upper dam and at the end of the writer's stay were repairing the old house. The water in the upper pond was still 2 feet below the level of the top of the dam and was clear and full of trout, while the water in the lower pond where the beavers were raising the dam and enlarging the house was usually somewhat muddy as it flowed over the top of the dam.

For a couple of days the writer watched the construction of this new dam with great interest, visiting it in the dusk of the evening and before daylight to watch the work of the beavers. First they brought sticks and laid them on and then they brought up armfuls of mud from the bottom, pushing it in front of them up over the sticks and onto the edge of the dam. The sticks were thus securely plastered in and held the mud firmly as the water pressed against it from above. While the level of the middle part of the dam was raised both ends were being extended as the water in the pond spread out. These extensions were made along the nearly level surface of the ground by laying a row of willow stems, sticks, and leaves along on the ground and covering it with wet earth taken from under the advancing water. After this more sticks were laid on top and more mud shoved up from the bottom, all the work being carried on from the upper side of the dam.

At that time the dam averaged 2 or 3 feet high across most of the gulch bottom, but on the lower side where it crossed the old river bed it reached the height of 6 feet above the water. The deepest part of the pond was then about 8 feet, but the greater part of it was only 2 or 3 feet deep. The writer waded over much of the shallower part and found it cut up with channels or canals that the beavers used in swimming to and from their house and from which they apparently brought much of the earth for building the dam. The upper surface of the dam sloped well back into the pond, and the sticks were so thoroughly covered with mud that it seemed like solid earth, while the lower face of the dam showed no mud and looked like a tangle of willow stems.

A large part of the building material was willows that had been cut in the pond and floated down to the dam. Some of these were poles 20 feet long with the branches still attached, and others had been cut into shorter sections for convenience in handling. There were pieces of old logs and branches of trees, some of them 6 feet long and 6 inches in diameter, and many of smaller size. All the old dry sticks that they could handle were gathered for building material, but most of the wood was freshly cut or had been cut the year before for food, the bark having been eaten off before it was used for building purposes. Great clusters of diamond willow (*Salix cordata watsoni*) grew here and there in the new pond and also in the old pond above, furnishing abundant food and building material. They also afforded protection, partially concealing the animals while at work on their houses and dams.

Along the steep slope bordering the pond a dense grove of second-growth aspens 2 to 6 inches in diameter reached down to the water's edge. Many of these had been cut for building material and food, and both freshly cut and old stumps were standing from a few inches to a foot high. Most of the trunks and branches had been carried away. A few of the larger trees near the edge of the water had been recently cut down, and one tree about 8 inches in diameter had been cut about half way through at the base when the writer first saw it. The next night a log of about the same size was cut near by, but the tree was left untouched. The following night the tree was gnawed until it stood on a peg not over 2 inches through and during the day it fell of its own accord. The aspens and willows were of no particular value, and no other species of trees had been attacked by the beavers. In fact, there is little else in these mountains that they would cut in the way of timber, as they rarely touch any conifer.

A new beaver house was being built in the lower pond, but it was then only about 10 by 12 feet in diameter and 5 feet high above the surface of the water, but as the water was 2 or 3 feet around it, its actual height was 7 or 8 feet, and its diameter as it rested on the bottom somewhat greater than that at the surface of the water. It was well built, consisting mainly of fresh sticks thickly plastered with mud from the bottom of the pond, shoved up over the sides each night until the sticks were firmly bedded and almost covered. The house was so surrounded and concealed by the dense willows that in the dusk of evening the beavers could not be seen at work, but they could be heard in the water, and an occasional heavy splash was heard as one would slide off the house into the pond.

The old beaver house (pl. 11, B) in the upper pond was considerably larger, being approximately 30 feet long by 18 feet wide and 6 feet high above the water level. One end came close to the edge of the steep bank, but with that exception the house was surrounded by water, which was approximately 6 feet deep around the greater part of it, making the actual height of the house about 12 feet. It had been broken into at both ends and was only partly repaired. It was composed of sticks of all kinds and sizes from willow brush to the trunks and branches of small aspens, many of which had first been peeled for food and then used for building material. The sticks were embedded in a matrix of mud and débris from the bottom of the pond and in walking over the top of the house the writer found it as firm as solid earth. When first walking over the house he evidently disturbed a visitor inside, either a mink, which was later seen coming out of one of the openings, or possibly a muskrat that the next morning was found sitting on the edge of the house when the beaver

was inside. The lawful occupants of the house were not there at
the first visit, but early the next morning he found a big beaver inside
and for 10 or 15 minutes stood close to the opening used as a doorway
by the mink watching the animal as it filled the passage with sticks
and mud from within until it was securely closed. The sticks it
brought in were freshly peeled and it placed them crisscross against
the little window before plastering it over.

Although the writer never saw more than one of the beavers at
a time, from the amount of work they were doing he concluded that
there must be three or four and possibly five or six of the old animals
and probably one or two families of young in the colony. A half-
grown young of the year, weighing about 20 pounds, was collected for
a specimen, but otherwise the colony was not disturbed. They were
not very shy. One old fellow came up and shoved a load of mud
onto the dam within 20 feet of him well after daylight one morning,
swimming off under the willows with its whole back out of water.
A little later a big head bobbed up in the pond, passed along nearly
to the dam, and then disappeared under water. Again, close to the
shore a beaver swam past only 2 or 3 rods away, turning back when
it saw him on the shore, where it evidently wanted to land to finish
cutting down a tree. Before it was half light they became active
and could be heard splashing as they worked before they could be
seen, while at twilight when they were busily at work on both dam
and house they splashed noisily. The stomach of the one collected
was full of bark and green leaves, seemingly of the willow. Its flesh
was light colored and when cooked was tender and excellent. The flesh
of the tail, mainly white, fatty tissue, was rich and tender, and especially delicious in a well-done stew. Some of the pieces of beaver
meat had a musky flavor, which evidently came from the musk
glands. Even in this young male the abdominal musk gland was
well developed and the sacks filled with considerable musky material with a tenacious odor which could not be removed from the
hands for two or three days. The "pods," as the musk sacks are
called, lie under the skin along each side of the penis, and while in
an adult they are often 5 or 6 inches long, in this half-grown young
they were between 2 and 3 inches long. (For full accounts of the
beaver's habits see Bailey, 1927, and Warren, 1927.)

Breeding habits.—The female beaver has 4 mammae arranged
well forward on the breast, the anterior pair being almost on the
throat. The number of young seems to be normally 4, although
records of 2 and 3 embryos are common and as high as 6 or 8, have
been recorded. Evidently 4 is the usual number. The young are
brought forth in the house or bank nests and are well furred at
birth. Little is known, however, of the actual breeding habits of
beavers in spite of the fact that they are one of the most important,
best known, and longest studied of our North American mammals.

Food habits.—The beavers usually store large quantities of green
wood in the ponds within reach of their houses or bank burrows
where it can be brought up for food at any time during winter.
A large part of their food is evidently willow rootlets, which line the
stream banks and are always available as a perennial supply of
fresh and tender food. The remains of these rootlets are often

found in the houses, and the writer has watched the beavers diving along the banks for such food and then eating it on the surface of the water with only their ears and nose protruding. Bark from trees and bushes is the principal food at certain seasons, but in summer grass and green vegetation are extensively eaten.

Economic status.—Information gathered from many sources indicates that the beavers in certain localities are exceedingly injurious to crops, timber, and ditches. Over a large part of their range, however, they are absolutely harmless and could be protected and allowed to increase to great numbers without danger of any harm. Needless to say they are not desirable in agricultural valleys and especially in irrigated valleys.

In the pastures of the Victoria Land & Cattle Co. along the Rio Grande south of San Antonio, J. S. Ligon reported beavers as abundant in 1916. They were said to cut a great deal of timber and cause some annoyance by felling trees across the wire fences and allowing the cattle to escape. Ligon also reported that late in the winter of 1916 permits were issued for trapping 100 beavers from the Rio Grande in the outskirts of Albuquerque, where farmers were complaining bitterly of the damage they were doing.

During 1910 and 1911 more than 900 permits were issued to parties in New Mexico who claimed that beavers were doing damage to their property and requested the privilege of catching them. The following year an order was issued requiring the skins of all beavers thus taken to be turned in to the game department, and the complaints of damage from beavers suddenly ceased. (de Baca, 1914, p. 83.) At that time the water company of Santa Fe was offering $50 a pair for beavers to be placed in the upper part of Santa Fe Canyon to aid in conserving the water supply for the city.

On almost all the mountain streams they should be protected and encouraged. A series of beaver ponds and dams along the headwaters of a mountain stream would hold back large quantities of mountain water during the dangerous flood season and equalize the flow of the streams so that during the driest seasons the water supply would be greatly increased in the valleys. Beaver ponds not only hold water but distribute it through the surrounding soil for long distances, acting as enormous sponges as well as reservoirs. A series of ponds also increases the fishing capacity and furnishes a safe retreat for the smaller trout and protection from their enemies. In addition a protected beaver colony is one of the most interesting features of mountain or forest, as with protection the animals become less wary and more diurnal in their habits so that they can be readily observed and studied by those traveling and camping in wild regions. From an economic point of view the conservation of animals valuable for food and fur is of no small importance, even if many years are required for their increase to such numbers as the region will support. A legitimate amount of trapping should eventually yield large annual returns over extensive areas of the country from which they have been almost exterminated. If the darkest and most valuable beavers from northern Michigan and Wisconsin were used for stocking streams, the value of fur returns would be greatly increased.

Family ERETHIZONTIDAE: Porcupines

ERETHIZON EPIXANTHUM EPIXANTHUM Brandt

YELLOW-HAIRED PORCUPINE; SA MA-NA of the Taos Indians

Erethizon epixanthus Brandt, Mem. Acad. Imp. Sci., St. Petersbourg (6) 3: 390, 1835.

Type locality.—California.

General characters.—Body short and wide and legs very short. Surface, except on belly, feet, and nose, covered with sharp quills. Winter fur black, almost concealing quills, long overhairs yellow or yellow tipped. Summer fur concealed by the quills which are conspicuous through the scattering yellow hairs.

Measurements.—A large male from Montana measures in total length, 875; tail, 314; hind foot, 112 millimeters. Weight of adults, about 20 to 30 pounds.

Distribution and habitat.—Porcupines (pl. 12, A) are common throughout the mountains of northern New Mexico from the valleys up to timber line, and they are not infrequently found in the valleys along brushy streams or canyons and on cliffs. They are variable in abundance, some years being fairly numerous and others very scarce. In the Pecos River Mountains one was secured near camp at 8,500 feet, just above Willis on the head of the Pecos, in July, 1903, and a few old gnawings on the trees were seen, but at that time they were said to be scarce in that vicinity. In the Taos Mountains farther north they were found fairly common in August, 1904. A few skins were seen hanging in the Indian houses at the Pueblo of Taos, and at one of the Indian dances a striking headdress of porcupine skin was worn by one of the dancers. In the low country the porcupines were scarce, but on the head of Lake Fork of the Hondo a few of their characteristic gnawings were found on the pines in the mountains at 11,400 feet altitude. In the Jemez Mountains they were found common throughout the forest up to the tops of the highest peaks and down through the nut pines to the pueblo of Jemez. Their greatest abundance, however, seems to be in the Canadian-zone forests from 9,000 feet upward. Fresh signs were found on the mountain slopes, and winter signs were abundant, both in piles of dry pellets under the trees and bare patches where the bark had been gnawed from the trunks and branches of pines and firs. In the San Juan Mountains a large number of gnawed trees were seen, and the remains of a dead porcupine was found near camp at 9,900 feet. On the Jicarilla Indian Reservation in 1904 they were abundant in the timber near Horse Lake, where many trees had been gnawed to such an extent as to seriously injure them. In one gulch in close proximity the writer counted nine small-sized pines with the tops killed and the leaves turning brown from the loss of bark on their trunks and branches. Some were killed at the tops for 8 or 10 feet down and others for only 2 or 3 feet, but many others had the branches killed and in large spots the bark had been gnawed from the trunks. In neighboring gulches numerous other trees were seen similarly gnawed and often partly or wholly killed. In this vicinity there were probably 100 trees the tops of which had been killed by porcupines. One tree that had been partly peeled at the base by the Indians and at the top by porcupines had succumbed to its wounds and stood dead and brown. At Stinking Spring Lake (now Burford Lake) on the Jicarilla Indian Reservation the writer also found a few yellow pines with the tops gnawed and branches killed, and a few nut pines somewhat injured. One Douglas spruce had been gnawed near the top, but the yellow pine seemed to be the favorite food in this region.

General habits.—In the Taos Mountains near the head of Lake Fork of the Hondo, in August, 1904, in an abandoned miner's cabin, which the porcupines had evidently occupied during the previous winter, most of the furniture had been partly destroyed by them. The legs of the table were gnawed almost in two, and a large part of the top of the table had been cut away. A soap box that had evidently contained bacon had been gnawed until only a few strips and corners remained. Other boxes and shelves and even the ends of logs that the table stood on were greatly cut away by the big chisel teeth of porcupines. In the rocks a hundred feet above camp one had spent the previous winter and left a bushel of oval sawdust pellets to mark its entrance to a big cavity under the bowlders. Near by there were also several bare spots on the sides of spruce trees from which patches of bark had been eaten, and one Engelmann spruce had been so extensively peeled that it had died after one year of effort to heal its scars.

The only porcupine seen in the Jemez Mountains was a fine old male discovered at dusk as it started up a large yellow-pine trunk. It climbed so slowly that the writer was able actually to get to the tree and push it out before it got beyond reach and to collect it for a specimen. As he had to carry it for about a mile on horseback at arm's length it seemed very heavy, and at camp he was surprised to find that it weighed only 16 pounds. While the animal was on the ground the writer tried to roll it over with a stick, and although it did not try to run away or escape up the tree, it stubbornly resisted being turned over, as if it knew the vulnerability of its lower parts, and when pried up sideways would reverse ends quickly and strike the stick with its tail. Though most of its actions were slow and stupid, the strokes of the tail were quick and powerful and seemed to be its principal means of defense. Care was taken that its tail did not come within reach of the writer's feet, as the quills would have been driven through any leather. After its determined efforts to stay right side up, it gave a vigorous shake, such as a dog gives on coming out of the water, and a shower of loose quills that the writer had disturbed in poking it about flew in all directions to a distance of 4 or 5 feet. Though the quills did not go with any force, the action gave some color to the superstition that porcupines can throw their quills with serious results.

Food habits.—Porcupines do not hibernate, and in winter their food consists mainly of the inner bark of trees, obtained by means of the large chisel teeth, which first remove the rough outer bark and then cut out as much of the tender inner bark as is needed for food. Evidently the food value of this material is very low, as great quantities are required for sustenance, and the enormous stomach often contains a quart of ground-up bark fiber. If the animal feeds upon one tree for several days sufficient bark is sometimes removed to completely girdle the trunk, or large areas are taken from one side and then another until the tree is seriously injured or is killed. In rare cases the whole trunk of the tree and even the branches are denuded of bark and the death of the tree made certain, but more often the animal feeds first on one tree and then on another until many are injured. In New Mexico the yellow pine and nut pine suffer most, but the bark is also eaten from foxtail pine (*Pinus aristata*), Douglas spruce, blue and Engelmann spruces, and fir trees. In the Pecos River Mountains at 10,000 feet in April, 1917, M. E. Musgrave reported about a third of the trees barked in a 10-acre stand of foxtail pine, but at that time the porcupines had moved to other pastures. In summer when green vegetation is available it is preferred to tree bark, and the porcupines graze on a great variety of herbaceous plants. They also eat the leaves and twigs of many shrubs and are fond of fruit and berries. In winter their pellets of excrement, little oval briquettes of sawdust, accumulate in great quantities under the feeding trees or near their dens in the rocks, sometimes several bushels in a place, but in summer the pellets from the green food are of a very different appearance, more like those of deer or sheep.

Breeding habits.—In the females the mammae are arranged in 2 pairs of pectoral, or sometimes given as 1 pair of pectoral and 1 pair of abdominal, as they are close together in a square near the point of the sternum. One young seems to be the usual number, and this is very large at birth with a well-developed coat of hair and in most cases of spines.

Economic status.—When abundant porcupines are capable of doing great injury to the forest trees, but fortunately they are not usually of sufficient numbers in New Mexico to cause serious losses. Their slow rate of breeding is compensated by their comparatively few enemies and their efficient means of self-protection, but when they do become numerous, as in some localities they are known to do, every effort should be made toward their destruction. (Gabrielson and Horn, 1930.) E. R. Warren, of Colorado, reports that a few are killed by mountain lions, bobcats, and coyotes, but apparently the number is not very great as their quills are not often found in these animals. Most dogs soon learn to let them alone, and it is probable that most wild animals have a wholesome respect for their outer covering of spines. Generally they are shot or otherwise killed on sight by hunters and trappers and also by those especially interested in forest protection. Still they have a real value in their interest to campers and nature lovers who care to study the home habits of our native wild life and can see the good in each form and sympathize with the humblest.

ERETHIZON EPIXANTHUM COUESI Mearns

Arizona Porcupine

Erethizon epixanthus couesi Mearns, U. S. Natl. Mus. Proc. 19: 723, 1897 (advance sheets, July 30, 1897).

Type.—Collected at Fort Whipple, Ariz., prior to 1865, by Elliott Coues.
General characters.—Size smaller and colors paler than in typical *epixanthum*; skull with larger audital bullae and other characters.
Measurements.—A large male from the San Mateo Mountains measures: Total length, 780; tail, 195; hind foot, 102 millimeters.

Distribution and habitat.—Specimens of the Arizona porcupine from the Mogollon Mountain region, Zuni Mountains, San Juan Valley, and Chuska Mountains are provisionally referred to this southern form of porcupine, although the individual variation seems to cover most of the alleged characters of the subspecies, and no definite line can be drawn between the ranges of the two. Much of the range of this southern form is in the comparatively low country, and the animals are often as common in the nut pine and juniper areas as in the heavily timbered mountains. In the Sacramento Mountains near Cloudcroft in 1900 the writer found trees gnawed by porcupines, and in 1916, Ed. Anderson collected a specimen 5 miles south of Elk in this range. Throughout the Mogollon Mountain region, including the Mimbres, San Mateo, Magdalena, and Datil Ranges, they are generally common.

General habits.—Trees from which the bark had been gnawed were seen along the edge of the canyon of the east fork of the Gila near the head of the Rio Mimbres and about Beaver Lake. At the latter place a long-used porcupine den was found under the great bowlders of a little side canyon where bushels of old winter pellets filled the cavities among the bowlders at the foot of the cliff, and fresh pellets of the green summer food were scattered about over the surface. Along the edge of the cliff near by a dozen small yellow pines were so largely stripped of their bark that some of them were killed and others practically ruined for future development, while on many of the larger trees the limbs or tops had been partly peeled by these bark-eating rodents. It was impossible to obtain any specimens, as the porcupines kept well back in their little caves under the rocky strongholds upon which they had evidently depended for many years. In Luna Valley at the western edge of the Mogollon Mountains there were said to be a few that occasionally made trouble for the dogs, but at the time of the writer's visit in September, 1908, none was found.

In 1916, one was collected by Ed. S. Steel 15 miles north of Luna. In the San Mateo Mountains in 1909, E. A. Goldman found several dens in the crevices of the cliff about Indian Butte, at elevations of 7,800 to 8,000 feet. In some places more than a bushel of excrement was scattered in and about the cave doors, and one of the animals was trapped for a specimen. Goldman says:

The porcupine in the trap persistently turned his back toward me as I approached and held all the spines on the lower part of his back crisscrossed, pointing in every direction, and ready for attack; his tail laid close to the ground, and when I touched it light with a stick a quick, vigorous flirt upward was evidently calculated to repel the attack of any enemy. Along the cliffs near this den many pinyon pines had patches of bark stripped from their trunks and branches to such an extent that some of the trees had been killed. Two or three Arizona oaks and several junipers had been nibbled, but only to a slight extent.

In the Magdalena Mountains he also reported their gnawings on the pinyon pines.

Hollister reported a few porcupines in the Datil Mountains, and the writer found their characteristic gnawings on nut pines and yellow pines along Largo Canyon and in the Pinyon and West Datil Ranges. On the Zuni River just above the Arizona line the quills and bones of a dead porcupine were seen by the side of the road, and at Cibola (Zuni) Coronado reported " porkenspikes " among other animals in 1540. (Whipple et al., 1856, p. 110.) In the Zuni Mountains, Hollister reported them as fairly common, and E. A. Goldman reported them as common in both the Transition and the Canadian Zones and said that they worked mainly on the pines. Several young trees were noticed that had been entirely girdled and at least the tops killed. He also found where they had stripped the bark from pinyon pines in the hills north of Thoreau. Over the slopes of Mount Taylor in 1905 Hollister reported porcupine signs, and in 1906 the writer found gnawings on the blue spruce high up on the mountain and some fresh signs among the broken rocks at the very top of the main peak. On the great ridge north of Chaco Canyon porcupine gnawings were common on the pinyon pines and also those along the Kimbetoh and Escavada Washes. Other gnawings were seen on the nut pines over the ridge about 20 miles south of Chaco Canyon and others on the Hasta Butte Mountains. A dead porcupine that had been recently shot was found by the side of the road about 20 miles south of Chaco Canyon out in the open cactus-covered plain. Its rounded dentate footprints and the marks where its tail had dragged in the dusty road showed where it had wandered for at least half a mile from the nearest timber out across the open valley before meeting the ranchman who avenged his grievance on its innocent head. This valley bridges one of the widest gaps between the nut pine ridges, which evidently carry the range of the species continuously over the western part of the State.

In the San Juan Valley in 1908 Clarence Birdseye reported porcupines as occasionally seen along the river bottoms at Blanco, Farmington, Fruitland, Liberty, and Shiprock. At Blanco their characteristic pellets were abundant in holes in the sandstone cliffs on the north side of the river, and many of the pinyon pines along these cliffs had been more or less stripped of their bark. The porcupines frequently came down into the cultivated land along the river, and at Fruitland Birdseye saw the tracks of one that had come down the road during the night and walked through the dooryard without regard to the barking of the dogs.

In the Chuska Mountains early in October, 1908, porcupines were common over the pine-covered plateau. Fresh tracks were frequently seen in the trails, and great quantities of pellets were found in the little caves and niches in the rim rock of the mesa tops. Gnawed trees were seen all through the woods but most abundant near cliffs or in the side canyons. Three of the animals were taken near the writer's camp in the southern part of the range. They were found in or near the cliffs, where some of the accumulated pellets apparently dated back for many years. On October 4, 1908, a half-grown young of the year, weighing 7 pounds, was caught in a trap at the entrance of its little cave in the rocks, and in another cave a male and female were found together and both secured for specimens. The female weighed 11 and the male 16 pounds, and apparently they were full grown.

Food habits.—The most conspicuous food habits of these porcupines consist in stripping the bark from many species of pines, spruces, and firs for food; but this is mainly done in winter or during dry times when green food in scarce. During the summer they graze on a variety of green vegetation. In the San Mateo Mountains E. A. Goldman, in September, 1909, examined the stomach of one that was well filled with acorns of the little blue oak (*Quercus grisea*), ground up shells and all, and a small quantity of vegetable fiber apparently from the bark of a tree. The stomach of one examined south of Chaco Canyon in Ocober contained green vegetation, which appeared to be grass and other herbaceous plants. The stomachs of those collected in the Chuska Mountains in October contained in one case mainly bark of the yellow pine, but in the other two mainly green herbage.

A tame female porcupine brought from southern New Mexico and kept in captivity preferred sweetpotatoes and apples to any other food but was fond of acorns and mesquite-bean pods and would eat such green vegetation as the base leaves of a large purple aster, the green branches of Ephedra, and the leaves and twigs of shadscale (*Atriplex canescens*). The writer could obtain no conifers for her. Much to his surprise she refused salt in any form or combination, bacon or grease or any of the foods the animals are usually credited with liking. When allowed the great pleasure of an evening in the tent, she would inspect every object around the walls until the apple box or sweetpotato box was encountered, then dig and scratch and gnaw until an opening was made and one of the fragrant dainties obtained and eaten with evident relish.

Economic status.—In October when green vegetation is still abundant pine bark is evidently eaten from choice and not necessity. Fortunately the bark is usually gnawed from the branches or near the top of the trunk where the outer shell is not so thick and hard as the top of yellow pines than from the lower trunk, where the bark is thick and hard. Consequently these pines are not so seriously injured. In an arid region where tree growth is slow, an abundance of porcupines would seriously retard the development of the forest, but fortunately these animals are not usually abundant and their actual damage is of only local occurrence. It is important, however, that their numbers be kept down to a reasonable abundance.

They have few native enemies, but J. S. Ligon wrote from Socorro County in 1915:

It would seem impossible for any animal to kill and eat a porcupine, but I am told by ranchmen that the mountain lion does. Mr. Sam Hillyard tells me that while recently trailing a mountain lion in the deep snow he found where it had killed and eaten one. The porcupine had been torn open along the belly and the body eaten out of the skin.

Ligon was also told of a bobcat found dead on Fox Mountain with its mouth, feet, and body full of porcupine quills.

Family ZAPODIDAE: Jumping Mice

ZAPUS PRINCEPS PRINCEPS Allen

Rocky Mountain Jumping Mouse

Zapus princeps Allen, Bul. Amer. Mus. Nat. Hist. 5: 71, 1893.

Type.—Collected at Florida, La Plata County, Colo., June 27, 1892, by Charles P. Rowley.

General characters.—The jumping mice are distinguished by very long tails, narrow ears, long hind feet, and grooved upper incisors. *Zapus princeps* is the largest and darkest colored of the three forms inhabiting New Mexico. The

whole back from nose to tail is blackish with a yellowish tinge, broadly bordered along the sides with pale yellowish; the lower parts are pure white; the
ears blackish, with pale margins.

Measurements.—A typical adult male measures: Total length, 239; tail, 144;
hind foot, 32 millimeters.

Distribution and habitat.—Specimens of the Rocky Mountain
jumping mouse (pl. 10, B) from 8,800 feet altitude on the east slope
of the Taos Mountains, from 8,200 in Hondo Canyon on the west
slope of the Taos Mountains, from the San Juan Mountains near
Tierra Amarilla, and from close to the New Mexico line west of
Antonito, Colo., while giving only a few actual records for the State,
would indicate a range throughout the Canadian Zone of the San
Juan and Sangre de Cristo Mountains. These mark the southern
limit of range of the species, which extends northward through the
Rocky Mountains. (Fig. 40.)

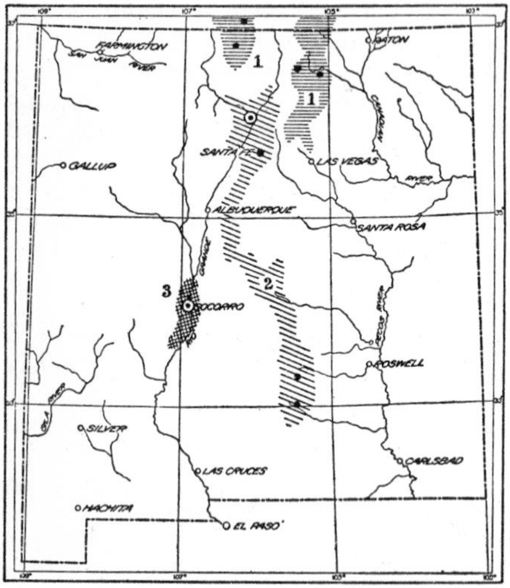

FIGURE 40.—Distribution of jumping mice in New
Mexico: 1, *Zapus princeps princeps;* 2, *Z.
luteus luteus;* 3, *Z. luteus australis.* Type
localities circled

General habits.—T h e
jumping mice are timid,
gentle little animals, somewhat like rabbits in disposition. They depend upon
their long legs and rapid
flight for protection and
even when caught in the
hands rarely show an inclination to bite or defend
themselves. Their l o n g
hind feet and the heavy
muscles of back and legs are
strongly contrasted with
the small and delicate hands
and light forward parts.
In fact, their build is more
kangaroo-like than that of
the kangaroo rats. They
usually live in g r a s s y,
weedy, or bushy places
where there is abundant
cover through which they can progress by long leaps. They are partial to dry meadows or the dry grassy borders of marshes and are
rarely found in the woods. Being unable to climb, they live on or
under the surface of the ground. They do not make roadways like
many of the ground mice, but go skipping about from place to place,
and since they leave few signs are difficult to catch. They are usually
caught by accident in traps set for other animals. They are generally
much more common than the few specimens collected would indicate
but are rarely so common that their presence can be readily detected.

In feeding they cut down the tall grass, beginning at the bottom
and cutting the stem at intervals as high as they can reach until
the seed part of the grass is brought down. This leaves little heaps
of grass stems about 3 or 4 inches long, easily distinguished from
the similar but shorter cuttings of the meadow mice, piled crisscross

in the meadows. In many places farther north and in a few places in the mountains of New Mexico the writer has found these grass heaps on their feeding grounds. Where these cuttings are common in the meadows Zapus can usually be caught in considerable numbers by scattering traps baited with rolled oats in the open spaces under the miniature forest of grass stems. It is necessary, however, to use a large number of traps in order to secure a few of these mice. Sometimes 40 or 50 traps will yield only two or three, while the same number of traps might yield a large number of other mice.

Food habits.—Their food consists almost entirely of seeds and very largely of the seeds of grass and grasslike plants. Their food habits are not easily studied, however, as they have no external cheek pouches in which food may be found, and they evidently do not store seeds for winter use. Their stomach contents almost always show a perfectly clean white mass of dough from the carefully shelled and cleaned kernels of the small seeds eaten, and only the cut stems of the various grasses indicate which plants are preferred for food. In examining the stomach contents of a great number of specimens the writer has never been able to detect any other food than seeds or the rolled oats used for trap bait.

Breeding habits.—Little is known of the breeding habits of this species except that the adults and sometimes the half-grown young are found during the summer living in grass nests on the surface of the ground under cover of grass or other vegetation. The nests are neat and well built. They are in the form of a ball consisting of soft grass fibers with one or sometimes two small openings at the sides to admit the occupants to the soft-lined chamber within. The mammae of the females are arranged in 3 or 4 pairs—2 pairs of abdominal and 1 or 2 pairs of pectoral. The number of young is usually 4 to 6.

Hibernation.—Unlike most mice the jumping mice hibernate long and securely. Before the cold weather begins they accumulate fat, most of which is deposited in a thick layer over the inside of the skin and furnishes ample food and fuel to carry them through five and possibly six months of inactivity. September 20 is the latest date at which any of the New Mexico specimens were taken, and these were very fat and probably ready to hibernate at the first cold wave. In fact, most of the individuals had evidently hibernated at that date, as no more were caught where their little piles of cut grass stems were abundant. There is little evidence as to the date of their emergence from hibernation, but at their altitude in the mountains the snow does not usually disappear until some time late in March, and as they enter hibernation after the first few frosts in autumn it is probable that they would not come out until freezing weather was practically over. Their winter nests are in burrows well underground, but little is known of their actual winter quarters.

Economic status.—The Rocky Mountain jumping mice are usually not sufficiently numerous to be of any serious economic importance. With a host of other mice they are constantly taking their slight toll from the grass crop, and in the aggregate this sometimes amounts to a considerable loss. So long as their natural enemies, the hawks, owls, and weasels, remain normally abundant, they will not do any great harm, but if their natural enemies were destroyed they might become very destructive in the meadows.

ZAPUS LUTEUS LUTEUS Miller

Yellow Jumping Mouse

Zapus luteus Miller, Biol. Soc. Wash. Proc. 24 : 253, 1911.

Type.—Collected at Espanola, N. Mex., June 24, 1904, by McClure Surber.

General characters.—A small slender species of the jumping mouse, with rich yellow sides and the dark band along the back from nose to tail less sharply defined and lighter than in *princeps*.

Measurements.—The type measures: Total length, 224; tail, 138; hind foot, 24 millimeters.

Distribution and habitat.—The beautiful yellow jumping mouse is represented in the Bureau of Biological Survey collection by specimens from Espanola at 5,500 feet altitude, from Penasco Creek 12 miles east of Cloudcroft in the Sacramento Mountains at 7,500 feet, and from the yellow-pine forest of the Sacramento Mountains at a point 10 miles northeast of Cloudcroft at 8,500 feet. (Fig. 40.) This seems to indicate a range covering both the Transition and the Upper Sonoran Zones, but the localities are too few for satisfactory determination of their zone limits. At Espanola, the type locality, McClure Surber collected four specimens in June, 1904, but gives no further notes than that they were collected in a large patch of weeds. His work at that locality was mainly along the bottom of the river valley, and evidently the specimens were taken at that level in the middle of the Upper Sonoran Zone. Those taken in the Sacramento Mountains were in grassy parks within the limits of the Transition Zone.

General habits.—Nothing is known of the habits of this species other than from the few specimens taken, but it apparently occupies the same kind of ground and has largely the same habits as the other forms of the group.

ZAPUS LUTEUS AUSTRALIS Bailey

Pale Jumping Mouse

Zapus luteus australis Bailey, Biol. Soc. Wash. Proc. 26 : 132, 1913.

Type.—Collected at Socorro, N. Mex., August 23, 1909, by E. A. Goldman.

General characters.—This small pallid form of the jumping mouse is well marked by its pale colors and very narrow slender skull. The sides are pale buffy yellow and the dorsal area is but slightly darker and not sharply defined. As usual the lower parts are pure white.

Measurements.—The type, an adult female, measures: Total length, 205; tail, 124; hind foot, 29.5 millimeters.

Distribution and habitat.—The type and only known specimen of the pale jumping mouse was collected by E. A. Goldman near Socorro in the Rio Grande Valley near the river. (Fig. 40.) It was taken in a trap set for cotton rats in a thicket of Baccharis, small willows, and grass on moist ground that is often overflowed from the river floods. The specimen, taken August 23, was a nursing female and shows such marked characters that it is impossible to place it with any other known species. Its closest affinities are evidently with *luteus*, of which an isolated colony may have been stranded in this

Lower Sonoran locality for so long a time as to develop marked characters. It is certainly the only species of jumping mouse known to inhabit the Lower Sonoran Zone and might well be expected to differ from its relatives of the Boreal zones.

Family GEOMYIDAE: Pocket Gophers

THOMOMYS FOSSOR ALLEN

COLORADO POCKET GOPHER; PAH-NA of the Taos Indians

Thomomys fossor Allen, Bul. Amer. Mus. Nat. Hist. 5 : 51, 1893.

Type.—Collected at Florida, La Plata County, Colo., June 25, 1892, by Charles P. Rowley.

General characters.—Small, dark-brown pocket gophers of the higher mountain ranges. Like all their family, they are sturdy, compact, little animals entirely adapted to underground life and burrowing habits. The eyes are very small, the ears short and almost concealed by the fur, the tail short and useful mainly as an organ of touch in guiding the animals backward through their burrows. The front legs are heavily muscled and the claws of the front feet long and well curved for digging. The ample fur-lined cheek pouches are used for carrying food.

Measurements.—Adult males measure, in total length, about 220; tail, 64; hind foot, 32 millimeters.

Distribution and habitat.—Of the nine species of the genus of pocket gophers (pl. 13) occurring in New Mexico, *fossor* is the most northern and has the highest range in the mountains, occupying the Canadian and the Hudsonian Zones and extending into the Arctic-Alpine Zone in

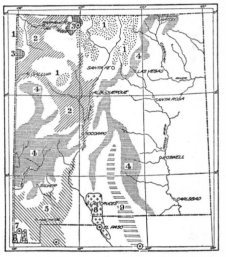

FIGURE 41.—Distribution of pocket gophers of the genus *Thomotys* in New Mexico: 1, *Thomomys fossor fossor*; 2, *T. perpallidus aureus*; 3, *T. perpallidus apache*; 4, *T. fulvus fulvus*; 5. *T. fulvus toltecus*; 6, *T. fulvus intermedius*; 7, *T. mearnsi*; 8. *T. lachuguilla*; 9. *T. baileyi.* Type localities circled

favorable situations on the higher peaks. (Fig. 41.) In the Taos Mountains these pocket gophers were abundant throughout the spruce and fir forests from 8,300 feet in Hondo Canyon to above timber line on the well-soiled slopes. A few of their old hills were seen on the very top of Wheelers Peak at 13,600 feet altitude, the highest point in New Mexico. The upper slopes of these mountains were in many places simply plowed over by the burrows of the pocket gophers, and the green turf was dotted with fresh black mounds of earth. Specimens caught above timber line in August had very long fur partly carried over from the previous winter coat. In the Culebra Mountains a little farther north they were equally abundant throughout the Canadian Zone and upward to the top of Culebra Peak at 13,500 feet, and farther south in the Pecos River Mountains throughout the same zones extending to the top of Pecos Baldy at 12,000 feet and as far up on the Truchas Peaks as the mellow soil extended, or to about 12,200 feet. In no part of this Sangre de Cristo Range were they found below the extreme lower limits of the Canadian Zone. In the San Juan and Jemez Mountains the pocket gophers are equally abundant throughout Canadian Zone and in cold meadows down to what seems to be the edge of the Transition Zone at 7,800 feet, but what is really the Canadian for temperature and species. Specimens of *fossor* were also taken on the Canadian Zone caps of Mount Taylor and the central part of the Chuska Range. The species is quite distinct from any of those occupying the adjoining lower country, and in many places there seems to be a narrow border line between their range and that of the next lower species, in which no pocket gophers occur.

General habits.—The Colorado pocket gophers avoid hard or clay soils, but collect in great numbers in the mellow, rich, mountain loam of the parks, meadows, and openings generally, and also occupy the open forests where there is sufficient vegetation for food. They are rarely found in the dense growth of conifers, although to some extent they are distributed through the aspen groves. In the parks and meadows their burrows seem to honeycomb the ground, the mounds dotting the surface so thickly that toward the close of summer they often cover from a tenth to a fifth of the surface. As fresh hills are thrown up the old ones are gradually sinking and disappearing beneath the rich carpet of vegetation. In this way the ground is constantly being plowed and the vegetation buried beneath the surface, which in many places greatly increases the fertility of the mountain slopes. The network of burrows underneath the surface also serves to hold and carry the water into the soil and store it for use. While the pocket gophers uproot, cover, or eat a great deal of the mountain vegetation, it all returns to the soil with a distinct gain in fertility.

In these high, cold, mountain regions the pocket gophers are largely diurnal in habits. A line of traps often remains untouched overnight, but as the sun begins to warm the ground about 8 or 9 a. m. the pocket gophers begin to spring the traps. As the ground often freezes slightly at night during the summer, it seems probable that the animals take advantage of the cold hours to enjoy their comfortable nests in the burrows and of the warmer hours of the day for their excavations and the collection of food. When the burrows are first opened more or less of the green vegetation about the doorway is collected for food, but after the earth is thrown out, the burrows are usually closed promptly.

Food habits.—A large part of the food of these miners consists of underground bulbs, tubers, and edible roots encountered as the burrows are extended. Little wild onions, camas, and lily bulbs are favorite foods. So many onions are eaten that the flesh of the pocket gophers often smells of them. Apparently most of the tender roots encountered contribute to their food. Of green vegetation they seem especially fond of the leaves and stems of the little clovers and vetches that abound in their mountain meadows, but a great variety of plants are eaten, including the many species of grass and sedges. Leaves, stems, roots, and bulbs are all tucked into their pouches as gathered and carried back into the burrows to be eaten at leisure or stored for future use. Frequently the specimens caught in traps are found with their pouches filled with leaves and stems cut by the sharp chisel teeth into convenient lengths. The finely masticated contents of the stomach and intestines gives little clue to the species of food plants, except as it has occasionally the strong odor of onions or some peculiarly scented plant.

The pocket gophers do not become fat and are evidently active all winter under the cover of deep snows, although probably less active during the very cold weather. They may depend in part on their summer stores but also get the roots and vegetation along the lines of their tunnels. They make long burrows under the snow and later pack them full of earth from deeper down, leaving snakelike casts of earth to mark their winter work. These extensive earth plugs remain after the snow is melted away and well into the summer to show the amount of work carried on during the winter.

Breeding habits.—In *Thomomys fossor* the mammae are arranged in 4 pairs—2 pairs of inguinal and 2 of pectoral. The young are probably about 4 in number and born sometime in May or June, as with other closely related species of the same group. There seem to be no actual dates, however, for this part of the country, even of embryos taken from specimens collected, but the nearly half-grown young are caught in July about the time they begin to move about and make burrows for themselves. There is evidently but one litter raised in a year, so that the increase is not more rapid than the normal decrease in numbers.

Enemies.—A host of enemies are constantly on the watch for these little animals as they are apparently a favorite food with hawks, owls, weasels, foxes, bobcats, badgers, and even bears. Weasels enter the burrows and capture the occupants without trouble if they can succeed in getting into the securely closed doorways. This is usually accomplished by hunting through the pocket-gopher meadows until a doorway is found through which the animal is throwing out earth, when there is no escape for him. Foxes and bobcats also pounce upon them when they are throwing out earth, and hawks and owls pick them up when they appear above ground. Badgers dig for them, but probably with little success, as it might take several days to dig out the total length of one burrow and make sure of the occupant. The rough holes where bears have dug for them are occasionally seen, but it is doubtful if they often meet with success or if the game is worth the candle.

Economic status.—This species of pocket gopher is perhaps of the least economic importance of any in the State, as it lives entirely above the zones of agriculture and as its work is mainly beneficial rather than injurious to man's interests.

For a recent account of the habits and economic status of the pocket gophers, see Scheffer (1931).

THOMOMYS FULVUS FULVUS (Woodhouse)

Fulvous Pocket Gopher

Geomys fulvus Woodhouse, Acad. Nat. Sci. Phila. Proc. 6: 201, 1852.

Type.—Collected at San Francisco Mountain, Ariz., October, 1851, by S. W. Woodhouse.

General characters.—Medium-sized pocket gophers, dark, rich, rusty brown in color, corresponding well with the color of the lava soil on which they are commonly found. In fact, the whole distribution of the species corresponds closely with the area of old lava flows in New Mexico and Arizona.

Measurements.—The males average in total length, 219; tail, 70; hind foot, 30 millimeters.

Distribution and habitat.—The widest range of the fulvous pocket gopher (pl. 13, B) is in the plateau country of Arizona, but it extends into western New Mexico throughout the Mogollon and Zuni Mountain region west of the Rio Grande and over the Sacramento, San Andres, and Manzano Mountains and northward along the eastern base of the Sangre de Cristos and into the Ratons. (Fig. 41.) The range lies mainly in the Transition Zone, but in the higher mountains not occupied by others this species extends into and in some cases practically through the width of the Canadian Zone. This is in such limited areas, however, that the range may be considered as mainly Transition. The pocket gophers are especially abundant throughout the open yellow pine forests where the grassy parks and openings are thoroughly plowed and worked over by their numerous burrows and mounds. They are partial to mellow, rich soil and the vicinity of moist and fertile valleys, but are often found on stony mesas where the soil is so scarce that a burrow sometimes has to be abandoned and a new one started on better ground.

General habits.—Like other species of the genus, the fulvous pocket gophers are great burrowers and spend almost their entire lives underground. They are industrious workers, as shown by the numerous mounds of earth thrown up at frequent intervals along the line of their underground tunnels. Their industry, however, seems to depend on the abundance of food, and in places where large edible roots are to be found the burrowing is less extensive and the mounds less numerous than in areas where vegetation is not so abundant and where it is necessary to cover more ground to obtain their food supply. Around some favorite plants a cluster of small mounds will remain for many days, while in other places a line of mounds will be extended at the rate of three or four a day, and at intervals of 6 to 10 or possibly 15 feet apart. At this rate the pocket gophers travel from place to place, always exploring for food and rarely leaving a place where it is found in abundance. During warm weather they seem to be active both night and day, as the morning will sometimes show a number of fresh mounds thrown up overnight, and at any time of day one may encounter a fresh mound that is being built up, the burrow being still open, the pocket gopher having been frightened away by approaching footsteps. On rare occasions one may approach so cautiously as not to disturb the worker and be able to watch its operations as each load of fresh, dark earth is pushed to the entrance of the burrow and given a final quick shove that sends it over the bank. Sometimes it will come entirely out of the burrow or a little more to push the load of dirt well out of the way of the next load, but more often only its head and shoulders appear for a twinkling as it throws out the dirt and dodges back out of sight of its numerous enemies.

At Cloudcroft, in the Sacramento Mountains, the writer succeeded in taking a dozen snapshots while one was making its mound by the side of his tent. During the 15 or 20 minutes between the opening of its burrow at the surface and the closing of its doorway after the mound was built up, when its pockets were stuffed with food from the growing vegetation, it did not get more than its full length, including tail, from the entrance of its burrow. Before throwing out any of the earth it gathered the stems and leaves of as many plants adjoining the burrow as it could stuff into its pockets. Then it would disappear for half a minute and reappear with a load of earth, which in the first instance was pushed well out, later loads being left nearer the opening until finally a few loads were pushed into it and left there to barricade the entrance. There was no scratching or kicking of the earth, but the pocket gopher brought out each load under its chin half-encircled by its arms while it wheel-barrowed itself along by pushing with its hind feet. Its motions were so quick that the dirt would often actually be thrown from it, and its retreat was so rapid that only a snapshot could register the animal distinctly. The pictures unfortunately were so small as to be of little interest and some were blurred by the swiftness of its motions. It was a rare occasion, however, for most people who live in pocket-gopher country have never seen the animal alive unless when one has been forced out of its burrow by irrigation water, at which time the wet and muddy pocket gopher is a most unattractive animal compared with the clean, smooth-furred, little miner seen in its normal dress.

Food habits.—As with all pocket gophers, the food is determined by the species of plants that are available in their habitat. Almost all bulbs and tender roots are eaten, but certain kinds prove more acceptable than others. The little wild onions and the bulbs of numerous lilies seem to be favorite food, but the big, fleshy root of a thistle or burdock or some of the perennial sunflowers, and even the poison parsnip, are all eagerly eaten. Leguminous plants seem to be favorites, both root and top, and one is often followed to the surface and the whole plant devoured or carried away. Cultivated plants, including potatoes, and all root crops, as well as all kinds of clover and alfalfa, are evidently preferred to the native food, as the pocket gophers seem to gravitate toward them and rarely leave them for outside forage. To some extent they store up food for future use, but as they are active throughout the winter they do not provide a complete winter store.

Breeding habits.—Like all the species of the genus occurring in New Mexico, these pocket gophers have the mammae arranged in 4 pairs—2 pairs of inguinal and 2 of pectoral. The writer has but one record of the number of young in a litter for the State: A female taken on May 12, 1906, on the head of the Mimbres River contained 6 embryos. This is probably about the maximum for the species, as other species with the same number and arrangement of mammae usually have from 4 to 6 young. Evidently but 1 litter is raised in a season, as the half-grown young began to get into the writer's traps in June and July, and no small ones were caught late in the season. Practically nothing is known of the breeding habits of the animals, however, as their life is mainly underground. By the first cold weather in October the young are nearly full grown and are each living in separate burrows.

Economic status.—As the greater part of the range of this species covers valleys or open grazing country, there is little damage that they can do. In the lower part of their range, however, they come in conflict with many small ranches and gardens, where they cause great annoyance and considerable loss by destruction of crops. Wherever opportunity offers they quickly find a potato patch or garden, and if left alone a few of them will almost destroy either. They also do considerable damage in grainfields by cutting the growing grain or covering it with their mounds. In gardens and small fields a few traps or a little poison administered in pieces of potato will soon eliminate the pocket gophers where, if left to themselves, they would do serious harm. When it is necessary to destroy them from larger areas more systematic methods must be used. Advice in this respect may be obtained from Bureau of Biological Survey.

THOMOMYS FULVUS PERVAGUS Merriam

Espanola Pocket Gopher

Thomomys aureus pervagus Merriam, Biol. Soc. Wash. Proc. 14 : 110, 1901.

Type.—Collected at Espanola, N. Mex., January 4, 1894, by J. Alden Loring.
General characters.—A rather large species averaging somewhat larger than *fulvus*. In color it is bright, rusty brown all over, but slightly paler below.
Measurements.—Adult males measure: Total length, about 239 ; tail, 73 ; hind foot, 32–33 millimeters.

Distribution and habitat.—The Espanola pocket gopher is found throughout the upper Rio Grande Valley from Santa Fe north to the southern part of the San Luis Valley in Colorado, mainly in the Upper Sonoran Zone. There are specimens from near Santa Fe, from Espanola, Chama River, Abiquiu, Rinconada, Hondo River near its junction with the Rio Grande, Questa, and from Antonito just over the Colorado line. It is an abundant species over the valley bottoms and along the valleys of the side streams that cut through the numerous lava fields into the Rio Grande. The soil in this part of the valley is generally a mixture of lava and sand, as the Rio Grande cuts through a long lava canyon above Rinconada, and the many side streams bring in their contributions from sandstone cliffs and many varieties of soil and rock. In places the valley where these pocket gophers occur has a surface of deep loose sand, but more generally it is firm and rather dark brown soil, which seems to bear a close relation to the color of the pocket gophers. The species is not very widely distributed and apparently is but a local valley form of *fulvus*, which reaches in almost typical form to Glorieta only a short distance from Santa Fe, where *pervagus* has been taken. In habits *pervagus* is more like *aureus* from the fact that it occupies the same type of valley country, and it is not improbable that intergradation may some time be traced from *fulvus* through it to *aureus*. For the present, however, there are no specimens showing direct connection.

Food habits.—In the Santa Clara Canyon just west of Espanola they were common along the bottom of the narrow wide valley extending up to the edge of the yellow-pine forest. Many of these little flats have been cultivated for ages by the cliff dwellers and Pueblo Indians and support an abundant growth of small wild potatoes (*Solanum tuberosum*), of which the pocket gophers seem very fond. They were constantly digging among these plants, and a number of the tubers were found in their pockets. The little tender roots that bear the tubers as well as the potato tops were found cut off at the entrance of the burrows. Other plants, including a little Chenopodium and a juicy Senecio were also found in their pockets.

Economic status.—Much of the valley land occupied by *pervagus* is good agricultural and fruit land, so that the presence of these pocket gophers is highly detrimental both in destroying crops and injuring irrigation ditches. At Espanola and along the Hondo River they were abundant in the alfalfa fields, where an attempt was made to flood their burrows and force them out. As no other method was used to destroy them, there seemed to be little check on their abundance.

THOMOMYS FULVUS TOLTECUS Allen

Toltec Pocket Gopher

Thomomys toltecus Allen, Bul. Amer. Mus. Nat. Hist. 5:52, 1893.

Type.—Collected at Colonia Juarez, Chihuahua, Mexico, autumn of 1890 by A. D. Meed on the Lumholtz Expedition.
General characters.—A large, pale-colored form of the *fulvus* group. It is slightly larger than *fulvus*.
Measurements.—An adult male measures: Total length, about 221; tail, 72; hind foot, 31.5 millimeters.

Distribution and habitat.—The Toltec pocket gopher occupies the valley country of southwestern New Mexico, southeastern Arizona and northern Chihuahua, mainly in the Lower Sonoran Zone. (Fig. 41.) Specimens from the Upper Sonoran Zone are generally more or less intermediate between *fulvus* and *toltecus*. Considerable variation is shown over a rather wide range, but in its typical form the species agrees very well in color with the dull-clay or sandy desert valleys that it occupies. Locally these pocket gophers are abundant in the more fertile spots where vegetation is sufficient to furnish an adequate food supply. They are absent, however, over wide spaces of barren mesa where plant life is poor and scattered.

General habits.—In the sandy mellow soil where these pocket gophers are generally most abundant their mounds and burrows are large and numerous. If vegetation is scarce they dig farther and faster and so seem always able to maintain an adequate supply of food. As with all mammals, and in fact all other forms of life, desert conditions require special adaptations and modify both tastes and habits. As many of the plants grow largely underground with extensive root systems, the pocket gophers must find those that are acceptable as food and adapt themselves to their manner of growth. The barren surface and scorching heat of the summer months also call for special adaptations, but the pocket gophers in their subterranean galleries have many advantages over other mammals with less protected homes. They are to a great extent nocturnal, though usually active during the cooler morning and evening hours. Water in a free state seems unnecessary, and the desert has little terror for them.

Nothing specific is known of the breeding habits of this species except that the mammae are arranged in four pairs, and evidently but one litter of young is usually raised in a season.

Food habits.—Little is known of the actual species of food plants selected by these pocket gophers, except that they often collect around patches of cactus and feed upon the stems and fleshy pads where they come in contact with the ground and can be reached from the burrow entrance. Often a number of pocket-gopher mounds are thrown up in and around a patch of pricklypear and sometimes the inside is hollowed out of some large fleshy cactus. Roots of various kinds seem to furnish most of their food, and it is probable that an abundance of moisture is found in them.

Economic status.—Though the pocket gophers are but moderately prolific, their enemies are numerous in the desert as elsewhere, and they are constantly preyed upon by coyotes, foxes, bobcats, badgers, and numerous hawks and owls. Their numbers are thus kept down to a harmless stage in the open country, but where they are given special protection and can work under the cover of ample vegetation or in fields of grain and alfalfa they increase more rapidly than in the open. In their constant search for better and more abundant food they also tend to collect in cultivated or protected grounds where they often do serious damage to farm products. They fairly revel in alfalfa fields, where their large mounds cover many of the growing plants while they feed on both the roots and tops. A large number of pocket gophers in an alfalfa field seriously reduce the yield, their mounds make it necessary to cut the crop at a higher level than would otherwise be necessary, and the stones and gravel in the mounds dull and break the knives of the mowing machines.

At Garfield and Cuchillo E. A. Goldman found them very abundant and destructive in the alfalfa fields. He says:

At Cuchillo, owing to the uneven surface of the ground, the checks are usually small and little land can be flooded at a time. The gophers are therefore able to escape to the check borders and when the water has soaked away are ready to resume active operations in the alfalfa. In several of the fields belonging to W. W. Martin considerable alfalfa had been killed by the gophers. A slight pull on the dried tops sufficed to draw the plants out of the ground and show that the roots had been eaten. Some alfalfa tops were also bitten off at the surface of the ground within reach of the holes that had been temporarily opened and the tops were drawn into the holes and eaten. As alfalfa hay is worth $25 per ton at Cuchillo, the injury to the crop is a serious matter. Mr. Martin also complained of breaks in ditch banks through the gopher burrows. At Garfield there were also complaints of the breaking of large ditch banks by the water escaping through gopher burrows.

At Redrock, Goldman also reported many complaints of damage by the pocket gophers, both in destroyed crops and in the weakening of levees and ditch banks by their burrows. In grainfields they cause some trouble and loss, but they seem less attracted to fields of grain than to alfalfa. In vegetable gardens they always create great havoc, and in orchards and nurseries their mischief is perhaps the most serious of all. The roots are cut from the small trees in rapid sequence and even old, bearing fruit trees are often seriously injured or killed by having their roots destroyed. In many cases this loss could be avoided by simple methods of trapping or other control methods.

THOMOMYS FULVUS INTERMEDIUS Mearns

INTERMEDIATE POCKET GOPHER

Thomomys fulvus intermedius Mearns, U. S. Natl. Mus. Proc. 19:719, 1897.

Type.—Collected at summit of Huachuca Mountains, Ariz., September 6, 1893, by E. A. Mearns and F. X. Holzner.

General characters.—A small southern mountain form of the group, considerably smaller and slightly darker than *fulvus,* with a distinctly blackish dorsal line in typical specimens.

Measurements.—Adult males measure: Total length, about 200; tail, 66; hind foot, 26 millimeters.

Distribution and habitat.—These pocket gophers have a scattered distribution on the tops of numerous mountain ranges in southeastern Arizona and southwestern New Mexico. (Fig. 41.) A few specimens from the higher slopes of the Animas Mountains constitute the only New Mexico records. They were taken in the Transition Zone from near the base to the summit of the Animas Peaks, or from about 5,800 to 8,000 feet. They occupy the more open slopes and timbered tops of the ridges, but are not found to any extent in the dense chaparral covering a large part of the range. Nothing was learned of their habits to show whether they differed in any way from other species. In their practically uninhabited area they seem to be of no economic importance.

THOMOMYS MEARNSI Bailey

MEARNS'S POCKET GOPHER

Thomomys mearnsi Bailey, Biol. Soc. Wash. Proc. 27:117, 1914.

Type.—Collected at the Gray ranch, in Animas Valley, southwestern New Mexico, August 10, 1898, by E. A. Goldman.

General characters.—Externally this species closely resembles *fulvus* to which it is perhaps nearest related. It is slightly smaller and lighter colored and is especially characterized by its slender projecting incisors.

Measurements.—The type, an adult male, measures: Total length, 220; tail, 67; hind foot, 31 millimeters.

Distribution and habitat.—A few specimens of the very peculiar Mearns's pocket gophers were collected in the moist soil along the edges of a large marsh in the bottom of the Animas Valley at the Gray ranch. (Fig. 41.) They are so decidedly different from those collected in the dry parts of the valley or in the adjoining mountain ranges that it seems necessary to recognize them as distinct from either. The extent of their range is entirely unknown, but it is not improbable that they follow down the Animas and possibly through the San Simon Valley into Arizona. The strongly alkaline soil of this valley bottom may have some bearing on the modifications of the animals through a long period of time, but it seems more probable that the hard and clayey character of the soil when dry, making it necessary for the pocket gophers to use their incisors in extending their tunnels, has played a large part in the modification of the teeth and cranium. The actual distribution and habits of the species remain to be worked out.

THOMOMYS BAILEYI Merriam

Sierra Blanca Pocket Gopher

Thomomys baileyi Merriam, Biol. Soc. Wash. Proc. 14: 109, 1901.

Type.—Collected at Sierra Blanca, Tex., December 28, 1889, by Vernon Bailey.

General characters.—In external appearance not very different from *lachuguilla*, but the skull indicates an animal of a very different type, with a short, wide cranium and very protruding incisors.

Measurements.—An adult male measures: Total length, 215; tail, 64; hind foot, 31 millimeters. Average of five females: 212; 69; 29 millimeters, respectively.

Distribution and habit.—The species *baileyi* is known from only two localities, by a series of specimens collected at Sierra Blanca, Tex., in 1889; and another series collected near Tularosa, N. Mex., in 1902. (Fig. 41.) It is apparently an Upper Sonoran form occupying the open mesa country about Sierra Blanca and extending up the western foothills of the Sacramento Range along the eastern border of the Great Tularosa Valley.

General habits.—At Sierra Blanca these pocket gophers were abundant but harmless, as no agriculture was possible in that region, but at Tularosa, Gaut reported them as very abundant along the foothills of the Sacramento Mountains east of town and in the alfalfa fields on the different ranches about Tularosa where they did serious damage to the alfalfa and to the irrigation ditches. He says:

One rancher tells me that his alfalfa crop is about half as large as it should have been this season, owing to the fact that the gophers prevented him from irrigating it sufficiently. They have made underground tunnels that carried the water off in streams and wasted what was needed for the crop.

These few notes show practically all that is known of this species.

THOMOMYS LACHUGUILLA Bailey

Lechuguilla Pocket Gopher

Thomomys aureus lachuguilla Bailey, Biol. Soc. Wash. Proc. 15: 120, 1902.

Type.—Collected at El Paso, Tex., September 24, 1901, by Vernon Bailey.

General characters.—This little, pale, buffy-yellow gopher, which was described from specimens collected at El Paso, Tex., as a subspecies of *aureus*, apparently is not closely connected with either the *aureus* or *fulvus* groups, and until more is known of its range and characters its affinities will remain in doubt, and it had better stand alone.

Measurements.—Adult males measure: Total length, about 202; tail, 61; hind foot, 27 millimeters.

Distribution and habitat.—The little desert Lechuguilla pocket gophers are common in the gulches of the lower foothills of the Franklin and Organ Mountains. (Fig. 41.) They have a more extensive range farther down the Rio Grande Valley in Texas, but reach their northern limit, so far as known at the present time, along the foothill slopes of the Organ Mountains in New Mexico. Gaut collected specimens near the Cox ranch on the east side of the mountains, and some small pocket-gopher hills that the writer saw on the west side of the range were probably made by this species. Some pocket gophers seem to be abundant over the higher slopes of the Organ Mountains, but as no specimens have been collected. it is very doubtful whether they are this species or the larger, darker colored *fulvus*, which occupies the San Andres Mountains farther north.

General habits.—These are typical desert pocket gophers, occupying the mellowest spots they can find on arid mesas and in sandy gulches over the hot Lower Sonoran Zone. They have a very interrupted range. One may travel for miles over barren mesas where no trace of their mounds is seen, and then find a few in a sandy gulch where a little moisture collects and plants can live. In color as well as food habits they are thoroughly adapted to their desert environment and probably lead as comfortable lives as other species in richer surroundings. In the region about El Paso and farther south they feed quite extensively on the tender and starchy heart of the lechuguilla (*Agave lecheguilla*). This plant is so protected by hooks and spines from other animals that it grows in abundance in many parts of the desert but is readily attacked by the pocket gophers from underground and its whole inside store of plant food is eaten out. Many species of cactus are also used for food. The large devil's-head cactus is burrowed into from beneath and the inside is eaten out, while the green pads and stems of pricklypear are eaten aboveground. Apparently yuccas and many other desert plants are also eaten by these pocket gophers, but in reality very little is known of their habits. As they rarely live where there are ranches or settlements, there are no complaints against them.

THOMOMYS PERPALLIDUS AUREUS Allen

GOLDEN POCKET GOPHER; NAZUZA of the Navajo Indians

Thomomys aureus Allen, Bul. Amer. Mus. Nat. Hist. 5: 49, 1893.

Type.—Collected at Bluff, Utah, May 12, 1892, by Charles P. Rowley.
General characters.—One of the largest pocket gophers occurring in New Mexico, with upper parts normally of a beautiful golden-buff color and underparts pale buff or whitish.
Measurements.—The males measure: Total length, about 240; tail, 73; hind foot, 31 millimeters.

Distribution and habitat.—The golden pocket gophers are valley dwellers, partial to mellow sandy soil and to some extent associated with the region of bright-red and yellow sandstone cliffs occupying so much of northwestern New Mexico (fig. 41), northeastern Arizona and southern Utah. As with other species, the color of the soil in which they live is to a great extent imitated in their pelage. In New Mexico they occupy the Great San Juan Valley and the Rio Grande Valley from Socorro to Bernalillo. These areas are probably connected through the valleys of the Puerco and San Jose with the San Juan and Zuni River Valleys. In New Mexico and throughout the range of the typical form it is a purely Upper Sonoran species. Two specimens collected on the Chama River near the little village of Gallina and another near El Vado seem to be referable to *aureus* rather than to any other of the surrounding forms, although these localities are apparently cut off from the main range of the species. Their characteristic large holes were also seen in the Quemado Valley south of the Zuni Mountains, and specimens were taken though not saved. It is not improbable that they have a continuous range from the San Augustine Plain through the narrow gap between the east and west Datil Ranges to the Zuni River Valley. They are most abundant in the mellowest, and most fertile valleys, but their big, sandy mounds are often seen through the dry parts of the valleys and in sandy washes, even where vegetation is scant and poor.

General habits.—In no radical way do the habits of these pocket gophers differ from those of others of the genus. In the mellow soil of their habitat their burrows are large, and the mounds of loose sand thrown out often contain a bushel, or, in some cases, several bushels of material. Digging is easy and rapid, and they cover more ground with their burrows and mounds than any species of equal size on less mellow soils. On poor soil the burrows are extended in direct lines until more fertile areas are encountered, when they congregate and remain as long as food is abundant. In some cases where food is scarce, it is possible that they even leave their burrows and travel overland until more favorable locations are found, but there is little evidence to show that any of them ever leave the burrows, except males in search of mates during the mating season. Two pocket gophers are seldom caught in one burrow, but occasionally this happens during the early spring. If they were in the habit of moving about at any distance from their burrows, their peculiar tracks would certainly show in the very mellow sand where they live. During years of trapping and observation of their habits, the writer has never detected their tracks at more than a foot from the freshly opened burrows. They seem to be about equally active during the day and night, but during the daytime are most active in the morning and evening hours, and it is very probable that their nocturnal activity is also mainly near evening and morning.

In trapping for them along the Rio Grande, Loring in 1894 reported them as especially abundant at Bernalillo, Albuquerque, Belen, Socorro, and Marcial. They were abundant over the valleys, but seemed partial to the railroad bank, where he said they would throw up their mounds at distances of about 20 feet apart, or again in groups, close together. In removing the earth from their burrows in some, one might find the hole near the surface and in others be compelled to dig from 1 to 2 feet before finding the open burrow. When caught, several specimens had small pieces of roots in their cheek pouches. On being released from the traps, he says, they would fight like little bulldogs. At Socorro, E. A. Goldman found them especially abundant in alfalfa fields on the river flats, where they were doing considerable damage to the alfalfa and other crops, and there were some complaints of their burrowing into ditch banks.

Food habits.—As in other species, the food of the golden pocket gopher includes a great variety of vegetation, both roots and tops of such wild and domestic plants as they encounter. Evidently the greater part of their food comes from underground vegetation, but the material in the alimentary canals the writer has found decidedly green. In some cases, however, the stomach is filled entirely with the white pulp of roots and underground vegetation. At the base of the Bear Spring Mountains and on the San Augustine Plains, Hollister, while collecting series of specimens, reported numerous cuttings of roots and grass and wheat stems found in digging out the burrows. These were evidently food caches put away for future, if not for winter, use, as they were found late in September and early in October.

Economic status.—This species of pocket gopher is peculiarly destructive to farm crops, not only from its large size, but from its abundance in some of the most fertile agricultural valleys of the State, and in a region where irrigation ditches are depended upon for practically all the agriculture. The pocket gophers congregate in fields, gardens, and orchards but are especially partial to alfalfa fields where they do considerable damage. In the San Juan Valley in October of 1908 they were abundant over most of the farms and orchards of the valley. At Fruitland, Clarence Birdseye was told by L. C. Burnham, who had lived there for some years, that in one day he had driven out and killed 130 pocket gophers by turning the water from the irrigation ditches into their burrows. Mr. Collier at Fruitland also said that many of his fruit trees leaned in one direction or another, because the pocket gophers had cut off part of the roots. In spite of irrigation the animals were still common in his orchards and fields and no effort was being made to destroy them. There were also many complaints of their injury to ditches in this rich farming and fruit valley. Near the pueblo of Zuni when the writer was camping there in September, 1908, a large Government irrigation ditch had been recently completed. The banks of the ditch had been finished for some time, but the water had not yet been turned in, and at frequent intervals pocket gophers as well as other rodents had taken up their residence in the banks of the ditch and were throwing out mounds of earth on both sides, showing that their burrows must penetrate back and forth from the inner to the outer surface. As the ditch followed for miles along the side of the valley the ground on the lower side was below the water level of the ditch, so that as soon as the water was turned in and found its way to the pocket-gopher burrows there would be numerous breaks in the bank. This is the inevitable history of sidehill ditches in a pocket-gopher country, as long as the animals are allowed to remain within reach of them. In small local ditches the pocket gophers also fill a great part of the ditch by throwing their earth out of the banks along its sides and when the ditches are dry by throwing up their mounds along the bottom as well as sides. It is especially important to be able to control their abundance on irrigated farms. The Bureau of Biological Survey is always ready to give directions for controlling pocket gophers in special cases that are not easily handled.

THOMOMYS APACHE Bailey

Apache Pocket Gopher

Thomomys apache Bailey, Biol. Soc. Wash. Proc. 23 : 79, 1910.

Type.—Collected at Lake La Jara, on the Jicarilla Apache Indian Reservation, N. Mex., September 10, 1904, by James H. Gaut.

General characters.—The largest and darkest colored pocket gopher in New Mexico; it is very dark buffy gray and in some specimens almost black.

Measurements.—The type, an old male, measures: Total length, 250; tail, 85; hind foot, 34 millimeters.

Distribution and habitat.—These big Apache pocket gophers were found in Transition Zone at Lake La Jara, Stinking Spring Lake

[Burford Lake], and Horse Lake on the Jicarilla Indian Reservation and on top of the southern end of the Chuska Mountains on the Apache Reservation. (Fig. 41.) In every locality where collected they were found occupying the rich, black soil along the borders of little, inland lakes. Apparently they represent a Transition Zone form of the *T. perpallidus aureus* group, which has locally become strongly modified by environment and adapted to a higher zone than their nearest relative, *aureus*. Two localities from which they have been taken are separated by 150 miles of Upper Sonoran desert where *aureus* occurs. There can be no possible continuity of range between these localities and evidently the form has developed independently along so exactly parallel lines as to be indistinguishable from the different localities. Large series of specimens are very uniform in character and in neither locality do they seem to intergrade with other species outside of their lake borders.

General habits.—In the moist earth surrounding the shores of a large number of shallow desert lakes these pocket gophers throw up numerous large mounds of black earth. The burrows as well as the mounds are large, and in trapping the animals the writer found it necessary to fasten the traps so they would not be drawn down the burrows. Often the ground was wet and the mounds muddy, and in some cases the bottoms of the burrows contained water that had seeped through from the edge of the lake. An abundance of plant food is always available along these lake borders where the pocket gophers have grown to a large size compared with surrounding species. No specific notes were obtained on their food habits, but in the midst of abundant vegetation they evidently obtained an ample supply. In the areas where they were taken there is no attempt at agriculture, so that they are practically harmless and possibly of some benefit to the soil and grazing.

CRATOGEOMYS CASTANOPS (Baird)

Chestnut Pocket Gopher [22]

Pseudostoma castanops Baird, Rpt. Standsbury's Expedition to Great Salt Lake, p. 313, 1852.
Geomys clarkii Baird, Acad. Nat. Sci. Philadelphia Proc. 7: 332, 1855. Type from El Paso.

Type.—Collected near Bents Fort (Las Animas), Colo., prior to 1860 by Lieutenant Abert.
General characters.—Size slightly larger than that of any other pocket gopher in New Mexico; colors dull yellowish brown above, slightly lighter below; skull broad and heavy; each upper incisor with a single middle groove.
Measurements.—An adult male topotype measures in total length, 295; tail, 95; hind foot, 37 millimeters.

Distribution and habitat.—The big pocket gophers, *C. castanops* (pl. 13, C), occupy practically all of the Lower Sonoran valleys of New Mexico east of the Rio Grande and extend in a few places up

---

[22] The name " chestnut-faced pocket gopher " is entirely inappropriate as a common name, as its Latin equivalent was applied to the type specimen on the supposition that the molt line, which had progressed to the back of the head and left the fresh dark pelage of the head and face in sharp contrast to the old faded pelage of the rest of the body, was a permanent color pattern. The whole upper parts are practically uniform in color when in the same condition, but the molt begins at the nose and progresses backward to the tail with a sharply defined margin. The fresh pelage is a dull yellowish chestnut; the faded coat at time of molting is much paler.

the valleys into the edge of the Upper Sonoran. (Fig. 42.) Specimens from El Paso and Albuquerque mark the western border of
their range. They are partial to the mellow rich soil of the valleys,
and are especially abundant throughout the Pecos Valley and locally
in parts of the Rio Grande and Tularosa Valleys. In two localities
they occur in the Upper Sonoran Zone—near Weed on a branch of
Penasco Creek and from somewhere near Chico in Colfax County.
The specimens from both of these localities are abnormally small,
which probably indicates an unsuitable environment. There seems to
be no appreciable variation in the species throughout the United
States part of its range. A series of specimens from the type locality
near Las Animas, Colo., and from El Paso, Tex., near the type
locality of Baird's *clarkii* are indistinguishable. At Albuquerque
Loring collected specimens and found them common in 1894, and
the writer has several times
observed numerous large
earth mounds over the mellow soil of the Rio Grande
Valley in that vicinity.
At Eddy (now Carlsbad)
Dutcher collected them in
1892, and in 1901 the writer
traced them all over that
part of the Pecos Valley.
The following year Hollister
and he collected two specimens on the east slope of
the Sacramento Mountains
at 6,000 feet altitude and
found their big mounds
lower down on both sides of
the range. They were also
found common about Ros-
well, and Hollister collected
specimens and reported
them at various localities
along the Pecos River Val-

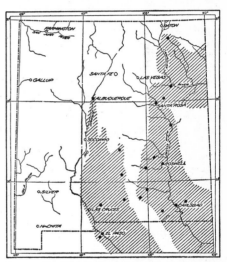

FIGURE 42.—Distribution of the chestnut pocket
gopher. *Cratogeomys castonops,* in New Mexico

ley north to Santa Rosa. Gaut collected one specimen at the west
base of the Jicarilla Mountains but could find no trace of others
in that region. He found them abundant, however, in the Tularosa
Valley, and collected series at points 9 miles south of Tularosa and
near Parker Lake at the east base of the Organ Mountains. They
are common along both sides of the Rio Grande Valley, at El Paso,
Tex., and southward through western Texas into Mexico, but their
range does not extend eastward beyond the region of mesquite.

General habits.—In the rich mellow soil of the valleys these large
chestnut pocket gophers multiply until their great mounds often
cover a large part of the best agricultural land. They avoid the
hard soil of the arid mesas and the upper slopes but extend their
range as far as possible along the valleys and side streams, which
furnish moisture and fertility. At Santa Rosa they were especially
numerous and active in the mellow sand of the valley along the river
flats and in the big meadows east of town. A few were scattered

along the Piedras Negras Creek Valley and thence eastward through the low gap to the valley of the Red River, where they were again abundant in the mellow soil of its valley. So long as the soil is mellow and rich and full of succulent vegetation and tender roots, they seem to have no choice between loose sand and rich black loam. In the sandy soil, however, their hills are larger and apparently more numerous, either because it is necessary to dig farther to find their food supply or because the digging is easier and the same amount of work carries them farther along and turns up more fresh earth. Their mounds are often 2 or 3 feet in diameter and 6 or 8 inches high and are scattered along the line of the underground burrows at intervals of 10 to 20 feet.

Food habits.—Like other members of the genus, these pocket gophers feed largely on roots obtained from their underground tunnels, but they also gather green vegetation from about the openings that they make in throwing the loose earth from the burrows. Any plants within reach are cut off at the bottom and drawn down until they can be cut into suitable sections for carrying in the cheek pouches, which are stuffed until widely distended. A great variety are eaten, but the clovers and related plants seem to be favorite foods. At Carlsbad the pocket gophers were found sparingly in the edges of the alfalfa fields, but irrigation kept them out of the central part of the best fields. The stomachs of those examined sometimes showed only green vegetation, but usually contained a large portion of light-colored pulp from the roots and underground vegetation ground so finely that the species could not be determined. The plants, leaves, and stems found in the pouches give a good idea of the food list, and the damage done in gardens and orchards adds additional species.

Breeding habits.—Little is known of the breeding habits of this species or of their underground habits in general. The females have three pairs of mammae, which is the usual number in Geomys, and it is probable that the young vary in number from three to six. It is only when the young are old enough to leave the nest and travel about the burrows that they are caught in traps, and then they are rarely less than half grown. When nearly full grown they evidently leave the parental burrows and start new tunnels for themselves, as a burrow rarely contains more than one adult. They do not hibernate but are active throughout the year.

Economic status.—The fact that these pocket gophers occupy the most fertile parts of the valleys, together with their large size and the large quantities of earth that they throw out of their burrows, makes them especially obnoxious tenants on well cultivated farms. In places they do considerable damage in orchards, gardens, and potato fields by eating the roots, tubers, and other underground parts of trees and plants. In alfalfa fields and meadows their earth mounds cover and destroy a part of the crop, and in addition they eat the stems and roots. Their mounds are very troublesome to the farmer in mowing, as the sickle, if lowered to obtain the full cut, is sure to run through the heaps of sand and gravel and be seriously dulled. The pocket gophers are easily trapped, however, and with a little effort the farm land can be kept clear of them.

GEOMYS ARENARIUS MERRIAM

DESERT POCKET GOPHER

Geomys arenarius Merriam, North Amer. Fauna No. 8, p. 139, 1895.

Type.—Collected at El Paso, Tex., December 14, 1889, by Vernon Bailey.

General characters.—Size, medium; tail rather long for a pocket gopher; colors pale buffy brown above; lower parts pale buffy or whitish, in many specimens with irregular patches of pure white over throat, breast, and belly. Upper incisors with a deep middle and shallow inner groove down the front of each.

Measurements.—The type, an adult male, measures: Total length, 258; tail, 88; hind foot, 33 millimeters.

Distribution and habitat.—The pale, sand-colored desert pocket gopher (pl. 13, A) inhabits the Rio Grande Valley from El Paso north to Las Cruces and probably somewhat farther, and specimens have been taken as far west as Deming and to latitude 30° 15' on the Mexican boundary. (Fig. 43.) Specimens from Monahans, Tex., are also referred to this species, which very probably follows up the sand-dune area into southeastern New Mexico. This is a sand-loving species of the Lower Sonoran valleys and in distribution is probably cut off from any other species of the genus.

General habits.—In December, 1889, the writer found these pocket gophers abundant over the sandy river valley below El Paso, and up to nearly Christmas

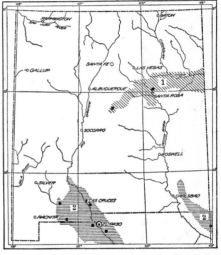

FIGURE 43.—Distribution of pocket gophers of the genus *Geomys* in New Mexico: 1, *Geomys breviceps llanensis;* 2, *G. arenarius.* Type locality circled

they were actively extending their burrows and throwing up fresh mounds of the moist light sand. A. K. Fisher also collected them on these sandy bottoms in 1894, and Loring found them in the same year on both sides of the Rio Grande. At Deming they were common in the mellow sand along the Rio Mimbres in December, 1889, and several specimens were collected. At Las Cruces, Loring caught a series of specimens in June, 1894, where he found them abundant in the railroad grade about 2 miles north of town. In 1909 E. A. Goldman found them common about Las Cruces, especially in alfalfa fields and orchards. He reported one caught in gravelly soil on the mesa 3 or 4 miles east of Las Cruces but found that they generally preferred the softer soil in the bottom of the valley. The hills thrown up were so large that the loss of alfalfa covered by them was considerable. There were also complaints of damage from breaks in ditch banks where they were at work.

At Mesilla Park in November, 1909, the writer found them numerous all over the valley bottoms, especially in fields and along irrigation ditch banks. The experiment-station fields, orchards, and grounds were full of them. In a 10-acre alfalfa field there were approximately eight pocket gophers to the acre, with an average of 50 mounds to a gopher. On one sandy place the writer counted 40 mounds in a row, pushed up by one big pocket gopher after the last rain, probably within two weeks. These mounds averaged about 5 feet apart, with a peck of sand to each. A pocket gopher at work in the lawn of the farm at Mesilla Park had thrown up about two dozen hills and if left alone would have plowed over most of the lawn by spring. The writer set a trap and caught the animal with about 5 minutes work and could just as easily have caught others in the lawns about the other buildings.

In many of the fields and meadows over the valley the pocket gophers were equally numerous, and a series of their fresh mounds was found along the outer banks of irrigation ditches that had been raised to a considerable level above the fields. In some places the burrows evidently reached clear through the banks of dry ditches, as in one place the hills were thrown out on both the outer and inner sides of the bank, and in other places the burrows evidently ran under the bottom of the ditch and came out on both outer banks. There were numbers of old breaks in the ditch banks undoubtedly caused by pocket-gopher burrows. Meadows from which the hay had been cut were thickly dotted over with mounds, and in places the pocket gophers were working extensively in the orchards and gardens. Apparently there was no attempt to get rid of them or to keep them out, except where the land could be irrigated and then they were driven to higher levels. At that time, however, there was no adequate supply of water for irrigation and the pocket gophers were flourishing over most of the valley. After talking with a number of farmers who complained that they did a great deal of damage, especially in the orchards, but that they knew of no means by which they could be destroyed, the writer had no trouble in catching a number in traps, and to test them on poisons he placed a little strychnine in two pieces of potato and two pieces of sweetpotato and put them into occupied burrows. The next morning three of these burrows remained open, which indicated that the strychnine had done its work in them, while the other hole was closed, having no doubt been closed before the potato was eaten. The pocket gophers are so easily trapped or poisoned that there is little excuse for leaving them in the fields in any locality where they can do damage. Much remains to be learned of the underground habits of these animals, but the results of their depredations are only too evident.

GEOMYS BREVICEPS LLANENSIS Bailey

Mesquite Plains Pocket Gopher

Geomys breviceps llanensis Bailey, North Amer. Fauna No. 25, p. 129, 1905.

Type.—Collected at Llano, Llano County, Tex., May 15, 1899, by Vernon Bailey.
General characters.—About the size of *arenarius* but darker and richer colored; upper parts, light cinnamon brown; lower parts, paler cinnamon; upper incisors with large and small groove down the front of each.

Measurements.—The type, an adult male, measured: Total length, 270; tail, 88; hind foot, 32 millimeters.

Distribution and habitat.—A few specimens of the bright-colored mesquite plains pocket gopher carry its range west to Santa Rosa and the north end of the Mesa Jumanes, in the vicinity of Progresso. It evidently finds its way up the Red River Valley from northwestern Texas. (Fig. 43.) The Santa Rosa specimens are practically typical of the species, although slightly pale, while the Jumanes specimen is equally pale and rather small. The specimen that Gaut collected at Santa Rosa was not recognized as different from *Cratogeomys*, which he had been collecting there, and his note refers to both species. In 1903 the writer picked up a dead pocket gopher of this species on the sandy river flats near Santa Rosa, but it was not in condition to be saved and no others were taken. On May 10, 1910, Lantz caught two on sandy ground near Santa Rosa and found that one had been feeding on yucca roots. On the Mesa Jumanes, Gaut caught one in a sandy location among the greasewood and tall grass, but no signs of others were found there. These pocket gophers are widely distributed around the eastern edge of the Staked Plains through central Texas and have evidently penetrated through the Red River Valley to the Upper Pecos and westward, but for some reason they have not become generally distributed in this extreme western corner of their range. In Texas they are abundant on the arid Lower Sonoran plains, where the mesquite forms a scattered scrubby growth. Their habits are similar to those of other pocket gophers, and they do considerable mischief in agricultural areas.

Family HETEROMYIDAE: Kangaroo Rats and Pocket Mice

DIPODOMYS SPECTABILIS SPECTABILIS Merriam

Arizona Banner-Tail; Large Kangaroo Rat

Dipodomys spectabilis Merriam, North Amer. Fauna No. 4, p. 46, 1890.

Type.—Collected at Dos Cabezos, Ariz., November 22, 1889, by Vernon Bailey.
General characters.—One of the largest and most spectacular of the 4-toed kangaroo rats; body short and compact; hind legs and feet long and powerful; front legs and feet small and weak; tail very long and slender with long brush at tip; head short and broad; eyes prominent, owl-like, appearing black but really with dark-brown irises; vibrissae long and full; external cheek pouches ample, fur lined and used for carrying food and stores; a small external gland concealed by fur on top of shoulders. Upper parts clear dark buff with dusky band across top of nose; tail gray along top and bottom, becoming black all around toward end and with abrupt white tip 1 or 2 inches long, white base, and broad white stripe along each side to beyond middle; lower parts, feet, band across hips, and spots over eyes and back of ears white.
Measurements.—Adults from the type locality: Total length, 350; tail, 211; hind foot, 52 and 53 millimeters. Weight of a large male, 123 grams.

Description.—Some of the anatomical characters and adaptations of these beautiful animals (pl. 14, A) are so interesting as to be worth recording. The large, rather prominent, owl-like eyes are apparently very keen in catching the least movement at night, but are not so keen in the daylight. They shine at night with a light-red or amethyst glow, very large and luminous, usually only one at a time but sometimes both, at 6 to 30 feet from a powerful flash light.
The external ears are remarkably well adapted to aboveground as well as underground life, since quick sight and hearing and great

speed are the only modes of defense against numerous enemies. Instead of having long ears like jack rabbits, which would not be good for underground life, they have wide ears with large auditory openings and hooded tips to keep out the dirt. For still further protection from earth and dust in which they are often enveloped, there is a crescentic lobe below the opening that closes valvelike when the ear is drawn down or folded back in digging or working in the loose earth of the burrow.

There is still much speculation about the greatly inflated mastoids and audital bullae, which surround the inner ear passages with large air chambers of thin, almost transparent bone. These inflations occupy more than half of the total bulk of the very wide triangular skull and give the peculiar form of wide, short heads of the animals, which causes their owl-like appearance. It is a development found in less marked degree in pocket mice, pocket gophers, and other animals that live much underground, and reaches its extreme of development in the gnome mice of the genus Microdipodops. It is generally supposed to be a form of ear trumpet for catching slight sound waves or magnifying the sound vibrations that come through the ground, a sort of seismograph, although other functions have also been suggested.

Stirling Bunnell, who has studied the animals in captivity and made experiments in passing sound through enlarged air chambers, has found that the tones are clarified and made more distinct by the process, but there is still something to be learned of the adaptations of these animals.

A small dermal gland on top of the shoulders is normally concealed under the hair, but when the hair is parted above it is conspicuous as a warty excrescence about a quarter of an inch long. It has a mild musky odor, which undoubtedly serves as a recognition character to individuals or species of the group and may be an important registration or property mark. It also seems to secrete a slightly oily substance, which in a few days causes the hair all over the animal's body to become mussy and rough and to lose its natural glossy appearance if the animal is kept too long in a clean box without sand or dust. Given a box of sand or pulverized earth, the animal at once and with evident relief and enjoyment rolls and rubs and wallows in the sand or dust until its fur is again as glossy and smooth as silk. The use of this oil is undoubtedly to render the fur waterproof, while the sand bath serves to regulate the excess of oil and keep the fur clean and beautiful.

The cheek pockets, or pouches, open from below along the sides of the lower jaws and extend back under the skin to the line of the ears. They are rather short but elastic, holding about a teaspoonful each and controlled by thin bands of muscle from their inner surface to the back of the animal's neck, so that when emptied of their contents they are instantly drawn back in place. They are lined with fine short hairs and used entirely for carrying food. Often they are found well filled with seeds or plants that are being gathered for food or for storage. They are deftly filled by the hands and instantly emptied by a single motion of the hands from the back pressing forward.

The very long tail is at first sight a surprise and something of a puzzle. It tapers but little, and a long crest near the tip makes it seem largest toward the end, but the crest is along the top and much higher than wide, a veritable rudder of excellent design. Its use is well illustrated as the animal runs in long leaps, merely striking the ground with the hind feet while its course is held straight and even or quickly turned by the long rudder tail. Also on the revolving wheel, on which the animals in captivity are fond of exercising, the tail is held curved to the inside of the circle or in the arc of the circle, in which the animals are running, thus enabling them to spin the wheel very rapidly under their feet without being thrown off by centrifugal force.

The very long hind legs and feet and the powerful hind leg and hip muscles need no explanation, especially if the animals are seen hopping about on the hind feet like a robin, with as much ease and grace as if walking on four legs, the little front feet or hands held up under the chin where they are mainly useful in holding the food or putting it in the pockets or emptying it out. The soles of the hind feet are well cushioned with coarse hairs, almost like rabbits' feet.

The nails of the four long hind toes are straight, long, sharp spikes used in digging, running, and fighting. They can be curled down sufficiently to catch in the ground for greater speed, or for quick turns, as is shown by the tracks of running animals in the trails. They are also excellent digging tools.

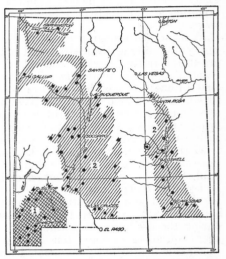

FIGURE 44.—Distribution of the large kangaroo rats in New Mexico: 1, *Dipodomys spectabilis spectabilis*; 2, *D. spectabilis baileyi*. Type locality circled

Distribution and habitat.—These big kangaroo rats occupy most of the upper division of Lower Sonoran Zone and the lower edge of Upper Sonoran Zone from Tucson, Ariz., east to the western edge of the Rio Grande Valley in New Mexico. (Fig. 44.) They are generally absent from the immediate valleys of the Rio Grande and Gila Rivers, but seem to prefer the dry hard soil of the barren mesa tops and foothill slopes of the desert ranges. They are common about Deming, Silver City, Lordsburg, and Hachita, and over the side slopes of the Playas and Animas Valleys.

Generally their mounds are widely scattered, but on favorite slopes in the Playas and Animas Valleys they may be counted in large numbers all around. In places they will average one or two mounds to an acre over extensive areas. Sometimes several animals are caught at a mound, but generally there seems to be only one adult to a mound or group of burrows at one time.

General habits.—Like all the kangaroo rats, this large species is strictly nocturnal. The animals are rarely seen by the local ranch people who live among them, but they are well known by their mounds and burrows. Even by digging out the burrows it is difficult to capture or get more than a fleeting glimpse of the animals, but they are easily caught at night in traps set near the burrows and baited with rolled oats or rolled barley. For study they are easily taken alive in tin-can traps with drop doors and may be kept indefinitely in suitable cages or pens properly supplied with nest boxes, exercise wheels, and the right kinds of food.

They are timid but very gentle animals and easily handled if not alarmed or excited. They almost never bite, and if held loosely in the hollow hands will soon cease struggling to escape and can be as easily handled as any domestic animals. Once on the ground, however, they are not easily recaptured and quickly revert to their wildest ways.

Fighting.—Although gentle with human beings, they have proved unfriendly among themselves, and only occasionally will two that are strangers live together without severe and often fatal fighting. Sometimes in cold weather two old males will live peaceably for some time in one nest box, but more rarely will a male and female live together in the same nest. In a large cage with plenty of nest boxes several can sometimes be kept without much fighting, but sooner or later there will surely be trouble and usually serious trouble. For such gentle animals they are most vicious fighters.

After persuading two old male kangaroo rats to live together peaceably for a few days, the writer put a third very large and beautiful old male in with them, but gave him a separate nest box, which he occupied quietly until evening. Then he investigated the other nest box and both of the other animals burst out in great excitement, and there were many little tilts and passes as they came near together during the evening, but nothing serious. In the night they were heard squeaking in angry tones, and turning on the flash light the writer saw the two largest animals locked in a fierce struggle on the floor. Each had a firm grip on the other, and they were using their hind feet in furious kicks and jabs and tears. Neither made any vocal sound, but the thumping and tearing of the long sharp toenails could be heard, as flat on their sides they fought like bulldogs. He pulled them apart and scared them into separate nest boxes and blocked the door to the box the newcomer was in, but later in the night the animal forced it open, and while the writer was asleep they fought it out. Next morning all was quiet, but the newcomer was found in its nest box terribly bruised, torn, bitten, kicked, scarcely able to move, and its hips paralyzed. As it was evident that it could not live, it was given a soft bed in a warm place with food and juicy cactus to eat. It was thirsty and feverish and ate the watery cactus pulp eagerly. During the evening it died without a sound or struggle, as silently as it had fought to a finish.

Post-mortem examination showed that the kangaroo rat was bitten around the head and shoulders and in many places along the tail.

The skin was punctured and torn over the back and hips and the skin of the whole back was like a sieve where the spikelike toenails had been driven through it and into the flesh below. This was apparently the main cause of death, but was not done during the clinched fighting witnessed in the night.

On other occasions the method of fighting was noted as two animals faced each other and jumping high in the air endeavored to strike each other straight down from above. At first both would jump at once and meet in the air, and little damage was done; but if one was knocked over or became tired or frightened so that the other got a fair stroke at it, the deadly blows reached home with great force and accuracy, and sometimes one would be seriously injured before anyone could intervene. If one turns and runs, its fate is sealed, for the pursuer has all the advantage and rains blows on its back from the rear and above.

On several occasions the writer felt the force of their kicks, if a forward thrust can be called a kick, when slipping his hand into the nest box and suddenly touching a nose only to be met on the tip of a finger by a sharp stab of the toenails shot under the body and forward with surprising force and accuracy.

The object of fighting seems to be generally sexual supremacy or protection of food stores, although they use their weapons against their hereditary enemy, the small kangaroo rat, and possibly against other enemies.

On one occasion the writer brought in two of the large *spectabilis* and one little *Dipodomys merriami* in his morning round of the live traps. All were cold and glad to be dumped into a soft cloth bag together, but the mistake was made of leaving them in a small box together while suitable cages were being prepared. After they had warmed up a loud thump in the box was heard, followed by a shriek of pain, and rushing to the box he found the little *merriami* on its side with a broken back and the skin torn off half its body by a single stroke of the hind foot of the big fellow. It was fatally injured and had to be killed.

Later the writer learned of the deadly enmity with which these little cousins were regarded and the evident cause. Though the big mound-building *spectabilis* lay up large stores, the little *merriami* usually do not store food but evidently steal from the stores of the larger species. They are so quick, however, that in the open they seem never to be caught, but if cornered in close quarters they are never spared. In a large cage where two of the small species were kept with two of the large form the little fellows were not in the least alarmed but always watchful. Frequently one of the large animals would jump across the 5-foot cage and land, toes down, exactly where a little one was sitting, but when it landed the place was always vacant. Sometimes one would spring from a revolving wheel to the feed box where both little ones were feeding, or again suddenly light on the revolving wheel where they were running, but always with the same fruitless efforts. For a week this was kept up with no harm done, but the enmity between the species was well demonstrated. The little ones were given nest boxes with small holes where they could be safe while sleeping, and seemed to rather enjoy the game of dodging.

Mounds.—The large mounds with big round holes in the sides are conspicuous objects over the open slopes where these big kangaroo rats live. A fair-sized mound measured 10 by 12 feet in extent and 18 inches high above the ground level and about the same depth below the surface, but some are larger and some smaller. Some of the largest are evidently very old and have been used for many years, while some of recent origin are small and have but a few holes. Sometimes a single hole is found at a distance from any mound, but the mounds are the real homes of these animals.

Each mound is a well-developed structure with numerous rooms or cavities for nests, storerooms, feeding places, halls, stairways, and winding tunnels. Usually there are three or four levels of rooms all more or less connected by tunnels or passageways, and the lowest and deepest may be 2 or 3 feet below the surface. On the outside there may be three or four to a dozen open doorways and several that are closed from within each morning as the animals retire for the day. The openings are large, even for the size of the animals, and readily admit the owner on a dead run.

Though generally in the open, a mound is occasionally built around a bunch of bushes, usually mesquite, catclaw, or blue thorn, of which the stems and roots serve to strengthen the walls and support an unusually high and symmetrical structure; also to shade and protect it and to serve as some protection against larger animals that might try to dig into the burrows.

The closed burrows are usually the ones occupied during the day, and by closing several passageways the animals shut themselves in and shut out some of their enemies. Snakes are probably the main enemies to be excluded.

The play spirit.—As with most desert animals, life is a serious matter with the banner-tails, and little real levity is shown, even by the young and immature. Hard work and strenuous exercise seem to cover most of their requirements, and if given a revolving disk they will keep it spinning half the night and occasionally come out of the nest box to take a run on it in the daylight. The fascination of running on one of these inclined wheels begins the moment they discover that it runs backward as fast as they run forward, and great skill is quickly attained in making it spin and in fairly dancing over its blurred surface. Occasionally one will get going so fast that centrifugal force throws it against the side of the cage, but that only increases the enthusiasm. Some will learn to make the wheel spin at high speed and then stop and ride several times around on the edge, or jump to the center and sit spinning round and round enjoying a free ride until the wheel runs down.

Whether from the play spirit or not, the exercise is evidently enjoyed, just as fast riding in automobiles appeals to many persons.

Food habits.—Like all their family, these big kangaroo rats are dainty feeders, living mainly on small seeds neatly shelled, only the clean inner kernels being eaten. Many if not most of the small local plants furnish them food, even those with such minute seeds as the pigweeds and purslanes. The seeds are gathered and tucked into the cheek pockets with the hands, many of the small kinds in the capsules or heads, and carried into the dens to be eaten at leisure, and any excess of present needs is laid away in the storerooms for future use.

Some green or succulent food is eaten, and the contents of the stomachs often show a trace of green or some moist pulpy material from sprouts, roots, or bulbs. In captivity a little green grass, clover, or cactus pulp, or juicy vegetables or fruit are eaten, and when such food is available no water is required. When the food is dry grain, seeds, or rolled oats, little water is necessary to keep them in good condition, and even to keep them alive. Several, however, that were kept entirely without water on dry food, grain, and rolled oats died in two or three weeks.

The quantity of food eaten by one captive individual in 24 hours was 5.5 grams of seeds and 7.7 grams of green clover and grass. Dried out, the same quantity of green clover and grass lost by evaporation 5.7 grams of water, so that for one day this test showed 7.5 grams of solid food and 5.7 grams of water for an animal weighing 121 grams. Other tests showed about the same results, indicating approximate proportions of food and water accepted when both are abundant.

In captivity all kinds of grains and seeds obtainable were eaten by the animals, but the rich sunflower and hemp seeds seemed to be preferred. In the wild state also the oily seeds of many composite plants are sought for food. The seeds of native plants identified in the food stores, in feeding rooms, and in the cheek pockets of the kangaroo rats include those of most of the grasses and other plants of the immediate vicinity and could be greatly extended by covering more numerous localities.

Some of the most important food plants aside from grasses found in their stores, including those recorded by Vorhies and Taylor (1922),[23] are as follows: *Plantago patagonica ignota* (desert plantain), *Sideranthus gracilis* (Aplopappus), *Machaeranthera asteroides* (tansy aster), *Bahia dissectifolia*, *Astragalus nuttallianus* (milkvetch), *Prosopis velutina* (mesquite), *Boerhaavia wrightii* (four-o-clock), *Eschscholtzia mexicana* (Mexican poppy), *Eriogonum abertianum* and *E. polycladon* (buckwheat bush), *Anisacanthus wrightii* (purple tube flower), *Lupinus parvifolius* (lupine), *Anisolotus trispermus* (birdsfoot trefoil), *Mollugo verticillata* (carpetweed), *Solanum elaeagnifolium* (trompillo), *Sida diffusa* (spreading mallow), *Oenothera primiverus* (evening primrose), *Martynia altheaefolia* (unicornplant), *Apodanthera undulata* (melon loco), *Chamaecrista leptadenia* (partridge pea).

Of grasses the following are important in the food: *Bouteloua rothrockii* (crowfoot grama), *B. aristidoides* (six-weeks grama), *B. radicosa* (grama), *B. eriopoda* (black grama), *Aristida divaricata* (Humboldt's needle grass), *A. bromoides* (six-weeks needle grass), *A. scabra* (rough needle grass), *Festuca octoflora* (fescue), *Panicum arizonicum* (panic grass), and many other grasses and other plants in less abundance. A few traces of green leaves of Evolvulus, Atriplex, Chenopodium, and such succulent plants had been brought in to be eaten and the animals in captivity were eager

---

[23] An intensive study of the nature of the storage of *Dipodomys s. spectabilis* on the U. S. Range Reserve in Arizona.

for these leaves. In fact the little Evolvulus plants on their range were never allowed to grow to more than flat mats on the ground on account of the leaves being eaten off as fast as they grew. A small sod 6 inches square of almost any green grass kept in the cage with a banner-tail and watered would be eaten off as fast as the grass grew and supplied all the moisture needed by one animal.

In places the kangaroo-rat trails ran to the base of Baccharis bushes growing in sandy washes where the deep roots bring up moisture and the underground sprouts around the base of the stems were dug up and eaten. These are like blanched celery but are more juicy and supply abundance of moisture for rodents. Other little sprouts and roots and tiny bulbs were dug up and eaten in places, and many little pits dug in their feeding grounds show where such juicy food is obtained by the kangaroo rats.

The cheek pouches of an adult animal will hold a teaspoonful each of seeds or grain, and apparently more when filled by the animal, instead of with a spoon. One let out of a cage in the tent made its home under the woodpile beside the stove and regularly gathered up all scattered grain from the floor and around the cages for its chache under the woodpile. To see how fast it could work, the writer placed a medicine glass (5 teaspoonfuls) of rolled oats on the tent floor about 8 feet from the woodpile. The animal soon found it and carried the oats to its cache in 2 trips, averaging 40 seconds to a trip, including the time of filling and emptying the pockets.

The measure proved to be one-twentieth of a quart, or one six-hundred-and-fortieth of a bushel. It would therefore take it 853 minutes (14½ hours) to carry away and store a bushel of rolled oats or grain. Gathering grass heads and various seeds would be usually slower work, but the animals are exceedingly quick and industrious.

Breeding habits.—With these remarkable animals breeding has become well adjusted to desert conditions. The families are small and the time of breeding very irregular and apparently regulated by weather and food conditions. The mammae of the females are in 3 pairs, 2 pairs of inguinal on 2 elongated mammary glands well back on the abdomen and 1 pair of pectoral on the breast on a pair of smaller pectoral glands. The young are usually three or four in number, born early or late in the spring when the weather conditions insure a good crop of seeds and food plants. During long dry periods young are scarce and breeding probably delayed.

A few young have been dug out of the nests deep in the mounds, and one pair kept in captivity for several years in the writer's vivarium bred once only, and the three young were successfully raised to maturity. The old male and female were kept through the winter in separate cages, as they would fight savagely if put together, and even when allowed the range of a screened sleeping porch would usually fight so much that one would have to be shut up before morning. After the middle of winter the male became highly developed sexually and so energetic that it chewed up several wheels and nest boxes. If a wheel stuck or became blocked in the night so that he could not run on it, he would chew it half into sawdust before morning. By running on its wheel for several hours every night, it kept in good condition and ate heartily and slept well through the day. The female was more quiet, and in the fights was always on the defensive.

On April 15 they were put in a cage together but fought so that they had to be parted, but on April 20 they were more friendly and began to sleep in the same box and run together on one wheel. From April 25 they were perfectly mated and the breeding season had begun, but actual date of impregnation could not be determined. On May 6 they were heard fighting in the night, and the next morning the male was found torn and bruised and badly bitten and so seriously injured that it died a couple of days later. Its head, feet, and tail were bitten full of holes, and the skin of the back was torn and punctured and the flesh underneath lacerated by the spiked claws of the female's hind feet. The inside of the cage was bloody, where it had tried to escape but was unable to get away, as it would have done from its native mound home. The female was uninjured and quietly sleeping in her nest box.

Though surprised and shocked at the tragedy, the writer learned some of the customs and requirements of the lives of these animals and is recording it for the benefit of others who may try to keep them in captivity. Like all rodents they are fully polygamous, and immediately after the mating the male is expected to go away and have no more to do with the family affairs until another breeding season comes around.

Six days later, at 7 p. m. on May 12, the writer slipped his hand into the nest and felt a young, just born, wet and mussy, and at 10 p. m. there were three young in the nest, all dry, clean, warm, pink, and helpless, carefully guarded, and covered by the mother. As nearly as he could tell the period of gestation was about 17 days, but there is a possibility of an error of several days either way, and further checks may show a different period.

Next morning, when 12 hours old, the young were examined, weighed, measured, photographed, and their peculiarities noted. They were hairless, pink, and semitranslucent, very soft, helpless, and tender. A slight trace of the color pattern of the adults was shown by light and dark pink areas; the eyes and ears were securely closed, the tips of the ears folded over to cover the future openings. There were no traces of teeth and the toenails were small and soft.

They weighed at 12 hours of age 9.3, 8.9, and 5.3 grams, and the largest one measured, in total length, 60; tail, 20; and hind foot, 9 millimeters.

At 3 days of age the backs and heads had begun to darken, but no hair had come out on the skin except the tips of the silvery whiskers, which were about a quarter of an inch long. When a week old a soft coat of fur appeared over the bodies, plumbeous gray over the dark parts, and white over the light parts in the same pattern as in adults. There were no teeth, and the eyes and ears were not yet open, although the tips of the ears had straightened up. The claws had become well hardened, and those on the front feet were curved, and were used in climbing about the nest and clinging to the mother's fur.

At 8 days old they weighed 19.5, 19, and 13.3 grams, and the largest one measured in total length, 110; tail, 45; and hind foot, 29 millimeters.

On May 23, at 11 days, the incisor teeth appeared through the gums as hard points or edges but not curved or hooked as in the young of some rodents. Their eyes opened on May 26, at 14 days.

On May 28, when 16 days old, the color pattern was well marked, as shown in the photographs, and the largest young weighed 29 grams and measured in total length, 165; tail, 85; and hind foot, 40 millimeters. At 23 days old it weighed 42 grams and measured 220, 120, and 46 millimeters, respectively. At 2½ months old they were almost full grown but still showed a color difference from the mother. When 4 months old they were apparently fully adult in size and color, the largest a male weighing 132 grams, 6 grams more than its mother, and the largest female young 125 grams, only 1 gram less than its mother.

Their growth and development were very rapid for animals of their size, and in this manner they are especially fitted to desert conditions, where life may depend upon storing a year's supply of food from the crop of seeds produced by one rain, and the same rain that awakened the sexual impulses in their parents.

The care of the mother banner-tail for her young was remarkable throughout their growing period. For the first few weeks she hovered them as a bird would its young, spreading her body wide and covering them under her in the nest and pushing away the hand if anyone tried to get them from under her.

She made a beautiful nest of cotton, filling the nest box over and under and all around them and closing the doorway securely so that she and the young were in the middle of a soft globe or ball of cotton. No wonder a big-footed old male was not wanted around the house at this time. Even after their eyes were open she watched the young closely, and if one was taken out and left in the cage outside of the nest box she promptly brought it in and closed the door securely behind her.

If the writer persistently annoyed her by removing the young and opening the nest, the mother would dig down into the corners of the nest box and bury them, one in a place, out of sight under the nest material, and sometimes even carry them outside and hide them under the wheel until he was gone and she could safely bring them back. Up to the time they were 16 days old and weighed 19 grams she would pick them up in her mouth with her jaws well around a large part of their bodies and carry them anywhere with ease, but only one at a time. As they grew larger and up to half her own size she would pick them up with her mouth, but also use her hands in holding and carrying them, sometimes reaching her arms around their bodies much as a human mother would carry her baby. On one occasion when the mother and a half-grown young were being photographed in a box she got excited and picked up the young one in her mouth and arms and jumped over the top of the box about a foot high and started to run away with it to some safe place where she would not be bothered.

When the young were being carried they held perfectly still in any position, and if laid down for a better hold they did not move or try to get away, seeming to understand that their lives might depend upon obedience. If hidden and covered by the mother they remained motionless while small, but as their strength and experience increased they would not always stay where put, and the mother had many worries.

The play instinct began to show at about 20 days old, soon after they began to venture out of the nest box by themselves. They began to hop about, trying their long and rather wabbly legs, rolled in the sand, and tried in an amateurish way to run on the revolving disk. When 24 days old they could run fairly well on the wheel if alone, but when the mother was also running they got all mixed up and fell off or got in the way of their mother and spoiled all the fun. Sometimes one or more would get in the middle of the wheel and ride around for a while, but usually their long tails or legs got out on the side and tripped up the mother until she became exasperated and would grab one in her mouth and arms and carry it to the nest box and push it inside. Sometimes she would put all three inside of the box and then start to run on the wheel, but they would soon be out and under her feet again. Sometimes she got almost cross with them and pushed them off the wheel or into the nest box so roughly as to discourage them for a little while, but it would not last. Before long the young gained such skill on the wheel that they could run with and keep in step with their mother, and sometimes the whole family would be dancing up one side of the wheel and down the other, their long tails all curved to one side to keep their balance in a circular course. By the time the young were a month old they had attained great skill on the wheel and would do the most difficult stunts, jumping off and on the revolving wheel without stopping it, jumping from the spinning wheel into the nest box and back again without interfering with the other members of the family running on the wheel.

Sometimes the young when not on the wheel would reach up with their hands and try to catch the bobbing white tip of their mother's tail as she danced along the side of the wheel, and they showed many little playful, childish ways that were later lost with maturity. Their passion for running the wheel, however, only increased with age.

When nearly full grown the young were given a new cage with a wheel and nest box, plenty of food, and more fresh, clean sand than they had ever seen before. They tried the wheel and the eats, inspected the nest and corners of the box, took a roll in the sand and then began to hunt for a place to get out, jumping at the top and showing great dissatisfaction. It was not home and did not smell or look natural, and their mother was not there. After an unhappy hour or so they were returned to the old cage, much to their satisfaction and that of the mother.

When 24 days old the young were given a fresh supply of dry clean sand in which they had a regular frolic, immediately rolling and playing and digging in it, rubbing their bellies, stretching their legs forward and back, rolling halfway over and rubbing their sides and almost onto their backs, kicking and pushing the sand and poking their noses into it in a friendly sort of way. Such antics are often recorded on wind-blown sand beds in a medley of tracks and strange marks that have puzzled naturalists for years.

After playing in the sand the young would make elaborate toilets, shaking the dust out of their fur, scratching and combing with the front claws over all parts of the body, smoothing out the long whiskers, and carefully combing the tail from base to tip with special care to get every hair in the long white brush straight and free.

On June 6, when 25 days old, the young were first noticed filling their cheek pouches with rolled oats to be carried into the nest box before retiring early in the morning. They had been seen eating rolled oats, seeds, clover, and lettuce leaves for several days and were probably being weaned. Each new kind of food was tested. A piece of watermelon rind was given them and they licked and nibbled it a little but got their hands wet and immediately ran to the sand pile and rubbed them in the sand until dry and clean. They did not eat any more and evidently decided it was no fit food for desert habitants.

When first born, the young made fine complaining little cries if disturbed, and as they grew up they often gave vocal expression to their feelings of hunger, impatience, pain, or anger. One at 36 days old, while waiting on the desk to be weighed, ran into a corner where there was nothing to interest it, and feeling lost and lonesome began to cry, making two or three whining little calls, probably intended to reach its mother's ever-attentive ears. When fully grown they rarely make any vocal sounds unless two are quarreling and scolding at each other; on rare occasions, if one is injured, it makes a sharp squeak of pain. Their calls and signals are generally tappings or drumming or thumping with the feet.

Sanitation with the young was soon as carefully observed as in the adults. The nest was always kept clean and neat, but the little dry, hard, black pellets were scattered carelessly anywhere outside of the nest box and soon became mixed with the sand and food refuse and eventually were kicked into the corners just as in their native homes the refuse is thrown out and used to build up the mounds. The rather copious urine was carefully deposited by all the members of the family in one place, a far corner of the cage or on one place in the sand under the wheel, and when the cage was cleaned out a cake of wet sand was found in its proper place. Either purposely or accidentally dry sand was kicked over the wet spot, and it was left as inoffensive as possible. When given a nest box half buried in sand, they soon completely buried the box in sand and then used the roof as a urinal and built it up by kicking more sand over the top.

Storing food by the young was begun in the middle of July when they were about 2 months old and nearly full grown. All the surplus food given them would be gathered in the cheek pouches, the leaves and stems cut in short sections, and neatly placed under the wheel and sand banked up around one side to hide it from view, and later when given empty boxes these were filled with the food that was not needed for immediate use. Apparently the mother and young stored together or in close proximity, a fact that would indicate the continuance of this part of the family life through the fall and winter and that may also account for the several storage chambers and food caches found in most of the mounds. Seeds, grain, rolled oats, and green plants were stored together, but the seed and grain formed most of the stores. Sometimes the nest boxes would be filled so full of food that the nest and finally the animals were crowded out.

Their relation to other animals was slightly suggested when a deer mouse got out of its cage and evidently went into the nest box of the family of kangaroo rats. Next morning its body was found torn half in two just outside the door to the nest box, evidently kicked and killed by the mother banner-tail.

Later when the young banner-tails were fully grown an old grasshopper mouse got out of his cage and ran into the nest box where the four big fellows were sleeping. In a moment one of the banner-tails came rushing out, shaking its head and acting very peeved, then another came out on a run. Opening the nest box, the writer saw the nest material boiling about in a lively manner, and soon the other two banner-tails left it in full possession of Onychomys. On reaching into the nest to take it out, the writer was met by a savage bite on the end of a finger that made the blood run. After evicting the four owners of the nest, each three times its own weight, the savage little grasshopper killer evidently was ready to "lick its weight in wild cats" or anything else.

Economic status.—The injury to the stock range where these mound-building, food-storing rodents are abundant has been so fully set forth by Vorhies and Taylor (1922) that little need be added. The injury to the range is mainly from the consumption of large quantities of seeds of grasses and other forage plants, which in good years may be of little consequence, but in dry years may take a large part of the available seed and leave little for reproduction.

There are many areas in southwestern New Mexico where the kangaroo rats are so numerous that their mounds and the bare patches of desert around them are conspicuous features of the landscape. When they are in great abundance on range lands it would undoubtedly be well worth while to reduce their numbers. Their rate of breeding is so slow that where this is done they will not soon return sufficiently to do serious damage.

DIPODOMYS SPECTABILIS BAILEYI Goldman

New Mexico Banner-tail

Dipodomys spectabilis baileyi Goldman, Biol. Soc. Wash. Proc. 36: 140, 1923.

Type.—Collected 40 miles northwest of Roswell, N. Mex., June 13, 1899, by Vernon Bailey.

General characters.—Size decidedly larger than typical *spectabilis* and body colors slightly paler, with stronger contrast of black markings; skull more massive with more expanded zygomatic arches.

Measurements.—Type, adult male: Total length, 385; tail, 283; hind foot, 58 millimeters. Weight of large male, 176 grams.

Distribution and habitat.—These largest and handsomest of all the kangaroo rats occupy most of the Upper Sonoran Zone of New Mexico and northwestern Texas in the open plains country below the level of the nut pines and junipers, and in places come slightly into the upper edge of Lower Sonoran valleys. (Fig. 44.)

In the Pecos Valley they are common across the valley from at least 30 miles east of Carlsbad to the foot of the Guadalupe Mountains 30 miles west, and up to 5,000 feet to the extreme upper limit of the Lower Sonoran Zone. Near Roswell the characteristic mounds of the species were first seen along the east side of the valley about 15 miles northeast of town. None were observed in the immediate vicinity of Roswell, but from about 12 to 50 miles northwest their burrows and mounds were abundant over the grassy plain in 1899. From the railroad their mounds were also observed in many places between Roswell and Carlsbad, and in 1902 Hollister found them abundant from 15 miles north of Roswell to north of Fort Sumner; in 1903 the writer found them common over the valley about Santa Rosa and 8 or 10 miles farther north. Gaut found a few dens and collected two specimens of the animals at the northwest base of the Jicarilla Mountains. Their mounds were common along the eastern border of the Tularosa Valley and near Jarilla at the southern end and at the eastern base of the Franklin Mountains. Along the east side of the Rio Grande Valley the big mounds and burrows were common on the mesa from 8 miles east of Mesilla Park at 4,800 feet to the base of the Organ Mountains at 5,200 feet altitude. No trace of them was seen in the lower part of the valley about Mesilla or Las Cruces. There were many mounds through the Jornado Valley, and at Albuquerque specimens were caught on the mesa 3 miles east of town. In 1889 E. W. Nelson found their mounds common on the mesa 6 miles east of Algodones. West of the Rio Grande Valley Hollister found them abundant on the edges of the San Augustine Plain and up to the foothills of the Datil and Gallina Mountains; in places actually extending up to the edge of the yellow-pine forest. He also found them abundant around the base of the Bear Spring Mountains and Jara Peak and thence over the plain to near Magdalena. Their characteristic mounds and burrows were seen in the valley of Salado Creek both east and south of Cabezon, and a few specimens were secured at Juan Tofoya at the eastern base of the Mount Taylor Range, and tracks and burrows were seen near Laguna, Cubero, and Chavis. A few of their mounds were found in a valley 15 miles southwest of Acoma. Specimens were collected a little west of Gallup, and the big mounds and burrows were found in the San Juan Valley along the east base of the Chuska Mountains and scattered over the valley bottom to near Fruitland on the San Juan River; also along the sandy bottoms of the Blanco and Largo Canyons farther east, and in the Chaco Canyon and the Escavada and Kimbetoh Valleys and north of the Hosta Butte Mountains. A few burrows and tracks were also seen near Bloomfield on the north side of the San Juan River, but none along the bottom part of the river valley. Farther south they are common along the west side of the Rio Grande Valley from Socorro north. None were found in the immediate vicinity of Socorro, but E. A. Goldman found mounds and burrows on the barren mesa 3 or 4 miles to the northwest. Along the upper part of the Alamosa River he found them abundant; also on the mesas about Cuchillo and a few on the mesas near Las Palomas. A few burrows were noted along the road from Garfield to Rincon, but none in the vicinity of either place. At Lake Valley they were rather common.

General habits.—In no important way do the habits of the New Mexico banner-tails differ from those of typical *spectabilis*, and like that species they are mound builders and are recognized over their range by the large mounds with open or closed holes in the sides. Near Santa Rosa on May 28, 1903, one of these mounds was dug out in the hope of finding the young and nest, as the old nursing female had been caught at the entrance of one of the burrows the previous morning. This mound was about 3 feet high and 8 feet wide and was built around a cluster of low mesquite bushes that rose a foot or so above the surface. It had nine holes leading into many galleries, which ran close to the surface. On digging into the mound, the writer found the walls thin and the partitions between the chambers and tunnels merely thick enough to support the weight of the structure. The whole was veritably honeycombed with tunnels and chambers irregularly arranged in three tiers one above the other. The materials of the partitions of the mound were a mixture of earth and old food and nest material, resembling the adobe walls of the Mexican houses, which are built of earth and chopped straw. This is the result of the occasional house cleaning when old nests and chaff are scraped out with the fresh earth, this material from time to time being added to the top of the mound. With time and rain the whole mass becomes packed and matted together, making a stronger and lighter structure than would the solid earth. The large burrows wind about through the mound in ascending and descending tunnels, apparently all connected and in many places widening out into chambers. In three of the larger cavities were found nests of soft grass and leaves, and in the largest of these nests a young kangaroo rat probably a week old. Its eyes and ears were not yet open, and its soft, almost naked, skin was distinctly marked with the pattern of the adult, all of the white markings of the old one appearing in pinkish-white lines and areas and the dark colors in plumbeous. If there were other young in the den, they could not be found, and the two other nests were empty. The nest chambers were 6 to 8 inches in diameter and about half filled with the soft nests of grass fibers.

Although strictly nocturnal and closely shut in their dens during the daylight hours, they are evidently not entirely inactive. If you tap or scratch on the earth at the closed doorways there is sometimes a prompt response in a low drumming or thumping noise from within. The actual method of producing this sound has been a matter of much discussion but of very little observation. E. A. Goldman, while camping one night near the Burro Mountains, heard this drumming sound during the evening and describes it carefully. He says:

I took a lantern and approached the nest cautiously until within 10 feet. The kangaroo rat was just outside the entrance to one of its holes and showed but little fear and kept up the drumming or thumping at intervals. When making the sound the animal was standing with fore-feet on the ground and the tail lying extended. I could see the vibration of the hind feet, and the noise seemed to be made with the hind feet only. The tapping was kept up for a second or two at a time, the sounds coming in two beats close together repeated after a very short interval rhythmically and suggesting the distant galloping of a horse. After tapping a short time the animal turned quickly about and began moving its head up and down in the opposite direction. It appeared to pay little attention to my light, but finally gave a sudden bound and entered one of its holes about 4 feet from where it was standing. Except for this drumming the animals are usually silent, and it is probable that their drumming is a signal code of special value to them in their partially underground life.

Unlike the smaller species, these kangaroo rats seem to prefer a firm and solid soil for their habitat, and rather avoid the mellow sands. The open mesa top with short grass and scattered vegetation is often dotted over with their mounds.

The mounds (pl. 14, B) are often 3 feet high and 10 or 12 feet in diameter at the base. They are built up mainly from the earth thrown out in excavating the burrows, but some of the surrounding surface soil is also scraped back upon them to increase their size. The numerous doorways, often six or eight in number, enter the sides and lead downward to the underground chambers. Usually part of the doorways are closed during the daytime, apparently those last entered by the animals.

The mounds are not only residences but also storehouses, where sometimes a bushel or more of seeds of various plants are stored in numerous cavities for future use, not only for winter but also to provide food for long dry periods when little or nothing grows. In time of abundance some of the food caches are not used but become moldy and later are discarded or thrown out to make room for fresh stores.

Numerous well-worn trails lead from one mound to another or from the mounds to the nearest weed and seed patches and across wide stretches of bare ground are often as conspicuous as where they run through the short grass and low desert vegetation. The long paired tracks of the hind feet show in sandy or dusty spots, but rarely is a print of the delicate little hands seen on the ground.

Food habits.—The banner-tails are dainty feeders, the small stomachs showing mainly the white starchy dough from numerous small seeds, the shells and hard parts all removed so there is little to show what kinds of seeds are eaten. The contents of the food caches and the refuse in the feeding chambers in the mounds, however, serve to identify a great variety of food plants and the list includes seeds of most of the grasses and other seed-bearing plants of the vicinity.

Several chambers in one house near Santa Rosa contained stores of food, mainly thickened bases of grass, including several species of Bouteloua, probably *hirsuta, oligostachya,* and *curtipendula,* and a few seeds and seed capsules and some flowers of snakeweed (Gutierrezia). There were several quarts of the grass bases forming the principal part of the food stores. These little grass stems, each in its husk of base leaves, are slightly swollen, almost bulblike, and although dry are sweet and starchy with a nutty flavor. At this particular place the excrement of the kangaroo rats was largely composed of minute fibers such as are contained in these grass stems, and the stomach contents of the animals, although finely pulverized, agreed well with the texture of the grass.

The food evidently varies at different times of year according to the local supply. In September Gaut found the animals with leaves of the thread-leafed sagebrush (*Artemisia filifolia*) tucked in the cheek pouches, and E. A. Goldman examined the pouches of two specimens that contained seeds of pigweed and whole heads of a wild sunflower (*Ximenesia exauriculata*), seeds and capsules of common purslane (*Portulaca oleracea*), and the seed heads of several grasses, including *Bouteloua oligostachya* and *Munroa squarrosa.* At another locality in November, he found one whose pouches contained about a dozen heads of the little wild sunflower (*Ximenesia exauric-*

ulata). In other places it was very difficult to attract them with rolled oats or grain bait when there was an abundance of wild sunflower seeds to be had, and it is evident that these are a favorite food with the kangaroo rats as with many other species of rodents.

In November, in the San Juan Valley, Birdseye reported Gutierrezia heads as forming the principal contents of the cheek pouches of specimens taken and of the food débris scattered around the mounds. In September the writer found the pouches containing the seeds of tumbleweed or Russian thistle (*Salsola pestifer*). Near Albuquerque in July the animals were feeding to a great extent on the seeds of a little plantain (*Plantago patagonica*), which was abundant over the mesa, and the ripe heads of which were found scattered about the mounds and mixed with the earth thrown out of the burrows.

Economic status.—In very little of their range do these kangaroo rats affect agricultural pursuits other than grazing. There are many complaints against them from cattlemen who object to riding over the burrows and being thrown as the horses break through into the underground chambers. This is a real danger, as low mounds may be ridden over without being seen, and in some cases the burrows enter the ground without noticeable mounds. A horse will often break through and drop a foot or two into the ground without warning, with serious results to both horse and rider. Riding after stock over ground where kangaroo rats are common is especially unpleasant.

Another matter of serious importance is the quantity of grass destroyed by these kangaroo rats about their dens. In places it is evidently considerable, and some of the best range grasses are dug up by the roots and carried to the dens to be eaten in rather large quantities throughout the winter months. The ground is usually almost denuded of grass for some distance around the dens and in places these bare spots may be seen dotting mesas which otherwise afford good grazing. From a slight elevation the writer has counted more than a hundred of these bare patches. In the total this injury to the range must be of serious consequence, and as range improvement progresses it will probably be necessary to reduce the number of the animals in many places.

DIPODOMYS MERRIAMI MERRIAMI Mearns

Merriam's Kangaroo Rat

Dipodomys merriami Mearns, Bul. Amer. Mus. Nat. Hist. 2: 290, 1890.

Type.—Collected at New River, Ariz., May 16, 1885, by E. A. Mearns.
General characters.—This little, dull-colored kangaroo rat of the 4-toed genus Dipodomys is the smallest of the kangaroo rats in New Mexico.
Measurements.—Adult specimens measure: Total length, about 248; tail, 150; hind foot, 38; ear from notch, 14 millimeters; weight, 40 to 50 grams.

Distribution and habitat.—Merriam's kangaroo rat (pl. 15, A) occupies the whole Lower Sonoran area of southern Arizona and New Mexico and extends into Mexico and western Texas. (Fig. 45.) In New Mexico it occupies the same ground with the very similar little *Perodipus ordii*, which, however, can always be distinguished by its minute thumb, or fifth toe, on the inner side of the hind foot. In habits as well as habitat the two species are very similar and are often caught in the same traps and even at the same burrows. Of the 4-toed species there are specimens in the Biological Survey collection from Carlsbad in the Pecos Valley, from Jarilla and Tularosa in the bottom of the Tularosa Valley, and from Las Cruces to Socorro in the Rio Grande Valley over the Deming Plain, from about Deming and Hachita, in the Animas and Playas Valleys, and from Redrock in the Gila Valley. They do not extend up into the mountains to any extent, but may be found wherever the mesquite tree grows and the soil is sufficiently mellow for their burrows.

General habits.—These small kangaroo rats are most abundant in the sandy and mellow soil of the desert valleys, where their characteristic burrows, trails, and tracks are conspicuous each morning before the sand has blown over them. Among the sand dunes and open sandy areas during the day the tracks and trails and even the burrows are often obliterated by shifting sands.

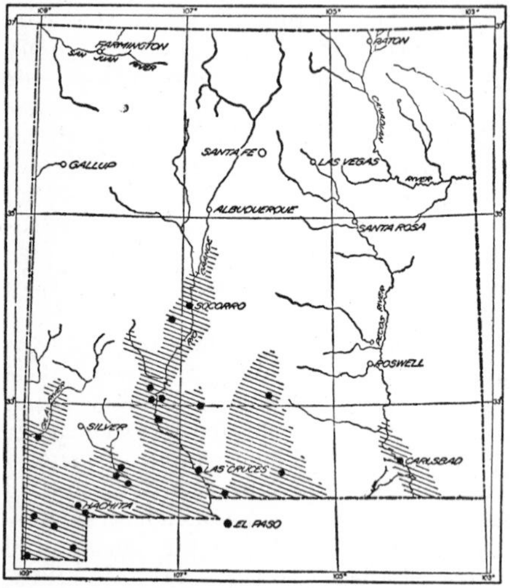

FIGURE 45.—Distribution of Merriam's kangaroo rat, *Dipodomys merriami merriami,* in New Mexico

As usual in this group, the animals are strictly nocturnal and are never seen moving about in the daytime. The burrows are usually closed before daylight and not opened again until after dark. They are generally placed under the edges of sheltering bushes, cactus, or other desert plants, which afford shade and probably other protection. In the Tularosa Valley, Gaut reported them as usually found under mesquite or creosote bushes or in some cases under cactus. In the Rio Grande and Gila Valleys E. A. Goldman reported them under creosote, mesquite, and other bushes, and under the edges of sotol and bunches of cholla cactus. There seems to be no preference, however, of one bush over another, as the choice is evidently for shade and the protecting roots or spines, which make it difficult for enemies to dig out their shallow burrows. Like the rest of the group, the animals are timid and without means of defense other than their long legs and rapid flight and the protection of their dens.

Food habits.—Their menu, as shown by the contents of cheek pouches, consists mainly of seeds, but probably to some extent of other vegetation. At Tularosa, in November and December, Gaut found mesquite beans and the seeds of the creosote bush in their pockets. At Deming, in September, and at Cuchillo, in October, E. A. Goldman found several with their cheek pouches partly filled with the seeds and seed capsules of purslane. At Socorro, in August, he recognized the seeds of ocotillo in their pockets, and at Las Palomas, in October, he found the seed-bearing heads of grama grass (*Bouteloua oligostachya*) in their pockets. Many other seeds were found that could not be identified and some fragments of grass and other material that may have been intended for nest building rather than for food.

Breeding habits.—One specimen collected by E. A. Goldman at Socorro in August contained two embryos, but others have been taken containing three, which is probably the normal number of young produced at a birth. There seems to be nothing to indicate that they breed more than once during the season.

Disposition.—These little 4-toed animals are the most gentle and attractive as well as the most delicate and graceful of the kangaroo rats. When caught in the hands or taken out of " live " traps they are generally quiet and unafraid, rarely struggling to escape and never offering to bite. As pets they are the gentlest, most interesting, and most easily kept of our small rodents, apparently perfectly contented and happy if given a warm nest box, a revolving disk for exercise, a box of sand in which to roll and dust their coats, a few seeds, a little green grass, and a very small dish of water. They are the cleanest, neatest little animals imaginable and seem to enjoy being held in the hands and stroked or petted. Several will usually live harmoniously together in close quarters and snuggle up in the nest box, but some care must be used in mating them, as they have strong individual likes and dislikes.

Economic status.—As they are strictly desert animals, avoiding water and dense vegetation, Merriam's kangaroo rats come but little into contact with cultivated crops. In irrigated valleys, however, they often burrow into the banks of ditches, occasionally producing leaks and breaks, while also carrying away some of the grain or other seeds from the fields. As most of the grain taken is the scattered or waste seeds left on the ground and of no especial value, their relation to agriculture is not important. On the stock range, however, they may have a serious effect in carrying away and consuming the seeds and heads of numerous grasses and other forage plants, thus slightly reducing the carrying capacity of the range. Apparently they do not store food for winter use, but their food habits are not so well known as those of some of the storing species of kangaroo rats.

PERODIPUS ORDII ORDII (WOODHOUSE) [23]

ORD'S FIVE-TOED KANGAROO RAT

D[ipodomys] ordii Woodhouse, Acad. Nat. Sci. Phila. Proc. 6: 224, 1853.
Perodipus ordi Merriam, Biol. Soc. Wash. Proc. 9: 115, 1894.

Type locality.—El Paso, Tex.
General characters.—The long tail, long hind legs and feet, small hands, and fur-lined external cheek pouches serve to distinguish the kangaroo rats from other rodents. The general buffy or yellow-brown color with pure-white underparts and black and white markings are more or less similar in the differ-

---

[23] In the present paper the genus Perodipus is used for the 5-toed kangaroo rats, notwithstanding the fact that two subspecies in California sometimes fail to produce a toenail on the first digit of the hind foot, and that the genus is considered invalid by some authors who employ Dipodomys for the entire group.

ent species, but in most cases vary sufficiently for recognition. This is the smallest of the four species of 5-toed kangaroo rats found in New Mexico. The length of the hind foot will readily distinguish the species from the larger *longipes, montanus,* or *richardsoni,* but the color and markings of all are very similar. The resemblance is so close, however, to the little *Dipodomys merriami,* which occupies the same ground, that it is usually necessary to count the toes to tell them apart, the small inner fifth toe of the hind foot being present in Perodipus and absent in Dipodomys.

Measurements.—Adults: Total length, 240; tail, 134; hind foot, 38 millimeters.

Distribution and habitat.—*Perodipus ordii* (pl. 15, B) inhabits the Lower Sonoran valleys of southern New Mexico, extending northward as far as Carlsbad in the Pecos Valley, Tularosa in the valley of that name, Socorro in the Rio Grande Valley, and up the Gila and San Francisco Rivers to Cliff and Alma. (Fig. 46.) The animals are abundant throughout practically all of the Lower Sonoran area of the State, but do not extend to any distance into the Upper Sonoran Zone. Their range in Texas, Mexico, and Arizona is also mainly Lower Sonoran. At Carlsbad, in 1892, Dutcher wrote of them: "Exceedingly common, swarming among the sandhills where the hillsides afford an opportunity to dig their horizontal burrows. Also common on hard and stony ground of the mesas." At Jarilla and up through the great Tularosa Valley Gaut reported them as "common and living in the same situations with *Dipodomys merriami.*" In fact, he often caught them at the entrance of the same burrows and found them with much the same habits. In the Rio Grande Valley at Mesilla Park and Las Cruces they are especially abundant in the dunes and sandy soil of the valley bottom, but they are also found in many places over the surrounding mesas to the foot of the adjoining mountain slopes. At Socorro, E. A. Goldman reported them rather scarce. One was taken among dalea (Parosela) bushes on a sand drift just above high water level on the west side of the river, and another at a hole in the bare ground in the little valley of Ojo de la Parida, 10 miles northeast of Socorro at an altitude of nearly 5,000 feet. Specimens have not been taken further up the Rio Grande Valley, but it is probable that a few may extend somewhat farther, as they extend out onto the San Augustine Plain, where a few burrows were seen and a specimen collected. Over the great Deming Plain they are abundant everywhere, especially in the mellow soil of the washes and sandy bottoms.

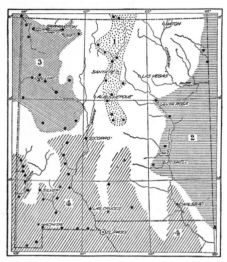

FIGURE 46.—Distribution of 5-toed kangaroo rats in New Mexico: 1, *Perodipus montanus montanus;* 2, *P. montanus richardsoni; c, longipes;* 4, *P. ordi ordii.* Type locality circled.

General habits.—Though these small kangaroo rats are often found in hard or gravelly soil, into which they burrow with considerable freedom, they seem to prefer and often fairly revel in the mellow sand of dunes and valley borders. Here their burrows are also more conspicuous and their trails and peculiar tracks are seen in great numbers over the surface of the shifting sands. In many cases the burrows enter the ground under the edge of cactus or some of the low bushes or spreading plants that seem to offer them shelter and protection, but in other cases they are in the most exposed and unprotected situations. A sand bank or sloping dune is a favorite site for the burrow, which always enters the ground at a nearly horizontal position, often with the doorway slightly lower than the main shaft of the burrow. They do not, as some other species, build mounds over their dens, but the burrows are often in groups of three or four or even more, radiating from a common underground center. For the size of the animal the burrows are rather large, and at times considerable earth is thrown out, usually to quite a distance from the entrance. Part of the burrows are closed during the day, apparently to keep out snakes and other enemies, but some are always left open, and it is probable that the closed burrows are the ones occupied. The little animals are strictly nocturnal, very timid, and practically defenseless, but in times of danger the speed of their long legs must generally enable them to reach their underground dwellings. Their method of progress is by long leaps, the hind feet only being used for running or hopping about. The delicate little hands are used mainly in gathering and holding food, in filling and emptying the cheek pouches, and in digging for food or extending their burrows. The loose earth from their burrows is brought out and kicked backward to considerable distances from the entrance by means of the strong hind feet, but the front feet are used in loosening the earth and also to support the weight of the animal's body when the hind feet are being used to throw the earth backward from the burrow. If the closed doorway is opened during the daytime it is usually closed again in a short time, showing that the animals are alert while shut in their dens and usually supposed to be sleeping. On several occasions the writer has watched them bring the earth to the entrance of a freshly opened burrow and kick it back of them until the doorway was again closed. From the entrance of the occupied burrows there are usually runways or well-beaten trails leading away to the feeding grounds or from one burrow or group of burrows to another. These trails may sometimes be followed for many rods as they extend in straight lines across the open or wind about to avoid obstructing vegetation. The peculiar paired tracks of the long hind feet may also be seen over the surface of fresh sand, and in places the distance of 3 to 5 feet between these tracks shows with what speed the frightened animals can progress.

Food habits.—The principal food of the 5-toed kangaroo rats consists of seeds of a great variety of desert plants. As much of it is gathered and carried in the cheek pouches and stored and eaten in the burrows, the nature of it is easily determined. The animals caught in traps for specimens usually have more or less food material in their pockets, which is readily identified. At Deming, in

December, 1889, the writer found that their pockets contained a great number of the fallen seeds of wild sunflowers; also the little hard beans of a dalea (Parosela), and in August, 1908, Goldman found them at the same place gathering in the seeds of the common mesquite (*Prosopis glandulosa*). In some localities it is very difficult to trap them as they find an abundance of seeds, which they prefer to rolled oats or any other bait that can be offered them. At Glenwood on the San Francisco River, in early November, the writer was unable to catch them for this reason, as they were evidently feeding on the abundant wild-sunflower seeds (Helianthus and Ximenesia), which covered the ground. Near Redrock in the Gila Valley, in September and October, E. A. Goldman found the cheek pouches containing seeds of sandbur (Cenchrus) and sunflower seeds (*Ximenesia exauriculata*), and at Gila the pouches of one were partly filled with the prickly seeds of rag bush (*Gaertneria acanthicarpa*). Near there the pockets of another contained stems of grass cut into sections one-half to three-fourths of an inch in length and laid parallel in bundles in the pockets. A specimen caught at Cliff in November had one seed of a croton in one pocket and a section of green grass stem in the other. At Pleasanton, in October, E. A. Goldman collected another specimen that had some sections of grass stems in one pocket and the seeds of an amaranth in the other, and at Deer Creek in Grant County he found in the pouches of one the ripening seeds of the desertwillow (*Chilopsis linearis*). At Las Cruces in November he found pockets filled with seeds of tumbleweed (*Atriplex expansa*), a few of the spiny seeds of rag bush (*Gaertneria acanthicarpa*), and a few leaves of marsh fleabane (*Pluchea sericea*). These were in addition to the rolled oats from the trap bait, which is usually found in their pouches. At Lake Valley he found pockets containing seeds of the common wild sunflowers (*Ximenesia exauriculata*) and a few capsules and seeds of a purslane. At Cuchillo he again found the capsules of common purslane (*Portulaca oleracea*) and seeds of Compositae and other plants in the pouches, and at Rio Alamosa one well filled with the capsules and seeds of the same purslane. In December, Gaut collected specimens near Tularosa whose pouches were well filled with the seeds of creosote bush (*Covillea tridentata*), which at that time of year had dropped most of its seeds on the ground. It is evident that most of the food is carried to the burrows to be eaten at leisure or stored for times of scarcity, as large quantities of seed shells and other refuse are thrown out from the entrances. Like the other kangaroo rats, Perodipus does not hibernate and seems to be active even in the coldest weather.

Breeding habits.—In adult females the mammae are arranged in 3 pairs—2 pairs of inguinal and 1 pair of pectoral. One female collected by E. A. Goldman at Gila, October 12, 1908, contained three embryos, which very probably represents the normal number of young in a litter. Of 10 adult females that the writer caught at Deming from November 29 to December 6, 1889, 4 were apparently nursing young, as the teats were full of milk. At the same time numbers of nearly full-grown young were being caught.

Economic status.—Over most of their habitat these little kangaroo rats inhabit open desert country, where they can do no possible harm to crops but may seriously reduce the grazing capacity of stock ranges. In the irrigated valleys where crops of small grain are raised, they feed to some extent on the grain and may carry away and store considerable quantities. Their mischief in this respect is rather local and not very serious, but the constant menace of their burrows to the banks of irrigation ditches is a more serious matter. With other species of burrowing rodents, they must be constantly watched, for if allowed to inhabit the ditch banks frequent breaks are sure to occur. Their preference for burrowing into sidehills often leads them to select the bank of any ditch running along the edge of a valley where the ground on one side is lower than the level of the water. Fortunately, they are easily controlled, and in areas of special danger they can be reduced to practically harmless numbers.

PERODIPUS MONTANUS MONTANUS (BAIRD)

SAN LUIS KANGAROO RAT; Tua-pena of the Taos Indians

Dipodomys montanus Baird, Acad. Nat. Sci. Phila. Proc. 7 : 334, 1855.

Type.—Collected at Fort Garland, Colo., in 1853 by Mr. Kreutzfeld under Lieut. E. G. Beckwith.

General characters.—Very similar in general appearance to *ordii* but slightly larger.

Measurements.—Adult males measure: Total length, about 253; tail, 141; hind foot, 40 millimeters.

Distribution and habitat.—From the San Luis Valley in southern Colorado, where it was first discovered, *montanus* extends southward along the upper Rio Grande Valley in New Mexico to Santa Fe southward in the high valleys east of the Rio Grande to Gran Quivera and the Jicarilla Mountains. (Fig. 46.) It is restricted to the Upper Sonoran Zone and inhabits both the open valley and plains country and the juniper and nut pine foothills of its region. It prefers the mellow soil and is usually most abundant where sandy ground is available for its burrows. In many places, however, it is found dispersed over the hard mesas and in soil that must require considerable strength and skill in digging. It is especially abundant over the sandy bottoms of the Rio Grande Valley about Espanola and along the lower Chama River.

General habits.—In habits this species does not differ from *ordii* except as the slightly different environment makes necessary its adaptation to different types of food and cover. In a cooler and less arid climate the more northern animals have slightly different conditions to meet. At Espanola in January, 1894, Loring found them common on the weedy flats along the valley bottom and on January 5 found their tracks in a light snow that had fallen the night before. To just what extent they are active during the time of deep snows, which occur in the San Luis Valley, is not known, but it is probable that their stores of food will carry them through considerable periods when the ground and seeds are buried.

Food habits.—Apparently the kangaroo rats feed to some extent on grass as well as seeds of various plants, as the writer has taken them with the heads of grama grass in their pockets. In the vicinity of Taos they would not touch traps baited with rolled oats, apparently on account of the abundance of seeds of wild sunflowers (Helianthus and Ximenesia) over the surface of the ground. Usually, however, they are very fond of rolled oats and are easily caught by setting the trap near their burrows or at the edge of their runways and sprinkling this bait over the trigger. Where there are no well-defined runways in which to set the traps, a long mark may be made by dragging the foot along the ground to make a smooth trail. Any kangaroo rat that finds such a trail is almost sure to follow it, and a trap set across it and baited with rolled oats will usually secure a specimen.

Breeding.—The breeding habits of this species are little known, but probably do not differ from those of *ordii* or other closely related members of the genus.

Economic status.—A large part of their range lies within a region where agriculture is largely dependent on irrigation. For this reason the burrows of the animals are a menace to the banks of many of the ditches that follow the valley borders. But for their natural enemies, hawks, owls, foxes, coyotes, cats, and weasels, they would undoubtedly be present in such numbers that they would do far greater damage. By the application of control measures in localities where they are especially troublesome, in addition to the wise protection of some of their natural enemies, serious trouble from these rodents can probably be avoided.

PERODIPUS MONTANUS RICHARDSONI (ALLEN)

RICHARDSON'S KANGAROO RAT

Dipodops richardsoni Allen, Bul. Amer. Mus. Nat. Hist. 3 : 277, 1891.

Type.—Collected at Beaver River, Beaver County, Okla., October 26, 1887, by Jenness Richardson and John Rowley, jr.

General characters.—Slightly larger and brighter yellow than *P. m. montanus*, with which it apparently intergrades in the region west of the upper Pecos Valley. The dark stripe on the lower surface of the tail reaches only about half the length of the tail, while in the other species it reaches the whole length.

Measurements.—Average of adults: Total length, 258; tail, 139; hind foot, 42 millimeters.

Distribution and habitat.—Richardson's kangaroo rat is a wide-ranging species of the Great Plains, in the Upper Sonoran Zone, extending from Montana to west-central Texas and covering practically all New Mexico east of the Pecos River Valley and Sangre de Cristo and Raton Mountains. (Fig. 46.) Specimens from Clayton, Raton, Santa Rosa, Fort Sumner, and the region about Roswell are referable to this species, while at Carlsbad the smaller and apparently distinct *ordii* almost, if not quite, meets its range. The animals are especially abundant where the soil is mellow and sandy, but in many places they burrow into fairly firm prairie soil. Generally they are on the open plains, but in many localities they are found among the scattered junipers and nut pines where soil and other conditions are suitable.

General habits.—The habits of *richardsoni* are very similar to those of other species of the genus. The animals make long, horizontal burrows usually in groups of two or three radiating from a common center and opening out sometimes 6 or 8 feet apart. The occupied burrows are usually closed during the day and not opened until after dark. Well-worn trails often lead from the doorways to a consider-

able distance, especially where the low vegetation is sufficiently dense
to make traveling easier in trails than in the standing grass, but
even on sandy and open ground the trails are often well worn and
conspicuous.

Food habits.—Apparently these kangaroo rats also live mainly
upon the seeds of various plants and grasses, but in many cases the
leaves and stems of grass and other plants have been found in their
pockets. At some of the burrows the chaff, remains of grass stems,
and heads are thrown out in considerable quantities, which indicates
that their food is not entirely seeds but comprises some of the green
foliage or dried parts of plants. Near Santa Rosa the pockets of one
specimen contained a few leaves of a little saltbush (Atriplex), some
yellow leaves apparently of loco weed (Oxytropis), and a few seeds
of juniper berries. Oatmeal from the trap bait is commonly found
in their cheek pouches and occasionally a little wheat or other grain
from the fields. The grain, however, seems to have been picked up
from scattered or sown grain, and the writer knows of no evidence
that they pull or cut down the stalks of growing grain.

Breeding habits.—As with other members of the genus, the mammae are arranged in 3 pairs, 2 pairs of inguinal and 1 pair of pectoral,
and there are records of two and four embryos. Out of a large number of specimens collected, there are no very small young taken late
in the season, and it seems probable in their zone and climate that
not more than one litter is raised in a year.

Economic status.—For many years the country occupied by this
species has been mainly stock range, but in recent years the "dry-
farming" methods have made little ranches possible and carried considerable agriculture into their area. The kangaroo rats undoubtedly
take a small toll of planted seeds and possibly of ripening grain, but
their depredations are of little consequence by themselves. Added to
those of many other species of rodents, however, they help to swell
the total, which means a steady drain on the returns of farm labor.

PERODIPUS LONGIPES (MERRIAM)

MOKI KANGAROO RAT; BAR-HU of the Moki Indians (Fisher); NAUSHESTOYI
of the Navajo Indians

Dipodops longipes Merriam, North Amer. Fauna No. 3, p. 71, 1890.

Type.—Collected at foot of Echo Cliffs, Painted Desert, Ariz., September 22,
1889, by C. Hart Merriam.

General characters.—Largest of the 5-toed kangaroo rats occurring in New
Mexico. In color it differs but little from the bright buffy *richardsoni* further
east, but the dark stripe runs the whole length of the lower surface of the
tail.

Measurements.—Total length, about 275; tail, 165; hind foot, 42 millimeters.

Distribution and habitat.—The species *longipes*, which was first
described from the Painted Desert, in Arizona, extends over a large
area of high arid plains in·northwestern New Mexico. (Fig. 46.)
It occupies the great San Juan Valley and the Zuni Plains south to
the northern base of the Datil Mountains and east to Laguna and
Riley on the western edge of the Rio Grande Valley. It probably
fills the whole Upper Sonoran Zone of this region, but the borders
of its range and its relationship with neighboring species have
not been fully determined. There are specimens from Blanco,

Fruitland, Fort Wingate, Gallup, Juan Tofoya, Laguna, Quemado, Riley, Shiprock, Thoreau, Wingate, and Zuni River.

General habits.—The large size of these kangaroo rats makes it possible to distinguish their burrows and tracks from those of smaller species. The burrows often seem unnecessarily large for the size of the animal, especially in the mellow sand, where digging is easy and where natural mounds are abundant, into the sides of which the burrows penetrate in almost horizontal positions. In sandy places in the San Juan Valley there is often a suggestion of an artificial mound over and around the entrance of the burrows. The earth that is brought out of the burrows is thrown backward to build up an artificial mound evidently to protect the underground den from which the burrows open out on all sides. The mound-building habit is but slightly developed in this species and is only occasionally noticeable, while in some other species, as in *Perodipus panamintinus* and *Dipodomys spectabilis*, it is highly developed. As a general thing, however, the burrows enter the ground singly or in groups in the ordinary way and show the same type of structure with the same radiating trails as in other species of the genus. The animals are often abundant, and early in the morning the barren areas of sand show networks of their tracks and trails. These are usually wiped out before night by the drifting sands, only to be reprinted with some variety in each early morning edition. The doorways of occupied burrows are usually closed during the day, and the animals are rarely seen unless one's horse breaks through into the underground den and a startled kangaroo rat pops out of the end of some burrow that leads almost to the surface but had been left with a thin covering of earth.

Food habits.—As in other species of the genus, their food is gathered and apparently most of it carried to the burrows in the cheek pouches to be eaten in greater safety at home. In places they are eager for rolled oats or almost any grain offered them as trap bait, but again they will not touch any of these or any kind of bait that can be offered, evidently because they are finding their favorite seeds abundantly scattered over the ground. At Gallup in September, 1908, the writer found them numerous, but at that season they would not touch the trap bait and only one specimen was secured. This one had a small collection of seeds of tumbleweed, or Russian thistle (*Salsola pestifer*), in its cheek pouches. In June, of 1905, Hollister found them abundant at Wingate, where he says their dens were commonly placed near the base of some bush where the sand was built up in a mound, but many were found in open places with no protection. Numbers of the animals were seen running about soon after sundown, scampering from one bush to another. They seemed to be busy gathering seeds of plants, and specimens shot often had their cheek pouches filled with seeds. In October of the same year he found them in the edge of the Gallinas Mountains, when the cheek pouches of the specimens taken were partly filled with seeds of various common plants of the vicinity. In the San Juan Valley in October and November, 1908, Clarence Birdseye found them abundant but very difficult to trap, as they did not care for the trap bait. By using an abundance of squash seeds, wheat, oats, and rolled oats, he succeeded in catching a few, but was obliged to set small steel traps in their runways to get a series of the animals. The traps were sunk in the runways and covered with tissue paper, over which sand was sprinkled, and in several cases parts of the tissue paper were found in the pockets of the rats, evidently being carried away for nest material. The pockets of those caught contained seeds of the Russian thistle (*Salsola pestifer*), rabbit brush (Bigelovia and Gutierrezia), and bee plant (*Cleome serrulatum*).

Breeding habits.—In the latter half of June, near Wingate, Hollister caught numbers of half-grown young, and one female taken on June 20 contained four good-sized embryos. In September and October the specimens taken were all nearly full grown, and it is probable that but one litter of young is raised in a season.

Economic status.—In a great part of the country covered by these kangaroo rats there is no agriculture and but little white population. In the San Juan Valley, however, there is a large area of valuable agricultural land that has been developed under the irrigation system, and here the kangaroo rats do some slight damage to the banks of irrigation ditches. In other localities where irrigation is possible they do considerable mischief, although they are not so serious a pest as the pocket gophers. In passing through the valley at Zuni in September, 1908, the writer found an abundance of these kangaroo rats and their large burrows in the mellow soil of the valley. The great ditch for carrying the water from the reservoir to the farm land of the valley had at that time just been completed, but the water had not yet been turned in. This ditch ran for many miles along the sloping side of the valley, and its lower bank was built up in such a manner that the bottom of the ditch was as high as and in places higher than the slope below. The kangaroo rats had gathered along this new embankment of mellow sand as if it had been placed there especially for their habitations. They had come from far and near and taken up their quarters in the mellow bank and were rapidly perforating it with big, round burrows that began near the bottom and went straight back into the bank. In places there were three or four of these burrows in 8-foot sections of the bank that the writer's little camera would include at a distance of 10 feet. Most of the burrows were in the lower bank of the ditch. The writer was not present when the water was later turned into the ditch, but probably many breaks occurred. In such cases it would not be difficult to protect the ditches by killing the animals that had collected there.

PEROGNATHUS FLAVUS FLAVUS Baird

BAIRD'S POCKET MOUSE

Perognatus flavus Baird, Acad. Nat. Sci. Phila. Proc. 7: 332, 1855.

Type.—Collected at El Paso, Texas, in 1851 by J. H. Clark.
General characters.—A small, smooth-furred, yellow mouse with short, rounded ears, and rather short, smooth tail. Upperparts rich pinkish buff clouded with dusky; spot back of the ear and a band along the side clear buffy; underparts white.
Measurements.—Adult specimens average: Total length, about 112; tail, 50; hind foot, 15.8 millimeters. Weight of male, 7.3 grams; of female, 6.5 grams.

Distribution and habitat.—Baird's pocket mouse (pl. 12, B), apparently the smallest rodent in America, is an abundant species over a great part of New Mexico, occupying the valley country in both the Upper and the Lower Sonoran Zones. (Fig. 47.) Specimens have been taken at Carlsbad, Santa Rosa, Clayton, Chico Springs, Raton, Ribera, Taos, Manzano Mountains, Mesa Jumanes, Carrizozo, Tularosa, Deming, Hachita, Playas Valley, Glenwood, Diamond Creek, Fairview, San Augustine Plain, Riley, Datil Mountains, Quemado, Rio Puerco, Laguna, Grant, Fruitland, and Liberty. The species is also abundant at the type locality, El Paso, Tex., and extends south into Mexico, west into Arizona, and northward into Colorado and Nebraska. It is partial to mellow soil of the valley bottoms, where it lives among the scattered weeds and bushes and burrows in the sand. Occasionally it is found on the sidehills and even among the stones and on rocky ground, but always where there is mellow soil in which to burrow.

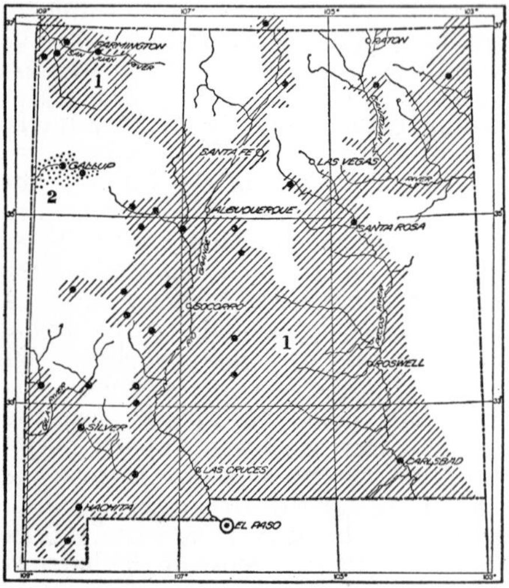

FIGURE 47.—Distribution of Baird's and Yavapai pocket mice in New Mexico: 1, *Perognathus flavus flavus;* 2 *P. flavus bimaculatus. Type* locality circled

General habits. — At Deming in December, 1889, Baird's pocket mice were abundant among the scattered mesquite bushes a mile east of town. Their t i n y b u r r o w s, usually closed during the day, were common, and little runways or lines of tracks led from them to neighboring patches of wild sunflower and o t h e r seed-laden plants. The little animals were evidently finding an abundance of choice food at that season and carefully avoided all traps and such bait as the writer could offer them. As the old cyclone traps were the only available mouse catchers at that time, he was obliged to remodel them by taking off one spring and bringing the other back to one side and flattening the trigger so they could be used as runway traps. With these carefully concealed in the runways, specimens were readily caught as they ran over the trigger. In the same way a little later he secured a series of topotypes at El Paso, where the mice were common on the sandy bottoms below town. Their burrows were generally in groups of three or four near together, evidently connecting below in a regular den. Often they were placed around the edges of a little tuft of desert brush, which afforded some shelter and protection. On warm December mornings their tracks were numerous in the light dust around the burrows and led away in trails from the burrows to the nearest sunflower or pigweed patches.

At other times of year, when there are fewer ripe seeds on the ground, they take rolled oats with avidity and are easily caught in traps set near their burrows or in artificial trails made by drawing the foot over the ground. Their tiny burrows are easily recognized, and if specimens can not be secured in traps they can be driven out of the burrows and caught in the hands. The burrows are not extensive and in mellow soil can be opened with a stick or with the fingers and the animals forced out. In Canyon Largo the writer secured one by turning over a flat stone under which the burrow led, and as the sleek little creature popped out of its den underneath he caught it in his hands and had a good opportunity to examine it closely. Few small mammals are more beautiful than these silky, bright-eyed mice. They are timid and when caught in the hands will struggle to escape, but make no attempt to bite or scratch. If held gently they soon become quiet and may be stroked as they sit in the open hand. On the San Augustine Plains E. A. Goldman caught specimens at burrows in the loose sand under a saltbush (Atriplex), and while digging for pocket gophers in September he dug into another of their dens and in a handful of earth threw out a young Baird's pocket mouse, which started off in short jumps but which he quickly caught in his hands. In the Datil Mountains Hollister found many of their burrows in the sandy soil, all with the entrances closed during the daytime.

Food habits.—So far as known, the food of this little mouse consists mainly of seeds, the pure white contents of the stomach indicating that they are carefully shelled and only the inner parts eaten. In captivity the mice eat a little green leaves, cactus pulp, lettuce, or other moist vegetation. In the Datil Mountains Hollister found the cheek pouches usually filled with small grass and weed seeds. At Santa Rosa in May and June, the writer found several with their pockets filled with seeds of juniper berries. Their partiality to the patches of seed-laden wild sunflowers and other composite plants, and patches of Croton would indicate that the seeds of these were favorite food, but their menu evidently varies with the season and the seed supply. At times they are very fond of rolled oats and will stuff their pockets full and carry it away to their dens. Very often, however, when more palatable seeds are available they refuse this bait.

Breeding habits.—The mammae of the females are arranged in 3 pairs, 2 pairs of inguinal, arranged so far forward that they might almost be considered abdominal, and 1 pair of pectoral. A specimen examined at Santa Rosa on May 28, 1903, contained two half-developed embryos. This evidently is not the full number, however, as another female taken June 5 had lately given birth to six young. The normal number of young is more probably three to six. There seems to be great irregularity in the time of their breeding, or possibly two or more litters are raised in a season. At Higbee, Colo., Ned Dearborn took a less than half-grown young on April 16, and at La Junta, Lantz took two half-grown young on April 23. At Ribera, N. Mex., the writer caught a half-grown young on July 3. On the San Augustine Plains E. A. Goldman caught a quarter-grown young on September 15, and two half-grown young the next day. At Riley, Hollister caught a half-grown young September 23. At Deming and El Paso the writer found females with milk in their teats in December.

Economic status.—Some claims have been made that these mice dig up the planted grains, but among the many other species of rodents to which the charge is also applied it is difficult to fix the guilt. Undoubtedly they do, where opportunity offers, consume some grass seed on the range and carry away a little of the planted grains from the edges of fields. Alone their depredations would be of little consequence, but added to that of many other rodents their mite adds to the tax levied upon the products of the soil. Their burrows often penetrate the banks of irrigation ditches, but in most cases are too small and shallow to be of serious consequence. On the other hand their destruction of weed seeds may well offset all their debts to agriculture.

PEROGNATHUS FLAVUS BIMACULATUS Merriam

Yavapai Pocket Mouse

Perognathus bimaculatus Merriam, North Amer. Fauna No. 1, p. 12, 1889.

Type.—Collected at Fort Whipple, Yavapai County, Ariz., May 21, 1865, by Elliott Coues.

General characters.—A robust form of the *flavus* group, readily distinguished by its larger size and darker coloration. The young or half-grown specimens of *flavus* are of a blue-gray color while of *bimaculatus* they are conspicuously dusky gray. None of the New Mexico specimens are perfectly typical *bimaculatus*, but those from Fort Wingate and Gallup, while somewhat intermediate, are decidedly nearest to this form. Those from the San Augustine Plain and San Juan Valley, while somewhat intermediate in characters, are referred to *flavus*.

Measurements.—Adult specimens of typical *bimaculatus* measure: Total length, 118; tail, 53; hind foot, 17 millimeters.

Distribution and habitat.—With most of its distribution in the plateau region of Arizona the Yavapai pocket mouse extends up the Rio Puerco branch of the Little Colorado River into western New Mexico and may well have a wider distribution over the surrounding plateau country. (Fig. 47.) It seems to be mainly an Upper Sonoran form.

General habits.—In habits these mice seem to be identical with the small *flavus*. At Fort Wingate, in June, Hollister found them common and easily trapped at their burrows under the edge of bushes on the sandy flats of the Puerco Valley. Unfortunately most of the specimens caught were devoured by other mice, probably by the grasshopper mice, which were taken at the same locality. Hollister says their cheek pouches were nearly always filled with tiny seeds. At Gallup, in September, the writer found abundant traces of them all over the valley in sandy soil, but only one specimen was caught. They refused to touch any kind of bait at this season, and the one caught accidentally got its tail in a trap in running across it. Their little burrows both closed and open, were common under and around bunches of sagebrush, rabbit brush, and saltbush. On still mornings the tiny tracks were seen all around the traps, but the traps were carefully avoided. The one specimen taken had a few seeds of tumbleweed, or Russian thistle (*Salsola pestifer*), in its pockets. At this season, however, there was an abundance of other ripe weed seeds on the ground, and the mice were evidently busy storing a supply of their favorite foods.

Breeding habits.—These are probably identical with those of *P. flavus* as the mammae are of the same number and arrangement. There is one record from the type locality of a female containing four embryos.

Economic status.—As the range of the species is mainly over a region of grazing land where there is little attempt at agriculture, it has little economic importance. Its consumption of weed seeds may even prove of some benefit to the range, especially if it succeeds in checking the abundance of such injurious plants as the tumble-weed.

PEROGNATHUS APACHE APACHE Merriam

Apache Pocket Mouse

Perognathus apache Merriam, North Amer. Fauna No. 1, p. 14, 1889.

Type.—Collected in Keam Canyon, Apache County, Ariz., May 22, 1888, by J. Sullivan.

General characters.—This buffy or pale yellow pocket mouse is noticeably larger than *flavus* or *bimaculatus* and has relatively smaller ears and longer tail than either. It is clear light buff above and pure white below.

Measurements.—Adults average: Total length, 139; tail, 67; hind foot, 18.5 millimeters.

Distribution and habitat.—In distribution the Apache pocket mouse is mainly an Upper Sonoran desert plains species, occupying the higher levels of the Rio Grande and San Juan Valleys and the plateau country of northeastern Arizona. (Fig. 48.) Deming, in the edge of the Lower Sonoran Zone, is the southernmost locality from which the species is known. Hollister took specimens among the yellow pines in the Gallina Mountains, but most of the

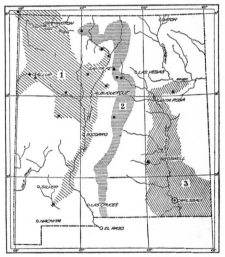

Figure 48.—Distribution of three little pocket mice in New Mexico: 1, *Perognathus apache apache;* 2, *P. apache melanotis;* 3, *P. merriami gilvus.* Type locality circled

known range of the species lies on the open plains from 5,000 to 7,000 feet.

General habits.—In December, 1889, the writer collected three specimens of the Apache pocket mouse on the sandy river bank near Deming. These were caught at one group of burrows in the mellow sand, and from the burrows their trails led away to the nearest patches of wild sunflowers and other seed-laden plants. They carefully avoided the traps and refused to take rolled oats as bait, probably because they could get an abundance of better food in the form of little dalea beans, wild sunflower, and other fallen seeds. In July of the same year the mice were caught in traps baited with rolled oats at San Pedro. Here they were living in the open park among scattered junipers. In the sandy valley of the Chama River near Abiquiu in October their burrows and tracks were common, but the mice persistently avoided the traps. As a last resort the writer dug one out and caught it in his hands. A little later near Espanola Gaut succeeded in catching a few in traps, and in June of the following year Surber collected three more there. In the river valley a few miles above the pueblo of Jemez early in September, their tracks and burrows were numerous, but even then the animals were not easily caught. One specimen that blundered into a trap had its cheek pouches well filled with the seeds of spurge (*Croton texensis*) and some seeds of a composite, probably tarweed (Grindelia). Near Laguna two were caught but were so badly eaten by insects that only the skulls were saved. At Wingate, in June, Hollister collected four specimens at little burrows under the bushes on the sandy plateaus of the Puerco Valley. The cheek pouches were nearly always filled with tiny seeds. In habits this species does not differ materially from the several other species of small, smooth-tailed pocket mice in New Mexico, and it is usually impossible to tell from the burrows or tracks which to expect in your traps. Like the others, it is mainly nocturnal and almost never seen alive except as forced out of its burrows.

Apparently nothing is known of its breeding habits or of its economic status.

PEROGNATHUS APACHE MELANOTIS Osgood

BLACK-EARED POCKET MOUSE

Perognathus apache melanotis Osgood, North Amer. Fauna No. 18, p. 27, September 20, 1900.

Type.—Collected at Casas Grandes, Chihuahua, Mexico, May 21, 1899, by E. A. Goldman.

General characters.—A dark form of *apache*, with deeper yellow of the upper parts and with inner surface of the ears blackish instead of buff.

Measurements.—Though the measurements are about the same as those of *apache*, the skull is conspicuously smaller with narrower mastoids.

Distribution and habitat.—The type and only known specimen of *melanotis* at the time of its description was from Casas Grandes in northern Chihuahua. Specimens taken since at Gran Quivera, Pecos, Glorieta, Santa Fe, and at Stinking Spring Lake [Burford Lake] on the Jicarilla Indian Reservation, are so nearly identical with the type of *melanotis* that they can not well be referred to any other form. The range thus shown is illogical and can only be accounted for by predicating a much wider former range, at present unknown. (Fig. 48.) All the localities represented are in the Upper Sonoran Zone and several of them at the extreme upper edge of the zone. A specimen of *apache* from San Pedro, in the Sandia Mountains, shows a tendency toward *melanotis* in the dusky inner surface of the ears, but it is too young to show good skull characters.

General habits.—Near the old pueblo of Pecos and at Glorieta, at respectively 6,800 and 7,200 feet altitude, these little mice were common among the junipers and nut pines of the Upper Sonoran Zone. They were living in dry, sandy, or mellow soil in burrows among scattered weeds, under the edges of stones or along the cut banks of the creek. Their little burrows were numerous in favorite places, part of them standing open and others closed during the day. As usual, the closed burrows were the ones where earth was thrown out, and the open ones, those not in recent use, or else they were partly concealed back doors from which the animals, if disturbed, could easily make their escape. Similar burrows made by this species were found near Santa Fe, and one specimen was taken. Near Stinking Spring Lake [Burford Lake] the mice were fairly common and two were caught in traps close to camp. One of these was caught in the daytime by opening its burrow and setting a trap inside, for it soon came out to close the burrow. The one caught near Santa Fe in July had its cheek pouches full of seeds of ryegrass (*Lolium perenne*). At Pecos the mice were eager for the rolled oats with which the traps were baited, and, during July and August, 17 specimens were collected. Four half-grown young were taken on August 26 and larger young of the year on July 4 and August 25 and 26.

In habits as well as distribution there is still much to be learned of this interesting little animal.

PEROGNATHUS MERRIAMI GILVUS Osgood

DUTCHER'S POCKET MOUSE

Perognathus merriami gilvus Osgood, North Amer. Fauna No. 18, p. 22, 1900.

Type.—Collected at Eddy (now Carlsbad), Eddy County, N. Mex., September 18, 1892, by B. H. Dutcher.

General characters.—This sleek, little yellow mouse, with white belly, short rounded ears, and short, smooth tail, is slightly larger than *flavus*, which it resembles, but it belongs to a distinct group, and occurs at the same localities with *flavus*.

Measurements.—Total length, about 122; tail, 60; hind foot, 16.5 millimeters.

Distribution and habitat.—There are specimens of *gilvus* from the type locality, Carlsbad, from 40 miles west of Roswell in the Pecos Valley, and from 25 miles west of Tucumcari at the northernmost point of the Llano Estacado. (Fig. 48.) Most of the range of the species, however, lies in western Texas and is practically all within the Lower Sonoran Zone. At Carlsbad, Dutcher found these little pocket mice inhabiting the low stony mesas, and at Cedar Point, about 40 miles west of Roswell, the writer took one specimen on the open prairie. Near the northern end of the Staked Plains, about 25 miles west of Tucumcari, two were collected among the low mesquite bushes at the edge of the valley.

General habits.—In habits *gilvus* is very similar to *flavus* with which it occurs at Carlsbad, but it is more often found on stony or hard ground than in the mellow sandy valley bottoms. Nothing is definitely known of its food and breeding habits.

PEROGNATHUS HISPIDUS PARADOXUS Merriam

KANSAS POCKET MOUSE

Perognathus paradoxus Merriam, North Amer. Fauna No. 1, p. 24, 1889.

Type.—Collected at Banner, Largo County, Kansas, October 17, 1884, by A. B. Baker.

General characters.—A large, stout pocket mouse with harsh fur and rather long but not bushy tail. The upperparts are grizzled buff with clear buffy stripes along the sides, and the underparts are white.

Measurements.—Adults measure: Total length, 222; tail, 108; hind foot, 26.5 millimeters.

Distribution and habitat.—The Kansas pocket mouse is a plains species covering the Pecos Valley and eastern New Mexico and occurring in the Tularosa, Rio Grande, and Gila Valleys. (Fig. 49.) Though most of its range lies in the Upper Sonoran Zone, it also comes into the edges of some Lower Sonoran valleys. Specimens have been taken at Las Vegas, near Roswell and Carlsbad, at Tularosa, near Mesilla Park, near Redrock, at Gila, and on Dry Creek betwen the Gila and San Francisco Rivers. They have also been taken just outside of New Mexico near the northeastern, southeastern, and southwestern extremities of the State.

General habits.—Over a wide range of open plains country these pocket mice burrow in any convenient place without regard to shelter or cover. Often their smooth, round burrows go into the bare earth, where it would seem that the animals must inevitably be picked up by owls and nocturnal enemies as soon as they appear on the surface. Even in the desert valleys, where low shrubby vegetation is abundant, they make their burrows in the open more often than under the shrubbery. They are not even particular about sandy soil, as their burrows are often found in firmly packed and rather hard soil formations. The burrows of this species are apparently left open during the daytime, and they usually go almost straight down instead of on the gradual slope, as with most species of the genus. Often it is difficult to locate the burrows or find where the animals run, but a long mark simulating a runway commonly attracts them and they will follow it for its full length or until caught by a trap. Though apparently a common species, not many specimens were taken, owing to the difficulty in finding where they live.

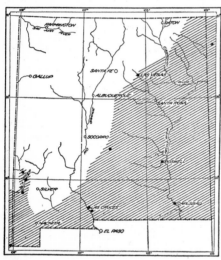

FIGURE 49.—Distribution of the Kansas pocket mouse, *Perognathus hispidus paradoxus*, in New Mexico

Food habits.—Generally these mice are fond of rolled oats, which seems to be the most successful trap bait used. In the cheek pouches of specimens caught are found a great variety of seeds. Near Gila E. A. Goldman found those of Johnson grass (*Holcus halepensis*) and wild morning-glory (Ipomoea) in the pockets of one. Wild sunflowers, parsnips, and other seeds have also been reported in their pockets. Of their breeding habits apparently nothing is known.

Economic status.—These pocket mice may have some economic importance, owing to their large size and their occupation of extensive areas of farming land. In grainfields they are said to carry off some of the grain, but this is not well authenticated and in any case would naturally be mainly the scattered and waste kernels. Some grass seed is undoubtedly destroyed on the range, but the destruction of weed seed would partially compensate this loss. Their burrows may in rare cases injure ditch banks, but the mice are not sufficiently abundant to be considered an important pest.

PEROGNATHUS PENICILLATUS EREMICUS Mearns

DESERT BRUSH-TAILED POCKET MOUSE

Perognathus (*Chaetodipus*) *eremicus* Mearns, Bul. Amer. Mus. Nat. Hist. 10: 300, 1898.

Type.—Collected at Fort Hancock, El Paso County, Tex., June 27, 1893, by E. A. Mearns.

General characters.—So similar to *intermedius* in size, color, and general appearance that the two are often mistaken, but the skulls show the two species to be entirely distinct. *P. eremicus* is readily distinguished in the flesh, however, by the pink instead of dusky soles of the hind feet.

Measurements.—Adult specimens: Total length, about 176; tail, 98; hind foot, 22 millimeters.

Distribution and habitat.—The desert brush-tailed pocket mouse is a Lower Sonoran species extending into New Mexico from the south. It is common at El Paso and thence north to Garfield and Tularosa. It is probable that it occupies the southern part of the Pecos Valley in New Mexico, as it comes close to the line at Pecos and Monahans, Tex. To the westward it extends over the Deming Plain to Playas Valley. Unlike *intermedius*, which is mainly restricted to rocks and cliffs, *eremicus* occupies the sandy desert valleys, where bushes and small plants afford some protection. At Tularosa, Gaut collected a series of 31 and reported them as living in burrows under the creosote bushes in the valley. At Garfield, E. A. Goldman found them living along the edge of the sandy valley in burrows under the bushes. Near Deming he caught specimens at burrows under the weeds and bushes bordering the sink of the Mimbres, and at the Cienega Ranch in the Playas Valley he took them among bushes on sandy soil. The species probably has a considerably wider range in the State than these few localities show, as only the most expert trapping produces specimens.

General habits.—In its occupation of mellow valley soils *eremicus* has a less restricted habitat than the rock-loving *intermedius*. The reason for this division of the ground between the two species is not entirely apparent, but it does not serve to keep them entirely apart, as specimens have been taken in the same traps at burrows near the cliffs. In habits the two may differ in some points, but the difference is not known. The closed burrows from which the sand has been thrown well out on one side are easily recognized, but little else is known of their habits. It is even doubtful if they are strictly nocturnal, as they seem to be active in their dens during the daytime, and if a burrow is opened it is quickly closed from within. They may thus be caught at any time of day by setting traps inside the burrows and leaving them open.

Food habits.—These pocket mice are usually eager for rolled oats and when caught often have their cheek pouches stuffed with those used as trap bait. At Garfield, in November, E. A. Goldman caught one with 92 seeds of mesquite in its pockets. At Tularosa, in November, Gaut reported their cheek pouches containing mainly seeds of creosote bush and snakeweed (Gutierrezia). These few notes, however, do not indicate a limited menu, as many undetermined seeds are also found in their pockets.

Breeding and economic status.—Of breeding habits apparently nothing is known. The economic status of the species is of little importance, owing to its scarcity and limited distribution in occupied lands.

PEROGNATHUS INTERMEDIUS Merriam

Intermediate Pocket Mouse

Perognathus intermedius Merriam, North Amer. Fauna No. 1, p. 18, 1889.
Perognathus obscurus Merriam, North Amer. Fauna No. 1, p. 20, 1889. Type from near Hachita, N. Mex., collected April 30, 1886, by A. W. Anthony.

Type.—Collected at Mud Spring, Mohave County, Ariz., February 26, 1889, by Vernon Bailey.

General characters.—This large pocket mouse has a long tufted tail and pointed ears, rather harsh buffy-gray fur and the lower parts clear salmon buff. From the very similar *eremicus* with which it is often associated it is conveniently distinguished in the flesh by the dusky soles of the hind feet. From all the smaller species occurring in New Mexico it is distinguished by the long and bushy tail.

Measurements.—Total length, 185; tail, 102; hind foot, 22 millimeters.

Distribution and habitat.—The pocket mouse *intermedius* extends into southwestern New Mexico and up the Rio Grande Valley to Isleta. There are specimens from El Paso, from the San Andres Mountains, Lake Valley, Las Palomas, Socorro, Rio Puerco, Isleta, and from old Camp Apache and near the Hatchet Mountains in Grant County. The range of the species is entirely within the Lower Sonoran Zone, but as the animals are partial to rocks and cliffs they are most often found along canyons or at the foot of the mountains and edges of the valley. They do not occur in the open part of broad, mellow valleys, so the range is by no means continuous. In the Franklin and San Andres Mountains, Gaut collected specimens about the rocks and cliffs in canyons and foothills up to 4,800 feet altitude. Near Isleta, Hollister collected a fine series of specimens on the rocky hillsides. Near Hachita, E. A. Goldman collected specimens among the loose rocks and cliffs along the adjoining hills and in similar situations in the foothills of the Big Hatchet Mountains. At Lake Valley, Las Palomas, and Socorro he also collected them in rocky situations along hillsides or cliffs.

General habits.—The mice live in burrows of their own construction and seem to prefer the mellowest sandy soil, but for greater protection they take special pains that these burrows shall enter the ground under some rock or between the narrow layers in cliffs. The burrows are small, inconspicuous, and often closed during the daytime, while tiny trails and lines of tracks lead away over the sandy ground to feeding places among the plants. The little animals are easily caught in traps baited with rolled oats and set along these trails or where their tracks are found near the bases of the cliffs. They are nocturnal, and little is known of their habits save what is shown by the specimens taken from the trap lines in the morning.

Food habits.—The food of this as of other related species apparently consists mainly of seeds of small plants. They usually are eager for the rolled-oat trap bait, and are often found with their cheek pouches well stuffed with the crushed grains. At Isleta, Hollister reported the pouches of trapped specimens well filled with seeds of various weeds.

Breeding habits.—Of their breeding habits practically nothing is known except that by midsummer the well-grown young are caught more frequently than adults. The number of young in a litter and the number of litters in a year are unknown except as may be judged from other related and better-known species.

Order CARNIVORA: Flesh Eaters

Family FELIDAE: Cats

FELIS ONCA HERNANDESII (GRAY)

JAGUAR; EL TIGRE of Mexico

Leopardus hernandesii Gray, Zool. Soc. London Proc. 278: 1857.

Type locality.—Mazatlan, Sinaloa, Mexico.

General characters.—Largest of the American cats and closely resembling the leopard in color and marking, but heavier and more powerful.

Measurements.—A specimen collected near Center City, Tex., is reported to have measured in the flesh 6½ feet from tip of nose to tip of tail; 36 inches around chest; 26 inches around head; and 21 inches around the forearm; and to have weighed 140 pounds. A skin belonging to Governor Otero measured from tip of nose to tip of tail, 7½ feet; tail, 27 inches; width between tip of ears, 11 inches; spread across narrowest part of skin, 21 inches; across front legs, 5 feet.[24]

Distribution and habitat.—A few large spotted cats (pl. 16, A) have been found over southern New Mexico, where they seem to be native, although generally supposed to be wanderers from over the Mexican border. Probably the first record of jaguars for New Mexico was made by Coronado, in 1540, when on his way north to Zuni he reported both " tigres " and " ounces " among the mammals of that region, probably intending one name for the jaguar and the other for the cougar. (Whipple, et al., 1856, p. 110.) One was reported at Santa Fe in 1825 (Baird, 1859, p. 7), and in recent years a few have been killed and many reported in the southern part of the State. In 1855 (?) one was reported as seen by J. Weiss, of the Mexican boundary survey party, in Guadalupe Canyon in or near the southwest corner of New Mexico. (Baird, 1859, p. 7.)

In May, 1900, Nat Straw, a hunter and trapper in the Mogollon Mountains, is reported to have trapped a jaguar near Grafton on Taylor Creek, Socorro County, N. Mex. He gave the length of this animal as 8 feet, 3 inches, but C. M. Barber, who saw the skin and made the report, did not say whether the measurement was taken from the skin or from the animal in the flesh. Barber (1902, p. 192) also reported several others that had been seen or killed in that region. In 1903 Governor Otero in his house at Santa Fe showed the writer a beautiful skin of a jaguar, which had been killed the

---

[24] Measurements of skins are very unsatisfactory, and it is greatly to be regretted that there are not on record more definite measurements and weights of these large cats.

previous year in Otero County, made into a rug and presented to him. His brother, Page B. Otero, State game warden of New Mexico at that time, also reported a jaguar seen on Ute Creek in San Miguel County during the winter of 1902–03 and one seen in the region of Cow Springs a few miles southwest of Fulton during the summer of 1903. He had perfect confidence in these reports, as he knew the men who saw the animals. He said that jaguars also had been reported from the San Andres and Sacramento Mountains in previous years. In 1905 Hollister saw and photographed a skin that had been mounted as a rug and was in the possession of O. Reddeman, at Magdalena. The original skull was mounted in the skin and showed the animal to be an adult with well-worn teeth. Reddeman had purchased the skin from a Mr. Manning, whose wife poisoned the animal in the Datil Mountains in August, 1902. A little later, when in the Datil Mountains, Hollister visited Manning and obtained an account of the killing of the animal. Mrs. Manning had been in the habit of putting out poison to kill the predatory animals about their ranch, in the mountains 12 miles northwest of Datil, and among the victims of the poisoned baits was this jaguar, which had been killing stock on the ranch for some time. It had killed 17 calves near the house during a short period before it was secured. The ranch was located at about 9,000 feet altitude in the pine and spruce timber of this exceedingly rough range of mountains. At the time Hollister was there another jaguar was supposed to be at large in the general neighborhood. In 1908, while in the Animas Valley in extreme southwestern New Mexico, the ranchmen told the writer of a jaguar killed in 1903 in Clanton Creek Canyon about 6 miles west of the Gray ranch. It had killed a bull that had wandered back in the canyon and was shot while feeding on him. W. P. Burchfield told the circumstances of its capture and where the skin had been sent for mounting. E. A. Goldman also secured a record of one that had been killed by a hunter named Morris on the west slope of Sierra de los Caballos about 1904 or 1905.

In Baird's report on the Mammals of the Mexican Boundary Survey (1859, pp. 7–8) there is a long and bloody account translated by Kennerly from Spanish records of a " tigre " that entered the Convent of San Francisco in Santa Fe, April 10, 1825, and without provocation attacked and killed four men before it was finally shot through a hole bored in the door of the sacristy. The narrative has an artificial sound throughout, and, even with the plausible explanation at the end that the animal had been driven by high water in the river to take refuge in the convent garden and had then entered an open door into the convent and made the attacks because it knew escape was impossible, the story sounds very improbable. Apparently there is no other record of the jaguar attacking human beings in either New Mexico or Texas, where a good many have been killed. One killed near Center City, Tex., in 1903 was treed at night by some boys and dogs, shot with a revolver, driven into some brush, surrounded by dogs and men, and, after it had killed one dog and one horse, finally killed; but during all this time it did not attack any of the men even when surrounded in the dark. (Bailey, 1905, p. 165.)

FELIS CONCOLOR HIPPOLESTES Merriam

ROCKY MOUNTAIN COUGAR; MOUNTAIN LION; PANTHER; THAM-MENA of the
Taos Indians

Felis hippolestes Merriam, Biol. Soc. Wash. Proc. 11: 219, 1897.

Type.—Collected at head of Wind River, Wyo., November, 1892, by John
Burlingame.

General characters.—Largest of all the mountain lions and distinguished not
only by its great size but also by its dark reddish-brown color and the relatively
long and massive skull and narrow, elongated audital bullae.

Measurements.—The type specimen, measured from a well-made skin, shows
a total length of 2,600; tail, 930; and hind foot, 270 millimeters. A still
larger male killed by Colonel Roosevelt, in Rio Blanco County, measured in
the flesh 8 feet (2,440 millimeters) from tip of nose to tip of tail and weighed
227 pounds. (Roosevelt, 1901, p. 435.) His largest female measured 6 feet
9 inches (2,059 millimeters)
and weighed 124 pounds.

Distribution and habitat.—In the Biological
Survey collection there is
but one specimen from New
Mexico that can be readily
referred to *hippolestes*.
This is the skull of a fine
large male, picked up in the
Jemez Mountains near
camp on the head of Santa
Clara Creek; but the writer
has seen several dark-
brown skins from the Taos
and Pecos River Mountains
that were undoubtedly of
this species. On the
strength of this material he
is referring all the notes
from the mountains of
northern New Mexico to
hippolestes, and it is not
improbable that some of

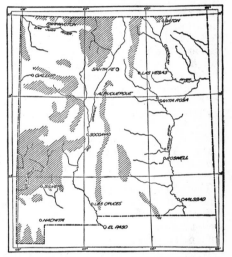

FIGURE 50.—Shaded area showing approximate
distribution of the estimated 400 mountain
lions in New Mexico in 1917, from map prepared by J. Stokley Ligon

the very large individuals recorded from the Sacramento Mountains
might also be referred to this form. There is even some doubt as to
whether those from the mesas and canyons of the San Juan River
Valley may not prove to be nearer to *aztecus* than *hippolestes*.
Much additional material is needed, however, before the ranges of
the different forms can be satisfactorily determined. (Fig. 50.)

Though these animals belong mainly to the forested mountains or
rock-rimmed canyons and cliffs, they often wander considerable
distances and have been recorded from localities well out on the
plains and in the open valleys. Their distribution depends mainly
upon the supply of game, and they are generally most abundant
where the deer are plentiful. In times past they also fed extensively
upon elk wherever they were available within their range. Probably
the first record for New Mexico was by Coronado in 1540, when on
his journey to Zuni he spoke of the "lions," among other animals.

In 1903 they were common in the Pecos River Mountains, especially
along the gulches and canyons on the roughest slopes of the headwaters of the Pecos, where their tracks were often seen.   The following year they were found fairly common in the Taos and Culebra
Mountains, where a few were killed every year.   One was killed
near camp at 9,400 feet altitude on the Costilla River in the latter
part of August.   In 1905 Hollister reported a few in the Mount
Taylor Range north of Laguna and a few in the Zuni Mountains, and
in 1909 E. A. Goldman again reported them in the Zuni Mountains
and learned of one being killed a short time before he was there.
In the San Juan Valley the ranchmen told the writer that they were
common on the mesas and in the canyons, both north and south of the
river, where they did considerable damage to stock.   In 1910 officials
of the Forest Service reported mountain lions as fairly abundant on
the Carson National Forest and as still very common in the Jemez
Mountains.   In 1914 they reported 3 killed on the Carson, 3 on the
Pecos, and 2 in the Jemez National Forest; in 1915, 4 on the Carson
and 4 on the Santa Fe National Forests; and in 1916, 4 on the Carson
and 7 on the Santa Fe National Forests.

General habits.—Mountain lions, even where common, are rarely
seen unless trapped or hunted with dogs.   They are among the most
cautious, secretive, and wary of the animals hunted by man, who is
perhaps their only enemy worth considering.   Their presence is
generally made known by their tracks, which are often seen along the
trails and sometimes close to camps where they come prowling at
night.   To a great extent they seem to be nocturnal, but when hunting under the stimulus of hunger they are fully diurnal and apparently keep moving or watching for game until a good meal is secured.

There is ample evidence both of their skill as hunters and also of
their great strength.   At the junction of Mora Creek with the Pecos
River a Mexican, Christine Rivera, who lived there, showed the
writer the gray winter skin of a large lion that he had caught
during the preceding winter (1903) in a No. 6 bear trap.   The lion
had killed a full-grown horse in Willow Creek Canyon near there
and was caught in the trap when it returned for a second meal of
horse meat.   The bear trap in which it was caught must have weighed
at least 40 pounds, and the lion had carried it, together with a heavy
green pole as a clog, a distance of about half a mile and had broken
one of the springs of the trap in its struggles before being overtaken
and shot.   The great cats are said to kill many horses and colts
and some cattle in this vicinity.   At the pueblo of Taos, the same
year, one of the Indians was tanning a very large skin of a mountain
lion that he had killed a short time before in Lucero Creek Canyon
back of the pueblo.   This was probably one of the lions that earlier
in the spring had killed and partly eaten one of the largest and
strongest work horses belonging to the pueblo.   Two other horses
had come running into the pueblo with their necks severely bitten
and torn and with long cuts and gashes down their sides, and when
the Indians followed up the canyon whence the horses had come
they found one that had been killed and partly eaten and buried
under leaves, sticks, and earth.   There were evidently two of the
mountain lions that had attacked the horses, but they did not return
to the carcass.

Economic status.—As deer and other native game animals become scarce, the mountain lions turn their attention to domestic stock and seem especially to relish colts, but if these are not to be found they take horse meat of any kind. In spite of the bounty usually paid for their destruction and the efforts of stockmen and hunters, they have until recently held their own in the rougher parts of the country, but with the present organized effort it will not be long before they are sufficiently reduced in numbers to prevent any great losses. Any system of adequate game protection or the restocking of the mountain forests with elk and large game animals will make it imperative that the mountain lions be kept well under control.

FELIS CONCOLOR AZTECUS MERRIAM

MEXICAN COUGAR; MOUNTAIN LION; PANTHER

Felis hippolestes aztecus Merriam, Wash. Acad. Sci. Proc. 3: 592, 1901.

Type.—Collected at Colonia Garcia, Chihuahua, Mexico, October 17, 1899, by H. A. Cluff.

General characters.—A large gray form of the group, but smaller than *hippolestes*, with relatively shorter, wider skull and more rounded audital bullae.

Measurements.—The type, an adult male, measured: Total length, 2,268; tail, 731; hind foot, 270 millimeters. An adult female topotype measured 1,814, 630, and 230 millimeters respectively.

Distribution and habitat.—A large series of specimens from the desert ranges of southern New Mexico are all referred to *aztecus*, of which they seem to be fairly typical. A skull of an old male from the Datil Mountains is rather large and heavy and shows evident gradation toward *hippolestes*, but the writer is referring the specimens to *aztecus*, as an arbitrary division between the two forms seems necessary. (Fig. 50.)[25] A series of 24 skulls from the Gila National Forest includes 10 adult males, 9 females, 2 half-grown individuals (unsexed), and 3 skulls of newly born kittens. These and the large series of mountain-lion skulls brought together by the trappers of predatory animals are especially important in the study of this rather difficult group. Mountain lions are or have been common over practically all of New Mexico, but they are rapidly decreasing in numbers and at present are rare or absent from most of the open plains country, but are still found in many of the rough or timbered mountain ranges, which afford them cover and game. In his report for May, 1917, J. S. Ligon estimates 84 killed during the year and 400 remaining alive, in New Mexico, distributed as shown on the accompanying map. (Fig. 50.)

At the present time they are probably most common in the Mogollon Mountain region, and in the Animas, San Luis, and Sacramento Mountain Ranges, with a few scattered through some of the small desert ranges over the southern and western parts of the State. In 1899 they were reported common in and around the Capitan and White Mountains, and in 1900 one was seen near Cloudcroft while the writer was there. In 1902 the track of a large mountain lion was seen in the road near his camp on the head of Silver Springs Creek, 10 miles north of Cloudcroft. In 1903, Gaut found cougars in the

---

[25] In the absence of specimens from more generally distributed localities over the State, the notes from the southern half of New Mexico are arbitrarily referred to *aztecus*, and those from the mountains of the northern part of the State to *hippolestes*.

Capitan Mountains and learned of one that was killed near Jarilla
during the previous autumn. In 1902 he reported them as common
about Corona and at Carrizozo and a few at Tularosa. In the San
Andres Mountains he reported two seen only a few years previously
in the range south of Salinas Peak, and a few seen near Bear Canyon
in the middle part of the range. In the Manzano Mountains in 1903
he reported them as scarce, but on December 8 he struck a fresh track
of one in the snow and followed it for two days without being able
to start the animal. In 1905, Hollister reported them as of regular
occurrence through the Datil and Gallina Ranges, where they were
doing considerable damage to stock and were much complained of by
the ranchmen.

   In 1906 the writer found them fairly common through the canyons
and rough country on the head of the Mimbres, Sapello, and Diamond
Creek region of the Gila National Forest and in the Tularosa Mountains north of the Mogollon peaks. Tracks were frequently seen,
a good many lions had been recently killed in that region, and late in
the fall the writer followed the tracks of one over the upper slopes
of the Mogollon peaks. In 1908 in crossing this same region, he
found that they were still rather numerous over the Gila and Datil
National Forests. Hotchkiss showed him where he had caught two
on Apache Peak at the head of Apache Creek the previous winter,
and gave him their skulls for the Biological Survey collection. On
the Negrito Creek the writer secured the skull of one recently caught
there and saw the skin of another tacked on the barn of a Mr.
Keener. There were said to be a few also in the San Francisco Mountains, where they were doing considerable damage to stock. Late in
October of the same year E. A. Goldman found their tracks common
in the snow in several places from 9,000 to 10,000 feet on the Mogollon peaks. He also reported them as occasionally found in the
Burro Mountains, and tracks seen along the bottom of the canyon of
the Gila 3 or 4 miles above Redrock, and he was told that they also
occurred in the hills north of Gila. The same year he reported them
as occurring sparingly in the Florida Mountains and in the San Luis,
Animas, and Cloverdale Mountains. At Hachita, on August 3, 1908,
the writer saw two nearly full-grown young of the year, said to be 10
months old. They had been caught in the Animas Mountains when
young and were quite tame and of the light-gray *aztecus* type. A
few days later he saw tracks of mountain lions high up in the canyons of the Animas Mountains. In 1908 officials of the Forest Service
reported for the preceding year 1 shot in the Magdalena National
Forest; 6 in the Lincoln National Forest; 2 trapped on the San Mateo
National Forest; 6 killed during the previous year on the Sacramento
National Forest; 3 killed on the Peloncillo National Forest; 6 killed
on the southern division and 4 on the northern division of the Gila
National Forest. In the autumn of 1909 E. A. Goldman reported a
few in the Mimbres Mountains west of Kingston, and in the San
Mateo Mountains near Monica Spring. In 1910 the Forest Service
reported some damage each year to stock, particularly colts, by mountain lions, but stated that hunters had kept the numbers reduced.
In 1915 they reported 3 killed on the Datil, 4 on the Alamo, and 1 on
the Lincoln National Forests; during 1916 the hunters of the Bureau

of Biological Survey killed 9 in the Guadalupe Mountain region, and the Forest Service reported 3 killed in the Manzano, 1 on the Alamo-Lincoln, 8 on the Gila, and 25 on the Datil National Forests. This number does not represent all, but probably does represent a large part of those killed in New Mexico during the year.

In 1917 the predatory-animal hunters in New Mexico killed 17 mountain lions; in 1918, 14; in 1919, 41; in 1920, 63; and in 1921, 29. Most of these were killed in the Mogollon Mountain Region where a few still remain.

General habits.—These big cats are hunters, and their prey is such species of deer, mountain sheep, and domestic stock as come within their reach. They are generally found where the deer are most numerous, and apparently deer are their favorite game. In the roughest, more inaccessible areas of mountain canyons and rim rock they find not only their prey but also secure retreats where they can live and breed with least disturbance. They are great wanderers and will cover long distances when hunting for food. In the Mogollon Mountains on the morning of October 23, 1906, the writer struck a fresh track in the snow at 10,000 feet altitude on the north side of the Mogollon peaks. It was so fresh that he followed it as rapidly as possible for several miles, confident of overtaking the animal soon or certainly in case it should capture a deer and stop to feed, but finally he gave it up, for the track turned across a deep canyon below the snow. The cat was not far ahead of him but was traveling steadily and was stepping just as far as the writer could step whether walking up hill or down. Evidently it was hunting deer, as there were abundant tracks in the snow and several of the deer had taken hasty flight. While following this track he found three places where the mountain lion had scratched up a little heap of earth and spruce needles from beneath the snow. At least two of these were evidently old scratching places that he had scented and was in the habit of visiting on his rounds.

In the Manzano Mountains Gaut followed a track for two days, and estimated that the lion covered 30 miles without making a kill or stopping for any appreciable length of time, and as he then gave up the pursuit there was no telling how much farther it went before stopping. There is no knowledge of the actual distances they travel or the length of time they can go without food when necessary. In all this region where mountain lions are most common there seems to be no report of their having ever attacked any person, even when wounded or treed by dogs. In 1825, at the hot springs near the head of the Gila River, one came into the camp of a party of trappers at night and was shot in the midst of the camp, but apparently had no intention of making an attack. (Pattie, 1905, p. 88.)

At that time they were evidently unaccustomed to firearms, but now they are one of the most wary and difficult animals to hunt, except by the use of dogs. Almost any good dog will chase one up a tree and keep it there until it can be shot. Though not easily trapped, sometimes by setting a trap at one of their fresh kills they may be caught on their return for a second meal. The scent baits that attract wolves and foxes seem to have no attraction for these cougars, either in the wild state or in captivity in zoological parks.

Judging from their return to regular scratching places in the woods, it would seem possible to trap them by using for bait the urine and scent of their own species, especially of the females.

Food habits.—There are probably no more strictly carnivorous animals than these large cats, and most of their food seems to be of the larger game animals or domestic stock. It is probable that at times they catch rabbits and birds, but very little is known of their actual everyday habits. When venison and mountain sheep are not to be had they readily turn their attention to horses, cattle, and sheep, seeming to prefer colts among all domestic stock.

Breeding habits.—Little is known of the breeding habits of these animals, but a litter of four kittens was taken by Hotchkiss on the head of Sapello Creek, April 9, 1908, and the skulls of three of these sent to the Biological Survey. They were very small, and none of the teeth had yet appeared, but no notes were furnished as to their condition or where found. Those seen in captivity at Hachita on August 3, 1908, were about half grown and were said to be then 10 months old.

Economic status.—These big cats are among the most destructive of predacious animals, not only to game but to a great variety of domestic animals. As the writer admired a beautiful large gray skin at the G. O. S. ranch in the Mogollon Mountains in 1906, Vick Culberson told him that just before the animal was shot it had killed a cow. At that time he said the cougars were becoming scarce in the mountains, although they had formerly been very abundant there and had done great damage to the livestock industry. A week later, on the head of the Mimbres, while trapping for wolves the writer saw the fresh tracks of a rather small mountain lion in a canyon below camp and one morning found it had dragged a 2-month-old calf, which it had recently killed, across the canyon and about a quarter of a mile up the steep slope and had partly covered it with sticks and earth. Hotchkiss, who was with him at the time, told him that he had previously found where one had dragged a full-grown cow and in another case a 2-year-old steer for a considerable distance. He also said that on Thanksgiving Day, 1897, while hunting at the head of Terry Canyon, he found a horse that had just been killed and buried in leaves and snow. On examining the horse he found that the heavy bell strap on its neck had been bitten nearly in two. He followed the tracks of the lion and toward night came upon it in the Mimbres Canyon and shot it while it was eating a calf that it had killed for supper. While following this track in the snow he said he had crossed the tracks of at least a dozen other lions, which had been hunting in the canyon. Some of the ranchmen in the country had given up trying to raise colts because lions were so numerous that they took practically all the increase. In October, 1890, he had helped Robert H. Bulwer, of Silver City, to put 70 brood mares and 40 saddle horses in the community pasture, a 40,000-acre tract partly inclosed by drift fences, near the headwaters of the Gila. The following May they found only 19 of the saddle horses, only a part of the mares, and no colts. The mountain lions had taken the rest, including all the colts. For the next 10 or 12 years a special effort was made by the ranchmen of the region to destroy the lions, and they were vigorously trapped and hunted with dogs until their numbers were greatly reduced.   Around the Capitan Mountains, in 1899, the writer was told that they killed a good many sheep and calves and still more colts for the ranchmen located near the foothills.   In the San Andres Mountains, in 1902, Gaut reported a few mountain lions, and the ranchmen of the vicinity complained of their killing some horses. In the Franklin Mountains, in 1903, just below the New Mexico line, he secured a skin of one that had been killed there and saw a mule that had been recently killed by another.   The deep gashes in the neck of the mule he attributed to both teeth and claws.   Many colts were being killed each year by the mountain lions in the Franklin Mountains.   In the Datil Mountains, in 1905, Hollister reported the destruction of many colts, but said that the ranchmen agreed that few calves were destroyed by mountain lions.   In 1908 E. A. Goldman reported them as occasionally killing stock in the San Luis and Cloverdale Mountains, and in 1909 as killing some stock, mainly horses, on the range west of Rio Alamosa.   In 1893 Townsend reported them as numerous in the Organ Mountains where he gave records of their having killed in one place five colts and numerous calves and sheep. (Townsend, 1893, p. 310.)

LYNX RUFUS BAILEYI Merriam

Plateau Wild Cat; Bobcat

Lynx baileyi Merriam, North Amer. Fauna No. 3, p. 79, 1890.

Type.—Collected at Moccasin Spring, Kanab Plateau, Ariz., December 28, 1888, by Vernon Bailey.

General characters.—The examination of much more material than was available when the species was described shows the form to be a rather large bobcat, yellowish gray in winter and pale yellowish in summer. Although variable in markings, the upper parts are generally much spotted and often have one or two black stripes along the back with lateral bands over the shoulders, while the buffy throat and white belly are thickly marked with large black spots.   The tail has, invariably, a white tip with black subterminal bar above and traces of several narrower bars back of this.   The skull is short and wide with full-rounded audital bullae.

Measurements.—The type, medium-sized female, measures: Total length, 745; tail, 132; and hind foot, 165 millimeters.   A young adult male from the Hualpai Mountains, Ariz., measured 820, 175, and 170 millimeters, and two adult males from Blue River, Ariz., each measured 838, 152, and 178 millimeters, respectively.   Weight of a rather small but fully adult female, collected at Fruitland by Clarence Birdseye, 20 pounds, and another at Embudo, collected by McClure Surber, 21 pounds.

Distribution and habitat.—Bobcats (pl. 16, B) are common over practically every part of New Mexico, and specimens from all the southern and western parts of the State are referred to this form, while those of the higher mountains in the north and down to the Manzano and Sacramento Mountains are referred to the slightly larger *uinta*.   Until the group is thoroughly studied the finer details of distribution can not be satisfactorily given, as the two forms blend into each other, and many of the specimens are intermediate in characters.   The greater part of the range of *baileyi* is in the Upper Sonoran Zone, but zone limits are not strictly observed by these cats. They are also common in the Transition Zone, where the limited areas of the zone occur in the plateau region of Arizona and western New Mexico.   They are also occasionally found in the Lower Sonoran valleys.   Their local distribution depends mainly upon two factors, rough country and food supply. Though great wanderers and occasionally found in any of the open valleys, these cats are most abundant in the rough country, full of canyons, gulches, cliffs, and rocky slopes, and especially in the half-open juniper and nut-pine forests of the plateau country. Rocky situations, especially, appeal to them not only as furnishing dens and safe retreats but as yielding a rich harvest of the rodents and other small game on which they constantly prey.

General habits.—These, like other cats, are largely nocturnal but are also perfectly adapted to daylight hunting, and in case of need they are often out looking for game during the brightest days. Normally however, they sleep during the day either in their rocky retreats or well hidden in thickets of brush or weeds or among old logs and tops of fallen trees. Occasionally one is frightened from its retreat and goes bounding away with almost rabbitlike motions, rather than with the smooth, soft running of the bushy-tailed animals, such as foxes and coyotes. Even at a distance they may be distinguished by their bobbing motion as they run. Though they show considerable speed for a short distance, they can not continue a long rapid flight. Usually they are quickly treed or run to cover by an ordinary dog and on good ground are easily overtaken by a man on horseback. Rabbitlike, they generally lie closely and depend on seclusion rather than flight. They are timid and even when caught in traps or closely cornered show little disposition to fight or defend themselves. If actually caught by a dog and forced to fight they do so with both vigor and execution, often tearing and biting the dog severely, but they are lightly built and have not much strength or endurance. A dog of their own size will often kill one, while a large dog or two or three dogs will dispatch one with very little trouble. Those taken for specimens are usually in good condition and occasionally are covered with a layer of fat, indicating that they are good hunters and generally able to find an abundance of game. Like all the cats, they are active throughout the year and in winter put on a thick coat of long light fur in contrast with their summer coat, which is thin and harsh.

Food habits.—The natural food of these cats is largely rabbits and other small rodents, including wood rats, kangaroo rats, pocket gophers, ground squirrels, chipmunks, and a great variety of mice and as many birds as they are able to catch. It is probable that their food also includes the young of many larger animals, such as deer, mountain sheep, and antelope, and in places they are very destructive to the smaller domestic stock, such as sheep and goats.

Breeding habits.—Sets of 2, 3, and 4 embryos have been found in the females and the usual number of young is probably four, as with other closely related species. On August 3, 1908, at Hachita in southwestern New Mexico there were three sizes of young bobcats kept as pets at a store. One half-grown individual kept in a cage was very vicious, while a quarter-grown kitten running at large in the house was as gentle and playful as any domestic kitten. A third, about 2 weeks old, was too young to take much interest in life, but gave promise of being a gentle and interesting pet.

Economic status.—In the San Juan Valley near camp at Fruitland on October 26, 1908, Clarence Birdseye caught two bobcats, an adult female and a half-grown young, by setting the traps along trails in the brush on river bottoms and baiting them with pieces of rabbit. C. J. Collyer, on whose ranch the party was staying, had recently lost 11 fine large turkeys out of a flock of 12 that had been in the habit of roosting in the low trees back of his house, and it was not hard to imagine what had become of them. At Pleasanton, in October, 1908, E. A. Goldman secured the skull of a bobcat that had been recently killed at the ranch. This animal had been feeding regularly on chickens, and when finally captured it had just killed five full-grown hens which were scattered around on the ground and left uneaten. The chickens were killed during the day among weeds and bushes, which grew close to the farm buildings. At the Dalgar ranch, just below Joseph on the Tularosa River, the bobcats had been catching chickens for some time, and one day as the writer drove out of the gate a fine large bobcat came out of the weed patch near the barn and went bounding over the ridge into the juniper woods beyond. In the Organ Mountains in January, 1903, Gaut reported bobcats numerous among the rocks of the mountain slopes, and a ranchman near Globe Spring told him that they came down to his ranch and caught his chickens and were especially troublesome in cold weather. In many places the bobcats kill so many of the lambs that certain rough areas are avoided by the sheep herders. In many cases they do not restrict themselves to lambs, but will kill any old sheep that is left unprotected, and some large individuals get in the habit of killing sheep and seem to prefer them to small game. The type of this species was caught by the side of a freshly killed and partly eaten full-grown sheep, which was still warm when found, and a trap set by the side of the sheep contained the bobcat the following morning. Constant care on the part of herders and dogs is necessary to protect the sheep from these cats as well as from coyotes. In spite of care the annual loss through their depredations is considerable.

The loss in game animals is not easily determined, but undoubtedly amounts to a greater drain on the game resources of the country than is generally supposed. Among the ranchmen and residents of the country every effort is made to destroy the bobcats when possible, local bounties are generally paid for their scalps, and at the present time the Biological Survey hunters and trappers are carrying on control operations against them, together with other predatory animals. During past years the officials of the Forest Service have made a special effort to catch and kill as many as possible, and in 1908 reports were made by the supervisors of the number of bobcats killed on each of the national forests in New Mexico during the previous year. The reports are incomplete and in many cases include those killed by others as well as officers of the Forest Service.

Those reported to the Bureau of Biological Survey by the Forest Service as killed in 1908 are, by national forests, as follows: Sacramento, approximately 95; Guadalupe, 5; Lincoln, 98; Manzano, 30; Gila, 26; Magdalena, 1; San Mateo, 14; Mount Taylor, 2; total, 271. This number represents but a small part of those killed in the region, however, as large numbers are trapped for fur as well as for the bounty, and many are killed just for the protection of stock and poultry. They are easily trapped by using feathers or rabbit fur or rabbit meat for bait.   They are much less suspicious than wolves and coyotes and usually will take bait readily if it is placed near the trails that they follow, where it can be plainly seen.   During 1916 the predatory-animal trappers of the Biological Survey killed 177 bobcats in New Mexico, most of which were of this subspecies.

LYNX RUFUS UINTA Merriam

Mountain Wild Cat; Pean-muse-ana of the Taos Indians

Lynx uinta Merriam, Biol. Soc. Wash. Proc. 15: 71, 1902.

Type.—Collected at Bridger Pass, Carbon County, Wyo., May 11, 1890, by Vernon Bailey.

General characters.—Distinguished from *baileyi* by its slightly larger size and relatively longer skull, slightly darker color with more conspicuous markings, the yellowish summer coat of *baileyi* being slightly darker and more rusty in *uinta*.

Measurements.—The type specimen, an adult male, measured: Total length, 1,030; tail, 195; and hind foot, 200 millimeters; and weighed 31 pounds. An adult male from Conejos River near the Colorado-New Mexico line measured 1,009, 203, and 196 millimeters, respectively, and weighed 29 pounds. One collected by Gaut in the Sacramento Mountains east of Tularosa measured 980, 194, and 203 millimeters, respectively, and weighed 31 pounds.

Distribution and habitat.—The New Mexico specimens of the large bobcat of the Rocky Mountain region are referred to *uinta* from Conejos River close to the Colorado-New Mexico line, and from La Jara Lake, Dulce, Chama, Tres Piedras, Embudo, Velarde, Cienega, Martinez, Halls Peak, Manzano Mountains, Capitan Mountains, and Sacramento Mountains.   One skull from the Pecos Valley 35 miles north of Roswell suggests intergradation with *texensis*, but it is not sufficiently typical of that species to warrant its inclusion in the New Mexico list.   Apparently this large Rocky Mountain bobcat extends southward in the higher mountains of northern New Mexico and along the Manzano and Sacramento chain of ranges between the Pecos and the Rio Grande Valleys.   Over a large part of its range it is a Transition Zone species, but it also occupies the adjoining Upper Sonoran country.   It is in a slight degree more of a forest animal than is *baileyi*, simply because more of the area that it occupies is covered with either open yellow-pine forest or juniper, nut-pine, and scrub-oak forests of the foothill country.   The animals are by no means restricted to forests, however, and wander well into the open and occupy rocky cliffs and canyons wherever they occur far out into the plains.

General habits.—In habits these cats do not differ materially from *baileyi*.   Their homes are generally in rocky caverns, dense thickets, or forest windfalls.   From these safe retreats the cats wander out over the surrounding country, as shown by their tracks, which are frequently seen in trails and sandy spots along creek margins and in the dust of caves and shelves of the cliffs and canyons.   They are mainly night prowlers but are also found abroad hunting in the daytime, creeping through the weeds and bushes in quest of rabbits, prairie dogs, squirrels, and small game, or watching the sheep herds for an opportunity to pounce upon some strayed or lost member of the flock.   Unless forced out of cover they are rarely seen.   In the Gallinas Mountains of Rio Arriba County the writer almost stepped on one in the low brush at 10,400 feet while hunting rabbits on a fresh snow. The cat was evidently hunting rabbits also, and as the writer stepped into a patch of low bushes it bounded out from his very feet but disappeared so quickly into the next thicket that he had no time to get a bead on it. At the base of the Jicarilla Mountains, Gaut found their tracks common in the soft earth about the dens of the big *Dipodomys spectabilis*, for which they were evidently hunting. He trapped a number of these rats, and with the exception of one specimen they were all eaten in his traps by the bobcats. At the pueblo of Taos their fresh tracks were found on the trails up to 9,500 feet, and in one place along the line of fresh cat tracks the stomach and intestines of a freshly eaten cottontail were seen. Half a dozen skins of bobcats hanging in the store at Taos were of this large, strongly marked species. One caught in a trap at Lake La Jara on the Jicarilla Indian Reservation had its stomach full of the mutton with which Gaut had baited his trap, but the lower intestines were also filled with rabbit fur from the previous meal. At Tres Piedras Gaut obtained a specimen of a fine old female that was brought to him by some boys who had killed it a short distance from there while it was carrying a prairie dog in its mouth, evidently to its young. In the Jemez Mountains the cat tracks were especially abundant along the canyons where the rock walls furnish the animals ideal homes and an abundance of wood rats and other small game for food. Along the canyon of Coyote Creek on the east slope of the Taos Mountains their tracks were unusually common along the basaltic cliffs, where the numerous cracks and crevices afforded large variety of choice homes for such cliff dwellers. The abundant excrement scattered along the rocky shelves showed mainly remains of rabbits and wood rats. In the Raton Range, A. H. Howell reported a few in Oak Canyon and one that was seen to steal a hen from the ranch a short time before he was there. In the Manzano Mountains, Gaut caught a series of specimens in traps from the foothills to the summit of the range. A trap set within 50 yards of his camp at Box Spring caught several specimens. One caught October 24 on the east slope of the mountain at 8,000 feet showed signs of having recently eaten a small owl. One foot of the owl had been swallowed whole and served to identify the species. In the canyons near Santa Rosa a few cat tracks were seen in 1903, and near Cuervo the writer scared a large lynx out of the cliff and watched it run across the valley at a rapid pace, though with a very bobbing motion. Along the Pecos Valley above Roswell, Hollister reported them as fairly common in 1902, and at Carlsbad in 1901 the writer found a few of their tracks along the river bottoms and in the mud around irrigated fields but did not secure any specimens to show what form of cat occurs in that vicinity. It is not improbable that the Texas species may occur along the valley bottom. Mr. Webster on the Vineyard stock ranch there reported that the previous year one of his men found a nest of young bobcats while mowing in the alfalfa field. The young were taken and kept for some time at the ranch.

Charles Springer, chairman of the executive committee of the Council of National Defense, in a letter of January 6, 1919, to E. W. Nelson, then chief of the Bureau of Biological Survey, reported 177 bobcats captured by one trapper on the Bartlett ranch in Colfax

County during the preceding six months. These were probably all of this large species, as also was one reported in June, 1918, by J. S. Ligon in the Pecos Valley 50 miles north of Roswell, where a herder discovered it standing with its front feet on a ewe that it had just killed.

Economic status.—The wide distribution and the abundance of these large cats over much of the best stock country in the West make them a rather serious factor in the livestock industry, especially with sheepmen. Though they undoubtedly have a certain value as a fur animal and locally serve as a check to the abundance of rodents, they are on the whole one of the most destructive of predatory animals. The extent of the damage they do in destroying young game animals is not easily estimated, but the tribute they lay on the sheep herds is second only to that of the coyote. Local bounties are usually paid for their destruction, and they are persistently hunted by ranchmen and almost every resident of the country. In spite of all efforts they hold their own surprisingly well and are not likely to be soon exterminated in any area well suited to their habits.

Family CANIDAE: Wolves and Foxes

VULPES MACROURUS BAIRD

WESTERN RED FOX; CROSS FOX; SAL-PEEN-E-ANA of the Taos Indians

Vulpes macrourus Baird, Rept. Stanbury's Expedition to Great Salt Lake, p. 309, 1852.

Type.—Collected in Wasatch Mountains, bordering Great Salt Lake, Utah, in 1849 or 1850, by Captain Stansbury's expedition.

General characters.—The western red, or cross, fox is the Rocky Mountain form of the group of red foxes, the relationships of which have not yet been thoroughly established. It is larger and yellower than the eastern red fox and more often of the dark-color variety known as the cross fox. In the light phase the general color is usually of a straw yellow, becoming slightly darker and more reddish over the shoulders, while the dark phase varies from a dusky band, along the back and another across the shoulders with the rest of the animal yellow, to the almost black but white-banded fur of the silver-gray and the entirely black, or melanistic, phase of the black fox. In all cases, however, the tip of the tail is strongly marked with white, and the feet and the back of the ears are black, even in the lightest color phase and in the young.

Measurements.—The males are slightly larger than the females, one from Liberty, N. Mex., measuring: Total length, 1,080; tail, 422; hind foot, 175 millimeters. A female from the Taos Mountains, measured 992, 388, and 173 millimeters, respectively.

Distribution and habitat.—Western red, or cross, foxes are fairly common throughout the higher mountains of northern New Mexico in the Canadian Zone, and in a few places they have been found in the lower valleys, even down to the Upper Sonoran Zone. They are fairly common throughout the Sangre de Cristo Range above 10,000 feet altitude, where the writer found them around Pecos Baldy and in the higher mountains back of the pueblo of Taos. In the Pecos Mountains an old female was caught August 1, 1903, near a 11,000-foot camp, and they were frequently heard barking near camp in the evenings. Their tracks and burrows were often seen in these mountains and their pungent odor was frequently noticed along the trails. Their droppings, composed mainly of the hair of meadow mice and conies, were common on the top of Pecos Baldy at 12,600 feet, where they were in the habit of hunting over the bare peaks above timber line. Dyche found them common around the Truchas peaks in this southern end of the range in 1881.

Farther north in the Taos Mountains in 1904 a den of these foxes was apparently located among the rocks at 12,400 feet on the west slope of Wheeler Peak well above timber line. The old fox was frequently seen here among the rocks and would sit on a large bowlder and bark at the writer and party as they were setting traps over the mountain side. Fresh tracks and droppings were also seen along the crest of the range up to 13,600 feet, and the strong characteristic fox odor could be noticed wherever they had been along the trails. Several skins seen at a miner's cabin near there were of the same light-yellow color as the fox seen on the rocks, and other skins that had been brought down into the valley were of the same character. Most of the droppings examined along the trails were composed largely of the fur of meadow mice, probably *Microtus mordax*, which were abundant over the high mountain slopes. At Twining, not far from there, the foxes were common about the garbage pile back of the mining camp at 10,000 feet altitude. During October, 1903, McClure Surber reported as many as six seen at one time fighting over the garbage.

In the Jemez Mountains west of the Rio Grande the strong odor of a fox was noticed near camp at 8,500 feet in the Canadian Zone near the head of Santa Clara Creek. No specimens were taken or seen, but it seems probable that the foxes in these upper valleys are of the red, or cross, group, as the odor is noticeably different from that of the gray foxes inhabiting the country lower down. While camped in the Mogollon Mountains near the head of Willow Creek at about 8,000 feet at the junction of the Transition and the Canadian Zones, the writer saw foxes pass along the canyon near camp on several nights. Besides their tracks they left a strong odor that was apparently of the cross fox. Their droppings noticed along the trail were composed mainly of mouse and pocket-gopher fur. In the San Juan Valley in northwestern New Mexico, Clarence Birdseye, in 1908, reported red foxes at Farmington, Fruitland, Liberty, and Shiprock and obtained from a trapper at Liberty a skin and skull and 11 extra skulls of foxes that had been trapped for fur near there. The trapper had caught 20 foxes during the previous season, and a trader at Shiprock told Birdseye that he had bought a very good silver-gray fox from a Navajo Indian for $50.

There seem to be no records of black foxes for New Mexico, but they have been reported from southern Colorado, where, however, they may have been only very dark silver grays. The light-yellow skins are the least valuable of any, but the dark cross-fox skins in good fur usually bring good prices. The number of these foxes caught in New Mexico is limited, owing to the restricted range of the species in the State, but much of the high mountain country is well adapted to fox farming and the artificial rearing of many other fur-bearing animals that require a cold climate.

Food habits.—The droppings along the trails where these foxes hunt are usually composed of the hair and bones of meadow mice, pocket gophers, conies, and rabbits, but these by no means cover the range of species preyed upon. It is safe to assume that almost every small mammal and bird that can be procured serves as food, besides such berries and fruits as may be found.

Breeding habits.—A few records of four young in a litter indicate small families among these foxes, but the 6 mammae arranged in 2 pairs of abdominal and 1 pair of pectoral suggest 4 as the minimum and 6 as the normal maximum number of young.

VULPES MACROTIS NEOMEXICANA Merriam

New Mexico Desert Fox

Vulpes macrotis neomexicanus Merriam, Biol. Soc. Wash. Proc. 15: 74, 1902.

Type.—Collected in San Andres Mountains, N. Mex. (about 50 miles north of El Paso, Tex.), April 4, 1899, by C. M. Barber.

General characters.—Slightly larger than *macrotis* of the deserts farther west, but much smaller than the gray or red fox. Compared with the kit fox or swift of the Great Plains, it is distinguished by its much larger ears and slenderer skull with large audital bullae. In color it is plain buffy gray with clear buff along the sides, middle of belly, and lower surface of tail, and white on throat and posterior part of belly. The tip of the tail is black. The original description of the species was based on a skull, and no measurements of typical specimens were then available.

Measurements.—An adult male since collected near the type locality at Parker Lake on the east slope of the San Andres Mountains measures: Total length, 831; tail, 335; hind foot, 131 millimeters. A female from the San Augustine Plain measures 850, 325, and 140 millimeters, respectively. The ears in dried skins average about 70 millimeters from crown to tip. Two young adult males collected near Cliff, N. Mex., weighed 5¼ and 5½ pounds, respectively.

Distribution and habitat.—The little, large-eared desert foxes (pl. 17, A) are nowhere abundant, but seem to be generally distributed in the Pecos Valley and westward through the more arid valleys of New Mexico in both the Lower and the Upper Sonoran Zones. Most of the localities where specimens have been taken are along the edge of the Upper Sonoran Zone, however, and apparently this is a slightly larger and higher ranging form of the Lower Sonoran *macrotis* farther west. Its range corresponds closely to that of the large kangaroo rat, *Dipodomys spectabilis*, in New Mexico, but does not extend into the mountains and probably not onto the plains east of the Pecos Valley. A specimen from Carlsbad in the Wright collection was sent to the Biological Survey for identification and proved to be typical *neomexicanus*. So far as known, this is its easternmost record. Other specimens in the collection are from the San Andres Mountains, Parker Lake, Tularosa, Loveless Lake (10 miles north of Capitan Mountains), San Augustine Plains, Faywood, Cliff, and Cloverdale ranch in Animas Valley. The foxes have also been recorded from the south end of Animas Valley, Playas Valley, Deming, Jarilla, Engle, and Albuquerque. They have also been reported in the San Juan Valley near Fruitland and Shiprock, but no specimens from that region have been obtained to substantiate the reports. A little fox has also been reported from Santa Rosa, but more probably this may prove to be the plains swift, or kit, fox.

General habits.—These foxes generally occupy the open mesa country along the borders of the valleys, where they burrow into banks and the sides of ridges. They apparently hunt in the open and depend for protection on their extreme quickness and speed and the cover of such burrows as they are able to reach if hard pressed. Their motions are the consummation of grace and speed as they glide cautiously from place to place and dart with wonderful quickness across the mesas or from one concealing gulch to another. They are mainly nocturnal in habits and are not often seen during the day, unless one is accidentally discovered curled up in its bed near the den. Out in the open Jornado Valley a couple of miles west of the little town of Engle, the writer noticed not far from the roadside a furry ball near a low mound of earth. Its color blended perfectly with the desert soil, and the object would have been overlooked except for two sharp points that were conspicuously unearthlike. Keeping it in view until nearer, he became convinced that it was a little fox, but it did not move until he drew up the team a few rods from it, when the ball of fur quickly unrolled and the fox glided like a flash into the burrow near by. Near Cliff, a little town on the Gila River, while out setting traps toward sunset on the mesa top, the writer saw two of these foxes playing about their burrows evidently just waking up for their night of hunting. There were several large burrows close below the crest of the ridge that evidently constituted a breeding den, as there were signs of long occupation with well-worn trails and scattered remains of food.

On the San Augustine Plains E. A. Goldman found a den of these foxes out in the open about 12 miles northwest of Monica Spring. There were two holes or entrances about 30 feet apart somewhat larger than prairie-dog burrows. In describing it he says:

At about 5 o'clock in the evening while riding across the valley my attention was attracted by a fox sitting at the entrance of each burrow. They moved about restlessly, watching me intently meanwhile, and allowed me to approach on foot to within about 100 yards, when one suddenly disappeared and the other was shot as it ran across toward the other hole.

Traps were set, and the following morning they held a fox at the entrance of each hole. At the southern end of the Animas Valley Goldman found another den of these foxes and saw one sitting at the entrance of its burrow near the international boundary line. This fox was shot and another trapped at a hole near by.

At Albuquerque, in July, 1889, the writer saw a Mexican boy leading a fox by a string along the streets. A number of skins were also seen in the fur stores there, and they were said to be frequently brought in for sale. At that time they brought from 25 to 50 cents apiece. He also saw the track of a little fox, probably this species, on the mesa back of town. At Parker Lake in the Tularosa Valley, Gaut caught two of these foxes in traps baited with prairie dogs. Another specimen was secured at the edge of an alkaline arroyo 9 miles south of Tularosa. Near Liberty, in the San Juan Valley, Clarence Birdseye was told by a trapper that these desert foxes were quite common in the open valley, and in the sand near Fruitland and Shiprock small tracks were noticed that may have been made by them, but no specimens were obtained.

Food habits.—Very little is known of the actual food habits of this fox, but at a den near Cliff there were scattered bits and bones of jack rabbits, cottontails, and part of the skeleton of a bird that had served as food. The foxes are readily caught in traps baited with carcasses of prairie dogs, rabbits, or the small animals that have been skinned for specimens, but their regular fare undoubtedly includes most of the small nocturnal rodents of the region. The fact that their range corresponds so closely to that of the large kangaroo rat would suggest this as one of their favorite varieties of game.

Breeding habits.—Judged from the dens where these foxes have been found at various seasons, the young are not only raised in the burrows but remain in them throughout the greater part of the year. The male apparently remains with the family and does its share in hunting and providing for the young. Apparently there is but one record indicating the number of young in a family—that of a set of four embryos noted in a female collected by Dutcher, February 8, 1898, at Fort Grant, Ariz.

Economic status.—The winter fur of these little foxes is soft and pretty but is of a pale color with no marked character of beauty. The skins are ranked of little value, and the scarcity of the animals renders them of slight importance as a fur-bearing species. Their scarcity also may be responsible for the absence of any complaints of mischief to poultry, and over most of their range they are not in a position to injure game to any great extent. In places they might serve as a check on the abundance of valley and scaled quail, but otherwise their food habits are largely of a beneficial nature.

VULPES VELOX VELOX (SAY)

KIT FOX; SWIFT

[*Canis*] *velox* Say, Long's Expedition to the Rocky Mountains 1: 487, 1823.

Type locality.—South Platte River, Colo.

General characters.—Resembles closely the New Mexico desert fox, but is readily distinguished by its much smaller ears, its pure-white belly, and by its relatively short heavy skull. In general color it has the same buffy-gray upper parts, bordered by a band of clear buff on the sides and neck and the black tip to the otherwise buffy tail.

Measurements.—In dried skins the ears measure about 50 millimeters from crown to tip.

Distribution and habitat.—So far as the writer can learn there is no specimen of the kit fox, or swift, available from New Mexico, but the species was reported to him at Santa Rosa as fairly common over the adjoining plains. There is, however, a chance that this may be the New Mexico desert fox, but the probabilities seem to be in favor of its being the swift of the Great Plains, which is commom in southeastern Colorado and over the Staked Plains of northwestern Texas, and undoubtedly occupies the Upper Sonoran plains east of the Pecos Valley and the Sangre de Cristo Mountains.

General habits.—These little foxes live in burrows in the open plains country, usually selecting sidehills or the sunny slope of a bank in which to make their dens. They are mainly nocturnal, are wonderfully swift and graceful in their motions, but, unlike the red foxes, are so unsuspecting in their natures as to be readily caught in traps baited with the carcasses of mice or birds and are so unable to cope with the advanced civilization that they are rapidly disappearing from the face of the earth.

UROCYON CINEREOARGENTEUS SCOTTII Mearns

Arizona Gray Fox ; Too-wha-tsu-le-ana of the Taos Indians

Urocyon virginianus scottii Mearns, Bul. Amer. Mus. Nat. Hist. 3 : 236, 1891.

Type.—Collected in Pinal County (probably Oracle, at north base of Santa Catalina Mountains), Ariz., October 28, 1884, by W. E. D. Scott.

General characters.—Slightly smaller than most of the red and cross foxes, with shorter, coarser fur. Further distinguished from the red foxes by the black tip of the tail and from both the red and the kit fox by the flattened or laterally compressed tail and the black stripe along its dorsal crest, as well as by pronounced skull characters. The clear gray back and orange-bordered sides and throat further distinguish this group from other foxes.

Measurements.—Six adult males measured in the flesh show an average total length of 1,028; tail, 441; hind foot, 141 millimeters. The female is slightly smaller. Three females weighed 8, 9, and 12 pounds, respectively.

Distribution and habitat.—The Arizona form of the gray fox (pl. 17, B) is generally distributed over the greater part of New Mexico and is most abundant in the Upper Sonoran Zone, to which it properly belongs. A few individuals are found here and there throughout the open yellow pine forest of the Transition Zone, and on some of the isolated and barren ranges of mountains they wander back and forth from the base to the summit. They are not usually found in the open nor in the Lower Sonoran valleys, except where neighboring canyons, cliffs, and rough country provide them with especially favorable homes and protection. Their greatest abundance is in the foothill region of nut pines and junipers, cliffs, canyons, and rocky gulches. Their occasional presence in higher and lower zones may be attributed largely to the natural wanderings of a predatory species.

General habits.—These gray foxes, not having the fleetness of the plains foxes, closely associate themselves with cliffs and rocky or timbered country, where they can quickly take refuge among sheltering rocks or climb trees to escape from swifter foes. Their abundance depends largely on the character of the country. In such mountains as the Mogollon, Black, Sacramento, Guadalupe, Jemez, Zuni, and Chuska Ranges they find plenty of cliffs that furnish favorable cavities for dens and shelter and afford choice hunting grounds for their small prey. In these sections they are particularly numerous, often causing much inconvenience to the trapper by getting into his traps ahead of more desirable game, and also to the collector of small mammals by eating or carrying off a considerable part of his catch during the night. Their tracks and sign are seen along trails, in dusty places among the rocks and along the bases of cliffs, where they hunt and prowl at night. Under the cover of low brush and chaparral they often make well-worn trails along their regular hunting courses or follow the rabbit trails to such an extent that it is difficult to say which is the more frequent traveler. In places the foxes are hunted for sport but rarely lead the hounds for a long chase. If possible they make for the nearest ledge or rock pile in which they can find safe shelter, but if hard pressed take to the nearest tree and hide among its topmost branches, so that the sport is apt to be short-lived and to end in a baffled pack or in a short scrimmage when the fox is shaken or dislodged from the tree top. Occasionally they were heard barking around the camps at night with a short, sharp yap, yap, like some little dog.

Food habits.—These gray foxes are almost as omnivorous as the raccoon. Their droppings along the trail show in places a large percentage of juniper berries, cactus fruit, insects, and the fur and feathers of small game. The stomach of one taken in the canyon of the Mimbres contained a pocket gopher and some maggots, and another a mouse, some grasshoppers, crickets, and beetles. In the Manzano Mountains the stomach of one examined by Gaut contained a pocket gopher and that of another the feathers of some small bird, probably a white-crowned sparrow (*Zonotrichia leucophrys*). Near Redrock, in the stomach of one, E. A. Goldman found the skins and seeds of several fruits of a pricklypear, some of the small spines from which were sticking in the lining of the stomach. In a canyon in the Organ Mountains the fox sign scattered along the trails was made up almost entirely of seeds and skins of cactus fruit, apparently of the big purple pricklypears of *Opuntia engelmanni cyclodes*. The stomach of one that Hollister examined in the Datil Mountains contained a mass of hair and fur from some rats or mice and a few blades of grass. At Blanco in the northwestern part of the State, Clarence Birdseye examined the stomach of an old female that contained the remains of a kangaroo rat and a white-footed mouse, while the stomach of a young one contained pieces of skin and feathers, which may have been from chicken or turkey from the neighboring ranch, and another contained remains of grasshoppers. The stomach of one examined by Gaut in the San Andres Mountains contained parts of a wood rat, and the stomachs of several others were found to contain bird feathers. In the Sandia Mountains these foxes ate several wood rats and rock squirrels in the writer's traps, and in some cases carried off the traps with their catch. As nearly as can be judged from the examinations made, fruit and small game in about equal quantities supply the food of these foxes, and the matter of choice depends largely upon what is available. They are especially attracted to traps by bird feathers, and in some cases they prey upon poultry, but over most of their range the small mammals, such as rats, mice, squirrels, and rabbits, seem to be their principal game.

Breeding habits.—The young are born and reared in such safe retreats among the rocks or in hollow trees or logs that they are rarely discovered until old enough to come out and hunt for their own food. They are usually three or four in number and are born early in the spring, but few data are available on either number or dates. In the Black Range at the head of the Mimbres, during May, 1906, three pairs of these foxes got into the traps that the writer had set for wolves and coyotes. The three females were all nursing young, and each was accompanied by a male that either got into another trap near by or was caught the following night in the same trap. They were evidently hunting in pairs, the male taking a full share in the family care and responsibilities, and sacrificing his life through his devotion to his mate. The three females had their bellies covered with fur of a peculiar pinkish purple, probably from some stain in connection with nursing their young. Their 6 mammae were arranged in groups of 2 abdominal on each side, borne on continuous mammary glands, and 1 pair of pectoral, each on a mammary gland isolated from the abdominal sets.

Economic status.—Few complaints are heard of damage to poultry by these foxes, but at Blanco in the San Juan Valley Clarence Birdseye found what he believed to be remains of chicken or turkey in the stomach of one, and at Kingston E. A. Goldman was told by a ranch owner that they carried off over 40 of his chickens in one season, climbing the trees in which the chickens roosted, scaring them to the ground, and then catching and carrying them away. Most of the country where they are numerous is not thickly populated, and the damage to poultry is therefore comparatively slight, but the loss in small game, such as wild turkeys, quail, and possibly the young of deer and antelope, by these foxes is undoubtedly serious in some localities. In other localities their destruction of rodents and small mammal pests doubtless compensates for their inroads on game and poultry.

Their value as a game and fur animal is unimportant, as but little of the sport of hunting the red fox with hounds can be obtained with this species, and the fur is of inferior quality and brings a low price. As other furs become scarce these will doubtless have a greater value, but the matter of adjusting their abundance to man's best interest is one of local control rather than protection or extermination. In localities where small game is abundant, and especially where wild turkeys and quail are protected, the numbers of these foxes should be reduced to a minimum. In other localities where there is little game and where the loss from rodents is serious the foxes can well be protected to a reasonable extent and still yield some returns in their fur value.

CANIS LYCAON BAILEYI Nelson and Goldman

Mexican Wolf

Canis nubilus baileyi Nelson and Goldman, Jour. Mammal. 10: 165, 1929.

Type locality.—Colonia Garcia, Chihuahua, Mexico.
General characters.—A rather small dark-colored wolf, in summer dull tawny, and in winter coat yellowish gray, heavily clouded with black over back and tail. The skull is smaller and slenderer than in the larger, lighter colored wolf of the Great Plains region.
Measurements.—Type, adult male; Total length, 1.570; tail, 410; hind foot, 260 millimeters.

Distribution and habitat.—Until the North American wolves (pl. 18, A) can be more thoroughly studied as a group, it seems best to refer all the specimens from southwestern New Mexico to this Mexican form, although many are far from typical and show evident gradation into the larger, paler wolf of the Great Plains region. A large series of skulls and a few skins from the Mogollon Mountain region show some specimens that might almost be referred to the larger Plains wolf, but the majority are rather small and dark, while specimens from Animas Valley and one broken skull from Fort Filmore in the Rio Grande Valley, 40 miles north of El Paso, show more clearly the characters of the southern form. There are specimens from the head of the Mimbres, Black Range, Black Canyon, Negrito, Reserve, Upper Gila River, Diamond Creek, Mule Spring, and others labeled merely Gila National Forest. There is one skull from Cloverdale ranch in the Animas Valley, a pup in the National Museum collection from the San Luis Mountains, and two skins sent in by B. V. Lilly from near the Mexican line but without definite locality. The range of the species is mainly within the Upper Sonoran and the Transition Zones, and their greatest abundance has long been in the open grazing country of the Gila National Forest. Here their range occupies both the open yellow-pine forests and the orchardlike growth of juniper, nut pine, and oak foothills. Apparently they are not known in the Lower Sonoran valleys of this region. The one old skull labeled Fort Filmore, by C. Wright, undoubtedly came from some of the neighboring mountain ranges.

General habits.—In the spring of 1906 the writer spent several weeks in the Gila National Forest studying the wolf problem, which at that time was serious with the local stockmen. Wolves were then abundant on the Sapello Creek, head of the Mimbres, and the Diamond Creek Ranges, and were reported equally bad over the rest of the stock range of that region. Most of his time was spent in testing various scents that might prove useful for baiting traps, and a good opportunity was afforded for observing some of the habits of the wolves. While camped on the head of the Mimbres he could count on about four wolves passing his station every two or three nights and learned to recognize their individual tracks and sometimes followed them along the roads or trails for as far as 15 miles at a time. In this rocky country they were traveling almost entirely in the trails and roads to save their feet from the sharp, stony surface outside. They had little fear of the ranches and often passed close to the buildings and killed stock as freely within the pasture as outside. At one ranch on the Mimbres below camp several wolves had been shot in the pasture from the house. A huge black, half wolf and half dog, which was kept chained in the corral at the Mimbres store, had been raised from a large mongrel bitch that had been visited by a male wolf at night, and this only remaining member of her litter was unmistakably as much wolf as dog, except for the color. It was a savage brute and considered too dangerous to run at large.

During the writer's stay on the Mimbres in May one pair of wolves was hunting together and evidently had a den of young at no great distance from where he was camped, but he was too busy experimenting with scents to hunt for the dens at that time. There were no packs or family parties of wolves at that season, but later they were found in bands of six or eight or more, according to the size of the families. In 1908 he was again over the Gila National Forest and Mogollon Mountain region and found the wolves still common, although many had been caught and killed during the interval. Near Black River he saw fresh tracks of three or four together, old and young, on August 24, and at the same time they were said to be killing stock along Diamond Creek. On August 28 he struck the tracks of another family of wolves with their headquarters on the mesa east of the Elk Mountains. Tracks were also found along the Negrito Creek Valley and on the high mesa east of Reserve. The wolves were also reported as more or less common in most parts of this region where stock was ranging, but they were never heard howling during the spring and summer months.

Food habits.—So far as the writer could learn, the wolves in this region were feeding on nothing but fresh meat of their own killing.

Stock was abundant, and they had no trouble in finding cattle of any age or condition they preferred, but they seemed to show little choice in their selection of beef. Cows, steers, or calves seemed to be killed indiscriminately as the wolves happened to come upon them when hungry. Cattle are killed throughout the year and seem to be preferred to deer, which are more nimble and not so easily caught. In the wolf droppings along the trails cattle hair was almost the only recognizable constituent, but occasionally some jackrabbit fur could be detected.

Breeding habits.—On March 13, 1907, on the Gila National Forest, Hotchkiss killed an old wolf and captured a litter of eight pups, which he thought were not more than 1 day old. He reported them from a den about 6 feet deep, but did not give the exact locality. Another litter of seven was taken by him the same spring, and two specimens were sent to the Biological Survey, but the date was not given. He collected four more pups on Diamond Creek in September when they were nearly half grown, but the skulls of these show only milk dentition, except for the first appearance of a few of the incisor teeth. Early in May, 1908, Hotchkiss found a den under a couple of big bowlders on Rocky Creek a mile above his camp. The young left the den when it was found, but one was caught near there that was about the size of a fox. In April, 1916, on the Gila National Forest, Dan Fowler caught an old wolf containing eight embryos. A specimen in the United States National Museum collected by Mearns in the San Luis Mountains, June 4, 1902, is a good-sized pup, probably 2 months old, with only milk dentition.

Economic status.—In the spring of 1906 the writer estimated the number of wolves then ranging on the Gila National Forest at not more than 1 to a township, or possibly 100 wolves to the region. The following year, 1907, the Forest Service reported 41 killed on the southern division and 31 on the northern division of the forest, or what are now the Gila and the Datil National Forests. These were killed by forest guards, rangers, and local and outside trappers, and probably do not represent the total number actually killed during that year. Forty-one of these were killed by Hotchkiss, employed as forest guard for the destruction of predatory animals. For a few years the loss of stock was much reduced, and the wolves through this region were too scattered to make professional trapping for the bounty profitable, although large bounties were paid by both counties and local stockmen. The lapse in vigorous trapping after a few years brought back the wolves to their original numbers, with proportionate loss of stock, a loss that has been fairly estimated as at least $1,000 a year per wolf.[26] It has been clearly demonstrated that if persistently followed up by expert trappers the wolves can be controlled on any area, but unless the control operations extend over the whole wolf country the animals will keep returning to their old haunts. The region along the Mexican border is the most difficult to control, as wolves keep coming across the line into southern New Mexico and Arizona, and only by constant vigilance can they be kept down and serious losses prevented.

---

[26] In 1916, J. Stokley Ligon estimated that, with the current high prices of beef, an adult wolf would cost the ranchers $1,200 to $1,500 a year.

The accompanying map (fig. 51) prepared by J. S. Ligon shows the approximate area infested by wolves in May, 1918.

Trapping wolves.—In November, 1916, J. S. Ligon and his assistant, M. E. Musgrave, began a trap line for some wolves that were ranging on the Continental Divide, 15 miles northwest of Chloride. Tracks were found along an old road where a year previously Ligon had trapped three wolves in four nights. Ten traps were scattered along this road for a distance of 6 miles and baited with the urine of a female dog. On the second night one of the traps contained a female wolf, apparently a pup of the year not fully grown. It was taken to camp alive, and after being kept 24 hours weighed 49 pounds. Two other wolves had followed the road that night, but although they approached several of the traps they were not caught.

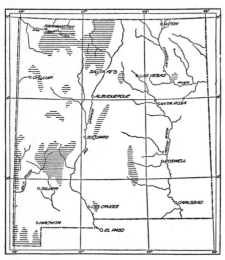

FIGURE 51.—Shaded area showing approximate distribution of the wolves in New Mexico in 1917. From map prepared by J. S. Ligon

Two nights later a male wolf returned and followed the round of the traps, but did not go near any of them. On its next round two days later, however, it was caught in one of the traps. It was apparently an adult and not very fat, for when it was taken to camp alive it weighed only 57 pounds. The trap was reset in a new place and baited with wolf dung and the urine of the female. Two days later three wolves struck the road, and a male was caught in one of the traps. The tracks showed that the other two stayed by and tramped about and scratched for some time before leaving. The traps were again set and baited with wolf dung and urine, and although the other two wolves came about the next night they did not venture near any of the traps. Two days later, however, they returned to the line, and the old female was caught in one of the traps and a young male in another. The female was fat and weighed 58 pounds, and had previously lost one toe in a trap. The male was evidently a pup of the year and not very fat, but it weighed 50 pounds. These five wolves were caught from November 6 to 17 in No. 14 traps fastened to 16-inch swivel pins, and none escaped, although one male was caught by only two middle toes of a front foot. All were caught by the front feet, and in each case the trap was set about 12 inches back from the scented place. All the wolves were carried to the camp alive, so that no carcasses and no odors of dead wolves were left to obstruct the trap line. The traps were set with great care and baited from horseback after they were first set. As no further wolf signs were seen in this vicinty, the traps were pulled up and the line abandoned.

In this way Ligon, with his corps of trappers, pursued the wolves from place to place over the worst infested areas of New Mexico until their numbers were very much reduced. His estimates were 103 adult wolves for New Mexico in May, 1917, and 45 in July, 1918. In 1927 he said that they were practically eliminated from New Mexico and that he was then concerned only with reinfestation from Mexico.

In his report for 1918 he gives the following valuable directions for locating wolf dens:

Hunting wolf dens.—The successful hunting of wolf dens is a science that few have mastered; by successful, I mean involving the destruction of both adults and pups. As a general thing it is an easy matter to get the pups provided they are found and taken without delay—before the parent animals have a chance to move them after being disturbed. The getting of the adult animals is the problem, and failure to do this has been the occasion, in the past, of much criticism of the bounty system, not always because the adults could not be taken, but too often because there was no effort made—for selfish reasons—to get them. Wolves use much caution about their dens, especially the older animals that have experienced difficulties in raising their young in former years. Their whole nature seems to be based on "safety first." They display much cunning in trying to mislead intruders. To the experienced hunter, however, their methods really betray the whereabouts of the den.

It is of interest to know that out of the seven dens that were located in New Mexico in the spring of 1918, the young and both adults were secured in six cases, and at the seventh den the adults were both trapped but made their escape with the traps. In another instance, in the Animas Mountains in February, both adults and five unborn pups were destroyed. Two—or probably three—litters of young are still at large in the State. We have a very close check on the number of wolves at the present time, as well as knowledge of their exact range. While we are not sure just where any young may be, it is probable that there is a litter in the southern portion of the Black Range and very likely one in the Animas Mountains in the southwest portion of the State.

Information regarding trapping wolves and coyotes may be found in a leaflet of the Biological Survey (Young, 1930), issued by the United States Department of Agriculture.

Wolves persistently cling to certain localities in their range for raising their pups. A hunter who knows their range generally knows where to go for the pups when the time comes. If disturbed one year, and the adults are not secured, they are likely to locate a new den for the next season not far from the former site—probably less than a mile away. When the female wolf is killed, leaving the male alone, he often returns to the old breeding sites of former years and works out the different dens, seemingly preparing for the return of his missing mate. This is a case of the strongest manifestation of the instinct in the wild animal to perpetuate its kind.

In going to and from the den the animals may follow the same general routes, but near the den tracks are likely to be confusing, as the wind direction will govern their approach. They generally lie about the den during the day and keep a close watch. In leaving the den on the approach of man, they will usually move off over the highest points in order to command a back view. They very often howl when their young are approached or molested. Both young and old wolves sleep much in midday, but at other times they are very active.

At night they make long trips into distant localities where they make their kills. When the young are small the food is always swallowed and later disgorged at the den for the little fellows. The food is thus partly masticated and is more easily digested. As the pups become stronger, large pieces of calves and yearlings, as well as antelope and other game, are carried to the den. The heads of calves and game animals, as well as other bones, are brought in great numbers, no doubt chiefly for the young to play with and for the necessary development of teeth and jaws.

Wolf dens are placed in various kinds of places but are always in a cavity or burrow of some description. In rough country they are generally found in a crevice or natural cavity, usually in the rim of a mesa. Even where there are suitable places among the rocks, badger burrows are often enlarged to the desired size and depth. Sometimes the den is prepared under the roots of an upturned tree, and it is common to find the young in holes in solid rock, where they can be obtained only by blasting.

In the sand hills of the Staked Plains the den is generally worked out underneath a mesquite or other brush that serves as a blind and where the roots of the shrub holds the soil or sand together. The writer knows of only two instances where they have burrowed into large and conspicuous mounds out in open flats. Dens are always placed in the most out-of-the-way places, with seemingly little regard for convenience as to water or food.

Number of pups to a litter.—The age of the animal governs the number of young. A young female, or one very old, will not have as many pups as one that is in the prime of life. The number in a litter varies from 1 to 12—the average about 6. The writer has been informed by reliable hunters that they have seen litters of 14; personally, he has never known of this number. The seven dens found in New Mexico, in the spring of 1918, contained 1, 2, 4, 4, 7, 7, and 8, respectively; or an average of less than 5 to the den. This, however, is not representative of the animals in general or of the offspring of fully adult females.

CANIS LYCAON NUBILUS SAY

GRAY WOLF; LOAFER; LOBO; BUFFALO WOLF; KAH-LE-NA of the Taos Indians

Canis nubilus Say, Long's Expedition to the Rocky Mountains, 1 : 169, 333, 1823.

Type locality.—Engineer Cantonment near present town of Blair, eastern Nebraska.[27]

General characters.—These large light-gray wolves occupy the Plains area of eastern New Mexico. There are specimens from the Sacramento Mountains; Capitan Mountains; Gallo Canyon, 40 miles southeast of Corona; near Santa Rosa; and from the Datil Mountains. The writer has seen several typical skins and some of the animals alive on the plains west of Roswell, and those of the San Augustine Plain and Datil Mountain region are large and light gray. He is also assuming, in the absence of specimens, that the wolf of the Zuni and Chuska Mountains is also of this northern form. The greater part of the range of this species is over the Upper Sonoran and the Transition Zones, but they readily follow stock into the mountain forests in summer and up to any altitude where stock ranges furnish them a food supply. Formerly they were abundant over the whole Plains country, but now they are mainly restricted to the rough and least-inhabited areas.

---

[27] In the writer's report on the mammals of Texas (Bailey, 1905), he referred the big gray plains wolf to *Canis griseus* Sabine, but, as Bangs has shown, the name *griseus* can not be used for any wolf, as it was applied by Boddaert in 1784 to the gray fox (Bangs, 1898, p. 505). The writer is, therefore, taking *nubilus*, the next name, which seems possibly applicable to this plains wolf, but the present status of the wolf names is much involved and will remain so until the wolves are studied as a group.

General habits.—In 1899 the big wolves were said to be common throughout the Pecos Valley, and at Portales one was kept at a hotel as a pet. When the writer saw it on June 7 it was a big, good-natured puppy with only its milk teeth and no idea of being cross or dangerous. It was the only survivor of a litter of seven dug out of a burrow near there before their eyes were open. In 1901 there were still some wolves in the Pecos Valley, and a short time before the writer's visit they had killed several sheep on a ranch only 3 miles from Carlsbad. In September of the following year three fine big gray fellows were seen on the plains 20 miles west of Roswell, but just out of rifle range, and Hollister saw another about 5 miles south of Santa Rosa in the Upper Pecos Valley. At Santa Rosa in 1903 there were said to be a few wolves, and a little east of there at the northern end of the Staked Plains in June they came and howled around the camp. Their fresh tracks were seen every day in that vicinity, but they were said to be less common then than four years previously when about 50 had been killed during one year. In the mountains around the head of the Pecos River in 1903 the writer was told that there were a few wolves, and one of the forest rangers reported having seen one just before the writer was there. In the Taos Valley he was told by the Indians that long ago there used to be many big wolves, but that now all are gone, none having been seen for many years. In the Jemez Mountains in 1906 he could get no trace of wolves.

In 1903 Gaut reported a few in and about the Capitan Mountains, and in the Manzano Mountains he was told that they were still fairly common, doing considerable damage to stock, but that they had formerly been much more numerous and troublesome. On the Mesa Jumanes he was told there were a few and was shown the scalp of one that had been recently taken there. He also obtained some rather vague reports of their occurrence in the San Andres Mountains farther south. On a trip from Laguna to Magdalena, west of the Rio Grande in 1905, Hollister reported wolves as formerly abundant in the Bear Spring Mountains and westward, and a few still there. The ranchers of this region had kept professional wolf hunters in the district for parts of several years and had succeeded in killing more than 20 of the "loafers," as large wolves were called. Most of these were said to be very pale colored, almost whitish. In the Datil Mountains Gaut was told that they were common and very destructive to cattle over the whole Datil and Gallinas country, where they were said to have been increasing rapidly during the previous five or six years. The wolves were said to be very light in color, some of them nearly white, although the light-gray shade predominated.

At Acoma in 1906, one of the Indians said that there were wolves on the high mesa country west of the pueblo, but no tracks or signs of them were seen except in Largo Canyon, south of Quemado. Here on October 5 the writer began to see fresh wolf tracks and followed them up the road through Jewetts Gap to the divide over the Datil Mountains. Here he camped and set a line of wolf traps along the road. No wolves came along for two nights, but then their heavy howling began to be heard in the valley not far from camp, and the next morning the line of tracks in the road showed where a family of two old and two young wolves had come back from the south. The leader, a huge fellow, was evidently an old and experienced wolf, for he not only kept out of the traps but kept his pack out of them; the female was a moderate-sized wolf; and the pups were nearly full grown. They came to two of the traps baited only with scent and tramped around them for some time but were too wary to step into either of them, although both were well concealed. They then came near camp and during the middle of the night howled melodiously for some time but finally swung off from the trail so that they missed the main line of traps. As they were not likely to return for several days and as the writer was hurrying through to work in the Mogollon Mountains before the cold weather began, he took up the traps and moved on. In the Chuska Mountains in October, 1908, wolf tracks were found common in the trails over the top of the mountains where most of the cattle and great numbers of Navajo sheep ranged during the summer. They were evidently thriving here unmolested by the Indians and with an abundance of food.

In 1852 Doctor Woodhouse reported the wolves as very common throughout New Mexico. (Woodhouse, 1854, p. 45.) In 1541, Coronado, on his trip across New Mexico and out onto the plains of Kansas, reported among the Indians " great dogs which will fight with a bull and will carry 50 pounds weight in sacks when they [the Indians] go on a hunt or when they move from place to place with their flocks and herds." (Whipple et al., 1856, p. 112.)

Economic status.—In 1907 the Forest Service reported 76 wolves killed in the Lincoln National Forest, 22 in the Sacramento National Forest, and 7 in the Manzano National Forest, most of them by professional trappers and wolf hunters. Of these a fine series of skulls was sent to the Biological Survey by Acting Supervisor A. M. Neal. In the Bear Spring Mountains region the ranchmen told Hollister in 1905 that the wolves were doing great damage to stock by killing many cattle, often including full-grown cows. In the Manzano Mountains in 1903, Gaut reported them as preying considerably on cattle and sheep, and in the Capitan Mountains he was told that they did enormous damage to stock, sometimes killing large numbers of goats when the herds were left unprotected. At the northern end of the Staked Plains in 1903 the ranchmen told the writer that the wolves killed many yearling cattle and some nearly full-grown cattle but very few calves, seeming to prefer beef to veal, but in the Datil Mountain region he was told that more calves were killed than grown cattle. A Mexican ranchman living near the Datil Mountains told him that during the summer of 1906 wolves had killed 16 or 17 head of his cattle that he knew of and that they had undoubtedly killed many more that he had not found. Their feces along the roads and trails were composed almost entirely of cattle hair.

In 1916, J. S. Ligon reported wolves very destructive to stock in the Jemez, Carson, Manzano, Datil, and Gila National Forests and on the Jicarilla and Mescalero Indian Reservations, and as preying heavily upon the deer that had been forced down out of the mountains in the Tres Piedras region. On the crusted snow the wolves were able to catch and kill the deer. Wolves do not often attack sheep if cattle are available, but in December, 1916, Inspector M. E. Musgrave received a letter from J. B. Archuletta, of La Jara, stating that wolves had attacked a bunch of 200 sheep on the bed ground at night, and in the morning only 130 of the sheep could be found alive. A few had been killed by falling over a high bank, but the letter implied that the rest had been killed by the wolves. Near Haynes two wolves killed seven purebred rams in one night.

In August, 1916, on the Lincoln National Forest, J. S. Ligon reported that wolves and wild dogs had long been a menace to all kinds of livestock until one of his trappers, T. L. Ritchie, succeeded in catching two hybrids, half wolf and half dog, and one wild dog. In 1916 A. B. McMillan, manager of a large ranch on the northwestern part of the Cebolleta Grant in the Mount Taylor region, wrote to Ligon that the wolves were so troublesome that he had refrained from putting any young cattle on the great mesa where they ranged and that they were coming down onto the lower country and killing stock. Seven calves were found killed in one week. Ligon examined the ground and found traces of four or five old wolves. He put two trappers on the range in July, and within 10 days they caught four wolves and later caught another of this family that had baffled all previous efforts toward capture. This was not the end of wolves in that region, however, as in 1918 Ligon reported that a Federal hunter on April 25 located a den about 12 miles northeast of Mount Taylor and about 1½ miles south of the denning site of the previous year. This den, 6 feet deep, had been recently worked out and was situated on a small, grassy knoll a short distance to the northwest of one much larger and higher, which was covered with extensive oak thickets. The den was under a large bowlder in thick oak brush, just off the crest and on the northwest slope of the knoll. A large dry lake bed, surrounded by rather abrupt rims, lay to the northwest. The top of the knoll afforded a commanding view in all directions. The den contained 4 pups—3 females and 1 male. When taken (April 28) their eyes were not yet open. One was kept alive for a few days and its eyes opened May 3, making the date of birth about April 24, more than five weeks later than the birth of two puppies in the Jicarilla Reservation. The eight pups taken on March 21, east of Carlsbad in the sand country, at an elevation of 4,000 feet, were probably born March 1. The birth of the other pups taken during the season was between these two extremes—Carlsbad, March 1, and Mount Taylor, April 24.

In the report of the district forester of district No. 3, Aldo Leopold gave the number of wolves killed in the national forests in New Mexico in 1915 as 57, distributed as follows: Alamo, 10; Datil, 25; Santa Fe, 19; Carson, 3. He also reported 20 others killed near the Carson National Forest. During the calendar year of 1916 the predatory-animal trappers operating under the direction of the Bureau of Biological Survey killed in New Mexico 100 wolves, 33 of which were April and May pups. The rest were adults or old enough to help kill cattle. For the same period the Forest Service officers reported 117 wolves killed on or near the national forests (including those reported by the Biological Survey), as follows: Carson, 9; Santa Fe, 37; Manzano, 5; Alamo-Lincoln, 1; Datil, 55; Gila, 10. The estimate, in January, 1917, by J. S. Ligon, then inspector of the Biological Survey predatory-animal trappers in New Mexico, was 100 adult wolves remaining in the State, and in July, 1918, he counted 45 and mapped their ranges. (Fig. 51.)

In his report on the wild life of New Mexico, Ligon (1927, p. 52) says that the wolves are no longer a menace to game, as they are practically eliminated from the State.

CANIS LATRANS TEXENSIS BAILEY

TEXAS PLAINS COYOTE; PRAIRIE WOLF

Canis nebracensis texensis Bailey, North Amer. Fauna No. 25, p. 175, 1905.

Type.—Collected at Corpus Christi, Tex., December 14, 1901, by John M. Priour.

General characters.—Distinguished from the very pale *nebracensis* of the Great Plains area by slightly smaller size and darker, richer colors in both summer and winter pelage, and a heavier clouding of black-tipped hairs over the back, tail, and on the front legs.

Measurements.—Type, adult male: Total length, 1,143; tail, 355; and hind foot, 180 millimeters.

Distribution and habitat.—This coyote, a rather large, dark form, occupies the mesquite and juniper country of middle and western Texas and southern and central New Mexico. Specimens are referred to it from Carlsbad, Fort Sumner, Santa Rosa, near Santa Fe, and Embuda and west to the Rio Grande Valley and throughout the Mogollon Mountain Range and south to the Mexican border. In the southwestern part of the State its range is overlapped to some extent by the small *mearnsi*, but along the eastern border it grades into *nebracensis*, in the mountains of the northern part into *lestes*, and apparently in the San Juan Valley region into the smaller *estor*. The actual limits of the range of the species in New Mexico can not be shown in hard and fast lines but rather by an average of characters that blend insensibly from one distribution area to another. Although a large number of specimens are available from many localities in the State, there are still many gaps in our knowledge of the actual subspecific variation over considerable areas. This form occupies both the Lower and the Upper Sonoran Zone areas and locally extends through limited areas of the Transition Zone without any apparent change of characters. Specimens from Gallo Canyon and the Sacramento Mountains are noticeably large and might almost be referred to *lestes* of the mountain country farther north, but in these limited areas of the Transition Zone the writer has referred them all to *texensis*.

Abundance.—It is not easy to give an adequate idea of the numbers of coyotes in a State like New Mexico, where they inhabit practically every part. After many years of persistent hunting, trapping, and poisoning for fur and for the bounties usually offered, and of the constant warfare of stockmen and ranchers, who never miss an opportunity to kill a coyote, the numbers in most localities are apparently as great to-day as they were in 1889, when the writer first collected over a considerable part of the State. They have been reported by the field collectors of the Biological Survey as common or abundant at almost every locality where work has been done in New Mexico, and a large number of specimens have been taken. In 1907 the Forest Service supervisors reported 77 coyotes killed on the Lincoln National Forest, 50 on the Sacramento, 81 on the Manzano, 242 on the Gila, 51 on the Magdalena, and 9 on the San Mateo National Forests, or 510 during the year. These represent but a part of those that were known to have been killed on a few of the forests and give no idea of the much greater numbers killed in the valley country and over other parts of the State.

In 1915 the Forest Service reported 80 coyotes killed on the Alamo, 22 on the Lincoln, 59 on the Santa Fe, 222 on the Carson, and 62 on the Datil, making 445 for these five national forests. In 1916 the Biological Survey predatory-animal trappers turned in 430 coyotes from many localities scattered over New Mexico and including the several subspecies found in the State. During the same period the Forest Service reported 1,084 coyotes killed in the State, including those of the predatory-animal trappers and all other trappers, hunters, and ranchers.

General habits.—Coyotes adapt themselves to every kind of environment, from the open valleys and plains to brushy and mesquite-covered slopes and into the rough foothill country of juniper and nut pine and even into the open yellow-pine timber of the mountain plateaus. During the daytime they generally hide in gulches or find some cover of brush or weeds in which to sleep after a full meal, but if their meals have been scanty they travel far and wide during both day and night in search of food. Occasionally one is startled out of its bed, but more often they are seen loping across the open country on their foraging expeditions, and still more frequently their tracks are seen in trails and roads and on sandy ground. At night they are especially active and during the summer and autumn usually furnish doleful music around the camp fires. Occasionally their yapping calls are heard during the daytime, but more commonly in the evening or at any time of night when there is anything of interest to bring them together. Their rapid falsetto barking mixed with short howls often has the effect of sounding as if several were engaged in a chorus, when there is really only one. When two or three join together in simultaneous calls the effect is that of a great number, and the tenderfoot generally supposes that he is surrounded by a large pack. There is usually a sort of hilarity in their calls, which is amusing and rather pleasing to experienced campers. They are inquisitive and rather bold, often coming close to camp or ranches when there is no gun in sight, but usually keeping well out of rifle range unless suddenly surprised in a turn of the road or at the top of a ridge. Even then their swiftness and skill in taking advantage of the lay of the land for protection often save them from even an expert with the rifle, and it requires a good rider and a good horse to overtake one if it has a fair start and some rough ground over which to run.

Food habits.—Besides many sheep and goats on the range, some pigs and chickens at the ranches, and any dead animals that are found, the coyotes have a standard, native diet consisting largely of rabbits, prairie dogs, ground squirrels, kangaroo rats, pocket gophers, frogs, salamanders, some insects, pine nuts, and many kinds of fruit and berries. At Jarilla, Gaut found that they had been digging out kangaroo rats in considerable numbers, evidently making a business of hunting the little animals. Near Parker Lake, on the flats east of the Organ Mountains, he watched one hunting prairie dogs. It started at one end of the prairie-dog town and ran at full speed until it had succeeded in cutting off one of the prairie dogs from its burrow, when it caught and shook it as a dog would a rat and carried it away as a choice prize. The writer has seen two at a time hunting in a prairie-dog town, well apart, creeping up in places, making short dashes where they would see a possible chance to cut one off, and systematically hunting throughout the town until they had obtained a meal or scared all the prairie dogs into their burrows. A patch of rabbit fur on the desert is often seen where a coyote has captured either a cottontail or jack rabbit and made a meal, leaving only the fur to mark the spot. In the droppings found along the trails, rabbit fur is one of the most common and conspicuous elements, but fur and bones of smaller rodents are often detected, together with traces of some insects and often the skins and seeds of cactus fruit and berries and the seeds and pods of mesquite beans, and the seeds of juniper berries. Coyotes always gather where food is abundant, whether it be jack rabbits in the valley, ripe cactus fruit in the gulches, sweet juniper berries on the ridges, or dead cattle on the range after a hard winter, but they are most strongly attracted by the sheep herds.

Breeding habits.—The coyote pups are generally born in March or April, and their number varies from four to eight. The young are usually born in natural cavities in banks or gulches, among the rocks, or not infrequently in burrows in the ground. Many of the dens are found by watching the parents returning with food or by noticing the numerous tracks heading in certain directions in rough country such as they select for breeding purposes. It is a fair assumption that any coyote seen during the spring or early summer carrying food is heading straight for the den where its young are hidden. At Conchas Creek, some 35 miles north of Santa Rosa, on June 23, 1903, an old female coyote came past the camp carrying a cottontail rabbit in its mouth. With a field glass the writer watched the coyote until it came to some rocks at the far end of the valley, and a family of half-grown young quickly surrounded it and made short work of the rabbit. A little later, as he approached the den, they all disappeared in a large burrow in the rocks, and the old one, watching until he was almost within rifle range, sneaked off behind the rocks and quietly disappeared. Rabbit fur was the only indication of food that could be found around this den, but the young were then large enough to begin to run about and were evidently not so well fed as to leave any scraps of possible food. By midsummer the young are half grown and leave the dens, and by the time their fur is good in autumn they are practically full-grown coyotes and capable of killing any game of their own size and considerably larger.

Unfortunately coyotes do not hibernate, but are active throughout the year and require as much food in winter as in summer, but their fur is then long and of some value, and they are extensively trapped and hunted for their coats.

Economic status.—As New Mexico is one of the important sheep-grazing States of the West the coyote problem is there one of the most serious of those relating to predatory animals. The coyotes gather and follow the herds of sheep and pick up all strays, and especially in lambing time kill not only the lambs but the ewes that have fallen out of the herds to give birth to their young. The constant presence of herders and dogs are necessary to protect the sheep, but even these are not always adequate, as a coyote will occasionally catch and kill a sheep that wanders at the edge of the herd farthest from the dogs. There are constant complaints of losses from the coyotes wherever sheep are ranged in the State. The total annual loss can not be definitely stated, but it is often estimated at 1 to 3 per cent of the herds.

In June, 1918, J. S. Ligon reported coyotes in the Pecos Valley as common but less abundant than in some other portions of the State. He said:

I have always had the idea that the abundance or scarcity of natural food supply governed to a great extent the amount of damage to domestic stock by coyotes. This idea has been greatly modified by facts learned at the McKenzie ranch in the Pecos Valley. During the past spring the loss in cattle has been very heavy, probably 1,000 out of 6,000 head having died of starvation, thus spreading a feast that one would think sufficient for coyotes. Rabbits are also extremely abundant. Even with this supply of food so easily obtainable, the coyotes rarely eat the dead cattle, but continue to take lambs and even older sheep from the flock that is kept on the McKenzie place. Our hunter, George W. Pope, has cleaned this range of coyotes during the past two months, and it is probable that but two coyotes remain about the range. The last one taken had but three feet and those still at large are very shy and seem to have had experience in traps. During April and on May 18 adult coyotes were secured, of which several were mother animals whose puppies probably perished.

It appears that the coyote's appetite for sheep is too strong to be resisted. He can not forego the temptation of a fat lamb. That he follows sheep from range to range can hardly be doubted. Apparently he can smell a flock for a distance of many miles. The following interesting account was given to me by R. E. Dunlap. He left the Pecos River a few miles north of Roswell, with a band of sheep and traveled across the sandhills to Portales, a distance of 75 miles. Cockleburs were very plentiful along the Pecos River, but there were none in the country except in the immediate proximity to the river. The second night after the arrival of the sheep at Portales a trapper in the locality caught a coyote that had great numbers of cockleburs in its hair. This coyote had evidently trailed the sheep from the river.

Mr. Dunlap is lambing and shearing his sheep this season 50 miles above Roswell on the Pecos River. This locality is swarming with both jack rabbits and cottontails, and dead cattle and horses are strewn over the country. He began to lamb April 20, and within 2 weeks thereafter coyotes began to take the lambs. From 1,400 ewes, only 600 lambs were reared to safe living age, and coyotes later took 50 of these. Lanterns kept burning at night about the bed grounds were apparently little protection to the sheep. About 4 days before my visit to Mr. Dunlap's camp, coyotes got into a small corral, where a bunch of ewes were held for the night, and killed 4 of the lambs, though Mr. Dunlap was sleeping near by to guard the sheep. I had the satisfaction of catching one of these coyotes in a trap and made sets for others.

This persistent killing of sheep in the presence of such an abundance of food, including young rabbits, undermines my theory that natural food conditions govern the damage done to domestic stock. The fact is, wild animals choose what they like best, and they run much risk to get it.

In parts of New Mexico goat raising is an important industry, and the coyotes levy a tribute on the goat herds, although not to such an extent as on the sheep. Goats are more pugnacious and the males are better able to protect the flock, but the young and females fall easy prey to the coyotes when they stray from the flocks. Coyotes are generally accused of killing some young calves, but actual data on this subject are not easily obtained. It is evident, however, that the loss is considerable. Pigs are killed by them and poultry is always in danger if allowed to run at large at a distance from the ranch buildings. The destruction of game animals, young deer, antelope, and mountain sheep is not usually taken into consideration, but the coyotes are always abundant where these animals occur and the loss is evidently one of the potent causes of the rapid decrease of large game. The destruction of game birds by coyotes, especially of the eggs and young, undoubtedly acts as a severe check on the increase of such game.

In November, 1915, at the Doby station on the V+T ranch about 30 miles northwest of Chloride, Mr. Ligon reported the young ducks and other water birds abundant in the marshes after the hay was cut in July, but apparently the coyotes got them all. In the evenings the coyotes could be seen coming into the meadows and then the alarm cries of the mother ducks could be heard. He also records the destruction of a whole flock of wild turkeys by them. To these actual losses through the depredations of coyotes may be added the heavy expense incurred by the State and most of the counties and many ranchmen through the payment of bounties. Though the bounties usually paid on coyotes are not large, ranging in most cases from $1 to $5 each, the number of scalps presented for bounty usually brings the cost up to the limit of the appropriations for bounty purposes, and in the annual total amounts to a very large sum. On the credit side of the coyotes stands a minor account. They constantly prey upon the rabbits, prairie dogs, and other rodent pests and serve as an important check in keeping down their increase, thus saving the crops of the farmer and conserving the grazing capacity of the stock ranch. They also yield considerable fur of moderate value and in this way partly pay to the trappers what they take from the proceeds of the stockmen. A leaflet has been issued by the Department of Agriculture on methods of trapping coyotes with a view to their better control. (Young, 1930.)

CANIS LATRANS LESTES MERRIAM

ROCKY MOUNTAIN COYOTE; TOO-WHA-NA of the Tcos Indians

Canis lestes Merriam, Biol. Soc. Wash. Proc. 11:25, 1897.

Type.—Collected in Toyabe Mountains, near Cloverdale, Nev., November 21, 1890, by Vernon Bailey.

General characters.—A very large and rather brightly colored coyote, corresponding in the Rocky Mountain region to *latrans*, the brush wolf of Iowa, Wisconsin, and Minnesota, and differing from it externally in clearer, brighter coloration. In size it was originally described as slightly smaller than *latrans*, but additional material has shown that individuals attain almost, if not quite, the proportions of typical *latrans*.

Measurements.—The type specimen, an adult male, measured: Total length, 1,116; tail, 320; and hind foot, 200 millimeters. A male collected on the headwaters of Costilla River at 9,500 feet in New Mexico measured: Total length, 1,260; tail, 310; hind foot, 200 millimeters.

Distribution and habitat.—In New Mexico specimens of coyotes from the head of Costilla River at 9,500 feet are referred to *lestes*, as are also those from near Twining in the Taos Mountains at 8,500 feet, Halls Peak and Martinez on the eastern slope of the Sangre de Cristo Range, specimens secured at Espanola without a definite locality, and one from Laplata in the mountains north of the San Juan River. The notes on these coyotes reported at localities throughout the Sangre de Cristo Range south to the Pecos Mountains and in the San Juan and Jemez Mountains are also included. A series of four skins and skulls collected by Gaut at Gallo Canyon, 40 miles southeast of Corona, are very large and suggest a tendency toward *lestes* in general characters. A series of 17 skulls collected in the Sacramento Mountains by A. M. Neal are also very large, but until a more exhaustive study can be made of the group both of these localities are included within the range of *texensis*. *Canis latrans lestes* throughout its wide range occupies the more or less timbered mountain ranges mainly within the Transition Zone, but at least in summer often ranges high into the Canadian Zone in following the herds of stock and game. Near Pecos Baldy one was seen at 11,500 feet altitude on an open ridge near timber line, and their tracks were frequently seen at this level. The fact that one seen in August was carrying a brown weasel, which it had just caught, would indicate that the young were also in that vicinity, although they may have been born far down the mountain side. In Moreno Valley at Black Lake and on the head of Coyote Creek their large tracks were often seen, and one coyote seen in the yellow-pine forest was so large and dark that at first it was mistaken for a lobo. Their voices at night were also noticeably heavier and more prolonged than those of the valley coyotes lower down. A large old male shot by Sun Elk near camp at 9,700 feet on the head of Costilla River, August 22, was in the short, rusty summer coat. Its stomach was found to be full of freshly-killed mutton, including pieces of skin, wool, and well-crushed bones, and the lower intestines showed that the previous meal had been of the same nature. There were also several sheep ticks found alive on the coyote, all of which gave evidence of his reason for being up in the mountains.

In a letter of January 6, 1919, from Charles Springer to E. W. Nelson, the statement was made that 438 coyotes had been caught during the preceding six months by one trapper on the Bartlett ranch in Colfax County. These were probably largely of this mountain species. Several skins obtained at Espanola probably came from the Jemez Mountains just west of there, where coyotes were found common in the open sheep-grazed parks at 9,000 feet, and where they are said to cause considerable loss among the flocks. In the Gallinas Mountains a little farther north they were also common, and two were one day chased by a couple of hounds near camp at 9,000 feet altitude. The hounds ran slowly along the brushy mountain side, and the writer could watch the coyotes keeping at an even distance in front and occasionally turning back a little way to make sure that the hounds were coming. Through the field glass they appeared to be the large, dark, mountain coyote. In the San Juan Mountains they were heard almost every night around camp at 9,900 feet and were frequently seen at a safe distance during the day. One with a conspicuous white tip to its tail was seen several times near camp, but always it kept out of rifle range, except on one evening when Gaut had left his gun at camp and then he followed closely while the traps were being set.

General habits.—This large mountain coyote differs from the valley species, if at all, in being more of a forest animal and big-game hunter. The great herds of sheep that are ranged every summer throughout the mountains of the Southwest are its chief attraction at high altitudes, but the presence of a large coyote in this habitat strongly suggests a descent from game-killing ancestors. Deer and elk were formerly abundant over its range, and the young undoubtedly suffered as the sheep herds are suffering to-day from their depredations. Fortunately they are not so numerous as the smaller forms of the valley country below, but their greater size and strength probably make up for smaller numbers.

CANIS LATRANS NEBRACENSIS Merriam

PLAINS COYOTE

Canis pallidus Merriam, Biol. Soc. Wash. Proc. 11:24, 1897. (Not of Rüppell, 1826.)
Canis nebracensis Merriam, Science (n. s.) 8: 782, December 2, 1898. (Substituted for *pallidus* Merriam.)

Type.—Collected at Johnstown, Nebr., March 12, 1896, by E. E. Fast.
General characters.—This large and very pale coyote of the Great Plains region apparently occupies the eastern edge of New Mexico from north to south.

Distribution and habitat.—A specimen from Monahans, Tex., near the southeastern corner of New Mexico, seems to be typical *nebracensis*, while skulls of coyotes from Clayton in the northeastern corner can readily be referred to this form, but the specimens from the mesquite country and the Pecos Valley are all referred to the darker *texensis*. Typical *nebracensis* apparently occupies only the short-grass plains along the eastern border of the State, where there is a minimum of shade and cover and where its pale-yellowish coloration harmonizes well with the glowing summer light of the open plains and its whitish winter coat with either the bleached winter grass or the snow fields of its habitat.

General habits.—In habits one coyote is like another, except as environment and opportunity may adapt it to local conditions. The great advantage that the coyote has over many animals is its adaptability to very different types of environment and even to change of conditions such as are produced by the gradual settlement of a region. As the abundant native game disappears the coyotes turn their attention to domestic stock and thrive just as well under conditions of civilization as they ever did in the days of the supremacy of the Indian and buffalo. It is only by well-planned and concerted action that their numbers and depredations can be successfully controlled by man.

CANIS LATRANS ESTOR Merriam

SAN JUAN COYOTE; MAI of the Navajo Indians

Canis estor Merriam, Biol. Soc. Wash. Proc. 11: 31, 1897.

Type.—Collected at the Noland ranch, San Juan River, southeastern corner of Utah, November 20, 1893, by J. Alden Loring.
General characters.—A rather small and pale coyote of the interior desert valleys. Winter specimens are almost as white as *nebracensis*, while in summer they are light but bright ochraceous, with very little clouding on back at any season and scarcely a trace of black on the front legs.
Measurements.—Type, a very small female: Total length, 1,052; tail, 300; hind foot, 179 millimeters. An adult male from Fruitland, N. Mex., measured in total length, 1,180; tail, 385; hind foot, 195 millimeters and weighed 25½

pounds in the flesh. This and a 23½-pound female from the same place are apparently typical *estor.*[28]

Distribution and habitat.—Eleven skulls from Liberty, 2 skins and skulls from Fruitland, 1 from Largo, 1 from Blanco, a skull from Canyon Blanco, and 6 skins and skulls from the Chuska Mountains in extreme northwestern New Mexico are referred to *estor*. All these are considered typical *estor*, although some of the males run almost as large as *texensis*. Other specimens referred to this form but possibly somewhat intermediate are from Stinking Spring Lake [Burford Lake], Lake La Jara, Dulce, Zuni Mountains, Wingate, Fort Wingate, Gallup, Blue Water, San Raphael, Copperton, and near Quemado. These are mainly from the very arid Upper Sonoran valleys of northwestern New Mexico. Those from the Chuska and Zuni Mountains had undoubtedly followed the sheep herds to the mountains for the summer and would probably return to the valleys with them in the fall, so the species, so far as known in this area, may be considered mainly Upper Sonoran. Coyotes are abundant over the region, both in the open, hot, and extremely arid valleys and over the rough juniper and nut pine covered slopes of the foothill and low mountain country. They are always most numerous where the sheep herds are ranging but are scattered at large all over the region.

General habits.—Many coyote tracks were seen in the roads and trails in the San Juan Valley; the animals were frequently seen along the roads and a few were shot, while Clarence Birdseye trapped two at Fruitland. At night they howled about the camps and were especially vociferous during the evening and morning hours. One reason for their abundance is undoubtedly the superstition of the Navajo Indians, the principal inhabitants, and of sheep herders of the country, who generally refuse to kill or touch one because of their belief that the coyote man was one of their mighty ancestors. At Shiprock at Baker's trading store Clarence Birdseye saw a man chase a Navajo all over the store, behind the stove, over the counter, and finally out of the door just by poking a coyote hide at him. During the time of the writer's visit to the valley in October, 1908, there was no bounty on coyotes and the fur was worth very little, so the animals had every opportunity for increase and abundance. At Liberty Birdseye found a bright 14-year-old boy who had caught about 40 during the previous season, using only the ordinary meat bait. By using scent bait the writer had no trouble in catching a considerable number in the valley and on the Chuska Mountains. Early in October in the Chuska Mountains the coyotes were numerous, although the thousands of sheep that had been running there in summer had been removed to the Indian villages in the valleys. After six good specimens were shot and trapped, the coyote chorus around the camps at night was still long and loud. On the Jicarilla Indian Reservation around the

---

[28] The type of *estor*, and the only specimen from anywhere in the type region at the time the species was described, is a fully adult but very small female and was at that time considered a member of the *microdon* group related to *microdon* and *mearnsi.* Series of specimens from Liberty and Fruitland in the San Juan Valley, about 50 miles north of the type locality of the species, are evidently typical *estor*, but none are quite so small as the type. They evidently represent a small pale Upper Sonoran desert form of the *latrans* group related to *nebracensis* and *texensis.*

Stinking Spring and La Jara Lakes the coyotes were especially numerous, their fresh tracks were in every road and trail, and a number of animals were shot and trapped. Farther south they were just as numerous around the Zuni Mountains, in the lower part of Largo Canyon near Quemado many were seen singly or in twos, and one family of eight was seen crossing the gulch in single file just below camp. This was evidently a grown litter that early in October was still hunting under the leadership of the head of the family, and evidently the collecting party had camped on their hunting ground, as they serenaded the camp vociferously every night. The writer was busy with other traps, but he set one coyote trap by the side of a trail the last night he was there and baited it with wolf scent. Evidently he placed the scent too close to the trap, for the next morning it was sprung, with a bunch of hair from the back of a coyote between the jaws, showing that it had rolled in the trap instead of stepping into it.

Food habits.—On the Chuska Mountains the coyotes were finding a variety of small game, and the writer watched one hunt along the edge of one of the numerous lakes. It was wading in the shallow water near shore and every few minutes would make a grab at something under water. After watching it for half an hour he shot it for the special purpose of finding out what it was eating and found in its stomach 15 salamanders (Ambystoma), and a piece of old horsehide. The stomach of another one shot contained 4 pocket gophers, 1 salamander, and a frog. One shot near Quemado at 9 a. m. had in its stomach 1 kangaroo rat (Perodipus), 1 white-footed mouse (Peromyscus), 2 pocket mice (Perognathus), about half a pint of juniper berries, and a little green grass. Another, only some fresh cow manure. This was in October when the coyotes were fat, 2 males weighing 25½ and 27 pounds, and 3 females 26, 23½, and 20 pounds. Down in the San Juan Valley a few days later they were found feeding on an occasional carcass of a dead cow or horse, and besides stock and poultry they were evidently catching many of the rodents of the valley. At Fruitland, Clarence Birdseye found where one had been feeding on pears and squashes, and their droppins along the trails often contained juniper berries.

Economic status.—Everywhere throughout the range of this species the ranchmen complained of their depredations on sheep and poultry, and some accused them of killing many young calves. At Blanco Birdseye reported a great deal of damage to calves and sheep, and was told of several instances where 12, 15, or 20 were killed in a single night. At San Raphael, Charles M. Grover told of a herd of yearling lambs that on December 10, 1907, had strayed during a storm, 150 of them being killed by coyotes during the night. The Indians with their hundreds of thousands of sheep are the heaviest losers, but they say little about it and suffer the loss patiently in a spirit of religious tolerance. In the San Juan Valley in 1908 the coyotes were especially destructive to poultry, and in some places made it almost impossible to raise turkeys. At Blanco a Mrs. Amiot told the writer that she had had a fine flock of turkeys but they had all been killed, and that she had to give up further attempts at turkey raising. At

Fruitland and Liberty, Birdseye reported that many of the ranch-men had to give up raising poultry on their account. Around the Stinking Spring Lake [Burford Lake] they had evidently gathered during the breeding season of the ducks and waterfowl to feed on eggs and such birds as they could capture, but in September, 1904, they seemed to be killing only an occasional wounded duck. In a range and stock country such as these coyotes inhabit there is little to offset the heavy losses through their depredations. Their great numbers are a good illustration of unrestrained increase.

CANIS MEARNSI MERRIAM

MEARNS'S COYOTE

Canis mearnsi Merriam, Biol. Soc. Wash. Proc. 11: 30, 1897.

Type.—Collected at Quitobaquita, Pima County, Ariz., February 5, 1894, by E. A. Mearns.

General characters.—One of the smallest of our coyotes, with especially light dentition and bright, rich coloration; described by Doctor Merriam as the handsomest of the coyotes.

Measurements.—Adult male from Playas Valley, N. Mex.: Total length, 1,100; tail, 300; hind foot, 190 millimeters. Adult female from type locality: 1,100, 330, 180 millimeters, respectively. Weight of adult male from Playas Valley, 22 pounds after bleeding copiously and being carried all day in the wagon; live weight probably 25 pounds.

Distribution and habitat.—Specimens in the United States National Museum collection carry the range of Mearns's coyote across the Lower Sonoran valleys of New Mexico. There is a good skin and skull from Playas Valley, one from Redrock, one from Salt Valley at the west base of the Guadalupe Mountains, and others from near El Paso, Tex.; also skulls from Pratt and Lordsburg. Apparently it is not an abundant species over this area, where its range is over-lapped by the larger and more numerous *texensis*.

General habits.—On a trip from Deming to Hachita, thence through the Playas and Animas Valleys and back over the San Luis Pass and between the Big and Little Hatchet Mountains, the writer saw a few coyotes and a moderate number of tracks along the roads and trails. One old male (pl. 18, B), shot from the wagon in Playas Valley, August 6, was in fine, fresh summer pelage of coarse, short hair, which made its big ears stand out in high relief. Its stomach contained only the afterbirth of a cow. In Animas Valley a few were seen but no specimens secured, although at Pratt in the northern end of this valley a series of 10 skulls was sent to the Biological Survey by Hotchkiss, two of which prove to be of this little species. At Redrock, E. A. Goldman shot one that came and barked near his camp and found in its stomach the remains of a recently eaten jack rabbit. There is nothing to indicate that the habits of these little coyotes differ from those of other species except that their habitat in the hot Lower Sonoran deserts gives them a different set of native food animals and different species of cactus and other fruits from which to draw their food supply. In voice and general habits the writer has not been able to detect any difference between them and their larger relatives.

Family MUSTELIDAE: Wolverenes, Martens, Otters, Minks, Ferrets, Weasels, Skunks, and Badgers

GULO LUSCUS (LINNAEUS)

WOLVERENE

[*Ursus*] *luscus* Linnaeus, Syst. Nat., Ed. 12, 1: 71, 1766.

Type locality.—Hudson Bay.

General characters.—A sturdy little animal, somewhat larger than a raccoon, with long, coarse hair and short, bushy tail; general color dark brown or blackish, face gray, throat usually spotted with white, and a yellowish band along each side and across the hips to rump. Although more nearly related to the martens, it has somewhat the appearance of a small bushy-tailed bear.

Distribution and habitat.—The range of the wolverene lies mainly over the northern part of the continent, but extends southward in the Rocky Mountain region to Colorado and probably into the higher Canadian Zone mountains of northern New Mexico. There seem to be no specimens or definite records for the State, but Coues in his monograph of the fur-bearing animals (1877, p. 49–50) says:

Its extreme limit is even somewhat farther [south] than this, reaching in the mountains to the borders of Arizona and New Mexico and corresponding latitudes in California. Of this I was assured by hunters whose statements I had no reason to doubt, and who were evidently acquainted with the species.

Although this reference lacks any specific record for New Mexico it seems to be based on verbal reports that Coues had from the residents in northern New Mexico, where he came more or less in contact with the local hunters and trappers in 1864.

Much of the high area of the Sangre de Cristo Mountains is entirely suitable to the wolverene's range, and there is no reason to doubt their former occurrence here, or that Doctor Coues's record was actually based on reports to that effect.

MARTES CAURINA ORIGENES (RHOADS)

ROCKY MOUNTAIN MARTEN

Mustela caurina origenes Rhoads, Acad. Nat. Sci. Phila. Proc. 54: 458, 1902.

Type.—Collected at Marvine Mountain, Garfield County, Colo., September 16, 1891, by Ernest Thompson Seton.

General characters.—Martens are about the size of minks, but with longer, softer fur and more bushy tails. In color they are more auburn or golden brown, usually with orange throats.

Measurements.—An adult male from Montana measures: Total length, 615; tail, 200; hind foot, 95 millimeters; and a female from the same locality, 565, 180, and 83 millimeters, respectively.

Distribution and habitat.—Rocky Mountain martens occur in New Mexico only in the high mountains of the northern part of the State. A specimen in beautiful winter fur was collected December 25, 1893, by Loring near Chama, a station on the Denver & Rio Grande Railroad, just south of the Colorado line in the San Juan Mountains. In 1881, at his camp near Truchas Peaks, Dyche saw some martens catching conies in the rocks, and succeeded in getting two of them. (Edwords, 1893, p. 64.) In 1874 a marten skin was reported at Taos by Doctor Coues (Coues and Yarrow, 1875, p. 61).

In 1903, Surber reported a few in the vicinity of Twining but did not secure a specimen. These few records show that the animals occur, but are by no means common in the Canadian Zone forests of the Sangre de Cristo and San Juan Mountains. It is very doubtful if they occur in any of the ranges farther south, and these localities undoubtedly mark the southern limit of the range of the genus in North America. There are extensive areas in these mountains well adapted to their habits and mode of life.

General habits.—Martens are forest dwellers and roam through the woods in search of their prey, which consists of the small mammals and birds that they are able to catch. They are expert tree climbers and make their homes in hollow trees as well as hollow logs and rocky ledges. They are great wanderers, and in their search for food cover extensive areas over the winter snow, in summer following along old logs and well-known runways from one hunting ground to another.

Food habits.—The greater part of the food of martens apparently consists of conies, pine squirrels, chipmunks, wood rats, and mice, some of which they seem to be always pursuing. They are easily attracted to traps by the feathers of birds, and it is not improbable that their catlike quickness enables them to catch many birds, either by surprising them when asleep at night or by pouncing upon them in the daytime.

Economic status.—The unusual beauty and high market value of marten fur make it one of the most desirable of the trapper's harvest. As a result martens are always scarce and hard to find. Many of the skins taken are not at their best and bring much less than they would if fully prime. More effective laws regulating the taking of fur bearers would not only enable the animals to increase more rapidly but greatly increase the quality and value of the fur crop. To those interested in artificially rearing fur-bearing animals, the marten offers one of the most tempting species. As yet they have not been reared with much success, but experiments are being carried on with a view to overcoming the difficulties in the way of their domestic control and propagation.

LUTRA CANADENSIS SONORA Rhoads

Arizona Otter; Pah-hua-pe′na of the Taos Indians

Lutra hudsonica sonora Rhoads, Amer. Phil. Soc. Trans. (n. s.) 19:431, 1898.

Type.—Collected at Montezuma Well, Ariz., December 26, 1886, by E. A. Mearns.

General characters.—Otters are semiaquatic animals with long lithe bodies, long tapering tails, short legs, half-webbed feet, and short glossy hair covering a dense underfur. Their color is chestnut brown with sometimes a grayish wash on throat.

Measurements.—An adult female from the type locality measures in the flesh in total length, 1,300; tail, 815; hind foot, 146 millimeters; it weighed 19½ pounds.

Distribution and habitat.—In 1906 the writer was told that there were still a few Arizona otters along the headwaters of the Gila River in southwestern New Mexico, and in 1825 the Pattie brothers recorded one among other animals caught along the Gila near where the Arizona-New Mexico line now crosses it. (Pattie, 1905, p. 107.)

These records undoubtedly refer to the typical Arizona form, but no more records are available in New Mexico except for the upper Rio Grande and Canadian Rivers in the northeastern part of the State, where the species is probably different. There is, however, not a specimen from the State available for study and comparison, and, until specimens are obtained, no definite decision can be arrived at in regard to the subspecies. In the Canadian River, near the mouth of the Mora River, Mr. Hatcher killed an otter on August 28, 1845, but the specimen seems not to have been saved. (Abert, 1846, p. 24.) A few are reported along the Rio Grande near Espanola, Rinconada, and Cienequilla. The Taos Indians are familiar with them, and bits of otter fur were seen on their clothing and ornaments as well as on those of the Jicarilla Apaches farther west.

General habits.—Otters are largely aquatic, doing most of their hunting and traveling in the water, where they are wonderfully expert. They travel on land slowly and with considerable effort, unless there is soft snow, over which they slide with great rapidity. The wide stretches of waterless area in New Mexico are complete barriers to their distribution, and apparently they are not found even along the main lines of some of the larger streams. Their principal food consists of fishes, crawfishes, and such other forms of animal life as they can pick up in or under the water. In New Mexico they are so rare as to be of little economic importance.

LUTREOLA VISON ENERGUMENOS (BANGS)

ROCKY MOUNTAIN MINK; SLA-MU'NA of the Taos Indians

Putorius vison energumenos Bangs, Boston Soc. Nat. Hist. Proc. 27:5, 1896.

Type.—Collected at Sumas, British Columbia, September 23, 1895, by Allan Brooks.

General characters.—Long-bodied, short-legged, short-eared, little animals, with coarse hair covering the very soft, dense fur; in color, dark brown all over except occasionally a white streak on chin or breast. The anal glands produce a fetid musk as offensive but less powerful than that of the skunk.

Measurements.—An adult male from Colorado measures: Total length, 579; tail, 189; hind foot, 69 millimeters; and a female from the same place, 451, 150, and 55 millimeters, respectively.

Distribution and habitat.—Minks are fairly common along the streams in northern New Mexico but rare or entirely absent from other parts of the State. On August 24, 1904, an immature male was collected by Gaut at 9,600 feet altitude on Costilla River in the Sangre de Cristo Mountains, and their tracks were common along this river down to 8,000 feet near the town of Costilla in the Rio Grande Valley. At 9,400 feet their tracks were seen in the mud around an old beaver house, and a family were evidently living in the beaver house, where they had well-worn entrances and trails. In the Pecos River Mountains a few mink tracks were seen along the river at 8,000 feet, and a skin was seen hanging in one of the houses at Willis on the upper Pecos at 8,500 feet. Others were reported at 8,600 feet along the trout streams of the upper Pecos, but they were by no means common at that time, July and August, 1903. The trappers along the Rio Grande above Santa Fe usually catch a few minks during the winter, and from one of these trappers during the winter of 1904–5 four skulls were obtained. In 1908 Clarence

Birdseye reported minks as formerly common along the Animas and San Juan Rivers near Farmington but at that time rather scarce. One trapper reported the diminishing numbers of 20, 12, and 10 taken there during the three preceding winters. A few were also reported at Liberty and Fruitland, and in 1893 Rowley reported them as quite plentiful along the streams in the vicinity of Laplata. (Allen, 1893, p. 83.) Over the rest of the State there seem to be no thoroughly substantiated records of the mink.

General habits.—Permanent water with a supply of fishes, frogs, and crustaceans seems to be a necessity with these animals, as their range does not extend into desert places where the water supply is uncertain. Their hunting is usually combined with fishing; hence they follow the stream courses or prowl about the borders of lakes and ponds, where a large part of their food is obtained. They are expert swimmers and divers and will catch small fishes in the water and bring up such foods as they can find below the surface or even under the ice. Their homes are usually in the banks of streams or under drift heaps or broken rocks, but they are great wanderers and seem to be constantly on the move up or down the streams.

Food habits.—Minks are voracious little carnivores, killing everything of their own size or under that comes in their way, and feeding on such game as muskrats, mice, birds, fishes, frogs, and crawfishes. In captivity they will eat any kind of fresh meat, but always seem to prefer killing their prey. They will also eat bread soaked in milk, and even dry bread, if forced by hunger, but seem not to relish anything but meat.

Breeding habits.—Minks breed once a year and bring forth the young in spring or early summer in litters usually numbering five or six.

Economic status.—In places where minks often raid poultry yards and do considerable damage it is commonly such an easy matter to fence against them that their depredations can be almost entirely prevented. They undoubtedly destroy some game birds and quickly clean out colonies of muskrats wherever the two species come in contact. Their value as fur bearers, however, makes them one of the most important sources of income to the trappers and usually warrants their inclusion in such laws as are made for the protection of fur-bearing animals. Their fur, if taken when prime, generally brings a high market price and is one of the durable and standard types of the fur market.

MUSTELA NIGRIPES (Audubon and Bachman)

BLACK-FOOTED FERRET

Putorius nigripes Audubon and Bachman, Quadrupeds of North America 2: 297, 1851.

Type.—Collected at Fort Laramie, Wyo., by Alexander Culbertson prior to 1851.

General characters.—Large, short-tailed weasels of a general creamy or buffy-gray color, with black feet and tip of tail, a black mask across face and eyes, and generally an indistinct patch of brownish over the middle of back.

Measurements.—An adult male from Oakley, Kans., measures: Total length, 529; tail, 130; hind foot, 65 millimeters.

Distribution and habitat.—Black-footed ferrets are found over the Staked Plains country of western Texas and undoubtedly occupy the plains region of all eastern and northern New Mexico, but few specimens have been taken. A lower jaw was found in 1903 in a prairie-dog town at Santa Rosa. In 1915, J. S. Ligon took 1 in Socorro County, 15 miles north of Reserve, and in 1916 and 1917, Joseph Crick reported ferrets frequently seen near Old Fort Wingate and on Center-fire Creek (10 miles northeast of Luna), and one 14 miles north of Luna. On Center-fire Creek 4 or 5, including young, were seen. In 1918 Ligon caught 1 in a trap set for a coyote near San Mateo, 10 miles northeast of Mount Taylor. On October 15, 1918, M. E. Musgrave took one 2 miles north of Bluewater; on March 22, 1918, J. S. Felkner took 1 at Garcias Ranch, 75 miles southwest of Magdalena.

General habits.—These big weasels are almost invariably associated with prairie-dog towns, where they live among the burrows and feed on the prairie dogs, going down the burrows and capturing the occupants at will. Had they not been very scarce they would long since have exhausted their favorite food supply. High living on easily obtained fat prairie dogs seems to be the only explanation of their scarcity, as they are vicious little animals with few enemies.

MUSTELA FRENATA NEOMEXICANA (BARBER AND COCKERELL)

NEW MEXICO BRIDLED WEASEL

Putorius frenatus neomexicanus Barber and Cockerell, Acad. Nat. Sci. Phila. Proc. 1898: 188, 1898.

Type.—Collected at Armstrongs Lake, near Mesilla, N. Mex., February 1, 1898, by A. C. Tyson.

General characters.—A large weasel, yellowish brown above and orange below, with dark-brown face and ears, white markings between and back of the eyes, black tip of tail, and no white pelage known.

Measurements.—The type specimen, an adult male, measured: Total length, 500; tail, 205; hind foot, 50 millimeters. Another male from Albuquerque measured in total length, 459; tail, 200; hind foot, 49 millimeters. The females are much smaller.

Distribution and habitat.—Specimens of the northernmost form of the bridled weasel group have been taken at the type locality, at Mesilla Park, Las Cruces, Albuquerque, Berino, on Eden Creek at 7,800 feet altitude in the White Mountains, and on Willow Creek at 8,500 feet in the Mogollon Mountains. There are other records from Arizona and Kansas. Other reports that undoubtedly apply to this species are from near Las Cruces, where E. A. Goldman was told that weasels were found about the fields in the bottom of the valley; at Kingston, where he was told that they were occasionally killed or seen; and at Garfield, where the farmers described them as strange little animals for which they had no name. They were said to be seen usually near irrigated alfalfa and sometimes to be driven out by the irrigation water. At Redrock on the Gila a few were reported, and a ranchman told Goldman about killing seven, all forced out of one hole by irrigation water. His description of the animals fitted these weasels perfectly. The principal range of the species seems to be in the Lower Sonoran valleys of the Rio Grande and Gila Rivers, but the fact that specimens have been taken high in the mountains and as far north as Kansas would indicate a wandering species or a ready adaptation to higher zones. The specimens taken in the White and Mogollon Mountains were both in the Transition Zone near the lower edge of the Canadian Zone. The question is whether these animals were raised in the mountains or whether during the summer they wander up from the lower valleys, as do many other free-ranging mammals and birds.

General habits.—These weasels apparently occupy the fields and fertile bottom lands of stream valleys, where they hunt for mice and pocket gophers in the burrows and under the cover of rich vegetation. The great abundance of small rodent life in these valleys is undoubtedly the attraction that keeps them in this mild climate, which the northern species do not enter.

Food habits.—The type specimen was shot February 1, 1898, by A. C. Tyson in the grass on the shore of Armstrongs Lake at Mesilla. An examination of the stomach showed that it had eaten some small rodent, which appeared to be a grasshopper mouse. (Barber and Cockerell, 1898, p. 189.) The instance recorded by E. A. Goldman from Redrock of seven specimens being forced out of a burrow in an alfalfa field by water would indicate the usual weasel habit of entering pocket-gopher burrows and, after feasting on the occupants, using the burrows as dens. The individual caught on Willow Creek in the Mogollon Mountains was taken in a trap set on a log for owls and baited with a meadow mouse. It got into the trap during the daytime, and, though caught by the neck and instantly killed, its stomach was empty.

Breeding habits.—The flat skin of an old female that Gaut obtained from Edward Baker at Berino shows the arrangement of mammae to be one pair of inguinal and three pairs of abdominal, all close together and well back on the abdomen. Barber and Cockerell (1898, p. 189) give a note by J. J. Roese, of Mesilla Park, who reported four specimens seen together in a road early in the morning about the end of January or the beginning of February. This, with the development of the sexual organs of a specimen obtained at that time leads them to believe that the mating season was the cause of the four being seen together. The specimen caught by the writer in the Mogollon Mountains on October 27, 1906, was a slightly immature female or a nearly full-grown young of the year, but still in the very dark-brown coat of the young, and with a white belly, which may be a sign of immaturity or possibly the beginning of a change to a white winter pelage in conformity with the snow fields on which it was taken. Goldman's note of seven individuals killed as they came out of one burrow at Redrock is without date, but this may well have been a family of one old and six young that had not yet separated.

Economic status.—Although of limited distribution and generally scarce, these weasels are undoubtedly of great benefit to agriculture because of their habitual destruction of rodent pests. There seem to be no complaints of their destruction of poultry, although the habit might be acquired if opportunity was offered; and there is also a possibility of some injury to the small game of the valleys, especially quail.

MUSTELA ARIZONENSIS (Mearns)

Arizona Weasel; Hah-nah-u'na of the Taos Indians

Putorius arizonensis Mearns, Bul. Amer. Mus. Nat. Hist. 3 : 234, 1891.

Type.—Collected near Flagstaff, Ariz., June 20, 1886, by E. A. Mearns.

General characters.—A medium-sized weasel, in summer plain brown above with orange belly; in winter pure white, except tip of tail, which is always black.

Measurements.—Average of males: Total length, 385; tail, 144; hind foot, 44.5 millimeters; of females, 358, 130, and 40 millimeters, respectively.

Distribution and habitat.—There are specimens of Arizona weasels from Ribera and Willis on the Upper Pecos and from Pecos Baldy in the Sangre de Cristo Mountains and Twining, and there are also many records over the State that indicate a much wider distribution. Near Twining, at 10,000 feet altitude in the Sangre de Cristo Mountains, McClure Surber caught one specimen on November 19, 1904, and reported a number of others seen. At that time they were changing from the brown to the white coats, and the miners said that they became snow white later in the winter. In the Taos Mountains in July and August, 1904, weasels were seen at 8,000, 11,400, and 12,400 feet, but none was secured. In all cases they were running through rock slides, and at the two higher localities were starting a panic among the conies, which at their discovery squeaked far and near with alarm. In the Pecos Mountains one was seen among the rocks at 12,000 feet, and Weller saw a coyote carrying one in its mouth through the park at 11,500 feet. A load of fine shot scared the coyote so that it dropped the weasel, which was secured for a specimen. In the San Juan Valley Clarence Birdseye reported a few weasels at Farmington, Fruitland, Liberty, and Shiprock, but did not secure a specimen. One caught the previous winter near Farmington was reported as pure white, except for a yellow strip along its back, which merely indicated that the spring molt had set in and the brown fur was appearing along the back before spreading over the rest of the body. From these records it seems that the range of the species is mainly in the higher mountains of the State, but the one taken at Ribera was among the junipers in the Upper Sonoran Zone. On July 2 it was nursing young, which were probably secreted in the rocky ledges near by. It was shot while running over the rocks at the edge of a little flat where numerous pocket gopher mounds suggested good trapping ground, but several days' work in the vicinity proved that not a pocket gopher was left in all the burrows. The weasel had evidently entered the burrows and cleaned them out.

General habits.—These are sprightly, active little animals, darting quickly from one rock pile to another, under bushes and logs or through the grass in pursuit of such prey as mice, chipmunks, ground squirrels, and pocket gophers. They are great travelers, apparently always seeking something to kill. Their slender form enables them to pass readily through the burrows of most of the small mammals, and they kill many that are much larger than themselves.

Food habits.—Blood and fresh meat from their own killing form the principal part of their diet, and it is rare to find anything in their stomach contents that can be identified, as they reject bones and fur and quickly digest the blood or well-masticated flesh that is eaten.

Occasionally their droppings show mouse hair, or their lower in-testines contain a little identifiable hair of chipmunks, pocket gophers, or ground squirrels. Their constant and eager pursuit of game would indicate that much is killed for the pleasure of killing rather than for the necessity of food.

Breeding habits.—The females have usually five pairs of mammae, all far back on the abdominal and inguinal areas. Of the number of young and breeding habits in general there seems to be little known.

Economic status.—To many persons the name weasel is associated with the destruction of poultry by some species of the genus, and some of the larger weasels occasionally do serious damage. Even these small weasels may kill poultry, but so rarely that the danger is insignificant. If overabundant they might become a menace to small game, but as they are never even common, the mischief they may do is insignificant, while the benefit from their constant war on rodents is of considerable importance.

MUSTELA CICOGNANII LEPTUS (MERRIAM)

DWARF WEASEL

Putorius streatori leptus Merriam, Biol. Soc. Wash. Proc. 16: 76, 1903.

Type.—Collected at Silverton, Colo., October 20, 1893, by J. Alden Loring.

General characters.—Size very small with tail short; color in summer plain brown above, white below, in winter pure white, except the tip of the tail, which is black at all times.

Measurements.—Type specimen, male: Total length, 243; tail, 64; hind foot, 31 millimeters. Another male from Twining, N. Mex., measures 211, 54, and 30 millimeters, respectively. The females are much smaller.

Distribution and habitat.—The little dwarf weasel is widely dis-tributed throughout the high mountains of Colorado and northward, but only one specimen has been recorded from New Mexico. This was caught in a mouse trap in a small meadow at 10,700 feet altitude a few miles east of the mining camp of Twining in the Taos Moun-tains, near the headwaters of the Hondo River, at the upper edge of the Canadian Zone.

General habits.—An interesting account of the habits of this weasel is given by Cary (1911, pp. 33, 187) in his list of the mammals of Colorado. To these notes can be added only the one instance of its capture in New Mexico previously mentioned. The trap in which Gaut took his specimen was baited with a bit of pine-squirrel meat and set in the runway of the mountain meadow mouse (*Microtus mordax*), under overhanging grass near a little stream. The pre-vious night the trap had caught a water shrew, and other traps in similar situations near by caught the meadow mice, which were evi-dently attracting the weasel. The trap was the ordinary mouse size, but proved sufficiently strong to kill this enemy of the mice.

After the publication of Cary's report on Colorado mammals (1911), a female of this little weasel was shot by a Mr. Page on April 18, 1913, and found to contain four small embryos. This note, which was obtained by Lantz, is of especial importance, because of the meager information on the breeding time and habits of weasels.

MEPHITIS MESOMELAS VARIANS Gray

LONG-TAILED TEXAS SKUNK; Cue-u-lu'na of the Taos Indians

Mephitis varians Gray, Charlesworth's Mag. Nat. Hist. 1 : 581, 1837.

Type locality.—Texas.

General characters.—Size rather large, tail very long, and normally the two white stripes on the back rather narrow.

Measurements.—Average of typical adult males: Total length, 758; tail, 393; hind foot, 71 millimeters; of adult females, 681, 376, and 69 millimeters, respectively.

Distribution and habitat.—The range of the long-tailed Texas skunk covers more than the eastern half of New Mexico, mainly in the Upper and Lower Sonoran Zones. (Fig. 52.) Many of the specimens from the Rio Grande Valley are grading toward *estor*, but all are referred to *varians*. The species is fairly common over the whole of this area, but in favorable localities of good cover and abundant food they are conspicuously more numerous than in the open and more exposed a r e a s. Brushy and weedy bottoms along the streams, gulches, and canyons are favorite situations for skunks, but many are found in the open country where, if cover is not provided, they burrow into any bank or even level ground to obtain retreats, and hence are able to occupy almost any type of land. In places they extend upwards into the Transition Zone in the mountains, but most of the range is over the lower zones.

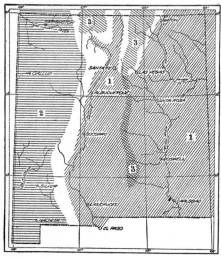

FIGURE 52.—Distribution of 2-striped skunks in New Mexico: 1, *Mephitis mesomelas varians;* 2, *M. mesomelas estor;* 3, *M. hudsonica*

General habits.—The skunks are exceedingly independent and adaptable in their habits and seem to thrive in any part of the country where there is an abundant food supply. Though mainly nocturnal, they are often seen abroad early in the evening or after daylight in the morning, but rarely during the full glow of daylight. Their peculiar little plantigrade tracks are conspicuous along the trails and roads, in sandy ground, or along the margins of streams, where they travel at night in search of food or wander from place to place over their range. Usually the tracks lead to some burrow of their own construction or one that some passing badger has made in search of ground squirrels. More often, however, they lead to cavities in the rocks where there are safe and comfortable retreats in which to sleep during the day. Again, a cactus patch or dense thicket will furnish temporary cover from which to make their nightly rounds. Occasionally one will take up its residence under the floor of some settler's cabin or among the outbuildings and stacks of the farmyard. Like many hunting animals, skunks are great wanderers and do not necessarily return to the same retreat each night. Their short legs and slow racking gait make impossible the rapid journeys of many of the other hunting mammals, but the lines of tracks are often found following a trail or road for several miles at a steady pace that would indicate considerable perseverance in these handicapped travelers. Their confidence in their ever-ready weapon of defense seems to make them free to go and come as they choose. On meeting any larger animals in the trail they generally consider it unnecessary to turn aside, apparently expecting everyone to get out of their way. This may be partly due to their limited range of vision and the fact that most animals do get out of their way. Their principal enemies are dogs and man, but they are occasionally attacked by eagles, owls, and some of the larger carnivores.

Food habits.—Along the east side of the Organ Mountains, where Gaut collected a number of specimens and reported them numerous about the edges of Parker Lake at night, the stomach of one skunk was found to contain meat and hair of some dead horse or cow. In Water Canyon, on the side of the Magdalena Mountains, E. A. Goldman caught one and found its stomach well filled with meat, which had been used for baiting the trap, but in addition a number of fragments of black beetles and a small quantity of chewed sticks, which had been swallowed while trying to make its escape. At Carlsbad in September, 1901, they were found abundant along the Pecos River Valley among the ranches, and their tracks were seen every morning along the roads and trails; wherever there was rich mellow soil the little holes where they had dug beetles and grubs dotted the ground. In an old stack yard on one of the ranches they were digging over the decayed hay at night, and one caught there had its stomach full of larvae and beetles. Near Albuquerque, M. E. Musgrave examined a skunk that had been robbing a beehive and found in its stomach 150 honeybees. The examination of many stomachs of this species shows a considerable portion of its food to consist of mice and other small rodents, in addition to any fresh or stale meat that they can pick up and a large proportion of insects and insect larvae. The scattered excrement along their trails, which gives a better summary of their food material, is very largely composed of insect remains, such as legs and wings of grasshoppers, shells of beetles, and the hard parts of a great variety of ground-dwelling insects. On rare occasions poultry and eggs are included in their diet, and they are also fond of berries and cactus fruit.

Breeding habits.—The mammae in this species of skunk are arranged in 6 pairs—1 pair of inguinal, 2 pairs of abdominal, and 3 pairs of pectoral. The average number of young is not definitely known, but, judged from the number of mammae, it is probably at least six to a litter.

Hibernation.—In autumn the skunks all become very fat, and in the northern part of their range generally hibernate during the cold part of winter. They undoubtedly do so through the more elevated parts of New Mexico, but in the lower valleys they are apparently active throughout the year. On the west slope of the Organ Mountains skunk tracks were common in the canyon in November, 1908, and, on the east slope of these mountains and around Parker Lake, Gaut found them common and collected specimens in January, 1903, and also in the vicinity of Tularosa during December, 1902. The same year in the San Andres Mountains on the north slope of Salinas Peak at 6,000 feet altitude, where they were reported as common, he was unable to find any trace of them in December. It is probable that they do hibernate even in the valleys during any unusually cold winter weather, but that the duration of the hibernating period is generally short and irregular.

Economic status.—In their food habits and relation to agriculture the skunks are mainly beneficial, doing far more good in their destruction of small rodents and great numbers of insects than could be balanced by the little mischief they do at rare intervals in the poultry yard and in the slight destruction of the eggs of game birds. In number of individuals they probably outrank all other fur-bearing animals of New Mexico, and, while their skins are not very valuable, skunk fur for the State probably yields the highest cash return of any fur. Skins with the maximum of black and minimum area of white bring the highest price. The flesh of the skunk is tender, rich, and of good flavor and by many persons is considered a delicacy. There is generally, however, a strong prejudice against using it for food, but there should be no objection to such use. At times when skunks get too friendly around ranch buildings and cause disturbance by their powerful and offensive odor it is necessary to kill them, but, on the whole, they are extremely interesting and valuable animals that should be given the intelligent protection of popular sentiment.

Method of killing.—By shooting a skunk through the spinal column back of the shoulders or breaking its back with a blow of a club, it is quickly killed and the posterior muscles are paralyzed so that the scent glands can not be discharged. When properly killed a skunk has no more odor than a rabbit.

MEPHITIS MESOMELAS ESTOR Merriam

Arizona Skunk

Mephitis estor Merriam, North Amer. Fauna No. 3, p. 81, 1890.

Type.—Collected at San Francisco Mountain, Ariz., August 7, 1889, by Vernon Bailey.

General characters.—Size rather small, tail conspicuously shorter than in *varians* and white stripes on back wider.

Measurements.—Average of adult males: Total length, 639; tail, 208; hind foot, 69 millimeters. Females: 580, 273, and 63 millimeters, respectively. Weight of type, adult male and very fat, 6½ pounds. Four males caught November 2 at Fruitland, N. Mex., by Clarence Birdseye weighed 3, 4, 6, and 6 pounds, respectively.

Distribution and habitat.—The small and very white Arizona skunks are common over practically all extreme western New Mexico, and in the Rio Grande Valley grade into the larger darker *varians* of the eastern part of the State. (Fig. 52.) Specimens from the San Juan Valley, Zuni, Datil, Mogollon, and Animas Mountain regions are all referred to *estor*, although in a large series of skulls from the Gila National Forest the variation in size is considerable, and a number of individuals can be selected that could better be referred to *varians*. In the Rio Grande Valley, San Andres and Manzano Mountains there are also small specimens that could be referred to *estor*, but the greater number are intermediate or typical *varians*. The intergradation seems to extend over a wide area and to be very gradual, so that no dividing line can be drawn, and it is only in the western part of the State that all the specimens can be considered typical *estor*.

At Deming, in December, 1889, their tracks were found along the sandy borders of the Mimbres River, and in 1908 E. A. Goldman reported them there but not very common. In the Animas Mountains he found them rather scarce, although more numerous around ranch buildings. A specimen was taken in the canyon at 5,800 feet and tracks were seen up to 7,500 feet. In the Burro Mountains Goldman found them abundant along cliffs and rocky ravines, where their tracks and other signs were seen in sandy places and where they had been digging over the ground in search of insects. The stomachs of those caught contained only meat used for trap bait, but their excrement found around the entrance of their dens was composed largely of insect shells. In the Mogollon Mountains he caught one at 8,000 feet and saw their tracks and found where they had been digging for insects still higher on the range. They were said to occur at Alma, Dry Creek, Pleasanton, and Glenwood in the upper Gila Valley and at Joseph still farther up the San Francisco River. In the Gila National Forest region they were found common throughout the Transition and the Upper Sonoran Zones, and tracks of skunks were seen commonly along the trails in the gulches and canyons. In Luna Valley they were especially numerous, and dead carcasses were often seen where poison bait had been put out for wolves and coyotes. In the Datil Mountains, Hollister reported them as occasionally seen, and he collected one skull high up in the range. E. A. Goldman collected one high up in the Zuni Mountains, and at Wingate he reported them as very scarce. At San Raphael near the eastern end of the Zuni Mountains the writer found them rather common around the old adobe houses of the village, where they often left unpleasant reminders of their presence. In the Chuska Mountains they were common, and their tracks and signs were seen in the canyons and up to near the top of the mountains at 8,800 feet. In the San Juan Valley they are common along the brushy river bottoms, along the ranches, and along the cliffs at the sides of the valley.

General habits.—In habits these skunks do not differ essentially from *varians*, except as they occupy different types of country and adapt themselves to local conditions. They seem to prefer rocky situations along the base of cliffs or in canyons, where they find safe retreats and comfortable dens in which to live. At night they hunt along the trails and the banks of streams and lagoons for their varied mammal and insect food. They are great burrowers, but apparently do not climb trees. Their presence is most frequently made known by their tracks in the dusty trails or by the strong odor left where some unfriendly dog or other animal has disturbed them. They are not infrequently seen lying dead along the sides of the road or trail, where some passerby has tried his rifle or revolver on them just for the fun of shooting something. Many of the people in the country formerly believed that the bite of the skunk conveyed hydrophobia and use this as an excuse for killing them on every possible occasion. Though any skunk affected with rabies may convey the disease to any animal it bites, this is no more true with skunks and is much less common with them than with dogs, coyotes, and other animals that after inoculation give the disease to others. The writer has many times slept on the ground in camp where these skunks were often heard pattering about his bed at night, but in no case did they ever offer to bite or molest him or any other member of the parties with which he camped. Through many seasons of field work within the range of these skunks the negative evidence of hydrophobia being endemic among them seems of considerable weight.

Near Fruitland, Clarence Birdseye reported them as unusually abundant in November, 1908, and said that at least one man was regularly engaged in trapping them for their fur. Birdseye caught 3 specimens in traps, 1 on a trail through a piece of brush near the river, 1 in an unused house near the ranch, and another in a trap set near the edge of a prairie-dog burrow at the edge of town. At wood-rat nests in the sandstone ledges a mile back from the river at Fruitland and Shiprock, he reported much skunk excrement, composed principally of the remains of various insects. At Blanco a few days later he reported them as common and said that they did considerable damage on the ranches by killing chickens and eating eggs. The stomach of one caught among the willows near the river contained principally insects, mostly grasshoppers.

Breeding habits.—There are records of four and five fetuses in this species, but probably these do not represent the normal number of a litter in adult breeding females. Evidently but one litter is raised in a season, and the young are almost full-grown skunks by the time their fur is prime in October and November.

Hibernation.—Like other species these skunks become extremely fat in autumn and in the higher and colder parts of their range undoubtedly hibernate for a considerable length of time during winter. In the valleys, however, they seem to be active throughout the winter, at least during mild weather. At Deming their tracks were found in the sand in December, and specimens were collected on the Gila National Forest by Hotchkiss in December and February, and in the San Juan Valley at Fruitland and Blanco by Birdseye in November.

Economic status.—The skins of this species are less valuable than are the larger and blacker *varians* and *hudsonicus* farther east, but a large number are marketed each year for fur, and the abundance of the animals makes them one of the most important fur bearers of the region. A great part of their range is grazing land or national forest, but in places, as in the San Juan Valley, where extensive agricultural areas are intensively cultivated by irrigation, the skunks may do some slight damage to poultry and cause some unpleasant odors around the ranch buildings. On the other hand, they are constantly destroying great numbers of injurious insects and rodents, so that on the whole their record may stand as mainly beneficial.

MEPHITIS HUDSONICA Richardson

Northern Plains Skunk

Mephitis americana var. *hudsonica* Richardson, Fauna Boreali-Americana 1: 55, 1829.

Type locality.—Plains of Saskatchewan, Canada.

General characters.—Size very large; tail heavy, black at end; back with two white stripes of medium width and length; skull heavy and wide.

Measurements.—Typical adult males: Total length, 726; tail, 268; hind foot, 82 millimeters. Females: 602, 250, and 71 millimeters, respectively.

Distribution and habitat.—The large dark Northern Plains skunk (pl. 19, A) occupies an extensive area over the plains country and extends southward through the high valleys of Colorado into northern New Mexico. (Fig. 52.) Specimens from Moreno Valley at 7,800 feet on the east slope of Taos Pass, from Lake Burford (Stinking Springs Like) on the Jicarilla Indian Reservation, and from the Capitan Mountains are referable to this species. The skunks reported from the Transition Zone in the Pecos, San Juan, and Jemez Mountains are undoubtedly of this form, but no specimens were taken. It is also probable that those reported on the Transition Zone top of the Sacramento Range may be of this form, as the country is very similar to the rest of the area occupied by the species, and those from the Capitan Mountains would indicate their continuation through the rest of the range. Apparently they do not go below the Transition Zone, nor to any extent into the Canadian Zone above. Near the headwaters of the Pecos they were reported up to 8,000 feet in the yellow-pine forest.

General habits.—In Moreno Valley one was caught September 13 at the edge of the yellow-pine forest, where it had been digging in the mellow earth for insect larvæ and possibly for mice. It was then very fat, and the fur was dense and full. At Stinking Springs Lake (now Lake Burford), in September, 1904, their tracks were abundant along the rocky cliffs, in the trails along the gulches and along the edge of the tule-bordered lakes. Four specimens that were trapped were all very fat, and their food was shown by the examination of the stomach contents to be mainly insects, chiefly grasshoppers, crickets, and beetles. Their excrement scattered along the trails was also composed mainly of the hard parts of insects. The abundance of these skunks around the lakes where great numbers of ducks and other waterfowl breed in summer suggest a possible danger to the eggs and young of the birds in this important breeding ground. The same species in North Dakota, where they congregate in unusual numbers along the borders of the lakes in summer, is known to be very destructive to eggs and young of breeding water birds, and in the evenings the writer has watched them frantically searching through the tules and tall grass for nests.

Breeding habits.—These skunks are prolific breeders, although they raise but one litter of young in a season and have none too much time for that between their long winter sleeps. The mammae are arranged in 6 pairs—1 pair of inguinal, 2 of abdominal, and 3 of pectoral—and litters of 4, 6, and 7 young have been recorded. It is probable that at times the families are even larger than this, but in any case they seem to multiply rapidly enough to maintain their abundance.

Economic status.—On account of their large size, dark color, and very full pelage, these skunks are among the most valuable for fur. Some individuals are almost entirely black, and occasionally one may be found with no trace of white. They probably offer the best stock from which to select choice breeding skunks for fur farms, and if properly handled are easily raised in considerable numbers.

MEPHITIS MACROURA MILLERI Mearns

Northern Hooded Skunk

Mephitis milleri Mearns, U. S. Natl. Mus. Proc. 20: 467, 1897.

Type.—Collected at Fort Lowell, near Tucson, Ariz., November 13, 1893, by F. X. Holzner.

General characters.—Compared with other species of Mephitis, this is a small, slender skunk with a very long tail. The long hairs of the neck and back of head often form a cape or hood, which is usually white. In some species the whole back, top of tail, and a narrow stripe along each side are white. In others the white is reduced to a narrow stripe along each side, and the whole back and top of tail are black. The diverging white lines on the back of the common skunk are rarely seen in this species, but a white stripe between the eyes is usually present.

Measurements.—Average of typical adult males: Total length, 672; tail, 359; hind foot, 65 millimeters. Females: 668, 357, and 61 millimeters, respectively.

Distribution and habitat. — Specimens of the northern hooded skunk have been collected in New Mexico at Redrock and Gila and at Cloverdale ranch in the Animas Valley, and in 1906 the writer saw a dead one, which was not saved, in the valley of the Mimbres, about 7 miles above Mimbres post office. Apparently this is a Lower Sonoran species occupying the valley country of southwestern New Mexico and southern Arizona.

General habits.—In habits these white-sided skunks are rather more active and sprightly than are the heavier species of Mephitis, but they do not approach in weasellike motions the little spotted skunks. They are generally found along the stream valleys or in canyons, where they follow the trails and resort to rocky ledges or brushy bottoms for cover and concealment during the day. At Redrock E. A. Goldman collected four specimens in September and October, 1908, in the woods along the river and along the base of cliffs. At Gila, farther up the river, he collected three specimens October 11, 1908, and reported their tracks numerous in fields and along the trails in the valley bottom. The stomach of one of these caught near the river was well filled with fragments of large black beetles, but the stomachs of the others were all empty, except for bark and sticks, which they had chewed up while in the traps. The food habits are apparently not very different from those of other skunks of the genus, but little is actually known concerning them.

Breeding habits.—In this group the mammae are arranged in 5 pairs—2 pairs of inguinal, 1 pair of abdominal, and 2 pairs of pectoral—and 5 embryos have been recorded in females taken for specimens.

Hibernation.—There seem to be no data as to the hibernation of these skunks, but specimens have been taken in November, December, and February, and it seems doubtful whether they do regularly hibernate in the warm valleys which they occupy.

Economic status.—The fur of this species is very long and light, and while generally considered of no great value, it is, however, in prime individuals very soft and fine and probably well worth cultivating for its length and airy texture. The good that these skunks may do in destroying insects is probably of considerable importance locally and may overbalance their occasional mischief in destroying poultry or the eggs of game birds.

CONEPATUS MESOLEUCUS MEARNSI Merriam

Hog-nosed Skunk; Mearns's Conepatus

Conepatus mesoleucus mearnsi Merriam, Biol. Soc. Wash. Proc. 15:163, 1902.

Type.—Collected at Mason, Tex., February 20, 1886, by Ira B. Henry.

General characters.—Conepatus is a large skunk, with long naked nose, very long claws, brownish-black body, and solid white back and tail.

Measurements.—Adult male: Total length, 670; tail, 290; hind foot, 75 millimeters. Adult female: 628, 243, and 72 millimeters, respectively.

Distribution and habitat.—There are specimens of the hog-nosed skunk in the Biological Survey collection from the San Andres, Capitan, and Jicarilla Mountains; from Lake Valley, Hillsboro, head of Mimbres, and Diamond Creek. A specimen recorded by Barber (1902, p. 192) from the west base of the Sandia Mountains in a canyon 18 miles east of Albuquerque gives the northernmost limit of the known range of the species in the State. It is mainly confined to the Lower Sonoran valleys and the hot canyons around the foothills of the desert mountains.

General habits.—Near the head of the Rio Mimbres Valley, in the bottom of the canyon, the writer found two of these skunks dead, evidently from eating poison put out for wolves. A few scattered mesquite bushes at this place showed that they were not much out of their zone. At Lake Valley E. A. Goldman collected one at the edge of a wet field. In the northwest foothills of the Jicarilla Mountains, Gaut collected one at a crevice in the rocks, where great numbers of chicken feathers were scattered about, and at a ranch near by chickens had been missing at frequent intervals. In the canyon east of Albuquerque, Barber caught an immature specimen in a trap baited with carrion, but was not able to catch any more in several weeks' trapping at the locality. (Barber, 1902, p. 192.)

Although these skunks seem to be common over most of the lower Sonoran area of New Mexico, they are not often collected, as they seem to prefer their natural food supply of beetles and larvae to the ordinary trap bait. Occasionally one is seen in the evening trotting along the trails in a very skunklike fashion, and if closely approached the familiar method of defense is exhibited. This natural weapon is fully as powerful and effective as that of any skunk and in no way distinguishable from them. Their peculiar, long, flexible nose apparently adapts them to the successful capture of an abundant supply of ground beetles, which make shallow burrows in the mellow soil of the valleys. In this habit they perhaps differ somewhat from the skunks in a more exclusive diet, but they are by no means restricted to this fare.

Food habits.—In Texas, where the writer had a better chance to study the habits of these skunks, their food was found to be mainly large beetles and their larvae, mingled with grasshoppers, crickets, and the ripe fruit of the pricklypear. It is evident that they will eat any kind of meat, fresh or stale, and capture poultry or small game that comes in their way, but apparently their food is mainly insects.

Breeding habits.—Of the actual breeding habits of this species little seems to be known. The arrangement of mammae in 3 pairs— 1 pair of inguinal and 2 pairs of pectoral—would indicate small litters of young.

Hibernation.—These skunks sometimes become moderately fat, and it is not improbable that they hibernate for a brief time in the colder parts of their range. In most of the warm valleys that they occupy, however, there is little excuse for their taking a winter vacation except for short periods of unusual cold.

Economic status.—With their short, harsh fur, nearly half of which is white and the rest a rusty black, their skins are of little value. Their insectivorous habits make them of considerable value to agriculture and probably more than counterbalance the occasional mischief they do to poultry and some possible destruction of eggs of game birds. Most of their range, however, is over the desert valleys where no agriculture is possible and where they are of no great economic importance.

CONEPATUS MESOLEUCUS VENATICUS Goldman

ARIZONA HOG-NOSED SKUNK

Conepatus mesoleucus venaticus Goldman, Jour. Mammal. 3:40, February, 1922.

Type.—Collected at Blue River (12 miles south of Blue), Ariz., September 1, 1914, by E. A. Goldman.

General characters.—Similar to *C. m. mearnsi* but small and with relatively narrow skull.

Measurements.—Type specimen, old male: Total length, 630; tail, 230; hind foot, 76 millimeters.

Distribution and habitat.—The Arizona hog-nosed skunk barely comes into the southwestern corner of New Mexico, where a specimen from the Animas Valley and one from Dry Creek near the Gila River are referred to it. Others from the Mimbres Valley show characters grading toward it, but are referred to *mearnsi*.

SPILOGALE ARIZONAE Mearns

ARIZONA SPOTTED SKUNK

Spilogale phenax arizonae Mearns, Bul. Amer. Mus. Nat. Hist. 3: 256, 1891.

Type.—Collected at Fort Verde, Ariz., March 13, 1886, by E. A. Mearns.

General characters.—Much striped and spotted, and light, slender, active, little animals, quite different from the slow heavy Mephitis and Conepatus, but with the same bushy tails and powerful odor. There are usually four narrow white stripes along the front half of the back, while the rump is variously spotted with white and usually the terminal half or quarter of the tail is white. Body color black.

Measurements.—Typical male specimens: Total length, 422; tail, 151; hind foot, 45 to 46 millimeters. Adult females: 380, 148, and 40 millimeters, respectively.

Distribution and habitat.—Specimens examined in the Biological Survey collection from the Animas Mountains, Hachita, Deming,

Burro Mountains, Redrock, and head of Mimbres River show the range of the Arizona spotted skunk to cover at least the southwestern part of New Mexico. (Fig. 53.) Farther limits of its range are not known, but as some form of spotted skunk is found over practically all the low country of the State, the range of some of the species is more extensive than is shown by the present limited series of specimens. These little skunks occupy both the Upper and the Lower Sonoran Zones and within their limits are generally found where there is any protecting cover. They prefer rocky canyons and cliffs, but are common also in brushy gulches and the timbered foothill country, where occasional thickets or rock piles afford protection. They even wander in the open valleys to some extent and make use of any weed patch, cactus bed, or burrow in a gulch bank for protection from enemies and the midday heat and glare of a desert region. At Cliff and Glenwood they were said to be fairly common along the brushy bottoms of the Gila and San Francisco Rivers, and near the head of the Mimbres the writer found one dead in the bottom of the canyon, where it had evidently eaten poison placed for wolves. E. A. Goldman caught one at a ledge of rocks on the slope of a low hill near Hachita, another among some rocks at the base of the Little Florida Mountains just south of Deming, and one in a cliff in the Burro Mountains. In the Animas Mountains Goldman and Birdseye

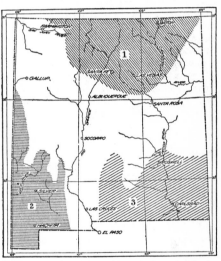

FIGURE 53.—Distribution of spotted skunks in New Mexico: 1, *Spilogale tenuis; 2, S. arizonae arizonae; 3, S. leucoparia*

caught them in the canyon at 5,800 feet, others higher up, and one near the summit of Animas Peak.

General habits.—In the arrangement and practical use of their powerful and offensive odor, these little animals are very like the other skunks. It is possible that there is a difference in their odor from that of Mephitis, but in its full strength this difference is obscured. In a light trace of the odor there is perhaps a foxlike suggestion. In general habits they are bright, quick, and active, with larger eyes and more intelligent expression than the other skunks have. They climb trees readily, and about old cabins or even occupied log houses they will run over the logs and walls and roofs with great freedom, sometimes giving considerable annoyance to the occupants. In the woods they seem to enjoy running over logs and sometimes make their homes in hollow trees or under logs or brush heaps, but more often in the little caves and cavities among the rocks. They are mainly nocturnal but are sometimes seen out hunting early in the twilight or at dawn. They are easily caught in traps baited with any kind of meat, bird feathers, or rabbit fur set among the trails or cliffs where they run. In traps they rarely discharge their scent, and if killed by shooting through the spinal column or with a quick blow across the back they usually may be taken out of the trap without any perceptible odor. Naturally they seem to be gentle and not much afraid, and often when trapped they will allow one to approach quietly to within a few feet without using their weapon of defense.

Among the residents of the country they are often spoken of as hydrophobia skunks or sometimes as " phoby " skunks, and there is a very general belief that their bite will always convey rabies. At Lordsburg it was reported that a man there who was bitten on the arm by a skunk died of hydrophobia five or six years later. Many of the old residents will tell you of cases where the bite has resulted in rabies, but generally after the story has passed from one to another there is no tracing it to any specific case. Undoubtedly at times individuals become affected with rabies and in such case would readily convey it to man or other animals by their bite. In many years' experience in camp among this and other species of the genus, the writer has often heard them pattering on the leaves around his blankets at night, but even where they were common has never known personally of their attempting to bite anyone sleeping on the ground.

Food habits.—In the Animas Mountains, Clarence Birdseye reported the food as consisting largely of grasshoppers and other insects, including the remains of a scorpion found in one of the stomachs examined. These skunks are said to catch the mice around cabins and it is probable that their food consists of a great variety of small rodents as well as of insects. They are attracted to traps by any kind of meat, fur, or feathers.

Breeding habits.—Very little is known of the breeding habits, but the mammae are arranged in 4 pairs, 1 pair of inguinal, 1 pair of abdominal, and 2 pairs of pectoral.

Hibernation.—In autumn these spotted skunks become exceedingly fat and probably, in at least a part of their range, hibernate for a brief period, but much of the country they occupy is characterized by mild winters, and it is doubtful if hibernation is very regular or of long duration with them.

Economic status.—The fur of these little skunks is very soft and fine and is quite fashionable and extensively worn. A great many are trapped for their skins during the late fall and in winter. In the destruction of insects and rodents they are locally of some importance to agriculture. In some cases they may do slight mischief to ranch poultry, and it is very probable that they destroy a few eggs and young of native birds. On the whole, however, they are probably more beneficial than injurious, and their value as fur bearers renders them of considerable importance.

SPILOGALE LEUCOPARIA Merriam

Rio Grande Spotted Skunk

Spilogale leucoparia Merriam, North Amer. Fauna No. 4, p. 11, 1890.

Type.—Collected at Mason, Tex., December 2, 1885, by Ira B. Henry.
General characters.—In external characters scarcely distinguishable from *arizonae*, but the skulls differ conspicuously in being relatively higher and narrower and with more swollen mastoid capsules.
Measurements.—Adult males average: Total length, 402; tail, 145; hind foot, 47.7 millimeters. Adult females 377, 147, and 41 millimeters, respectively.

Distribution and habitat.—The Rio Grande spotted skunk is mainly a Texas and eastern New Mexico species, of which there is one specimen from near Tularosa, N. Mex. (Fig. 53.) "Hydrophobia cats" reported from the Pecos Valley and other localities in eastern New Mexico can probably all be safely referred to this species, which is common just below the line in western Texas, but the limits of its range are entirely unknown and much material is needed before it can be satisfactorily worked out.

General habits.—Near Tularosa, Gaut collected a specimen close to an irrigation ditch in the foothills of the Sacramento Mountains, but he said that the species was considered rare there by the ranchmen. The stomach of this individual was examined and found to contain flesh and feathers apparently from a chicken. In Texas, where the writer has been familiar with the species, their general habits apparently do not differ materially from those of *arizonae*. So little is on record of their actual breeding or food habits that a note by Howard Lacey from Kerrville, Tex., in 1906 is of especial interest. He found a little spotted skunk in a hollow log with two young ones, together with the remains of young rabbits and the shell of a wild turkey's egg. A careful study of the habits of these little animals would well repay some local naturalist.

SPILOGALE TENUIS Howell

Rocky Mountain Spotted Skunk

Spilogale tenuis Howell, Biol. Soc. Wash. Proc. 15: 241, 1902.

Type.—Collected at Arkins, Colo., November 13, 1899, by R. S. Weldon.
General characters.—Externally this little spotted skunk is not noticeably different from *leucoparia* and *arizonae*, but the long, narrow skull readily distinguishes it from any other species in the State.
Measurements.—The type, an adult male, measured: Total length, 450; tail, 165; hind foot, 51 millimeters. A female from near Folsom, N. Mex.: 400, 160, and 47 millimeters, respectively.

Distribution and habitat.—The Rocky Mountain spotted skunk is a rather local form that has been taken along the eastern foothills of the Colorado Mountains and in the mountains of northeastern New Mexico. (Fig. 53.) There are specimens in the Biological Survey collection from Oak Canyon near Folsom, Bear Canyon near Trinchera Pass, and the eastern base of Sierra Grande. These localities give only a suggestion of its range within the State, as there are no more specimens from northern or eastern New Mexico until we strike *leucoparia* at Tularosa. Most of the localities where it has been taken are at the upper edge of the Upper Sonoran Zone or at the lower edge of the Transition Zone. The species probably belongs to the Sonoran Zone, but extends up on warm canyon slopes to the extreme limits of Sonoran environment. They are generally found among rocks or in timbered gulches and sometimes take up their residence around cabins or in abandoned shacks. In the Raton Range, A. H. Howell reported two specimens trapped among big rocks high up on the side of Oak Canyon, where they were said to be common, and at Bear Canyon he secured a skull where two had been killed in a garden a few days before his arrival. An old skull that he picked up at Sierra Grande is very small and may possibly represent another species, but until more material is obtained is provisionally referred to *tenuis*. At Chama, N. Mex., Cary reported little spotted skunks as not uncommon, and it is probable that these also were *tenuis*, although no specimens have been taken in that region to prove it. Specimens from Coventry, Colo., show a close approach to *tenuis*, so the range of the form has been mapped across most of the mountain country of northern New Mexico.

SPILOGALE AMBIGUA [29] Mearns

Chihuahua Spotted Skunk

Spilogale ambigua Mearns, U. S. Natl. Mus. Proc. 20: 460, 1897.

Type.—Collected at Eagle Mountain, Chihuahua, about 4 miles south of monument 15 on the Mexican boundary line, March 23, 1892, by E. A. Mearns and F. X. Holzner.

General characters.—A very well-marked southern form and easily recognized by the high, narrow brain case of the skull.

Distribution and habitat.—There are no typical specimens of the Chihuahua spotted skunk from New Mexico, but the fact that the type came from only 4 miles south of the New Mexico boundary in a region where the little spotted skunks are common would indicate that eventually, when more material is obtained, this species will be added to the New Mexico list with a range covering at least a part of the southwestern border of the State.

New Mexico seems to be the center for the meeting of several forms of this group, but until specimens have been collected from a great number of localities throughout all parts of the State where they occur the details of distribution and relationship must remain in a very unsatisfactory condition. An interesting season's field work for some naturalist with time to devote to local problems would be the field study of the skunks of New Mexico, the collection of sufficient specimens to define their ranges, and the accumulation of notes fully to illustrate their habits. Such a study would yield results of both scientific and economic value.

TAXIDEA TAXUS BERLANDIERI Baird

Mexican Badger; Cald-na-una of the Taos Indians

Taxidea berlandieri Baird, Mammals North Amer., p. 205, 1859.

Type.—Collected at Llano Estacado, Tex., near border of New Mexico, May 8, 1855, by Capt. J. Pope.

General characters.—The badger is a sturdy little animal, short and wide, with short tail and legs and very long front claws. The body hair is long and

---

[29] Specimens from the Animas Mountains show a tendency toward the characters of *ambigua,* but are referred to *arizonae.*

coarse and of a yellowish-gray color, while that of the feet, nose, and face is black. The cheeks are marked with white, and a white stripe extends from the nose over the crown to the shoulders or sometimes along the center of the back to the base of the tail.

Measurements.—An old male from Lake Valley measures: Total length, 730; tail, 120; hind foot, 120 millimeters. There seems to be but little difference in the size of the sexes. The longest front claw measures usually from 1 to 1½ inches in length, varying greatly with the degree of wear from digging. Weight estimated at approximately 20 to 30 pounds, although there are records up to 42 pounds.

Distribution and habitat.—The badgers [30] are generally distributed over the whole of New Mexico without much regard to climate or physiographic features, except as these modify the abundance of their food supply. Their numbers are greatest in the valleys where prairie dogs and ground squirrels abound and least in the timbered and rocky mountain areas where there are no burrowing rodents. Locally they are abundant in the Lower Sonoran as well as the Upper Sonoran valleys, and likewise in the open Transition Zone areas where food is available. As much of the Canadian Zone is timbered, they are least abundant there but are often common near or above timber line in the open spaces of Hudsonian Zone and even Arctic-Alpine Zone where they wander, at least in summer, through the meadows and over the open slopes in search of small game. It seems doubtful, however, whether they spend the winters at these higher altitudes; it is more probable that their natural wandering habits carry them up there during the brief summer period. Their center of abundance is certainly within the Austral Zones, and their breeding area is probably restricted to them.

General habits.—The badgers are pugnacious little animals with as much confidence in their fighting powers as the skunks have in their weapon of defense. Their powerful muscles, tough hide, and often a coat of thick fat, together with their long, dense fur, make them practically immune from the attacks of other animals of their own and generally of much greater size. Their powerful jaws and sharp teeth give them deadly weapons of defense and also a confidence in their powers of self-protection that enables them to wander without fear over wide stretches of open country where there is no external protection except the burrows that they dig. But few dogs unassisted can kill a badger, and a badger will often kill a dog two or three times its own size. Besides having a rank odor and being tough and unpalatable, they are evidently not popular with the larger carnivores, so that man is practically their only important enemy. They are hunters, and their prey is almost entirely the burrowing rodents of the open country, their structure and habits fitting them for unearthing these little animals with the greatest ease and celerity. As the rodent colonies are thinned out in one locality the badgers do not hesitate to strike off over unknown areas for fresh hunting grounds, so that wandering individuals may be found at almost any spot. They are both nocturnal and

---

[30] The finer subspecific relations in this group have not been worked out, and it is probable that more than the one form is included in the specimens from New Mexico. The darker colored individuals from the northern part of the State may belong to the Colorado form, which has been named *Taxidea taxus phippsi* by Figgins, but the rapid accumulation of material renders the present time inopportune for the final working up of the group.

diurnal and apparently keep traveling until a good meal is obtained and then sleep until they are again hungry and it is time to start out in search of the next meal. The last burrow dug in pursuit of some fat ground squirrel or prairie dog usually serves for temporary lodgings until hunger drives the animal out, but if no burrow is available one is quickly made to serve as a resting place. So rapidly do they dig that even while fighting off a dog one will often gain a few moments time in which to sink a well and bury itself before the very eyes of the hesitating enemy. Once below ground the badger's escape is almost assured, for it digs rapidly and turning around pushes out loads of the loose earth in front of its breast without emerging from the burrow, and when it is well down, instead of shoving its loads outside, it packs the earth into the entrance and closes the door, and continues the burrow indefinitely with only a narrow chamber between the point of excavation and the closed door behind it. So rapidly does the animal work that a man with a spade is rarely able to overtake it when once started in extending its burrow.

Food habits.—As previously stated, the principal food of the badgers is burrowing rodents, but this is varied by insect and other animal diet. Their favorite game consists of prairie dogs and ground squirrels. A fat prairie dog makes a good meal for a badger, and usually where prairie dogs and ground squirrels are common the badgers are as fat as the little animals on which they live. On a ranch near Carlsbad in the Pecos Valley one was found living with a colony of prairie dogs in an irrigated alfalfa field. For over two weeks while the writer was observing this colony the badger dug out a few burrows every night. When finally shot for a specimen it was found to be very fat, and although the stomach was empty, the intestines contained nothing but wads of prairie-dog fur. On a trip from Deming to Animas Valley in August, 1908, the writer found badgers' burrows and tracks all along the way and numerous excavated burrows where prairie dogs, ground squirrels, kangaroo rats, and mice had been dug out. In the Datil Mountains in 1906, he caught a badger near camp in Jewett Gap, where it had been digging out prairie-dog burrows at night, but when taken from the trap its stomach was empty and only the hair and bones of meadow mice (*Microtus mogollonensis*) could be identified in the lower intestines. Its last meal had evidently consisted of these mice, which were abundant about the vicinity and with which it occasionally varied its prairie-dog diet.

At Fairview E. A. Goldman found one nosing about among the drift material at high-water mark in an arroyo from which the water had recently receded, apparently in search of insects. Its stomach, however, contained a pocket gopher besides at least one grasshopper and a quantity of unidentified material. Not far from there Goldman also found six groups of pocket-gopher burrows in each of which there was a fresh badger hole; and in only one of these groups was there any recent work. The badger had evidently succeeded in capturing most of the pocket gophers. In other places, however, the writer had found where a great deal of time and hard work had been wasted in pursuit of these rival burrowers. On the Jicarilla Indian Reservation a badger shot at 6 p. m. had part of a prairie dog in its stomach, and another shot at 9 a. m. as it came out of the water after swimming across a wide pond at Lake Burford had a prairie dog and part of a young cottontail in its stomach. In the San Juan Valley in 1908 badgers were common throughout the valley and over the surrounding country, where they were busily digging out prairie dogs, ground squirrels, kangaroo rats, and pocket gophers. At Lake Valley, E. A. Goldman found one with a garter snake in its stomach, and near Cuervo at the northern end of the Staked Plains McClure Surber caught one near camp with its stomach full of pupae of cicadas, which were especially numerous in that vicinity. The badger diggings had previously been noticed under the cactus bushes where these insects were rapidly coming out of the ground. At the base of the Capitan Mountains in 1903 Gaut trapped a badger in a chicken house at Hunt's ranch, where it had been getting a chicken every night for some time. At Wingate, Hollister reported a number of badger skins at one of the ranch houses where they were said to be very destructive to poultry, sometimes cleaning out a chicken house in one visit.

Breeding habits.—The badgers breed early in the summer in their underground dens, where the young are fed and cared for until they are old enough to come out and dig for their own food. There are little data as to the number of young or the breeding habits, but the 4 pairs of mammae in the females, arranged in 2 pairs of inguinal, 1 pair of abdominal, and 1 pair of pectoral, would indicate moderate sized families as the rule. Four to five young have been reported.

Hibernation.—In the more elevated and northern localities with the first freezing weather of early winter the badgers dig deep burrows and begin a long winter's sleep well supplied with a thick blanket of fat on which to draw for nourishment. They do not usually enter hibernation, however, until long after most of their prey have begun their winter sleep, and only when the ground becomes so frozen that digging out the sleeping rodents is no longer a pleasant pastime. In spring they commonly emerge from hibernation with the first heavy thaw that softens the ground sufficiently to render the opening of their burrows an easy matter. From that time until the appearance of the rodents considerably later in spring they wander about over the country picking up any food that is available, still depending largely on their last year's supply of fat, while the males hunt for mates over a wide area of country. In the lower valleys of southern New Mexico it is doubtful if they hibernate at all or for more than the brief period of some cold storm, but the winter store of fat is evidently useful in carrying them through the cold weather when food is not so easily obtained as in the warm seasons.

Economic status.—In the irrigated valleys badgers occasionally do some damage to the elevated banks of ditches when digging after the pocket gophers, ground squirrels, and mice, their large burrows occasionally tapping the water level and letting the ditch banks cut through and the water escape. These occasional accidents are, however, insignificant in comparison with their activities in destroying rodents along the ditches, which thus prevent more numerous and equally serious disasters to the banks. The fact that they occasionally kill poultry in unprotected situations is well known, but this is not serious, as they can not climb, and a strip of poultry netting close to the ground is usually ample protection for the fowls. The most serious complaint against the badger is of the large burrows it leaves scattered over the plains and along the roads, burrows made in the continual destruction of rodent pests, but no less a danger and source of annoyance and anxiety to horsemen riding over the plains. So serious is this menace to the cowboy that an opportunity to shoot, rope, and drag the badgers is rarely lost. The ranchmen commonly share this feeling toward them, although the more intelligent usually recognize their great economic value in keeping down rodent pests. Within certain limits badgers are among the most harmless and useful of all our carnivorous animals, but over much of the country they have been so wantonly destroyed that their numbers are greatly reduced, and it becomes necessary to use artificial means to control the pests that they would have destroyed.

Family BASSARISCIDAE: Cacomistles

BASSARISCUS ASTUTUS FLAVUS Rhoads

Bassaris; Civet Cat; Cacomistle; Ringtail

Bassariscus astutus flavus Rhoads, Acad. Nat. Sci. Phila. Proc. 1893: 417, 1894.

Type.—Collected in Texas in 1861 by A. L. Heermann.

General characters.—The beautiful little cacomistle has the face of a fox, the body of a buffy-gray marten, and a long bushy tail with a black tip and about seven black and seven white bars or rings. The tail is approximately the same length as the head and body, and the broad black bands give it a striking character shared by no other North American animal except in a slight degree by the raccoon.

Measurements.—An adult male measures in total length, 796; tail, 415; hind foot, 70 millimeters; and a female 756, 383, and 67 millimeters, respectively.

Distribution and habitat.—The civet cat or, as often called, ring-tailed cat or ringtail is fairly common over all of the Upper Sonoran part of New Mexico except the open plains and valleys. Although it may in places occupy the Lower Sonoran areas, it does not usually extend beyond the upper limits of the Upper Sonoran Zone. It inhabits the cliffs and canyons and does not stray far from these haunts on which it depends for protection and hunting ground. There are specimens in the Biological Survey collection from near Redrock, Jarilla, and the Guadalupe Mountains, and many reports of their occurrence. They are reported as occurring in all the warm deep canyons of the Mogollon Mountains and in the foothills of the Black Range and along both slopes of the Sacramento Mountains. There are fewer reports of them in the northern part of the State, but they occur in western Texas, southern Colorado, and in Arizona, although nowhere in great numbers.

General habits.—These bright-faced little animals are nocturnal in habits and rarely seen except when they are caught in traps or occasionally come into cabins or camps. They have, however, a wide range and are often present where not suspected. Along the dusty shelves and in the caves of the cliffs and canyons their little round catlike tracks are often seen where they have been prowling for cliff mice and wood rats. Occasionally one gets into a trap set for some other animal and baited with the carcasses of birds, mice, or rats. Near Jarilla, Gaut caught one in a trap baited with the body of a small bird and set under an engine house at the copper mine. At Redrock near the Gila River, E. A. Goldman caught one in a trap at the base of a cliff of Box Canyon about 3 miles above town. When approached in the trap it screamed loudly and jumped at him in a threatening manner, trying to bite his foot and struggling violently to escape. At Glenwood on the San Francisco River these animals were said to be rather common in the canyons well back into the Mogollon Mountains, and a Mr. Kit told the writer of several young ones that he had caught and tamed. He had kept them in camp and said that they were very interesting pets. It seems to be a common practice of the miners to catch and tame these animals and keep them in their cabins for protection against the rats and mice, which often are troublesome. They are said to be better mousers than house cats and are certainly much more attractive animals.

Food habits.—Though mainly carnivorous, the bassaris also eats fruit and a variety of other articles. Apparently it is also fond of poultry when it is easily available.

Breeding habits.—Little is known of the actual breeding habits of this species, but in Texas an old female collected on May 26 contained three large fetuses. Another was reported with four young, so that the normal number of young would probably vary from two to four.

Economic status.—The fur of these animals is soft and lax and of no great beauty or value. The skins are usually saved by the trappers but bring an insignificant price. As a check on the overabundance of rodent pests they doubtless have considerable economic value, but to what extent this is counterbalanced by their possible destruction of game, especially of game birds and nests, is not at present known. They have a possible value as pets, but probably could not be allowed to run at liberty where poultry and birds could be reached. Their scarcity and scattered distribution under present conditions render them of little economic importance.

Family PROCYDONIDAE: Coatis and Raccoons

NASUA NARICA PALLIDA ALLEN

COATI; CHOLUGO of the Mexicans

Nasua narica pallida Allen, Bul. Amer. Mus. Nat. Hist. 20:53, 1904.

Type.—Collected in vicinity of Guadalupe y Calva, Chihuahua, Mexico, by Carl Lumholtz.

General characters.—The coatis are about the size of raccoons, with long flexible noses, long hairy tails, plantigrade feet, short ears, and coarse stiff hair. Their general color is rusty brown, with indistinct light markings on nose, face, and shoulders, and usually about 10 distinct dark and 10 light-brown rings on the tail.

Measurements.—A female from Alamos, Sonora, collected by E. A. Goldman, measured: Total length, 1,133; tail, 590; hind foot, 109 millimeters. The males are somewhat larger.

Distribution and habitat.—In the southern end of the Animas Valley in August, 1908, Goldman was told of a strange animal that had been killed by Charles Yarber at his ranch just north of the international boundary and 4 miles southeast of the Culberson ranch. The description of the animal fitted so perfectly with Nasua, with which Goldman had long been familiar in Mexico, that he considered evidence of the occurrence of the species at this locality unmistakable. Although an extension of the known range of the species, the record is not strange as specimens have been taken in south-eastern Arizona equally far north. The deep barrancos of the Rio de Batepito, cutting southward through Sonora from near the border of New Mexico, bring a number of southern forms into this vicinity.

PROCYON LOTOR MEXICANUS Baird

Mexican Raccoon; Pah-su-de'na of the Taos Indians

Procyon hernandezii var. *mexicana* Baird, Pacific Railroad Rpts. 8 : 215, 1857.

Type.—Collected at Espea, Sonora, Mexico, April, 1855, by C. B. R. Kennerly.

General characters.—In general appearance the raccoon somewhat resembles a little gray bear with a pointed nose, black mask, bushy tail encircled by five or six black rings, and large plantigrade feet with naked soles. This Mexican form is decidedly paler than the eastern form, *lotor*.

Measurements.—Adult males: Total length, 865; tail, 300; hind foot, 135 millimeters.

Distribution and habitat.—Raccoons (pl. 19, B) are common along practically every permanent stream in New Mexico up to the lower border of the Canadian Zone. They are not often found far from water, and in many sections of the State are unknown over wide areas where water is scarce or in only scattered localities. They are most abundant along the immediate valleys of the Pecos, Rio Grande, and Gila Rivers, and a few are found along the San Juan River Valley, where they seem to be rather scarce.

General habits.—Throughout most of their range in New Mexico the raccoons depend upon cliffs and broken rocks for cover and dens in which to spend the day, and in localities where canyon walls afford ample protection and streams supply their favorite food they are especially numerous. In the lower mountain regions they find some hollow trees in which to make their homes, but over most of their range in the State they are mainly cliff and canyon dwellers. They are strictly nocturnal in habits and their fondness for the water is proverbial. Though rarely seen, except when hunted by dogs at night or caught in traps for their fur, they are most in evidence by their characteristic babylike tracks along the borders of streams and water holes.

Food habits.—In choice of food the raccoons are almost as omnivorous as the bears, although they show the taste of epicures in choosing such dainty morsels as crawfish, mussels, and a variety of fruits, nuts, and game. Any kind of meat seems to attract them readily to traps, even when it is not very fresh, and it is probable that they catch some small game for themselves. Much of their time is spent along the shores of streams and lakes fishing for crawfishes and other crustaceans, the shells of which are conspicuous in their droppings along the trails. The fresh-water mussels are eagerly sought and eaten and the shells piled on the banks, while acorns and many other nuts are favorite food where they can be obtained. The ripe sugary pods of the mesquite bean, which they find on the ground under the trees along the river valleys, often form their principal diet during the late summer and autumn months, while cactus berries and other fruits are gathered whenever available. They are noted for their raids upon fields of green corn and are also fond of watermelons. At Carlsbad, in 1910, Dearborn reported complaints of their robbing both chicken yards and watermelon patches. To get into the watermelons they were said to make a small hole through the rind and through this remove the ripe inner flesh of the melon. In the Raton Range A. H. Howell reported them in 1903 as common in Bear Canyon and very destructive to growing corn. At Deming in 1908 E. A. Goldman reported them common along the Mimbres River, where they did considerable damage in cornfields. In the Magdalena Mountains at the mouth of Water Canyon in September, 1909, he caught one near a cornfield, where the owner had complained of something destroying his crop. Many of the stalks were pulled down and the green ears eaten, while the stomach of the raccoon caught was found well filled with a pulpy mass of green corn. One was trapped in a field where over an area of several acres more than half of the stalks had been stripped of the ears, which had been partly eaten and left scattered over the ground.

Hibernation.—Over the northern part of their range the raccoons hibernate for the greater part of the cold winter, depending on their ample stores of fat under the skin and in the body cavities. Few data are available as to their hibernation in New Mexico, but the fact that they are trapped for fur during a great part of the winter would indicate that they hibernate for only a short time or during the periods of lowest temperatures. From Alcalde in the Rio Grande Valley above Santa Fe there are specimens collected January 26, February 5, 6, and 25, and March 1, 3, and 12 of 1905, and from Velarde and Senega in the same general region specimens collected November 28 and 30, January 6 and 29, February 6, 8, and 28, and March 2 and 11 of the same year. At higher elevations it is probable that they hibernate for a considerable part of the winter, but in the lower valleys they are active at least during the mild weather.

Economic status.—In New Mexico the raccoon is one of the principal fur-bearing animals, and its pelt while of moderate value forms an important share of the trapper's annual harvest. Usually the oil and flesh are thrown away, but sometimes the oil, which has considerable value as a dressing for leather and for other domestic purposes, is saved, and the flesh is by many considered a great delicacy. Though in certain localities there are many complaints of damage in cornfields and occasionally of a raid on the chicken yard by raccoons, in most cases the damage is not of a serious nature and when discovered can be quickly checked by a night hunt with the dogs. The game and fur value of these animals seems to outweigh the mischief they occasionally do, and the general feeling is against their unnecessary destruction. They are one of the few animals, however, that apparently need no artificial protection, as they are very keen in protecting themselves.

Family URSIDAE: Bears

EUARCTOS AMERICANUS AMBLYCEPS [31] (BAIRD)

NEW MEXICO BLACK BEAR; CINNAMON BEAR; OSO NEGRO of the Mexicans; SHAS of the Apache and Navajo Indians; [32] KUA-PUNA-ANA of the Taos Indians

Ursus amblyceps Baird, Rpt. U. S. and Mex. Bound. Survey 2 (pt. 2): 29, 1859.

---

[31] Other forms of the black bear may occur within the State but until the group is more thoroughly studied the specimens are all referred to this form.
[32] On the Navajo Indian Reservation the bears have, until recently, been very little molested, as the Indians associate Shas, the bear, with the spirit world in a manner that has effectually protected it as a nongame species.

Ursus cinnamomeus Baird, Rpt. U. S. and Mex. Bound. Survey 2 (pt. 2): 29, 1859. Applied to brown specimens from Copper Mines, N. Mex.
Ursus machetes Elliot, Field Columb. Mus. Pub. 80 (Zool. ser.) 3:235, 1903, from Casa Grande, Sierra Madre, Chihuahua, Mexico.

Type locality.—" Copper Mines " (near Santa Rita), N. Mex.
General characters.—Size large for a black bear of the *americanus* group; color black or brown, skull short, wide, and high, teeth small.

Distribution and habitat.—Specimens of the small-toothed form of the black bear have been examined from the type locality and various places in the Mogollon and Mimbres Mountains, the Manzano, Capitan, and Raton Mountains; from Ute Park, Colfax County, and Boulder Lake on the Jicarilla Indian Reservation, besides skulls from eastern Arizona and northern Chihuahua just below the New Mexico boundary line.

Black bears are still more or less common in most of the mountain ranges in New Mexico, where there is timber or chaparral to afford them cover and food. In the more open areas they are becoming scarce, and in some of the heavily timbered areas have been trapped and hunted until no longer abundant. (Fig. 54.) In the early pioneer days of the State they were extremely abundant in certain areas where the food supply was unlimited.

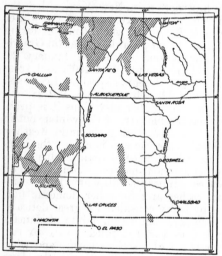

FIGURE 54.—Approximate distribution of the estimated 157 black and brown bears in New Mexico in 1917, from map prepared by J. Stokley Ligon

In 1540 Coronado (Whipple et al., 1856, p. 110; Winship, 1896, pp. 512, 560) reported large numbers of bears before reaching Zuni from the south and saw their " paws " at the pueblo of Zuni, but some of these were undoubtedly grizzly bears. In 1825 the Pattie brothers (Pattie, 1905, p. 118) on a trapping expedition through New Mexico reported killing a large number of bears at their camp one day northward from the copper mines. In 1854 John R. Bartlett (1854, v. 2, p. 556) reported bears extremely abundant at the copper mines. The references to the type and three other specimens collected near the copper mines in 1855 by J. H. Clark are so confused with those of the grizzly bears encountered on the same trip that the relative abundance of these animals at that time can not be told with certainty, for the brown grizzly and brown blacks were not always distinguished in the notes, and apparently not in the field. But even to very recent times the black and cinnamon bears have been abundant in these mountains. In 1894 A. K. Fisher reported black bears abundant in the Mogollon Mountains 80 miles north of Silver City, and in about equal numbers with the grizzlies of that region. In 1909 E. A. Goldman reported a few black bears in the San Mateo Mountains (near Monica Springs) and also a few in the Magdalena Mountains, and in 1905 Hollister reported them as rather scarce in the region west of Burleigh and north of the Gallina Mountains, where they had formerly been common. They were also becoming scarce in the Datil Mountains, only four or five individuals being reported in the range at that time.

In 1906 Victor Culberson, of the GOS ranch on Sapello Creek, about 30 miles north of Silver City, said that since 1885 he had killed 46 bears and helped to kill 70 more. These included what he considered four species—black, cinnamon, brown, and silvertip. The greater part of these were the black, or cinnamon, bears, which were then common in the mountains about there. Throughout these mountains the aspen trees still show the greatest abundance of bear scratches on the white bark seen in any part of the country. In 1908 the writer covered a large part of the Mimbres (or Black) Range and Mogollon Mountain country and found only scattering traces of black bears, which were then restricted to the forested canyons and were rarely seen except as caught in traps. Apparently a few have been killed each year since then, but they are no longer abundant. In 1910 the Forest Service officials reported extensive bear hunting still carried on each year in these mountains and a few animals killed each year. In 1906 the black and cinnamon bears were said to be fairly common in the Tularosa Mountains, where the writer saw a few old signs up to 8,500 feet.

Hollister, while in the Zuni Mountains, in 1905, reported bears as common and at times destructive to stock, and in 1909 E. A. Goldman reported a few in the Zuni Mountains, where he saw some tracks and where one bear was seen near Mount Sedgwick. He reported bear scratches on the aspen trees and along the top of Bear Ridge many stones turned over by bears in search of food. In 1909 Dearborn reported a bear and two cubs shot within 2 miles of Sawyer. In 1905 Hollister reported a few bears still remaining in the Mount Taylor Range, where both black and brown were said to occur, and a few tracks seen near his camp in August. In the Chuska Mountains in 1908 the writer found a few fresh black-bear tracks and an abundance of old bear excrement, but as there were no acorns or pine nuts that year the bears were scattered, and he was not able to locate one. At Fort Defiance the skin of one that had been recently killed in the southern end of the Chuska Range was seen, but its skull had been thrown into the pigpen and destroyed. In the Jemez Mountains in 1906 black and brown bears were said to be fairly common, and many places were seen at altitudes ranging from 8,000 to 11,200 feet where they had turned over stones in search of insect food.

In 1904 in the Gallinas Mountains of Rio Arriba County bears were said to be numerous and destructive to stock, but no tracks or signs could be found save the old scratches on aspen bark. This local scarcity was probably due to the failure of the acorn crop that year and to the fact that the country had been so thoroughly denuded of vegetation by sheep herds that the bears had scattered out for other pastures. In the San Juan Mountains Loring reported bears as common in 1892, and in 1904 the writer was told that they were still fairly common in the Brazos Canyon, where many of their scratches were seen on the bark of aspens. On the Jicarilla Indian Reservation, in 1904, an old skull of a black bear was picked up at a spring near Boulder Lake, which was the only evidence of bears that could be found in that region, but they were reported to be occasionally seen through the timbered part of the reserve. In the Taos Mountains in 1904 a number of fresh bear tracks were seen near camps on Lake Fork of the Hondo and the head of Lucero Creek, while on the east slope of these mountains they were said to be common. The aspens showed numerous claw marks and some old bear feces were found on the timbered slopes of the range. A few black bears were also said to be found in the Culebra Mountains farther north.

In the Raton Mountains in 1903 A. H. Howell saw a few fresh tracks and signs and obtained one skull. A few other black bears were reported and Charles Youngblood, an old trapper living in Bear Canyon, said he had killed 18 in this canyon within the preceding five or six years. In the mountains about the head of the Pecos River in 1903, black and brown bears were fairly common, and fresh signs were frequently seen near the camps. One day at about 11,000 feet on the southeast slope of Pecos Baldy a bear was caught sight of in the spruce forest, but it made such a frantic rush to get out of range that only a blurred streak of black could be detected between the trees. In the Manzano Mountains in 1903, Gaut reported a few bears still inhabiting the higher part of the range and was informed that an old trapper had a few years previously captured quite a number near the Box Spring northwest of Mountainair. A. Rea, from his ranch on the summit of these mountains due west of Tajique, reported a number of bears killed near his place, and he later sent to the survey three good skulls. In 1905 Hollister was informed that there were still a considerable number of bears in this range. In 1902 in the San Andres Mountains Gaut was told by a ranchman near Salinas that two bears had been killed two years previously near his place. In 1889 black bears were numerous in the Capitan Mountains, and in going up the north side of the range the writer found many places where stones had been turned over and saw some fresh bear signs. While he was camped at the east base of these mountains on June 14, a Mexican hunter killed an old bear and two cubs near camp. The cubs were said to be about as big as raccoons and were both black, while the old bear was brown and in the old worn winter fur.

In 1903 Gaut found an abundance of bear signs in the Capitan Mountains and on the west side reported them as common also near Carrizozo. In 1902 in the White Mountains the writer saw several fresh tracks of black bear and several skins that had been lately taken along the headwaters of Ruidoso Creek. In 1900 M. H. Webb, of El Paso, Tex., told E. W. Nelson that bears were becoming scarce in the Sacramento Mountains where they had formerly been common. In 1901 black bears were common in the Guadalupe Mountains near the New Mexico and Texas line, where they lived in security in the dense scrub-oak chaparral and where they are likely to persist for a long time. In 1908 numerous bear signs were seen in the Animas

Mountains, and black and brown bears were said to be common. In 1909 officials of the Forest Service reported bears in the middle and southern portion of the Guadalupe Mountains. In 1914 they reported 8 killed on the Jemez National Forest, 11 on the Pecos, and 12 on the Carson; in 1915, 12 on the Carson, 26 on the Santa Fe, 5 on the Lincoln, and 4 on the Datil; and in 1916, 7 on the Carson, 21 on the Santa Fe, 2 on the Alamo-Lincoln, 3 on the Datil, and 4 on the Gila. These were mainly black or cinnamon, but the species were not separated. In his report for May, 1917, J. S. Ligon estimated 33 black bears killed in the State during the year and 157 remaining in the forests, as indicated on his map of approximate range. (Fig. 54.)

Early records indicate that bears were more generally distributed over the State before it became so fully occupied by settlers and stock and that they wandered farther from their timbered areas of cover and protection than at the present time. Apparently they have no zonal limits in this region and adapt themselves to conditions where food and shelter are obtainable. The principal part of their present distribution, however, is in the heaviest timber of the Transition and the Canadian Zones, although this may be a purely superficial distribution. Their actual breeding range, which is the range of their hibernating area, is mainly within the Canadian Zone in the deep spruce-filled gulches of the mountain slopes. From this level, however, they wander downward in the spring wandering back again and even higher later in summer in their constant search for food, in a few days easily covering any vertical range that is available.

General habits.—Bears are great wanderers, drifting in search of food from one area to another and making long and rapid journeys when a sufficient food supply is not available, but they are among the most timid and wary of the wild animals, and so far as possible keep within the protection of dense cover of timber, brush, and tall vegetation. They are both nocturnal and diurnal in habits, but from long persecution have become largely nocturnal in regions where they are scarce. Their senses of hearing and smell are wonderfully acute, which render them extremely difficult to approach in their dense cover. Even where abundant they are rarely seen except as driven out of some gulch or thicket, and even then they generally keep out of sight in making their escape. They are easily trapped, however, in any place that they are in the habit of passing or where they have located some food supply, such as a dead animal; and trapping has done more to reduce their numbers than all other methods of hunting. They have, however, been successfully hunted with hounds in certain parts of the country, especially in the Mogollon Mountains, where large numbers have been killed by this means.

Food habits.—Although the bears are so omnivorous that almost any food is welcomed, it is interesting to note the different materials chosen for food in different parts of the country. In the Animas Mountains the bear excrement along the trails was made up almost entirely of manzanita berries, acorn shells, and in one instance of well-felted balls of black pig hair. Near the top of these mountains a black cherry tree full of ripe fruit had the branches pulled in and broken all through the top where the bear had been gathering the fruit. In the Datil Mountains, Hollister reported them as feeding at times largely on acorns, pine nuts, and juniper berries, which, when obtainable, they seemed to prefer to any other food.

In the Chuska Mountains, in 1908, the acorn and pine-nut crop had been an entire failure, and the bears had gone in pursuit of such other foods as they could obtain. They were then feeding on bear-berry (*Arctostaphylos uva-ursi*), rose haws, grass, other green vegetation, and insects. Great numbers of stones were turned over by the bears in search of insects, and numerous old dead pine trees had the bark clawed off in search of the borers that work underneath. Several trees were photographed with the broken bark piled on the ground around the base, and bear scratches showing on the naked trunks, which they had climbed in tearing off the bark. Some bear excrement of the previous year showed mainly acorn shells. In the Jemez Mountains, in 1906, the excrement was made up largely of green vegetation, chokecherry pits, acorn shells, seeds of various berries, and fruits that had been eaten, and also ants and beetles. Throughout these mountains great numbers of stones had been turned over in search of insects and larvae. In the Taos Mountains old bear feces near timber line were made up mainly of ants, pine needles, and old dried vegetation, evidently from the early spring food, when anything to fill up would answer the purpose. In these mountains also the stones had been turned over in many areas in search of food.

McClure Surber caught a skunk near the Twining mine at 10,000 feet altitude on October 31, and after killing it left it in the trap until the next day, when skinning it would be less disagreeable. During the night, however, a bear came along and ate the skunk. In the Capitan Mountains, in July, 1889, the writer found numerous stones turned over where the bears had been feeding on insects. In the same mountains, in 1903, Gaut reported them feeding in early summer around the rock piles on raspberries and strawberries, but later turning over rocks in search of insect food. The local hunters reported that the bears in autumn fed largely on the sweet berries of the alligator juniper, upon which they became very fat. The great abundance of these sweet berries throughout the Capitan, White, Sacramento, and Guadalupe Mountains, and in the Manzano and Mogollon regions have undoubtedly been a great attraction to bears.

In the Capitan Mountains, Gaut was told by one of the ranchmen that the bears occasionally killed a few kids from the goat herds. In the Zuni Mountains, Goldman reported several sheep killed by bears near Mount Sedgwick while he was there in 1909. A trap set by a woodcutter was baited with a partly eaten sheep and the bear returned and managed to get the bait without springing the trap. In the Datil Mountains, in 1905, Hollister was told by the ranchmen that the bears in that region live largely on cattle at certain times of year, but these probably were not black bears.

Breeding habits.—Little is known of the actual breeding habits of these bears except as an old female is occasionally seen, shot, or trapped with her cubs, which are usually two in number. In August, 1907, Hotchkiss wrote the writer from Fierro, N. Mex., that he had two cubs, male and female, which had been captured in the mountains near there. They were both black, but their mother, who was killed at the time of their capture, was a brown bear. The young are known to be born late in winter or early in spring while the mother is still in her winter den and are nursed until they are sufficiently grown to come out in the warm spring weather and follow their mother in her search for food. A specimen in the Biological Survey collection from the Mogollon Mountains taken in August, 1907, was about the size of a small dog, and others taken at the same time, judged by their skulls, were apparently over a year old and as large as a good-sized Newfoundland dog, but the full growth is not attained for several years.

Hibernation.—Even in the milder sections of the State these bears become extremely fat in autumn, and with the first heavy snowstorms and cold weather in the mountains they seek their winter quarters in some hollow bank, cave, or scooped-out hollow under a big log or bowlder, where they pass the winter in a state of inactive lethargy. When they first appear early in spring they are said to be still fat, but at this season food is often scarce and their store of fat is usually needed to carry them through until the more abundant summer food is available. Their fur as they enter hibernation is very long and full, but it is said to be more perfectly prime when they first emerge from their winter den. It is then beautifully long, full, wavy, and with a luster that soon begins to wear away with their outdoor activity.

Economic status.—There has been much controversy as to the value of the black and brown bears as fur and game animals, considered in the light of their occasional destruction of domestic stock. In 1910 the Forest Service, at the request of the Bureau of Biological Survey, addressed a circular letter to its supervisors over the Western States, asking for information as to the abundance and depredations of black bears on the national forests and also as to the opinions so far as obtainable from the stockmen and sportsmen of the country in regard to destroying this animal as a predatory species or giving it limited protection as a game animal. The following extracts from replies to this circular from New Mexico are of interest:

From the Jemez National Forest, May 3, 1910, Acting Forest Supervisor B. M. Thomas reported:

The field force on the Jemez seem to be about equally divided on the question as to whether black bears are detrimental to the interests of the forest. They reported only three cattle killed during the past grazing season, and it is certain that losses incurred by stockmen from this source are very small. The sheepmen would probably disapprove of any protection for black bears, though aside from the sheep owners it would not meet with general disapproval and would be gladly received by many, especially those interested in the forest as a recreation ground.

From the Pecos National Forest, April 27, 1910, Forest Supervisor Thomas R. Stewart reported:

I have never known of one single instance where black bears have done any damage to stock on this forest, and I agree with the Biological Survey that they should be considered a game animal and that there should be a closed season on them, the same as on deer and other game animals. I have talked the matter over with stockmen in this vicinity and also with Mr. Gable, Territorial game and fish warden. While Mr. Gable is of the opinion that black bears should be classed as predatory animals, the stockmen, who are most interested in the subject, are generally of the opinion that they do little or no damage to stock and should be considered as game animals and protected.

From the Lincoln National Forest, May 16, 1910, Acting Supervisor James A. Scott reported:

After receiving reports from the officers on this forest, it is found that no damage was done to stock grazed upon the forest the past season by black bears. The majority of officers report that it would not be detrimental to national-forest interests to discontinue the killing of black bears, but such action would be generally disapproved by the people interested in the forest.

From the Manzano National Forest, May 24, 1910, Supervisor W. R. Mattoon reported:

Replies received from the forest officers on the Manzano strongly indicate that very little, if any, damage has been done to stock by black bears. The number of bears on this forest is limited to a few and it is my belief that they do practically no damage to stock except possibly to ranchmen's hogs. The latter is small in amount, since the bear lives high in the mountains where there are scarcely any ranches and hogs are usually not kept on the ranches at high altitudes. I wish to express myself strongly in favor of the bear being classed as a game animal and being hunted and killed only under regulations.

From the Zuni National Forest, May 14, 1910, Acting Supervisor Frederic Winn reported:

The reports received from forest officers indicate that practically no damage has been done to stock on this forest by black bears. One officer on the Mount Taylor division reports that two black bears have been killed by ranchmen within the past two years. Aside from this none has been reported killed and no stock has been reported lost from this cause. The people interested in the forest, from all reports obtainable, are not inclined to class the black bear as a predatory animal. The majority of the forest officers are in favor of classing it as a game animal.

From the Gila National Forest, April 20, 1910, Supervisor Douglas Rodman reported:

Black bears in this vicinity do slight damage only to stock. While they may, of course, be considered to some extent a predatory animal, it is my opinion that the damage done by them is of little importance compared with that done by lions and wolves. I have never heard a permittee in this locality express the opinion that the black bear was seriously detrimental to stock interests. I do know, however, that certain people in this vicinity hunt bear on a large scale during the fall and that the extermination of this animal would be considered by them as a loss.

From the Alamo National Forest, May 6, 1910, Supervisor A. M. Neal reported:

At the present time there are only a few black bears within the boundaries of the Alamo Forest, and consequently the detriment to stock is reduced to a minimum. Even when this species of game was more plentiful their destructive qualities were never much in evidence. In the Mescalero Indian Reservation, where most of the big game is found, no reports have ever reached me which indicated that the black bear had done any damage. It is my firm belief that the people generally and forest officers certainly, in this section, would prefer this animal to remain as a game animal protected by law, and not have it considered as a predatory animal.

From the Datil National Forest, May 14, 1910, Supervisor W. H. Goddard reported:

It is impossible to obtain the exact amount of stock killed by black bears during the past grazing season, but a number of stock that are known to have been killed by predatory animals were supposed to have been killed by black bears. During the year 1909 there were four black bears killed by forest officers and five by forest users. It is impossible to ascertain the number killed in past years. The opinion of forest officers in general is that black bears are a predatory animal, and in one instance the forest officer cites that a black bear with two cubs killed a cow and was found a short time afterwards by cowboys and killed at the carcass. On the Datil National Forest about six months of each year there is no mast and the black bears are compelled to live on other animals which they can kill, and they have been known to follow the grizzly or silvertip in many instances and eat what is left of their kill, thus getting in the habit of eating fresh meat, which soon encourages them in killing what they require for their own food. The public sentiment generally on this forest is in favor of regarding the black bear as a predatory animal and killing it whenever and wherever possible, and it is believed by this office that the discontinuance of the killing of black bear by forest officers would be detrimental to the users of the National Forest and would be disapproved generally by the people interested in the forest.

Thus opinions differ locally as to the relative merits of these bears. At times they undeniably destroy some stock, but it is evident that a part, and probably a large part, of the stock supposed to have been killed by black bears has been killed by grizzlies or silvertips and the remains of their feasts finished up by the more harmless blacks. In the Datil and Mount Taylor Ranges especially is this probable, as until quite recently stock-killing grizzlies have been known to occupy these areas.

In 1927, J. S. Ligon reported black and cinnamon bears as rather evenly distributed throughout the more extensive mountain areas of the State in numbers that would rapidly increase and fill their old range if given proper protection.

URSUS HORRIAEUS BAIRD

COPPERMINES GRIZZLY; Oso of the Mexicans; SHAS of the Apache Indians

Ursus horribilis var. *horriaeus* Baird, Mammals North Amer., p. 224, 1857.
Ursus horriaeus Merriam, North Amer. Fauna No. 41, p. 85, 1918.

Type.—Collected at old copper mines, near present site of Santa Rita, Grant County, N. Mex., by J. H. Clark, about 1852.[33] A skull of adult male, No. 990, U. S. Nat. Mus., catalogued November 1, 1852.

General characters.—Size, considerably smaller than *Ursus horribilis* and dentition much lighter; skull short, wide, and massive, with moderate sagittal crest; molar teeth small for a grizzly, with the posterior upper molars acutely triangular. This was called the brown bear or brown grizzly by the collector.

Measurements.—Basal length of type skull, 312; zygomatic breadth, 207 millimeters.

Distribution and habitat.—At the present time there is no known specimen of the Coppermines grizzly except the type skull, and the species is probably extinct. Other grizzlies collected in the type region in recent years have all proved to belong to other forms, which have occupied the same region or been driven into it from other areas, and *horriaeus* may not improbably have been the form of grizzly occupying the foothill and valley country around the Mogollon Mountains, where in 1852 bears were reported common in the open country by Clark and other collectors, even into the Rio Grande Valley of southern New Mexico. In his journal notes of December 3, 1824, in the Rio Grande Valley below Socorro, Pattie (1905, p. 86) records "great numbers of bear, deer, and turkeys—a bear having chased one of our men into camp; we killed it." Again on October 28, 1826, while in the Rio Grande Valley above El Paso he says:

At a very short distance from The Paso I began to come into contact with great bears and other wild animals. In one instance a bear, exceedingly hungry,

---

[33] There is no date on the skull, but it was catalogued in the National Museum on Nov. 1, 1852, and Clark was in the vicinity of the copper mines in 1851 and 1852.

as I supposed, came upon my horses as I was resting them at midday and made at one of them. I repaid him for his impudence by shooting him through the brain. I made a most delicious dinner of the choice parts of his flesh. (Pattie, 1905, p. 158.)

Later near the copper mines in July, 1825, Pattie says: "We passed our time most pleasantly in hunting deer and bear, of which there were great numbers in the vicinity "—" an Apache chief [called Mocho Mano] had one hand bitten off by a bear " (pp. 111 and 117). While near the copper mines in November, 1826, Pattie again speaks of an old grizzly with three cubs that attacked him and a companion. They fired from a tree and killed the old bear, but the cubs bit and fought off the hunters and escaped. Another bear killed a Mexican and his burro, and they were said to destroy corn and often to kill people. The country, Pattie says (p. 159), "abounds with these fierce and terrible animals." Again on January 25, 1825, between the Frisco and the Gila Rivers (near the spot now known as Cactus Flat), he found a bear in a cave and shot it. "The largest and whitest bear I ever saw. It took four men to drag it out of the cave. It was very fat and yielded ten gallons of oil " (p. 93). "On January 31 another bear that attacked us on the Gila was killed [apparently near Cliff] " (p. 94).

In 1851 Bartlett, while at the copper mines, wrote of the bears:

The grizzly, black, and brown varieties are all found here; and there was scarcely a day when bear meat was not served up at some of the messes. The grizzly and brown are the largest, some having been killed which weighed seven to eight hundred pounds. These are dangerous animals to approach, unless there are several persons in the party well armed. * * * I have known a grizzly bear to receive twelve rifle or pistol balls before he fell; though in one instance a huge animal was brought down by a single shot from a well-directed rifle, which passed through his entire length, killing him instantly (Bartlett, 1854, v. 1, p. 236).

In the vicinity of the copper mines (now Santa Rita) J. H. Clark reported (Baird, 1859, p. 28) : "A brown bear occurs here also, which I think can hardly be identical with the brown or grizzly of northern Chihuahua and Sonora." He says the brown bear of the former place is smaller and usually met with about watercourses, which furnish both cover and food, while the black or grizzly was found abundant in all the mountainous regions traversed west of the Rio Grande. Late in the summer, he says, they leave the mountains for the open prairie to get some plant that ripens at this season and is much relished, but what the plant is he was never able to ascertain.

Thus it appears that in the early days the grizzly bears were common at times over the open-plains country around the base of the mountains, where food and water were obtainable, but whether these were one or more than one species it is now impossible to tell.

Food habits.—Besides occasionally attacking burros, horses, and men, and raiding the fields of green corn, the grizzlies were credited with feeding on acorns, pinyons, and cedar berries, and even coming into camp after nightfall for offal. They also were reported as tearing up the soil in pursuit of roots and turning over stones for insects they could find underneath. There seems to be no mention of their feeding on the sugary pods of mesquite beans, which abound in the valleys where they roamed and which were undoubtedly as important a food for the bears as for the other animals of the region. Presumably this grizzly was still in existence when domestic animals were brought into this grazing paradise, and wholesale destruction of superabundant carnivores became necessary to protect the stock industry.

Breeding habits.—Pattie's record of an old grizzly with three cubs the size of coons in November is apparently the only record throwing any light on the breeding habits of this species.

Hibernation.—Pattie's account of great numbers of bears in the Rio Grande Valley below Socorro on December 3, 1824, and other accounts of the activity of bears in the valley country in November and December, would indicate that hibernation was not very regular or extensive in this warm part of the State. The bear that he killed in a cave near Cactus Flat on January 25 may have been in a state of hibernation at the time, as no mention is made of its being active when shot, and the fact of its being exceedingly fat and yielding 10 gallons of oil would indicate hibernation or a condition that would render hibernation possible during cold weather. But another grizzly, which attacked them and was killed on January 31 on the Gila near Cliff, must have been decidedly active.

On April 2, 1827, one day out from "Alopaz" on his 5-day trip back to the copper mines, Pattie saw a fresh bear track and, finding that he had but one bullet, was greatly worried for "fear of the bears which, thawed out, were emerging from their dens with appetites rendered ravenous by their long winter fast." (Pattie, 1905, p. 173.)

URSUS ARIZONAE MERRIAM

ARIZONA GRIZZLY

Ursus arizonae Merriam, Biol. Soc. Wash. Proc. 29: 135, 1916.

Type.—Skull of an adult male, collected at east side of Escudilla Mountains, Apache County, Ariz. (about 6 miles west of the New Mexico line), September 3, 1911, by C. H. Shinn.

General characters.—Size, rather large; color, dull brown with yellow tips to the long hairs; skull long, well arched, and with relatively small molar teeth.

Measurements.—Basal length of type skull, 326; zygomatic breadth, 208 millimeters.

Distribution and habitat.—Although the Arizona grizzly was collected on the very border of New Mexico, there were until recently no authentic specimens from the State that could be considered typical *arizonae*. Two skulls picked up on the headwaters of the Rio Mimbres in 1906 show most of the characters of this species, but are remarkably short. They, however, have the arched cranium and rounded frontal shield so characteristic of the species to which they are provisionally referred. On December 16, 1916, an old female and three yearling cubs were killed on the west side of the Black Range by T. T. Loveless, and all were secured by C. Hart Merriam for the National Museum collection and identified as *arizonae*. According to John A. Gatlin, Biological Survey leader of predatory-animal control in New Mexico, in a letter dated May 12, 1930, G. W. Evans, of Magdalena, N. Mex., killed a large grizzly bear in April, 1930, on the east slope of the Black Range just north of Hillsboro Peak after following the trail about 10 miles from the extreme headwaters of the Mimbres on the south slope of Reeds Peak.

According to local residents this bear had been killing livestock in the vicinity for the past many years. The skull shows that it was a very old bear with much worn teeth, possibly 15 or 20 years old. At the time this bear was killed tracks were found of a smaller grizzly that had been traveling with it, but the smaller one had not been reported as killing stock, so it could not then be legally killed.

It seems probable that many grizzlies killed in the Mimbres and Mogollon Mountains of New Mexico within recent years are also of this species. It is very desirable that more skulls and skins should be obtained from this region to satisfactorily clear up the distribution of the forms of bears found there.

In 1908 a few grizzlies or silvertips were said to be still in the Mimbres, Mogollon, and San Francisco Ranges. In 1905, a large female silvertip was killed in the Tularosa Mountains, and a large male was said to be still at large in the range. In 1894, A. K. Fisher was told that grizzly bears were common in the mountains about 80 miles north of Silver City, and he saw a large skin that belonged to Joe Sheridan, of that town, and another skin, which was of a light straw color, at a tannery. In 1906, at the GOS ranch on Sapello Creek north of Silver City, the handsome skin of a large grizzly that had been made into a rug was shown the writer by Culberson. This skin was of a uniform dark-brown color, with yellowish tips to the long hairs and had the typical long grizzly front claws. Culberson said that he killed many of these bears in the early days in the surrounding country and mentioned particularly one old male that had killed cattle for a long time before it was finally hunted down. It led the dogs and hunters on a persistent hunt for nine days before it could be brought to bay, and during this time it killed seven head of cattle that were found along the trail. Two other bears were killed while this one was being followed and a wide stretch of country was covered in the 9-day hunt.

Culberson told of another grizzly that he had shot with a revolver in the open where he found it while riding for cattle. He described the place so accurately that a few days later as the writer went past there, he was able to find the skull, which was badly weathered from lying on the ground for several years, but still makes an interesting specimen in the Biological Survey collection. Culberson said that the destruction of these grizzlies was absolutely necessary before the stock business of the region could be maintained on a profitable basis, and that one of the ranchers on the Gila had brought in a pack of good bear dogs, and during the years previous to 1906 the ranchmen had combined and destroyed a large part of the bears of the region. The black and cinnamon bears were considered comparatively harmless, but the grizzlies were at one time almost as bad as the big wolves in their depredation on the range cattle.

URSUS NELSONI Merriam

NELSON'S GRIZZLY

Ursus nelsoni Merriam, Biol. Soc. Wash. Proc. 27 : 190, 1914.

Type.—An adult female, collected at Colonia Garcia, Chihuahua, Mexico, November 13, 1899, by H. A. Cluff. A series of topotypes were collected by E. W. Nelson and E. A. Goldman in June and July of the same year.

General characters.—Smallest of all the grizzly bears. Color, pale buffy yellow to grayish white and yellowish brown; skull of male the size of that of a female *texensis*, to which species it is very closely related.

Measurements.—Basal length of skull of old male topotype, 284; zygomatic breadth, 199 millimeters.

Distribution and habitat.—The only actual New Mexico specimen of *nelsoni* is the skull of a young but nearly full-grown male, collected by B. V. Lilly in northwestern Chihuahua. On March 10, 1911, Lilly started this bear in the Animas Mountains in extreme southwestern New Mexico and followed it south through the San Luis Mountains into Chihuahua, across into Sonora, and back into Chihuahua before it was finally killed. Lilly was sure that he was following the same bear all this time, because it had lost two toes from one foot and made a track that could be easily recognized. Though the specimen was actually collected in Mexico, it was first driven out of New Mexico and serves to identify the bears of that corner of the State as *nelsoni*.

General habits.—In 1855 Kennerly reported these animals observed in greater or less numbers in the San Luis Mountains near the Mexican boundary line and further says (Baird, 1859, pp. 28–29):

We were assured by the Mexicans of Sonora, who also distinguished this animal from the grizzly, that it was feared by themselves, as well as by the Indians, more than the latter, on account of its ferocity. This, however, admits of a considerable degree of doubt; for, notwithstanding some very good proofs of its boldness within our own knowledge, we also observed almost unexampled evidence of its cowardice. While on one occasion a very old male rushed unexpectedly from the bushes and made a fierce and unprovoked attack upon a gentleman of the Boundary Commission, who probably only saved his life by a fortunate escape into a neighboring tree, we observed on a subsequent occasion in the same vicinity a female entirely forsake her cubs by a rapid retreat, and without being wounded; and this, too, notwithstanding the cries of the little ones while we pursued and captured them; she only looking around once, at a distance of half a mile, raising herself on her hind feet in a menacing manner, then again fled rapidly over the hills and disappeared. In the same region a very large female grizzly defended her young with great desperation, and only fled after the cubs were entirely beyond the reach of the hunters, when she made her escape, covered with wounds. * * * The food of these animals, in this country, consists of acorns, walnuts, piñones (the fruit of *Pinus edulis*), manzanillas, the fruit of an ericaceous shrub, and such animals as they are able to capture.

Another note in the same connection, apparently from W. H. Emory's own observations, states that:

Near the highest crest of the Sierra Madre, called " San Luis mountains " I had an opportunity to witness a rare butchery, by which, in less than one hour, a whole family of grizzlies was killed, without one offering the slightest resistance. It was about noon on the 11th of October, 1855, when our long trains, coming from the Guadaloupe Pass, in the Sierra Madre, toward the San Luis springs, met on the plains these unexpected mountaineers. When surprised, they were lying on the ground not far from each other digging roots. The position in which they performed this work naturally caused long narrow strips of grassy lands to be turned up and searched as if it had been done by a bad plough. I could not learn what kind of roots they had been looking for. After taking off the thick skin of these root-diggers, we found them all in a very poor condition, and this may account for the want of that resistance which they failed to offer. The ungrizzly-like behavior of these poor brutes induced the majority of our party to doubt their being grizzlies at all. They evidently had descended from the surrounding mountains, where they have their stronghold in the rough trachytic recesses of this part of the Sierra Madre, the highest crest of which is densely crowned by a dark growth of pines. There their fruit stores had probably given out in the late season, and they were obliged to resort to roots to satisfy their hunger. (Baird, 1859, p. 29.)

In August, 1908, while E. A. Goldman, Clarence Birdseye, and the writer were camped in the Animas Mountains they found abundant bear signs in the dense chaparral covering the upper slopes of this range and saw some large tracks that were undoubtedly those of grizzlies. Several silvertips were reported to have been killed there in recent years, and evidently some were then living there. The dense chaparral with abundance of acorns and manzanita berries make of this range a sort of bear's paradise, and there are plenty of cattle and hogs just below the chaparral. In one place along the bear trail a lot of black pellets were found, which, on examination, proved to be made up of felted balls of black pig hair. In other places the bear sign was composed mainly of manzanita berries and acorn shells, but we could not be sure whether these signs were to be credited to the grizzlies or to black bears, which also occurred there. The grizzly which Lilly chased out of these mountains in March, 1911, stopped twice to feed on the sotol plant (*Dasylirion wheeleri*).

On May 20, 1851, while going through Guadalupe Pass in the Cloverdale Hills of the extreme southwestern corner of New Mexico, Bartlett writes (1854, v. 1, p. 252):

Two bears were observed to-day after entering the defile; they were so large as to be taken at first for mules. When their real nature was discovered several of the horsemen gave chase but without success * * *

The size of these bears suggests that rather than the smaller *nelsoni* they may have been the species later collected a little farther west in Sonora by Kennerly, a species which now bears his name.

URSUS TEXENSIS TEXENSIS Merriam

Texas Grizzly; Oso blanco of the Mexicans

Ursus horriaeus texensis Merriam, Biol. Soc. Wash. Proc. 27:191, 1914.
Ursus horribilis horriaeus Bailey, North Amer. Fauna No. 25, p. 192, 1905.

Type.—Skull of adult male collected in Davis Mountains, Tex., by C. O. Finley and J. Z. Means, October, 1890. Biological Survey collection, United States National Museum.

General characters.—About the same size as *horriaeus* or slightly smaller, with lower and flatter skull and many detailed characters separating it from that form. No skin of this bear has ever been seen by a naturalist, nor any reliable data obtained as to its coloration, but from the notes on the osos blancos of the Mexicans, and the gray bear of Pattie and its close relationship with the light-yellow *nelsoni* of Chihuahua, it is evident that this was also a light-colored or yellowish bear.

Measurements.—Basal length of type skull, 308; zygomatic breadth, 218 millimeters.

Distribution and habitat.—So far no specimen of the Texas grizzly has ever been obtained from New Mexico, but the type from the Davis Mountains, a short distance south of the New Mexico line, and another specimen from southwestern Colorado, indicate a probable range for the species along the Guadalupe, Sacramento, White, Capitan, Manzano, and possibly the Jemez Mountains through the State; and as grizzly bears are known to have occupied these ranges, the notes from various localities along this line are referred to this species. At the present time grizzlies are extremely scarce throughout these ranges, and it is not impossible that the species has already become extinct, but until comparatively recent years they have been found in considerable numbers. In 1889, while camped in the Capitan Mountains, the writer was told by a Mexican hunter of osos blancos, or white bears, that were occasionally killed there. Other hunters in that region reported grizzly bears in the mountains and also formerly out in the Pecos Valley and even on the east side of the Pecos Valley. In 1900, E. W. Nelson was told by a Mr. Webb, of El Paso, Tex., that silvertips had been common in the Sacramento Mountains, but were then becoming scarce. In 1901, while camped at the head of Dog Canyon in the Guadalupe Mountains near the New Mexico and Texas boundary line, the writer found tracks of very large bears that were evidently of the grizzly group, though apparently no grizzlies had been killed there for some time. In this very rough part of the range, with deep canyons clothed in dense chaparral, the species may still be found and may even hold its own for years to come. It was reported by the Forest Service in the Sacramento Mountains in 1907 and in the Guadalupes in 1909.

In December, 1826, Pattie wrote that along the Rio Grande Valley below the mouth of the Puerco "We killed plenty of bears," and that while in the mountains west of the upper Puerco River "We killed several bears, the talons of which the Indians (Navajos) took for necklaces." (Pattie, 1905, pp. 160, 166.) The following month— on January 2, 1827—in making a journey from Perdido to "San Tepec" (from the Puerco to the Rio Grande Valley), he says (p. 169):

We saw plenty of bears, deer, and antelope. Some of the first we killed, because we needed their flesh, and others we killed for the same reason that we were often obliged to kill Indians, that is, to mend their rude manners in fiercely making at us and to show them that we were not Spaniards, to give them the high sport of seeing us run.

On November 2, 1824, between Taos and Abiquiu in the Rio Grande Valley, he reports (p. 75):

We killed a gray bear that was exceedingly fat. It had fattened on a nut the shape and size of a bean which grows on a tree resembling the pine, called by the Spanish, pinion. We took a great part of the meat with us.

Thus a gray bear seems to have occupied these valleys and low ranges up through the State, and the notes on it can probably best be gathered under the species *texensis*.

General habits.—Little is known of the habits of this species except from the type of country it inhabited, where scrub oak furnished abundant acorn crops, the pinyon pine nuts, and the alligator juniper great quantities of sweet berries, besides other abundant bear food, which rendered these low, open mountain ranges full of brushy canyons and gulches a natural paradise for bears. As the country settled up the stockmen found it necessary to protect their herds from the bears, and in the open part of the country they were easily hunted on horseback and rapidly destroyed. The bear whose skull serves as the type of this species was found in the Davis Mountains of Texas, where it had killed a cow and eaten most of the carcass, and was trailed for about 5 miles by the hounds until the horsemen caught up and killed it. These bears of the open country at an early date paid the penalty of their fondness for beef.

URSUS TEXENSIS NAVAHO Merriam

Navajo Grizzly; Shas of the Navajo Indians

Ursus navaho Merriam, Biol. Soc. Wash. Proc. 27: 191, 1914.
Ursus texensis navaho Merriam, North Amer. Fauna No. 41, p. 37, 1918.

Type.—Collected near Fort Defiance, Ariz., probably from the Chuska Mountains, which lie mainly within New Mexico.

General characters.—The type, a badly broken skull of an old male, is very similar to the type skull of *texensis*, rather small, short, and wide.

Distribution and habitat.—Of the original distribution of *navaho*, which apparently is now extinct, nothing is known, unless it should be considered conspecific with *texensis*, to which it is certainly very closely related. The type, which consists of an old skull lacking the posterior part, is accompanied by no other data than the locality, Fort Defiance, which lies close to the Arizona-New Mexico line, and the name Möllhausen, which would indicate that the specimen was collected by Möllhausen on the Whipple expedition through New Mexico and Arizona in 1854. In 1908 the writer was at Fort Defiance and followed the whole length of the Chuska Mountains lying just east of there, but could get no clew to any grizzly bears occupying the region at that time, although black bears were fairly common. It is not impossible, however, that grizzlies may still occupy some of the remote canyons in this range, and if the species is not extinct it is greatly to be hoped that specimens may be obtained to show more perfect characters.

URSUS PERTURBANS Merriam

Mount Taylor Grizzly

Ursus perturbans Merriam, North Amer. Fauna No. 41, p. 64, 1918.

Type.—An old male, collected in a canyon on Mount Taylor, N. Mex., 12 miles east of San Mateo, July 9, 1916, by Eddy Anderson, and sent to the Bureau of Biological Survey by J. S. Ligon.

General characters.—Size large; color dark brown, with grizzled tips to the long hairs; skull very long and narrow with high sagittal crest; molar teeth not very large. Another skull of a large old male killed at Kid Springs, 10 miles northeast of Datil in the Datil Mountains, about 1900, is very similar.

Measurements.—Basal length of skull (type), 338; zygomatic breadth, 210 millimeters.

Distribution and habitat.—The two specimens of *perturbans* mentioned are all that remain to show the range and characters of this large grizzly, but it seems safe to assume that at least some of the numerous bears reported from the region lying between the Mount Taylor and Datil Ranges, including the Zuni Mountains, and a number of small scattered ranges, may be referred to this species. In 1853 Kennerly reported great numbers of bears, both the black and the huge grizzly, among the bushes on the hillsides after leaving the " Rio Rito " on his trip from Albuquerque to Zuni. West of these mountains along the valleys that stretch toward Zuni he says:

We found the grizzly bear (*Ursus ferox*) abundant. When impelled by hunger they become very fierce and, descending into the valleys, frighten off the *pastores*, who, in their terror, abandoned their flocks to these huge monsters. (Kennerly, 1856, p. 5.)

This may have been the source of the "bear paws" that Coronado mentions among the Zuni Indians when he first visited the pueblo in 1540.

In 1905 Hollister reported many bears seen and killed in the San Mateo or Mount Taylor Range in past years and a few still remaining there. Much damage to stock, especially sheep, had been reported from time to time, and only the previous summer a sheep herder had been nearly killed by a large bear. Black, brown, silvertips, and grizzlies were all reported there. In 1906 the writer camped in these mountains and found a few old bear signs, but in the short time he was there he could not discover any bears. The dense forest growth in the old crater, however, forms an ideal rendezvous in which they are comparatively safe and from which they can make their raids among the herds over the stock ranges.

During the summer of 1916 one of these old grizzlies had become so bold and active in killing stock that a large bounty was offered for its destruction. For a long time the local hunters and trappers made every effort to win the bounty, but they were unsuccessful and finally gave up the attempt, when a Biological Survey trapper, Eddy Anderson, was sent for. He soon found and killed the bear, which had been feeding on a recently killed cow. The skin and skull are now among the treasured types in the National Museum collection, and at last the specific characters of the bears that Coronado reported nearly 400 years ago at Zuni are known.

In 1905 Hollister reported grizzly bears as still occupying the region north of the Datil and Gallina Mountains, where they were formerly more common and had done immense damage to cattle. In the Datil Mountains in the same year he found that a few of these cattle killers had been taken by professional hunters for the large bounties that had been offered, but that they were then becoming scarce, although at least one old bear was known to be at large. In 1906 the writer ran across an old prospector at a well north of Quemado, on whose pack burro was the skin of a large grizzly that he had shot in the mountains south of there—as nearly as could be made out from his description, in the Horse Spring Mountains at the east end of the West Datil Range. He had not saved the skull, but the fur was in good condition, long and dull brown with yellowish tips. It is quite possible that a few of these bears still remain in the region lying between Mount Taylor and the Datils, and if so, every remaining specimen should be procured for the National Museum collection for the light that it might throw on the specific characters and distribution of these almost extinct species.

General habits.—Apparently these grizzlies have belonged largely to the half-open country of mountains, plains, and scattered juniper and nut pine forest. Kennerly reported them feeding on pine nuts, but said that when hungry they became fierce and visited the flocks of the peaceful Zuni Indians in the valleys. Evidently they became stock-killing animals at an early date, and as the country filled up with domestic herds they wrought their own destruction by setting the hand of every man in self-defense against them.

URSUS APACHE MERRIAM

APACHE GRIZZLY ; SILVERTIP ; KUA-PAHTZYA A' NA of the Taos Indians

Ursus apache Merriam, Biol. Soc. Wash. Proc. 29: 134–135, 1916.

Type.—Collected at Whorton Creek, south slope of White Mountains, near Blue, eastern Arizona, April 3, 1913, by B. V. Lilly.

General characters.—Size medium; skull short, wide and massive, with short nose and spreading zygomatic arches; dentition moderate; color dark brown or blackish, much grizzled with yellow-tipped hairs over back and sides.

Description of a female and cubs.—Old female, in little-worn midsummer fur. Color over most of the body grizzled-brownish black, darkest on rump, mane, ears, and legs; forehead, throat, and belly light-yellowish brown; nose and face light brown; front claws long and white; hind claws short and brown.

Cub of about 6 months, killed with its mother on the same date, is similar in color, although slightly more blackish over rump, legs, and mane, but with the same brown nose and yellow wash over face and lower parts. Front claws slender, very sharp, and light horn color, hind claws short and sharp.

Live cub at National Zoological Park February 24, 1919, in winter fur, lighter and more yellowish than its mother and brother in midsummer fur with more striking contrasts of dark brown. Color pattern striking with straw-yellow face, crown, throat, belly, and worn rump patch; grizzled brown sides, back and mane; dark-brown ears, sides of neck, legs, and feet; and a light-brown circle the size of a silver dollar around each eye; nose almost as light yellow as the rest of the face. Nails long, slender, and still sharp and of the same light-horn color as those of the other cub. Weight probably 75 or 80 pounds.

Measurements.—Skull of type, adult male: Basal length, 325; zygomatic breadth, 234 millimeters; skull of adult female from Taos Mountains: Basal length, 277; zygomatic breadth, 195 millimeters.

Distribution and habitat.—In referring the grizzly bears of the Sangre de Cristo Range of northern New Mexico to this species, the writer is aware that one or two other forms may be included in the notes. It is not improbable that the larger, darker *Ursus horribilis bairdi* Merriam, described from Blue River, Summit County, Colo., may also range down through these mountains, and it would not be strange if *U. texensis navaho* Merriam, described from Fort Defiance, Ariz., shares some parts of the range. A single adult female and one of her cubs from the head of Rio Chiquito, Taos County, are the only available specimens from the range for determination, and they agree so perfectly with the type of *U. apache* that there can be no question of their identity. The distribution seems unreasonable, but the few scattered remnants of the species have been so chased by hunters from range to range over the State that there is no certainty of their being at the present time within their original habitat. There is no other record of the species in New Mexico, although at one time grizzly bears were abundant in every group of mountains from the Sangre de Cristo to the White Mountains of Arizona. In the collection of the University Museum at Lawrence, Kans., there are mounted specimens of several grizzlies from the headwaters of the Pecos and Mora Rivers, and it is to be hoped that some day the skulls will be removed from them for identification. There are still, however, some grizzly bears in this range of mountains, and there is still the possibility of getting specimens, or at least skulls, to clear up the status of the different forms that probably occur.

On July 22, 1918, T. J. McMullin caught an old grizzly and killed one of her two cubs, on the head of Rio Chiquito, Taos County. With the help of Bob Reed, a cowman from Taos, the other cub was roped from the top of a small spruce tree that it had climbed and was brought to camp alive. A few days later M. E. Musgrave came along and persuaded the men to send the cub to the National Zoological Park, to which they agreed on condition that he should be given the name of "McReed." Musgrave packed him out 25 miles

on his burro and shipped him to the Zoo, where he arrived in good
health on August 10, 1918.

Through the cordial cooperation of Charles Springer, the skins
and skulls of the mother and other cub were obtained for the Biological Survey collection, so supplying identification characters for the
live cub at the National Zoological Park, while it in turn furnishes
information concerning all the age and seasonal phases of color and
markings for the species.

In 1881, Dyche collected a number of specimens in the mountains
west of Mora and Las Vegas. (Edwords, 1893, pp. 68–75.) Judged
from his account, the grizzly bears were then abundant in these
mountains, but they have since become scarce. In 1903, while the
writer was camped on the headwaters of the Pecos River, there were
said to be a few old grizzlies in a big windfall near Jack Creek at
10,000 feet altitude, and later in the season others were reported in
the Taos Mountains, one especially large old fellow being said to
range in the dense second growth of aspens and spruces on the ridge
west of Black Lake. In 1904 a few were reported among the Culebra
and Costilla Peaks just south of the Colorado boundary, and a hunter
told of a big gray bear that had recently chased three Mexicans out
of the canyon on the east side of Culebra Peak. In 1903, A. H.
Howell, while in the Raton Range, was told that only one grizzly had
been killed in Bear Canyon during the previous five or six years.
In the Gallinas Mountains of Rio Arriba County, in 1904, the writer
was told that there were still a few silvertips, but in the San Juan
and Jemez Mountains in 1906 he could get no definite records of
them. In this region the grizzly bears seem to be almost entirely
mountain-forest animals, keeping in the dense growth of timber,
especially in the deep canyons and almost impenetrable jungles of
windfall and second growth, which follow the burning of forest
areas. Their present distribution, however, may be entirely artificial
and forced from their long and vigorous persecution by hunters.
Though they range up and down the slopes of the mountains from
timber line to the lowest timber, they are said usually to " den up "
and hibernate on the higher slopes of the mountains among the
spruces of the Canadian Zone. As the young are brought forth
before the mother leaves the winter den this becomes also the breeding zone of the bears.

General habits.—While camped in the Pecos River Mountains
in 1903, Page B. Otero, then State game warden, and long familiar
with the game conditions in that region, told the writer that near
the headwaters of the Pecos River when the first snows came he had
seen broad roadways made by the grizzlies in moving up the mountains toward their winter quarters. In some cases he had known of
their making their dens in hollow cavities among the rocks and in
others by merely scooping out a big hollow in a sidehill and letting
the snow drift deeply over the entrance through the winter. During
years of hunting in these mountains Otero has gathered many interesting incidents in regard to bears, both from his own and other
hunters' experiences. The one grizzly that came nearest to getting
him died at his third shot within 20 feet of him, but some of his
friends fared worse. An Indian of San Miguel was fearfully torn
and bitten by a huge grizzly he had wounded. The bear caught

him by the left arm and tore his face and breast into strings before he could kill it with his knife. After the encounter the Indian dragged himself to a road and was picked up, and went back in the mountains hunting. " The Pueblo Indians," Otero said, " were great bear hunters, even before they had guns," and numerous arrowheads and obsidian chips are still found over the mountains, especially near springs.

In 1910 Forest Service officials reported a few grizzlies in the Taos, San Juan, and Gallinas Mountains, and in May, 1916, J. S. Ligon reported a large cow-killing bear trapped on the headwaters of the Pecos during the latter part of the month, and six or seven others in that district.

A tentative estimate by J. S. Ligon in his report for May, 1917, of 48 grizzly bears in New Mexico is probably as near the facts as anyone could come at that time. (Fig. 55.) In his report for 1927,

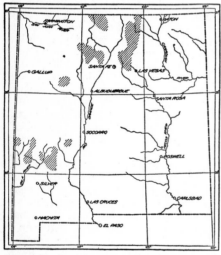

he stated that the predatory habits of the grizzlies had resulted in their almost total extermination in the State.

With their cattle and man killing instincts, it is not strange that these bears should have been brought to the verge of extinction during a progressive occupation of the country, but they are now so far gone that the occasional individual hiding in the deepest recesses of the mountains is no longer a terror to people or stock, but should afford a source of deep interest as a remnant of big game now becoming a thing of the past.

FIGURE 55.—Shaded area showing approximate distribution of the estimated 48 grizzly bears in New Mexico in 1917, from map prepared by J. S. Ligon

ORDER INSECTIVORA: INSECT EATERS

Family SORICIDAE: Shrews

NOTIOSOREX CRAWFORDI CRAWFORDI BAIRD

EARED SHREW

Sorex (*Notiosorex*) *crawfordi* Baird, MS. published by Coues, Bul. U. S. Geol. and Geogr. Survey Terr. 3: 651, 1877.
Notiosorex crawfordi Dobson, Mon. Insectivora, part 3, fig. 20, pl. 23, 1890.

Type.—Collected near old Fort Bliss, about 2 miles above El Paso, Tex., by S. W. Crawford. The type is labeled New Mexico, but Fort Bliss is on the Texas side of the river. It was entered in the National Museum catalogue April 28, 1857.

General characters.—The genus Notiosorex is characterized by three upper and two lower unicuspid teeth and prominent ears. In external characters *crawfordi* resembles a little Sorex, but has a relatively shorter tail, thinner fur, and more conspicuous ears. Its tail is not so short, however, as that of the little *Cryptotis berlandieri*, which has never been taken in New Mexico, but may come into the State in the Rio Grande Valley. The upper parts are clear plumbeous or slightly tinged with sepia; the lower parts paler and somewhat silvery plumbeous. The measurements serve to distinguish it from either *Sorex* or the little *Cryptotis*.

Measurements.—An adult male: Total length, 96; tail vertebrae, 29, hind foot, 10 millimeters.

Distribution and habitat.—Two specimens of the widely ranging and rarely collected eared shrew carry its known range well up the Rio Grande Valley into central New Mexico. (Fig. 56.) One of these was taken by Gaut at the northwest base of the Capitan Mountains; the other was taken near Juan Tofoya at the east base of the Mount Taylor Plateau not far from the Puerco River. The range of

the species has generally been supposed to be strictly Lower Sonoran, but these two localities both lie just beyond the edge of the zone and fairly within the edge of the Upper Sonoran. It is probable, however, that they mark only the extreme limit of range and that a species occurring at El Paso and along the lower Colorado River really belongs to the lower zone.

General habits. — There are few species of North American mammals of whose habits less is known than this rare shrew. The type, from old Fort Bliss, was long unique, but occasionally a specimen, usually picked up by accident, has been added from some

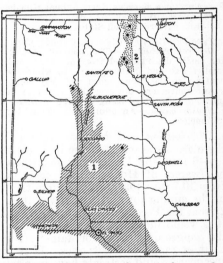

FIGURE 56.—Distribution of eared shrew and masked shrew in New Mexico: 1, *Notiosorex crawfordi crawfordi*; 2, *Sorex cinereus cinereus*. Type locality circled

widely isolated locality. The one that Gaut collected was found partially decomposed at the base of a rocky bluff on the edge of the Tularosa Valley. There was no water anywhere near and no clew as to where the animal had lived. The only one the writer has taken in many years of field work was caught under the canvas of his tent floor on breaking camp one morning in a sandy juniper gulch at the east base of the volcanic plateau surrounding Mount Taylor. The small alkaline creek near by was at that time almost dry, and its cut banks seemed to offer neither cover nor protection for such animals as shrews. The tracks and burrows of desert species, such as pocket mice and kangaroo rats, were common in the sand, and it was a great surprise to see a member of this forest and water-loving family dart from under the canvas. The writer quickly caught it in his hands and at once recognized the genus from its proportions and conspicuous ears, and examined with great care and interest an animal that he had never before seen alive. A careful search of the ground gave no clew as to where it came from. Some rain had fallen in the night and the shrew may have taken refuge under the tent floor just to keep dry, or it may have been seeking insects for food; or possibly had burrowed up through the mellow soil until it came to the impassable barrier of canvas. An examination of its stomach contents showed its food habits to be those of the shrews in general, the stomach containing the remains of insects too finely chewed for identification.

SOREX CINEREUS CINEREUS Kerr

CINEREOUS SHREW

Sorex arcticus cinereus Kerr, Animal Kingdom, p. 206, 1792.
Sorex personatus Geoffroy, Mem. Mus. Nat. Hist. Paris 15: 122, 1827. Type from eastern United States

Type locality.—Fort Severn, Ontario, Canada.
General characters.—The smallest species of Sorex found in New Mexico and easily distinguished from *obscurus*, with which it occurs, by its slightly smaller size and darker color. In winter pelage the back is sooty in strong contrast to the brown sides and gray belly, making a tricolor pattern. The surest characters, however, are found in the relative size of the five upper premolars, the third being as large or larger than the fourth.
Measurements.—An adult male: Total length, 100; tail, 40; hind foot, 12 millimeters.

Distribution and habitat.—In the Biological Survey collection there are 9 specimens of the little cinereous shrews from New Mexico—6 from the Taos Mountains, where they were caught along the headwaters of Hondo River, near Twining, at altitudes ranging from 10,500 to 10,700 feet; 1 from the mountains a few miles north of the mining town of Red River at an altitude of 10,700 feet; and 2 from the Pecos Mountains at 8,000 and 11,000 feet. These localities would indicate a range completely filling the Canadian Zone in the Sangre de Cristo Mountains. (Fig. 56.) This is the southern limit of range of the species. If it were a common species more specimens would certainly have been taken and a wider range would probably have been shown. Those caught were taken along the banks of cold streams, in springy meadows, or under logs in the cool spruce woods. Usually they were caught in traps set in the runways of Microtus or in little cavities under logs and rocks. One of the specimens, taken August 8, 1904, at 10,700 feet in the Taos Mountains, was already getting well into the winter pelage.
Food habits.—Apparently these shrews are caught at all times of the day and night for they seek their food mainly under cover and in the dark and seem to be tireless in their search for prey. The stomachs of those collected were as usual filled with the finely masticated parts of various insects, and the meat used for trap bait, showing that in food habits they are highly carnivorous as well as insectivorous.
Breeding habits.—E. R. Warren (1910, p. 264) says that they have from four to eight young and that five embryos were found in a female taken July 15 at Mud Springs, Colo.

SOREX OBSCURUS OBSCURUS Merriam

Dusky Shrew; Pah-ka-che-una of the Taos Indians

Sorex obscurus Merriam, North Amer. Fauna No. 10, p. 72, 1895.

Type.—Collected at Timber Creek, Salmon River Mountains, Idaho, August 26, 1890, by Vernon Bailey and B. H. Dutcher.

General characters.—Although a tiny animal, *obscurus* is noticeably larger than *cinereus* and duller or more plumbeous in color. The tooth formula also differs in the third upper premolar being very much smaller than the fourth. The winter pelage is not represented in any of the New Mexico specimens, but Colorado specimens collected in October and November have the upper parts decidedly darker, more blackish and less plumbeous than in summer. One specimen collected in the Manzano Mountains October 18, 1903, has the dorsal area well marked for about half the length of the back where the dark winter fur is coming in, but the more grayish summer pelage is still retained over the rest of the body.

Measurements.—An a d u l t male: Total length, 115; tail, 45; hind foot, 13 millimeters.

Distribution and habitat.—There are specimens of the dusky shrew in the Biological Survey collection from the Pecos River Mountains at 11,000, 11,600, and 11,700 feet; from the Taos Mountains at 7,400, 9,800, 11,300, 11,400, and 12,500 feet; and from the Jemez and Manzano Mountains at about 9,000 feet. These localities show a range completely filling the Canadian Zone and extending into and probably through the Hudsonian in the mountains of northern

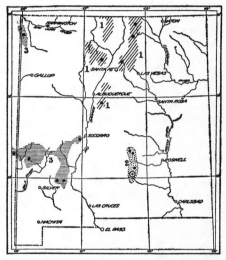

FIGURE 57.—Distribution of three little shrews in New Mexico: 1, *Sorex obscurus obscurus*; 2, *S. obscurus neomexicanus*; 3, *S. vagrans monticola.* Type locality circled

New Mexico. (Fig. 57.) They also mark the southern limit of a wide-ranging species. Though some of the localities given may seem low in altitude for the Canadian Zone, it is of interest to note that these are invariably along the banks of cold mountain streams, where the Canadian Zone plants are also brought down by the proximity of cold water.

The shrews are generally caught under old logs, in moist cold woods, along creek banks, about springs, in mountain meadows, or under and among broken rocks.

General habits.—Most of the shrews taken for specimens are caught by accident in traps set for Microtus, Clethrionomys, and other ground mice and baited with rolled oats; but by baiting the traps with bits of fresh meat almost as many shrews as mice are sometimes taken. In their favorite haunts of cold moist ground with abundant cover they seem to be active both day and night and are as often found in the evening round of the traps as in the morning. The question of more or less light evidently does not matter, especially as much of their food is found under cover of leaves and grass or in underground burrows, where their long sensitive noses are probably of more assistance than their minute eyes. They are rarely seen alive, but occasionally one darts across an open space or over a rock or swims across the creek or pool in front of you, disappearing as soon as cover is reached.

In the moist rich mold of woods' earth their tiny burrows can often be found in great numbers, usually where the material is so soft and light that they can push their way through without the effort of digging, for their tiny feet are poorly adapted to burrowing. They are caught in the burrows of other small mammals so commonly as to suggest that they are hunting larger game than insects or that the owners of the burrows may have been evicted.

Shrews rarely show much fat, and that they do not hibernate is shown by their tiny tracks seen on the snow in the coldest winter weather. They run into and out of the soft snow with ease and rapidity, but spend most of the winter under its cover on the surface of the ground under leaves and grass or in burrows and natural openings among logs or rocks.

Food habits.—The stomachs of these shrews are usually found filled with the finely masticated remains of various small animals popularly classed as insects but probably including worms, myriapods, bugs, and spiders. Occasionally traces of the flesh of some animals are found in the stomachs and more frequently a mouse is found in the traps with the skin torn and the flesh half eaten. By resetting the trap and baiting it with meat a shrew is almost invariably taken, often in a very short time. In the Manzano Mountains Gaut found a pocket gopher in one of his traps with a small hole eaten into its side, and setting a small trap baited with a bit of the animal's intestine on the spot he an hour later found a shrew in the trap. They are voracious feeders and the quantity of small animal life they destroy places them on the list of highly beneficial mammals.

Breeding habits.—The mammae of the females are arranged in three pairs close together on the posterior part of the abdomen.

SOREX OBSCURUS NEOMEXICANUS Bailey

New Mexican Dusky Shrew

Sorex obscurus neomexicanus Bailey, Biol. Soc. Wash. Proc. 26: 133, 1913.

Type.—Collected at Cloudcroft, N. Mex., May 29, 1900, by Vernon Bailey.

General characters.—The southern form of the *obscurus* group is easily recognized by large size, dull coloration, and brownish suffusion over belly, but most readily by its relatively large, heavy skull.

Measurements.—The type, an adult male: Total length, 118; tail, 45; hind foot, 15 millimeters. A female topotype: 115, 45, and 14 millimeters, respectively.

Distribution and habitat.—In the Biological Survey collection there are 4 specimens of *neomexicanus* from Cloudcroft—3 from the top of the range 10 miles northeast of Cloudcroft, 1 from the southwest, and 1 from the northwest slope of the Capitan Mountains.

(Fig. 57.) All were taken in a mixture of Canadian and Transition Zone forests, but the shrews undoubtedly represent the Canadian element, as they were always found in cold locations.

General habits.—At Cloudcroft they were caught in traps set under old logs on the highest cold slopes above 9,000 feet altitude. They evidently blundered by accident into traps set and baited for ground mice. In the Capitan Mountains Gaut caught them high up on both slopes of the range about cold springs, where they were trapped under old logs. In habits they seem to be identical with their nearest relative, *obscurus*, farther north.

SOREX VAGRANS MONTICOLA MERRIAM

ROCKY MOUNTAIN SHREW; TSE-NIS-NA-SA of the Navajo Indians

Sorex monticola Merriam, North Amer. Fauna No. 3, p. 43, 1890.
Sorex vagrans monticola Merriam, North Amer. Fauna, No. 10, p. 69, 1895.

Type.—Collected at San Francisco Mountain, Ariz., at 11,500 feet, August 28, 1889, by C. Hart Merriam and Vernon Bailey.

General characters.—Slightly smaller than *obscurus*, which it resembles in both external and tooth characters, but the teeth are much smaller and especially narrower. In size *monticola* falls between *obscurus* and *cinereus*, but from the latter it can be readily distinguished by the third upper premolar being smaller than the fourth. In summer the upper parts are sepia brown and the lower parts ashy gray. Specimens from the Mogollon Mountains taken in late October are in complete winter coat. The upper parts are blackish with a minute silvery frosting that in certain lights gives almost a gray appearance; the lower parts are silvery white; the tail is sharply bicolor with a blackish tip.

Measurements.—Average of four topotypes: Total length, 108; tail, 44; hind foot, 12.7 millimeters.

Distribution and habitat.—Specimens from the central part of the Mogollon Mountains, from near Kingston in the Mimbres Mountains and from the Magdalena Mountains carry the range of the Rocky Mountain shrew well over from Arizona into New Mexico. A single specimen taken in the highest part of the Chuska Mountains is also referred to this species, and it is very probable that the shrews of the Zuni and Mount Taylor groups also belong to this form. (Fig. 57.) No specimens have been taken in these ranges, but a little shrew seen at the edge of a creek on Mount Taylor shows that some species occurs there and the Zuni Mountains are perfectly adapted to their requirements. In the Mogollon Mountains they were taken at 8,500 feet; in the Magdalena Mountains at 9,000 feet, near Kingston at 6,200 feet, and in the Chuska Mountains at 8,800 feet. All these localities except Kingston are in the Canadian Zone, as are most of the Arizona localities where the species has been taken. Cold streams and springy places will probably serve to carry their range across some of the intervening valleys and may account for their rather scattered distribution.

General habits.—Near the headwaters of Willow Creek in the Mogollan Mountains the writer caught two of these little shrews under logs where he was trapping for Microtus and Clethrionomys. One was partly eaten in the trap, probably by another shrew, but could still be saved as a specimen. Several of the Microtus and Peromyscus caught in this line of traps were also partly eaten, probably by other shrews. The mice were so abundant in that locality that they quickly filled the traps, or more shrews would probably have been taken, as they were evidently common there. The following year, E. A. Goldman caught another specimen under a grassy bank a little farther up Willow Creek. In the Magdalena Mountains he caught three along the banks of a small stream in Copper Canyon at elevations ranging from 8,200 to 9,200 feet. Near Kingston he caught one at 6,200 feet on a moist bank of Percha Creek well down in the Transition Zone. This low altitude can only be accounted for by the influence of cold weather and a rapid mountain stream. In the Chuska Mountains, Clarence Birdseye and the writer trapped especially for shrews, and Birdseye finally secured one specimen on a cold slope near the highest point of the range. They were evidently not common or generally distributed in that region.

SOREX PALUSTRIS NAVIGATOR (BAIRD)

MOUNTAIN WATER SHREW

Neosorex navigator (Cooper Ms.) Baird, Mammals North Amer., p. 11, 1859.
Sorex (*Neosorex*) *palustris navigator* Merriam, North Amer. Fauna, No. 10, p. 92, 1895.

Type.—Collected near head of Yakima River, Wash., August 31, 1853, by J. G. Cooper.

General characters.—The large, long-tailed water shrew can not be confused with any other species in New Mexico. Its hind feet are relatively large and are fringed along the edges with stiff hairs much like those of the muskrat for swimming, and the eyes, while very small, are relatively less minute than those of the little shrews. The fur is dense and velvety; the upper parts in winter are glossy black and in summer brownish black and the lower parts usually silvery whitish.

One collected at 9,000 feet on the east slope of Costilla Pass September 25, is nearly half through the molt from summer to winter pelage. The short brownish-black summer coat is strikingly contrasted with the long black winter fur, which was progressing forward along a sharp line and had reached the middle of back and edges of belly, making the posterior half of the animal appear twice the size of the anterior half. Others collected on the east slope of the Taos Mountains, September 18 and 19, show the darkening fur of the posterior half of back, but it has not reached its full length. One from St. Elmo, Colo., collected at 10,100 feet by Cary October 10, is in full winter pelage, which is not shown in any of the New Mexico specimens. The fall molt evidently progresses forward over the body along a sharp line. Other specimens collected July 5 at 6,400 feet in the canyon west of Coventry, Colo., are losing the dark winter fur apparently in the reverse order, as the shorter, browner summer fur has extended back over the head and neck and replaced the dark but worn-out winter fur along a sharp line of demarcation, while the change has extended with ragged margins along the whole length of the belly. The brownish summer coat is evidently of brief duration, but New Mexico specimens of July 19 and 20, August 7, and September 8 are fully covered by it.

Measurements.—Average of eight specimens from Montana: Total length, 148; tail, 71; hind foot, 20.4 millimeters. An adult male from Jemez Mountains, N. Mex.: 150, 74, and 21 millimeters, respectively. A female from the San Juan Mountains: 151, 74, and 20 millimeters, respectively.

Distribution and habitat.—There are specimens of the water shrew in the Biological Survey collection from Costilla Pass, the east and west slopes of the Taos Mountains, head of Coyote Creek in Mora County, Santa Clara Creek in the Jemez Mountains, and the summit of the San Juan Mountains in New Mexico. In other words, they extend southward from the mountains of Colorado through the Canadian Zone of the Sangre de Cristo Range and the San Juan and Jemez, on the two sides of the Rio Grande Valley, and reach here the extreme southern limit of range of the species. (Fig. 58.)

General habits.—On the east slope of Costilla Pass A. H. Howell took one specimen at the edge of the creek at 9,000 feet altitude; on the east slope of the Taos Mountains a few miles west of Elizabethtown the writer caught one at the edge of a mountain stream at 8,900 feet altitude and on the head of Coyote Creek another at 8,000 feet. On the west slope of the Taos Mountains Gaut caught one by the creek in a little meadow on the head of the Rio Hondo at 10,700 feet in a trap set for Microtus, and in the San Juan Mountains another near a little stream at 10,000 feet altitude. On Santa Clara

Creek in the Jemez Mountains the writer caught one in the canyon at 8,000 feet just at the lower edge of the Canadian Zone, where a little stream of cold water came out from under the high bank. All these specimens were taken in the Canadian Zone and at localities ranging from its lower to its upper edge.

The species is probably much more common than these few scattered records would indicate, as the habits of the water shrews render them somewhat difficult to locate or capture. They are principally caught in traps set at the water's edge along cold mountain streams, where they swim back and forth

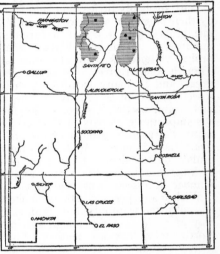

FIGURE 58.—Distribution of the mountain water shrew, *Neosorex palustris navigator,* in New Mexico

and land at certain places along the margins. But traps set at the water's edge, half submerged and baited with fresh meat, only occasionally catch one. To some extent they use the numerous burrows of meadow mice that perforate the stream banks, as they are occasionally caught in traps set in the runways of these mice. The only way to secure even a few specimens is by keeping out a large number of traps set in places where they are most likely to live. They are rarely seen alive, but they are known to be expert swimmers and divers and to spend much of their time in the water. They are also active on the shore, but to what extent they travel on land is not known; indeed, very little is known of their habits.

Food habits.—The examination of stomach contents of those collected for specimens always shows a mass of the finely masticated remains of insects and the very small animal life, but the specific identification of this material is very difficult, if at all possible.

Order CHIROPTERA: Bats

The great order of Chiroptera, or bats, highly specialized flying mammals, is represented in New Mexico, so far as at present known, by two families, the Vespertilionidae, with 8 genera and 17 species and subspecies; and the Molossidae, with a single genus and species (*Tadarida mexicana*). Among their many peculiarities the bats are wholly nocturnal, hiding away during the hours of daylight in caves and clefts of the rocks, in dark places in buildings or trees, or under cover of dense foliage, coming out only in the twilight to begin their eager quest of insect prey.

The food of our northern bats is composed entirely of insects, as none of the fruit-eating bats or the blood-sucking vampires of the Tropics reach the borders of the United States.

With probably little or no help from their minute eyes, but guided by their large and sensitive ears and by the expanse of sensitive wing membranes, they find and capture on the wing vast numbers of flying insects. With such highly beneficial food habits the bats are probably almost as essential to successful agriculture as are the birds. Though comparatively few in species, their individual numbers are great, and in many localities greatly in excess of the number of insectivorous birds. Many of the night-flying insects, especially moths and beetles, are not easily found by the diurnal birds, and the importance of bats in thus keeping a check on the increase of many destructive groups of insects is beyond calculation. Great quantities of guano, composed entirely of insect remains, often accumulate on the floors of caves where the bats roost during the day or hibernate during the winter, and give some idea of the enormous number of insects consumed in the locality. (Nelson, 1926.)

With many persons bats are looked upon with aversion, but they are not often wantonly destroyed, as there seems to be no convenient way of even securing enough specimens for study and comparison. Fortunately, they are neither edible nor ornamental, nor is any money value likely to be attached to them that will help to exterminate any of the species.

At present, the habits of the species are known mainly by what may be gathered from the individuals seen flitting about at twilight and around the camp fire at night, or occasionally fluttering about lighted rooms to which they have gained entrance by open doors or windows, or else from examination of those shot for specimens during the early evenings or found hanging head downward from the roofs of caves or dark attics, or tucked away in hollow walls or under boards or the bark of trees. Occasionally one or two young are found clinging to the mother, both in their roosting places and also when the old ones are shot on the wing, and the embryos in pregnant females collected for specimens give some clew to the number of young and to the breeding time.

A close and patient study of bat colonies or of groups or even of single bats found roosting in accessible places would be well repaid in new and useful information regarding these valuable and much-maligned animals.

Family MOLOSSIDAE: Free-tailed Bats

TADARIDA MEXICANA (SAUSSURE)

MEXICAN FREE-TAILED BAT

Molossus mexicanus Saussure, Rev. et Mag. Zool. (ser. 2) 12: 283, 1860.
Nyctinomus mexicanus Bailey, North Amer. Fauna No. 25, p. 215, 1905.
Tadarida mexicana, Miller, U. S. Natl. Mus. Bul. 128: 86, 1924.

Type locality.—Ameca, Jalisco, Mexico.

General characters.—Size medium with short, wide ears joined at base over nose, and naked tail extending about three-fourths of an inch beyond membranes; fur short and velvety, sooty or dull blackish.

Measurements.—Forearm, 40–45 millimeters; spread of wings, about 12 inches.

Distribution and habitat.—The only representative of the free-tailed bats (pl. 20) found in New Mexico occupies the Lower Sonoran area of the State in the Pecos and Rio Grande, and probably the Gila Valleys. Specimens have been taken at El Paso, Tex., and at Mesilla Park, Deming, Animas Valley, Cloverdale Hills, west of Animas Valley, and near Monica Spring on the San Augustine Plains. Vast numbers occupy the Carlsbad Cave, and at Roswell and Carlsbad they are numerous in some of the old buildings of the towns.

General habits.—These bats, while mainly cave dwellers, seem to be always abundant in towns and settlements in their range and to occupy the cracks and open spaces in old houses and buildings as roosting places. They emit a very strong musky odor, which so permeates the buildings they inhabit that even from the outside a good bat colony can usually be detected. They are especially numerous and noticeable along certain streets of El Paso in warm evenings, and in 1908 at Mesilla Park the peculiar odor of the species was very noticeable among the buildings, and in some of the old adobe structures the guano, which has much the same odor as the bats, had in places accumulated in little heaps under the window casings. The bats also occupy caves and clefts in rocks. Near Monica Spring, E. A. Goldman collected one in a small opening in the face of a cliff. and others were seen flying about. In the Cloverdale Hills, just west of the Animas Valley, the writer found a small bat cave on the head of Whitmire Creek in which there were large numbers of other species, and a few of these musky, free-tailed bats, but whether they had been in direct company with the others could not be determined. At the Lang ranch in the Animas Valley, not far from the bat cave, they were also common about the ranch buildings and over the pond, where they came to drink early in the evening. Although rapid-flying bats, they are not so difficult to shoot as many of the smaller, quicker forms, but in many places where they are abundant specimens are not obtained because shooting is not allowed within the city limits, where they are most numerous.

Some light on the habits of these bats was gained in 1924 by a study of the colony living in the Carlsbad Cave where for ages they had roosted by millions under the great arched roof of this remarkable cave. Early in autumn they gather in vast numbers for winter sleep and as the frosty nights come and stop the flight of nocturnal insects outside the bats hang up by their hooked hind claws in a dense mass over the inner surface of the roof where they remain in a state of torpor until the warm air outside in March and April penetrates sufficiently to arouse them for their summer season of activity. (Bailey, 1928, p. 108–120.)

On March 11, 1924, they were still quiet and mostly asleep. By the 15th a warm evening brought out a few, but not until the warm days of April did they come out by thousands every evening and scatter widely over the lower country, many of them not to return until the following August or September. Still great numbers remain in the cave during the summer days and raise their young there, foraging over the surrounding valleys for food each night and pouring back to the gaping mouth of the cave just before daylight each morning. On May 5 the writer estimated about 12,000 leaving the cave in the evening, and this was probably the summer resident colony. Late in August of the previous summer they were said to leave the cave each evening in a black cloud visible 2 miles away at early dusk and to continue to pour out of the 50-foot throat of the cave for two hours. The numbers were estimated by millions, and such numbers would be necessary to account for the vast deposits of guano found in the cave.

The guano had been in places a hundred feet deep when the work of shipping it began in 1901, and it was roughly estimated from partial records of shipments that 100,000 tons had been taken out in the 20 years following. This guano from the indigestible particles of insect remains may have been accumulating for thousands of years, and the mass of insects it represents is beyond conception.

The guano was shipped mostly to California and sold for fertilizer at $20 to $80 a ton, which represented considerable profit, when the low cost of taking it out of the cave and shipping it is considered. This, however, is mainly a wintering cave for the bats, and the deposit of guano is relatively much less rapid than in caves farther south, where the bats are active for a longer period, and where a larger proportion of the numbers spend the summer also.

Food habits.—The stomach contents of these bats show always a mass of finely masticated insect remains, but the minute particles can not be identified except by expert entomologists. W. D. Hunter, of the Bureau of Entomology, found on examination of a series of stomachs 95 per cent moths, the rest being carabid beetles, hymenopterous insects, and a few crane flies. Though but a fragmentary report this gives some definite idea of the great value of these insect-destroying mammals. The droppings of the bats at the Carlsbad Cave were found to be made up largely of particles of beetles and moths, and the bats kept for a time in captivity lived comfortably on the supply of large gray "candle moths" inhabiting the writer's cabin. The quantity of insects destroyed must be enormous, as each bat fills its stomach to its utmost capacity, appearing to feed actively during a great part of the night. Where the bats are abundant, their total destruction of insects must be of decided economic importance. (Bailey, 1928.)

Breeding habits.—As usual in most bats the females have two mammae, one on each side of the breast a little back of the shoulders, and the single large young is carried clinging to its mother until old enough to fly. Mating probably takes place in July or August, but during the hibernation period the embryos develop very slowly and the young are not born until May or June of the following summer. At birth the young weigh 3 or 4 grams, or about a quarter as much as the mother; as they grow rapidly and can fly before full grown, the mother's burden is not of long duration.

Family VESPERTILIONIDAE: Common Bats

ANTROZOUS PALLIDUS PALLIDUS (LeConte)

Large Pale Bat

V[espertilio] pallidus LeConte, Acad. Nat. Sci. Phila. Proc. 7: 437, 1856.

Type.—Collected at El Paso, Tex., by J. H. Clark; entered in United States National Museum Catalogue May 19, 1853.

General characters.—Easily recognized by its pale-buffy fur and light-brownish wings, by its very long ears extending forward an inch or more in length, by only two upper incisors, and a total of only 28 teeth.

Measurements.—The forearm, or long bone of the wing, measures about 50 millimeters, and the entire spread of wings is considerably more than a foot.

Distribution and habitat.—In New Mexico the large pale bat occupies all the lower Sonoran area and in places extends slightly into the Upper Sonoran Zone. There are specimens from Carlsbad, Slaughter Canyon, Las Cruces, Mesilla Park, Animas Valley (Lang ranch and near the Mexican line), Cloverdale Mountains, base of Big Hatchet Mountains, Silver City, near the San Mateo Mountains, and Laguna. These few specimens from scattered localities give only a suggestion of the actual range and abundance of the species in the region, as it is often impossible to secure specimens where the bats are most abundant. The species will undoubtedly be found over a much larger part of the Upper Sonoran Zone, as a flying mammal has the same opportunity of wandering from its regular breeding ground as have the birds.

General habits.—Though inhabitants of the hottest deserts, these big bats are not subjected to the maximum heat of the region, as they roost during the day in caves or cracks in the cliffs, hollow trees, or dark places in buildings and are active and flying about during the cool evenings and nights. They usually come out of their roosting places early in the evening and fly about on their big soft wings before many of the other species of bats appear and before it is too dark to use a shotgun effectively. They are therefore among the easiest bats to collect, although generally less numerous than many of the smaller species. Near Carlsbad, late in July, 1901, they were abundant about the ranch where the writer was staying, many being seen flying about in the evenings. They were living under the casings of the house, where they were often heard squeaking during the day, and with a pair of long forceps five were taken from behind one of the casing boards. A few of their bones were found in Carlsbad Cave and a lot of drowned bats in a large water tank in Slaughter Canyon. At Silver City in July, 1894, A. K. Fisher collected four specimens, including one half-grown young, and reported them as common about the buildings and cottonwoods every evening. Their long ears were conspicuous against the sky as they flew about.

In the Cloverdale Hills in the extreme southwestern corner of New Mexico the writer found a bat cave where large numbers of smaller bats were congregated, and, after securing all the specimens he wanted, as he was coming out of the cave he found five of these big pale bats flying about in the bright sunlight hunting for cover. He had evidently driven them out without knowing it. One of them returned to a small crevice in the rocks above the cave and others entered an old hollow tree near by, but he shot one before it got under cover. At the Lang ranch, where E. A. Goldman and the writer were staying at the time, the former picked several from cracks in the roof and several more were found suspended from a roof in the open corridor along the side of the house. These seemed rather stupid and were easily knocked down and secured as specimens. Although evidently common here, none was seen flying about in the evenings, although other species of bats were being shot near the water holes. At Monica Spring, near the San Mateo Mountains in September, 1909, Goldman found about 25 of these bats living in a deep hollow in the face of a cliff bordering the Indian Butte, and at Laguna in August, 1905, Hollister reported them common along the river bottom, where he secured a specimen.

Breeding habits.—In June, 1907, J. M. Gunn sent the Bureau of Biological Survey 30 more specimens from near Laguna. Among these only three were males and about half of the females contained one embryo each and the others two each. Those containing only one embryo were smaller and probably only a year old, while those containing two embryos were larger and evidently fully matured individuals. Some of the embryos were about ready for birth and so large that it is almost inconceivable how their birth could be accomplished. Others were not more than half developed. The mammae in all the females are in one pair that might be called subaxillary, as they are so far out on the sides as to be just back of the armpits. The advantage of this position can be readily seen by holding the bat head downward in the position in which it roosts during the day and noticing the ample pocket formed by the folded wing just below each nipple where the young can rest without even holding on. In this warm-zone species only the bottom of the pocket or cradle is fur lined, but the nipples are surrounded with soft fur to which the young can safely cling. Unfortunately the actual date of capture of this series of specimens was not ascertained, but Mr. Gunn writes that it was in May. He also states in a letter of February 2, 1917, that the bats were taken from among the rafters and next to the wall of an adobe mill building and were so numerous that he could have filled a 50-pound flour sack with them if he had cared to. The half-grown young that Doctor Fisher shot at Silver City on July 4 would indicate the 1st of June or earlier for their date of birth.

CORYNORHINUS MACROTIS PALLESCENS Miller

Long-eared Bat

Corynorhinus macrotis pallescens Miller, North Amer. Fauna No. 13, p. 52, 1897.

Type.—Collected in Keam Canyon, Navajo County, Ariz., August 3, 1894, by A. K. Fisher.

General characters.—Size large, with ears over an inch long; upper incisors, four; fur light drab gray; ears and membranes slightly darker. The only other long-eared bat of New Mexico with which this might be confused is *Antrozous pallidus*, from which it can readily be distinguished by its four instead of two upper incisors.

Measurements.—Forearm, about 44 millimeters; spread of wings, about 12 inches.

Distribution and habitat.—The only actual records of the long-eared bat (pl. 21, A) for New Mexico seem to be an old alcoholic specimen (No. 5232, United States National Museum collection) collected at Santa Fe by W. J. Howard in 1861; [34] three alcoholic specimens in the State college collection taken by Barber in 1900 from the cliff dwellings on Mule Creek; and others from McKitterick Cave, 20 miles west of Carlsbad. Specimens have been taken, however, on all sides of New Mexico, and the species undoubtedly ranges over all the Lower and Upper Sonoran Zone area of the State. The distribution is usually local and largely determined by the presence of rocks, as it is preeminently a cliff and cave dwelling species.

General habits.—In canyons these large, light-colored bats may be seen flying about early in the evenings, when they are comparatively easy targets, especially if it is light enough to see the long ears projecting well in front of their heads. They are, however, more often found hanging from the walls of caves or mine shafts, where they spend the daylight hours, often in large clusters.

Breeding habits.—One young seems to be the usual number to each female, and the mammae are a single pair of pectoral or subaxillary.

EUDERMA MACULATUM (J. A. ALLEN)

SPOTTED BAT

Histiotus maculatus J. A. Allen, Bul. Amer. Mus. Nat. Hist. 3: 195, 1891.
Euderma maculata H. Allen. Monograph Bats of North America, U. S. Natl. Mus. Bul. 43: 61, 1893.

Type.—Collected near Piru, Ventura County, Calif., March, 1890, by E. C. Thurber.

General characters.—A rather large bat with very large ears; fur black with three large white spots on back and underparts washed with white.

Measurements.—Type: Total length, 110; tail, 50; hind foot, 9; forearm, 50; ear from notch at base of opening, 34 millimeters.

Distribution and habitat.—The four known specimens of the spotted bat (pl. 21, B) are from Piru and Mecca, Calif.; Yuma, Ariz.; and Mesilla Park. N. Mex. In September, 1903, E. O. Wooton found an adult male of this species dead in the biological laboratory of the College of Agriculture and Mechanic Arts, at Mesilla Park, and although this was the second specimen ever taken, the species was recognized and it was carefully preserved in alcohol and forwarded to the United States National Museum. The skull was removed and figured with an account of the capture and full measurements of the specimen by Gerrit S. Miller, jr. (1903, p. 165.) This very rare bat should be collected and studied wherever possible, as at present very little is known of its distribution or habits.

NYCTERIS CINEREA (BEAUVOIS)

HOARY BAT

Vespertilio cinereus Beauvois, Cat. Peale's Mus., Phila., p. 15, 1796.

Type locality.—Philadelphia, Pa.

General characters.—A very large bat, with short furry ears and furry upper surface of tail membrane; fur dark brown, frosted with white-tipped hairs.

---

[34] This specimen is no longer to be found unless it is one of several that have lost their labels.

Measurements.—Total length, 140; tail, 60; foot, 13; forearm, about 50 millimeters; spread of wings, about 15 to 16 inches.

Distribution and habitat.—Specimens of the hoary bat have been taken at Gila, at Lang ranch, Dona Ana, Dog Spring, Magdalena Mountains, and San Luis Mountains in New Mexico, but this gives no clew to the actual range of the species, which is well known to be migratory and to breed mainly within the boreal zones and after the breeding season to wander southward over the lower zones. Undoubtedly it breeds in all the higher mountains of the State. In the Bear Spring Mountains, in September, 1905, Hollister wrote:

A large bat flew over our camp high in the mountains early one evening. Having killed numbers of this species in the Northern States, I am quite sure of the identification as *Nycteris cinerea*. The appearance and manner of flight were unmistakable.

In the Moreno Valley east of the Taos Mountains at 8,400 feet on September 20, 1903, Weller found a bat of this species hanging to a barbed-wire fence, where it had been caught by one wing on the barbs and was unable to escape. In the Magdalena Mountains on August 30, 1909, E. A. Goldman shot one near his camp at 6,500 feet in Water Canyon at dusk as it circled about in pursuit of insects. On October 7, 1908, he shot another at Gila near the Gila River as it circled about over a cornfield. In the southern end of the Animas Valley at the Lang ranch on August 10, 1908, Clarence Birdseye shot two of these big bats as they circled about a pond. At Dog Spring on September 18, 1893, Mearns secured a male and female of this species, and in November, 1855, T. C. Henry collected a specimen at Dona Ana in the Rio Grande Valley. A few old wing bones were found in the Carlsbad Cave in 1924, and one of the bats was reported near there the previous September.

Most of these records are undoubtedly of migrating individuals that had left their higher mountain homes and were working southward.

General habits.—These bats are usually found within reach of timber, where they spend the day hanging in the dense foliage of the trees. They are not usually numerous, but their large size and rapid flight readily distinguish them from the smaller, faster-flying bats. The real habits of this, as of most bats, are little known, except for the few suggestions in connection with specimens taken.

Breeding habits.—The mammae of the females are four in number, two close together on each side a little back of the shoulders, so that when the bats hang head downward, as they do through the day, the folded wings form two beautifully fur-lined cradles just underneath the nipples. In most bats the wing membranes are entirely naked but in this cold-zone species they are well furred underneath at the base, apparently as a protection for the young. There are records (McAtee, 1907, p. 8; Jackson, 1908, p. 33; Bailey, 1926, p. 208) of old bats taken with two young clinging to the mother, and while two seems to be the regular number of young, there are other records of four.

LASIONYCTERIS NOCTIVAGANS (LeConte)

Silver-Haired Bat

V[*espertilio*] *noctivagans* Leconte, McMurtrie's Cuvier, Animal Kingdom 1: 431, 1831.
Lasionycteris noctivagans H. Allen, Monograph Bats North Amer., p. 105, 1894.

Type locality.—Eastern United States.
General characters.—A medium-sized bat, with small ears and long soft fur of a blackish color, with a silvery wash of white-tipped hairs over the back; ears and membranes blackish.
Measurements.—Total length, 100; tail, 40; foot, 9; forearm, about 41 millimeters; spread of wings, about 10 or 11 inches.

Distribution and habitat.—A few specimens of this northern bat have been taken in New Mexico. In the higher part of the Zuni Mountains near Mount Sedgwick, E. A. Goldman secured one on June 25, 1909, which would indicate a breeding locality. At Rinconada, in the Rio Grande Valley north of Santa Fe, McClure Surber took one on April 15, 1904, and at Lake Burford (Stinking Spring Lake), on the Jicarilla Apache Indian Reservation, the writer collected two males on October 1 and 2, 1904. Both the Rinconada and Lake Burford bats may have been migrants to and from their breeding grounds in the higher mountains near by, as were undoubtedly those taken at Carlsbad Cave in April, 1924. So far as known, their breeding range is confined to the boreal zones of the mountains or the northern part of the United States; but, like other boreal species, they evidently migrate after the breeding season is over. Cary (1911, p. 211) records specimens from Colorado at 8,500 to 10,000 feet altitude.

General habits.—These soft-haired black bats are mainly forest dwellers and are usually found in the open parks surrounded by timber or in localities where trees are abundant. They have been found in summer living under the loose bark of dead trees and in hollow or broken trunks that afford dark roosting places for the daylight hours. Their flight is rapid but rather steady, and they often come out before it is too dark for effective use of the shotgun.

Food habits.—Insects, caught on the wing among the branches of trees, in the open spaces of the forest, or over the surface of the water, form the entire food of these bats, but as to the species of insects nothing is known.

Breeding habits.—The females have the usual number of mammae, one on each side just back of the shoulders. As with other bats, when hanging head down the folded wings form fur-lined pockets just below the nipples; but it is not known whether the young occupy these furry cradles, as apparently no young have been found clinging to the old bats when shot for specimens. The usual number of young of this species is shown by the embryos to be two and less commonly only one at a birth. (Merriam, 1884, p. 191.)

EPTESICUS FUSCUS FUSCUS (Beauvois)

Brown Bat

Vespertila [sic] *fuscus* Beauvois, Cat. Peale's Mus., Phila., p. 14, 1796.
Eptesicus fuscus Mehely, Magyarorszag Denevereinek Monog. (Monog. Chiropterorum Hungariae), p. 206, 338, 1900.

Type locality.—Philadelphia, Pa.

General characters.—Size rather large; ears small; fur bright hazel-brown; ears and membranes naked, black.

Measurements.—Total length, 119; tail, 50; foot, 11; forearm, about 45 millimeters; spread of wings, about 13 inches. Weight, 12 to 15 grams.

Distribution and habitat.—The brown bat (pl. 22, B) is one of the most abundant of the bats over the higher parts of New Mexico. Its center of abundance seems to be in the Transition Zone, but specimens are often taken somewhat above and below this level. They are rarely taken, however, in the low, hot valleys, but late in summer they may be found in the mountains well up in the edge of the Canadian Zone. In the yellow-pine forests they are almost invariably found during the whole summer, and often where conditions are favorable and open water is available they are extremely abundant. In April they were common in Slaughter Canyon of the Guadalupe Mountains, and two old skulls were found in the Carlsbad Cave. In the White Mountains in September the writer found them common among the yellow pines, and a few specimens were taken at his camp on Ruidoso Creek. In the Pecos River Mountains they were common at Glorieta and at the junction of Mora Creek with the Pecos River. At camp on the east side of the Pecos Mountains in the yellow-pine forest 10 miles south of Mora on September 3 one was shot. Others of apparently the same species were seen there and also at Black Lake and in Moreno Valley. They were abundant in the Santa Clara Canyon on the east side of the Jemez Mountains at 8,000 feet in the yellow-pine forest and over the Jicarilla Indian Reservation, at Lake Burford, Lake La Jara, and throughout this pine-covered plateau they were found at every camp.

In the San Juan Mountains these bats were common up to at least 7,800 feet altitude along the Las Tusas River and also in Brazos Canyon near Tierra Amarilla. Along the Hondo Canyon on the west side of the Taos Mountains they were common from 7,900 to 8,200 feet and probably much lower and somewhat higher than our camps in the canyon. In the Mogollon Mountains these were the commonest bats throughout the Transition Zone area, and they were abundant at the camps on Rocky Creek, Diamond Creek, at Beaver Lake, Negrito Creek, and Luna Valley. In the Magdalena Mountains E. A. Goldman reported a few seen and one collected in Water Canyon at 6,500 feet altitude, and in the Zuni Mountains he found them common at 8,200 and 8,600 feet altitude near Mount Sedgwick. Hollister collected two specimens at Wingate in June and reported a few others seen. Gaut reported them common in the Capitan Mountains and about Tres Piedras, and in the Manzano Mountains, near Eastview, while chopping down a dead stump, he found one in a crevice of the wood.

General habits.—The brown bats are often found during the daytime under pieces of loose bark on dead trees, and being mainly forest bats this is evidently their common roosting place. They also come into houses, barns, and outbuildings, where they occupy open spaces under roofs, casings, cornices, or the hollow spaces between walls. Apparently they are not fond of crevices in the rocks, as they are less apt to be common in rocky situations than in the forest or around buildings. The large size and steady flight of these bats make them rather easy targets for the collector, but they usually do not begin

flying until twilight has well advanced, and it is only after considerable practice with the shotgun that specimens are obtained as they
dart back and forth across the sky.

Breeding habits.—The females have the usual arrangement of
mammae, one on each side, and the young, as shown by embryos and
occasionally one clinging to the mother in flight, are apparently
never more than one at a birth.

PIPISTRELLUS HESPERUS HESPERUS (H. ALLEN)

PIGMY BAT; LITTLE CANYON BAT

Scotophilus Hesperus H. Allen, Monograph, Bats North America, p. 43, 1864.
Pipistrellus hesperus Miller, North Amer. Fauna No. 13, p. 88, 1897.

Type.—Collected at old Fort Yuma, Calif., by Maj. G. H. Thomas, United
States Army; entered in National Museum catalogue October 31, 1861.

General characters.—A tiny gray bat, with very small ears; fur pale buffy
gray; naked ears and membranes black.

Measurements.—Total length, 75; tail, 30; foot, 7; forearm, about 30 millimeters. Spread of wings, 8 inches. Weight, 4 to 5 grams.

Distribution and habitat.—The little pigmy bats occupy the whole
Lower Sonoran Zone area of New Mexico, wherever there are cliffs
or canyons to be found for roosting places. There are specimens from
Carlsbad, Carlsbad Cave, Santa Rosa, Guadalupe Mountains,
Laguna, Jemez, Socorro, Florida Mountains, Dog Spring, Big
Hatchet Mountains, and Animas Valley. Some of these localities
are just beyond the edge of pure Lower Sonoran, but all are close
enough for many traces of the zone. The species is so abundant that
it seems to fill the zone to its utmost limits.

General habits.—These perhaps more than any other bats are
canyon dwellers, being rarely found far from the rocky walls of
canyons or cliffs. At Laguna one was shot as it came from the big
cliffs back of the pueblo early in the evening on its way to the river
for water, and in the Jemez Canyon one was shot early in the evening
of September 8 as it flew between the high walls of the river canyon.
Others were reported by Hollister about the cliffs at the junction
of the San Jose with the Rio Puerco, but no specimens were taken.
At Socorro, E. A. Goldman shot two in August, 1909, and reported
them common over the river bottoms in the evenings. In the Gila
Valley he found them common in a little canyon 3 miles above Redrock and on October 2, 1908, collected a specimen. In the Florida
Mountains south of Deming on the morning of September 8, 1908, he
shot one as it flew about camp at daylight. Near Carlsbad on July
30, 1901, the writer found them abundant in Dark Canyon and
secured one specimen.

A few miles north of Santa Rosa in a little side canyon of the
Pecos River in 1903, pigmy bats were numerous, and a number of
specimens were obtained. They began to fly early in the evening;
sometimes before the sunlight had entirely disappeared above they
would be flying about in the shadow of the walls of the canyon and
they were occasionally found even at midday flying about in shadowy
places. They are extremely quick and fly with short abrupt turns,
making it very difficult to shoot them on the wing, but the added
advantage of fairly good light enables the collector to secure more

specimens than of many others that begin to fly only in the deeper twilight. All those shot for specimens had the stomachs well filled with insects, which they had gathered on the wing in the short time in which they had been flying before being killed. In some cases they could not have been hunting for more than 15 or 20 minutes.

Breeding habits.—One female collected at Santa Rosa on May 27 contained two small embryos, which seems to be the usual number of young, although the writer has examined others that contained only one embryo. The mammae are as usual one pair of subaxillary.

MYOTIS VELIFER VELIFER (J. A. ALLEN)

CAVE BAT

Vespertilio velifer Allen, Bul. Amer. Mus. Nat. Hist. 3: 177, 1890.
Myotis velifer Miller, North Amer. Fauna No. 13, p. 56, 1897.

Type.—Collected at Santa Cruz del Valle, near Guadalajara, Jalisco, Mexico, September 7, 1889, by A. C. Buller.

General characters.—One of the largest of the genus Myotis in the United States, measuring almost a foot across the spread wings, with small ears, the tips reaching about to the nostril when laid forward; color of fur dull sepia; ears and membranes about the same or slightly darker.

Measurements.—Total length, 90; tail, 40; foot, 9; ear from crown, 12; forearm, about 42 millimeters.

Distribution and habitat.—Apparently the only specimen of the cave bat (pl. 22, A) from New Mexico is an immature individual in alcohol, collected at Fort Wingate by R. W. Shufeldt, in July, 1915, but there are specimens from the southeastern corner of Arizona, from western Texas, and from farther east and south, so that a considerable range over southern New Mexico may be expected when more is learned of its distribution. Apparently it is an habitual cave dweller, and this may account in part for its erratic and very scattered distribution.

MYOTIS VELIFER INCAUTUS (J. A. ALLEN)

HOUSE BAT

Vespertilio incautus Allen, Bul. Amer. Mus. Nat. Hist. 8: 239, 1896.
Myotis incautus Miller, Proc. Biol. Soc. Washington 15: 155, 1902.

Type.—Collected at San Antonio, Tex., October 10, 1896, by H. P. Attwater.

General characters.—About the size of *Myotis velifer*, but paler in coloration; fur dull brownish; ears and membranes dark brown or blackish.

Measurements.—Total length, 93; tail, 41; foot, 9; ear from crown, 12; forearm, about 42 millimeters. Weight, 6 or 7 grams.

Distribution and habitat.—House bats have been taken at several localities over western Texas, eastern Mexico, and at Carlsbad, N. Mex., but as yet little is known of their distribution or habits.

General habits.—At the old water tower 3 miles west of Carlsbad, where a large pool formed from the mountain water pumped up to supply the town, on the evening of July 29, 1901, these bats came in over the dry plains from some limestone hills several miles away. They were flying straight for the water pool without a crook or turn, and the writer shot four without missing, a rare occurrence in bat shooting. These were all females, but four taken on September 17 at the Bolles Ranch 6 miles south of Carlsbad were all males. Three of these were shot in the evening as they flew about the house, and one was caught in the daytime in the corner of an outhouse. In the original description of the species, based on a series of five specimens taken at San Antonio by H. P. Attwater March 12 and October 10, Doctor Allen says (1896a, pp. 239–240) : "It is a ' house ' bat, all of the specimens having been taken in the house, except one, which was caught in a barn."

Evidently they are also cliff and cave bats, as in some of the localities where taken they apparently came from the cliffs, as no houses were near; and in a cave near Sun City, Kans., hundreds were found by Theo. H. Scheffer on March 8, 1911, in a largely dormant condition. Live specimens that he sent to the Bureau of Biological Survey arrived in good condition although still torpid, but when brought into a warm room they soon came to a condition of normal activity.

Twenty-three years after the four bats were shot at the water tower near Carlsbad, the writer entered a cave on top of a limestone ridge half a mile northwest of there and found about a thousand of these bats hanging to the low roof of the cave. A considerable deposit of guano on the floor of the cave indicated many years of use by the bats. All but one of the specimens collected in this cave on May 2, 1924, were females, as were the four taken near there in 1901, indicating a breeding colony and the cave as their breeding home.

One other specimen was collected in McKitterick Cave, 20 miles west of Carlsbad, and an old skull was found in the farthest, deepest room of the Carlsbad Cave.

MYOTIS THYSANODES THYSANODES MILLER

FRINGED BAT

Myotis thysanodes Miller, North Amer. Fauna No. 13, p. 80, 1897.

Type.—Collected at Old Fort Tejon, Kern County, Calif., July 5, 1891, by T. S. Palmer.

General characters.—One of the larger species of the genus Myotis, with moderately large ears reaching slightly beyond tip of nose, and with hairy margin of tail membrane; fur dull yellowish brown; ears and membranes dusky.

Measurements.—Total length, 87; tail, 37; foot, 9; ear from crown, 15; forearm, about 42 millimeters.

Distribution and habitat.—An old specimen of the fringed bat (No. 5413, U. S. Nat. Mus.), collected by Captain Pope, is labeled "mountains of New Mexico," with no definite locality given. There are specimens from Carlsbad Cave, Sacramento Mountains, Gallup, Agua Fria Spring (Copperton), Mimbres Mountains, San Luis Mountains, Cloverdale Hills, Gran Quivera, and Espanola.

This species has been reported as occupying mainly the Lower Sonoran Zone, and it has a wide range over Mexico, southern California, and southern New Mexico. Most of the New Mexico localities where the specimens have been taken, however, are in the Upper Sonoran Zone, and it seems probable that the breeding range of the species covers both the Lower and the Upper Sonoran Zones, where suitable localities are found. In the old ruins of the Gran Quivera, on September 28, 1903, Gaut collected three specimens and reported them even at that late date flying about the buildings. At Espanola, on June 15, 1904, Surber collected a specimen but gave no notes on its habits. At the south base of the Zuni Mountains, on July 23, Hollister collected one at the Agua Fria Spring, where he reported them as not common. At the west base of the Mimbres Mountains, on August 23, 1908, Birdseye collected a specimen at 8,000 feet altitude on Rocky Creek, at the extreme upper limit of the Upper Sonoran Zone, where the junipers came up only on the hot slope of the canyon. On August 9, 1908, the writer found a colony of these bats in a cave in the Cloverdale Hills west of the Animas Valley, evidently a breeding colony, as many of the bats were not fully grown and had doubtless been raised in the cave or its vicinity.

General habits.—The fringed bats seem to be largely colonial in habits and especially partial to caves and old buildings. The cave in the Cloverdale Hills where the colony was found was near the head of Whitmire Creek among the live oaks and Chihuahua pines. It was in a cliff of baked volcanic ash with the entrance only 6 feet above the base. It was a dry cavern washed out of the soft rock 10 to 20 feet wide and 4 to 8 feet high, reaching back 100 feet into the mountain side. The bottom of the cave sloped upward and was dry and half filled with earth and bat guano. Back about 40 feet from the entrance was a mass of bats a yard across hanging from the roof like a swarm of bees. The writer's approach disturbed them, and as he came near enough to see in the half light some were fluttering away and others lighting, all were in motion, and there was much squeaking and disturbance. A couple of light charges of dust shot brought down showers of bats, from which many were gathered up for specimens. Most of the bats flew at the report, but a few remained hanging head down from the rocky ceiling, and the writer picked off as many more as he wanted, until all pockets were bulging. The cave was alive with flying bats, but no other species could be detected except a few free-tailed bats, four of which were secured for specimens. When the catch was examined outside the cave, 87 *thysanodes*, were counted all of which were carried back to camp for specimens.

At one of the cabins near the entrance of the Carlsbad Cave one of these bats was found drowned in a rain barrel half full of water and was saved for a specimen.

MYOTIS OCCULTUS Hollister

HOLLISTER'S BAT

Myotis occultus Hollister, Biol. Soc. Wash. Proc. 22: 43, March 10, 1909.
Myotis baileyi Hollister, Biol. Soc. Wash. Proc. 22: 44, 1909. Type from Ruidoso Creek at 7,500 feet altitude, White Mountains, N. Mex.

Type.—Collected at Needles (10 miles above), Calif., May 14, 1905, by Ned Hollister.

General characters.—A medium-sized bat often lacking one or two upper premolars; fur glossy or burnished, rich brown above, yellowish buff below; ears and membranes dark brown or blackish.

Measurements.—Type: Total length, 96; tail, 40; foot, 10.5; ear from crown, 10.6; forearm, 33 millimeters.

Distribution and habitat.—Four specimens of Hollister's bat from Ruidoso, in the White Mountains, three from Luna Valley near the head of the San Francisco River in extreme western New Mexico, and four from the Zuni Mountains, mark the only known records of the species from New Mexico. These were all taken in the Transition Zone among the yellow pines and Douglas spruce, but across central Arizona and in southern California they range or migrate into Lower Sonoran Zone also.

General habits.—On Ruidoso Creek near the town of Ruidoso, Hollister and the writer collected three specimens, shooting them as they flew up and down the creek between the tall trees. They flew rapidly in short zigzags, and it was only against the little patches of sky between the branches of the trees that they could be seen at all. In Luna Valley, Clarence Birdseye and the writer had the same experience, and secured only three specimens out of the large numbers that darted about the camp and along the edge of the woods. Though they came to drink from the little pools along the creek early in the evening when it was comparatively light in the open, it was almost impossible to shoot them, for they darted back and forth over the water in the low shady gulch of the creek bed and did not come out from the shadow of the trees until the dusk was so far advanced that it was impossible to see the gun sights or the bats except as they crossed the patches of sky. In the Zuni Mountains E. A. Goldman reported them as apparently the most abundant bat, and he secured four specimens at 8,200 and 8,600 feet altitude among yellow pines on the slopes of Mount Sedgwick. Though undoubtedly an abundant and wide-ranging species, these few fragments of knowledge concerning habits are all that are available.

MYOTIS EVOTIS CHRYSONOTUS (J. A. ALLEN)

LITTLE LONG-EARED BAT

Vespertilio chrysonotus J. A. Allen, Bul. Amer. Mus. Nat. Hist. 8:240, November 21, 1896.

Type.—Collected at Kinney ranch, Sweetwater County, Wyo., July 21, 1895, by W. W. Granger.

General characters.—A small bat, with relatively large ears that reach well beyond tip of nose; fur of upperparts golden brown; lowerparts buffy or whitish; ears and membranes blackish.

Measurements.—Total length, 96; tail, 48; foot, 9; ear from crown, 20; forearm, 40 millimeters.

Distribution and habitat.—The only specimens of the little long-eared bat from New Mexico are one from Vermejo River collected June 26, 1885, by W. L. Carpenter; one collected on the east slope of the San Luis Mountains in June, 1902, by Mearns; and two alcoholic specimens collected at Fort Wingate in July, 1885, by R. W. Shufeldt. Though these little bats apparently are not numerous anywhere, they are widely scattered over the Western States from the Rocky Mountains to the Pacific. They range from the Lower Sonoran Zone to at least the lower edge of the Canadian Zone in summer, but how much of this is migratory or wandering range there are at present insufficient data to determine.

General habits.—Little is known of the habits of this bat, except that occasionally one is shot while flying among the trees in some open forest or caught in a house entered through an open window in pursuit of flying insects. On the wing it is not distinguishable from many other species of small bats which flit about during the twilight hours. It is a beautiful little animal and when obtained is easily recognized by its big black ears and golden-brown fur.

MYOTIS CALIFORNICUS CALIFORNICUS (Audubon and Bachman)

Little California Bat

Vespertilio californicus Audubon and Bachman, Jour. Acad. Nat. Sci. Phila. 8 (part 2) : 285, 1842.
Myotis californicus Miller, North Amer. Fauna No. 13, p. 69, 1897.

Type locality.—California.
General characters.—A very small bat with a spread of wings only about 8 inches, with small ears, bright-tawny or hazel-brown fur, and blackish ears and membranes.
Measurements.—Total length, 77; tail, 37; foot, 6; ear from crown, 11; forearm, 32 millimeters.

Distribution and habitat.—The little California bats are found over most of the Lower Sonoran Zone area of New Mexico. There are specimens from Carlsbad Cave, San Andres Mountains, San Mateo Canyon, Animas Valley (Lang ranch), and Apache [35] (near Hachita).
General habits.—In a canyon of the San Mateo Mountains E. A. Goldman collected two of these little bats on October 6 as they were flying about at dusk near the creek. In the San Andres Mountains Gaut caught two in an old stone house in Bear Canyon during a cold storm on January 12, 1903. As his fire warmed the stone walls of the old house, the bats came out and began flying around in the room, evidently aroused from winter quarters in the walls. An old skull found in the deepest room of the Carlsbad Cave suggests the usual bat habit of spending the winter's hibernation in such retreats.

A specimen referred by Miller and Allen (1928, p. 158) to the pale desert form, *Myotis californicus pallidus* Stephens, from old Fort Defiance close to the New Mexico line in northeastern Arizona, suggests that this pale form probably occurs in the Gallup and San Juan country of northwestern New Mexico. It is merely a slightly paler desert form, scarcely recognizable in the field.

MYOTIS SUBULATUS MELANORHINUS (Merriam)

Black-Nosed Bat

Vespertilio melanorhinus Merriam, North Amer. Fauna No. 3, p. 46, September 11, 1890.
Vespertilio nitidus henshawii Harrison Allen, Monog. Bats North Amer., U. S. Natl. Mus. Bul. 43 (1893) : 103, March 14, 1894. Type from Fort Wingate, N. Mex.

Type.—Collected at Little Spring, north base of San Francisco Mountain, Ariz., August 4, 1889, by C. Hart Merriam and Vernon Bailey.
General characters.—Size small with small ears, sooty-black nose and face, light buffy brown back and pale buffy belly.
Measurements.—Total length, 81; tail, 39; foot, 6.5; ear from crown, 12; forearm, 33 millimeters.

Distribution and habitat.—One of the common small bats over the arid region from eastern Oregon and southern Colorado to southern

---

[35] This locality, not found on any map, was the name applied by A. W. Anthony to a locality in southwestern New Mexico, near what is now Hachita, where he collected a large number of specimens for Doctor Merriam in 1886.

California and Mexico, including most of New Mexico. There are specimens from Las Vegas, Hot Springs, Santa Rosa, Guadalupe Canyon,[36] Capitan Mountains, Camp Burgwyn (near Taos), Pecos, Tres Piedras, Zuni Mountains, Wingate, Silver City, and San Luis Mountains.

At Silver City, in June, 1894, A. K. Fisher secured one specimen and reported that they were common about the streets but were not seen outside the city limits. At the east base of the Capitan Mountains on June 15, 1899, the writer found them common among the junipers and nut pines at 6,500 feet, but they flew so rapidly among the trees in the twilight that he secured only one specimen. At Santa Rosa in the latter part of May, 1903, they were abundant with other species of bats in the canyon and juniper country just north and east of town, and a few specimens were secured, but much ammunition was wasted in attempts to hit the rapid, crooked-flying midgets in the dusk of evening. They flew noticeably among the trees and in open spaces, while the little canyon bats were mainly restricted to the vicinity of canyon walls, but apparently they roost during the day in cracks among the rocks and in little openings that reach farther back into the dark. At Tres Piedras in July, 1904, Gaut secured two specimens that were flying among the yellow pines in that locality, which is just at the edge of the Upper Sonoran and the Transition Zones. In the Zuni Mountains on June 20, 1909, E. A. Goldman collected one at dusk when flying among the yellow pines at 8,200 feet altitude, well up in the Transition Zone.

Food habits.—Like most bats, they are thirsty when they first emerge from their roosts and at once seek some still pool or open water from which they can drink by skimming over the surface, dipping down repeatedly and scooping up the water as they fly. Little ripples are made as they touch the water's surface, and often these are in series a few feet apart along their line of flight. A few minutes at the water pool satisfy the bats' thirst; then they scatter out to feed on the insects in the air. In a very short time after their first appearance their stomachs are found well distended with food, so that under normal conditions their rapid flight and quick motions enable them to obtain an ample food supply. Almost invariably when shot their stomachs are found to be full of food, but of so finely pulverized insect remains that very little can be determined as to the species eaten.

Breeding habits.—One female collected at Santa Rosa on May 29 was found to contain one small embryo and, so far as known, only one embryo has been found in the species. The mammae are arranged in a single pair too far back on the sides to be called pectoral and more accurately described as subaxillary. This is the usual position in most species of bats, so that when hanging up by the hind claws, as they generally are during the day, the folded wings make a little pocket just below each of the mammae in which the young can easily sleep without even having to hold on with their hooked claws. In this, as in other species of the genus Myotis, the armpits are furry, but the wing membranes, which enfold the young, are thin and naked.

<hr>

[36] The specimen from Guadalupe Canyon collected by Captain Pope in 1856 apparently came from some canyon on the east slope of the Guadalupe Mountains near the New Mexico and Texas line.

Hibernation.—Little is known of the winter habits of these bats, except as they are occasionally found in tunnels and mine shafts in winter in a quiet, and probably dormant, condition of hibernation. It is well known that great colonies of bats gather in caves during the cold winter months and hibernate for considerable time, but the actual species composing these colonies are not often determined. The extent and nature of hibernation and migration among bats are subjects little understood at the present time.

MYOTIS YUMANENSIS YUMANENSIS (H. ALLEN)

YUMA BAT

Vespertilio yumanensis H. Allen, Monogr. Bats North Amer., p. 58, 1864.
Myotis yumanensis Miller, North Amer. Fauna No. 13, p. 66, 1897.

Type.—Type series collected at Old Fort Yuma, Calif., in 1855 by Maj. G. H. Thomas.

General characters.—Size rather small; ears moderately long, reaching to tip of nose; fur lax and woolly, dull buffy gray above, buffy white below; ears and membranes light-grayish brown; tail membranes edged with lighter.

Measurements.—Total length, 77; tail, 35; foot, 8; ear from crown, 11; forearm, 34 millimeters.

Distribution and habitat.—The little pale Yuma bats cover both Upper and Lower Sonoran areas of the more arid parts of the Western States and south into Mexico. From New Mexico there are only three records, one collected in Apache Canyon, near Clayton, by A. H. Howell, August 10, 1901; one collected at Rinconada, in the Rio Grande Valley above Santa Fe, by Surber, May 29, 1904; and four collected by Merrill, at Mesilla Park, in September, 1916.

General habits.—Over much of the country these desert bats seem to be very scarce, but again where conditions are favorable they are found in great numbers established in large breeding colonies in caves or old buildings. Females have been shot flying about with one young clinging to the breast.

MYOTIS VOLANS INTERIOR MILLER

Western Little Brown Bat; TSE'LE-YAH-AH'NA of the Taos Indians

Myotis longicrus interior Miller, Biol. Soc. Wash. Proc. 27: 211, 1914.

Type from Taos Mountains, 5 miles south of Twining, at 11,300 feet altitude, collected July 23, 1904, by Vernon Bailey.

General characters.—A small bat, with small ears, rich chestnut brown fur, and dusky ears and membranes.

Measurements.—Total length, 91; tail, 32; foot, 8; ear from crown, 10; forearm, 38 millimeters.

Distribution and habitat.—Specimens of the western little brown bat have been taken in New Mexico near Twining in the Taos Mountains, Costilla River, Raton Range, Cantonment Burgwyn (near Taos), Santa Clara Canyon in the Jemez Mountains, Santa Fe, and Willis. From a wide range over other Western States—Montana and Washington to southern California and northern Mexico—it seems to have at least its center of abundance in the Transition Zone of mountain areas, and some specimens, including the type, have been taken well up in the Canadian Zone. It is largely a mountain species, and most of the specimens secured were shot among the yellow pines or spruces and aspens. In the Taos Mountains specimens were taken at 10,700 feet and others up to 11,400 feet, where frost covered the ground nearly every morning from July 23 to August 5.

General habits.—This is a late, quick-flying species, difficult to shoot, and the few specimens taken do not necessarily indicate a scarcity of individuals. They are largely forest dwellers, and many times in forest localities the writer has wasted all his powder on them and returned to camp empty handed, and has frequently seen much better wing shots do the same. Their flight is extremely rapid, quick, and erratic, and they usually keep close to the trees, only darting across the little open patches of sky where a snapshot occasionally brings one down. But on quiet evenings a dozen or more would often be seen circling about the campfire after it had become too dark to shoot.

In the Culebra Mountains farther north these bats were common at a 10,700-foot camp among the aspens and along the Costilla River lower down. In the Pecos River Mountains, on July 14 and 19, two specimens were secured at Willis, at 8,000 feet altitude, near the head of the Pecos River. One of these was shot at noon on a clear day as it was seen flying over the river among the trees, and the other was secured in the evening as with many others it was flying among the trees. In the Jemez Mountains two specimens were taken in Santa Clara Canyon at 8,000 feet, one of them as it was flying about among the trees at 4 p. m. The habit of occasionally flying in the daytime is observed among many species of bats, but probably indicates only that they have been disturbed in their roosting place and have been obliged to get out and hunt for new quarters.

Food habits.—Five specimens secured in the vicinity of the type locality are more than from any other locality in the State, but from the numbers seen around each of the camps there must be many thousands, if not millions, of these bats in the Sangre de Cristo Mountain forests. The stomachs of those killed were always well filled with finely pulverized insect remains, but the actual species eaten remains to be determined by some patient naturalist, who can give years of critical study to bat food. From their constant gleanings about the branches of the trees it is not improbable that the very existence of the forest growth may depend on the protection from insect enemies afforded by these busy night hunters. Fortunately bats will never need protection from hunters, and the species that do not gather in caves or buildings are not likely to be seriously interfered with through human agencies.

Breeding habits.—Of the breeding habits of this particular species apparently nothing is definitely known, except that the females have the usual number and position of mammae, one pair of subaxillary, which indicates the common number of one young.

MYOTIS LUCIFUGUS CARISSIMA Thomas

YELLOWSTONE BAT

Myotis (Leuconoë) carissima Thomas, Ann. and Mag. Nat. Hist. (7) 13: 383, May, 1904.

Type.—Collected at Yellowstone Lake, Yellowstone National Park, Wyo., September, 1903, by J. ffolliott Darling.

General characters.—Size medium for the small species of Myotis, ear medium, color of upper parts rich buffy brown or golden buff; lower parts pale buffy; ears and membranes dusky brown, the tail membranes tending to light edges.

Measurements.—Total length, 90; tail, 40; foot, 9; ear from crown, 12; forearm, 38 millimeters.

Distribution and habitat.—Mainly in semiarid Transition Zone from Montana and Oregon to California and New Mexico. The one New Mexico record is based on a skull from Sierra Grande, Union County, of which Miller and Allen (1928, p. 52) say "identification not positive," but another specimen collected on the Conejos River, Colo., close to the New Mexico line in the Rio Grande Valley, brings a positive record practically to the edge of the State.

General habits.—To a great extent these are mountain and forest dwellers sometimes found hanging up during the day in caves, buildings, or bridges, but usually flying about water or among the tree tops in the evening. In the Devils Kitchen, a warm cave at Mammoth Hot Springs, in Yellowstone Park, they hang up on the dry walls during summer days, but leave for some cooler place in which to hibernate for winter. A summer colony also visited the attic of the Yellowstone Lake Hotel. (Bailey, 1930, p. 184.)

LITERATURE CITED

ABERT, J. W.
  1846. MESSAGE FROM THE PRESIDENT OF THE UNITED STATES, IN COMPLIANCE
    WITH A RESOLUTION OF THE SENATE, COMMUNICATING A REPORT OF AN
    EXPEDITION LED BY LIEUTENANT ABERT, ON THE UPPER ARKANSAS AND
    THROUGH THE COUNTRY OF THE COMANCHE INDIANS IN THE FALL OF
    THE YEAR 1845 . . . 75 pp., illus. (U. S. Cong. 29th, 1st sess.,
    Senate Doc. 438.)
  1848. REPORT ON AN EXPEDITION IN NEW MEXICO IN 1846–7. (U. S. Cong. 30th,
    1st sess., House Ex. Doc. 41:417–548.)
ALLEN, J. A.
  1874. NOTES ON THE MAMMALS OF PORTIONS OF KANSAS, COLORADO, WYOMING
    AND UTAH. Bul. Essex Inst. 6: 43–66.
  1876. THE AMERICAN BISONS, LIVING AND EXTINCT. Ky. Geol. Survey Mem.
    1 (pt. 2): 1–246, illus. [Also issued as Mem. Mus. Comp. Zool.
    4 (10).]
  1893. LIST OF MAMMALS COLLECTED BY MR. CHARLES P. ROWLEY IN THE SAN
    JUAN REGION OF COLORADO, NEW MEXICO, AND UTAH, WITH DESCRIPTIONS
    OF NEW SPECIES. Bul. Amer. Mus. Nat. Hist. 5: 69–84.
  1896a. DESCRIPTIONS OF NEW NORTH AMERICAN MAMMALS. Bul. Amer. Mus.
    Nat. Hist. 8: 233–240, illus.
  1896b. LIST OF MAMMALS COLLECTED BY MR. WALTER W. GRANGER, IN NEW
    MEXICO, UTAH, WYOMING, AND NEBRASKA, 1895–96, WITH FIELD NOTES
    BY THE COLLECTOR. Bul. Amer. Mus. Nat. Hist. 8: 241–258.
BACA, T. C. DE
  1914. REPORT OF THE GAME AND FISH WARDEN OF NEW MEXICO, 1912–1914.
    116 pp., illus. Santa Fe.
BAILEY, (MRS.) F. M.
  1928. BIRDS OF NEW MEXICO. Published by N. Mex. Dept. Game and Fish.
    807 pp., illus. Santa Fe.
BAILEY, V.
  1905. BIOLOGICAL SURVEY OF TEXAS . . . North Amer. Fauna No. 25, 222 pp.,
    illus.
  1913. LIFE ZONES AND CROP ZONES OF NEW MEXICO. North Amer. Fauna No.
    35, 100 pp., illus.
  1926. BIOLOGICAL SURVEY OF NORTH DAKOTA. North Amer. Fauna No. 49, 229
    pp., illus.
  1927. BEAVER HABITS AND EXPERIMENTS IN BEAVER CULTURE. U. S. Dept. Agr.
    Tech. Bul. 21, 40 pp., illus.
  1928. ANIMAL LIFE OF THE CARLSBAD CAVERN. 195 pp., illus. Baltimore.
    (Monog. Amer. Soc. Mammal. No. 3.)
  1930. ANIMAL LIFE OF YELLOWSTONE NATIONAL PARK. 241 pp., illus. Spring-
    field, Ill.
BAILEY, V., and SPERRY, C. C.
  1929. LIFE HISTORY AND HABITS OF GRASSHOPPER MICE, GENUS ONYCHOMYS.
    U. S. Dept. Agr. Tech. Bul. 145, 20 pp., illus.
BAIRD, S. F.
  1857. MAMMALS OF NORTH AMERICA. Pacific R. R. Rept. v. 8, 757 pp., illus.
  1859. MAMMALS OF THE BOUNDARY. In United States and Mexican Boundary
    Survey, under the Order of Lieut. Col. W. H. Emory. v. 2, pt. 2,
    62 pp., illus.
BANGS, O.
  1898. A LIST OF THE MAMMALS OF LABRADOR. Amer. Nat. 32: [489]–507,
    illus.
BARBER, C. M.
  1902. NOTES ON LITTLE-KNOWN NEW MEXICAN MAMMALS AND SPECIES APPAR-
    ENTLY NOT RECORDED FROM THE TERRITORY. Biol. Soc. Wash. Proc.
    15: 191–193.
BARBER, C. M., and COCKERELL, T. D. A.
  1898. A NEW WEASEL FROM NEW MEXICO. Acad. Nat. Sci. Phila. Proc. 1898:
    188–189.

BARTLETT, J. R.

    1854. PERSONAL NARRATIVE OF EXPLORATIONS AND INCIDENTS IN TEXAS, NEW MEXICO, CALIFORNIA, SONORA, AND CHIHUAHUA, CONNECTED WITH THE UNITED STATES AND MEXICAN BOUNDARY COMMISSION, DURING THE YEARS 1850, '51, '52, AND '53. 2 v., illus. New York.

CARY, M.

    1911. A BIOLOGICAL SURVEY OF COLORADO. North Amer. Fauna No. 33, 256 pp., illus.

COPE, E. D.

    1875. REPORT ON THE GEOLOGY OF THAT PART OF NORTHWESTERN NEW MEXICO EXAMINED DURING THE FIELD SEASON OF 1874. Geogr. Expl. and Surveys West of 100th Meridian in California, Nevada, Nebraska, Utah, Arizona, Colorado, New Mexico, Wyoming, and Montana. Ann. Rpt. Appendix G1, p. 61–97, illus. Washington, D. C.

COUES, E.

    1877. FUR-BEARING ANIMALS: A MONOGRAPH OF NORTH AMERICAN MUSTELIDAE. U. S. Geol. and Geogr. Survey Terr., Misc. Pub. 8, 348 pp., illus. Washington, D. C.

    1895. THE EXPEDITIONS OF ZEBULON MONTGOMERY PIKE . . . v. 2. Arkansaw Journey—Mexican Tour., pp. 357–855. New York.

COUES, E., and YARROW, H. C.

    1875. REPORT UPON THE COLLECTIONS OF MAMMALS MADE IN PORTIONS OF NEVADA, UTAH, CALIFORNIA, COLORADO, NEW MEXICO, AND ARIZONA DURING THE YEARS 1871, 1872, 1873, AND 1874. In Wheeler, G. M., Report Upon Geographical and Geological Explorations and Surveys West of the One Hundredth Meridian. 5: 35–129. Washington, D. C.

DAVIS, W. W. H.

    1869. THE SPANISH CONQUEST OF NEW MEXICO. 438 p. Doylestown, Pa.

EDWORDS, C. E.

    1893. CAMP-FIRES OF A NATURALIST; THE STORY OF FOURTEEN EXPEDITIONS AFTER NORTH AMERICAN MAMMALS, FROM THE FIELD NOTES OF LEWIS LINDSAY DYCHE. . . 304 pp., illus. New York.

GABRIELSON, I. N., and HORN, E. E.

    1930. PORCUPINE CONTROL IN THE WESTERN STATES. U. S. Dept. Agr. Leaflet 60, 8 pp., illus.

GOLDMAN, E. A.

    1910. REVISION OF THE WOOD RATS OF THE GENUS NEOTOMA. North Amer. Fauna No. 31., 124 pp., illus.

GRIGGS, J. W.

    1909. HYBRIDIZING THE VIRGINIA DEER. Amer. Breeders' Assoc. Ann. Rpt. 5: 212–213.

HENDERSON, J., and HARRINGTON, J. P.

    1914. ETHNOZOOLOGY OF THE TEWA INDIANS. Bur. Amer. Ethnol. Bul. 56, 76 pp.

HODGE, F. W. (editor)

    1907–10. HANDBOOK OF AMERICAN INDIANS NORTH OF MEXICO. Bur. Amer. Ethnol. Bul. 30, 2 v., illus. Washington, D. C.

HOLLISTER, N.

    1911. A SYSTEMATIC SYNOPSIS OF THE MUSKRATS. North Amer. Fauna No. 32, 47 pp., illus.

    1916. A SYSTEMATIC ACCOUNT OF THE PRAIRIE-DOGS. North Amer. Fauna No. 40, 37 pp., illus.

HORNADAY, W. T.

    1889. THE EXTERMINATION OF THE AMERICAN BISON, WITH A SKETCH OF ITS DISCOVERY AND LIFE HISTORY. Smith. Inst. Ann. Rpt. 1887 (pt. 2): 367–548, illus.

    1901. NOTES ON THE MOUNTAIN SHEEP OF NORTH AMERICA, WITH A DESCRIPTION OF A NEW SPECIES. N. Y. Zool. Soc. Ann. Rpt. 5: [77]–122, illus.

HOWELL, A. H.

    1914. REVISION OF THE AMERICAN HARVEST MICE (GENUS REITHRODONTOMYS). North Amer. Fauna No. 36, 97 pp., illus.

    1915. REVISION OF THE AMERICAN MARMOTS. North Amer. Fauna No. 37, 80 pp., illus.

    1929. REVISION OF THE AMERICAN CHIPMUNKS (GENERA TAMIAS AND EUTAMIAS). North Amer. Fauna No. 52, 157 pp., illus.

HUMBOLDT, A. DE
    1811. ESSAI POLITIQUE SUR LE ROYAUME DE LA NOUVELLE-ESPAGNE [MEXICO].
        5 v. Paris.
JACKSON, H. H. T.
    1908. A PRELIMINARY LIST OF WISCONSIN MAMMALS. Bul. Wis. Nat. Hist.
        Soc. (n. s.) 6:13–34, illus.
    1928. A TAXONOMIC REVIEW OF THE AMERICAN LONG-TAILED SHREWS. North
        Amer. Fauna No. 51, 238 pp., illus.
JAMES, E. (compiler)
    1823. ACCOUNT OF AN EXPEDITION FROM PITTSBURGH TO THE ROCKY MOUNTAINS
        PERFORMED IN THE YEARS 1819, 1820 . . . UNDER THE COMMAND OF
        MAJ. S. H. LONG . . . COMPILED FROM THE NOTES OF STEPHEN H. LONG,
        THOMAS SAY, AND OTHER MEMBERS OF THE PARTY. 3 v., illus.
        London.
KENNERLY, C. B. R.
    1856. IN REPORTS OF EXPLORATIONS AND SURVEYS TO ASCERTAIN THE MOST
        PRACTICABLE AND ECONOMICAL ROUTE FOR A RAILROAD FROM THE MIS-
        SISSIPPI RIVER TO THE PACIFIC OCEAN. v. 4, pt. 6. Report on the
        Zoology of the Expedition., pp. 1–17. Washington, D. C.
LIGON, J. S.
    1927. WILD LIFE OF NEW MEXICO: ITS CONSERVATION AND MANAGEMENT.
        BEING A REPORT ON THE GAME SURVEY OF THE STATE 1926 AND 1927.
        212 pp., illus. N. Mex. State Game Commission, Santa Fe.
LYON, M. W., JR.
    1907. MAMMAL REMAINS FROM TWO PREHISTORIC VILLAGE SITES IN NEW MEX-
        ICO AND ARIZONA. U. S. Natl. Mus. Proc. 31: 647–649.
McATEE, W. L.
    1907. A LIST OF THE MAMMALS, REPTILES, AND BATRACHIANS OF MONROE
        COUNTY, INDIANA. Biol. Soc. Wash. Proc. 20: 1–16.
MEARNS, E. A.
    1896. PRELIMINARY DESCRIPTION OF A NEW SUBGENUS AND SIX NEW SPECIES
        AND SUBSPECIES OF HARES FROM THE MEXICAN BORDER OF THE UNITED
        STATES. U. S. Natl. Mus. Proc. 18: 551–565.
    1907. MAMMALS OF THE MEXICAN BOUNDARY OF THE UNITED STATES. . . .
        U. S. Natl. Mus. Bul. 56, 530 pp., illus.
MERRIAM, C. H.
    1884. THE MAMMALS OF THE ADIRONDACK REGION, NORTHEASTERN NEW YORK.
        WITH AN INTRODUCTORY CHAPTER TREATING OF THE LOCATION AND
        BOUNDARIES OF THE REGION, ITS GEOLOGICAL HISTORY, TOPOGRAPHY,
        CLIMATE, GENERAL FEATURES, BOTANY, AND FAUNAL POSITION. 316 pp.
        New York. [Reprinted from Linn. Soc. (N. Y.) Trans. 1:9–107,
        1882; 2: 1–214, 1884.]
    1889. DESCRIPTIONS OF FOURTEEN NEW SPECIES AND ONE NEW GENUS OF NORTH
        AMERICAN MAMMALS. North Amer. Fauna No. 2, 52 pp., illus.
    1890a. RESULTS OF A BIOLOGICAL SURVEY OF THE SAN FRANCISCO MOUNTAIN
        REGION AND DESERT OF THE LITTLE COLORADO IN ARIZONA. North
        Amer. Fauna No. 3, 136 pp., illus.
    1890b. DESCRIPTIONS OF TWENTY-SIX NEW SPECIES OF NORTH AMERICAN MAM-
        MALS. North Amer. Fauna No. 4, 60 pp., illus.
    1902. THE PRAIRIE DOG OF THE GREAT PLAINS. U. S. Dept. Agr. Yearbook
        1901: 257–270, illus.
MILLER, G. S., JR.
    1893. DESCRIPTION OF A NEW MOUSE FROM SOUTHERN NEW MEXICO AND
        ARIZONA. Bul. Amer. Mus. Nat. Hist. 5: 331–334.
    1903. A SECOND SPECIMEN OF EUDERMA MACULATUM. Biol. Soc. Wash. Proc.
        16: 165–166, illus.
MILLER, G. S., JR., and ALLEN, G. M.
    1928. THE AMERICAN BATS OF THE GENERA MYOTIS AND PIZONYX. U. S.
        Natl. Mus. Bul. 144, 218 pp., illus.
NELSON, E. W.
    1909. THE RABBITS OF NORTH AMERICA. North Amer. Fauna No. 29, 314 p.,
        illus.
    1925. STATUS OF THE PRONGHORNED ANTELOPE, 1922–1924. U. S. Dept. Agr.
        Bul. 1346, 64 pp., illus.
    1926. BATS IN RELATION TO THE PRODUCTION OF GUANO AND THE DESTRUCTION
        OF INSECTS. U. S. Dept. Agr. Bul. 1395, 12 pp., illus.

OSBORN, S. E.
  1892. COLORADO WOODCHUCKS. Observer 3 (1) : 32.
OSGOOD, W. H.
  1909. REVISION OF THE MICE OF THE GENUS PEROMYSCUS. North Amer.
        Fauna No. 28, 285 pp., illus.
PARKE, J. G.
  1855. REPORT OF EXPLORATIONS FOR THAT PORTION OF A RAILROAD ROUTE, NEAR
        THE THIRTY-SECOND PARALLEL OF NORTH LATITUDE, LYING BETWEEN
        DONA ANA, ON THE RIO GRANDE, AND PIMAS VILLAGES, ON THE GILA.
        28 p. In Reports of Explorations and Surveys to Ascertain the
        Most Practicable and Economical Route for a Railroad from the
        Mississippi River to the Pacific Ocean . . . v. 2. ([U. S.] Cong.
        33, 3d sess., Ex. Doc. 91.)
PATTIE, J. O.
  1905. THE PERSONAL NARRATIVE OF JAMES O. PATTIE, OF KENTUCKY, DUR-
        ING AN EXPEDITION FROM ST. LOUIS THROUGH THE VAST REGIONS BE-
        TWEEN THAT PLACE AND THE PACIFIC OCEAN, AND THENCE BACK
        THROUGH THE CITY OF MEXICO TO VERA CRUZ, DURING JOURNEYINGS OF
        SIX YEARS . . . [A reprint of the original edition of 1831] in R. G.
        Thwaites's Early Western Travels, 1748–1846 . . . v. 18, 379 pp.,
        illus. Cleveland.
POPE, J.
  1855. REPORT OF EXPLORATION OF A ROUTE FOR THE PACIFIC RAILROAD NEAR
        THE THIRTY-SECOND PARALLEL OF NORTH LATITUDE, FROM THE RED
        RIVER TO THE RIO GRANDE. 185 p., illus. In Reports of Explora-
        tions and Surveys to Ascertain the Most Practicable and Econom-
        ical Route for a Railroad from the Mississippi River to the
        Pacific Ocean . . . v. 2. ([U. S.] Cong. 33, 3d sess., Ex. Doc. 91.)
ROOSEVELT, T.
  1901. WITH THE COUGAR HOUNDS. Scribner's Mag. 30 : 417–435, 545–564,
        illus.
SCHEFFER, T. H.
  1931. HABITS AND ECONOMIC STATUS OF THE POCKET GOPHERS. U. S. Dept.
        Agr. Tech. Bul. 224, 27 pp., illus.
SETON, E. T.
  1909. LIFE HISTORIES OF NORTHERN ANIMALS. AN ACCOUNT OF THE MAMMALS
        OF MANITOBA. v. 1. 1, Grass-eaters. 673 p., illus. New York.
  1925–1928. LIVES OF GAME ANIMALS. 4 v., illus. Garden City, N. Y.
SILVER, J.
  1927. RAT CONTROL. U. S. Dept. Agr. Farmers' Bul. 1533, 21 pp., illus.
STONE, W., and REHN, J. A. G.
  1903. TERRESTRIAL VERTEBRATES OF SOUTHERN NEW MEXICO AND WESTERN
        TEXAS. Acad. Nat. Sci. Phila. Proc. 55 : 16–34.
TAYLOR, W. P.
  1930. OUTLINES FOR STUDIES OF MAMMALIAN LIFE HISTORIES. U. S. Dept.
        Agr. Misc. Pub. 86, 12 pp.
TAYLOR, W. P., and LOFTFIELD, J. V. G.
  1924. DAMAGE TO RANGE GRASSES BY THE ZUNI PRAIRIE DOG. U. S. Dept.
        Agr. Bul. 1227, 16 pp., illus.
TOWNSEND, C. H. T.
  1893. NOTES ON THE OCCURRENCE OF THE PUMA (FELIS CONCOLOR L.) IN
        SOUTHERN NEW MEXICO. Zoe 3 : 309–311.
VORHIES, C. T., and TAYLOR, W. P.
  1922. LIFE HISTORY OF THE KANGAROO RAT, DIPODOMYS SPECTABILIS SPECTA-
        BILIS MERRIAM. U. S. Dept. Agr. Bul. 1091, 40 pp., illus. [Also
        Ariz. Agr. Expt. Sta. Tech. Bul. 1.]
WARREN, E. R.
  1910. THE MAMMALS OF COLORADO. AN ACCOUNT OF THE SEVERAL SPECIES
        FOUND WITHIN THE BOUNDARIES OF THE STATE, TOGETHER WITH A
        RECORD OF THEIR HABITS AND OF THEIR DISTRIBUTION. 300 pp., illus.
        New York.
  1927. THE BEAVER: ITS WORK AND ITS WAYS. Amer. Soc. Mammal. Monog.
        2, 177 pp., illus. Baltimore.

WHIPPLE, A. W.
    1856. REPORT OF EXPLORATIONS FOR A RAILWAY ROUTE, NEAR THE THIRTY-FIFTH
        PARALLEL OF NORTH LATITUDE, FROM THE MISSISSIPPI RIVER TO THE
        PACIFIC OCEAN. PART 1. ITINERARY. 136 pp., illus. In Reports of
        Explorations and Surveys to Ascertain the Most Practicable and
        Economical Route for a Railroad from the Mississippi River to
        the Pacific Ocean. . . . v. 2. ([U. S.] Cong. 33, 3d. sess., Ex.
        Doc. 91.)
WHIPPLE, A. W., EWBANK, T., and TURNER, W. W.
    1856. REPORT UPON THE INDIAN TRIBES. 127 pp., illus. In Reports of Ex-
        plorations and Surveys to Ascertain the Most Practicable and Eco-
        nomical Route for a Railroad from the Mississippi River to the
        the Pacific Ocean. . . . v. 2. ([U. S.] Cong. 33, 3d sess., Ex. Doc.
        91.)
WINSHIP, G. P.
    1896. THE CORONADO EXPEDITION, 1540–1542. Bur. of Ethnol. Ann. Rpt.
        Sec. Smithsonian Inst. (1892–93) 14 : 329–613, illus. (Transla-
        tion of the Narrative of Castañeda reprinted in Winship's The
        Journey of Coronado, 1540–1542, 251 pp., illus., New York. 1922.)
WOODHOUSE, S. W.
    1854. REPORT ON THE NATURAL HISTORY OF THE COUNTRY PASSED OVER BY THE
        EXPLORING EXPEDITION UNDER THE COMMAND OF BREV. CAPT. L. SIT-
        GREAVES. . . . : Mammals. In Sitgreaves's Report of an Expedition
        down the Zuni and Colorado Rivers. 198 pp., illus. Washington,
        D. C. ([U. S.] Cong. 33, 1st sess., Senate Ex. Doc.)
WOOTON, E. O., and STANDLEY, P. C.
    1915. FLORA OF NEW MEXICO. U. S. Natl. Mus. Contrib. U. S. Natl. Her-
        barium 19, 794 pp.
YOUNG, S. P.
    1930. HINTS ON COYOTE AND WOLF TRAPPING. U. S. Dept. Agr. Leaflet 59,
        8 pp., illus.

PLATE 1

B310AM

TEXAS ARMADILLO (DASYPUS NOVEMCINCTUM TEXANUM)

An unborn young sent to the Bureau of Biological Survey by J. D. Mitchell, from Victoria, Tex.   Natural size.

PLATE 2

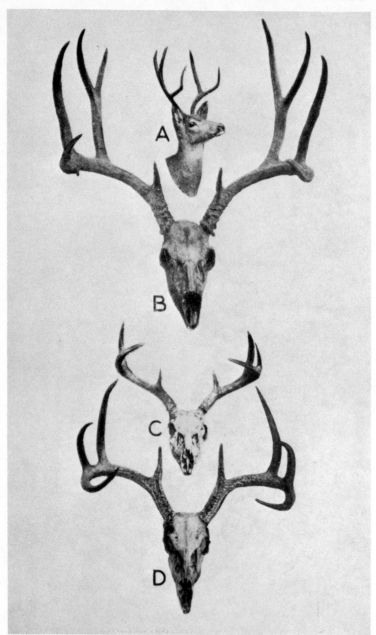

B4435M

ANTLERS OF DEER

A, Immature Rocky Mountain mule deer (*Odocoileus hemionus macrotis*) from Clayton, N. Mex.;
B, adult Rocky Mountain mule deer from the Gallinas Mountains, showing typical forked
antlers; C, little Sonora deer (*O. couesi*) from the Mimbres Range, on same scale as B and D;
D, plains white-tailed deer (*O. virginianus macrourus*) from Oklahoma, showing the single-beam
type of antlers.

PLATE 3

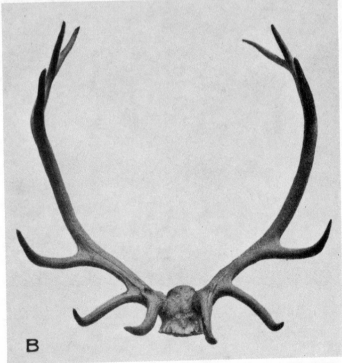

B5519   B1827M

ANTLERS OF ELK

A, Old antlers of Merriam's elk (*Cervus merriami*) photographed at a ranch in the Sacramento Mountains in 1903; B, antlers of a large bull of Merriam's elk taken in the same mountains in 1881, now in the United States National Museum collection.

PLATE 4

B3740   B4031M

A, Little cottontail (*Sylvilagus auduboni minor*) near a prairie-dog burrow at Carlsbad in the Pecos Valley; B, rock cony (*Ochotona saxatilis incana*) from Irwin, Colo. (Photos by E. R. Warren)

PLATE 5

B4032M   B1887M

A, Fremont's pine squirrel (*Sciurus fremonti fremonti*) of Colorado; B, larger Colorado chipmunks (*Eutamias quadrivittatus quadrivittatus*) from Colorado.   (Photos by E. R. Warren)

PLATE 6

B23272   B4033M

A, Gray-tailed antelope squirrel (*Ammospermophilus harrisi*) taken near Tucson, Ariz.; B, Say's ground squirrel (*Callospermophilus lateralis*) from Colorado.   (Photo by E. R. Warren)

PLATE 7

B23238   B18556

A, Spotted ground squirrel (*Citellus spilosoma canescens*) from Arizona; B, pale 13-lined ground squirrel (*C. tridecemlineatus arenicola*) on plains near Clayton, N. Mex.

PLATE 8

B23286   B4030M

A, Arizona grasshopper mouse (*Onychomys torridus torridus*) eating a grasshopper; B, long-nosed deer mouse (*Peromyscus nasutus*) from Colorado. (Photo by E. R. Warren)

PLATE 9

B23323   B4029M

A, White-throated wood rat (*Neotoma albigula albigula*) taken at base of Santa Rita Mountains, Ariz.; B, Colorado bushy-tailed wood rat (*N. cinerea orolestes*). (Photo by E. R. Warren)

PLATE 10

B4035M   B4034M

A, Dwarf meadow mouse (*Microtus nanus nanus*); B, jumping mouse (*Zapus princeps*). (Photos taken at Crested Butte, Colo., by E. R. Warren)

PLATE 11

B4544M   B7167A

A, Beaver (*Castor canadensis*) photographed by Ben East; B, beaver house in pond on head of Costilla River; the house is about 20 feet wide at the surface of the water and 6 feet high above, and about the same below the water line

PLATE 12

B23357   B23430

A, Yellow-haired porcupine (*Erethizon epixanthum*) photographed at Crested Butte, Colo., in 1903 by E. R. Warren; B, Baird's pocket mouse (*Perognathus flavus*), the smallest rodent in New Mexico, about natural size

PLATE 13

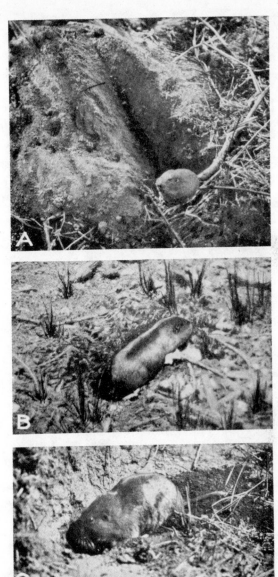

B10882   B450   B18559

THREE GENERA OF NEW MEXICO POCKET GOPHERS

A, Desert pocket gopher (*Geomys arenarius*) burrowing in irrigation
ditch bank at Mesilla Park; B, fulvous pocket gopher (*Thomomys
fulvus fulvus*) filling its pockets with green leaves near its burrow
at Cloudcroft; C, chestnut-faced pocket gopher (*Cratogeomys
castanops*) starting a new burrow on the prairie at Clayton.

PLATE 14

B23467   B10767   B5487

A, Large kangaroo rat (*Dipodomys spectabilis spectabilis*) from Tucson, Ariz., in captivity, filling its cheek pouches with rolled oats; B, mound of New Mexico banner-tail (*D. s. baileyi*); C, New Mexico banner-tails caught in traps near the mound of earth that protects their underground burrows and den near Valentine, Tex.

PLATE 15

B23449   B23457

A, Merriam's kangaroo rat (*Dipodomys merriami merriami*), captive photographed in glass box;
B, Ord's 5-toed kangaroo rat (*Perodipus ordii ordii*), photographed in captivity

PLATE 16

A, Skin of jaguar (*Felis onca hernandesi*) killed in the Datil Mountains in 1902 (photo by N. Hollister, 1905); B, bobcat (*Lynx rufus baileyi*) in sagebrush near Antonita, Colo.

PLATE 17

B12285   B8929

A, New Mexico desert fox (*Vulpes macrotis neomexicana*) taken by E. A. Goldman on the San Augustine Plains in 1909; B, Arizona gray fox (*Urocyon cinereoargenteus scottii*) on the rocky slopes of the Mimbres, 1906

PLATE 18

B134M   B10776

A, Two gray wolves (*Canis lycaon baileyi*) and two coyotes (*Canis latrans texensis*) taken by H. H. Hotchkiss in the Mogollon Mountains in 1907; B, Mearns's coyote (*Canis mearnsi*), in the thin August coat, shot in the Playas Valley in 1908

PLATE 19

B4573M   B23508

A, Northern Plains skunk (*Mephitis hudsonica*) at Crested Butte, Colo. (photo by E. R. Warren);
B, Mexican raccoon (*Procyon lotor mexicanus*) in hackberry tree near Tucson, Ariz.

PLATE 20

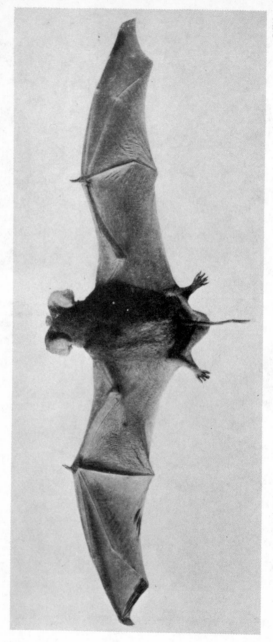

E499M

MEXICAN FREE-TAILED BAT (TADARIDA MEXICANA), FROM SKIN IN UNITED STATES NATIONAL MUSEUM COLLECTION

PLATE 21

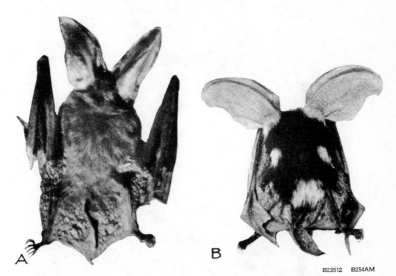

B23512   B254AM

A, Long-eared bat (*Corynorhinus macrotis pallescens*), photograph of fresh specimen; B, spotted bat (*Euderma maculatum*), from specimen in United States National Museum, collected at Mesilla Park, N. Mex., by E. O. Wooton

PLATE 22

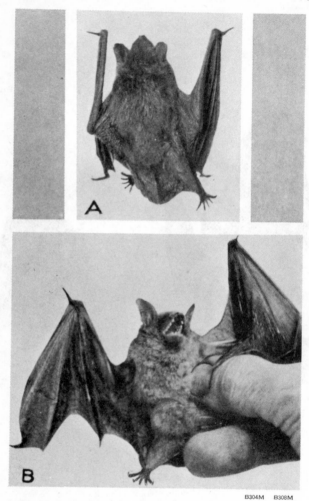

B304M   B308M

A, Cave bat (*Myotis velifer velifer*), from specimen taken at Sun City, Kans., by Theo. H. Scheffer; B, brown bat (*Eptesicus fuscus fuscus*) photographed alive at Washington, D. C.

INDEX

O

A CATALOGUE OF SELECTED DOVER BOOKS
IN ALL FIELDS OF INTEREST

A CATALOGUE OF SELECTED DOVER BOOKS
IN ALL FIELDS OF INTEREST

AMERICA'S OLD MASTERS, James T. Flexner. Four men emerged unexpectedly from provincial 18th century America to leadership in European art: Benjamin West, J. S. Copley, C. R. Peale, Gilbert Stuart. Brilliant coverage of lives and contributions. Revised, 1967 edition. 69 plates. 365pp. of text.

21806-6 Paperbound $2.75

FIRST FLOWERS OF OUR WILDERNESS: AMERICAN PAINTING, THE COLONIAL PERIOD, James T. Flexner. Painters, and regional painting traditions from earliest Colonial times up to the emergence of Copley, West and Peale Sr., Foster, Gustavus Hesselius, Feke, John Smibert and many anonymous painters in the primitive manner. Engaging presentation, with 162 illustrations. xxii + 368pp.

22180-6 Paperbound $3.50

THE LIGHT OF DISTANT SKIES: AMERICAN PAINTING, 1760-1835, James T. Flexner. The great generation of early American painters goes to Europe to learn and to teach: West, Copley, Gilbert Stuart and others. Allston, Trumbull, Morse; also contemporary American painters—primitives, derivatives, academics—who remained in America. 102 illustrations. xiii + 306pp. 22179-2 Paperbound $3.00

A HISTORY OF THE RISE AND PROGRESS OF THE ARTS OF DESIGN IN THE UNITED STATES, William Dunlap. Much the richest mine of information on early American painters, sculptors, architects, engravers, miniaturists, etc. The only source of information for scores of artists, the major primary source for many others. Unabridged reprint of rare original 1834 edition, with new introduction by James T. Flexner, and 394 new illustrations. Edited by Rita Weiss. 6⅝ x 9⅝.

21695-0, 21696-9, 21697-7 Three volumes, Paperbound $13.50

EPOCHS OF CHINESE AND JAPANESE ART, Ernest F. Fenollosa. From primitive Chinese art to the 20th century, thorough history, explanation of every important art period and form, including Japanese woodcuts; main stress on China and Japan, but Tibet, Korea also included. Still unexcelled for its detailed, rich coverage of cultural background, aesthetic elements, diffusion studies, particularly of the historical period. 2nd, 1913 edition. 242 illustrations. lii + 439pp. of text.

20364-6, 20365-4 Two volumes, Paperbound $5.00

THE GENTLE ART OF MAKING ENEMIES, James A. M. Whistler. Greatest wit of his day deflates Oscar Wilde, Ruskin, Swinburne; strikes back at inane critics, exhibitions, art journalism; aesthetics of impressionist revolution in most striking form. Highly readable classic by great painter. Reproduction of edition designed by Whistler. Introduction by Alfred Werner. xxxvi + 334pp.

21875-9 Paperbound $2.25

CATALOGUE OF DOVER BOOKS

VISUAL ILLUSIONS: THEIR CAUSES, CHARACTERISTICS, AND APPLICATIONS, Matthew Luckiesh. Thorough description and discussion of optical illusion, geometric and perspective, particularly; size and shape distortions, illusions of color, of motion; natural illusions; use of illusion in art and magic, industry, etc. Most useful today with op art, also for classical art. Scores of effects illustrated. Introduction by William H. Ittleson. 100 illustrations. xxi + 252pp.

21530-X Paperbound $1.50

A HANDBOOK OF ANATOMY FOR ART STUDENTS, Arthur Thomson. Thorough, virtually exhaustive coverage of skeletal structure, musculature, etc. Full text, supplemented by anatomical diagrams and drawings and by photographs of undraped figures. Unique in its comparison of male and female forms, pointing out differences of contour, texture, form. 211 figures, 40 drawings, 86 photographs. xx + 459pp. 5⅜ x 8⅜.

21163-0 Paperbound $3.00

150 MASTERPIECES OF DRAWING, Selected by Anthony Toney. Full page reproductions of drawings from the early 16th to the end of the 18th century, all beautifully reproduced: Rembrandt, Michelangelo, Dürer, Fragonard, Urs, Graf, Wouwerman, many others. First-rate browsing book, model book for artists. xviii + 150pp. 8⅜ x 11¼.

21032-4 Paperbound $2.00

THE LATER WORK OF AUBREY BEARDSLEY, Aubrey Beardsley. Exotic, erotic, ironic masterpieces in full maturity: Comedy Ballet, Venus and Tannhauser, Pierrot, Lysistrata, Rape of the Lock, Savoy material, Ali Baba, Volpone, etc. This material revolutionized the art world, and is still powerful, fresh, brilliant. With *The Early Work*, all Beardsley's finest work. 174 plates, 2 in color. xiv + 176pp. 8⅛ x 11.

21817-1 Paperbound $3.00

DRAWINGS OF REMBRANDT, Rembrandt van Rijn. Complete reproduction of fabulously rare edition by Lippmann and Hofstede de Groot, completely reedited, updated, improved by Prof. Seymour Slive, Fogg Museum. Portraits, Biblical sketches, landscapes, Oriental types, nudes, episodes from classical mythology—All Rembrandt's fertile genius. Also selection of drawings by his pupils and followers. "Stunning volumes," *Saturday Review*. 550 illustrations. lxxviii + 552pp. 9⅛ x 12¼.

21485-0, 21486-9 Two volumes, Paperbound $6.50

THE DISASTERS OF WAR, Francisco Goya. One of the masterpieces of Western civilization—83 etchings that record Goya's shattering, bitter reaction to the Napoleonic war that swept through Spain after the insurrection of 1808 and to war in general. Reprint of the first edition, with three additional plates from Boston's Museum of Fine Arts. All plates facsimile size. Introduction by Philip Hofer, Fogg Museum. v + 97pp. 9⅜ x 8¼.

21872-4 Paperbound $1.75

GRAPHIC WORKS OF ODILON REDON. Largest collection of Redon's graphic works ever assembled: 172 lithographs, 28 etchings and engravings, 9 drawings. These include some of his most famous works. All the plates from *Odilon Redon: oeuvre graphique complet,* plus additional plates. New introduction and caption translations by Alfred Werner. 209 illustrations. xxvii + 209pp. 9⅛ x 12¼.

21966-8 Paperbound $4.00

DESIGN BY ACCIDENT; A BOOK OF "ACCIDENTAL EFFECTS" FOR ARTISTS AND DESIGNERS, James F. O'Brien. Create your own unique, striking, imaginative effects by "controlled accident" interaction of materials: paints and lacquers, oil and water based paints, splatter, crackling materials, shatter, similar items. Everything you do will be different; first book on this limitless art, so useful to both fine artist and commercial artist. Full instructions. 192 plates showing "accidents," 8 in color. viii + 215pp. 8⅜ x 11¼.   21942-9 Paperbound $3.50

THE BOOK OF SIGNS, Rudolf Koch. Famed German type designer draws 493 beautiful symbols: religious, mystical, alchemical, imperial, property marks, runes, etc. Remarkable fusion of traditional and modern. Good for suggestions of timelessness, smartness, modernity. Text. vi + 104pp. 6⅛ x 9¼.
         20162-7 Paperbound $1.25

HISTORY OF INDIAN AND INDONESIAN ART, Ananda K. Coomaraswamy. An unabridged republication of one of the finest books by a great scholar in Eastern art. Rich in descriptive material, history, social backgrounds; Sunga reliefs, Rajput paintings, Gupta temples, Burmese frescoes, textiles, jewelry, sculpture, etc. 400 photos. viii + 423pp. 6⅜ x 9¾.   21436-2 Paperbound $3.50

PRIMITIVE ART, Franz Boas. America's foremost anthropologist surveys textiles, ceramics, woodcarving, basketry, metalwork, etc.; patterns, technology, creation of symbols, style origins. All areas of world, but very full on Northwest Coast Indians. More than 350 illustrations of baskets, boxes, totem poles, weapons, etc. 378 pp.
         20025-6 Paperbound $2.50

THE GENTLEMAN AND CABINET MAKER'S DIRECTOR, Thomas Chippendale. Full reprint (third edition, 1762) of most influential furniture book of all time, by master cabinetmaker. 200 plates, illustrating chairs, sofas, mirrors, tables, cabinets, plus 24 photographs of surviving pieces. Biographical introduction by N. Bienenstock. vi + 249pp. 9⅞ x 12¾.   21601-2 Paperbound $3.50

AMERICAN ANTIQUE FURNITURE, Edgar G. Miller, Jr. The basic coverage of all American furniture before 1840. Individual chapters cover type of furniture— clocks, tables, sideboards, etc.—chronologically, with inexhaustible wealth of data. More than 2100 photographs, all identified, commented on. Essential to all early American collectors. Introduction by H. E. Keyes. vi + 1106pp. 7⅞ x 10¾.
         21599-7, 21600-4 Two volumes, Paperbound $7.50

PENNSYLVANIA DUTCH AMERICAN FOLK ART, Henry J. Kauffman. 279 photos, 28 drawings of tulipware, Fraktur script, painted tinware, toys, flowered furniture, quilts, samplers, hex signs, house interiors, etc. Full descriptive text. Excellent for tourist, rewarding for designer, collector. Map. 146pp. 7⅞ x 10¾.
         21205-X Paperbound $2.00

EARLY NEW ENGLAND GRAVESTONE RUBBINGS, Edmund V. Gillon, Jr. 43 photographs, 226 carefully reproduced rubbings show heavily symbolic, sometimes macabre early gravestones, up to early 19th century. Remarkable early American primitive art, occasionally strikingly beautiful; always powerful. Text. xxvi + 207pp. 8⅜ x 11¼.   21380-3 Paperbound $3.00

ALPHABETS AND ORNAMENTS, Ernst Lehner. Well-known pictorial source for decorative alphabets, script examples, cartouches, frames, decorative title pages, calligraphic initials, borders, similar material. 14th to 19th century, mostly European. Useful in almost any graphic arts designing, varied styles. 750 illustrations. 256pp. 7 x 10.
21905-4 Paperbound $3.50

PAINTING: A CREATIVE APPROACH, Norman Colquhoun. For the beginner simple guide provides an instructive approach to painting: major stumbling blocks for beginner; overcoming them, technical points; paints and pigments; oil painting; watercolor and other media and color. New section on "plastic" paints. Glossary. Formerly *Paint Your Own Pictures*. 221pp.
22000-1 Paperbound $1.75

THE ENJOYMENT AND USE OF COLOR, Walter Sargent. Explanation of the relations between colors themselves and between colors in nature and art, including hundreds of little-known facts about color values, intensities, effects of high and low illumination, complementary colors. Many practical hints for painters, references to great masters. 7 color plates, 29 illustrations. x + 274pp.
20944-X Paperbound $2.50

THE NOTEBOOKS OF LEONARDO DA VINCI, compiled and edited by Jean Paul Richter. 1566 extracts from original manuscripts reveal the full range of Leonardo's versatile genius: all his writings on painting, sculpture, architecture, anatomy, astronomy, geography, topography, physiology, mining, music, etc., in both Italian and English, with 186 plates of manuscript pages and more than 500 additional drawings. Includes studies for the Last Supper, the lost Sforza monument, and other works. Total of xlvii + 866pp. 7⅞ x 10¾.
22572-0, 22573-9 Two volumes, Paperbound $10.00

MONTGOMERY WARD CATALOGUE OF 1895. Tea gowns, yards of flannel and pillow-case lace, stereoscopes, books of gospel hymns, the New Improved Singer Sewing Machine, side saddles, milk skimmers, straight-edged razors, high-button shoes, spittoons, and on and on . . . listing some 25,000 items, practically all illustrated. Essential to the shoppers of the 1890's, it is our truest record of the spirit of the period. Unaltered reprint of Issue No. 57, Spring and Summer 1895. Introduction by Boris Emmet. Innumerable illustrations. xiii + 624pp. 8½ x 11⅝.
22377-9 Paperbound $6.95

THE CRYSTAL PALACE EXHIBITION ILLUSTRATED CATALOGUE (LONDON, 1851). One of the wonders of the modern world—the Crystal Palace Exhibition in which all the nations of the civilized world exhibited their achievements in the arts and sciences—presented in an equally important illustrated catalogue. More than 1700 items pictured with accompanying text—ceramics, textiles, cast-iron work, carpets, pianos, sleds, razors, wall-papers, billiard tables, beehives, silverware and hundreds of other artifacts—represent the focal point of Victorian culture in the Western World. Probably the largest collection of Victorian decorative art ever assembled—indispensable for antiquarians and designers. Unabridged republication of the Art-Journal Catalogue of the Great Exhibition of 1851, with all terminal essays. New introduction by John Gloag, F.S.A. xxxiv + 426pp. 9 x 12.
22503-8 Paperbound $4.50

A HISTORY OF COSTUME, Carl Köhler. Definitive history, based on surviving pieces of clothing primarily, and paintings, statues, etc. secondarily. Highly readable text, supplemented by 594 illustrations of costumes of the ancient Mediterranean peoples, Greece and Rome, the Teutonic prehistoric period; costumes of the Middle Ages, Renaissance, Baroque, 18th and 19th centuries. Clear, measured patterns are provided for many clothing articles. Approach is practical throughout. Enlarged by Emma von Sichart. 464pp. 21030-8 Paperbound $3.00

ORIENTAL RUGS, ANTIQUE AND MODERN, Walter A. Hawley. A complete and authoritative treatise on the Oriental rug—where they are made, by whom and how, designs and symbols, characteristics in detail of the six major groups, how to distinguish them and how to buy them. Detailed technical data is provided on periods, weaves, warps, wefts, textures, sides, ends and knots, although no technical background is required for an understanding. 11 color plates, 80 halftones, 4 maps. vi + 320pp. 6⅛ x 9⅛. 22366-3 Paperbound $5.00

TEN BOOKS ON ARCHITECTURE, Vitruvius. By any standards the most important book on architecture ever written. Early Roman discussion of aesthetics of building, construction methods, orders, sites, and every other aspect of architecture has inspired, instructed architecture for about 2,000 years. Stands behind Palladio, Michelangelo, Bramante, Wren, countless others. Definitive Morris H. Morgan translation. 68 illustrations. xii + 331pp. 20645-9 Paperbound $2.50

THE FOUR BOOKS OF ARCHITECTURE, Andrea Palladio. Translated into every major Western European language in the two centuries following its publication in 1570, this has been one of the most influential books in the history of architecture. Complete reprint of the 1738 Isaac Ware edition. New introduction by Adolf Placzek, Columbia Univ. 216 plates. xxii + 110pp. of text. 9½ x 12¾. 21308-0 Clothbound $10.00

STICKS AND STONES: A STUDY OF AMERICAN ARCHITECTURE AND CIVILIZATION, Lewis Mumford.One of the great classics of American cultural history. American architecture from the medieval-inspired earliest forms to the early 20th century; evolution of structure and style, and reciprocal influences on environment. 21 photographic illustrations. 238pp. 20202-X Paperbound $2.00

THE AMERICAN BUILDER'S COMPANION, Asher Benjamin. The most widely used early 19th century architectural style and source book, for colonial up into Greek Revival periods. Extensive development of geometry of carpentering, construction of sashes, frames, doors, stairs; plans and elevations of domestic and other buildings. Hundreds of thousands of houses were built according to this book, now invaluable to historians, architects, restorers, etc. 1827 edition. 59 plates. 114pp. 7⅞ x 10¾. 22236-5 Paperbound $3.00

DUTCH HOUSES IN THE HUDSON VALLEY BEFORE 1776, Helen Wilkinson Reynolds. The standard survey of the Dutch colonial house and outbuildings, with constructional features, decoration, and local history associated with individual homesteads. Introduction by Franklin D. Roosevelt. Map. 150 illustrations. 469pp. 6⅝ x 9¼. 21469-9 Paperbound $3.50

THE ARCHITECTURE OF COUNTRY HOUSES, Andrew J. Downing. Together with Vaux's *Villas and Cottages* this is the basic book for Hudson River Gothic architecture of the middle Victorian period. Full, sound discussions of general aspects of housing, architecture, style, decoration, furnishing, together with scores of detailed house plans, illustrations of specific buildings, accompanied by full text. Perhaps the most influential single American architectural book. 1850 edition. Introduction by J. Stewart Johnson. 321 figures, 34 architectural designs. xvi + 560pp.
22003-6 Paperbound $3.50

LOST EXAMPLES OF COLONIAL ARCHITECTURE, John Mead Howells. Full-page photographs of buildings that have disappeared or been so altered as to be denatured, including many designed by major early American architects. 245 plates. xvii + 248pp. 7⅞ x 10¾.
21143-6 Paperbound $3.00

DOMESTIC ARCHITECTURE OF THE AMERICAN COLONIES AND OF THE EARLY REPUBLIC, Fiske Kimball. Foremost architect and restorer of Williamsburg and Monticello covers nearly 200 homes between 1620-1825. Architectural details, construction, style features, special fixtures, floor plans, etc. Generally considered finest work in its area. 219 illustrations of houses, doorways, windows, capital mantels. xx + 314pp. 7⅞ x 10¾.
21743-4 Paperbound $3.50

EARLY AMERICAN ROOMS: 1650-1858, edited by Russell Hawes Kettell. Tour of 12 rooms, each representative of a different era in American history and each furnished, decorated, designed and occupied in the style of the era. 72 plans and elevations, 8-page color section, etc., show fabrics, wall papers, arrangements, etc. Full descriptive text. xvii + 200pp. of text. 8⅜ x 11¼.
21633-0 Paperbound $4.00

THE FITZWILLIAM VIRGINAL BOOK, edited by J. Fuller Maitland and W. B. Squire. Full modern printing of famous early 17th-century ms. volume of 300 works by Morley, Byrd, Bull, Gibbons, etc. For piano or other modern keyboard instrument; easy to read format. xxxvi + 938pp. 8⅜ x 11.
21068-5, 21069-3 Two volumes, Paperbound $8.00

HARPSICHORD MUSIC, Johann Sebastian Bach. Bach Gesellschaft edition. A rich selection of Bach's masterpieces for the harpsichord: the six English Suites, six French Suites, the six Partitas (Clavierübung part I), the Goldberg Variations (Clavierübung part IV), the fifteen Two-Part Inventions and the fifteen Three-Part Sinfonias. Clearly reproduced on large sheets with ample margins; eminently playable. vi + 312pp. 8⅛ x 11.
22360-4 Paperbound $5.00

THE MUSIC OF BACH: AN INTRODUCTION, Charles Sanford Terry. A fine, nontechnical introduction to Bach's music, both instrumental and vocal. Covers organ music, chamber music, passion music, other types. Analyzes themes, developments, innovations. x + 114pp.
21075-8 Paperbound $1.25

BEETHOVEN AND HIS NINE SYMPHONIES, Sir George Grove. Noted British musicologist provides best history, analysis, commentary on symphonies. Very thorough, rigorously accurate; necessary to both advanced student and amateur music lover. 436 musical passages. vii + 407 pp.
20334-4 Paperbound $2.25

JOHANN SEBASTIAN BACH, Philipp Spitta. One of the great classics of musicology, this definitive analysis of Bach's music (and life) has never been surpassed. Lucid, nontechnical analyses of hundreds of pieces (30 pages devoted to St. Matthew Passion, 26 to B Minor Mass). Also includes major analysis of 18th-century music. 450 musical examples. 40-page musical supplement. Total of xx + 1799pp.
(EUK) 22278-0, 22279-9 Two volumes, Clothbound $15.00

MOZART AND HIS PIANO CONCERTOS, Cuthbert Girdlestone. The only full-length study of an important area of Mozart's creativity. Provides detailed analyses of all 23 concertos, traces inspirational sources. 417 musical examples. Second edition. 509pp.
(USO) 21271-8 Paperbound $3.50

THE PERFECT WAGNERITE: A COMMENTARY ON THE NIBLUNG'S RING, George Bernard Shaw. Brilliant and still relevant criticism in remarkable essays on Wagner's Ring cycle, Shaw's ideas on political and social ideology behind the plots, role of Leitmotifs, vocal requisites, etc. Prefaces. xxi + 136pp.
21707-8 Paperbound $1.50

DON GIOVANNI, W. A. Mozart. Complete libretto, modern English translation; biographies of composer and librettist; accounts of early performances and critical reaction. Lavishly illustrated. All the material you need to understand and appreciate this great work. Dover Opera Guide and Libretto Series; translated and introduced by Ellen Bleiler. 92 illustrations. 209pp.
21134-7 Paperbound $1.50

HIGH FIDELITY SYSTEMS: A LAYMAN'S GUIDE, Roy F. Allison. All the basic information you need for setting up your own audio system: high fidelity and stereo record players, tape records, F.M. Connections, adjusting tone arm, cartridge, checking needle alignment, positioning speakers, phasing speakers, adjusting hums, trouble-shooting, maintenance, and similar topics. Enlarged 1965 edition. More than 50 charts, diagrams, photos. iv + 91pp.   21514-8 Paperbound $1.25

REPRODUCTION OF SOUND, Edgar Villchur. Thorough coverage for laymen of high fidelity systems, reproducing systems in general, needles, amplifiers, preamps, loudspeakers, feedback, explaining physical background. "A rare talent for making technicalities vividly comprehensible," R. Darrell, *High Fidelity*. 69 figures. iv + 92pp.   21515-6 Paperbound $1.00

HEAR ME TALKIN' TO YA: THE STORY OF JAZZ AS TOLD BY THE MEN WHO MADE IT, Nat Shapiro and Nat Hentoff. Louis Armstrong, Fats Waller, Jo Jones, Clarence Williams, Billy Holiday, Duke Ellington, Jelly Roll Morton and dozens of other jazz greats tell how it was in Chicago's South Side, New Orleans, depression Harlem and the modern West Coast as jazz was born and grew. xvi + 429pp.
21726-4 Paperbound $2.00

FABLES OF AESOP, translated by Sir Roger L'Estrange. A reproduction of the very rare 1931 Paris edition; a selection of the most interesting fables, together with 50 imaginative drawings by Alexander Calder. v + 128pp. 6½x9¼.
21780-9 Paperbound $1.25

AGAINST THE GRAIN (A REBOURS), Joris K. Huysmans. Filled with weird images, evidences of a bizarre imagination, exotic experiments with hallucinatory drugs, rich tastes and smells and the diversions of its sybarite hero Duc Jean des Esseintes, this classic novel pushed 19th-century literary decadence to its limits. Full unabridged edition. Do not confuse this with abridged editions generally sold. Introduction by Havelock Ellis. xlix + 206pp.   22190-3 Paperbound $2.00

VARIORUM SHAKESPEARE: HAMLET. Edited by Horace H. Furness; a landmark of American scholarship. Exhaustive footnotes and appendices treat all doubtful words and phrases, as well as suggested critical emendations throughout the play's history. First volume contains editor's own text, collated with all Quartos and Folios. Second volume contains full first Quarto, translations of Shakespeare's sources (Belleforest, and Saxo Grammaticus), Der Bestrafte Brudermord, and many essays on critical and historical points of interest by major authorities of past and present. Includes details of staging and costuming over the years. By far the best edition available for serious students of Shakespeare. Total of xx + 905pp.
21004-9, 21005-7, 2 volumes, Paperbound $5.25

A LIFE OF WILLIAM SHAKESPEARE, Sir Sidney Lee. This is the standard life of Shakespeare, summarizing everything known about Shakespeare and his plays. Incredibly rich in material, broad in coverage, clear and judicious, it has served thousands as the best introduction to Shakespeare. 1931 edition. 9 plates. xxix + 792pp.   (USO) 21967-4 Paperbound $3.75

MASTERS OF THE DRAMA, John Gassner. Most comprehensive history of the drama in print, covering every tradition from Greeks to modern Europe and America, including India, Far East, etc. Covers more than 800 dramatists, 2000 plays, with biographical material, plot summaries, theatre history, criticism, etc. "Best of its kind in English," New Republic. 77 illustrations. xxii + 890pp.
20100-7 Clothbound $7.50

THE EVOLUTION OF THE ENGLISH LANGUAGE, George McKnight. The growth of English, from the 14th century to the present. Unusual, non-technical account presents basic information in very interesting form: sound shifts, change in grammar and syntax, vocabulary growth, similar topics. Abundantly illustrated with quotations. Formerly Modern English in the Making. xii + 590pp.
21932-1 Paperbound $3.50

AN ETYMOLOGICAL DICTIONARY OF MODERN ENGLISH, Ernest Weekley. Fullest, richest work of its sort, by foremost British lexicographer. Detailed word histories, including many colloquial and archaic words; extensive quotations. Do not confuse this with the Concise Etymological Dictionary, which is much abridged. Total of xxvii + 830pp. 6½ x 9¼.
21873-2, 21874-0 Two volumes, Paperbound $5.50

FLATLAND: A ROMANCE OF MANY DIMENSIONS, E. A. Abbott. Classic of science-fiction explores ramifications of life in a two-dimensional world, and what happens when a three-dimensional being intrudes. Amusing reading, but also useful as introduction to thought about hyperspace. Introduction by Banesh Hoffmann. 16 illustrations. xx + 103pp.   20001-9 Paperbound $1.00

POEMS OF ANNE BRADSTREET, edited with an introduction by Robert Hutchinson. A new selection of poems by America's first poet and perhaps the first significant woman poet in the English language. 48 poems display her development in works of considerable variety—love poems, domestic poems, religious meditations, formal elegies, "quaternions," etc. Notes, bibliography. viii + 222pp.

22160-1 Paperbound $2.00

THREE GOTHIC NOVELS: THE CASTLE OF OTRANTO BY HORACE WALPOLE; VATHEK BY WILLIAM BECKFORD; THE VAMPYRE BY JOHN POLIDORI, WITH FRAGMENT OF A NOVEL BY LORD BYRON, edited by E. F. Bleiler. The first Gothic novel, by Walpole; the finest Oriental tale in English, by Beckford; powerful Romantic supernatural story in versions by Polidori and Byron. All extremely important in history of literature; all still exciting, packed with supernatural thrills, ghosts, haunted castles, magic, etc. xl + 291pp.

21232-7 Paperbound $2.00

THE BEST TALES OF HOFFMANN, E. T. A. Hoffmann. 10 of Hoffmann's most important stories, in modern re-editings of standard translations: Nutcracker and the King of Mice, Signor Formica, Automata, The Sandman, Rath Krespel, The Golden Flowerpot, Master Martin the Cooper, The Mines of Falun, The King's Betrothed, A New Year's Eve Adventure. 7 illustrations by Hoffmann. Edited by E. F. Bleiler. xxxix + 419pp.

21793-0 Paperbound $2.25

GHOST AND HORROR STORIES OF AMBROSE BIERCE, Ambrose Bierce. 23 strikingly modern stories of the horrors latent in the human mind: The Eyes of the Panther, The Damned Thing, An Occurrence at Owl Creek Bridge, An Inhabitant of Carcosa, etc., plus the dream-essay, Visions of the Night. Edited by E. F. Bleiler. xxii + 199pp.

20767-6 Paperbound $1.50

BEST GHOST STORIES OF J. S. LEFANU, J. Sheridan LeFanu. Finest stories by Victorian master often considered greatest supernatural writer of all. Carmilla, Green Tea, The Haunted Baronet, The Familiar, and 12 others. Most never before available in the U. S. A. Edited by E. F. Bleiler. 8 illustrations from Victorian publications. xvii + 467pp.

20415-4 Paperbound $2.50

THE TIME STREAM, THE GREATEST ADVENTURE, AND THE PURPLE SAPPHIRE— THREE SCIENCE FICTION NOVELS, John Taine (Eric Temple Bell). Great American mathematician was also foremost science fiction novelist of the 1920's. *The Time Stream,* one of all-time classics, uses concepts of circular time; *The Greatest Adventure,* incredibly ancient biological experiments from Antarctica threaten to escape; The *Purple Sapphire,* superscience, lost races in Central Tibet, survivors of the Great Race. 4 illustrations by Frank R. Paul. v + 532pp.

21180-0 Paperbound $2.50

SEVEN SCIENCE FICTION NOVELS, H. G. Wells. The standard collection of the great novels. Complete, unabridged. *First Men in the Moon, Island of Dr. Moreau, War of the Worlds, Food of the Gods, Invisible Man, Time Machine, In the Days of the Comet.* Not only science fiction fans, but every educated person owes it to himself to read these novels. 1015pp.

20264-X Clothbound $5.00

LAST AND FIRST MEN AND STAR MAKER, TWO SCIENCE FICTION NOVELS, Olaf Stapledon. Greatest future histories in science fiction. In the first, human intelligence is the "hero," through strange paths of evolution, interplanetary invasions, incredible technologies, near extinctions and reemergences. Star Maker describes the quest of a band of star rovers for intelligence itself, through time and space: weird inhuman civilizations, crustacean minds, symbiotic worlds, etc. Complete, unabridged. v + 438pp. 21962-3 Paperbound $2.00

THREE PROPHETIC NOVELS, H. G. WELLS. Stages of a consistently planned future for mankind. *When the Sleeper Wakes*, and *A Story of the Days to Come*, anticipate *Brave New World* and *1984*, in the 21st Century; *The Time Machine*, only complete version in print, shows farther future and the end of mankind. All show Wells's greatest gifts as storyteller and novelist. Edited by E. F. Bleiler. x + 335pp. (USO) 20605-X Paperbound $2.00

THE DEVIL'S DICTIONARY, Ambrose Bierce. America's own Oscar Wilde— Ambrose Bierce—offers his barbed iconoclastic wisdom in over 1,000 definitions hailed by H. L. Mencken as "some of the most gorgeous witticisms in the English language." 145pp. 20487-1 Paperbound $1.25

MAX AND MORITZ, Wilhelm Busch. Great children's classic, father of comic strip, of two bad boys, Max and Moritz. Also Ker and Plunk (Plisch und Plumm), Cat and Mouse, Deceitful Henry, Ice-Peter, The Boy and the Pipe, and five other pieces. Original German, with English translation. Edited by H. Arthur Klein; translations by various hands and H. Arthur Klein. vi + 216pp.
20181-3 Paperbound $1.50

PIGS IS PIGS AND OTHER FAVORITES, Ellis Parker Butler. The title story is one of the best humor short stories, as Mike Flannery obfuscates biology and English. Also included, That Pup of Murchison's, The Great American Pie Company, and Perkins of Portland. 14 illustrations. v + 109pp. 21532-6 Paperbound $1.00

THE PETERKIN PAPERS, Lucretia P. Hale. It takes genius to be as stupidly mad as the Peterkins, as they decide to become wise, celebrate the "Fourth," keep a cow, and otherwise strain the resources of the Lady from Philadelphia. Basic book of American humor. 153 illustrations. 219pp. 20794-3 Paperbound $1.25

PERRAULT'S FAIRY TALES, translated by A. E. Johnson and S. R. Littlewood, with 34 full-page illustrations by Gustave Doré. All the original Perrault stories— Cinderella, Sleeping Beauty, Bluebeard, Little Red Riding Hood, Puss in Boots, Tom Thumb, etc.—with their witty verse morals and the magnificent illustrations of Doré. One of the five or six great books of European fairy tales. viii + 117pp. 8⅛ x 11. 22311-6 Paperbound $2.00

OLD HUNGARIAN FAIRY TALES, Baroness Orczy. Favorites translated and adapted by author of the *Scarlet Pimpernel*. Eight fairy tales include "The Suitors of Princess Fire-Fly," "The Twin Hunchbacks," "Mr. Cuttlefish's Love Story," and "The Enchanted Cat." This little volume of magic and adventure will captivate children as it has for generations. 90 drawings by Montagu Barstow. 96pp.
(USO) 22293-4 Paperbound $1.95

THE RED FAIRY BOOK, Andrew Lang. Lang's color fairy books have long been children's favorites. This volume includes Rapunzel, Jack and the Bean-stalk and 35 other stories, familiar and unfamiliar. 4 plates, 93 illustrations x + 367pp.

21673-X Paperbound $1.95

THE BLUE FAIRY BOOK, Andrew Lang. Lang's tales come from all countries and all times. Here are 37 tales from Grimm, the Arabian Nights, Greek Mythology, and other fascinating sources. 8 plates, 130 illustrations. xi + 390pp.

21437-0 Paperbound $1.95

HOUSEHOLD STORIES BY THE BROTHERS GRIMM. Classic English-language edition of the well-known tales — Rumpelstiltskin, Snow White, Hansel and Gretel, The Twelve Brothers, Faithful John, Rapunzel, Tom Thumb (52 stories in all). Translated into simple, straightforward English by Lucy Crane. Ornamented with headpieces, vignettes, elaborate decorative initials and a dozen full-page illustrations by Walter Crane. x + 269pp. 21080-4 Paperbound $2.00

THE MERRY ADVENTURES OF ROBIN HOOD, Howard Pyle. The finest modern versions of the traditional ballads and tales about the great English outlaw. Howard Pyle's complete prose version, with every word, every illustration of the first edition. Do not confuse this facsimile of the original (1883) with modern editions that change text or illustrations. 23 plates plus many page decorations. xxii + 296pp.

22043-5 Paperbound $2.00

THE STORY OF KING ARTHUR AND HIS KNIGHTS, Howard Pyle. The finest children's version of the life of King Arthur; brilliantly retold by Pyle, with 48 of his most imaginative illustrations. xviii + 313pp. 6⅛ x 9¼.

21445-1 Paperbound $2.00

THE WONDERFUL WIZARD OF OZ, L. Frank Baum. America's finest children's book in facsimile of first edition with all Denslow illustrations in full color. The edition a child should have. Introduction by Martin Gardner. 23 color plates, scores of drawings. iv + 267pp. 20691-2 Paperbound $1.95

THE MARVELOUS LAND OF OZ, L. Frank Baum. The second Oz book, every bit as imaginative as the Wizard. The hero is a boy named Tip, but the Scarecrow and the Tin Woodman are back, as is the Oz magic. 16 color plates, 120 drawings by John R. Neill. 287pp. 20692-0 Paperbound $1.75

THE MAGICAL MONARCH OF MO, L. Frank Baum. Remarkable adventures in a land even stranger than Oz. The best of Baum's books not in the Oz series. 15 color plates and dozens of drawings by Frank Verbeck. xviii + 237pp.

21892-9 Paperbound $2.00

THE BAD CHILD'S BOOK OF BEASTS, MORE BEASTS FOR WORSE CHILDREN, A MORAL ALPHABET, Hilaire Belloc. Three complete humor classics in one volume. Be kind to the frog, and do not call him names . . . and 28 other whimsical animals. Familiar favorites and some not so well known. Illustrated by Basil Blackwell. 156pp. (USO) 20749-8 Paperbound $1.25

EAST O' THE SUN AND WEST O' THE MOON, George W. Dasent. Considered the best of all translations of these Norwegian folk tales, this collection has been enjoyed by generations of children (and folklorists too). Includes True and Untrue, Why the Sea is Salt, East O' the Sun and West O' the Moon, Why the Bear is Stumpy-Tailed, Boots and the Troll, The Cock and the Hen, Rich Peter the Pedlar, and 52 more. The only edition with all 59 tales. 77 illustrations by Erik Werenskiold and Theodor Kittelsen. xv + 418pp. 22521-6 Paperbound $3.00

GOOPS AND HOW TO BE THEM, Gelett Burgess. Classic of tongue-in-cheek humor, masquerading as etiquette book. 87 verses, twice as many cartoons, show mischievous Goops as they demonstrate to children virtues of table manners, neatness, courtesy, etc. Favorite for generations. viii + 88pp. 6½ x 9¼. 22233-0 Paperbound $1.25

ALICE'S ADVENTURES UNDER GROUND, Lewis Carroll. The first version, quite different from the final *Alice in Wonderland,* printed out by Carroll himself with his own illustrations. Complete facsimile of the "million dollar" manuscript Carroll gave to Alice Liddell in 1864. Introduction by Martin Gardner. viii + 96pp. Title and dedication pages in color. 21482-6 Paperbound $1.25

THE BROWNIES, THEIR BOOK, Palmer Cox. Small as mice, cunning as foxes, exuberant and full of mischief, the Brownies go to the zoo, toy shop, seashore, circus, etc., in 24 verse adventures and 266 illustrations. Long a favorite, since their first appearance in St. Nicholas Magazine. xi + 144pp. 6⅝ x 9¼. 21265-3 Paperbound $1.75

SONGS OF CHILDHOOD, Walter De La Mare. Published (under the pseudonym Walter Ramal) when De La Mare was only 29, this charming collection has long been a favorite children's book. A facsimile of the first edition in paper, the 47 poems capture the simplicity of the nursery rhyme and the ballad, including such lyrics as I Met Eve, Tartary, The Silver Penny. vii + 106pp. 21972-0 Paperbound $1.25

THE COMPLETE NONSENSE OF EDWARD LEAR, Edward Lear. The finest 19th-century humorist-cartoonist in full: all nonsense limericks, zany alphabets, Owl and Pussycat, songs, nonsense botany, and more than 500 illustrations by Lear himself. Edited by Holbrook Jackson. xxix + 287pp. (USO) 20167-8 Paperbound $1.75

BILLY WHISKERS: THE AUTOBIOGRAPHY OF A GOAT, Frances Trego Montgomery. A favorite of children since the early 20th century, here are the escapades of that rambunctious, irresistible and mischievous goat—Billy Whiskers. Much in the spirit of *Peck's Bad Boy,* this is a book that children never tire of reading or hearing. All the original familiar illustrations by W. H. Fry are included: 6 color plates, 18 black and white drawings. 159pp. 22345-0 Paperbound $2.00

MOTHER GOOSE MELODIES. Faithful republication of the fabulously rare Munroe and Francis "copyright 1833" Boston edition—the most important Mother Goose collection, usually referred to as the "original." Familiar rhymes plus many rare ones, with wonderful old woodcut illustrations. Edited by E. F. Bleiler. 128pp. 4½ x 6⅜. 22577-1 Paperbound $1.25

TWO LITTLE SAVAGES; BEING THE ADVENTURES OF TWO BOYS WHO LIVED AS INDIANS AND WHAT THEY LEARNED, Ernest Thompson Seton. Great classic of nature and boyhood provides a vast range of woodlore in most palatable form, a genuinely entertaining story. Two farm boys build a teepee in woods and live in it for a month, working out Indian solutions to living problems, star lore, birds and animals, plants, etc. 293 illustrations. vii + 286pp.

20985-7 Paperbound $2.50

PETER PIPER'S PRACTICAL PRINCIPLES OF PLAIN & PERFECT PRONUNCIATION. Alliterative jingles and tongue-twisters of surprising charm, that made their first appearance in America about 1830. Republished in full with the spirited woodcut illustrations from this earliest American edition. 32pp. 4½ x 6⅜.

22560-7 Paperbound $1.00

SCIENCE EXPERIMENTS AND AMUSEMENTS FOR CHILDREN, Charles Vivian. 73 easy experiments, requiring only materials found at home or easily available, such as candles, coins, steel wool, etc.; illustrate basic phenomena like vacuum, simple chemical reaction, etc. All safe. Modern, well-planned. Formerly *Science Games for Children*. 102 photos, numerous drawings. 96pp. 6⅛ x 9¼.

21856-2 Paperbound $1.25

AN INTRODUCTION TO CHESS MOVES AND TACTICS SIMPLY EXPLAINED, Leonard Barden. Informal intermediate introduction, quite strong in explaining reasons for moves. Covers basic material, tactics, important openings, traps, positional play in middle game, end game. Attempts to isolate patterns and recurrent configurations. Formerly *Chess*. 58 figures. 102pp. (USO) 21210-6 Paperbound $1.25

LASKER'S MANUAL OF CHESS, Dr. Emanuel Lasker. Lasker was not only one of the five great World Champions, he was also one of the ablest expositors, theorists, and analysts. In many ways, his Manual, permeated with his philosophy of battle, filled with keen insights, is one of the greatest works ever written on chess. Filled with analyzed games by the great players. A single-volume library that will profit almost any chess player, beginner or master. 308 diagrams. xli x 349pp.

20640-8 Paperbound $2.50

THE MASTER BOOK OF MATHEMATICAL RECREATIONS, Fred Schuh. In opinion of many the finest work ever prepared on mathematical puzzles, stunts, recreations; exhaustively thorough explanations of mathematics involved, analysis of effects, citation of puzzles and games. Mathematics involved is elementary. Translated by F. Göbel. 194 figures. xxiv + 430pp.

22134-2 Paperbound $3.00

MATHEMATICS, MAGIC AND MYSTERY, Martin Gardner. Puzzle editor for Scientific American explains mathematics behind various mystifying tricks: card tricks, stage "mind reading," coin and match tricks, counting out games, geometric dissections, etc. Probability sets, theory of numbers clearly explained. Also provides more than 400 tricks, guaranteed to work, that you can do. 135 illustrations. xii + 176pp.

20338-2 Paperbound $1.50

CATALOGUE OF DOVER BOOKS

MATHEMATICAL PUZZLES FOR BEGINNERS AND ENTHUSIASTS, Geoffrey Mott-Smith. 189 puzzles from easy to difficult—involving arithmetic, logic, algebra, properties of digits, probability, etc.—for enjoyment and mental stimulus. Explanation of mathematical principles behind the puzzles. 135 illustrations. viii + 248pp.
20198-8 Paperbound $1.25

PAPER FOLDING FOR BEGINNERS, William D. Murray and Francis J. Rigney. Easiest book on the market, clearest instructions on making interesting, beautiful origami. Sail boats, cups, roosters, frogs that move legs, bonbon boxes, standing birds, etc. 40 projects; more than 275 diagrams and photographs. 94pp.
20713-7 Paperbound $1.00

TRICKS AND GAMES ON THE POOL TABLE, Fred Herrmann. 79 tricks and games—some solitaires, some for two or more players, some competitive games—to entertain you between formal games. Mystifying shots and throws, unusual caroms, tricks involving such props as cork, coins, a hat, etc. Formerly *Fun on the Pool Table*. 77 figures. 95pp.
21814-7 Paperbound $1.00

HAND SHADOWS TO BE THROWN UPON THE WALL: A SERIES OF NOVEL AND AMUSING FIGURES FORMED BY THE HAND, Henry Bursill. Delightful picturebook from great-grandfather's day shows how to make 18 different hand shadows: a bird that flies, duck that quacks, dog that wags his tail, camel, goose, deer, boy, turtle, etc. Only book of its sort. vi + 33pp. 6½ x 9¼. 21779-5 Paperbound $1.00

WHITTLING AND WOODCARVING, E. J. Tangerman. 18th printing of best book on market. "If you can cut a potato you can carve" toys and puzzles, chains, chessmen, caricatures, masks, frames, woodcut blocks, surface patterns, much more. Information on tools, woods, techniques. Also goes into serious wood sculpture from Middle Ages to present, East and West. 464 photos, figures. x + 293pp.
20965-2 Paperbound $2.00

HISTORY OF PHILOSOPHY, Julián Marias. Possibly the clearest, most easily followed, best planned, most useful one-volume history of philosophy on the market; neither skimpy nor overfull. Full details on system of every major philosopher and dozens of less important thinkers from pre-Socratics up to Existentialism and later. Strong on many European figures usually omitted. Has gone through dozens of editions in Europe. 1966 edition, translated by Stanley Appelbaum and Clarence Strowbridge. xviii + 505pp.
21739-6 Paperbound $2.75

YOGA: A SCIENTIFIC EVALUATION, Kovoor T. Behanan. Scientific but non-technical study of physiological results of yoga exercises; done under auspices of Yale U. Relations to Indian thought, to psychoanalysis, etc. 16 photos. xxiii + 270pp.
20505-3 Paperbound $2.50

Prices subject to change without notice.
Available at your book dealer or write for free catalogue to Dept. GI, Dover Publications, Inc., 180 Varick St., N. Y., N. Y. 10014. Dover publishes more than 150 books each year on science, elementary and advanced mathematics, biology, music, art, literary history, social sciences and other areas.

S.
NRY